About the Author

One of the world's foremost experts on the occult, Raymond Buckland has been studying fortune-telling, witchcraft, Gypsy magic, and other aspects of the supernatural for more than half a century and is credited with introducing modern witchcraft into the United States.

Of Romany (Gypsy) descent, Buckland was born in London in 1934. At an early age, an uncle introduced him to spiritualism, sparking a lifelong interest in the occult. He obtained a doctorate in anthropology and, in 1962, moved to America. His spiritual quest led him to the works of Wicca pioneer Dr. Gerald Gardner, who was living on the Isle of Man. Before long, Buckland and Gardner were corresponding on a regular basis, with Buckland serving as Gardner's spokesperson in the United States. Buckland was initiated into the Craft shortly before Gardner's death in 1964.

In 1969 Buckland published his first book, *A Pocket Guide to the Supernatural*. He has had more than thirty titles published (and translated into fourteen languages), including the definitive encyclopedia *The Witch Book*, published in 2002, and the classic *Buckland's Complete Book of Witchcraft*, first published in 1986. His *Gypsy Witchcraft and Magic* received the 1999 Visionary Award for nonfiction, and his *Buckland Romani Tarot* received the same award in 2002. He has designed a number of fortune-telling decks and has been reading cards and doing other types of fortune-telling for forty years.

Now living in Ohio, Buckland has been the subject of and has written countless newspaper and magazine articles, appeared on many television and radio shows, and lectured on college campuses nationwide. He has written five screenplays and acted as technical adviser for several films.

Also from Visible Ink Press

Angels A to Z

The Astrology Book: The Encyclopedia of Heavenly Influences

The Death and Afterlife Book:
The Encyclopedia of Death, Near Death, and Life after Death

The Dream Encyclopedia

The Fortune-Telling Book: The Encyclopedia of Divination and Soothsaying

Real Ghosts, Restless Spirits, and Haunted Places

The Religion Book: Places, Prophets, Saints, and Seers

The UFO Book: Encyclopedia of the Extraterrestrial

Unexplained! Strange Sightings, Incredible Occurrences,
and Puzzling Physical Phenomena

The Vampire Book: The Encyclopedia of the Undead

The Werewolf Book: The Encyclopedia of Shape-Shifting Beings

The Witch Book: The Encyclopedia of Witchcraft, Wicca, and Neo-paganism

The Fortune-Telling BOOK

The Encyclopedia of Divination and Soothsaying

The Fortune-Telling BOOK

The Encyclopedia of Divination and Soothsaying

RAYMOND BUCKLAND

VISIBLE INK PRESS

Detroit

THE FORTUNE-TELLING BOOK: The Encyclopedia of Divination and Soothsaying

Visible Ink Press®
43311 Joy Rd. #414
Canton, MI 48187-2075

Visible Ink Press is a registered trademark of Visible Ink Press LLC.

Most Visible Ink Press books are available at special quantity discounts when purchased in bulk by corporations, organizations, or groups. Customized printings, special imprints, messages, and excerpts can be produced to meet your needs. For more information, contact Special Markets Director, Visible Ink Press, at www.visibleink.com.

Art Director: Mary Claire Krzewinski
Typesetting: Graphix Group

Front cover image of *Astrologia*, 1865, by Sir Edward Burne-Jones reproduced by permision of The Bridgeman Art Library International.

Back cover image of *Palmistry* reproduced by permission of The Bridgeman Art Library International.

ISBN 1-57859-147-3
CIP data is on file with the Library of Congress

Printed in the United States of America

10 9 8 7 6 5 4 3 2 1

Contents

Signs of Things to Come: An Introduction

Raymond Buckland

The need to know what the future holds . . . most of us have that need at one time or another. Not necessarily simply wanting to know what horse will win a certain race, but desiring to glean at least an idea of where our lives are heading. The ability to divine the future is generally thought of as a gift. The very word *divine*—and its extension, *divination*—comes from "divinity," the belief that to be able to peer into the future is a gift of the gods. In many early civilizations, the diviner or soothsayer held a court position, with his or her utterances being sought for state matters and in cases of war and natural disasters.

There is evidence that some form of fortune-telling was practiced in ancient China, Egypt, Babylonia, and Chaldea from at least 4000 BCE. Divination, augury, and soothsaying all were part of everyday life in ancient Greece and Rome. The oracles at Delphi and elsewhere were freely consulted. Various forms of divination are mentioned throughout the Bible, in both the Old and the New Testaments. But seeking knowledge of the future almost certainly goes back much farther than any of these. Early humankind was undoubtedly anxious about the seasonal changes, about the success of the hunt, about fertility, and about the welfare of the coming harvest. By repeated observation over several generations of such things as weather, animal habits, and bird migration, such happenings were aligned with the later results to give the basics of prophetic lore.

The Roman statesman, writer, and philosopher Marcus Tullius Cicero (106–43 BCE) said that divination is a truly religious matter since it predisposes a belief in a deity that has arranged a destiny for all humankind. Pythagoras (c. sixth century BCE), the Greek philosopher, is known to have visited Egypt and parts of Asia, studying Magian and Chaldean lore; the so-called

Pythagorean form of numerology is ascribed to him. Philosopher Aristotle (384–322 BCE) wrote a treatise on physiognomy. Plato (428–348 BCE) is credited with a belief in fortune-telling.

Divination, or fortune-telling, is practiced in all cultures. What was once the prerogative of the shaman, and later became the jurisdiction of the priest, has today become the tool of anyone who has the inclination to try it. Tarot cards are read by all and sundry; astrological charts are cast and palms are scrutinized; crystal-gazers peer into the past, present, and future. For divination is not only the prediction of the future, but also the uncovering of secrets of the past and the present.

One of the earliest forms of divination was probably through dreams. Virtually everyone dreams, and many times a dream, on later reflection, turns out to have been a precursor of a coming event. From dreams, perhaps the path led to scrying—to gazing at a reflective surface and, through trance (light or deep), focusing onto events happening at a different time and place. Alongside these "internal" forms of divination are the "external" forms: observation of the actions of animals and birds, for example, and relating those actions to coming events. Other internal forms include automatic writing, use of pendula and dowsing rods, clairvoyance, cards, and tea leaves—all regarded as internal because their results depend upon sensory and motor automatisms and mental impressions. The external forms are dependent upon inference from external facts. Dice and other forms of sortilege, augury and omens, and casual meetings and overheard words are all beyond the immediate control of the diviner.

What induces people to turn to fortune-telling? It is usually fear, hope, or desire, along with simple curiosity. There is fear of future events not going the way you would like; fear of enemies, known or unknown; fear of illness, accident, hunger. There is also hope for what you desire. Many people also use divination for advice—to make an assessment of a career move or relocation, for example. A simple, daily card layout can smooth decision making. Much also has to do with an age-old belief that certain people are truly gifted with the ability to see the future, and then there is the desire to make use of their gifts. When the Romany, or Gypsies, first appeared in Europe in the fourteenth and fifteenth centuries, they found that they were looked upon as natural owners of such gifts. Persecuted as they were, the Roma did not hesitate to trade on any credulity of local populaces and to charge money to "tell the future." Over the centuries they did go on to develop true gifts for divination in many different forms. Even today Gypsies are viewed as specialists in this field.

The reason divination, or fortune-telling, has survived for so long is that it gives results. If it did not, it would have died out long ago. Obviously, individual results vary. This is also a field that is wide open to fraud. Yet despite the charlatans, there are innumerable instances of people learning of coming events and finding that what was prophesied actually came to pass. Many believe that certain people are truly gifted with the ability to see the future and desire to make use of their gifts. Documentation exists with a variety of professional societies, such as the (British) Society for Psychical Research, the American Society for Psychical Research, and the Parapsychology Foundation of New York, as well as at a large number of colleges and universities including the Duke Parapsychology Laboratory in North Carolina, the University of Saskatchewan, the University of Leningrad, and the A. S. Popov Scientific Technical Society in Moscow. Records of Spiritualist churches and societies, of small home circles, and the evidence of tens of thousands of professional psychics and readers all lend credence to the fact that divination, fortune-telling, prophecy, or whatever label is applied, actually works.

Having said that, it must be emphasized that human life is not fatalistic. What is seen in "future readings," from astrological horoscopes to tarot-card spreads, is not written in stone. It is all no more than an indication of what is *likely* to happen, with the current forces at work around you, if nothing changes. But, of course, things do change, and it is within the power of the person whose fortune is being told to make change. If, from a reading, indications are that something negative is going to happen, then it behooves that individual to focus his or her attention on the turning events and ensure that the negative does *not* happen. Would this then show that the divination was incorrect, since it foretold one thing but now that has not come to pass? Not at all, for it foretold what was going to happen if things had continued as they were at the time of the reading. A later reading, taken during rapidly changing times, would have shown a different outcome.

Christianity has had a confused, and confusing, attitude toward divination. As mentioned, the Bible is replete with examples of its use by the likes of Joseph, Jacob, Saul, Samuel, the Apostles, the Magi, and Pilate's wife. Jesus foresaw his own death and resurrection. In 1 Corinthians 12 and 14 some verses promote divination and prophecy (for example, chapter 14, verse 31: "For ye may all prophesy one by one, that all may learn, and all may be comforted," and in verse 39: "Wherefore, brethren, covet to prophesy, and forbid not to speak with tongues.)" Yet despite this, many Christians condemn any form of divination.

Over the centuries the different forms of divination have acquired technical names. For example: divining by numbers is arithmancy, by using arrows is belomancy, from the entrails of animals is haruspicy, from the movements of mice is myomancy, and by the movements of straws placed on red-hot iron is sideromancy. The problem with most books and articles on divination is that they do little more than acquaint the technical name with the object used. From the above examples, most writings define myomancy as "divination from the movements of mice" and haruspicy as "divination from the entrails of animals." They fail to tell any more than this. *How* are the arrows of belomancy used? *What* is done with a finger ring in dactyliomancy? *How* does one "draw lots" in sortilege? In this encyclopedia, I have endeavored to give full explanations of all the various forms.

Along with those explanations, I have, where possible, cited references to that particular form of divination from a variety of sources. One problem that I found was the distinguishing of similar forms. For example: divination using or connected with water could cover dowsing, rhabdomancy, lecanomancy, hydromancy, hydatoscopy, and pegomancy. Water could be used for scrying—much like using a crystal ball—but even that could be broken down into whether the water used was rain water or water from a well or a fountain. Similarly, scrying (gazing into a reflective surface and seeing visions) could be crystallomancy, hydromancy (and from there to hydatoscopy and pegomancy, as mentioned), or spheromancy. The studying of entrails, which seemed popular in many cultures, covered the entrails from humans (anthropomancy), from animals (haruspication), and from fish (ichthyomancy)—all of these coming under the general heading of extispicy. Then they could be supplemented by the observation of sacrificed things (hieromancy) and the observation of the actions of the victim leading up to the sacrifice (hieroscopy).

There are more than four hundred separate articles in this book. After going through it carefully, the reader may be excused for thinking that virtually *anything* can be used as a tool for divination. And indeed it can. Basically, the item used—be it a mouse, a feather, a bird, or the track made by a wheel—is no more than a focal point for the diviner. There is a lot of psychism in divination, sometimes some extrasensory perception, but always a large dose of divine inspiration. Fortune-telling has been with humankind for millennia; it is unlikely to go away. Perhaps, with the aid of this book, you can study an aspect of it and enjoy it.

ACKNOWLEDGMENTS

Many thanks go to my agent, Agnes Birnbaum, and to Martin Connors, Roger Jänecke, and Christa Gainor of Visible Ink Press.

My thanks also go to editor Susan Salter, proofreader Peggy Daniels, indexer Lawrence Baker, photo digitizer Robert Huffman, cover and page designer Mary Claire Krzewinski, typesetter Marco Di Vita of the Graphix Group, and Janet Bord of Fortean Picture Library.

Although my own personal library was able to furnish most of the research material, I would be remiss if I did not acknowledge the part that the World Wide Web now plays in bringing material straight to the writer's computer. Hours of laborious study are cut short with the click of a few keys.

Finally, my deepest thanks to my wife, Tara, for her continual encouragement, constructive criticism, and continuous support over a period of concentrated writing.

A

Abacomancy

Foretelling the future by observing patterns of dust. The way the dust is distributed, disturbed, or blown into layers is interpreted much as are the patterns left by tea leaves in a teacup, in **tasseography.** Sometimes the cremated ashes of the recently deceased were used instead of dust, sprinkled onto a silver tray.

Aberfan

The Aberfan tragedy took place in Wales at 9:15 a.m. on October 20, 1966. On that date a half-million-ton mountain of coal waste, saturated by days of unrelenting rain, slid down and buried the little Welsh village, covering dozens of houses as well as Pantglas Junior School. Sixteen adults and 128 schoolchildren died. There were so many reports of **dreams** prior to the tragedy, giving great details, that London psychiatrist J. C. Barker suggested a survey be conducted.

Many of the reported **premonitions** were rejected for lack of authenticating evidence, or because they were too vague, but at least thirty-six **prophetic** dreams could be fully documented and confirmed, together with twenty-four non-dream premonitions. As a result of this, the **British Premonitions Bureau** was established in 1966. The following year, the New York **Central Premonitions Registry** was also founded.

In Plymouth, on England's south coast, a female **psychic,** Mrs. C. Milden, was at a spiritualist meeting when she saw the avalanche of coal slag pour down the mountainside onto the village. A man in Yorkshire saw dozens of black horses pulling black hearses down a hill. Another person dreamed of young children's screams coming from a mountain of coal slag. Nine-year-old Eryl Jones of Aberfan told her mother that she had dreamed there was no school—literally no school—that day, but she went off to school anyway and died.

Sybil Brown, of Brighton, had a dream of a child screaming with fear, trapped in a telephone booth as a "black, billowing mass" advanced. One woman dreamed of a mountain flowing downward and a child running away screaming. An elderly man dreamed of the letters ABERFAN spelled out in bright light, though he had never before heard of the name or the village. A London woman dreamed that the walls of her bedroom were caving in. A woman dreamed of Welsh children, all dressed in national costume, ascending to heaven. A young man in Kent woke up two days before the event with a vague sense of tragedy that he couldn't get rid of. He told a female coworker that something terrible, connected with death, was going to happen that Friday. Another man, Alexander Venn, a retired Cunard Lines employee living in the southwest of England, told his wife the same thing, and he kept thinking of coal dust. A woman had a dream of suffocating in "deep blackness." This was probably one of the most large-scale documentations of premonitions, certainly in recent times.

Sources:

Holroyd, Stuart. *The Supernatural: Dream Worlds*. London: Aldus Books, 1976.
Mysteries of the Unknown: Psychic Powers. Alexandria, VA: Time-Life Books, 1987.

Abrams, Albert (1863–1924)

Albert Abrams was born into a wealthy family in San Francisco in 1863. Showing some brilliance, he qualified at medical school but was too young to receive his diploma. Consequently, he went to Europe where he studied extensively under some of the greatest scientists of the time. He quickly took an interest in the newly developing field of modern physics and, later, attempted to reconcile this to the laws of biology.

Returning to San Francisco, Abrams rapidly made a name for himself, earning an international reputation and making many important contributions to the field of neurology. He became director of the medical department of California's Stanford University. He then became interested in what Pierre and Marie Curie were doing in France with their discovery of radium. Abrams wondered about applying this to the treatment of his patients, and this set him off on a line of research that was to last until his death in 1924. It laid the foundation for what was initially labeled ERA, or the electronic reactions of Abrams. It later became better known as radionics.

It was a middle-aged man who had a chronic ulcer, or *epithelioma*, on his lip who sparked Abrams's exploration. When Abrams routinely tapped the man's stomach, he found that in one area there was a very dull rather than a hollow sound. Strangely, this only happened when the man was facing to the west. Abrams guessed that this phenomenon was somehow connected to the earth's magnetic field. He checked other cancer patients and found similar reactions, bringing him to the conclusion that the diseased tissue sent out some kind of radiation that affected certain groups of nerve cells, but only when the patient faced west. More than that, he found that different diseases offered different sounds produced by muscular contractions affected by the nerve fibers. He determined that the different sounds, and the areas from which they were emitted, could be used as a diagnostic tool.

Over the years Abrams formulated his theories. He found that a glass vial holding a diseased tissue, when held against a healthy person, would cause the same sound effects found in a diseased patient. He later found that just the use of a blood spot would also trigger the same results. From his experimenting Abrams reached the conclusion that the basis of disease was electronic rather than cellular and set out to construct equipment that could measure the radiations. This was based on the idea of receiving radio waves. With his equipment, he hoped to not only diagnose but also to treat abnormal radiations.

Based on a variable resistance box, Abrams constructed what he termed *reflexophones* for diagnosing, and *oscilloclasts* for treating. They became better known as "black boxes." With these, Abrams performed some amazing diagnoses and treatments. Upton Sinclair, the novelist, referred to his laboratory as a "House of Wonders."

In 1924 the British Medical Association formed a committee to investigate Abrams's work. The result was not only an endorsement of his work but also—as is typical with the monopoly of the medical profession—a condemnation of those who used his black boxes! Abrams died that same year, but his researches were taken up by Ruth Beymer Drown, who had been Abrams's secretary, and later by George de la Warr in England.

Sources:

Kingston, Jeremy. *The Supernatural: Healing without Medicine*. London: Aldus Books, 1975.
Shepard, Leslie A. (ed.). *Encyclopedia of Occultism & Parapsychology*. New York: Avon, 1978.
Wethered, Vernon D. *An Introduction to Medical Radiesthesia & Radionics*. London: C .W. Daniel, 1962.
Wethered, Vernon D. *The Practice of Medical Radiesthesia*. London: C. W. Daniel, 1967.

ACTIONS *see* **Hieroscopy**

Acultomancy

Divination using needles. Needles are a popular divination tool among the **Gypsies** of the British Isles, and are also used by others. One method is to take twenty-one new needles and place them in a saucer or shallow dish. **Water** is poured very slowly into the dish. As the dish fills, the needles move about. Some of them will invariably turn to lie across others. This is said to indicate enemies: the number of crossed needles shows the number of enemies at work against you. One needle crossing two (or more) others indicates a strong enemy who is capable of working against you time and again.

If the vast majority of needles remains straight and none, or very few, cross any others, it indicates that you have great inner strength and psychic defenses, and that few can harm you magically.

Another way to use a needle for divination is to utilize it as a **pendulum,** by threading it and then holding the thread so that the needle is suspended off the surface of the table. Asking questions of the needle will cause it to swing, indicating the answers. (see **Radiesthesia** for full details of this method.)

If you have a number of suitors and wish to find which one is best for you, there is a ritual that may be done at night when the **moon** is shining. Draw a large circle on a sheet of paper and write the names of your admirers anywhere within the circumference. Take up the paper in your left hand, and hold a needle in your right hand. Facing the moon, close your eyes and stab the needle into the paper. The name closest to the hole made by the needle is the one who is best for you. If the hole actually passes through the name—so that the moonlight flows through the hole and, therefore, through the name—then that person will be the very best match for you.

Adams, Evangeline (1865–1932)

Evangeline Adams (whose married name was Mrs. George E. Jordan) became one of America's most famous **astrologers.** She claimed to be descended from John Quincy Adams. Born in Boston, at age thirty-four she moved to New York. There Adams initially took a room in the Windsor Hotel on Fifth Avenue. She didn't stay long, however, telling proprietor Warren F. Leland that, after studying his natal chart, she knew the place to be "under one of the worst possible combinations of planets." The very next day a fire broke out in the hotel, burning it to the ground and killing the proprietor's daughter and other members of his family. Leland gave his account to the newspapers and they all headlined the story of Adams's **prediction.** Her name as an astrologer was made overnight.

Adams rented a studio over Carnegie Hall and quickly found herself with a long list of famous clients: movie stars, politicians, financiers, and others. They included Mary Pickford, Caruso, and J. P. Morgan. It is said that she was even visited by England's King Edward VII. Despite this, in 1914 she was prosecuted for **fortunetelling.** She refused to pay a fine and went to trial, loaded down with astrological reference books. The judge was so impressed with her interpretation of the birth chart of someone completely unknown to her (who turned out to be the judge's son) that he dismissed the case. He said, "The defendant raises astrology to the dignity of an exact science."

On April 23, 1930, Adams started her own astrology radio show, which gained a following of many thousands. She received over 150,000 requests for astrological charts. On the show the following year, 1931, she predicted that the United States would be at war in 1942. In 1932 she also predicted her own death later that year. When she did die that November, thousands of people, including many of the famous, went to see her body lying in state at Carnegie Hall.

Sources:

Cavendish, Richard (ed.). *Encyclopedia of the Unexplained*. London: Routledge & Kegan Paul, 1974.

Fishley, Margaret. *The Supernatural*. London: Aldus, 1976.

MacNeice, Louis. *Astrology*. Garden City, NY: Doubleday, 1964.

Aeromancy

Observation of atmospheric changes is an ages-old method of foretelling the future. With the approach of a storm, in seventeenth-century London, many soothsayers

Observation of atmospheric changes, or aeromancy, is an age-old method of foretelling the future. ***Fortean Picture Library.***

claimed to have seen the coming death of Oliver Cromwell. A violent thunderstorm shook the city on the night of September 3, 1658, and that was the night Cromwell died. He was suffering from malaria, but even so, his death was unexpected. Many claimed that the sudden storm was a presage of the event. The appearance of a comet, or shooting star (see **meteoromancy**), was generally believed to foretell the coming death of some great personage.

Aeromancy is a term often used for weather **prediction,** which is still practiced regularly in many areas of the United States. It is said that when tall grass is bone dry first thing in the morning it means that there will be rain before evening. However, what seems contrary to this is the belief that a very heavy dew in the morning also means there will be rain before evening. **Dogs** eating grass, rabbits playing in the road, and **cats** sneezing and licking their fur against the grain are all signs of coming rain. When a **horse** suddenly stops grazing and rubs itself against a tree or fence post, it's a sign of a coming cloudburst.

In some areas of Missouri and Arkansas it is believed that the first frost will come six weeks after the katydids start singing. Others claim as long as twelve weeks.

Æsculapius, Greek demigod of healing. ***Fortean Picture Library.***

Whatever the length of time, there is general agreement that there is a correlation between the first singing of the katydids and the first frost. Another old belief is that the number of fogs that are experienced in August is equal to the number of heavy snows that are to be expected in the coming winter. It is also said that the number of days the first snow remains on the ground indicates the total number of snows to be expected that winter.

Aeromancy also covers divination by the shape of clouds. Studying clouds was known to **Celtic shamans** as *neladoracht*. Much as vague shapes formed by tea leaves (see-**Tasseography**) can be indicators of coming events, so can the shapes formed by clouds. "Mares' tails" and "mackerel" skies may have specific meanings to some people, but it is the ever-changing shapes of cumulus clouds that lend themselves more to prognostication. For example, a cloud formed like a castle is a prediction of high office and excellent reputation to come for the observer. The shape of a fist is a warning to guard against impulsive actions. A lamb shape suggests new ideas are being born, with changes to come. A cloud shaped like a rabbit is a sign of timidity and a call for more assertiveness.

François de la Tour Blanche stated that thunder and lightning were "concerned with auguries, and the aspect of the sky and the planets belong to the science of astrology." He felt that aeromancy was fortune-telling by means of specters that are made to appear in the air, and he included images that seemed to be projected onto clouds as if by a magic lantern.

Sources:

Buckland, Raymond. *Secrets of Gypsy Fortunetelling*. St. Paul, MN: Llewellyn, 1988.
Randolph, Vance *Ozark Superstitions*. New York: Dover, 1964.
Shepard, Leslie A. (ed.). *Encyclopedia of Occultism & Parapsychology*. New York: Avon, 1978.

ÆSCULAPIUS

Also known as Asklepios (from the Greek), Æsculapius was the patron deity of physicians. He was the son of Apollo and Coronis. He was not only able to heal the sick but also to bring the dead back to life. It was for this reason that Zeus finally destroyed him with a thunderbolt, in case humankind should learn to evade death. Those who visited the Temple of Æsculapius in Epidaurus, Greece, would sleep in order to learn, in their **dreams,** the means of recovering their health. Eventually anyone could sleep in any of the temples dedicated to him and **divine** their cure through their dreams.

Sources:
Kaster, Joseph. *Putnam's Concise Mythological Dictionary*. New York: G. P. Putnam's, 1963.
Rose, H. J. *Religion in Greece and Rome*. New York: Harper & Row, 1959.

African Divination

Traditionally African spirituality is embodied in everyday life, with the connection between nature and spirituality defining life for the people. This is seen in many of the divination methods employed across the continent, and there is a very wide diversity of such methods employed there. For example, among the 11.5 million people in the ten provinces of Cameroon, divination methods include using **shells,** bones, seed pods, palm kernels, antelope and elephant dung, **bird** flight, the tracks of crabs, examination of **entrails,** and more.

The most popular form of divination in Africa seems to be **sortilege.** Casting bones is common, as is use of cowry and other shells, eggs, and kola nuts. The Yoruba, for example, will cast sixteen strings of palm kernels, the Nupe use eight strings of berries, the Yukun use six strings of calabash disks. A form of **Ifa** divination is based on the multiple permutations obtained from the manipulation of sixteen palm kernels, the interpretations based on stories from local mythology. The Menemo and the Ntim use palm wine, pouring it into a large shell and floating millet seeds on the surface. The Azande use leafy branches stuck into termite holes, interpreting by the amount of stripping done by the insects. The Bimbia cast pebbles and shells, the Bakweri gaze into heated palm oil, the Widekum cast seed pods, the Banso split kola nuts and cast them, and the Mambila use the hard fruits of the wild banana together with sixteen cowry shells. The Venda use four marked pieces of ivory; they also use divining bowls, as do the Karanga of Zimbabwe. Although many diviners refer to their tools as "bones," they are not necessarily actual bones. They might be stones, shells, nuts, pieces of wood, or any combination of these. The diviner usually "breathes his spirit" into his bones before using them by holding them in his cupped hands and blowing softly on them, asking the spirits to guide them as they are used.

Among the Azande, when searching for the truth following an accusation, two chickens would be fed poison. If the first chicken died, that indicated the charge was true; if it lived, that indicated a falsehood. In the event of the first chicken dying, the second chicken received poison but with the interpretation reversed: if the accusation was true then the chicken would live and, if false, it would die. This double poisoning would give a confirmation or denial of the charge.

Most diviners are male, though not all. Usually a diviner has an assistant who is much like an apprentice, watching and learning the various methods used. It is usually two to three years before such an assistant is allowed to do any divining him or herself. Secret societies of diviners (such as the *mbir* of the Kakas) are found across the continent, and membership is closely guarded. It is a great honor for an apprentice to be made a member.

Zulu oracle in South Africa. *Klaus Aarsleff/Fortean Picture Library.*

Good examples of divination types are those of the Zulus, Dogon, Ashanti, Venda, Masai, Yoruba, and the Kaka people of the Tikar tribe of Cameroon. Rather than attempt the impossible of describing all the many and varied methods found throughout the continent of Africa, here are the details of a selective representation.

NgáM, Or Tikar Spider Divination

This is practiced in the northeastern section of the Bamenda Province in southwestern Cameroon. As its name implies, it utilizes the actions of a relative of the trapdoor **spider.** The *Heteroscodra crassipes* is a very large, black earth spider, four to six inches in length with a three-inch-long body. It is sometimes confused with the tarantula, but although its bite is painful it is rarely fatal. The Kaka people believe that this spider, because it nests in the ground, possesses wisdom obtained from the earth deities.

The head man of a village is usually the owner of the spider, using it for daily divination to ascertain the will of the gods. All the villagers will gather at the head man's hut each morning to observe the daily ritual. The rite, and divination, is actually performed by the *nkú-ngám* or diviner (ngám means "divination," while ngàm means "spider"). He has a set of "**cards**" made from leaves of the African plum tree (*Pachylobus edulis*). There may be as many as two hundred of them, each with different signs and symbols marked on them by cutting or burning. These cards have been placed in a large calabash pot. A lid is on the pot, but the bottom of it is broken and placed over the home of the earth spider, the hole in the pot allowing the spider access to the leaves. When the lid is removed in the morning, the diviner will see how the cards have been disturbed and rearranged by the spider. Interpreting these movements constitutes the divination.

When not in use, the cards are kept in a special wooden container that is kept hanging from his bed or is carried slung over his shoulder. The container itself is wrapped in a piece of fur, usually from the civet cat. The cards may also be read at any time by the diviner throwing them down on the piece of fur in a certain way, or even having a spider move them around on the fur.

Venda Divination

The Venda are found in Zimbabwe and the Transvaal area of South Africa. Their main method of divination is by using a bowl that has been made especially for the purpose. The rim of the bowl is decorated with pictures representing god, goddess, home, danger, warnings, movement, sacrifice, injury, caution, and other qualities and objects. In the center of the bowl is a carved representation of a cowry shell, as a connection to the goddess.

The diviner casts five bones—knuckle bones, stones, or carved pieces of wood—into the bowl. Each of the bones represents something different, which might be positive or negative. Interpretation is based on the proximity of the bone to the symbols around the edge, and the relationship to the central cowry shell. The relationship of each stone to its neighbors is also of importance. There are a large number of interpretations that can come from any one throw.

Venda tablets are also used by these people. These may be made of wood, bone, ivory, clay, or rock. They are about an inch to an inch and a half in length and about three-quarters of an inch wide. The thickness varies. Each bears a particular symbol on one side, with the other side blank.

There are only four such tablets. One represents the Father, an Old Man, or Male/masculine. It also ties in with rain, semen, and the element of **water.** The second tablet is the feminine one: Woman/feminine, Mother, Old Woman, or Married Woman. This is associated with the element of earth, nurturing, and home life. It can also indicate caution. The third tablet is Youth, Son, or Unmarried Man, and is associated with the element of **fire.** It indicates rashness, but also boyhood, health, and energy. It shows a need for restraint and for further learning. The fourth tablet is Spirituality, Single Woman, or Young Girl. It is the element of air, innocence, luck, and artistic talent.

These four tablets, with their faces and plain backs, can give up to sixteen combinations: each one of the four tablets (together with three blanks), Father-Mother, Father-Daughter, Father-Son, Father-Mother-Daughter, Father-Mother-Son, Father-Mother-Daughter-Son, Father-Daughter-Son, Mother-Daughter, Mother-Son, Mother-Daughter-Son, Daughter-Son, and All Blank Sides up (indicating a definite negative).

Yoruba Seashell Divination

The coastal area of western Africa is home to the Yoruba people, which actually includes Yoruba, Oyo, and Ibadan. Seven million people speak the Yoruba language. They worship a large number of anthropomorphic deities known as the Orishas. These are closely connected to nature and have been compared to the ancient Greek deities. There are more than four hundred myths and legends connected with the deities. There is a belief in a division of light and dark, or good versus evil.

The ancient city of Ife, or Ilé-Ifé, used to be the holy city of the region. In the twelfth century it was ruled by a divine king, Ifa, who had lesser kings or chiefs known as Obas beneath him. Today there are still Obas, though their position is purely ceremonial. Ifa was a man-god who had come to Earth to put the world right. His oracle was to be used in giving guidance and helping humankind in times of trouble.

The Ife deities feature in the Yoruba seashell divination system, which has been adopted, and adapted, in many of Nigeria's neighboring countries. The divination is done on a board, known as the "Table of Ifa," usually decorated with figures of gods and animals around its outer edge. Ifa is a spirit identified with the god Orun-mila, who directed the creation of the earth. The board is sprinkled till the center is covered with white sand, or a fine white powder. Cowry shells or nuts are used for the casting. When cast, the shells may land on their faces, with the smooth, rounded side uppermost, or on their backs with the smoothly serrated, vulva-like openings (known as the "mouth") upward. To make it easier for the shell to lay flat when on its back, many diviners will break open the thin surface of the rounded side and make what is known as an "eye" there.

Combinations of four and sixteen shells are used. They are shaken in the hands and cast into the circle. The number of "mouths" is counted. The original casting was done with palm nuts and tied in with the myth of Fa, who had sixteen eyes. Fa lived on a palm tree in the sky, from the height of which he was able to see all that went on in the world. Every morning God's son, Legba, climbed the tree to open Fa's eyes. Fa didn't want to speak out loud of what he had seen, so he placed nuts in Legba's hands to indicate how many of his eyes should be opened. If men use the nuts (now shells) correctly, they may open all of Fa's eyes to see the future.

Zulu Divination

There are approximately four million Zulu people, living along the east coast of South Africa. Myths tell how the first Zulus were women from another planet.

There are several categories of divination among the Zulu. A sorcerer, who may be male or female, is known as a *Sanusis*. A healer is a *Znyanga Zokwelapha* or a *Znyanga Zemithi*. A **weather** worker is a *Znyanga Zezulu*, and a diviner is a *Sangoma*. A Sangoma is usually female, though not always. All begin as apprentices.

The Zulu bones divination system used by most Sangomas is worked with a set of oracle bones, which are actual bones plus other objects like hoof tips, teeth, or shells. They are usually collected together over a period of time, being chosen especially for their size and shape and, in the case of bones and teeth, the particular animal they belong to and what it means to the Sangoma. The objects are usually collected in twos, a large one representing male and a smaller one representing female.

The objects have specific meanings when cast, usually two possible meanings depending upon which side faces upward. When all are thrown down together they will give a multifaceted life reading, with the elements of friends, lovers, finances, obstacles, and so on. They are usually cast into a circle drawn on the ground or onto a small mat of leather or cloth. Any piece that falls outside the area is discounted. The areas of the circle or mat have specific meanings to which the bones can relate.

Sources:

Buckland, Raymond and Kathleen Binger. *The Book of African Divination*. Rochester, VT: Destiny Books, 1992.

Evans-Pritchard, E .E. *Witchcraft, Oracles and Magic among the Azande*. Oxford: Oxford University Press, 1937.

Gebauer, Paul. *Spider Divination of the Cameroons*. Milwaukee, 1964.

Lystad, Robert A. *The Ashanti*. New Brunswick, NJ: Rutgers University Press, 1958.

Parrinder, Geoffrey. *African Mythology*. London: Paul Hamlyn, 1967.

Tutuola, Amos. *The Palm Wine Drinkard*. New York: Grove Press, 1953.

AILUROMANCY

People have been divining by the movement and actions of cats for centuries. This is known as Ailuromancy. Traditionally there is a connection between a cat and the **moon.** Many pagan goddesses were similarly linked to the moon. The Scandinavian Freya—associated both with the moon and with fertility—rode in a chariot pulled by cats. The **Roman** Diana was able to take the form of a cat. Bast was the sacred cat-headed goddess of **Ancient Egypt.** The cat is considered the bearer of souls of the dead in parts of the East, and in some places it is thought that, at death, a human soul will pass into the body of a cat.

Both white cats and black cats are considered lucky, dependent upon their actions. It is considered lucky simply to see a white cat, except in some parts of Britain where the reverse is true. A black cat needs to be either sitting to the right of the observer or moving from left to right to indicate good luck to come. If it moves from right to left, it is portending bad luck to come. Part of the fear of black cats comes from the Middle Ages belief that witches could turn themselves into cats (Diana, mentioned above, was regarded as a witch goddess). There was also the belief that the cat was a familiar of the devil and a servant to the witch.

A black cat should be stroked gently along its spine to bring out the good luck and brush away the bad. To carry a stray cat into the house is to bring bad luck in with it. If a cat sits and washes itself, licking "against the grain," it is a sign of a coming shower. In many areas, if the cat carries its young to higher ground it indicates that a flood or severe cloudburst is imminent. If the cat sits with its back to the fire it means frost is on the way. A sneezing cat near a bride can indicate a happy marriage to come. But under other circumstances the cat's **sneeze** means a storm is coming. In New England it is said that if a cat stares out of the window for a long time, it is a sign that it is looking for rain. On the coast of that area it is believed that a cat's pupils will be nearly closed at low tide but will dilate at high tide.

Sources:

Leach, Maria (ed.). *Funk & Wagnalls Standard Dictionary of Folklore, Mythology, and Legend*. San Francisco: Harper & Row, 1972.
Randolph, Vance. *Ozark Superstitions*. New York: Dover, 1964.

AIR ***see*** **Chaomancy; Eromancy**

Akashic Records

This is a Theosophical term for a "filing system" of records of all events that have ever taken place and all thought that has transpired and been impressed upon the *âkâsa*, or astral plane. This is not unlike Carl Jung's idea of the collective unconscious. Helena **Blavatsky** refers to the âkâsa as "the subtle, supersensuous spiritual essence that pervades all space; the primordial substance erroneously identified with Ether. But it is to Ether what Spirit is to Matter . . . the Universal Space in which lies inherent the eternal Ideation of the Universe." It is also referred to as the cosmic memory. Psychics may access this information and thereby see into the past and, possibly, the future, foretelling probable events to come. Blavatsky, Rudolf Steiner and **Edgar Cayce,** among others, have claimed to have obtained information from the records. Many psychics say that they access the records through trance, **astral projection, clairvoyance,** self-hypnosis, and similar methods.

The idea of a Book of Life, or a storehouse of life's recordings, is found with the Arabs, Assyrians, Babylonians, Hebrews, and Phoenicians, among others. Cayce described the repository of the Akashic Records as being like a huge library, situated in a temple on a hill. He said (Reading 294–19): "I am conscious of seeing an old man who hands me a large book, a record of the individual for whom I seek information." When delving into such a book he remarked, "We have conditions that might have been, that are, and *that may be* [author's italics]" (Reading 304–5).

Sources:

Blavatsky, Helena P. *The Theosophical Glossary*. London: Theosophical Publishing Society, 1892.
Langley, Noel. *Edgar Cayce on Reincarnation*. New York: Paperback Library, 1967.

Shepard, Leslie A. (ed.). *Encyclopedia of Occultism & Parapsychology*. New York: Avon, 1978.
Todeschi, Kevin J. *Edgar Cayce on the Akashic Records*. Virginia Beach, VA: A.R.E. Press, 1998.

ALECTROMANCY; ALECTORMANCY; ALECTRYOMANCY

This is a form of divination that was popular in **Rome** and was frequently used as a method of identifying robbers. It was done when the Sun or the **moon** was in Aries or Leo. The name comes from the **Greek** *alectruon* ("cock") and *manteia* ("divination").

Letters of the alphabet are placed in a large circle, with small piles of grain in front of each letter. An all-white cockerel, or occasionally a hen, would then be placed in the center of the circle. The letters where the cock pecks at the grain are gathered and then laid out to form words or names. They are not necessarily laid down in the same order in which they were chosen by the cock. It was assumed that the word/name might be in anagrammatical form. If a simple "Yes" or "No" would suffice, then just two piles of grain would be placed on the ground.

Jean Baptiste Belot (1640) described the method:

> He then who desires to know concerning some matter, whether it be a robbery, a larceny, or the name of a successor, must make upon a very smooth spot a circle which he will divide into as many parts as there are letters in the alphabet. This done he shall take grains of wheat and shall place them on each letter, beginning with A and so on continuing, while he says this verse: *Ecca enim veritatem, etc*. The wheat then being thus placed, let him take a young cock or cockerel, perfectly white, and cut its claws; then, having set down this cock, he must take care to watch upon which letters he eats the grain of corn, and, having noted or written these letters upon paper, he must gather them together and then will find the name that he desires to know.

Other sources say that, before it begins to peck at the grain, the cock must be forced to swallow its own claws, which have been cut off. It must also swallow a small parchment scroll, made of lambskin, on which are written certain words. In addition to the magical verse mentioned, the diviner should also repeat the two verses of the Psalms that fall exactly in the middle of the seventy-two verses.

A well-known case of the use of alectromancy was when the Roman emperor Valens Cæsar wanted to know the name of his successor. The divining was performed by the magician Iamblicus. The cock spelled out the letters THEOD. Valens assumed it was short for Theodorus and proceeded to kill anyone with that name, so they couldn't take over from him. On his death, in 378 CE, he was succeeded by Theodosius!

Sources:

Buckland, Raymond. *A Pocket Guide to the Supernatural*. New York: Ace Books, 1969.
Leach, Maria (ed.). *Funk & Wagnalls Standard Dictionary of Folklore, Mythology, and Legend*. San Francisco: Harper & Row, 1972

ALECTRYOMANCY ***see*** **Alectromancy**

Aleuromancy

It is from this form of divination that the idea of **Chinese** fortune cookies may have come. The word is from the Greek *aleuron*, meaning "flour." One method was simply to mix flour and **water** in a bowl and then swill it around and tip it out. The residue on the bowl's sides would then be interpreted by the diviner, the images and patterns being read much as in tea-leaf reading (see **Tasseography**). But the more detailed, and more common, method was to write basic statements on small slips of paper and then roll each in a ball of flour paste and to bake it. The resultant "cookies" were mixed nine separate times then distributed among the seekers. On breaking open the baked balls, they would read the papers and learn their fates.

ALOMANCY—varient of Halomancy, which ***see.***

Alphitomancy

From the Greek *alphito* meaning "barley," this is a form of divination that utilizes barley, or wheat, made into a cake. Reaction to eating the cake would show whether or not the person was innocent or guilty of any crime charged. Severe stomach upset was taken as a sign of guilt. Even just finding the cake to be distasteful was an indicator.

In a certain sacred wood, close to Lavinium, the purity of women was tested using this barley cake together with the services of a snake. At a particular time of the year, blindfolded young women were sent along the path to the woods carrying the alphitomancy cake. The women who were chaste had their cakes devoured by the serpent, leaving the others to bear their cakes on to the meeting with the priests.

The use of cakes in connection with the gods was common in ancient **Greece.** A twelve-knobbed cake was offered to Cronus, in Athens, every spring. Circular cakes topped with candles were offered to Hecate, being placed at crossroads for her. Cakes and honey were offered to Artemis, and barley cakes to Zeus in the Eleusinian mysteries in Athens. Cakes of dough would be offered to the deities of the harvest, Demeter and Persephone.

Sources:

Leach, Maria (ed.). *Funk & Wagnalls Standard Dictionary of Folklore, Mythology, and Legend*. San Francisco: Harper & Row, 1972

Alveromancy

Divination by sounds. The louder the sound; the more danger is implied. The nearer the sound; the sooner the happening. What the actual sound is may vary. A sudden, unexpected cry from a crow, for example, would become the sound to be used, and the following cries would be noted and interpreted.

AMBULOMANCY

Divination by walking, from the Latin *ambulare*, "to walk." This could involve a number of other forms of divination, depending upon what is observed while walking. It could also be the walking itself: the number of paces, length of stride, speed, ascent or descent, and so on.

AMERICAN SOCIETY FOR PSYCHICAL RESEARCH

The oldest psychical research organization in the United States, the A.S.P.R. was founded in Boston in 1885, by Sir William Fletcher Barrett (1845–1926) of the British **Society for Psychical Research.** Barrett was visiting the United States at the time. The initial directors were astronomer Professor Simon Newcombe, president; N. D. C. Hodges, secretary; with vice presidents professors Stanley Hall, George S. Fullerton, Edward C. Pickering, and Charles S. Minot. One of the founding members was the renowned Harvard psychologist and professor of philosophy, William James. The aims of the society were to investigate apparitions, hypnosis, mediumship, telepathy, and all other fields of parapsychology.

In 1887 Dr. Richard Hodgson, the British S.P.R's chief investigator, was sent to America to act as secretary to the A.S.P.R. He continued in this position until he suffered a fatal heart attack, while playing handball at the Boat Club in Boston, on December 20, 1905.

In 1889, due to financial problems, the society affiliated with its British counterpart, under Professor S. P. Langley's presidency. In 1905, on Hodgson's death, the society was dissolved but was reestablished the following year as a separate entity from the British S.P.R. Dr. James Harvey Hyslop (1854–1920) was then elected president and took over where Hodgson had left off, as chief investigator for the society.

On Hyslop's death in 1920 Dr. Walter Franklin Prince assumed the presidency and stayed there until he resigned five years later. The society has enjoyed active participation from a number of outstanding scientists and philosophers, among them the physicists Sir William Barrett and Sir Oliver Lodge. By 1940 Gardner Murphy had become a vice president, and he assumed the presidency in 1962. He initiated the first telepathic experiments through wireless, in Chicago and New Jersey. He also focused the research of the society on scientific experiments, especially in **Extrasensory perception** working with Dr. **J. B. Rhine,** and on altered states of consciousness and survival after death.

Today the American Society for Psychical Research is headquartered in New York in an historical landmark building and maintains one of the world's largest libraries of books on parapsychology.

Sources:

Guiley, Rosemary Ellen. *The Encyclopedia of Ghosts and Spirits*. New York: Facts on File, 1992.
Shepard, Leslie A. (ed.). *Encyclopedia of Occultism & Parapsychology*. New York: Avon, 1978.

American Society of Dowsers

Founded in 1961, this is a nonprofit corporation based in Vermont. Its aims are to disseminate information on all forms of **dowsing, radiesthesia, water** witching, etc., and to promote the use and acceptance of this form of divination. The society estimates that there are approximately 50,000 dowsers who regularly operate in the United States.

The American Society of Dowsers issues a seventy-two-page quarterly journal, *The American Dowser*. In 1984, out of 200 newsletters, periodicals, and journals reviewed by the Parapsychological Association of the American Association for the Advancement of Science, it was cited as the best special interest journal in the field of PSI. (*See* also **British Society of Dowsers.**)

Sources:

http://dowsers.new-hampshire.net/

Amniomancy

The membrane that sometimes envelopes the head of a newly born infant is called a caul. Amniomancy is the examination of this caul—usually by the delivering midwife—to determine the future fortunes of the child. The basic interpretation goes by the amount of the color red in the membrane. A vivid red suggests a full, active life of energy. A dull, leaden color would suggest a similarly dull, uninspired life, probably with many misfortunes along the way.

Amon; Amun; Ammon

Amon was the ram-headed, ancient **Egyptian** god of fertility and reproduction, originally one of eight gods of Khum in Middle Egypt. It was believed that Amon would speak through an **oracle,** and the oracle temple was at Oasis Siwa, in the Libyan desert. The oracle was consulted by Alexander the Great in 332 BCE. There were also Amon oracles at Napata and Meroe. Contact with the main oracle (the oracle to Zeus), at Dodona, was maintained by message-carrying doves.

Sources:

Larousse Encyclopedia of Mythology. London: Paul Hamlyn, 1965.

Wilkinson, Sir J. Gardner. *The Ancient Egyptians: Their Life and Customs*. New York: Crescent Books, 1988.

ANGEL URIEL *see* Onimancy

ANIMAL BEHAVIOR *see* Zoomancy

Anthomancy

Divination by the use of flowers. Different flowers would have different meanings, which might vary depending upon the geographical area, and their placement and happenstance would determine the interpretation of that meaning in relation to the observer. The colors of the flowers would also be significant. For example, red ties in with passion, sexual desire, and warmth; pink with creativity; orange with freedom and independence; yellow with cheerfulness; gold with self-confidence; green with balance, judgment, self-control; pale blue with calmness and relaxation; darker blue with abstinence and conscientiousness; purple with mysticism, purification, spirituality; brown with stability and security; black with the unconscious; white with enlightenment and purity.

Examples of the meaning of flowers are the following:

Chrysanthemum—longevity, contemplation.
Daisy—innocence.
Lady's mantle—nurturing, feminine qualities.
Lily—purity, forgetfulness.
Morning glory—death, rebirth.
Narcissus—good fortune, new beginnings, numbness.
Rose—love, desire.
Rosemary—friendship, faithfulness, remembrance.
Violet—purification, modesty, fidelity.

Sources:

Jay, Roni. *Sacred Flowers*. Hillsboro, OR: Beyond Words, 1997.
Smith, A. W. *A Gardener's Handbook of Plant Names, Their Meanings and Origins*. Mineola, NY: Dover, 1997.

Anthracomancy

Divination by the inspection of burning coals. Anthracite is a hard, glossy-surfaced coal that burns without much smoke. This is the type of divination that many can relate to, if they have grown up with coal fires rather than wood-fueled fires. Sitting and looking into the red-hot ashes of the burning coal opens a wonderland of images, from dragons in caves to fish, birds, humans, and anything one is capable of imagining. Diviners of old would follow this pattern, gazing into the embers to see what the future might hold or to find the answer to any question posed.

One of the joys of "fire-gazing" of this sort is that, within a short space of time, the ashes can collapse and reposition so that there are ever-changing scenes.

Anthropomancy

A very ancient form of divination using human **entrails.** When referring to sacrificial victims, it was sometimes called *splanchomancy*. Herodotus, the fifth-century BCE **Greek** author, said that Menelaus, detained in Egypt by contrary winds, sacrificed two children in this manner in order to determine his destiny. Heliogabalus was one known practitioner of this type of divination as part of his worship of Baal. Originally called Varius Avitus (and known by the Greeks as Elagabalus), this Roman emperor (218–222 CE) was killed by the imperial guard for deviant and perverse practices.

In ancient Rome, Julian the Apostate (331–363 CE) has been described as "the last champion of a dying polytheism." His creed was a curious mixture of active polytheism combined with the emotional appeal of the mysteries. It is said that, in pursuit of magical knowledge, he caused a large number of children to be sacrificed so that he might consult and interpret the movements in their entrails. This he did at night, in the light of a full **moon.** One report has it that, on his last expedition, he shut himself in the Temple of the Moon, at Carra in Mesopotamia, and performed a ritual after which he emerged and sealed the temple doors. When he was later killed by the Persians, the doors to the temple were opened and the body of a woman was disclosed, hanging by her hair with her entrails torn out.

Both Diodorus Siculus and Tacitus mention a Druidic custom of divining with the entrails of sacrificed victims. Tacitus says: "The Druids consult the gods in the palpitating entrails of men" According to Spence, Strabo describes how they would stab a man in the back with a sword and then observe his convulsive movements and divine from those. Diodorus also mentions this and says that they augured from the posture in which the victim fell, from his contortions, and from the direction in which the spilled blood flowed away from the body (**hæmatomancy**).

Sources:

Encyclopedia Britannica. Chicago: William Benton, 1964.
Shepard, Leslie A. (ed.). *Encyclopedia of Occultism & Parapsychology*. New York: Avon, 1978.
Spence, Lewis. *The Magic Arts in Celtic Britain*. London: Rider, 1945.

ANTHROPOSCOPY ***see*** **Physiognomancy**

Apantomancy

Apantomancy is **divining** by whatever happens to come to hand—any objects that happen to present themselves. It can also include any unexpected happening. A chance meeting with a chimney sweep, for example, could be taken as indicative of some future event, as could opening a drawer and unexpectedly seeing a magnifying glass. (The **augurs** of ancient Rome would include such things as the fall of a stick in a temple, the squeak of a mouse, stumbling, or **sneezing.**) The way in which these objects and people are interpreted would depend entirely on the diviner. In the examples just given, if the diviner were familiar with **dream** interpretation, he or she might associate the chimney sweep with good luck to come and with the acquisition of useful knowledge, acquired bit by bit. The magnifying glass would be associated with the prospect of overextending yourself financially.

The actual interpretation, therefore, depends entirely upon the background of the diviner. It might be tied in with dreams, **tea leaves, colors,** actions, sounds, or anything else.

A branch of apantomancy especially considers chance encounters with animals. It is said to be especially fortunate to meet a black cat, hedgehog, goat, white horse, brown mouse, white rat, squirrel, flock of sheep, swallow, robin, dove, wren, kingfisher, owl, spider, or ladybug.

Sources:

Buckland, Raymond. *Gypsy Dream Dictionary*. St. Paul, MN: Llewellyn, 1999.
Smith, Christine. *The Book of Divination*. London: Rider, n.d.

Temple of Apollo in Delphi, Greece. ***Paul Broadhurst/Fortean Picture Library.***

Apollo

The Greek god associated with the wisdom of the oracles. He was also called Phœbus Apollo, from his maternal grandmother. He had many functions besides those connected with divination and **prophesy,** being associated especially with healing, light, music, and song, also with youth, protection from evil, protection of flocks and herds, alchemy, and other subjects.

Apollo intended to erect his first oracular temple at Bœotia but was dissuaded by Telphusa (variously also called Delphusa and Thelpusa), the local undine, and instead he built it farther north at Crisa. There was an ancient oracle to Gæa already at that place, guarded by a female dragon named Python. Apollo slew the dragon and went ahead and built his own shrine there. This became the well-known Oracle of Delphi with the diviners known as **Pythia.**

In looking for someone to administer his new temple, Apollo spied some Cretan sailors passing in their ship. He appeared to them in the form of a dolphin and conjured great winds to drive their ship ashore at the site of the temple. There he revealed himself to them. Since he had first appeared as a dolphin, they called him

Apollo Delphinius (the Greek word for dolphin), and the site of the oracular temple became known as Delphi.

A second oracular temple was built at the foot of Mount Cynthus. It is said that when the Persians passed by on their way to attack the Greeks, they left expensive gifts to Apollo and left the temple intact. Other oracles were in Asia Minor at Thymbra, Clarus, Grynia and Didymus, and all over Greece. Most famous were the Delphi and Cynthus ones mentioned, plus those at Tygera and Bœoita.

At Delphi, the Pythia would sit on a three-legged chair called a **tripod.** This was positioned in a deep cavern from which came what have been termed "prophetic vapors." Under Apollo's influence, the Pythia would pass into a trance state and begin to utter words and phrases that were then interpreted by the priesthood of the Delphi temple.

Apollo was the son of Zeus and Leto and, in the words of Edward E. Barthell, was hailed as "the most glorious of all of the sons of Zeus." He was a twin of Artemis and father of Orpheus, Asklepios, and Aristæus. His loves included Coronis, Psamathe, Clymene, Calliope, and Cyrene.

There was an instance when Hercules came to seek purification at the Oracle at Delphi for having murdered Iphitus. Apparently the Pythia remained silent. This so incensed Hercules that he seized the tripod, and Apollo had to fight with him to get it back. The struggle was finally resolved by the intervention of Zeus.

Sources:

Barthell, Edward E. Jr. *Gods and Goddesses of Ancient Greece*. Coral Gables, FL: University of Miami Press, 1971.

Guirand, Félix. *Greek Mythology*. Paul London, 1963.

APOLLO, TEMPLE OF *see* Apollo

Apollonius of Tyana

Apollonius of Tyana was born in Cappadocia, Asia Minor, c. 4 BCE. He was educated at Tarsus and at the Temple of Æsculapius, at Ægae. He was a neo-Pythagorean sage who gave away everything he owned to live by wandering from temple to temple, healing the sick, preaching, and giving advice as a **fortune-teller.** Most of what is known about Apollonius comes from a biography written, at the behest of the empress Julia Doman (second wife of Septimius Severus), by Philostratus the rhetorician. The biography was written about 200 CE and is loosely based on the work of Apollonius's disciple Damis, itself a dubious work. Philostratus's biography was aimed to please the empress rather than to present a true picture of the sage, but its appearance did lead to a certain veneration of Apollonius by the devout pagans of the later Roman Empire.

Of the reported deeds of Apollonius, one of the most notable was when he was said to have warned the people of Ephesus of the coming of a serious plague. They took no notice of his warnings until the plague was actually upon them, then they asked what they should do. He told them to stone to death a beggar who, he claimed, was the cause of the plague. The citizens did that, to the point where the unfortunate man was buried beneath a pile of stones. When these were later removed, there was only the dead body of a black dog to be found but the pestilence was gone. There were many other stories told of Apollonius's **clairvoyant** and magical powers.

Sources:

Encyclopedia Britannica. Chicago: William Benton, 1964.

Headon, Deirdre (ed.). *Quest for the Unknown—Charting the Future*. Pleasantville, NY: Reader's Digest, 1992.

Mead, George R. S. *Apollonius of Tyana—the Philosopher-Reformed of the First Century AD*. London: Theosophical Publishing House, 1901.

D'ARC, JEANNE (1412–1431)

At Joan of Arc's trial, judgment was to be based on seventy different points, including charges that she was a diviner, prophetess, **sorceress,** witch, and conjurer of evil spirits. Eventually these charges were dropped to twelve. Her judges were of the opinion that her visions were worthless and denied her the gift of **prophecy.**

In the countryside of Domremy, France, she had been known as Jeanette, with the surname of Arc or Romée. (She's also mentioned in contemporary documents as Jeanne, commonly called *la Poucelle*, the Maid.) Jeanne, or Jeanette, was born on January 6, 1412, to Jacques d'Arc and Isabelle de Vouthon, two devout Catholics. She had two brothers, Pierre and Jean du Lys. Her father owned **horses** and cattle and was the head man of his village of Domremy. Jeanne was very pious and, while the other girls her age were dancing, she chose to attend church.

When she was thirteen, Jeanne was in her father's garden when she heard a voice she believed came from God. During the next five years she heard voices two or three times a week and was able to distinguish those of Saints Catherine, Margaret, and Michael. They even appeared to her, wearing crowns. Jeanne determined to remain a virgin and lead a godly life.

The Hundred Years War between France and England, over who should rule France, was in full swing. The dauphin Charles, son of Charles VI, battled the English who had control of large portions of the country. Jeanne's voices told her to help the dauphin to be crowned King of France. In May 1428, about twelve miles from Domremy, Robert de Baudricourt, commandant at Vaucouleurs, was approached by Jeanne who was accompanied by Durand Lassois, a relative on her mother's side. She told Baudricourt that she had been sent by God to place the dauphin on the throne, and she would like to speak with him. The commandant sent her home again.

In July 1428 the village of Domremy was threatened by the English, and the inhabitants retreated to Neufchâteau. It was October before they were able to return, only to find the village burned to the ground. The English, meanwhile, had laid siege to Orléans. When news of this reached Domremy, Jeanne again set out to see the dauphin, and again, at Vaucouleurs, she encountered Robert de Baudricourt. She also met a young squire, Jean de Metz, in whom she confided. He lent her men's clothes. Baudricourt finally authorized her departure for Chinon, where Charles had his court. The people of Vaucouleurs bought her a horse, and she was given a sword.

Joan of Arc before the dauphin. *Fortean Picture Library.*

Louis de Bourbon, count of Vendôme, presented Jeanne to the dauphin, who talked with her for two hours. According to her confessor, Jean Pasquerel, Jeanne told the dauphin, "I am God's messenger, sent to tell you that you are the true heir to France and the king's son." Charles had her interrogated by a commission, presided over by the archbishop of Riems. They found her honest and ruled in her favor. Jeanne then assured Charles that she would raise the siege of Orléans and have him crowned.

In a suit of white, Jeanne, accompanied by Gilles de Rais, led 4,000 men and entered Orléans on the night of April 28. On May 5 they stormed the bastille and captured the Tourelles. On May 8 was held the first thanksgiving procession, the origin of what has become the great Festival of Orléans. Jeanne went on to Troy and then Reims by July 14. Two days later Charles was crowned King Charles VII of France, with Jeanne standing beside him. On December 29, 1429, she was ennobled and her village exempt from taxation.

The following May, Jeanne attempted to raise the siege of Compiègne. She and her forces made a sortie against the Burgundian camp, but Jeanne got cut off and was taken prisoner by the Duke of Burgundy, an English ally. He handed her over to the Bishop of Beauvais, also an English ally. On January 3, 1431, Jeanne was passed on to Pierre Cauchon, bishop of Beauvais, an ambitious man who hoped to obtain the vacant see of Rouen. Jeanne was to be tried by tribunal, which had been selected by Cauchon and consisted of ten Burgundian theologians, twenty-two canons of Rouen (all in the hands of the English), and some monks of different orders. Interrogation began on February 21. Judgment was to be based on seventy different points, including charges that Jeanne was a diviner, prophetess, sorceress, witch, and conjurer of evil spirits. Eventually these charges were dropped to twleve. Her judges were of the opinion that her visions were worthless and denied her the gift of prophecy. They censured her for dressing in masculine clothing and for "sinful pride" and believing that she was responsible only to God and not to the church, which the judges represented; this last was the charge that most incensed her accusers.

On May 23 Jeanne was taken to the cemetery of Saint-Ouen and sentenced to be burned at the pyre unless she submitted. Tired and worn out, she signed what was presented to her and was returned to her cell to serve life imprisonment. A woman's dress was given to her, but she either did not put it on or else she later returned to her men's clothing, for on May 27 Cauchon found Jeanne so dressed and declared her to have relapsed. He handed her over to the English secular arm. On May 30 Jeanne was made to appear in the Old Market Square of Rouen, though she had again been dressed as a woman. There she was burned for being a relapsed heretic.

It has been said that throughout Jeanne d'Arc's capture and imprisonment, Charles made no attempt to assist her or obtain her release. In fact, on December 15, 1430, hearing the news that she had fallen into the hands of the Duke of Burgundy, Charles sent an embassy to Philippe le Bon saying that if there was nothing that could be offered to set Jeanne free, then he, Charles, would exact vengeance for her upon Philippe's men that he held captive. There is correspondence that states, "The English wished to burn her (Jeanne) as a heretic, in spite of the Dauphin of France who tried to bring threatening forces against the English." But Charles's attempts seemed half-hearted. Finally, in 1450, he instituted a preliminary inquiry into Jeanne's trial and execution, but it was not fully followed through. It was not until June 16, 1456, that the judgment was annulled by Pope Calixtus III. Jeanne was finally beatified in 1909 and then canonized by Pope Benedict XV, in 1920.

Sources:

Buckland, Raymond. *The Witch Book: The Encyclopedia of Witchcraft, Wicca, and Neo-paganism*. Detroit: Visible Ink Press, 2002.

Barrett, W. P. (trans.) *The Trial of Jeanne d'Arc*. Gotham House, 1932.

Encyclopedia Britannica. Chicago: William Benton, 1964.

Murray, Margaret Alice. *The Witch Cult in Western Europe*. Clarendon Press, 1921.

ARITHMANCY; ARITHMOMANCY

see also Numerology

Divination by means of numbers, much akin to **numerology.** In ancient **Greece,** the number of letters in the names of competing contestants would be examined, along with the values of those letters. The one with the greatest total value would be declared the winner. By this method it was said that Achilles was predicted to overcome Hector in the Trojan Wars, according to diviners of the time. Anyone betting on the outcome of such contests would be sure to put his or her money on the one with the longest name!

According to the works of Diodorus, Herodotus, and Strabo, the Chaldeans also practiced arithmancy, dividing their alphabet into three parts of seven letters each. These seven were then each attributed to a planet, and predictions were so based. There was, therefore, a tie between arithmancy and **astrology** for the Chaldeans. The Pythagoreans and the Platonists also followed this method of divination.

Pythagoras is generally accepted as the father of the science of numbers, but it seems uncertain whether he invented arithmancy or merely made use of it. Aristotle said that the Pythagoreans believed that all things are numbers, "such and such a modification of numbers being justice, another being soul and reason, another being opportunity—and similarly almost all other things being numerically expressible."

Sources:

Encyclopedia Britannica. Chicago: William Benton, 1964.

Shepard, Leslie A. (ed.). *Encyclopedia of Occultism & Parapsychology*. New York: Avon, 1978.

ARITHMOMANCY *see* Arithmancy

ARMOMANCY

According to Thomas Blount's *Glossographia* of 1656, Armomancy is "divination by the shoulders of beasts." This was mainly done to determine the suitability of the beast for sacrifice to the gods. Upon sacrifice, further forms of divination would come into play, such as **Aurispicy, Extispicy, Haruspication,** and **Scapulomancy.**

ARROWS *see* Belomancy

ARUSPICATION *see* Haruspication

ASHES *see* Ceneromancy; Spodomancy; Tephramancy

ASP *see* Aspidomancy

Aspidomancy

A form of divination supposedly practiced in the East and West Indies. It is performed in the middle of a circle marked on the ground by the diviner. In the center of this circle is placed a buckler: a round shield, usually small, that was strapped to the arm. The diviner would sit on this shield in the center of the circle and chant certain ritual words. Through chanting, he or she would go into a trance. Certain things are witnessed in the trance, as in a dream, and future events are seen. When the diviner comes out of the trance, he or she is able to relate what was seen.

It has been written that aspidomancy is divining with a small snake called an asp, but this is possibly an uninformed guess based on the mere sound and spelling of the word.

ASS *see* Cephalomancy

Astragalomancy; Astragyromancy

This is a method of divination performed using knucklebones or dice. The small, uneven, four-sided bone found in the tarsal joint of most hooved animals is called the *astragal*, hence the term astragalomancy. Some definitions state that "huckle" bones are used, yet huckle bones are bones of the hip. Since the bones are mentioned as an alternate to dice, it would seem that the use of knucklebones is more likely.

Using dice, knucklebones, "Jackstones," or "Dibs" as a game is found around the world, especially in North America, Great Britain, China, Japan, Czechoslovakia, the Middle East, eastern Europe, and Egypt. It may be the oldest game known to humankind. The bones have been pictured on jars in ancient Greece and in prehistoric caves in Kiev. In addition to knucklebones, the anklebones of goats, sheep, and other animals have been used. Sophocles attributed the invention of dice to Palamedes during the siege of Troy, and Herodotus attributed them to the Lydians. However, both claims have been discredited. Dice that look much like our modern ones have been found in **Egyptian** tombs dating to earlier than 2000 BCE.

In ancient **Rome** the bones were marked like present-day dice, although each die was marked only on four sides. There were also pyramidal dice and pentahedral and octahedral dice. The Romans threw their dice from cylindrical cups much like modern dice cups. In early Greece the dice were shaken up and thrown from conical beakers. Along with bone, dice have been made from ivory, wood, stone, glass, amber, jade, and other gem stones.

West of the Gulf of Pagasæ in ancient Greece, in Achæa, was the temple of Hercules, where astragalomancy was a common practice. There the diviners would frequently cast the bones or dice to see what the future held. The details of such casting are not known but, with two or three such bones, the possible permutations would allow a wide variety of predictions. Grillot de Givry, in *A Pictorial Anthology of Witchcraft, Magic & Alchemy*, says that the twelve sides of a pair of dice were marked with letters of the alphabet representing the twelve principal divisions of human language. He refers to a book titled *Passe-temps de la fortune des dez, ingénieusement compilé pour response à vingt questions* by Maistre Laurens l'Esprit. In this book, according to de Givry, are given the various combinations possible and their meanings.

The first mathematical analysis of dice casting was made in 1526 and written by Gerolamo Cardano (or Cardani), an Italian physician, astrologer, and mathematician. Along with theoretical arguments on relative probabilities of separate combinations, he included tips on betting on the dice.

Sources:

Encyclopedia Britannica. Chicago: William Benton, 1964.
de Givry, Grillot. *A Pictorial Anthology of Witchcraft, Magic & Alchemy*. London: Spottiswoode, Ballantyne, 1931.
Line, David and Julia. *Fortune Telling by Dice: Uncovering the Future through the Ancient System of Casting Lots*. London: Aquarian Press, 1984.
Oxford English Dictionary. Oxford: Clarendon Press, 1989.
Shepard, Leslie A. (ed.). *Encyclopedia of Occultism & Parapsychology*. New York: Avon, 1978.

ASTRAGYROMANCY ***see*** **Astragalomancy**

Astral Projection

The physical body has an invisible double known variously as the spirit, ethereal body, or astral body. Astral projection (or OOBE—out-of-body experience) is the ability to send out, or cause to travel to a distance, this etheric double. The ability is inherent in most individuals and frequently occurs spontaneously. The majority of recorded cases of astral projections, however, have occurred after development of the skill by long and assiduous cultivation.

In astral projection, your physical body relaxes and rests while your etheric double departs from it, maintaining an apparently tenuous yet surprisingly strong connection in the form of an infinitely elastic silver cord. This silver cord is what draws you back to your physical body in case of any emergency.

The idea of the astral double is a very old one. There are descriptions, in ancient Indian writings, of the eight *siddhis*, or supernatural powers. These can be acquired through the yoga practice known as *Pranayama*. The sixth siddhi is astral projection or, as described, "flying in the sky." To the Hebrews, this astral body was the *ruach*. To the ancient **Egyptians** it was the *ka*. To the **Greeks** it was the *eidolon*. It is the etheric double, or astral body, that finally leaves the physical body, eventually breaking the silver cord, at death.

Some say that the astral body emerges from the physical through the solar plexus. Others say it is from the position of the Third Eye, or from the crown chakra. The person projecting often experiences what feels like a rapid shaking or vibration of the body at the moment of departure. From whatever point it leaves, the astral body floats up and away

Representation of astral projection, or out-of-body experience. ***Philip Panton/Fortean Picture Library.***

from the physical so that it is possible, for one versed in the art, to look back down at his own sleeping form. Then, the etheric double moves away rapidly to wherever it wishes to go. It travels with the speed of thought. If you decide you'd like to be halfway around the world, you will be there immediately; and can return just as fast.

Many **dreams** may be the remembrance of astral journeys undertaken while you are asleep. All people dream, though not everyone remembers his or her dreams. Frequently dreams seem ridiculously involved and mixed up. This is because you are remembering only the highlights of several dreams. The average person experiences a large number of dreams during the course of a normal night's sleep. Suppose that in the dream state—more correctly, on the astral plane—you take a trip to **Scotland** and do some salmon fishing. From there you travel to Asia and have a pleasant journey in a sampan. Then you may visit the pyramids in Egypt before rounding out the night reenacting a battle of the Civil War. On waking, you may have only a confused recollection of what seemed like one long, very strange, dream. In it, you were drifting down the Nile River in a Chinese junk that suddenly disappeared and left you fighting Confederate soldiers with nothing more than a salmon-fishing pole!

The steps to remembering astral journeys, and later directing them, start with remembering your dreams. These should be written down in as much detail as possible, *immediately* upon waking. You may remember very little to start with, but persevere. Slowly you will remember more and more of your dreams until you can separate them and note all the details. The next step is to decide, before going to sleep, what dream you would like to have. More exactly, where you would like your etheric double to travel on the astral plane. Tell yourself exactly where you want to go, and what or whom you want to see. The following morning, again record the details of your dreams, and see if there is any connection between them and what you wanted to do. After a very short period of training you will find that you can, in fact, go where you want to go.

There have been a number of cases where a person has undergone surgery and, on submitting to the anesthetic, has astrally projected and then watched the operation take place. Floating at ceiling level, they have seen their own body being operated on and, later, have given the full details to the surgeon.

There are hundreds of cases on record of people who have astrally traveled to a house they have never been to before, and later have given accurate details of the rooms, decorations, people, and actions taking place. Sylvan Muldoon was an accomplished projector. In 1924 he went to sleep and felt his etheric double take off, passing through the walls of his house. He was brought into a house he had never seen before and, in it, discovered an attractive young woman sewing a black dress. He stood for a while and studied her before returning to his physical body. Six weeks later he happened to see the same girl get out of a car. He approached her and asked where she lived. She told him it was none of his business, but he explained to her why he asked. He went on to describe the room where he had seen her sitting, and other members of her family. She confirmed all he said, and that was the start of a long friendship and even projection projects that they did together.

Robert Monroe, a Virginia businessman who is very accomplished at astral projection, has religiously kept a journal of his astral experiences over many years. This is one of the best-documented records. Charles Tart, professor of psychology at the University of California at Davis, worked with Monroe on several documented laboratory experiments. In his introduction to Monroe's book, Tart says:

> If we look to scientific sources for information about OOBEs we shall find practically none at all. Scientists have, by and large, simply not paid any attention to these phenomena. The situation is rather similar to that of the scientific literature on extrasensory perception (ESP). Phenomena such as telepathy, clairvoyance, precognition, and psychokinesis are "impossible" in terms of the current physical world view. Since they can't happen, most scientists do not bother to read the evidence indicating that they do happen; hence, not having read the evidence, their belief in the impossibility of such phenomena is reinforced. This kind of circular reasoning in support of one's comfortable belief system is not unique to scientists by any means, but it has resulted in very little scientific research on ESP or OOBEs.

One way some people first experience, and experiment with, astral projection is through what is known as the "false awakening." Most people have had the experience of half waking in the morning and knowing, or being told, that it is time to get up out of bed and get dressed. They get out of bed and sleepily start to dress. They may ponder what to wear, reach a decision, and then fully dress. They may even go into the kitchen to make a cup of coffee. Suddenly the alarm clock goes off again, or someone calls, and they realize they are still in bed! Yet they could have sworn they had actually got up and got dressed. This is a case of the astral body acting out the getting up and getting dressed. If you can realize, at the time, that this is only your astral body operating, and that your physical body is still asleep, then you can go on from there and direct yourself where you will.

Sources:

Crookall, Robert. *The Study and Practice of Astral Projection*. London: Aquarian, 1960.
Crookall, Robert. *The Techniques of Astral Projection*. London: Aquarian, 1964.
Fox, Oliver. *Astral Projection: A Record of Out-of-Body Experiences*. London: Rider, 1939.
Hart, H. *The Enigma of Survival*. London: Rider, 1959.
Monroe, Robert A. *Journeys Out of the Body*. New York: Doubleday, 1971.

Astrology

(See also Sun Signs)

The basic assumption of astrology is that every element of the cosmos influences the whole—that there is a very real relationship between the heavens and the earth. This is reflected in the saying, "As above, so below." The art or science of astrology forecasts events on Earth by observing the fixed stars, the sun, **moon,** and planets, and their interrelationship.

Astrologers claim that their art has been practiced for 5,000 years. Recognizable forms of it have been visible in ancient Babylonian, **Chinese, Egyptian, Greek, Indian, Mayan,** and Muslim civilizations, and it has attracted such men as Plato, Pythagoras, St. Thomas Aquinas, and Sir Isaac Newton. It originated in **Mesopotamia,** probably in the third millennium BCE, spreading from there to India and on to China by the sixth century BCE. It was much later that astrology attained its full development in the Greek civilization of the Hellenistic period. As it developed into a complex science, it came to influence religion, philosophy, and science throughout both pagan and Christian Europe. It was similarly absorbed into Islamic culture.

Initially it was a case of systematically observing the celestial bodies, keeping records, and using arithmetical procedures to correlate the data. Greek records of eclipses were available from as early as 750 BCE, and in the first millennium BCE there was accurate knowledge of the sun's annual course, of the phases of the moon, and of the periodicities of certain planets.

The Egyptians had constructed a calendar of twelve months of thirty days each, with five additional days. This was adopted and adapted by the Greeks as a standard of reference. The Egyptians also selected a succession of thirty-six bright stars that rose at intervals of ten days. This gave an indication of time throughout the year, and these intervals became known as *decans*. The Greek word *horoskopos* means decan star, and it is from this word that we get the word "horoscope."

"The tracing out of the annual path through the constellations of the sun with its attendant planets, the division of the belt into 12 signs of 30° each and the tailoring of the older constellations to fit so far as possible into the 12 signs, was an enterprise probably carried out in stages," according to *Encyclopedia Britannica*. The discovery of the precession of the equinoxes by Hipparchus in the second century BCE might well have depended on the completion of this enterprise.

For the casting of an individual horoscope, it is necessary to ascertain the configuration of the heavens at the moment of birth so that the influences of the planets upon the individual may be determined. This is known as a *natal* or **genethliacal** chart. From this "map" it is possible for the **diviner**—in this case, astrologer—to ascertain the likely influences on the individual's life in the future. The start of the calculation is finding the point where the ecliptic intersects the eastern horizon at the moment of birth. This is known as the *Ascendant*. The relative positions of the sun, moon, planets, and constellations are then recorded. Influence of the various components is modified by relative position: in conjunction (planets within 10° of each other), opposition (180° apart), square (90° apart), sextile (60° apart), and so on. The influence of the planets is further modified by the houses: preferred positions among the stars. There are twelve of these houses, and each concerns a particular aspect of life, such as health, wealth, family, or children. The houses do not have names; they are merely numbered, counterclockwise from the Ascendant position, as follows.

First house: Personal appearance and disposition; beginnings, childhood.

Second house: Possessions; money; values; investing.

Third house: Communication; brothers and sisters; close neighbors; short journeys; transport.

Fourth house: Home; property; roots; real estate; underground places; a man's mother or a woman's father.

Fifth house: Pleasure; love; sex; amusement; sensual pleasures.

Sixth house: Domestic animals; health and conditions affecting health; clothing; servants; physical comfort.

Seventh house: The spouse; partners.

Eighth house: Death; losses; wills; legacies.

Ninth house: Spirituality; religion; journeys to other lands; relatives by marriage.

Tenth house: Business; business affairs; honors; earnings.

Eleventh house: Friends and acquaintances; hopes; fears; wishes.

Twelfth house: Confinements: prison, deportation, exile; enemies; large animals.

The Greeks were the ones who perfected—over several centuries—the idea of a zodiacal belt. Pliny ascribes the first steps to Anaximander and Cleostratus, in the sixth and fifth centuries BCE. It was not until the third century BCE that the Mesopotamian practice of divination by the stars was adopted by the Greeks. They made it a means of ascertaining the future for anyone (which would be termed *mundane* astrology), not just for kings and countries.

The **zodiac** is an invisible belt indicating the orbit of the sun, moon, and planets around the earth. It is actually a band extending about eight degrees on either side of the *elliptic*, which is the apparent path of the sun across the sky. Looking up from the earth, the planets are always seen within this band of sky. The twelve divisions/signs of the zodiac are named Aries, Taurus, Gemini, Cancer, Leo, Virgo, Libra, Scorpio, Sagittarius, Capricorn, Aquarius, and Pisces.

The sun passes through each of these signs, taking thirty days to do so. The periods are as follows: Aries: March 21–April 19; Taurus: April 20–May 19; Gemini: May 20–June 20; Cancer: June 21–July 22; Leo: July 23–August 21; Virgo: August 22–September 22; Libra: September 23–October 22; Scorpio: October 23–November 21; Sagittarius: November 22–December 21; Capricorn: December 22–January 20; Aquarius: January 21–February 19; Pisces: February 20–March 20. In fact, these dates vary from year to year, so, when constructing a chart, it is necessary to check the exact time the sun passes from one sign to the next for the year in question. The dividing line between the signs is called the *cusp*.

The earth does not take exactly twenty-four hours to revolve on its axis (it is actually 23 hours, 56 minutes, 4.09 seconds). Similarly, it does not complete its orbit around the sun in exactly 365 days, which is why we have leap years. To determine exact positions of stars, astronomers calculate in star time, or *sidereal* time (ST), which is far more accurate. Astrologers similarly use sidereal time, based on the precise amount of time the stars take to complete a revolution around the earth. In astrology, then, all terrestrial time is converted to ST. In a sidereal day, the stars appear to make a complete circuit of the sky although the sun has not quite finished. The sidereal day, therefore, is a few minutes shorter than the ordinary day. This difference is known as the "acceleration on interval" and must be allowed for when calculating the ST at birth.

Charting a Horoscope

Most astrologers today use a computer program to produce an astrological chart; consequently, the majority of today's astrologers have lost the art of constructing one manually. Any true astrologer should know how to cast a horoscope without such mechanical means, even if he or she makes use of the computer technology.

From the above we can see that a horoscope is no more than a map of the heavens immediately above the place of birth, showing the positions of all relevant planets at the exact moment of birth. In order to draw, or cast, this horoscope it is therefore necessary to know two basics: time of birth (year, month, day, time of day) and place of birth.

A book called the *Ephemeris* gives the exact positions of the various planets through the year(s). Since it would be nearly impossible to give the ST for every single minute of every single day in every possible place, another book, the *Table of Houses*, shows only the ST for noon at GMT (Greenwich mean time). The difference to the actual birth time and place must then be calculated. These two books are essential for constructing the chart for the "native" (term used for the person whose chart is being constructed).

First of all, the sidereal time for noon on the birth date in question is found from the tables. The necessary hours and minutes to birth time are then added for births after noon and subtracted for births before noon, together with adjustment for

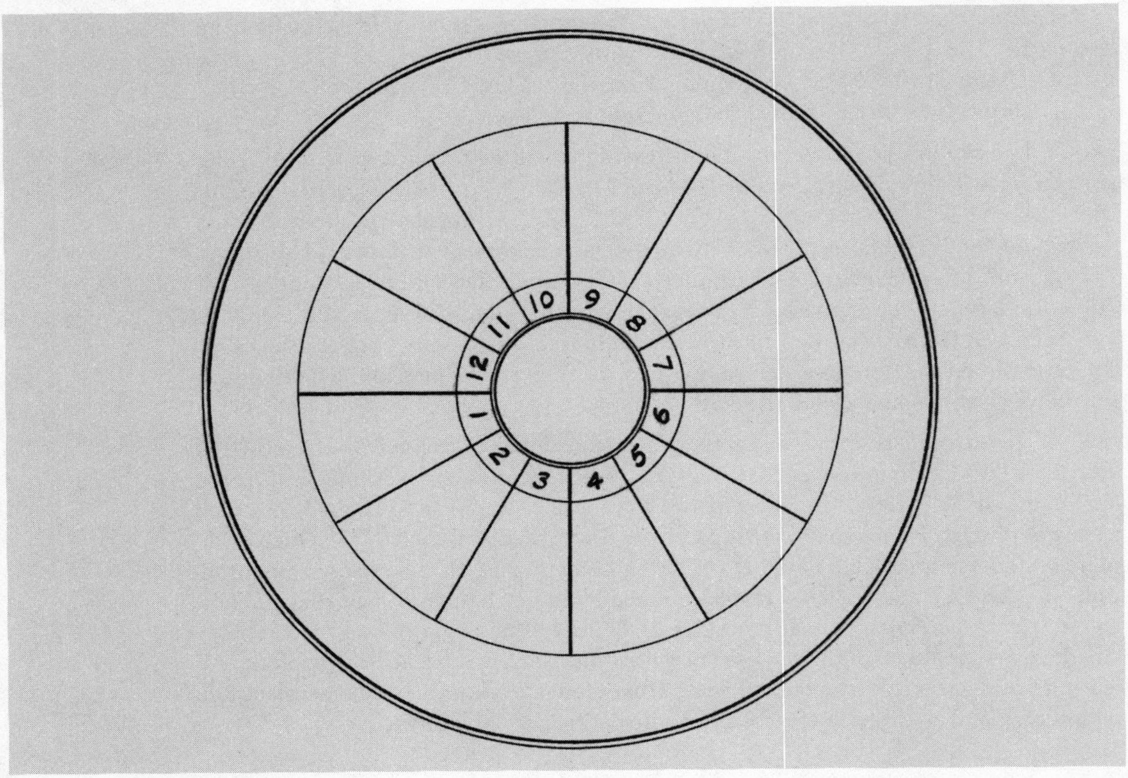

This template is used in casting an astrological birth chart in star time, or sidereal time. *Philip Panton/Fortean Picture Library.*

difference from GMT. For example, take someone born at 6:59 p.m. on March 19, 1955, in Dayton, Ohio. First, the time must be converted to GMT, which is the standard time given in the ephemeris. Cleveland would be EST, five hours slower than GMT. The birth at 6:59 p.m. would then be the GMT equivalent of 11:59 p.m. (6:59 p.m. plus five hours). The ephemeris states that at noon on that day the ST was 23 hours, 45 minutes, 2 seconds at GMT. Since the actual birth time was *after* noon, it is necessary to *add* 6 hours, 59 minutes. This is known as the "interval." This gives:

23	45	02
+ 6	59	0
30h	44m	2s

Now to consider the acceleration on the interval. This is found by subtracting or adding 10 seconds for every hour and one second for every six minutes of the interval time. In this case the interval was almost exactly seven hours. Acceleration, then, was 70 seconds, or 1 minute, 10 seconds. This gives:

30	44	2
+ 1	10	
30h	45m	12s

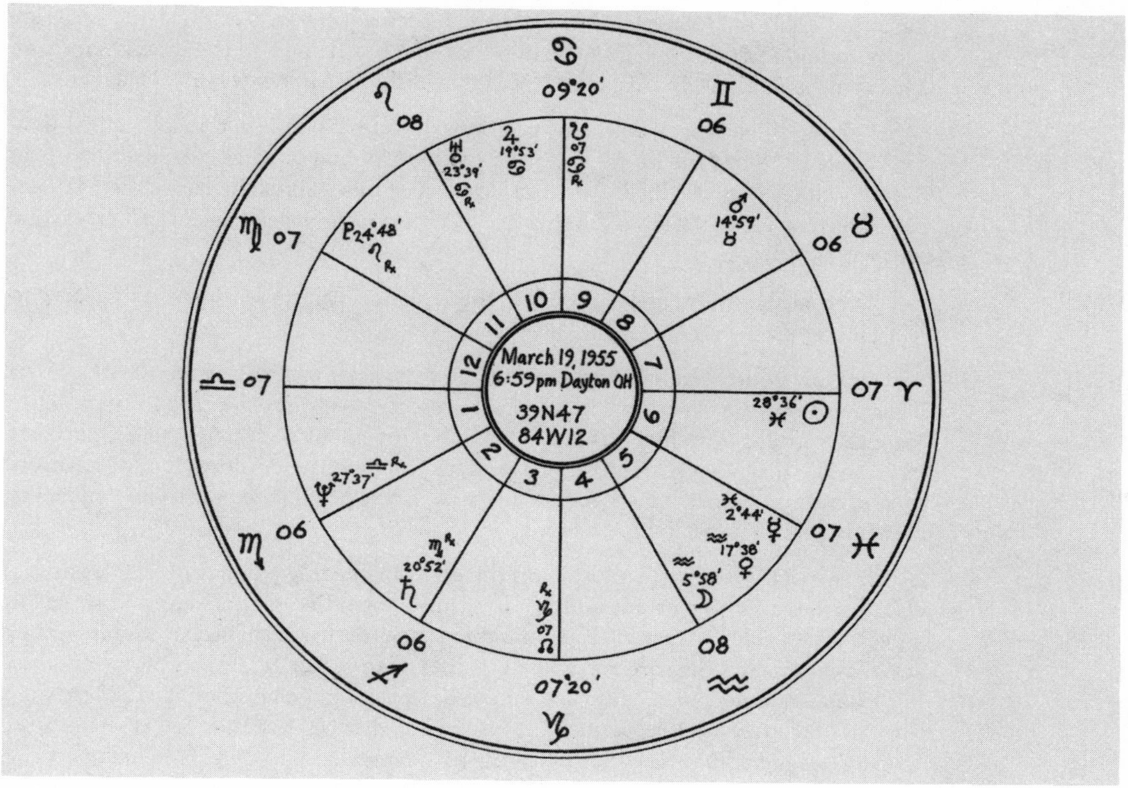

Sample of an astrological birth chart. ***Raymond Buckland.***

This is the sidereal time at GMT for the moment of birth. But this now has to be converted for the place of birth: Dayton, Ohio. This adjustment must be made by allowing for longitudinal difference from the Greenwich meridian. Degrees and minutes of longitude must be converted into minutes and seconds of time (giving the longitude equivalent in time), bearing in mind whether the location is east or west of Greenwich. The conversion is done by multiplying by four. Dayton is at 84°W 12' longitude. Multiplied by four (and divided by 60), the longitude becomes 5 minutes, 40 seconds of time. This is subtracted from the sidereal time at Greenwich, which was found above:

30	45	12
-5	40	
30h	39m	32s
-24h		
6h	39m	32s

This, then, is the local sidereal time at birth, which is needed to find the ascendant and the midheaven, or medium coeli, which is at 39°N 47' latitude. Looking at the Table of Houses for the established sidereal time, and at this latitude, a sign of the zodiac is shown as being the one that will be "rising" on the eastern horizon. This is the ascendant. In this case, 7°50' Libra with the Midheaven at 9° Cancer.

From the listing of planetary positions, it can be found (in the ephemeris) that, for March 19, 1955, the Sun is at 28°36' Pisces, Moon at 5°58' Aquarius, Mercury at 2°44' Pisces, Venus at 17°38' Aquarius, Mars at 14°59' Taurus, Jupiter at 19°53' Cancer, Saturn at 20°52' Scorpio, Uranus at 23°39' Cancer, Neptune at 27°37' Libra, and Pluto at 24°48' Leo.

From the information obtained, these planets can now be placed in their correct Houses on the chart.

Now comes the most important, and hardest, part of astrology—the chart interpretation. It is one thing to cast the horoscope, but quite another to interpret it. Here the astrologer/diviner has to use his or her judgment to decide which aspects are harmonious and which are obstructive. This is where the conjunction, opposition, square, trine, and other aspects come into play. Every possible relationship of planet to planet has its own specific meaning.

Aspect lines can be plotted on the chart by placing a dot close inside the circle, at the planet's position, and joining those dots. Two planets are said to be "in aspect" when there are specific angular differences between them. For example, they are in *conjunction* if they are very close together, within 8 or 10 degrees of one another. If they are separated by 90° they are said to be *square* to one another. At 120° they are *trine;* at 180° they are in *opposition;* 45° is *semi-square;* 60° is *sextile;* 30° is *semi-sextile;* 135° is *sesquiquadrate;* 150° is *quincunx;* 72° is *quintile;* and 144° is *bi-quintile*. The most powerful aspects are conjunction, opposition, square, and trine. Sesquiquadrate, sextile, and quincunx are regarded as moderate aspects; semi-square, semi-sextile, quintile, and bi-quintile are weak aspects.

The following tables show some of the glyphs plotted on a natal chart and what they indicate. Also plotted on a chart are the moon's nodes, defined as the two points in space where the path of the moon crosses the ecliptic. The north node refers to destiny, growth, future, and connections. The south node indicates knowledge of the past, memory, and karma. The ascendant describes personality or approach to life, and the midheaven indicates true vocation or activity in the world.

Planet	**Glyph**	**Keywords**
Sun	☉	The self; vitality; determination
Moon	☽	Sensitive; emotional; domestic
Mercury	☿	Quick-witted; researcher; active mind
Venus	♀	Physical attraction; love; peace-making
Mars	♂	Action; energy; courage; impulsive
Jupiter	♃	Harmony; morals; religion; education
Saturn	♄	Persevering; inhibited; taciturn
Uranus	♅	Excitable; erratic; sarcastic; occult
Neptune	♆	Mysticism; individuality; doubtful
Pluto	♇	Dislikes laws; selfish; enjoys children

Signs	**Glyph**	**Keywords**	**Ruler**	**Element**
Aries	♈	Leader; pioneer; impatient	Mars	Fire
Taurus	♉	Hard worker; perseverance; bull-headed	Venus	Earth
Gemini	♊	Adaptable; diplomatic; superficial	Mercury	Air
Cancer	♋	Home-lover; sensitive; traditional	Moon	Water
Leo	♌	Extrovert; self-confident; lover	Sun	Fire
Virgo	♍	Critical; conservative; intellectual	Mercury	Earth
Libra	♎	Intuitive; justice; peace-loving	Venus	Air
Scorpio	♏	Tenacious; self-opinionated	Pluto	Water
Sagittarius	♐	Kind; gentle; outspoken; fearless	Jupiter	Fire
Capricorn	♑	Ambitious; materialistic	Saturn	Earth
Aquarius	♒	Planner; honest; independent	Uranus	Air
Pisces	♓	Sensitive; sympathetic; vague	Neptune	Water

Aspects	**Glyph**	**Keywords**
Conjunction	☌	Consider relationship; may harmonize or conflict
Opposition	☍	Difficult aspect; tension; may be modified
Trine	△	Easy aspect; harmonious relationship
Square	□	Difficult aspect; uneasy struggle
Sextile	✶	Favorable aspect; more mental than physical
Quincunx	⚻	Unnatural aspect implying strain
Semi-Square	∟	Difficult aspect, like square; mildly irritating
Sesquiquadrate	⚼	Agitating; stressful; active
Semi-Sextile	⚺	Favorable but stressful; mildly supportive
Quintile	□	Promotes creativity
Bi-quintile	☍	Mildly positive

Starting with the Sun, draw lines to the Moon, Mercury, Venus, Mars, Jupiter, etc. Then draw lines from the Moon to the others; then from Mercury, from Venus, and so on. Study and measure these lines to see what aspects are on the chart. They can be listed in a side chart, using various symbols to show what the aspects are.

In addition to the aspects, interpretation follows through all that is on the chart, considering both the planets in the various houses and the planets in the different signs.

Planets in the Houses

Sun in First House: An inward-looking tendency. Possible selfishness. Well aspected—good health. Afflicted—chance of bad health.

Sun in Second House: Focus is on finances, with an urge to earn more money. There is a desire to gather material wealth; beware of becoming possessive. Try to share with others.

Sun in Third House: A competent writer and fascinating speaker. An interest in education. Communication is important. Develop persistence and try to be more patient.

Sun in Fourth House: Strong family ties. There is a tendency to be introspective. Security is sought after. Well aspected—great happiness in home life. Afflicted—discontent.

Sun in Fifth House: Very positive. Great enjoyment derived from home and family and from life in general. Fondness for children. Don't take risks, especially with family finances.

Sun in Sixth House: Good organizer. Possibility of advancement in business. Well aspected—excellent health. Afflicted—unsuitability for directing others; can be too demanding.

Sun in Seventh House: Excellent for partnerships, though there is a tendency to try to dominate. Social status is important.

Sun in Eighth House: Deep interest in the New Age; metaphysics. Involvement with others' financial affairs. Possible inheritance to come.

Sun in Ninth House: There is a continuing desire to study. Foreign languages come easily. A need for security. Possibility of travel abroad.

Sun in Tenth House: Enjoyment and satisfaction come from absorption in career. Can be power-driven, with a great need to succeed. Afflicted—a tendency to neglect duties.

Sun in Eleventh House: Opportunity to be elected to an important office. Well aspected—well suited for such an office. There will be a chance to demonstrate organizational abilities. Beware of becoming argumentative.

Sun in Twelfth House: Introspective, especially where business is concerned. Good at medical work and secretive work. A time to keep close-mouthed with partners.

Moon in First House: Strong maternal nature. Good imagination. Moody and changeable. A shrewdness in business matters; can be tenacious but beware of becoming too narrow-minded.

Moon in Second House: Instinct to save money. There is a need to learn to budget, especially at this time when there are fluctuations in income.

Moon in Third House: There is a need to communicate. There are changes in educational experiences. Travel-minded. Protective attitude to younger siblings.

Moon in Fourth House: An interest in history with an inclination to worship the ancestors. There is an urge to redecorate and even to relocate. Afflicted—a clinging attitude toward children.

Moon in Fifth House: An interest in gambling. If afflicted—avoid this. There is also a sport interest that could lead to fame. Love of large families and children. Possibility of love affairs.

Moon in Sixth House: Cleanliness in the home, and hygiene, are of great importance. There is reduced vitality. Try not to be too critical of others' work patterns.

Moon in Seventh House: Very status-conscious with a desire for social success. There is a need for a partner, though a tendency to be attracted to moody partners. Well aspected—firmness of business status. Afflicted—unsteadiness in business.

Moon in Eighth House: Preoccupation with sex. Psychic powers. Interest in the afterlife. Possible involvement with public finance.

Moon in Ninth House: Travel-minded. Foreign travel possible; even relocation. There is an attraction to ancient history and dead languages. Consider changing past-held religious ideas.

Moon in Tenth House: Changes in occupation considered. Brief fame possible. Concern with reputation and a desire to seek public recognition. Afflicted—loss of privacy.

Moon in Eleventh House: There is a multiplicity of interests and a large range of friends and acquaintances has developed. Well aspected—deep interest and involvement in various societies and organizations. Afflicted—many passing interests with superficial involvement.

Moon in Twelfth House: Need for retirement, if only temporary. Sabbatical, or some type of respite, is looked for. Strong psychic abilities. Retreating into the imagination: well aspected—beneficial; afflicted—detrimental.

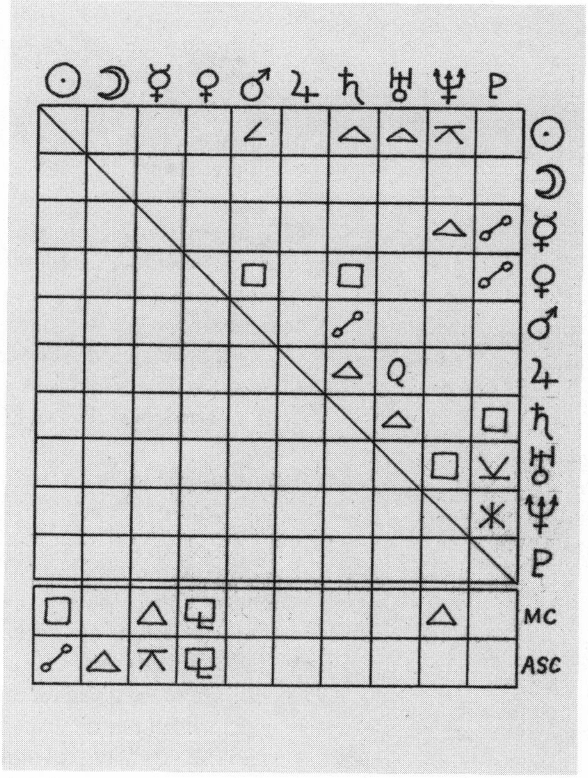

A side chart listing various aspects from a birth chart. *Raymond Buckland.*

Mercury in First House: Emphasis on intellectual energy. Highly strung with quick reactions. Excellent communication skills. Afflicted—beware of becoming too self-centered.

Mercury in Second House: Financial skills with strong business aptitude. Excellent bargaining powers. Possibility of becoming an excellent salesperson.

Mercury in Third House: Active yet restless. Looking for travel opportunities and a change in love. Talkative; intellectual. Afflicted—nervous system could become a concern.

Mercury in Fourth House: Tendency to hold on to old, often now-useless items. Could become overly domesticated. Home study and work are all around.

Mercury in Fifth House: Good at games involving mental activity and strategy. Teaching ability; creative. Good rapport with young people.

Mercury in Sixth House: Watch out for mental anxiety but don't become overly concerned with health matters. Possibility of intestinal problems. Afflicted—self-destructive tendencies.

Mercury in Seventh House: An attraction to those younger than self. Scientific, literary, and artistic interests with a need for intellectual stimulation.

Mercury in Eighth House: Interest in the occult. Scientific leanings. Study the fine print before signing anything. Afflicted—preoccupation with death.

Mercury in Ninth House: Broad-minded and intuitive. Interest in travel. There is a need for self-expression and an attraction to languages and higher education.

Mercury in Tenth House: There could be benefit from a connection with the literary world. A career in publishing would be good. Good communications. Keep busy.

Mercury in Eleventh House: Mental stimulation and a lively social life are needed. Afflicted—beware of unreliable friends.

Mercury in Twelfth House: Do not worry too much or be too secretive. There is an attraction to mysticism and a tendency to fantasize. Fix more on reality.

Venus in First House: Charming, good-looking and sexy. Fondness of music and drama. Afflicted—could become lazy and self-centered.

Venus in Second House: Sociable and pleasure-loving. Capable of increasing financial position but extravagant and obsessed with acquisitions.

Venus in Third House: Excellent at expressing ideas, with an ability to study. Good relationships with siblings and a happy disposition.

Venus in Fourth House: Able to express ideas and good at interior decorating. Beware of extravagance. A love of travel exists.

Venus in Fifth House: Inclined to have sexual affairs. Enjoy sports, creativity, and the arts. Musical ability and enjoyment of children.

Venus in Sixth House: Fond of animals. Good health. Get along well with coworkers.

Venus in Seventh House: Well aspected—excellent for starting personal or business partnership relationships. Afflicted—possibility of persecution complex developing.

Venus in Eighth House: Possible inheritance. Strong sex drive: well aspected—satisfied; afflicted—frustrated.

Venus in Ninth House: Good relationships with foreigners and a love of travel. Idealistic and sympathetic. May develop interests in religion. Good marriage.

Venus in Tenth House: Ambitions realized; popular and successful in business. Well aspected—good relationships with parents. Afflicted—problems with parents.

Venus in Eleventh House: Many friendships could lead to advantages and profits. Good time to work with groups and organizations.

Venus in Twelfth House: Interest in the occult. Love of animals. A need to be alone for a while. Possible secret love affair.

Mars in First House: Freedom-loving. Quick responder. A pioneer. Afflicted—quarrelsome and aggressive, with lack of forethought.

Mars in Second House: Can make or lose money very quickly. Don't try to appear to be a big spender. Learn to plan and budget.

Mars in Third House: Don't take so many risks. Not always logical and can be too hasty. Afflicted—could become aggressive.

Mars in Fourth House: Possible real estate losses. Well aspected—hardworking and handy at home. Afflicted—there is a yearning to get away and be independent.

Mars in Fifth House: Beware of self-indulgence and gambling desires. Get along well with children.

Mars in Sixth House: Subject to fevers, inflammations, and small wounds. Keep a careful watch on health. A good, industrious worker, but don't push coworkers too hard.

Mars in Seventh House: Well aspected—good cooperation with partners. Lots of energy. Afflicted—quarrels, disappointments, possible loss of partner.

Mars in Eighth House: Involvement with insurance. An interest in surgery. Well aspected—strongly sexed. Afflicted—legal problems.

Mars in Ninth House: Mentally alert. A good time to indulge in sports. A love of travel, but beware possible danger in foreign travel.

Mars in Tenth House: Ambitious and energetic. Desire to be own boss. Afflicted—trouble with parents.

Mars in Eleventh House: Control impulsive behavior because this could cause loss of friends, despite increased activity with them. Lots of energy and enthusiasm.

Mars in Twelfth House: Very secretive. Well aspected—desire to help others. Afflicted—watch out for treachery; possible loss of reputation.

Jupiter in First House: Great vitality; able to inspire others. Well aspected—optimistic, generous, and loyal. Afflicted—conceited, wasteful and self-indulgent.

Jupiter in Second House: Financially successful but inclined to extravagance. Afflicted—beware of financial carelessness.

Jupiter in Third House: Enjoyment of the learning process, with interest in literature and travel. Good communication and good relationship with family, especially siblings.

Jupiter in Fourth House: Good home conditions. Love of pomp and ceremony but possibility of vanity and lack of perspective.

Jupiter in Fifth House: Pleasure-loving. Ability in sport and enjoyment of art, literature, and theater. Well aspected—good time to take financial chances. Afflicted—stay away from gambling.

Jupiter in Sixth House: Loyal and cooperative. Well aspected—plenty of work can increase finances. Good health, though if afflicted—inclined toward hypochondria.

Jupiter in Seventh House: Good business relationships but not necessarily a happy home life. Afflicted—beware of sexual attraction outside marriage.

Jupiter in Eighth House: Possible inheritance. Ability to handle others' finances. Interest in the afterlife.

Jupiter in Ninth House: Broad-minded, optimistic and logical. Good time for study and travel. Excellent time for lecturing.

Jupiter in Tenth House: Can be influential, especially in politics and business. Good financial success in chosen career. Could do well in the theater.

Jupiter in Eleventh House: Popular. Enjoyment from many friends and acquaintances. Good social life. Plans falling into place.

Jupiter in Twelfth House: Psychic powers come to the fore. Good time to be philanthropic and help others without pushing self forward.

Saturn in First House: Self-confident and persistent. Well aspected—showing to be solid and reliable will be very constructive. Afflicted—don't let inhibitions cramp style. Possibility of ill health.

Saturn in Second House: There is a need to work hard to earn money. Learn to budget. Learn from experiences.

Saturn in Third House: It may be necessary to take on some responsibility for siblings. Possible difficulties associated with education. There is the ability to work at problems and find solutions.

Saturn in Fourth House: Anxiety about approaching old age. A feeling of restriction in the home life. Learn to discipline self.

Saturn in Fifth House: Little sense of humor. Difficulties with father, or another paternal figure, and with children. Afflicted—sexual inhibitions.

Saturn in Sixth House: Although good at chosen work there is little enjoyment from it. Afflicted—possibility of ill health and depression. Try not to be despondent.

Saturn in Seventh House: There will be a delay in partnership plans. Loyal and conscientious, also ambitious, but need to be more affectionate.

Saturn in Eighth House: Psychic powers come to the fore. Well aspected—responsibility demonstrated and ability to handle problems seemingly easily. Afflicted—can become moody and self-opinionated.

Saturn in Ninth House: Frustrated due to lack of education, yet good at studying and have a scientific mind. Afflicted—tend to mental exhaustion. There is a loss connected with long-distance travel.

Saturn in Tenth House: A demand for recognition and a demonstrated ability to hold a responsible position. A feeling of loneliness experienced. Afflicted—handicap self by carrying a grudge.

Saturn in Eleventh House: Friends may be small in number but they are all true and loyal. Frequent wrestling with mental problems.

Saturn in Twelfth House: There is a period of quiet; almost of disenchantment. A feeling of carrying the weight of the world on the shoulders. Possibility of seeking seclusion. Afflicted—feeling morbid.

Uranus in First House: Inventive, with scientific leanings. Independent, freedom-loving, but somewhat erratic. Dislike restrictions and can be eccentric. Afflicted—stubborn and have trouble getting along with others.

Uranus in Second House: Discover unusual ways to make money. There is good financial news. Well aspected—long-lasting advances.

Uranus in Third House: Love of travel. A lot of sudden, inventive ideas. Afflicted—can be too outspoken and ideas too scattered to be effective.

Uranus in Fourth House: Domestic upheavals and a need for emotional security. Possibility of relocation. Afflicted—much disruption.

Uranus in Fifth House: Constantly changing love life with unconventional views on sex. Love of gambling. Ability to inspire others.

Uranus in Sixth House: Highly strung and with the possibility of circulatory problems that may develop suddenly. Afflicted—problems with coworkers.

Uranus in Seventh House: Belief in open marriages and free love. A partner preferred who is eccentric in some way. Beware of entering any partnership too quickly. Afflicted—a tendency to cruelty.

Uranus in Eighth House: Psychic abilities with an unconventional interest in the afterlife. Well aspected—possibility of money coming from unusual and unexpected source. Afflicted—possible financial losses.

Uranus in Ninth House: Possibility of nervous breakdown. Accident prone at this time. Urge to travel: well aspected—could encounter very unusual and exciting events; afflicted—possible accident while traveling.

Uranus in Tenth House: Thoughts of self-employment. Difficult to take orders from others. Interest in unusual careers. Independent and original, with far-sightedness; would make a good leader.

Uranus in Eleventh House: Do not notice friends coming and going. Enjoy organizations and have unusual ideas for reform of groups.

Uranus in Twelfth House: Beware of deceit and treachery. Attraction to the unusual. Afflicted—interests could lead to misunderstanding and jeopardizing of reputation.

Neptune in First House: Need for firmness and decisiveness; it is easy to drift and dream. Plan the future with definite objectives. Think positive.

Neptune in Second House: Finances are uncertain; budget carefully. There is a tendency to spend needlessly.

Neptune in Third House: Imaginative and intuitive, with a great interest in the occult. Develop concentration since there is a failure to express well or display emotions.

Neptune in Fourth House: Increase security and look out for theft. Enjoy artistic surroundings. Afflicted—misunderstandings may arise in family matters.

Neptune in Fifth House: Overindulgence of sensual pleasures, inspired by movies and television. Susceptibility to seduction. Tendency to overlook faults in loved ones.

Neptune in Sixth House: Disorganization. A need to serve others, though a love of being alone. Afflicted—look out for unusual health patterns and beware of food poisoning.

Neptune in Seventh House: There is a need for companionship. Choice of partners is unusual. There is difficulty judging character of others. Afflicted—possibly unexpected problems; disappointment in marriage.

Neptune in Eighth House: Good imagination and powerful intuition. Unexpected fluctuations in finances, especially those involving a partner.

Neptune in Ninth House: Great interest in travel. Strong imagination. Intuitive and form own philosophies.

Neptune in Tenth House: Attracted by unusual careers, there are many possible career changes. Artistic and capable of becoming famous. Good leadership.

Neptune in Eleventh House: Can easily be led astray. Beware of deception and fraud. Idealistic, and open to seduction.

Neptune in Twelfth House: There are artistic abilities, especially strong in the field of poetry. Very creative, intuitive and psychic. Afflicted—tendency to live in a fantasy world and be subject to self-deception.

Pluto in First House: Tendency to skepticism. Idealistic, imaginative, and sensitive. Afflicted—possibility of minor crises.

Pluto in Second House: Unstable finances. Income may come from more than one source. There is an attraction to items for their aesthetic appeal. Don't spend too freely.

Pluto in Third House: Petty jealousies in the family. Don't be too sensitive. A searching, penetrating mind and strong intuition are in evidence.

Pluto in Fourth House: Great interest in family history. Learn to cooperate with the family; avoid being dictatorial. There is a tendency to untidiness in the home. Afflicted—sudden upheavals in family life.

Pluto in Fifth House: Love of adventure. Enjoyment of movies and video games. Beware of gambling tendencies. Afflicted—jealousy and domination in romantic affairs.

Pluto in Sixth House: Interest in the medical field. Don't abuse prescribed drugs. Watch what is eaten; beware of food poisoning.

Pluto in Seventh House: Possibility of a big change due to the influence of another. Possible involvement with a religious or artistic partner. Learn to work well with others.

Pluto in Eighth House: A number of small crises. Seek professional help with finances. There is good intuition and a powerful imagination.

Pluto in Ninth House: Seeker of adventure and travel minded. Involvement with the occult. Afflicted—beware of religious fanaticism.

Pluto in Tenth House: Wide variety of changes and opportunities possible with chosen career. There is a need to exert independence. Guard against scandal and becoming dictatorial.

Pluto in Eleventh House: Possibility of being caught up in cults and mass hysteria. Carefully examine all claims made by others. There is an urge to change the world. There are many friends but some of them could dissipate energies and lead astray.

Pluto in Twelfth House: Extremely sensitive. Try to understand self before judging others. Afflicted, subject to nervous tension and petty jealousies.

Planets in the Signs

Moon in Aries: An uneven temper and a changeable mind, with a headstrong temperament and dislike of discipline. Much enthusiasm but little patience. Possibility of accidents caused by being impetuous. A dislike of conventionality. Selfishness may be evident.

Moon in Taurus: Stability, with impulsiveness balanced by determination and persistence. Good financial vibrations. Can be fun-loving; generally very sociable and also sensual. Music and the arts may feature. A positive outlook. Afflicted—possessiveness can become a serious problem.

Moon in Gemini: Changeability and physical restlessness, unless balanced by other areas of the chart. Action and desire for action in a number of different areas at the same time. Avid reader and, frequently, a craftsman. Perseverance and decision-making need to be developed. Afflicted—nervous tension may develop.

Moon in Cancer: Strong family feelings with need to protect. Sensitivity and sympathy for others is very strong. A high emotional level with a powerful imagination.

Moon in Leo: Self confident and loyal, with a pleasing disposition. Prominent organizing ability. Prefers sophisticated pleasures. Personal limitations should be acknowledged. Afflicted—ostentatious and conceited.

Moon in Virgo: May be timid and reclusive. Health often affected by tendency to worry. Good business sense, with an analytical mind. Excellent attention to detail, though this can become too much if not carefully monitored. Ability to study and work hard. Beware of becoming overly fussy.

Moon in Libra: Friendly, easygoing and popular, with natural charm, courtesy and diplomacy. Enjoys music and poetry. Works very well with others, sharing decision-making, but needs to work on decisiveness. Afflicted—can be fickle, overly critical, and capricious.

Moon in Scorpio: High emotional levels. Intense, magnetic, and determined. Works and plays hard. Proud, but if afflicted—can become resentful, moody, and possessive. Frequently has inner passion and turbulence.

Moon in Sagittarius: Quickness of movement and giving a sense of urgency are common traits. Although often appearing off-handed, can be a fluent talker with a liking for freedom and a high sense of independence. Enjoys participation in sports to offset need for physical exercise.

Moon in Capricorn: Cautious and prudent with good common sense. Take care that these qualities do not develop into over-caution and austerity. Able to shoulder responsibility. Leans toward ostentation.

Moon in Aquarius: A tendency to value independence and to prefer the unconventional. There may be some eccentricity and even obstinacy. Ingenuity and originality are usually present, with an attraction to science, astrology and astronomy. Afflicted—nervous tension and erratic behavior. Conscious effort must be made to control what could become unpredictability.

Moon in Pisces: Kind, gentle, and amicable. Afflicted—can become lazy, restless and gullible, with a tendency to change his or her mind. Artistically inclined and imaginative but easily discouraged. Can be self-indulgent.

Mercury in Aries: Strong vitality combined with good business sense. Original ideas. Quick mind and speech, but with a tendency to be argumentative and to break into conversations. Need to cultivate tact and patience and to stick with projects. Serious study is usually put off till the last moment.

Mercury in Taurus: Does not like to be rushed. Decisions come slowly but, once made, are stuck to. Generally cheerful and appreciative of art and beauty, but physical pleasure is important. Not a glib talker but needs to become less opinionated and obstinate.

Mercury in Gemini: Versatility; a lively, inventive mind. Clever and shrewd, but with a tendency to become mentally and sexually restless. May be an excellent orator. Capable of scientific investigation. Avoids work that is boring and routine. Needs to check a tendency to be dishonest in presenting facts to others.

Mercury in Cancer: Love of home and family. An excellent memory and sharp mind, but can be overly emotional and super-sensitive. Appreciates praise but could easily be swayed by flattery. Strong tendency to live in the past and not think about the future. Frequently has irrational worries and phobias.

Mercury in Leo: Would make a good executive, though can be arrogant and bombastic. Has high ideals. Cheerful and optimistic, with a love of children. Can be creative and appreciates the arts. Broad-minded; would make a good teacher.

Mercury in Virgo: Intellectual and practical, he or she uses critical judgment freely. Loves to solve mysteries and delve into occult studies. Frequently has literary talent and can be good at linguistics. Also good with figures and may be skilled with his or her hands. Needs to avoid becoming overly critical.

Mercury in Libra: Slow to arrive at a decision but able to look at both sides of a question. Tender feelings and musical voice are characteristic. Frequently involved in charitable acts. Can be tactless and weak-willed.

Mercury in Scorpio: Possesses great vitality and intensity. Tendency to overdo things and then health can suffer from overindulgence. Quick mind but often suspicious. Tendency to sarcasm. May have the gift of healing.

Mercury in Sagittarius: Broad-minded with a zest for living. Has progressive ideas and high ideals, with a natural sense of justice. Frequently possesses a talent for writing. Can be too outspoken and sometimes rebellious. Likes to be the boss.

Mercury in Capricorn: Possesses a patient and practical mind that is not given to extravagance. Conversation is a serious subject, with words carefully chosen. Can be ambitious and patient. Scientific and mathematical abilities usually in evidence.

Mercury in Aquarius: Reluctant to change views once formed. May be eccentric. Interest in metaphysics, astrology and astronomy. Has humanitarian interests and can become devoted to the social welfare of others. Usually is excellent judge of human nature.

Mercury in Pisces: Extremely creative imagination. There is a tendency to be secretive. Charitable and kind, with a flexible mind but with the stumbling block of forgetfulness. There is a talent for entertaining others. Creative writing, such as poetry, is sometimes called for as an outlet for the emotions.

Venus in Aries: Frequently disappointed through having looked for the ideal. Sets very high standards. A natural ability to make friends and is popular with the opposite sex. Has a warm and loving nature and can fall in love quickly, with a strong erotic compulsion. Impulsive toward finances, frequently getting caught up in money-making schemes that come to naught. Afflicted—restless and quarrelsome with loved ones.

Venus in Taurus: Very loyal and devoted lover, but with tendencies to laziness and self-indulgence. Possessive of loved one(s). Makes friends easily. Love of luxury that, over time, may lead to becoming overweight. Lover of the arts, especially music.

Venus in Gemini: Frequently a lighthearted approach to love, with a great deal of flirting. There can be an attraction to a near relative, but nothing serious. Attitude to marriage may not be too serious either. Fickleness is apparent. The idea of love is more real than the actuality.

Venus in Cancer: High emotions and true affection are apparent. Loving can become smothering to the recipient. Homeloving is included in the package, with good housekeeping and usually good cooking. Emotions may need controlling, since they can run high.

Venus in Leo: Domination in love is often the keyword. Jealousy may play a part. There is sincerity in the love and pride in the home, though often with great drama that can lead to domestic scenes. Creative talents are apparent. Little interest in sex outside the marriage. A generous spender on items of quality and artistic merit.

Venus in Virgo: Marriage may come after a long platonic relationship. Can be overly critical of spouse, which may become a hindrance to romance. Minor faults may be seen as major ones when they are not.

Venus in Libra: Happiness and joy may be found in relationships but take care not to leap in too quickly; it is easy to fall in love with being in love. This is a true sentimentalist but sometimes with untidy personal habits.

Venus in Scorpio: Here may be found the extremes of love and hate. Deeply passionate and highly emotional, with a satisfying sex life, but jealousy is common and must be watched and controlled. There may be big business connections that can be lucrative.

Venus in Sagittarius: A desire not to be tied down in love. If the partner can accept an open relationship, the lovemaking can be exceptional. There is a nonchalance about money that needs to be watched, but such ventures as import-export can be rewarding.

Venus in Capricorn: Although faithful in love, can be most undemonstrative, leaving the lover feeling cold and abandoned. Business may come first. There can be a love of music and the arts and there is great money-making potential.

Venus in Aquarius: Sociable and with good artistic taste, personal magnetism may attract but detachment may repel. There is a lack of emotion despite a fondness for the opposite sex. It may be difficult to give the heart to only one. Unconventional in relationships but with a sensible financial attitude.

Venus in Pisces: Totally ruled by the emotions. Although able to show genuine feeling, may be over-sentimental. May also be too submissive, denying basic necessities as a sacrifice for a loved one or for a cause. Very generous with a desire to help the underdog.

Mars in Aries: Great intellectual energy that may be used to the point of strain. Aggression and impulsiveness must be controlled. May be forceful sexually. May be considered "pushy," but can be an inspiring leader. There is a love of independence and frankness.

Mars in Taurus: Although the temper is slow to arouse, it can easily get out of hand and become difficult to control. There is possessiveness and a stubbornness, but a practical approach to life. Financial reward comes from hard work but the money can be spent as quickly as it is earned.

Mars in Gemini: Mentally and physically alert. Frequently talkative. Agile and athletic. There may be a writing ability though this could show itself in personal correspondence rather than with books or short stories. Possibility of employment changes but a tendency to not finish jobs that are started, which must be overcome. Arguments with friends and neighbors should be avoided.

Mars in Cancer: There may be great ambition and tenacity, but also a lack of straightforwardness. There is strong intuition. Grudges are held and there is rebellion against authority. Holding in feelings may result in stomach upsets. There is a high emotional level. Afflicted—easy to become upset and bad-tempered.

Mars in Leo: There is a lot of ambition and enthusiasm that can become a driving force. There is also generosity and affection, and a love of sports and adventure. Emotions may be expressed through artistry and may also bring about a passionate love life. Small-mindedness and pettiness should be avoided if possible. There may be a sorrowful love affair.

Mars in Virgo: With good overseeing there can be excellent work, with a forte in detail work. Although there may be constant obstacles, these are overcome and progress continues. Emotional frustration can lead to tension, but there is lots of enthusiasm.

Mars in Libra: Energy goes up and down, with constant conflicts at work. There can be a need to create harmony that conflicts with a desire to get things done. They may be love disappointments, rivals, and secret enemies. Judgment gets better with age.

Mars in Scorpio: Passionate and highly sexed, this is a practical, hard worker who enjoys dangerous work. There is a love of good living that can run to excess. There are deep emotions that, if kept positive, can bring assured results.

Mars in Sagittarius: Lots of enthusiasm for new projects. Boisterous, with some ideas that seem outrageous. Can be independent. Skepticism is not uncommon and enjoys a good argument. Afflicted—there is a tendency to exaggerate.

Mars in Capricorn: Ambitious with a tremendous drive to carry out goals. There is a desire to be in the public eye. Little toleration for waste and incompetence.

Mars in Aquarius: Lack of patience for change can result in rebellion and fighting for a cause. Can be very unpredictable. Original and ingenious ideas may lead to great inventions but there is a need to be more open to input from others.

Mars in Pisces: A sensuous and emotional disposition with a desire to work for others. Efforts can be inadequate and confused. Can be overly influenced by others.

Jupiter in Aries: Characteristic are high spirits, generosity, and a love of freedom. Frequently found to be self-sufficient and to have income from more than one source. May hold an important, responsible position. Afflicted—bullying, extravagant, and over-optimistic.

Jupiter in Taurus: A big-hearted lover of good living who works hard for worthwhile causes. Usually devoted to family and home and likes peaceful, harmonious surroundings with little change. Afflicted—self-indulgence and indolence.

Jupiter in Gemini: Intelligence and versatility with broadmindedness. Often marries someone older; may marry twice. Humane and compassionate. Possibility of being superficial, with scattered interests. Can be very clever.

Jupiter in Cancer: Enjoys love of family and friends. Has a high emotional level. Is protective and understanding, charitable and devoted to public work. Interested in travel and enjoys most forms of art and entertainment.

Jupiter in Leo: Intelligent, ambitious, affectionate, and generous. Will make friends wherever he or she may go, garnering confidence from others. Possibility of being appointed to a government position. Afflicted—intolerant, egotistical, and snobbish.

Jupiter in Virgo: Possesses a critical outlook, choosing friends carefully. However, a marriage partner may be unconventional. Scientific and technical ability, with possible success in real estate and foreign interests. Afflicted—absent-minded and careless.

Jupiter in Libra: Gentle and lovable. Very sociable. Dislikes loneliness and seeks partnership. Does not work well, or live well, independently. Well aspected—artistic ability. Afflicted—laziness and self-indulgence.

Jupiter in Scorpio: Capacity for deep emotions. Has sharp, penetrating perception, with high ambition and pride. Stress can come about through too much mental work. Afflicted—tendency to be suspicious, together with conceit. Possibility of scandal.

Jupiter in Sagittarius: Maintains a dignified appearance but is very approachable. Optimistic; cannot bear restrictions. Good leadership qualities. There is a love of horses and other animals.

Jupiter in Capricorn: Conscientious and hardworking, with a resourceful mind and strong sense of responsibility. Popularity and ambition may lead to the gaining of power, though this would come gradually. Afflicted—stubborn and bigoted.

Jupiter in Aquarius: Sociable and cheerful, with empathy for others and feelings of brother/sisterhood. Humanitarian, interested in promoting peace. A good sense of justice. Afflicted—unpredictable, intolerant and tactless.

Jupiter in Pisces: Compassionate and benevolent. Powerful imagination and strong emotions, with an impressionable mind. Identifies with suffering;

would work well in a hospital or similar institution. Possibility of a gift of prophesy. Afflicted—self-indulgent, extravagant and unreliable.

Saturn in Aries: Ambitious and determined, but alternatively strong and weak. Afflicted—impatient, jealous, defiant and possibly cruel.

Saturn in Taurus: Patient and long-suffering, methodical and practical. Functions best when under pressure. Can be stubborn. Afflicted—avaricious and frugal.

Saturn in Gemini: Conscientious and impartial. Has an ability for literature, science, and mathematics. Can be overly serious. Afflicted—skeptical and cold.

Saturn in Cancer: Insecure, with fear of independence. Conservative and opinionated. Good at seeing things through to the end. Concerned with public welfare.

Saturn in Leo: Self-assured with strong will and good sense of humor. Has ability to be a good organizer. Tendency to jealousy. Often seen as standoffish. Has difficulty expressing pleasure.

Saturn in Virgo: Devotion to duty evident. Prudent, discreet and meticulous. Not afraid of hard work; extremely tidy. Tends to find fault with others easily, due to own high standards.

Saturn in Libra: Good judgment, patience and impartiality. A kind and pleasant personality. Good partnership needed for complete happiness. Afflicted—intolerant and over-emotional.

Saturn in Scorpio: Although lacking in flexibility, there is excellent business acumen. There are deep emotions and there may be occult leanings. Possibility of becoming unpopular. Afflicted—possible cruelty and ruthlessness.

Saturn in Sagittarius: Exhibits honest, plain speech, but sometimes shows seemingly contradictory attitudes. An attraction to philosophical and religious subjects. Prudent, fearless and dignified. Sometimes tactless and cynical.

Saturn in Capricorn: Practical and capable, with a sense of discipline. Can be very patient when necessary. Capable of self-sacrifice to achieve goals. There is a love of power. Afflicted—pessimistic and selfish.

Saturn in Aquarius: Freedom loving; interested in ideologies. Scientific interests. Given to studying, since objectives in life are important. Prefers to be independent but dislikes loneliness. Sociable yet reserved.

Saturn in Pisces: Sympathetic and flexible; philantropic and imaginative. Possesses a strong emotional nature that sometimes leads to his or her own undoing. Has a good imagination and has the ability to develop intuition.

Uranus in Aries: Freedom-loving and independent; unconventional and eccentric. Has a lively imagination. Can be impulsive and rebellious.

Uranus in Taurus: Headstrong, opinionated, obstinate and stubborn. Can be intense and resourceful, removing obstacles with force.

Uranus in Gemini: Inventive, versatile, interested in the scientific. Good at writing. May have psychic abilities. Afflicted—nervous tension.

Uranus in Cancer: Eccentric and unpredictable. May be emotionally unstable. Interested in home and domestic issues. Possibility of mediumistic abilities.

Uranus in Leo: Leadership skills that may be unconventional. Can be defiant and arrogant. Very independent.

Uranus in Virgo: Has teaching abilities and a scientific curiosity. Intellectual and critical faculties. May have unusual dietary ideas.

Uranus in Libra: A dual personality, which is sometimes disturbing but at other times quite charming. Very psychic and artistic, with literary abilities.

Uranus in Scorpio: Independent, energetic and emotional. Has original ideas for helping others. Has difficulty expressing emotions.

Uranus in Sagittarius: Revolutionary, desperately seeks freedom. Intuitive and imaginative; loves travel. Can become rebellious and reckless.

Uranus in Capricorn: Good leadership qualities and organizing ability. Has a serious, penetrating mind. Can be highly ambitious.

Uranus in Aquarius: Resourceful with strong mental capabilities. Intuitive and imaginative, liking to be independent. Seeks to change things for the better. A possible interest in mechanics and science.

Uranus in Pisces: Emotional and highly intuitive. Can be secretive. Has unusual dreams and visions. Idealistic with religious interests.

Neptune in Aries: Interested in psychic research. Very sociable. Loves to travel.

Neptune in Taurus: Creative and musical, with a good sense of rhythm.

Neptune in Gemini: Sensitive, imaginative and mystical, with the gift of prophesy.

Neptune in Cancer: Very imaginative, seeking to escape reality. Idealistic, with a love of the sea.

Neptune in Leo: Dramatic, with delusions of grandeur. Artistic and can be magnetic.

Neptune in Virgo: Analytical, intuitive and sensitive. Highly critical of orthodox religion.

Neptune in Libra: Charming and very easygoing. Refined and sensitive. Possibility of an attraction to drugs.

Neptune in Scorpio: Extremely sensitive with feelings and emotions running high. Tends to be secretive. Has mediumistic gifts.

Neptune in Sagittarius: A visionary with a mind of highest caliber. Optimistic in the extreme. Literary interests. Loves to travel.

Neptune in Capricorn: Good business sense based on intuition and inspiration. Practical ability.

Neptune in Aquarius: Searches for the inner meaning of life. Very independent.

Neptune in Pisces: Highly mystical and spiritual.

Pluto, only discovered in 1930, is so slow moving that it stays in each sign approximately twenty-five to thirty years. There is little research material yet available on its influences.

The progressions and the transits are examined. All have meanings and must be interpreted bearing in mind the relationships of one to the other and how some may modify others.

Sources:

Dernay, Eugene. *Longitudes and Latitudes throughout the World.* Washington, DC: National Astrological Library, 1948.

George, Llewellyn. *A to Z Horoscope Maker and Delineator*. St. Paul, MN: Llewellyn, 1970.
http://www.awakenings-inc.com/academics/symbols.htm.
Lewis, Ursula. *Chart Your Own Horoscope: For Beginner and Professional*. New York: Grosset & Dunlap, 1976.
MacNeice, Louis. *Astrology*. Garden City, NY: Doubleday, 1964.
Orion, Rae. *Astrology for Dummies*. Foster City, CA: IDG Books, 1999.
Parker, Derek and Julia. *The Compleat Astrologer*. New York: McGraw-Hill, 1971.
Raphael. *Raphael's Astronomical Ephemeris of the Planets' Places*. London: W. Foulsham (annual).

ASTROMANCY *see* Astrology

AUGURS

The augurs were found in ancient **Rome** and **Greece,** as well as in **Mexico** and Peru. Their job was to read and interpret signs (*auspicia* or *auguria*). They were members of a priestly class and generally performed their task as part of religious observances. The word augur comes from the Latin *augere*, "to increase," possibly indicating original duties tied into fertility rites.

In Rome, there was a large priestly college originally established around 300 BCE by either Numa or Romulus, with three priest/augurs. Originally it is thought that the king made up a fourth, though later he was not directly involved. By the time of Sulla the number had been increased to fifteen augurs and then, in the time of Julius Caesar, there were sixteen. The uniform of the augur was a toga with scarlet stripes and a purple border. This was known as the *trabea*. The augurs developed huge political power, since their pronouncements were unchallengeable. If they felt it necessary, they would not hesitate to give an unfavorable reading. Not unnaturally, the position of augur was highly sought after but it was bestowed only on persons of distinction and was a lifetime honor.

When doing a reading, the augur was accompanied by a magistrate who would verify the results. The magistrate was also the one who was officially entitled to ask the deities for signs. Rather than actually trying to see the future, the object was to ascertain whether or not the deities approved or disapproved of the course of action queried.

The augur used a straight staff bent at the top, known as a *lituus*, which was also a symbol of his office. With this staff, and after due prayer and sacrifice, the augur would mark a large circle, known as a *templum*, on the ground. This then became a consecrated area. A tent would be erected within the space, its entrance facing south. The circle was usually constructed on or near the top of a hill. Seated in the entrance to the tent, the augur would point his staff at the sky and describe a circle, also called a *templum*. It was then expected that the signs would appear within that space of the sky, since this was the domain of Jupiter. The magistrate would be inside the tent, observing. Signs in the eastern section of the sky, which would be to the observer's left, would be considered favorable; those to the west, unfavorable. Signs included shooting stars, thunder, lightning, **birds'** flight, or anything considered unusual. (In Greece the reading was reversed, with the augur facing north and seeing favorable signs on his right.) Lightning moving from left to right was considered favorable, while right to left was unfavorable. At the appearance of any form of lightning, however, all business in the public assemblies would be suspended for the day.

If there were proposed public meetings that the augur—or those close to him—did not support, it was not unusual for the augur to claim that he had seen lightning moving from right to left, and no one could doubt him. If, on his first day in office, a new consul or prætor prayed for good omens, then invariably the augur would report to him of having seen lightning flash from left to right.

The usual time for observing auspices was between midnight and dawn. If there was a particular undertaking for which signs were sought, then the augury was done on the morning of that undertaking. This applied to such diverse things as going to battle, building a temple, sitting in the senate, and any major decisions.

There was a book or manual that contained augural ritual, together with a collection of answers to questions that had previously been given to the college of the senate. The augur always announced his finding with a specific set of words, which were duly recorded by the magistrate. The complexity of interpretation of phenomena grew by degrees until it finally became unmanageable and the Roman college had to be abandoned. The **Aztecs** had a similar college of augurs, known as the *Calmecac*. Their interpretation was mostly limited to the flight and song of birds (*see* **Orniscopy**).

The term augury, meaning the observation and interpretation of omens, is especially applied to the observation of birds. This parrot in Jaipur, India, is being used as a fortune teller. *Klaus Aarsleff/Fortean Picture Library.*

Sources:

Adkins, Lesley and Roy A. *Dictionary of Roman Religion*. New York: Facts on File, 1996.

Buckland, Raymond and Kathleen Binger: *The Book of African Divination*. Rochester, VT: Destiny Books, 1992.

Encyclopedia Britannica. Chicago: William Benton, 1964.

Leach, Maria (ed.). *Funk & Wagnalls Standard Dictionary of Folklore, Mythology, and Legend*. San Francisco: Harper & Row, 1972.

AUGURY

The observation and interpretation of omens, or auspices, by the **augurs** of ancient **Greece** and **Rome;** also practiced in India, Africa, South America, and New Guinea.

It was especially applied to observation of the flight and song of birds (*see* **Orniscopy**). The term augury has come to be applied to divination in general, but originally it applied specifically to birds.

AURA

According to metaphysics, the human body is composed of seven distinct elements. The first three—solid, liquid, and gas—form the physical body. The fourth is the etheric body and interpenetrates the physical. Then there is the astral, the mental, and finally the spiritual body. The last two are virtually impossible to see, since they vibrate at rates too high for normal detection by the physical eye, but the others can be seen by sensitives. These energy patterns are termed the *aura*.

The etheric body, or inner aura, extends slightly beyond the physical, appearing to the adept as a thin, dark line no more than an inch thick. Beyond it extends the astral body, which may be several inches in thickness. The aura extends around the whole body but is most easily seen around the head, where it is termed the *nimbus*. The aura around the whole body is the *aureola*. The nimbus is what is shown in Christian art—especially from the fifth to the sixteenth centuries—as "halos" or "glorias." In paintings of Moslem prophets, the aura is often shown as a ring of flames. Crowns and priests' headdresses symbolize the aura. Some art of Ceylon, **Mexico,** Peru, and of Japanese Buddhism show light extending around the whole body of a holy person. Paracelsus, in the sixteenth century, said, "The vital force is not enclosed in Man, but radiates round him like a luminous sphere."

The aura changes color with the person's health, mood, etc., and so can be used by the sensitive as an instrument of **divination.** A person with a blue or lavender aura, for example, will be in a deeply spiritual state. Love shows as a pink aura, and anger as a vibrant red. Vortexes and holes in the aura or the aureola may indicate health problems and need for attention. Seeing a change of color, for example from dark pink to vibrant red, would indicate that the person's anger was increasing and could explode in the near future.

Sources:

Buckland, Raymond. *Color Magic—Unleash Your Inner Powers*. St. Paul, MN: Llewellyn, 2002.
Butler, W. E. *How to Read the Aura*. New York: Samuel Weiser, 1971.
Cayce, Edgar. *Auras*. Virginia Beach, VA: A.R.E. Press, 1973.
Spence, Lewis. *An Encyclopedia of the Occult*. London :George Routledge & Sons, 1920.

AURISPICY

(See also Scapulomancy)

Knuckle bones, ankle bones (from sheep and goats), and other animal and human bones have been used for centuries in the performance of divination. **Astragalomancy** is one form of this, where small bones are used like dice. Bones being so used have been pictured on jars in ancient Greece and in prehistoric caves in Kiev. In ancient Rome the bones were marked, like present-day dice, although each die was marked only on four sides. West

This representation of the Buddha shows an aura surrounding the holy man. ***Fortean Picture Library.***

of the Gulf of Pagasæ in ancient Greece, in Achæa, was the temple of Hercules, where astragalomancy was a common practice. There the diviners would frequently cast bones to see what the future held. The details of such casting are not known, but, with two or three such bones, the possible permutations would allow a wide variety of predictions.

One common method, found with a number of primitive peoples, is to toss a predetermined number of bones into a circle marked on the ground or on a table. Any bones that fall outside the circle are discounted. Of the others, their position in the circle, relationship to each other, and way of lying are significant. The circle itself may be divided—if only in the mind of the diviner—into sections, each with its own significance.

In the Transvaal area of South **Africa,** the Venda's main method of aurispicy divination is by using a bowl that has been made especially for the purpose. The rim of the bowl is decorated with pictures representing god, goddess, home, danger, warnings, movement, sacrifice, injury, caution, and other qualities and objects. In the very center of the bowl is a carved representation of a cowry shell, as a connection to the goddess.

The diviner casts five knuckle bones into the bowl. Each of the bones represents something different, which might be positive or negative. Interpretation is based on the proximity of the bone to the symbols around the edge, and the relationship to the central cowry shell. The relationship of each stone to its neighbors is also of importance. A large number of interpretations can come from any one throw.

Venda tablets are also used by these people. These are usually made of bone, although they may be made of wood, ivory, clay, or rock. They are about an inch to an inch and a half in length and about three-quarters of an inch wide. Four tablets are used, each of which bears a particular symbol on one side. (See the entry on **African Divination** for a detailed explanation of divination using Venda tablets.)

The Bushmen of the Kalahari Desert use fragments of bones—broken pieces of all types—each of which is especially marked. They are simply cast down on the ground, with no central circle, and interpreted by the method in which they fall and their placement. In the Congo, the *Mganga* or *Mufumu*—diviner and magician—uses bones to predict future events such as whether or not a sick person will get better, the state of the coming harvest, or the general lot for the tribe. Favorite bones are the leg bones of goats. These are highly polished and their ends are shaped to resemble the heads of various animals, such as hyenas, lions, and crocodiles. The Mganga will enter into a self-induced trance and, while in that state, vigorously fling down the bones. On coming out of the trance, he will review the bones. Some are often found to be standing upright, their ends imbedded in the ground. This is usually taken as a danger sign if the bones are representations of dangerous animals.

The Zulu bones divination system, used by most Zulu *Sangomas*, or diviners, is worked with a set of oracle bones that are actual bones plus other objects like hoof tips, teeth, or shells. (See the entry on **African Divination** for a detailed explanation of divination using Zulu bones.)

For at least one version of aurispicy found in Africa, fourteen knuckle bones are used, each representative of animal totems. Of the fourteen bones, ten are power animals and the other four emphasize human characteristics, as listed below.

Aardvark—Represents ancestral spirits thought to reside in the burial grounds. The aardvark represents this wisdom since it burrows deep into the earth to acquire its nourishment. Positive aspect: Look to the wisdom of the past and accept the status quo. Negative: Don't be too rigid or old-fashioned in your approach to things.

Antelope—Represents leadership and warns to not ignore a relationship you might have with a person of power and influence. Positive aspect: Take the lead in affairs and don't hold back. Negative: Do not ignore your superiors or revolt against them.

Baboon—The followers. Some African legends portray baboons as innocents who are easily led. Positive aspect: Follow the majority and don't try to lead. Negative: Don't imitate others and ape their antics.

Bird—The seeker. In countless societies the bird is the messenger of the gods. Positive aspect: Look beyond your immediate surroundings and fasten your sights on distant goals. Don't be afraid to follow your dreams. Negative: Don't flit from one idea to another but try to be more down to earth and concentrated.

Chameleon—The prevaricator. This creature represents slow reactions, indecisiveness, changeability, and indecision. Positive aspect: Seize opportunities when they arise, since they won't wait around for ever. Negative: Don't be impatient; observe, be adaptable and ready to act.

Elephant—Force and coercion, representing brute force and animalistic instincts. Resist persuasive forces that try to change your opinions and decisions. Positive aspect: Be strong and resist threats. Negative: Avoid riding roughshod over others.

Hare—Deception. The elusive, swift hare can usually outrun its predators. It can change direction extremely quickly, making its enemies believe it is going one way when it is going another. Positive aspect: Be prudent and secretive, quick and cunning, when necessary. Negative: Beware of broken promises and deception.

Jackal/Hyena—Mercenary actions. This animal is a scavenger and a trickster. Its appearance is an indication that you are becoming mercenary. Positive aspect: Try to be objective. Negative: Don't be inconsiderate of others.

Lizard—Lost opportunities. Tied into psychic visions, the lizard is frequently the bearer of news of a death. Positive aspect: Don't delay in working for your hopes and aspirations. Negative: Face the future head on. Don't prevaricate where important decisions are concerned.

Tortoise—Patience and determination, which will invariably bring victory. Positive aspect: Whatever the obstacles, stick to your plans and persevere. Negative: Don't be stubborn and try to react more quickly.

Senior Male—Authority and control; the father figure representing authority. Positive aspect: Take command and don't prevaricate. Negative: Don't be dogmatic; be open to suggestions.

Senior Female—Care and dependence. Representing motherhood, caring, nurturing, protection. Positive aspect: Be sympathetic without being overly critical. Negative: Don't be over-bearing and dictatorial.

Junior Male—Youthful optimism. Enthusiasm and new ideas. Positive aspect: Willingness to assist, forethought, patience. Negative: Don't fight authority or experience.

Junior Female—Co-operation, adaptability, compromise. Positive aspect: Share your ideas and enthusiasm. Negative: Don't be pressured or influenced against your will.

Sheep bones, and especially the shoulder bones, are thought in some regions to be especially good for divination. They have been used by Bedouins, Mongolians, Icelanders, Scots, and Slavs, among others. In Scotland, one method was to scrape the shoulder blade of a black sheep with a sharp stone. The resultant lines and ridges are interpreted, as is the toughness of the scraping action. In southern England, the way for a young woman to gain the return of an errant lover was to stab a sheep's shoulder blade with a knife and say the words:

It's not this bone I wish to stick,
But (Name)'s heart I wish to prick.
Whether he be asleep or awake
I'd have him come to me and speak.

There are many variations on this spell, many not using a bone. One, for example, involves the woman writing the man's name on a piece of paper, setting fire to it, and scattering the ashes, saying:

It's not this heart I mean to burn,
But (Name)'s love I wish to turn.
Be he asleep or be he awake
May he come to me before daybreak.

A length of kangaroo bone is used by the Australian *kurdaicha*, or diviner, to discover the identity of a murderer. If a murder has been committed in a village and the murderer has made off into the bush, the villagers do not immediately attempt to track down the perpetrator. Instead, they call in the kurdaicha and show him the scene of the crime. He will study it, then sit in the center of the village and sing and chant. As he works himself into a state of *ekstasis*, he comes to his feet and starts to swing the "pointing bone" in a circle about him. It is a length of bone attached, with a tarlike wax, to a length of plaited human hair. Swinging it about him, he causes the bone to point in all directions, thus sending out a projection of the bone to implant itself, invisibly, in the body of the murderer. Only then will the villagers set out to track the criminal through the bush. It is said that they always come upon the dead body of the man, since the pointing bone will have brought about his death.

The **Chinese** were believers in the power of bones to answer questions and to foretell events. This was especially prevalent in the 400–year Han dynasty, where everyone, from nobles to lay persons, used a wide variety of fortune-telling methods.

Sources:

Buckland, Raymond and Kathleen Binger. *The Book of African Divination*. Rochester, VT: Destiny Books, Rochester 1992.

Cavendish, Richard (ed.). *Man, Myth & Magic*. London: BPC Publishing, 1970.

Loewe, Michael. *Chinese Ideas of Life and Death*. London: Routledge, 1982.
www.angelfire.com/electronic/bodhidharma/bones.html.

Austromancy

Divination from observation of the winds. Winds blowing from the east and the south are generally positive, while those blowing from the west or north are negative, though different areas have different interpretations. In the southern United States, it is said that if the wind blows suddenly and strongly from the east, a heavy rain may be expected.

If a wind blows strongly from one direction then suddenly calms and starts up again from a different direction, it is a forewarning of some dire circumstance coming. Small whirlwinds on a dusty road indicate a coming rain.

The Ashanti of Ghana believe that you can talk to the wind to find out about the future. The wind is everywhere and therefore knowledgeable on all things. If, under the right circumstances, you speak to the wind and ask about the future, you can hear the answer by listening carefully to the sound of the wind blowing.

Automanzia

An obscure form of divination using ten straight pins and three bent pins. The exact method is unknown, but it is probably similar to the Romany practice of floating needles in a saucer of **water** and seeing how many of them cross the others. Obviously, the straight pins have a different meaning from the bent ones, with the latter probably indicating misfortune. The number of good to bad, and the relationship, would indicate the probable future.

Automatic Writing/Drawing/Painting

Performing the tasks of writing, drawing, and/or painting without control by the conscious mind is called automatic writing/drawing/painting. It is a not-uncommon phenomenon of **spiritualism.** To focus on writing (drawing and painting follow the same procedures), the operator uses the same muscles that would normally be used but in no way tries to govern what is actually written. The true "director" of the writing is believed to be a departed spirit attempting to communicate. The practice is followed to gain knowledge of the future, with the governing force being thought of as a deity, disembodied spirit, alien, or unknown force, depending upon the beliefs of the person acting as **medium** for the writing.

Looking at the spiritualist form, the operator or medium would take a pen or pencil and sit with a large sheet of paper on the table in front of, or beside, him or her. Because the writing produced is frequently voluminous, many mediums will use something like a roll of wallpaper or wrapping paper to ensure having enough paper available without having to look down or turn pages.

Usually the medium will first sit quietly, perhaps meditating on whose energy might be expected to materialize. Then the hand holding the pen is rested on the

This woman from Italy, although right-handed, holds a pen in her open left hand to write automatically. Messages she writes this way contain information unknown to her. ***Dr. Elmar R. Gruber/Fortean Picture Library.***

paper, and the medium directs his or her attention elsewhere. That might be to read a book, watch television, talk with another person, play a game of chess, or anything that will draw focus away from the hand holding the pen.

What usually happens is that the hand starts to move, initially in small movements, and seemingly of its own volition. The movements, of course, cause marks to appear on the paper. Initially these are no more than straight lines, developing into wavy lines, and then squiggles. Gradually it seems the force becomes aligned with the muscles of the hand and arm and able to direct the writing. Squiggles become circles and hooks, which slowly develop into letters and actual writing. As the spirit hand operator becomes more accustomed to the mechanics involved, the writing becomes clearer and is written much more quickly. Some automatic writing is done at incredible speed, with the medium's hand flying across the paper. Many times a normally right-handed medium will use the left hand for automatic writing, or vice versa. Usually the writing that is produced in no way resembles the normal handwriting of the medium.

While a neophyte needs to occupy the mind in order to disassociate from the writing, a medium/**diviner** who is skilled in automatic writing can separate from what is taking place sufficiently without needing outside stimulus to prevent him or her from influencing what is written. This can be done to the point where it is then possible to look at the paper and to put questions and receive answers through the writing. If necessary, however, a second person may sit beside the medium/diviner and ask the questions, so that the medium cannot see what is written in reply.

There are instances of a medium going into a trance and producing writing, but actually no trance is necessary. From the point of view of divining the future, this is a method that can be used by anyone with a little practice. But it has also produced some fascinating information concerning the past and the present. One classic case was when William Stainton Moses (1839–1892) produced a large number of such writings from various spirits, which were published under the title *Spirit Teachings* (London, 1883). Describing the procedure, Moses said:

> At first the writing was slow and it was necessary for me to follow it with my eye, but even then the thoughts were not my thoughts. Very

soon all the messages assumed a character of which I had no doubt whatever that the thought opposed my own. But I cultivated the power of occupying my mind with other things during the time that the writing was going on, and was able to read an abstruse book and follow out a line of close reasoning, while the message was written with unbroken regularity. Messages so written extended over many pages and in their course there is no correction, no fault in composition, and often a sustained vigour and beauty of style.

Another, perhaps better-known, automatic writer was Pearl Curran, who produced the writings of an entity calling herself Patience Worth. Pearl Curran was a St. Louis housewife who was persuaded by a friend, Emily Hutchinson, to use a **Ouija® board.** On July 8, 1913, it started spelling out a message that started, "Many moons ago I lived. Again I come; Patience Worth my name." The spirit identified itself as a seventeenth-century Englishwoman. Pearl Curran progressed from the Ouija board to automatic writing and eventually produced 2,500 poems, short stories, plays, and allegories, plus six full-length novels under the name Patience Worth—a total of over four million words within a period of five years.

Automatic writing has also been produced by such well-known people as Victor Hugo, Goethe, Charles Linton, Professor William James, and Mme. D'Esperance.

Sources:

Buckland, Raymond. *Doors to Other Worlds*. St. Paul, MN: Llewellyn, 2000.

Ebon, Martin. *True Experiences in Communicating with the Dead*. New York: New American Library, 1968.

Fodor, Nandor. *An Encyclopedia of Psychic Science*. London, 1934.

Moses, William Stainton. *Direct Spirit Writing*. London, 1878.

Mühl, Anita M. *Automatic Writing*. Dresden, Germany: Steinkopff, 1930.

AXE *see* Axinomancy

Axinomancy; Axiomancy

Divination using an axe head and a bed of red-hot coals. According to Sir Thomas Urquhart (*The Third Book of the Works of Mr. Francis Rabelais*, London, 1693): "To have the truth ... disclosed ... by axinomancy: we want only a hatchet and a jet-stone to be laid together upon a fire of hot embers." Possibly an adze could be used as well as an axe.

Two different methods of working with the axe have been suggested. The first method—which is to divine the location of buried treasure—is to build a fire then to stand an axe, or just the head of an axe, in the embers. The axe should be a single-bit axe and must be placed in such a way that the axe head will stand on its back with the blade in the air. When the blade is red hot, an agate stone or a piece of jet is balanced on the edge of the blade. If it remains balanced there, then there is no treasure in the area. However, if the stone should fall and roll into the embers, it must be replaced, and then again replaced if it falls a second time. If, on falling, the stone rolls to the same side each time, then that is an indication of the direction in which treasure lies.

A second method of using an axe, without the fire embers, is as an aid in tracking thieves. The axe is swung so that the head gets stuck into the ground with the handle sticking up in the air. There should be a number of people present and they should take hands and dance around the projecting axe handle until it topples and falls over. When it has fallen, the end of the handle will indicate the direction in which any thieves have gone.

According to Pierre de l'Ancre (*L'incrédulité et mécréance du sortilège*, Paris, 1622), the method was to stick the axe "into a round stake, and by the quivering or movement that it made they judged of thefts or other great crimes."

Sources:

de Givry, Grillot. *A Pictorial Anthology of Witchcraft, Magic & Alchemy*. London: Spottiswoode, Ballantyne, 1931.

Oxford English Dictionary. Oxford: Clarendon Press, 1989.

Shepard, Leslie A. (ed.). *Encyclopedia of Occultism & Parapsychology*. New York: Avon, 1978.

AZTEC *see* Mexico and Central America

B

Babylonian Zodiac

The Babylonians had a good knowledge of the heavens as long as four thousand years ago. They knew that the stars revolved above the earth once a day and that the sun, moon, and various planets also moved around at different speeds. They noted the spring equinox, with equal hours of day and night. Although it was known that the twelve constellations of the zodiac do not occupy equal segments of the sky, for convenience the circle of the zodiac was divided into twelve equal houses and named after those constellations that used to appear in them.

The Babylonians recorded their names for the signs of the zodiac over 2,500 years ago. Modern names are derived from these. They were:

Modern Name	Babylonian Name	Meaning
Aries	*hunga*	hireling
Taurus	*gudanna*	bull of heaven
Gemini	*mastabbagalgal*	great twins
Cancer	*allul*	crab
Leo	*urgula*	lion
Virgo	*absin*	furrow
Libra	*zibanitu*	scales
Scorpio	*girtab*	scorpion
Sagittarius	*Ninurta*	the god of war
Capricorn	*kusarikku*	fish-ram
Aquarius	*Enkidu*	giant water-carrier
Pisces	*zibbati*	tails

Sources:

Headon, Deirdre (ed.). *Quest for the Unknown—Charting the Future*. Pleasantville, NY: Reader's Digest, 1992.

Bagoe

The Erithryean sibyl or pythoness. Bagoe was believed to have been the first woman to practice the art of divination. She lived in Tuscany and used the diviner's art of **brontomancy**—judging events by the sound of thunder. Interpretation would depend upon volume and distance from the sibyl.

BARLEY ***see*** **Aleuromancy; Alphitomancy; Crithomancy**

Batrachomancy; Batraquomancy

Divination by frogs, toads, and newts. If a tree toad is heard, it is a sign of a coming rain shower. If a bullfrog's skin turns a dark color, there will be rain within twelve hours. These are old beliefs from the Ozark region of the United States. Frogs, toads, and newts are generally associated with **water,** so the sighting of such an amphibian would frequently be taken as a sign of approaching wet weather.

During the witch persecutions, many witches were accused of having a pet toad as a "familiar," or magical servant. It was certainly not uncommon for people to encourage toads to occupy space in their gardens to help exterminate insects. With the importance of rain for garden cultivation, many did carefully observe the activities of their toads for any possible indications of weather changes. Predicting weather by the actions of a toad, frog, or even a newt was a personal endeavor, with conclusions varying greatly from one person to the next.

In some areas of Europe the frog and toad are associated with water spirits, or undines. In Acton Barnett, in Shropshire, England, there is an ancient healing well where it is said three blessed spirits often appear in the form of frogs.

Sources:

Buckland, Raymond. *The Witch Book: The Encyclopedia of Witchcraft, Wicca, and Neo-paganism.* Detroit: Visible Ink Press, 2002.

BELLY ***see*** **Gastromancy**

Belomancy; Bolomancy

Dating from as far back as the Chaldeans, this is a form of divination done with arrows. It was popular with the **Greeks** and the **Romans,** among the latter being especially popular with the soldiers. It was also used by the Arabians, despite being forbidden by the Koran. The *Saturday Review of Science* of 1883 refers to "divining arrows, rods, or the knotched (*sic*) sticks of belomancy."

The arrows could be used in much the same way as the sticks of **rhabdomancy.** They could be loosely stuck into the ground, and the direction in which they later fell would be of significance. One method was to shoot arrows straight up into the air and see in which direction the shafts leaned when they came down and stuck into the ground. This would indicate the direction in which to go to find, for example, buried treasure. Another method was to mark various quadrants and circles of a target with different meanings then to shoot arrows or throw darts at the target, noting where the missiles struck. Of course a marksman could simply aim at the answer he wanted, but the majority of diviners were not particularly good archers. Sometimes just two arrows would be used, one marked "Yes" and the other marked "No." They would be shuffled and the diviner would then take an arrow without looking to see which one it was. He would then shoot at a target marked with specific questions. Yet another method was to mark arrows each with a different possible answer to a question. The arrows would be shuffled together and placed in a quiver. One arrow would be drawn out, and that was the pertinent answer.

In the **Bible,** Ezekiel 21:21, it says: "For the king of Babylon stood at the parting of the way, at the head of the two ways, to use divination: he made his arrows bright [one translation says 'he shakes the arrows'], he consulted with images, he looked in the liver."

Parapsychologist Hans Georg Bender. ***Dr. Elmar R. Gruber/Fortean Picture Library.***

Sources:

Headon, Deirdre (ed.). *Quest for the Unknown—Charting the Future*. Pleasantville, NY: Reader's Digest, 1992.

Oxford English Dictionary. Oxford: Clarendon Press, 1989.

Shepard, Leslie A. (ed.). *Encyclopedia of Occultism & Parapsychology*. New York: Avon, 1978.

BENDER, HANS GEORG (1907–1991)

Born in Freiburg, Germany, in 1907, Hans Bender was the son of a lawyer. He studied at a number of European universities and eventually, in 1954, became professor for the border areas of psychology at Freiburg. He was one of the few academics to seriously study **astrology** and astrologers, testing more than one hundred astrologers by giving them the charts of people unknown to them and asking them to interpret what was shown.

Bender edited the *Journal of Parapsychology and Border Areas of Psychology*. He did a lot of scientific research into the subject of poltergeist activity and wrote the book *New Developments in Poltergeist Research*.

Sources:

Fishley, Margaret. *The Supernatural*. London: Aldus, 1976.

BHAL *see* Kumalak

Bible

One of the best-known examples of divination in the Bible is the interpreting of **dreams** done by Joseph. In Genesis 41:14–36 he foretold of seven years of plenty coming to **Egypt,** to be followed by seven years of famine. This was based on the Pharaoh's dream of seven fat cows emerging from a stream and going to graze in a meadow. These were followed by seven thin cows that devoured the fat ones, although the second seven remained thin after the feasting. A second dream of the Pharaoh's was of seven fat ears of corn growing on a stalk, which were devoured by seven thin ears of corn. This confirmed Joseph's interpretation of plenty followed by famine.

But prior to that, in Genesis 40:1–23, Joseph had interpreted the dreams of both the Pharaoh's head butler and his head baker, who were imprisoned. The dream of the butler involved three grape vines that developed first leaves, then blossoms, then grapes. The grapes, when pressed, filled the Pharaoh's cup. Joseph showed this to mean that the butler would be released and restored to his place within three days. The dream of the baker was similar but involved three baskets of bread and other baked goods that were eaten by **birds.** This, according to Joseph, showed that the baker would be taken out and hung in three days. Both prognostications came true.

Joseph's dream interpretation had started early. In Genesis 37:5 it says: "And Joseph dreamed a dream, and he told it his brethren: and they hated him yet the more." What he dreamed was of a sheaf of wheat that, he felt, represented himself, and other sheaves that represented his brothers. The sheaves representing his brothers all bowed down to his sheaf. Then he had another dream that the sun, moon, and eleven stars "made obeisance to me."

Ancient **Hebrew** literature has a number of examples of portentous dreams. For example, when Jacob was fleeing from the wrath of his brother Esau, he had a dream at Bethel (possibly an ancient Canaanite sanctuary) of a ladder stretching from Earth up to heaven. At the top of the ladder the God of Abraham informed Jacob that he and his descendants would be given the surrounding land. In Judges 7:13–14 there is a man "that told a dream [about a cake of barley bread tumbled into the host of Midian] unto his fellow," which is then interpreted for him by the "fellow."

There are also many references in the Old Testament to casting **lots.** In Leviticus 16:7–9, after telling him to make various burnt offerings and sacrifices, God commands Aaron to take two goats to the Tabernacle door and to cast lots upon them. In Proverbs 16:33 it says: "The lot is cast into the lap; but the whole disposing thereof is of the Lord." In Proverbs 3:16 there is reference to palmistry: "Length of days is in her right hand; and in her left hand riches and honor." And in 1 Samuel 26:18 is found: "What have I done? Or what evil is in mine hand?" Revelation 14:9 has "If any man worship the beast and his image, and receive his mark in his forehead, or in his hand." And in Job 37:7: "He sealeth up the hand of every man; that all men may know his work," which, according to Cheiro (**Louis Hamon**), was originally rendered, "God placed signs and seals in the hands of men, that all men might know their works." (Cheiro apparently based this on Louis Isaac Le Maître de Sacy's seventeenth-century translation of the Latin text.)

In 1 Samuel 10:10 is found: "And when they came thither to the hill, behold a company of prophets met him (Saul); and the Spirit of God came upon him, and he **prophesied** among them." Next Samuel called a council at Mizpeh and carefully arranged things so that Saul was chosen "by lot," making use, presumably, of the *Urim* and *Thummim*. These are Hebrew words that translate as "Lights" and "Perfections" and are often mentioned when there is the casting of lots. No one seems to know exactly what were the Urim and Thummim, but it seems most probable that they were a form of lot used for guidance when divining the will of God. Possibly one indicated "Yes" and the other "No." Later, in 1 Samuel 28:6 it says that Saul asked a question of the Lord about the advance of the Philistines, and that he got no answer—"neither by dreams, nor by Urim, nor by prophets." The Revised Standard Version of the Bible, which is fuller and more explicit than the King James Version, in 1 Samuel 14:41 says: "If this guilt is in me or in Jonathan my son, O Lord, God of Israel, give Urim; but if this guilt is in thy people Israel, give Thummim."

In Ezekiel 21:21, it says: "For the king of Babylon stood at the parting of the way, at the head of the two ways, to use divination: he made his arrows bright [one translation says 'he shakes the arrows'], he consulted with images, he looked in the liver." In making "his arrows bright," and in consulting "with images," he could well have been using the shiny metal for **scrying,** or **mirror-gazing.** Shaking the arrows was **belomancy** or **rhabdomancy.** Looking "in the liver" was obviously **hepatoscopy** or **haruspicy.**

In the New Testament, in Acts 1:26 there is a choosing between Matthias and Joseph Barsabbas, to see which of them will take Judas's place: "And they gave forth their lots: and the lot fell upon Matthias, and he was numbered with the eleven apostles." However, poor Matthias is not mentioned again anywhere in the New Testament after that! In John 19:24, the Roman soldiers are deciding who shall get Jesus's garments and do so by casting lots: "They said therefore among themselves, Let us not rend it but cast lots for it, whose it shall be."

Sources:

Asimov, Isaac. *Asimov's Guide to the Bible*. New York: Avon, 1968.
Cheiro (Louis Hamon). *Cheiro's Language of the Hand*. Chicago: Rand, McNally, 1897.
Holy Bible—various editions.
Scott's Bible; Old and New Testaments with Notes, Observations, and References. New York: Samuel T Armstrong, 1827.

Bibliomancy

(See also Rhapsodomancy; Sortes)

One method of **divining** is to open a book at random and to read the first sentence your eye falls upon. That sentence is believed to have some relevance to the question being asked. This was also known as *sortes biblicæ*. Often the **Bible** is used for this (*sortes sanctorum*), but also, at one time, the works of Homer (*sortes Homericæ*) and Virgil (*sortes Virgilianæ*) were very popular. Virgil's *Æneid* was a book commonly used in the Middle Ages. The **Greeks** preferred to take from Homer's *Iliad* and the *Odyssey*, while the **Romans** favored Virgil. Mohammedans practice bibliomancy using the Koran.

The usual method is to close the eyes, possibly say a short prayer, and then open the book at random and place a finger on the page before opening the eyes. The sentence being touched is the one that will relate to the question, give some indication of what the future holds, or suggest some action to be taken. Some diviners will stick the passage with a pin or the tip of a dagger, rather than just with the finger.

One source defines bibliomancy as the "weighing against the Bible" found during the witchcraft persecutions. At that time most churches had huge, heavy Bibles. The accused would be placed on a stool suspended from a pivot, balancing against a platform on which rested the Bible. If the person weighed more than the Bible, he or she was deemed guilty.

Sources:

Grand Orient (A. E. Waite). *A Manual of Cartomancy*. London: William Rider, 1912.
Oxford English Dictionary, Oxford: Clarendon Press, Oxford 1989.

BIORHYTHMS

Over the period 1895–1902, Herman Swaboda, a professor of psychology at the University of Vienna, became interested in and worked with human rhythmic cycles. By studying the recurrence of pain and the swelling of tissues, he was able to detail a twenty-three-day cycle, which he termed the "physical cycle," in certain aspects of illness. He found a periodicity in fevers, heart attacks, and the initial outbreak of an illness. He was aware of the female twenty-eight-day menstrual cycle and so considered this twenty-three-day cycle a masculine rhythm. Swaboda published a number of scholarly books on the subject and even produced a slide rule that would easily reveal the critical days of anyone's life, based on their birth date. Independently, Wilhelm Fliess, a nose and throat specialist in Berlin, accumulated a vast amount of research on the same two rhythmic cycles; the twenty-three-day and the twenty-eight-day.

Nearly twenty years later, in 1920, an Innsbruck engineering instructor, Dr. Alfred Telscher, noticed a thirty-three-day periodicity for his students' high and low peaks. This was confirmed, again by independent studies, by Dr. Rexford Hersey at the University of Pennsylvania. There are, then, three basic human rhythms, known as *biorhythms:* a physical twenty-three-day cycle, an emotional twenty-eight-day cycle, and an intellectual or mental thirty-three-day cycle. Since all humans have male and female elements in their makeup, the "masculine" twenty-three-day cycle and the "feminine" twenty-eight-day cycle apply equally to both sexes.

Physicians and psychologists have observed and charted these physical, emotional, and mental changes for many years. They have observed that certain patterns cover these three rhythms and that each rhythm never varies. It therefore became possible to forecast "good" and "bad" days, or high- and low-energy days. More importantly, it became possible to forecast critical days in each of these cycles. These were days when accidents were most likely to happen, when there was the most likelihood of sickness, and when poor decisions were likely to be made. Critical days are the days when a cycle, in a sine-curve presentation, switches from high to low or low to high, crossing the midpoint, or zero, line of the graph. Articles on the subject have been published in *Psychology Today*, *Business Week*, *Science Digest*, *Human Behavior*, and other journals.

To find your cycles, it is necessary to add up the total number of days from your date of birth to the first of the month for which the chart is being constructed. This total is then divided by twenty-three, twenty-eight, and thirty-three respectively. These divisions indicate how many times each cycle has run a complete span. The remainders show the position of each rhythm on the first day of the month being studied. There are sets of tables, special instruments, and computer programs available for these calculations, although they can be done purely by mathematics.

As to the accuracy of these rhythms over a full lifespan, Thommen says:

> We might say that Nature has devised a way of doing two useful, but somewhat contradictory, things at the same time. First, each infant at birth automatically sets his clock to zero and times his rhythms from that day onward throughout the rest of his life. In this sense, the infants born on the same day, within a few hours of each other, form a human subspecies with their own "standard time." Second, all human beings, whatever their individual starting points may be, unconsciously keep their individual clocks from running fast or slow by daily reference to the twenty-four-hour cycle of light and darkness, activity and quiet, which results from the rotation of the earth on its axis. *Thus, although each individual has his own "standard time," all individuals have equally accurate clocks.*

Based on biorhythms, Switzerland and Japan have managed to reduce bus-driver accidents by over ninety percent by forecasting the critical days for the individuals involved and scheduling them for other than intense driving conditions. George Margolin, a science editor, claims that ninety percent of all accidents happen on biorhythm critical days and that the *Guinness Book of World Records* shows that eighty-four percent of all world records were created when the individual's physical curve was high.

Based on biorhythm charts, it has been proven possible to forecast, or divine with great accuracy, the moods and feelings of every person, including those that could lead to great success or great failure. Thommen's charts show that Carl Jung died (July 26, 1875) during what was a double-critical day for him; William Faulkner died of a heart attack (July 6, 1962) when his chart showed a critical day in his sensitivity rhythm; Robert Frost died (January 29, 1963) when his physical rhythm was at a critical point; General Douglas MacArthur died (April 5, 1964) on a physical critical day. There are many more examples. Muhammad Ali lost to Ken Norton on Ali's critical day; Robert Kennedy was murdered on a critical day; both Judy Garland and Marilyn Monroe committed suicide on their critical days. When planning ahead for some event or considering significant action, it would be well to look ahead and avoid any day that might be critical in any of the three cycles.

Sources:

Anderson, Russell K. *Biorhythm—Man's Timing Mechanism*. Park Ridge, IL: American Society of Safety Engineers, 1973.

Fliess, Wilhelm. *Der Ablauf des Lebens*. ("The Course of Life"). Liepzig-Vienna: Franz Deuticke, 1906.
Gittelson, Bernard. *Biorhythm: A Personal Science*. New York: Warner Books, 1980.
Swoboda, Hermann. *Das Siebenjahn* ("The Year of Seven"). Liepzig-Vienna: Orion-Verlag, 1917.
Thommen, George S. *Is This Your Day?* New York: Crown, 1973.
Ward, Ritchier. *The Living Clocks*. New York: New American Library, 1971.

BIRDS *see* Augury; Orniscopy

BLACK BOXES *see* Abrams, Albert

Blavatsky, Helena Petrovna (1831–1891)

Helena Petrovna Blavatksy was one of the best-known and most influential occultists in the world. As a spiritualist medium and a **seeress** she had no equal. With Colonel Henry S. Olcott, she became the cofounder of the world-renowned Theosophical Society.

Helena's father was Colonel Peter Hahn, a Russian officer and member of the Mecklenburg family. Her mother was Helena de Fadeyev, a noted novelist. On her mother's side, she was the granddaughter of the gifted writer and botanist Princess Helena Dolgorukov. Count Sergei Yulievich Witte, a Tsarist prime minister, was her cousin. Helena was born at Ekaterinoslav, a town on the river Dnieper, in southern Russia, on August 12, 1831. After the early death of her mother in 1842, she was brought up by her maternal grandparents at their house in Saratov. Her grandfather was civil governor there. An exceptional child, at an early age Helena was aware of being deeply sensitive and of possessing certain psychic powers. She could see spirits, invisible to her friends, and foresee certain events through various forms of divination. She was a natural linguist, a talented pianist, and a fine artist. She was also a fine horsewoman. According to her sister's memoirs, Helena had frequent bouts of somnambulism, walking in her sleep and speaking in unknown tongues. She could also cause hallucinations in her playmates through her vivid storytelling.

Helena received no formal education and, at seventeen, married a much older man, Nikifor (or Nicephore) Blavatsky, vice-governor of the Province of Erivan in Transcaucasia. Within a few months of the marriage she ran away to adopt a nomadic existence—a life that has been compared to the Victorian equivalent of a hippie—moving through Egypt, Greece, and Turkey. In London by the time she was twenty, Blavatsky met an individual whom she claimed to have known from her childhood visions. He was the Mahatma Morya (or "M," as he became known among Theosophists in later years), an Eastern Initiate of Rajput birth. He told Blavatsky of the spiritual work that lay ahead of her, and from then on she fully accepted his guidance. Later the same year, 1851, she embarked for Canada. Blavatsky then went on to travel various parts of the United States, Mexico, South America, and the West Indies.

In 1852 she went to India, traveling by way of the Cape and Ceylon. She was prevented from entering Tibet and so, in 1853, returned to England. Summer of the following year she again went to America, where she crossed the Rockies with a caravan of emigrants. In late 1855 Blavatsky again left for India, this time going by way of

Japan. On this attempt she succeeded in entering Tibet, doing so through Kashmir and Ladakh. By 1858 she was in France and then Germany, finally returning to Russia in the late fall of that year. She stayed a short time with her sister Vera at Pskov. By this time Blavatsky had developed strong mediumistic abilities and achieved considerable fame as a spiritualist medium with a spirit guide named John King. It was said that whisperings, rappings, and other strange phenomena were heard all over her house. From 1860 to 1865, she traveled through the Caucasus then left Russia again in the fall of 1865, going on to the Balkans, Egypt, Syria, Greece, and Italy.

In 1868 Blavatsky again went to Tibet, this time via India. On this trip she met "the Master Koot Hoomi" (K.H.) for the first time, and she stayed in Little Tibet and also in Great Tibet. She then underwent part of her occult training with her master. She later reported that she had been initiated by the "hidden masters," who were to become her driving force for the rest of her life. By late 1870 Blavatsky was back in Cyprus, then Greece. En route to Egypt, the *Eumonia,* on which she sailed, was shipwrecked on July 4, 1871, near the island of Spetsai. Blavatsky, saved from drowning, went on to Cairo where she tried to form a *Société Spirite,* but it failed. After further travels through the Middle East, she returned for a short time to her relatives at Odessa, Russia, in July of 1872.

In the spring of 1873, Blavatsky was instructed by her teacher to go to Paris and, on further direct orders from him, left for New York City where she landed July 7, 1873. Then forty-two years old and in possession of many spiritual and occult powers, she worked for a while as a dressmaker to earn a living. A year later, on a whim, Blavatsky traveled to Vermont to witness the much-publicized Eddy Brothers, William and Horatio, two spiritualists who produced a variety of phenomena. There she met Colonel Henry Steele Olcott, a man with a reputation for honesty. He had served in the Civil War and then, with distinction, for the U.S. government. Nandor Fodor says of her psychic abilities at this time: "Whereas there is a limit to the phenomena of every spiritualist medium, Mme. Blavatsky apparently knew none. From the materialization of grapes for the thirsty Colonel Olcott in New York to the duplication of precious stones in India, or the creation of toys for children out of nothingness, she undertook almost any magical task and successfully performed it to the stupefaction of her coterie."

Blavatsky launched into journalism, translating Olcott's articles into Russian and writing her own articles on spiritualism. In the opinion of the Mahatmas, or Adepts, Helena Blavatsky was the best available instrument for the work they had in mind, namely to offer to the world a new presentation of the age-old *Theosophia:* "The accumulated Wisdom of the ages, tested and verified by generations of Seers." Blavatsky's task was to challenge both the entrenched beliefs and dogmas of Christian theology and the equally dogmatic materialistic view of the science of her day. On September 7, 1875, Blavatsky and Olcott, together with several others, founded the Theosophical Society. The inaugural address by the president-founder, Colonel Olcott, was delivered November 17, 1875, also considered to be the official date of the founding of the society. They stated the aims of the society to be: "1: To form a nucleus of the Universal Brotherhood of Humanity, without distinction of race, creed, sex, caste or color. 2: To encourage the study of Comparative Religion, Philosophy and Science. 3: To investigate unexplained laws of Nature, and the powers latent in man."

Helena Petrovna Blavatsky, as drawn by Gordon Wain, with the symbol of the Theosophical Society above her head. *Fortean Picture Library.*

In September 1877 Helena Petrovna Blavatsky's first monumental work, *Isis Unveiled* was published, the 1,000 copies of the first printing being sold within ten days. It was her book on the divine wisdom, or body of truth, concerning god, man, and the universe. She claimed that, while writing it, she had glimpsed the goddess Isis herself. On July 8, 1878, Blavatsky was naturalized as a U.S. citizen, and in December of the same year she and Colonel Olcott left for India via England.

They arrived in Bombay in February 1879, and there established their Theosophical Headquarters. Added importance was given to their activities by the reporting of A. P. Sinnett, editor of the *Pioneer.* After a tour of northwestern India, the founders returned to Bombay and started, in October 1879, their first Theosophical journal, *The Theosophist* (still published today), with Blavatsky as editor. From then on the society experienced rapid growth. In May 1882, a large estate was bought in southern India at Adyar, near Madras, and the Theosophical Headquarters was moved there. It is during this period that Colonel Olcott engaged in widespread mesmeric healings until February 1884, when he left for London to petition the British government on behalf of the Buddhists of Ceylon (Sri Lanka). Blavatsky, then in very poor health, went to Europe with him.

Blavatsky produced many seeming marvels at séances she held over an extended period. So much publicity was generated by her mediumship that it provoked the Society for Psychical Research to send an investigator to Adyar. This was Richard Hodgson, who, after a superficial examination, claimed to find nothing but fraud. He also accused Madame Blavatsky of being a Russian spy. Alex and Emma Coulomb, a couple who had been with her since 1880, stated that they had been instruments in perpetrating much of the fakery. Blavatsky wanted to sue the couple but was overruled by a committee of leading Theosophical Society members. In disgust, she resigned as corresponding secretary of the society and, on March 31, 1885, left for Europe, never again to return to India. Blavatsky settled first in Italy and then, in August 1885, at Wurzburg, Germany, where she worked on *The Secret Doctrine*, much of which was written either by **automatic writing** or by inspirational writing.

The vicious attack on her had a most unfavorable effect on Blavatsky's health. In July 1886, she relocated to Ostend, Belgium, and in May of the following year, at the invitation of English Theosophists, she moved to a small house in London. After her arrival in England, Theosophical activities immediately began to move rapidly. The Blavatsky Lodge was formed and started publicizing Theosophical ideas. She continued to work on her book, which was finally completed and published in two volumes in October–December 1888. *The Secret Doctrine* was to become the crowning achievement of Blavatsky's literary career. It was an account of the root knowledge out of which all religion, philosophy, and science have grown. Also in October 1888, Blavatsky formed the Esoteric Section (or School) of the Theosophical Society "for the deeper study of the Esoteric Philosophy by dedicated students." In July 1890, she established the European Headquarters of the Theosophical Society in London. It was from there that Blavatsky, who had been suffering from Bright's disease, died on May 8, 1891, during a severe epidemic of flu in England.

Sources:

Blavatsky, Helena Petrovna. *Isis Unvieled*. New York: J. W. Bouton, 1877.

Blavatsky, Helena Petrovna. *The Secret Doctrine*. London: Theosophical Publishing Company, 1888.

Fodor, Nandor. *An Encyclopedia of Psychic Science*. London, 1934.

Harrison, Vernon. *H. P. Blavatsky and the SPR: An Examination of the Hodgson Report of 1885*. Pasadena, CA: Theosophical University Press, 1997.

http://www.blavatskyarchives.com/.

Sinnett, A .P. *Incidents in the Life of Madame Blavatsky*. London: George Redway, 1886.

Symonds, John. *Madame Blavatsky: Medium and Magician*. London: Odhams, 1959.

Williams, Gertrude Marvin. *Priestess of the Occult: Madame Blavatsky*. New York: Alfred A. Knopf, 1946.

Bletonism

The *Monthly Magazine* of 1821 stated that "bletonism is a faculty of perceiving and indicating subterraneous springs and currents by sensation; the term is modern, and derived from a Mr. Bleton, who for some years past has excited universal attention by his possessing the above faculty." In other words, in the early nineteenth century there was a well-known **water** diviner named Bleton, and his name came to be applied to **dowsing,** or **rhabdomancy.**

BLOOD *see* Dririmancy; Hæmatomancy

BOLOMANCY *see* Belomancy

BONES *see* Aurispicy; Ossomancy; Osteomancy

BOOK OF CHANGES *see* I Ching

BOOKS, RANDOM PASSAGES *see* Bibliomancy; Sortes; Stichomancy

Botanomancy; Botomancy

Edmund Chilmead's 1640 translation of Jacques Ferrand's *Treatise discoursing of the essence, causes, and cure of love, or erotique melancholy* includes the description: "Botanomancy is done by the noise or crackling of knee holme, box, or bay leaves when they are crushed betwixt one's hands or cast into the fire." François Rabelais (c. 1483–1553) mentions "to have the truth of the matter disclosed unto you by botomancy."

Botanomancy also covers having branches of various herbs, such as vervain and briar, carved with questions and then burned. The crackling made by the burning branches is then interpreted, giving answers to the questions.

Sources:
Oxford English Dictionary. Oxford: Clarendon Press, 1989.

Bouly, Abbé Alex (1865–1958)

Born in 1865, the Abbé Alex Bouly, a Roman Catholic priest, lived on the north coast of France near the English Channel. He became so well known as a **water dowser** that he was contacted to do **divining** work for industrialists in Belgium, Portugal, Poland, and Romania. At the end of World War I the city of Reims employed him to locate unexploded ordnance. Such was his ability with the **pendulum** and rods that he was not only able to locate the shells but could also state whether they were of German, Austrian, or French origin. He was recommended to the Ministry of War in Paris.

Bouly founded the Society of Friends of Radiesthesia. In 1927 he coined the word "radiesthesia" as an alternate for dowsing, taking the Latin *radius* for "radiance" and the Greek *aisthesis* for "sensitivity."

Bouly carried out experiments in the hospitals of Boulogne-Sur-Mer, Berck Plage, Lille, and Liege, where he demonstrated an ability to identify cultures of microbes in test tubes as easily as others did it using microscopes.

In 1950, at the age of eighty-five, Bouly was made a Chevalier de la Legion d'Honneur, France's highest decoration. He died in 1958.

Sources:
Lethbridge, Thomas C. *The Power of the Pendulum*. London: Routledge & Kegan Paul, 1976.

Brahan Seer (d. 1660)

Kenneth Mackenzie, or "Kenneth the Swallow" (*Coinneach Odhar Fiosaiche*) was known as the "Brahan **Seer.**" In Scotland his name is as well known as **Nostradamus** is elsewhere. Kenneth was born at the beginning of the seventeenth century on the Isle of Lewis, at Baile-na-Cille in the parish of Uig. He was a laborer on the Brahan estate but came to be regarded as the greatest of all Highland seers.

The "**second sight,**" the gift of **prophesy** or *an da shealladh*, is a centuries-old belief in the Highlands of Scotland, and the Brahan Seer's prophesies were recited from generation to generation for many years before they were actually fulfilled. Some have been fulfilled in recent years and more have yet to be fulfilled. A Festival of the Brahan Seer still takes place in Scotland every year.

According to legend, Mackenzie had a sharp tongue and a ready wit in his early teens. The wife of the farmer he worked for did not have much of a sense of humor and didn't care for the practical jokes that he sometimes played on her. Nor did she care for his mockery of her assumed airs. Eventually she came to despise Mackenzie so much that she actually planned to poison him. One day Mackenzie had been out cutting peats, or divots, to be used for fuel. He was very tired from his hard work and lay down to rest while he waited for the farmer's wife to bring out his lunch to the field where he was, as was her custom. Unknown to Mackenzie, he had fallen asleep on the side of a fairy hill.

Mackenzie woke up with a start, and the first thing he noticed was a white stone lying on his chest. When he picked it up he found that it had a hole through it. He held up the stone and squinted through it. Through the hole, he saw the farmer's wife approaching across the fields, bringing his lunch. It turned out to be a fairy stone and, by looking through it, Mackenzie was able to "see" that the food the woman was bringing to him was poisoned. After she had left the food with him and gone away again, Kenneth fed it to a collie. The dog died in agony.

According to one account, Mackenzie lost his sight in the eye he first used to look through the stone. Ever after he could hold up the stone to that blind eye and "see" the future.

Kenneth Mackenzie made a number of famous predictions. He said that "the time would come, and it is not far off, when full-rigged ships will be seen sailing eastward and westward by the back of Tomnahurich (Hill), near Inverness." A hundred years later the Caledonian Canal was built around the back of Tomnahurich Hill. Mackenzie also said that "the day will come when Tomnahurich (or, as he called it, *Tom-na-sithichean*—the Fairy Hill) will be under lock and key and the fairies secured within." In 1859 the following passage appeared in the *Inverness Advertiser:*

> Tomnahurich, the far-famed Fairies' Hill, has been sown with oats. According to tradition, the Brahan prophet, who lived 200 years ago, predicted that ships with unfurled sails would pass and repass Tomnahurich; and further, that it would yet be placed under lock and key. The first part of the prediction was verified with the opening of the Caledonian Canal, and we seem to be on the eve of seeing the realization of the rest by the final closing up of the Fairies' Hill.

In fact, a short time later a cemetery occupied the top of the hill, with the spirits of the dead securely chained within its gates.

Another prediction of Kenneth Mackenzie: "The day will come when there will be a road through the hills of Ross-shire from sea to sea, and a bridge over every stream." This prediction was made at a time when there were virtually no established roads anywhere in the Highlands. He also prophesied the Battle of Culloden, making the prophesy at Culloden itself: "This bleak moor, ere many generations have passed, shall be stained with the best blood of Scotland. Glad am I that I shall not see the day." The battle eventually took place in 1746, 116 years after Mackenzie had foreseen it. More than five thousand of Bonnie Prince Charlie's soldiers died there.

Strings of black carriages, horseless and bridleless, led by "a fiery chariot" would pass through the Highlands, predicted Mackenzie. It was not to be until Victorian times that this prediction came true, with the introduction of the steam train.

Memorial to the Brahan Seer at the place where he was burnt to death in a tar-barrel for witchcraft. ***Andreas Trottmann/Fortean Picture Library.***

He made many predictions about Scottish families: "The day will come when the Mackenzies will lose all their possessions in Lochlash. . . . We shall have a fair-haired Lochiel; a red-haired Lovat; a squint-eyed, fair-haired Chisholm; a big, deaf Mackenzie. . . . The old wife with the footless stocking will drive the Lady of Clan Ranald from Nunton House." All of these, and many more, predictions came true. But the greatest of them was the foretelling of the fall of the great House of Seaforth.

Mackenzie had become the personal seer to his patron, the Earl of Seaforth. In the 1660s, the earl traveled to Paris on the order of King Charles II. The Countess Isabella did not hear from her husband for many months. She repeatedly demanded of Mackenzie to know what her lord was doing in Paris. The prophet tried to be evasive but eventually had to tell her what he saw. He saw the third Earl of Seaforth enjoying himself with the ladies of the French court. In her rage at hearing this, the countess had Mackenzie taken away and burned to death as a witch in a tar barrel. However, just before he died, he predicted, in great detail, the end of Seaforth. He said that the last chief of the clan would be born deaf and dumb and would outlive his sons. This came true in 1815, when there were no more heirs on the death of Francis Humberstone Mackenzie, the last of his line."

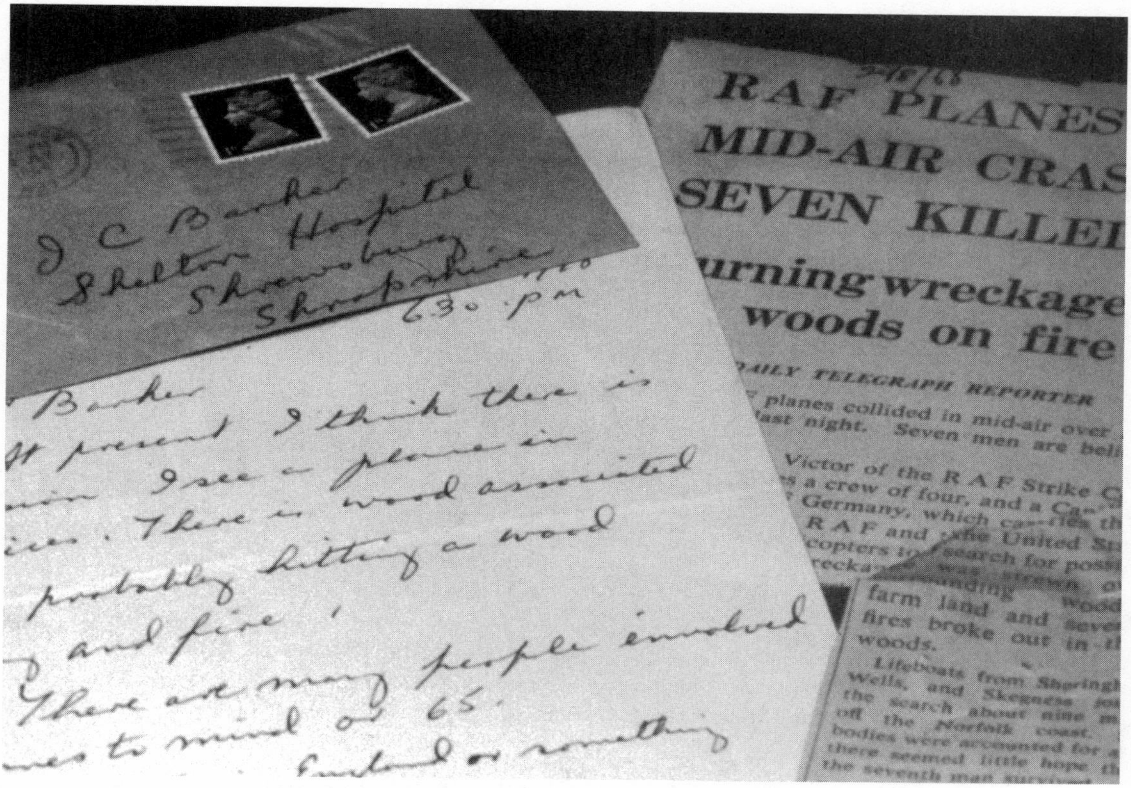

Premonitions sent to the British Premonitions Bureau. ***Fortean Picture Library.***

One of the outstanding prophesies of Kenneth Mackenzie is that Highlanders who had gone to other countries would finally return to their home, when "horrid black rains" begin to fall. Time will tell what that could mean.

Sources:

Buckland, Raymond. *Scottish Witchcraft*. St. Paul, MN: Llewellyn, 1992.

Campbell, John Gregorson. *Witchcraft and Second Sight in the Highlands and Islands of Scotland*. Glasgow: James MacLehose, 1902.

Headon, Deirdre (ed.). *Quest for the Unknown—Charting the Future*. Pleasantville: Reader's Digest, 1992.

Mackenzie, Alexander. *The Prophesies of the Brahan Seer*. Inverness, 1882.

BRAN *see* Alphitomancy

BRITISH PREMONITIONS BUREAU

This bureau was started in London in 1967 as a direct result of the large numbers of **prophetic dreams** experienced by people around Great Britain prior to the **Aberfan** tragedy, which took place October 20, 1966. On that date, in the little Welsh village of Aberfan, a half-million-ton mountain of coal waste, saturated by days of unrelenting rain, slid down over the village and buried dozens of houses and the village school. Sixteen adults and 128 schoolchildren died.

In Plymouth, on England's south coast, a **psychic** saw the avalanche of coal slag pour down the mountainside onto the village. One man who had never heard of the village dreamed of the word "Aberfan." Another man saw dozens of black horses pulling black hearses down a hill. Another person dreamed of young children's screams coming from a mountain of coal slag. Nine-year-old Eryl Jones of Aberfan told her mother that she had dreamed there was no school—literally no school—that day, but she went off to school anyway and died.

There were so many reports of detailed dreams prior to the tragedy that a London psychiatrist, Dr. J. C. Barker, suggested a survey be conducted. Many of the reported **premonitions** were rejected for lack of authenticating evidence or because they were too vague. At least twenty-six prophetic dreams could be fully documented and confirmed, together with twenty-four non-dream premonitions. Consequently, the British Premonitions Bureau was established, as was the New York Central Premonitions Registry.

Sources:

Buckland, Raymond. *Gypsy Dream Dictionary*. St. Paul, MN: Llewellyn, 1999.
Holroyd, Stuart. *The Supernatural: Dream Worlds*. London: Aldus Books, 1976.
Mysteries of the Unknown: Psychic Powers. Alexandria, VA: Time-Life Books, 1987.

British Society of Dowsers

(See also American Society of Dowsers)

The British Society of Dowsers was founded in 1933 by Colonel A. H. Bell, who served as its president until 1964. As one of the oldest **dowsing** societies in Great Britain, it attracts a considerable number of overseas members, particularly from the Commonwealth and from English-speaking nations. The stated objects for which the society is established include the search for subterranean watercourses, cavities, tunnels, ores, and other entities, concealed by natural or artificial means; the diagnosis of disease and restoration of health in human beings, trees, and plants; and the quest for lost or missing objects, animate and inanimate.

The society publishes a quarterly journal, *Dowsing Today*, plus other occasional papers and books, and holds lectures, conferences, courses, and meetings. It maintains a register of practicing dowsers and operates a free information service for the benefit of the public who seek the services of a dowser. As part of its charitable endeavors the society raises funds to help source water supplies for people in developing countries. For example, in southern India an outstanding dowser from the society has sited boreholes for more than 1,800 previously dry villages.

The society comprises over 1,400 active members. The mission statement adopted by the council states that The British Society of Dowsers exists to promote, encourage and safeguard the art of dowsing in its widest sense. It recognizes that dowsing is a personal and subjective activity based partly on physical principles, and partly on principles that science has not yet recognized.

Sources:

http://www.britishdowsers.org/.

Brontomancy

From the **Greek** word for thunder, brontomancy is divining by thunder. Interpretation depended upon intensity, direction, length, and distance from the observer. Generally, thunder heard to the left was unfavorable and to the right favorable. The longer and louder the rumble, the more ominous it was. Whether or not the thunder was accompanied by lightning made a difference also (see **Ceraunomancy**).

Rosemary Brown, automatic composer, composing a Mazurka inspired by Chopin, 1980. ***Guy Lyon Playfair/Fortean Picture Library.***

Brown, Rosemary (b. 1917)

For several decades Rosemary Brown received **spiritual** messages in the form of music from deceased composers. Brown's mother was supposed to have been a **psychic.** Brown claimed that since her childhood she has been in contact with such people as Chopin, Liszt, and Beethoven; Franz Liszt (1811–1886) first came to her when she was seven years old. She saw him only as a white-haired old man. It wasn't until ten years later that she saw a picture of Liszt and recognized him as that old man. All of these composers dictated new compositions to Brown, who dutifully copied them down.

In 1964 Brown suffered injuries, including broken ribs, in an automobile accident. She spent a large part of her recuperation sitting at the piano. She had not played for at least twelve years and had little formal musical training, but suddenly she found herself playing. She claims she felt the spirit of Liszt guiding her hands. Liszt went on to introduce Bach, Beethoven, Berlioz, Brahms, Chopin, Debussy, Grieg, Monteverdi, Rachmaninov, Schubert, Schumann, and Stravinsky to her.

On April 14, 1970, CBS television's "Sixty Minutes" carried a segment on Rosemary Brown. Notable musicians, among them André Previn and Virgil Thomson, were impressed with the material she had produced. Previn stated that it would require someone with a great deal of musical knowledge and technique to fake that kind of music, though he added that he felt the quality of the compositions was far below the usual standards of the attributed composers. Others have acknowledged that the works are in the style of the claimed composers but lack the quality of the masters. Some critics said that what they heard from Brown was simply reworkings of the composers' known works, but they admitted that it would take a person of considerable musical knowledge and ability to pull off such a feat. Brown did not have that ability. In fact, she had great difficulty playing the compositions she wrote down.

In the July 6, 1970, issue of *Time* magazine, British composer Richard Rodney commented: "If she is a fake, she is a brilliant one and must have had years of training. . . . I couldn't have faked the Beethoven."

As word spread about her **mediumship,** Brown started to give public performances. She received more than 400 compositions from the various dead composers. She issued a recording of some of the works in 1970 under the title *Rosemary Brown's Music*. She also authored three books: *Unfinished Symphonies*, *Immortals by My Side*, and *Look beyond Today*.

Sources:

Brown, Rosemary. *Unfinished Symphonies: Voices from the Beyond*. New York: William Morrow, 1971.
Fishley, Margaret. *The Supernatural*. London: Aldus, 1976.
Guiley, Rosemary Ellen. *The Encyclopedia of Ghosts and Spirits*. New York: Facts On File, 1992.
Litvag, Irving. *Singer in the Shadows*. New York: Macmillan, 1972.

Buchanan, Joseph Rhodes (1814–1899)

"The past is entombed in the present, the world is its own enduring monument; and that which is true of its physical is likewise true of its mental career. The discoveries of Psychometry will enable us to explore the history of the earth. There are mental fossils for psychologists as well as mineral fossils for the geologists . . . Aye, the mental telescope is now discovered which may pierce the depths of the past and bring us in full view of the grand and tragic passages of ancient history." So said Joseph Rhodes Buchanan who, in 1842, coined the term "psychometry": the measuring of the soul.

Buchanan was dean of the faculty and professor in the Eclectic Medical Institute in Covington, Kentucky. He was the pioneer of psychometric research. As early as 1838 Buchanan localized the "region of sensibility" in the brain, in which could be found traces of a then-unknown psychic faculty. In 1843 he published a neurological map showing a new distribution of the phrenological organs.

Experimenting with Bishop Polk (General Polk of the Civil War), Buchanan found that various senses could be stimulated by the very presence of atmospheric, electric, and other physical conditions. Bishop Polk could literally taste when there was brass in the vicinity, even in darkness. Through a series of experiments, Buchanan was drawn to the conclusion that some emanation is thrown off by all substances—even the human body—and that certain sensitives can feel and interpret these emanations. To the subtle emanation given off by the human body, he gave the name "nerve aura." Psychometry, to him, was essentially a human faculty that did not involve the intervention of spirits, despite the fact that he was a spiritualist.

Buchanan's work was picked up by a professor of geology named Denton who, with his sister Ann Denton Cridge, did similar experiments to those done by Buchanan with Polk. Denton wrote a book called *The Soul of Things*, which dealt with the psychometric faculty.

Sources:

Butler, William E. *How to Develop Psychometry*. New York: Samuel Weiser, 1971.

Shepard, Leslie A. (ed.). *Encyclopedia of Occultism & Parapsychology*. New York: Avon, 1978.

Buckland, Raymond (b. 1934)

Raymond Buckland. ***Raymond Buckland.***

Raymond Buckland was born in London, England, on August 31, 1934. At the age of five, Buckland moved to Nottingham where he remained for the war years, returning to the London area in 1949. His father, Stan, a full-blood Romany (**Gypsy**), was a higher executive officer in the British Ministry of Health. Stan was also a freelance writer of short stories, plays, and music, who encouraged his son to write. At twelve Raymond was introduced to **spiritualism** by his uncle George, Stan's brother. This was the start of Buckland's interest in all matters of the occult. He read voraciously and, in the 1950s, began to thoroughly research spiritualism. His interests then broadened to ghosts, ESP, magic, witchcraft, voodoo, and all aspects of the occult. Although raised nominally in the Church of England, Buckland's religious interest quickly focused on Wicca. He was educated at Kings College School, Wimbledon. From there he took a job as a structural engineering draftsman. He married in 1955, to Rosemary Moss, and spent two years in the Royal Air Force (1957–1959). He then worked as retail manager and book illustrator for James Brodie Ltd., an educational publishing company in London. Throughout the war years and for some years after, Buckland was heavily involved in both amateur and professional theater, appearing regularly at the People's Theater, Nottingham, and the Nottingham Repertory Theater.

In the late 1950s Buckland began a correspondence with Gerald Gardner and, later, with Gardner's high priestess, Monique Wilson (Lady Olwen). He later became Gardner's spokesman in the United States, emigrating there in February 1962.

At the end of 1963, on a trip to Perth, Scotland, Buckland was initiated into Wicca by Olwen. This was his first actual meeting with Gardner, just before the "Grand Old Man of Witchcraft" left for the winter for what was to be his last visit to Lebanon.

There was a big interest in witchcraft in America in the early 1960s, and Raymond and Rosemary, as the founders and instigators of Wicca in this country, were not short of coven candidates. But, as taught, they were cautious and did not initiate anyone without due process. Such was the demand for Wicca entry at that time that they received a great deal of criticism for this caution. But even today Buckland feels that he did the right thing, pointing to many problems he has seen resulting from indiscriminate initiations. However, many people—impatient and without coven contacts—decided to start their own covens without proper training or initiation, resulting in a number of pseudo-Wiccan groups based solely on misinformation gleaned from such sources as Ira Levin's novel *Rosemary's Baby*, from **ceremonial magic,** and from other nontraditional sources.

Buckland dedicated himself to straightening popular misconceptions about witchcraft through the press, radio, and television, but he tried to remain anonymous in so doing. *Betrayal*, by Lisa Hoffman, a journalist with the *New York Sunday News*, resulted in his name being published. This, in turn, led to a great deal of persecution for himself, his wife, and their two children. However, Buckland continued his self-appointed task of correcting the misconceptions. Gardner's books had, by this time, gone out of print, so Buckland wrote *Witchcraft from the Inside* (Llewellyn, 1971) to fill the gap. This was to be the first of many such books.

Buckland found his life paralleled Gardner's in many ways. One way was the building of a collection of artifacts that grew into a museum. Gardner had a Museum of Magic and Witchcraft on the Isle of Man, the first of its kind in the world. Buckland's collection, the first of its kind in the United States, formally opened in 1968. For two years prior to that it was housed in the basement of his Long Island home and was open by appointment only. Later, in 1973, it was moved into an old Victorian house in Bay Shore. There it was reviewed in many major newspapers and periodicals and was the subject of a television documentary. Artifacts from the collection were loaned to the Metropolitan Museum of Art for a special exhibit and to the New York Museum of Folk Art. Meanwhile, other covens eventually hived off from the original New York one, slowly spreading the Gardnerian branch of the craft throughout the United States. Gradually other traditions began to appear, joining with the various spurious ones, to establish the craft as a viable alternative religion in America.

Buckland's writing continued. In 1969, just prior to his witchcraft book, *A Pocket Guide to the Supernatural* had been published by Ace Books. This was followed by *Practical Candleburning* (Llewellyn, 1970), *Witchcraft Ancient and Modern* (HC, 1970), and many more. Buckland has been averaging approximately one book a year since 1969.

In 1973, Buckland's marriage broke up and the running of the New York coven was turned over to another couple. The author moved to New Hampshire and shortly after, in 1974, married Joan Taylor. The museum was established in a new building at Weirs Beach, and he continued with his writing. In 1978 a move was made to Virginia Beach, Virginia. Buckland became Educational Director for the Poseidia Institute, and the museum went into storage. At Poseidia he taught a number of psychic development classes.

While in New Hampshire, Buckland finally admitted to himself that he was not totally happy with the Gardnerian form of Wicca. It no longer met his religious needs, and he was dismayed at the blatant ego trips and power plays displayed by many of its later practitioners. After much thought and research he founded the Seax-Wica, based on a Saxon background. It was more democratically organized than the Gardnerian Degree System tradition. Although originally written for his own personal use, he found there was a big interest in it and was persuaded to publish the rituals in *The Tree: Complete Book of Saxon Witchcraft* (Samuel Weiser, 1974). Some irresponsible writers later suggested that the tradition was written as a joke, but their comments stemmed from ignorance. Buckland insists this is far from the truth, since it is a form of the religion to which he felt very strongly drawn.

By the early 1980s Buckland and his wife found their interests going in different directions and divorced. In 1983 he married his third, and present, wife, Tara Cochran. They lived for two years in Charlottesville, Virginia, where he worked as a licensed real estate appraiser. In December 1984 the couple moved to San Diego. While in Virginia they had founded the Seax-Wica Seminary and published the *Seax-Wica Voys*, a Wiccan magazine. The seminary, as a correspondence school, grew to more than 1,000 students worldwide. Eventually, however, Buckland found it took too much of his precious writing time and had to terminate it.

In San Diego, before turning to writing full time, Buckland worked for a few years for a theatrical and film casting company. He became very close friends with the actor John Carradine, working with him for the last few years of the actor's life. Buckland had also worked with Orson Welles (as technical consultant for *Necromancy*, later renamed *The Witching*), William Friedkin, Bert I. Gordon, and other movie actors and directors. He played character parts himself, appearing as a crazy psychiatrist in the cult movie *Mutants in Paradise*. While in San Diego, Buckland wrote and starred in the video *Witchcraft Yesterday and Today*. There, he also became good friends with Scott Cunningham, a fellow author and Wiccan.

In 1986 Buckland produced the first of a series of books about Romany life and practices. Since he is himself a half-blood Roma, it was a natural attraction. Among other things, he produced a deck of **fortune-telling** cards based on those he remembered his grandmother using. The **cards** became popular but Buckland wanted to do a true **tarot** deck, again based on Gypsy life.

While Buckland was in San Diego, his interest returned to spiritualism, and he did a number of very successful sessions acting as a medium. On various occasions he was able to make contact with the deceased relatives of a number of different people. He eventually wrote a book, *Doors to Other Worlds* (Llewellyn, 1993), detailing the history of spiritualism and the various methods of drawing out and developing **mediumship.**

In search of a house and some land, rather than living in a condominium, in 1992 the Bucklands moved to Ohio (Tara's home state) and bought a small farm. From there Buckland continued his writing, which by then included fiction as well as nonfiction.

Still wanting to do a full tarot deck, Buckland finally found the right artist to do the cards for him. It was **Lissanne Lake,** who had done the cover for his *Secrets of*

Gypsy Love Magick (Llewellyn 1990). In much the same way that **Arthur Edward Waite** worked with **Pamela Colman Smith,** and **Aleister Crowley** with **Frieda Harris,** Buckland got Lissanne to translate his ideas into vibrant cards depicting a wide variety of Gypsy scenes. He wrote a 240-page book to accompany the cards, and they were published at the beginning of 2001, to critical acclaim, as the *Buckland Romani Tarot*. The deck and book were awarded the Coalition of Visionary Retailers' 2002 Visionary Award. The partnership with Lissanne Lake worked so well that the publisher is now awaiting a second deck and book by the pair, this one based on witchcraft and magic.

Buckland's many spare-time interests have included flying ultralight aircraft and building unusual automobiles. He also is part of a musical group organized by Tara. Some of Buckland's best-selling books, from more than thirty written to date, have been *The Witch Book* (2002), *Wicca for Life* (2002), *Buckland's Complete Book of Witchcraft* (1986/2002), *Gypsy Witchcraft and Magic* (1998), *Scottish Witchcraft* (1991), *Doors to Other Worlds* (1993), *Advanced Candle Magic* (1996), and his two novels, *The Committee* (1993) and *Cardinal's Sin* (1996).

BUMPOLOGY

This is a modern slang term for **phrenology,** reading the bumps on the head.

C

CAKE *see* Critomancy

CANDLE

(See also Lampadomancy)

Before using any candle, whether for candle-burning rituals or simply as a tool of **divination,** it should be consecrated, or "dressed." This is done by rubbing it with oil from the center outward toward each of the ends. All surfaces should be lightly covered. The oil used should be pure olive oil, though it is possible to purchase "consecrated" anointing oil from occult supply stores. Consecrated means that the oil has been blessed in some ritual, be it religious or purely magical. While anointing the candle, the operator should concentrate on the purpose for which the candle will be used.

The candle itself may be of any type other than made from animal fat. (Virtually all candles these days are either paraffin wax or vegetable oil; very few, if any, are made of animal fat.) In many candle-burning rituals, it is the color that is important. If the candle is going to be used to represent a person, then the color (termed the "astral color") is chosen dependant upon the birth date of that person:

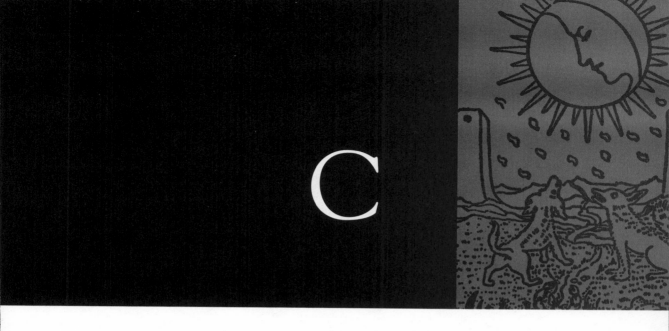

Aquarius (Jan. 20–Feb. 18): Blue and/or Green
Pisces (Feb. 19–Mar. 20): White/Green
Aries (Mar. 21–Apr. 19): White/Pink
Taurus (Apr. 20–May 20): Red/Yellow
Gemini (May 21–Jun. 21): Red/Blue
Cancer (Jun. 22–Jul. 22): Green/Brown
Leo (Jul. 23–Aug. 22): Red/Green
Virgo (Aug. 23–Sep. 22): Gold/Black
Libra (Sep. 23–Oct. 22): Black/Blue

Scorpio (Oct. 23–Nov. 21): Brown/Black
Sagittarius (Nov. 22–Dec. 21): Gold/Red
Capricorn (Dec. 22–Jan. 19): Red/Brown

Colors may also represent various qualities and properties, as follows:

Red: Courage, health, sexual love, strength, vigor.
Pink: Honor, love, morality.
Orange: Adaptability, attraction, encouragement, stimulation.
Yellow/Gold: Attraction, charm, confidence, persuasion, protection.
Greenish/Yellow: Anger, cowardice, discord, jealousy, sickness.
Green: Fertility, finance, healing, luck.
Brown: Hesitation, neutrality, uncertainty.
Light Blue: Health, patience, tranquility, understanding.
Dark Blue: Changeability, depression, impulsiveness.
Violet: Healing, peace, spirituality.
Purple: Ambition, business progress, power, tension.
Gray/Silver: Cancellation, neutrality, stalemate.
White: Purity, sincerity, truth.
Black: Confusion, discord, neutrality, loss, nothingness.

In Native American spirituality, the colors represent the following properties:

Red: Communication, faith.
Rose: Motivation, seeing.
Pink: Creativity, working.
Orange: Kinship, learning.
Yellow: all-conquering unconditional love.
Green: Living willfully, will.
Brown: Knowing, self-discipline.
Blue: Intuition, serving, teaching.
Purple: Gratitude, healing, wisdom.
Gray: Friendship, honoring.
White: Magnetism, sharing.
Black: Harmony, hearing, listening.
Crystal: Clarity, wholeness.

According to Asian symbolism, the candles' colors represent the following:

Red: Happiness, marriage, prosperity.
Pink: Marriage.
Yellow: Against evil, for the dead, geomantic blessings.
Gold: Strength, wealth.
Green: Eternity, family, harmony, health, peace, posterity.
Blue: Self-cultivation, wealth.
Purple: Wealth.
Gray: Helpful people, travel.
White: Children, helpful people, marriage, mourning, peace, purity, travel.
Black: Career, evil influences, knowledge, mourning, penance, self-cultivation.

Candles may be lit and the diviner will simply sit and stare into the flame, seeing and divining either by the way the flame flickers or just by the pictures that enter his or her head. Frequently **incense** is burned as an accompaniment to this **scrying.**

There are also full rituals to divine the future, and many are done to try to bring influence to bear on future events. These rituals are of the sympathetic magic variety: The candles represent people and things and are manipulated so that the candles' actions will be echoed by those persons and things.

In medieval Europe there was a practice in Jewish communities of using a candle to see into the future for the coming year. For ten days before Yom Kippur a candle would be burned, carefully shielded from any drafts. Traditionally, this was the period when each person's fate for the coming year was decided in heaven. If the candle burned all the way down, without going out, it indicated a year of continued life ahead. However, if the candle went out before burning down, it signified that death would come before year's end. Today if this form of divination is used, the candle is chosen by the astral colors given above, to give it a more personal connection.

Sources:

Buckland, Raymond. *Color Magic—Unleash Your Inner Powers*. St. Paul, MN: Llewellyn, 2002.
Buckland, Raymond. *Practical Candleburning Rituals*. St. Paul, MN: Llewellyn, 1982.
Buckland, Raymond. *Advanced Candle Magick*. St. Paul, MN: Llewellyn, 1996.

Capnomancy; Captromancy

(See also Empyromancy)

In John Healey's *St. Augustine; of the citie of God, with the learned comments of J. L. Vives* (1616) there is mention that "divination was done by smoke; capnomancy." Unfortunately there is no detail of exactly *how* it was done. Other works of the seventeenth century through the nineteenth century also mention capnomancy, but none of them gives details.

It seems probable that the smoke would be interpreted according to its volume, density, and the way in which it ascended. The direction it moved would be important, as would the consistency of it: whether it was continuous or sporadic, for example. Broiling, swirling, thick smoke might indicate troubles and problems, while thin, wispy smoke could indicate slight activity of an inconsequential nature. If the smoke assumed unusual shapes, this, too, would be significant.

Frequently the smoke would be from a special fire on which vervain and other special plants and herbs were burned. In ancient **Greece** the smoke would be from the burning of sacrificial animals. Special portions of the sacrifice were consumed by fire and **omens** read in the flame or smoke that ensued.

In *Etruscan Magic & Occult Remedies*, Charles Godfrey Leland gives details of a variety that he terms captromancy, where grains of sesame or black poppy were thrown on hot coals. From the smoke rising from it, omens were drawn. In addition to the suggestions of the smoke, "if (the grains) burst or pop well, it is a sign that the crop for the next year will be a good one. And if they do not burst it will be bad."

Psychical researcher Hereward Carrington. ***Fortean Picture Library.***

Sources:

Lawson, John Cuthbert. *Modern Greek Folklore and Ancient Greek Religion*. New York: University Books, 1964.

Leland, Charles Godfrey. *Etruscan Magic & Occult Remedies*. New York: University Books, 1963.

CARDS *see* Cartomancy

CARRINGTON, HEREWARD (1881–1959)

British-born Hereward Carrington had his interest in **psychic** matters aroused at the age of eighteen. His inclination was to disbelieve reported psychic phenomena, until he read *Essays in Psychical Research* by "Miss X" (London, 1899). Miss X was actually A. Goodrich-Freer, the Marquess of Buze. In 1900, at the age of nineteen, Carrington became a member of the **Society for Psychical Research** and from then on devoted his life to the study of the paranormal.

Carrington quickly established a reputation for his intellect and common sense. After Dr. Richard Hodgson died and Professor James Hervey Hyslop took over the leadership of the society, Carrington became Hyslop's assistant, a position he maintained until 1908. He was sent to Naples to investigate the **medium** Eusapia Paladino, on whom he reported favorably, saying: "genuine phenomena do occur and, that being the case, the question of their interpretation naturally looms before me. I think that not only is the **spiritualist** hypothesis justified as a working theory, but it is, in fact, the only one capable of rationally explaining the facts."

In 1921 Carrington was the American delegate at the first International Psychical Congress in Copenhagen. That year he founded the American Psychical Institute and Laboratory. In 1924 he sat on the committee of *Scientific American* for the investigation of the phenomena of spiritualism.

In 1929 Carrington wrote *The Projection of the Astral Body* after becoming acquainted with Sylvan Muldoon, the expert on **astral projection.** In all, Carrington wrote seventeen books.

Sources:

Buckland, Raymond and Hereward Carrington. *Amazing Secrets of the Psychic World*. New York: Parker Publishing, 1975.

Fishley, Margaret. *The Supernatural*. London: Aldus, 1976.

Shepard, Leslie A. (ed.). *Encyclopedia of Occultism & Parapsychology*. New York: Avon, 1978.

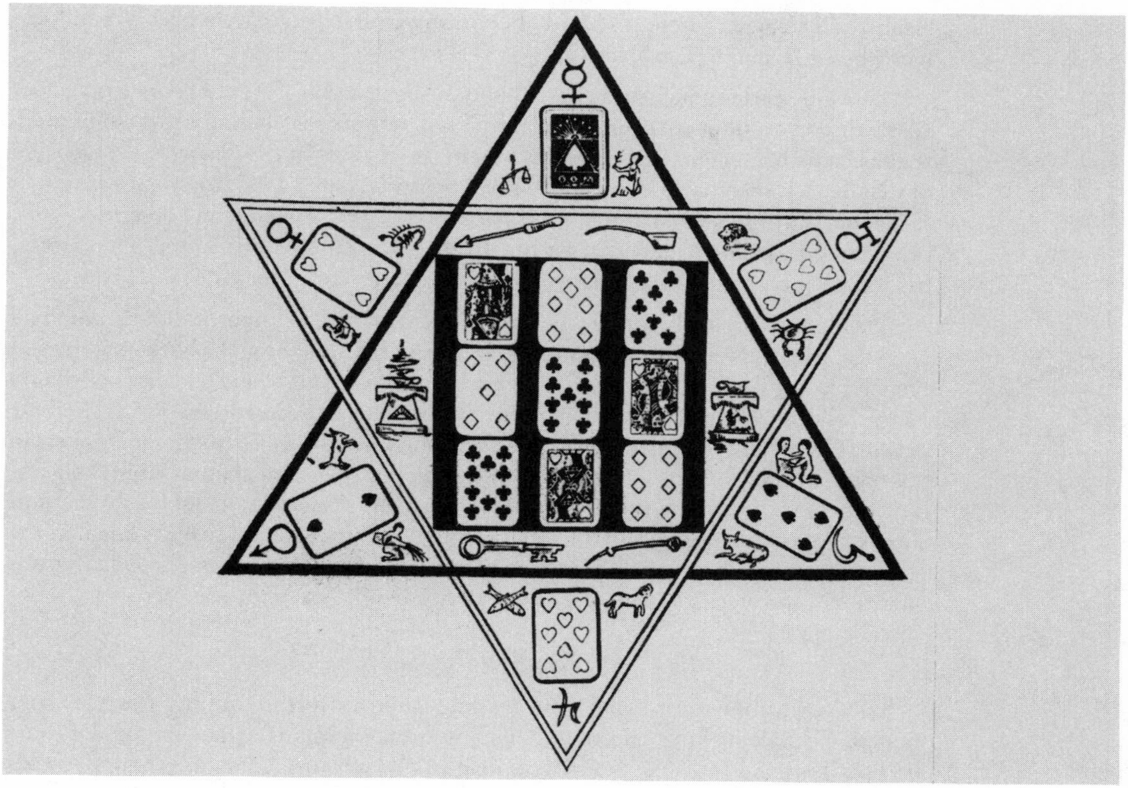

Cartomancy is the use of playing cards, such as these laid out in a hexagram, for purposes of prediction. ***Fortean Picture Library.***

Cartomancy

(Note: Although the ***tarot*** *comes under the general heading of cartomancy, or card reading, it will be looked at as a separate subject.)*

Regular playing cards have been used as tools for divination for hundreds of years, with more methods of using them than can be counted. One theory is that the cards derived from the use of arrows for divination (**Belomancy**). Certainly arrows were depicted as the symbols of one of the suits on early tarot cards. It is also interesting to note that Korean playing cards always bear a picture of an arrow on the reverse. The earliest playing cards were either Korean or **Chinese,** existing in that part of the world before the twelfth century. It was not until the fourteenth century that they were introduced into Europe, where they spread rapidly. T. F. Carter, in *The Invention of Printing in China* (1925), cites a reference to playing cards in China as early as 969 CE.

One theory is that playing cards were derived from the minor arcana of the tarot deck, the tarot having been brought from **India** (perhaps having arrived there from China) by the nomadic Roma, or **Gypsies.** This certainly seems most likely, since it was at that time that the Roma began to filter into Europe by way of Persia,

Arabia, and **Egypt.** There is record of Gypsies being in Yugoslavia by 1348, in Germany by 1407, and in Paris by 1427.

Many early Indian cards were round in shape and made out of very thin wood, ivory, or cotton fiber that had been lacquered. Wherever playing cards originated, they became firmly entrenched in France. In the register of the *Chambre des Comptes* of Charles VI, there is an entry of the royal treasurer, dated 1392, for money paid to a Jacquemin Gringonneur, painter, for three games of cards "in gold and diverse colours, ornamented with many devices, for the diversion of our lord, the King." These were, in fact, what are known as *atouts*, or tarot cards, as were introduced by the Gypsies.

It seems probable that in the early fifteenth century, English soldiers, who had been fighting in Normandy, Touraine, Poitou, and Anjou, brought back examples of French playing cards. They became very popular to the point where an edict of Britain's Henry VII forbade the use of playing cards by servants and apprentices during the Yule season. However, by the early seventeenth century there were so many card makers in London that they formed a guild under the protection of a royal charter. From their earliest appearance, playing cards were seized upon as a convenient tool for divination. They have remained that way through the years, being small and easily carried on the person. They were certainly so used by the Gypsies from earliest times. Today tarot cards have finally surpassed playing cards in popularity, but the latter are still used.

Reading the Cards

As with most card games, in reading cards for fortune-telling the ace ranks highest. Then come king, queen, jack, ten, nine, etc. Speaking in general terms, Hearts are usually tied to joy, happiness, and love in all its forms. Diamonds connect with money, but also with delays, excitement, gifts, and insight. Spades are the difficulties of life; problems, disappointments, sickness, and grief. Clubs tie into transformation, hard work, and the process of getting somewhere or achieving a goal. But these are generalizations and, like all generalizations, they can be modified by which specific card of the suit is being looked at and by the position that card has in a particular layout or spread. But if the vast majority of cards in a layout happen to be, for example, hearts, then the reading can be regarded as one focused on joy and happiness.

There are two basic systems used in divining with cards. One uses the full fifty-two cards of the deck; the second ignores those cards below seven, using just thirty-two cards. The fifty-two-card method is often referred to as the English method and the thirty-two-card as the Foreign method.

Before looking at layout, here is a listing of each of the cards and what, traditionally, it represents:

Hearts

Ace: The house or home. With Diamonds near, it means money and/or news of distant friends. With Spades near, it means misunderstandings, a possible quarrel to come. With clubs: a celebration.

King: A fair man who is good natured. Beware of rashness and hastiness overruling discretion.

Queen: A fair woman who is affectionate and faithful.

Jack: Can apply to either sex. A dear friend. Attuned to the thoughts of someone who is fair-haired.

Ten: Happiness and good fortune to come. Possible children, or concerning a large family. This card can counteract nearby negative cards.

Nine: Known as the wish card. Wealth and high esteem, or high social position. May be affected by the closeness of negative cards.

Eight: General conviviality. Good food; good friends.

Seven: Beware of a false friend who may betray you.

Six: Credulity; too open-minded and open-handed; an easy prey for swindlers. Can also mean a coming proposal.

Five: Problems caused by unfounded jealousy.

Four: A person who is difficult to please and, consequently, remains unmarried.

Three: Beware of the results of imprudence and lack of tact.

Two: Depending upon the neighboring cards, this could indicate great success and prosperity.

Diamonds

Ace: A letter, its contents dependent upon the neighboring cards. This can also signify a ring or paper money.

King: A fair but obstinate man with a quick, violent temper.

Queen: A fair, flirtatious woman who is vain and fond of society.

Jack: A self-opinionated, selfish, near relative. Attuned to the thoughts of someone who is fair-haired.

Ten: Money, family and home.

Nine: A person fond of roving, influenced by those cards near it. Connected with the eight of spades it means a coming quarrel.

Eight: A marriage or partnership late in life that will have its ups and downs.

Seven: Need for caution in all things. No hasty decisions. It could be linked with negative gossip.

Six: Early marriage and equally early death of the spouse. A second marriage should be approached with caution.

Five: Unexpected news, usually good.

Four: Betrayed trust; a breach of security. Trouble caused by those previously considered friends.

Three: Legal and domestic problems. Domestic disagreements.

Two: A love interest strongly advised against by friends.

Spades

Ace: Misfortune, which could be personal or business. Spite from a previous friend may be involved. This card is unaffected by nearby cards.

King: A dark, ambitious man who has gained considerable success.

Queen: A dark, malicious woman who might be a widow. She is fond of scandal and open to bribery.

Jack: An inept person who is unready to take action. Attuned to the thoughts of someone who is dark-haired.

Ten: Possible imprisonment; grief. Detracts from any good cards in the vicinity.

Nine: Sickness, trouble, losses, family disagreements.

Eight: Look out for enemies, especially if this card is close to one representing the querier (the enquirer) .

Seven: Loss of a friend, bringing problems and worries.

Six: Hard work is well rewarded.

Five: Curb a bad temper and seek comfort in the arms of your spouse or dear one.

Four: Possible sickness and need for attention to your business.

Three: A journey, plus the possibility of unfaithfulness while on a trip, causing problems with spouse.

Two: A sudden removal, or death.

Clubs

Ace: Wealth, peace of mind, general prosperity.

King: A dark, faithful, upright man who is affectionate.

Queen: A dark gentle woman, who is affectionate, charming and trusting.

Jack: A trustworthy, generous friend, who may be a little hasty at times. Attuned to the thoughts of a man who is dark-haired.

Ten: Unexpected inheritance, due to the loss of a dear friend.

Nine: To go against friends' opinions could cause problems.

Eight: Beware of speculation and love of money.

Seven: Good fortune and happiness. Any problems will come from the opposite sex.

Six: Great business success, for yourself and family.

Five: A marriage good for both spouses.

Four: Beware of lying and deceiving.

Three: Remarriage, with chance of increased fortunes.

Two: Possibility of a great disappointment.

Significance of different cards of the same suit

Four Aces, either coming together or following one another: Danger, business failure, possible imprisonment. If one or more is reversed it will simply lessen the severity.

Three Aces: Good news. One or more reversed indicates folly.

Two Aces: A plot. If one is reversed, it will not succeed.

Four Kings: An important business meeting with satisfactory results. Any reversed means the results may prove doubtful.

Three Kings: A number of small business meetings with the results uncertain. Any reversed, the results will be unfavorable.

Two Kings: A business partnership. One or both reversed—the partnership will not last long.

Four Queens: A social occasion. With one or more reversed, there will be an embarrassing situation.

Three Queens: Friendly visits from acquaintances. Any reversed indicate an amount of negative gossip.

Two Queens: A meeting between friends. One or both reversed—one or both of the friends needs help with a problem.
Four Jacks: A noisy party composed mainly of young people. Any reversed indicates a drinking problem.
Three Jacks: False friends. Any reversed—a violent quarrel.
Two Jacks: Danger. One reversed—evil intentions involved.
Four Tens: Plans will work out extremely successfully. Any reversed—there will be delays that are very frustrating.
Three Tens: Improper conduct on someone's part. Reversals—a failure to complete something important.
Two Tens: A change of profession. One reversed—the new job is not yet certain.
Four Nines: A big surprise. Reversals—an unexpected public presentation.
Three Nines: Joyful good fortune with excellent health. Reversals—Loss of wealth through poor planning and choices.
Two Nines: A small gain, financially. One reversed—a small loss.
Four Eights: A short journey. Any reversed—a visit from a friend or relative.
Three Eights: Thoughts of marriage. Reversals—a serious flirtation.
Two Eights: A brief love fantasy. One reversed—small pleasures accompanied by small pain.
Four Sevens: Threats and disputes, especially from employees or fellow workers. Any reversals—the threats against you will go back on those who are threatening.
Three Sevens: Sickness and premature aging. Reversals—a number of small sicknesses.
Two Sevens: Levity. One reversed—regrets.
Multiples below Sevens are not especially significant.

Note: With the court cards and with many of the other cards, especially even-numbered ones and most of the diamonds, it isn't possible to tell which is a reversed situation. In such cases it is recommended that you mark the card in some way—perhaps a dot at the bottom.

This table can be used to help remember some of the meanings, grouping together those with similar meanings:

Early marriage: 2 clubs; 3 clubs; 5 clubs; 6 diamonds.
Late marriage: 3 clubs; 8 diamonds.
Wealth: 2 hearts; 9 hearts; 7 clubs; 10 clubs; 10 diamonds.
Prosperity: 2 hearts; 10 hearts; 6 clubs; 7 clubs.
Prudence: ace clubs; 6 spades.
Unfaithfulness: 4 clubs; 7 hearts; 4 diamonds; king diamonds.
Discretion needed: 3 hearts; 2 diamonds; 7 diamonds; 2 clubs; 4 spades.
Possible misfortune: 2, 3, 7, 8, 9, 10 spades; 3 diamonds; 9 clubs.

Layouts

Various layouts are used for specific purposes. For example, the cards are used one way in instances where the querier is interested in marriage prospects, but a different way for questions of inheritance, lawsuits, traveling, and so on. Here we will look at the methods used for marriage and for inheritance as examples, then review some of the various layouts for general prediction.

For marriage, the cards are shuffled and cut three times. If an actual marriage (rather than general exploration) is being looked at, then two cards are withdrawn from the deck to represent the prospective bride and groom. Fair people are represented by diamonds, very fair people by hearts, dark people by clubs, and very dark people by spades. For older men and women, use the kings and queens; for younger people, use the jacks.

With those cards withdrawn, do the shuffling, then lay down the top three cards. If they are all of different suits, put them in a pile to one side for the moment. If there are two or three of one suit, then take the highest-valued one and lay it to the right of the cards representing the bride and groom. Place the others in the "reject" pile. Turn up the next three and do the same thing. Continue doing this until there are fifteen cards to the right of the querier. If you get to the end of the cards without having produced fifteen, then shuffle the reject pile and start going through that again, three at a time.

What is known as a "tierce" is three cards of one suit together in sequence. A tierce major is the three highest cards and a tierce minor is the three lowest cards. A "tierce to the King" is jack, queen, king; "tierce to the queen" is ten, jack, queen; etc. With this in mind, if the querier is the man he will not have his wish regarding the hoped-for marriage unless a tierce to the king in clubs or spades is among the fifteen cards. If the querier is a woman, then not only must there be a tierce to the queen in the suit used to represent the prospective bride, but there must also be an ace of that suit included somewhere in the fifteen cards.

Many other sequences and considerations are considered. For example, if the prospective bride or groom happens to be a widow or widower, then there must be a tierce to the queen of hearts or to the king of spades, respectively, for a favorable reading.

For questions of inheritance, choose a card to represent the querier and place it on the table. Then shuffle and cut the cards. As above, go through the deck in threes and draw off cards to lay out to the right of the querier's card until you have fifteen there. If the ace of spades is among these cards, right side up, this is an indication of an inheritance coming through death of someone close. If there are also the seven, eight, nine, and ten of clubs among the cards, the amount of money will be considerable.

Past, Present, and Future

A simple method of checking, in detail, past, present, and future may be used with the thirty-two-card deck. The cards must first be shuffled and cut. At the cut, before placing the lower half on top of the upper half, the top card of the lower half and the bottom card of the upper half should be removed and placed to one side. These two are known as the "surprise." The remaining thirty cards are dealt into three equal piles. The pile on the left represents the past; the middle pile is the present; the right-hand pile is the future.

The ten cards in the first (left: past) pile are spread out and read, taking into account the relative positions and whether or not any cards are inverted. Then the second (middle: present) pile is read, and finally the third (right: future) pile. The three cards of the "surprise" are read last. They may have bearing on any of the three piles.

The Pyramid Layout

This is done for a general reading. A *significator* is first chosen to represent the querier . . . remember: fair people are represented by diamonds, very fair people by hearts, dark people by clubs and very dark people by spades; for older men and women, use the kings and queens; for younger people, use the jacks. This significator is first chosen and laid down on the table, then the rest of the cards are shuffled. The first two cards are taken from the top and laid down below the significator. Beneath them go the next three cards. The next four below them, and so on until there are seven rows (twenty-eight cards in all). The significator is the querier. The second row deals with present strong influences around him or her. The third row is the power that may be drawn upon (i.e. friends, influences, etc). The fourth row is the forces working against the querier. The fifth row shows the past. The sixth row shows hopes, fears and dreams. The bottom row shows the final outcome. When reading these, or any cards, take note of pairs, triplets, quartettes—two, three or four of a kind lying side by side.

Now study the last card in each row, all seven of them. These cards will give a general idea of luck or good fortune for the coming month. Note which suit appears most in those seven cards. If it is hearts then there will be a lot of luck. If diamonds, then quite a bit of luck. Clubs means no more than usual. Spades indicates nothing but bad luck to come.

Sevens

Using the Foreign deck (the deck of thirty-two cards), shuffle and count out seven cards from the top. Lay just the seventh card on the table and discard the other six. Repeat this, counting out another seven and placing that seventh one beside the first selected card and discarding the other six. Continue through the deck in this fashion, placing each seventh card in a line across the table. After the fourth time there will not be sufficient cards left to do it again, so take up the discards and shuffle them all together with the remaining four cards in your hand. Then again go through, adding every seventh card to the four already on the table. Keep this up until you have a total of twelve cards in the line across in front of you. Study the cards to see if one of them is the card that should be the significator for the querier (see above). If it is not among the twelve cards, gather them all together, shuffle, and start all over. This must be repeated until the traditional significator is one of the twelve chosen cards.

From the twelve cards, take the significator and place it in the center, above the others in the line. Now count seven cards from the left of the line, take that card, and place it above and to the left of the significator. This card will represent the forces that have been at work around the querier in the past. Next take the card on the far left of the original line and the card on the far right, and place these under the significator. These two cards represent the querier's hopes and fears. Again count seven cards from the left and place that card below the previous two. This represents influences—a person or set of circumstances that will unexpectedly come into play in the near future, greatly influencing the querier.

A total of seven cards are now left in the original line. Take the middle three and place them at the bottom, and place the remaining four above them (below the influences card). The four represent forces now at work around the querier, and the bottom three represent what will be the final outcome.

SEVENS: ORIGINAL LINE OF DRAWN CARDS

Significator

1 2 3 4 5 6 7 8 9 10 11

CARDS DRAWN AND REARRANGED TO THIS PATTERN

7
S
1 11
9
2 3 8 10
4 5 6

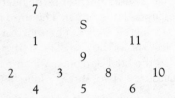

There are a great many different layouts, some extremely simple and some very complicated. They have names such as Wheel of Life Spread, Nine Square, Romani Star, Grand Star, and Lucky Thirteen. All cartomancy comes down to there being different meanings for the positions of the cards drawn and then the interpretation of the cards themselves in those positions. That interpretation must take into account the significance and modification, if any, of neighboring cards.

Specific questions can be answered using cards, and they do seem to have a degree of accuracy. That accuracy is perhaps not as great as with tarot cards, where there is far more latitude for the interpretation of each card, but a skilled reader can frequently astonish a querier.

Sources:
Buckland, Raymond. *Secrets of Gypsy Fortunetelling*. St. Paul, MN: Llewellyn, 1988.
Foli, Prof. P. R .S. *Fortune-Telling by Cards*. Philadelphia: David McKay, 1902.
Grand Orient (A. E. Waite). *A Manual of Cartomancy*. London: William Rider, 1912.
Hargrave, Catherine Perry. *A History of Playing Cards*. New York: Houghton Mifflin, 1930.
Sophia. *Fortune Telling with Playing Cards*. St. Paul, MN: Llewellyn, 1996.

CATOPTROMANCY; ENOPTROMANCY

(See also Mirror-Gazing; Scrying)

Catoptromancy, divination by means of a mirror, is an aspect of mirror-gazing. Sir Thomas Urquhart finds reference to it in *The Third Book of the Works of Mr. Francis Rabelais* (London, 1693), where it says: "Catoptromancy is held in such account by the emperor Didius Julianus," implying that it was practiced in ancient **Rome.** The

London *Annual Register* of 1758 says: "He understands all the mysteries of catoptromancy, he having a magical glass to be consulted upon some extraordinary occasions."

Pausanius, the fifth century BCE Spartan regent of the Greek forces and admiral of the Greek fleet, described how this form of divination was performed: "Before the Temple of Ceres, at Patras, there was a fountain, separated from the temple by a wall, and there was an oracle, very truthful, but not for all events—for the sick only. The sick person let down a mirror (*of bronze or silver*), suspended by a thread, till its base touched the surface of the water, having first prayed to the goddess and offered incense. Then looking in the mirror, he saw the presage of death or recovery, according as the face appeared fresh and healthy or of a ghastly aspect." The Romans and the Egyptians also used this form of divination.

Another version of catoptromancy is when young girls study the reflection of the moon in a mirror. They time how long it is, in minutes, before a cloud or a bird passes across the face of the moon. That number of minutes represents the number of years they may have to wait for matrimony. Staring into a mirror in the light of the moon will also bring the face of the future husband/lover—to be seen reflected over the girl's shoulder, it was believed. Some say that this last act had to be done at midnight on Halloween.

Mirror magic of one kind or another has been practiced from earliest times. As a tool for divination, the mirror, or any type of reflection, is considered one of the most infallible of methods.

Sources:

Leach, Maria (ed.). *Funk & Wagnalls Standard Dictionary of Folklore, Mythology, and Legend*. San Francisco: Harper & Row, 1972.

Oxford English Dictionary. Oxford: Clarendon Press, 1989.

CAT *see* Ailuromancy

CAUL *see* Amniomancy

CAUSIMANCY; CAUSIMOMANCY

(See also Xylomancy)

This is a form of divination by fire. Interpretation is of the speed and general combustibility of objects cast into a fire. If the object does not burn, it is a fortuitous sign. If it burns rapidly and spectacularly it is a sign of trouble and possibly of evil to come.

CAUSIMOMANCY *see* Causimancy

CAYCE, EDGAR (1877–1945)

Known as "The Sleeping Prophet" because he delivered his predictions while in trance, Edgar Cayce was one of America's most famous **psychics** and seers. He was a photographer by profession, though when his psychic abilities developed fully they left him with little time to pursue that career.

Cayce was born on March 18, 1877, near Hopkinsville, Kentucky. With four sisters, he grew up surrounded by uncles, aunts, and other relatives, all of whom lived close by. From the family background and atmosphere, Cayce developed an early interest in the Bible, an interest that remained with him throughout his life. At the age of six he told his parents that he was able to see visions and even talk with the spirits of dead relatives. His parents didn't believe him. At thirteen he had a vision of being visited by a goddess figure who asked him what he most wanted in life. He replied that he wanted to help others; in particular, he wanted to aid sick children.

For a short period Cayce demonstrated a special talent of being able to absorb knowledge by sleeping on books, papers, etc. He would sleep with his head on a book and, on waking, be able to tell everything about the material in the book, even repeating whole passages word for word.

When the family moved from their farm into the city of Hopkinsville, Cayce found employment in a bookstore. There he met Gertrude Evans, and the two became engaged in March 1897. For a short while he lived in Louisville, but he returned to Hopkinsville by the end of 1899, where he formed a partnership with his father, an insurance agent. Cayce started traveling and selling insurance, supplementing this with the sale of books and stationery. His sales job ended when Cayce developed a severe case of laryngitis, so severe that it lasted for months despite attention from a number of doctors. Having to give up the insurance job, he took a position as assistant to a photographer, where he wouldn't have to try to speak to anyone.

A traveling entertainer named Hart hypnotized Cayce and found that, under hypnosis, the young man's voice could be normal. But when out of a trance, Cayce's laryngitis returned. Hart moved on, but a local hypnotist named Al Layne took over. Cayce put himself into trance and had Layne give him suggestions. Layne asked Cayce what was wrong with his throat and Cayce responded with a full and detailed diagnosis. He further urged Layne to give the suggestion that the throat return to normal. When Cayce woke up, everyone was amazed to find that he now spoke normally for the first time in almost a year. The date was March 31, 1901. This was Cayce's first diagnosis while in a trance.

Al Layne, the hypnotist, had himself long been bothered with a stomach problem. Inspired by Cayce's recovery, he prevailed upon the young man to go into a trance and diagnose for him. Reluctantly Cayce did so, and he prescribed a dietary and exercise regimen to solve Layne's problem. Within a week it had worked, again after a number of doctors had been unsuccessful.

Although Cayce's personal desire was to be left alone to be a photographer and raise a family, he reluctantly gave in to pressure from his father, Layne, and others, and continued to give trance readings for people in need. He cured a five-year-old girl named Aime Dietrich, who had been seriously ill for three years. Cayce did not understand how it worked, having no medical knowledge and frequently, on waking, not remembering what he had said while asleep. But the cures continued.

On June 17, 1903, he and Gertrude married and moved to Bowling Green, Kentucky, where Cayce opened a photographic studio. Later a disastrous fire wiped out everything, and he and his wife, now with a son, returned to Hopkinsville. An association began with Dr. Wesley Ketchum, a homeopath, which eventually led to Dr. Ketchum reading a paper about Cayce's abilities to the American Society of Clinical Research. The *New York Times* picked up on this and featured an article: "Illiterate man becomes doctor when hypnotized." Soon Cayce was swamped with readings. He had earlier found that the person for whom he was reading did not have to be physically present; all he needed was a name and location of the person and he could focus on that person and the problem.

In the late summer of 1911 Gertrude contracted tuberculosis and almost died. Cayce's diagnosis and recommendation of revolutionary treatment brought about her complete recovery by the end of the year. He was able to perform a similar service for his son, Hugh Lynn, some time later. The family had moved to Selma where Cayce had a new photographic studio. Hugh was playing with flash powder when it exploded in his face. Doctors said that he had severely burned his eyes and recommended removing one of them. Cayce thought otherwise and, from a trance, prescribed for his son. Two weeks later Hugh could see again.

As Cayce's reputation grew, so did a problem with treating people. Doctors were reluctant to follow the diagnoses that the "Sleeping Prophet" recommended. Cayce began to dream of having a hospital, fully staffed with doctors and nurses, that would work solely on the cases he prescribed. He attempted to use his psychic talents to make the money to establish such a hospital, but very quickly it was made clear to him that he could not use his gift for making money.

In 1923 Cayce had to hire a secretary, Gladys Davis, to write down all the information he was producing in his readings. His wife Gertrude was, by this time, conducting the readings and asking him the necessary questions. About this time a man who had received successful readings for two of his nieces asked Cayce for a "horoscope reading." In the course of it, Cayce made mention of a past life that the man had once had. This opened the door to a whole new field of psychic investigation; however, Cayce's personal attachment to Christianity (he read the Bible and taught Sunday school) made him uneasy. Re-reading the Bible in its entirety, he finally realized that the concept of reincarnation was not incompatible with any religion and actually followed his own ideas of what it meant to be a good Christian. So began what became known as the "Life Readings," trance readings that looked at a person's past lives and the relationship to the present life. In time this further expanded into mental and spiritual counseling, philosophy, dream interpretation, and other avenues.

Finally, and very reluctantly, Cayce had to give up his photographic career for lack of time. He also began to accept donations toward the hospital he still wanted to build. Readings that he gave indicated that it needed to be established at Virginia Beach, Virginia. In September of 1925 the Cayce family, with secretary Gladys Davis, moved there; two years later the Association of National Investigators was formed to research the information that was now rapidly growing in volume. In 1928, on November 11, the Edgar Cayce Hospital was opened. Patients came from all over the country and were diagnosed and prescribed for by Cayce. They were then treated by the staff of doctors, nurses, and therapists.

The Depression forced the hospital to close in 1931 when financial backing was lost, but later that year the Association for Research and Enlightenment was formed as a research body for all the information in the readings.

Cayce himself continued to develop psychically, picking up information in the waking state as well as when in a trance, seeing auras around people and even diagnosing from these. With the onset of World War II Cayce was inundated with requests for readings and, despite warnings about his own health (given from his own readings), he began to grow weak from overwork. His readings continuously told him to rest, but he felt obliged to keep going. Finally, in 1944, he collapsed. His last reading was for himself, in September of that year, when he was told that he must rest until either he got better or he died. Shortly after, he had a stroke and became partially paralyzed. Cayce died on January 3, 1945. Within three months, Gertrude also died.

Copies of over 14,000 case histories of Cayce's readings, including all follow-up reports received from the individuals concerned, are available for reference at the Association for Research and Enlightenment, Inc. (A.R.E.), in Virginia Beach. This material represents the most massive collection of psychic information ever obtained from a single source. The organization has grown from a few hundred supporters in 1945 to one that today is worldwide.

Countless individuals have been touched by the life work of this man who was raised a simple farm boy and became one of the most versatile and credible psychics the world has ever known. He has been called "the father of holistic medicine." In history, the Cayce readings gave insights into Judaism that were verified a decade after his death; in world affairs, he saw the collapse of communism nearly fifty years before it happened. Even in the field of physics, a professor and fellow of the American Physical Society theorized a connection between the elementary-particle theory and the way in which Cayce received his information. Repeatedly, science and history have validated concepts and ideas explored in Edgar Cayce's psychic information.

Sources:
Cayce, Hugh Lynn. *Venture Inward*. New York: Paperback Library, 1969.
Langley, Noel. *Edgar Cayce on Reincarnation*. New York: Paperback Library, 1967.
Stearn, Jess. *Edgar Cayce: the Sleeping Prophet*. New York: Doubleday, 1967.
Sugrue, Thomas. *There Is a River: the Story of Edgar Cayce*. New York: Dell, 1970.
http://www.edgarcayce.org/.

Celtic Astrology

Robert Graves first visualized the Celtic lunar zodiac in his book *The White Goddess*. He arrived at the symbol or association of a tree with each of the lunar months. He further connected the thirteen months with the thirteen consonants of the Celtic Beth-Luis-Nion tree alphabet.

The **Celtic** Druids used a thirteen-month calendar working from the phases of the **moon,** which was the basis for their form of **astrology.** Rather than centering around the sun, they centered around the moon. Solar-oriented astrology has dominated Western astrological thought for centuries, yet the Celts had a concept that worked just as well and tied in with their native ideas of deities and mythology.

Rather than symbolizing the signs by the constellations, they were symbolized by tree images; Druids utilized trees in many of their workings. These run as follows:

Tree	Celtic	Dates
Birch	*Beith*	Dec 24–Jan 20
Rowan	*Luis*	Jan 21–Feb 17
Ash	*Nuin*	Feb 18–Mar 17
Alder	*Fearn*	Mar 18–Apr 14
Willow	*Saille*	Apr 15–May 12
Hawthorne	*Huathe*	May 13–Jun 9
Oak	*Druir*	Jun 10–Jul 7
Holly	*Tinne*	Jul 8–Aug 4
Hazel	*Coll*	Aug 5–Sep 1
Vine	*Muin*	Sep 2–Sep 29
Ivy	*Gort*	Sep 30–Oct 27
Reed	*NgEtal*	Oct 28–Nov 24
Elder	*Ruis*	Nov 25–Dec 23

The zodiac chart is divided by calculating the first twelve signs at 28°, to correspond to the twenty-eight days of the lunar month, beginning with Beith (birch). The thirteenth sign (Ruis—elder) contains the remaining twenty-four degrees. A second division of the zodiac is given by Paterson, which gives 28° each to Beis, Luis, Nuin, and Fearn; 27° each to Saille, Huathe, Druir, Tinne, and Coll; 28° again to Muin, Gort, and NgEtal; and 29° to Ruis.

Important on the zodiacs are the summer and winter solstices (*Alban Hefin* and *Alban Arthuan*) and the vernal and autumnal equinoxes (*Alban Eilir* and *Alban Elfed*). Also significant are the four major feast days of the Celtic calendar: *Samhain* (November Eve), *Lughnasadh* (August Eve), *Beltaine* (May Eve), and *Imbolc* (February Eve).

As Helena Paterson says: "The Druids . . . had observed and developed a zodiac that was both heliocentric and geocentric. . . . Their lunar division of the signs restores the soli-lunar balance and integration of the psyche which is lacking in the astrology of the Greeks. . . . It draws on the vast storehouse of astrological lore already collated by ancient Greek and Roman scholars with those theorems the Druids were apparently most intimately acquainted."

Sources:

Graves, Robert. *The White Goddes*. London: Faber & Faber, 1961.

Orion, Rae. *Astrology for Dummies*. Foster City, CA: IDG Books, 1999.

Paterson, Helena. *The Handbook of Celtic Astrology: The 13-Sign Lunar Zodiac of the Ancient Druids*. St. Paul, MN: Llewyllen, 1999.

CELTS

Celt, or Kelt, is derived from the **Greek** *Keltoi*, a name used to label a group of people spread across Europe and the Iberian Peninsula. Most authorities recognize the Celts as existing from the Black Sea across to the Atlantic Ocean and from the North Sea and

Denmark down to the Mediterranean. They were known as *Kelten* in Germany and *Celtes* (with the soft C) in France. Much of their expansion was due to their use of iron, rather than bronze, for weapons. The Celts were a distinctive group of people of related tribes who emerged in the eighth century BCE. Their social system was divided into three parts: king, warrior aristocracy, and freemen farmers. They introduced the use of iron to northern Europe. Their inventions and introductions were numerous: chain mail, soap, horse shoes, iron rims for wheels, the shapes of chisels, files, and handsaws.

The Celts measured time in nights rather than days, dividing months, or **moon** spans, into two halves: bright and dark. Even today, the language of the Celts survives in Brittany, Wales, the Isle of Man, and along the west coasts of both **Scotland** and Ireland. In recent years it has been revived in Cornwall, England. The Celtic revival in Cornwall has been intense, with renewal of celebrations of the past and big festivals, including the lighting of balefires on hill tops across the county on the main Celtic feast days.

Each of the various Celtic tribes had its own leader and its own laws, yet there was great similarity among all tribes. Originally the leaders were known as kings, but later, with the exception of Ireland, the title became chieftain. One form of their language, today known as P-Celtic, was spoken in Gaul and Britain while another form, Q-Celtic, was spoken in Ireland.

Although the Celts had knowledge of Greek writing, their laws, histories, and religious beliefs were not committed to writing but were passed on orally. Caesar commented on this when speaking of the Celtic priesthood, the Druids. In his *De Bello Gallico* he said, "(They) learn by heart a great number of verses, and therefore some persons remain twenty years under training."

There were four main festivals in the Celtic year—Imbolc, Beltane, Lughnasadh, and Samhain—which were celebrated at the main sacred site of each tribe. The priests and priestesses for these rituals were the Druids, though little is now known of them. It is known, however, that they were recruited from warrior-class families and were then regarded as of higher rank. The Druids were believed to be not only religious leaders and teachers but also magicians, shape-shifters, and **diviners** or **seers.**

The Celts practiced human sacrifice. Dr. Anne Ross refers to three of their gods, Teutates, Esus, and Taranis, commenting that the Roman poet Lucan told of people being drowned in a vat in sacrifice to Teutates, stabbed and then hung in a tree in sacrifice to Esus, and burned in sacrifice to Taranis. Animals were routinely sacrificed, and the bull-sacrifice (*tarb-feis*) was featured at the crowning of a new king. Anu (or Danu) was the Mother of the Gods. From her came the Irish gods known as the *Tuatha De Danann* (Tribes of the Goddess Danu). It is possible that the goddess Brigit is Danu known by another name. It was a custom to give a number of different names to any one deity, though some of these names were simply epithets.

The priesthood of the Celts was the Druids. The Greeks and the **Romans** first identified them, calling them variously *druidai*, *druids*, *drysidæ*, and *dryadæ*. Pliny the Elder suggested that the name might have derived from "oak tree." The Greek word for oak was *drus*. As Celtic priests, the Druids possessed tremendous knowledge, including knowledge of many forms of divination. These included **augury** by birds (**orniscopy**), insects, fire (**causimancy, empyromancy,** and **pyromancy**), dreams and visions (**oneiromancy** and **metagnomy**), examination of animals' shoulder blades (**omoplatoscopy** and **scapulomancy**), scrying, sacrifice (**hieromancy**), and water (**hydromancy** and **lecanomancy**).

The Sicilian Greek writer Diodorus Siculus said that the Druids divined by the flight and action of birds. They would note how many species flew within a marked area. Certain birds were considered lucky and others unlucky. Whether flying in from the left or the right would be relevant. The time spent within the designated space would also mean something. Even those birds that flew over the area without actually alighting were noted. The birds' cries were also significant.

John Toland, writing in 1697, related how he met two old Irish men who told him they knew their private business venture was going to succeed because they had seen a raven standing on the road in front of them. It had some white feathers in its plumage, and when it flew off it headed south, uttering a cry. This, they assured him, was all they needed to know their business would be successful. "Raven knowledge" was highly regarded in many parts of Great Britain. In Ireland it was said that if a raven sat on the roof of your house over the position of the head of your bed and cried out, a distinguished visitor would soon be at the house. Depending on the type of cry the bird made, the visitor might be a monk or some other of the clergy. If the raven called from the northeast corner of the house, there was a chance of thieves breaking in. If it called from near the door, there would soon be soldiers or strangers visiting.

In Wales the eagle was the bird of divination. In the north of England it was the cuckoo. In Scotland it was the crow and the rook. The wren was also viewed as a bird to be studied for omens, among the Celts. It was referred to as a *drui-en*, or "Druid bird." In fact, in Wales the name for the wren is *dryw*.

The Celts also considered the movement of animals of various sorts for their divination. The hare was especially auspicious and features in much British folklore. It is said that before Queen Boudicca (or Boadicea) faced down the Romans, she released a hare to see which way it would run.

In Celtic Devonshire, if a swarm of bees alights in a dead tree it means that within a year there will be a death in the house of the family that owns the tree. Even insects were studied. The actions of worms were noted, especially in parts of Scotland. If a certain worm in a medicinal spring in the parish of Strathdon was found alive, it augured the survival of the patient. In a well in Appin there was a similar belief: if a dead worm was found the patient would die; if a live worm, the patient would live.

The Celts would draw omens from the direction of smoke and flames of sacred fires. They would also study the shape of clouds. If an Irish Druid wished to track stolen property, he would sing a particular incantation through his half-closed fist, using it like a trumpet. He would then go to sleep and, in his dreams, would find what was sought.

Scapulomancy is found almost universally. It was practiced by the Celts, where divining by means of studying the shoulder blades of animals was a popular form of divination, though carried out only by certain people who made a profession of the study. The right blade bone of a black pig or sheep was considered the best for this form of augury. It was thoroughly boiled, so that no flesh remained on it, but was not scraped since it was important that only natural marks should be found. The bone was divided into a number of different sections corresponding to the geographical features of the local area. Author Lewis Spence says:

> Certain marks indicated a crowd of people, meeting at a funeral, a fight, sale, etc. The largest hole of indentation symbolized the grave of the beast's owner and, from its position, the problem of whether he should survive the current year, or otherwise, was resolved. It if lay near the side of the bone, the omen was fatal, but if in its centre, prosperity was indicated.

An unusual method of divining was found in the North of Scotland. It was known as "the swimming of names in water." Spence reports that it was "resorted to in cases of theft, in order to discover the guilty person." The names of those suspected were written on pieces of paper and thrown into a large vessel of water. Whichever one sank was the name of the guilty party.

Both Diodorus Siculus and Tacitus mention a Druidic custom of divining with the entrails of sacrificed victims. Tacitus says: "The Druids consult the gods in the palpitating entrails of men." According to Spence, Strabo describes how they would stab a man in the back with a sword and then observe his convulsive movements and divine from those. Diodorus also mentions this and says that they augured from the posture in which the victim fell, from his contortions, and from the direction in which the spilled blood flowed away from the body (**hæmatomancy**).

Sources:

Buckland, Raymond. *The Witch Book: The Encyclopedia of Witchcraft, Wicca, and Neo-paganism*. Detroit: Visible Ink Press, 2002.

Ross, Anne. *Pagan Celtic Britain*. London: Routledge & Kegan Paul, 1967.

National Geographic, "The Celts." May, 1977.

Norton-Taylor, Duncan. *The Emergence of Man: The Celts*. Alexandria, VA: Time-Life Books, 1974.

Spence, Lewis. *The Magic Arts in Celtic Britain*. London: Rider, 1945.

Toland, John A. *A Critical History of the Celtic Religion and Learning: Containing an Account of the Druids*. Edinburgh, 1815.

Ceneromancy

Ceneromancy is divination using ashes. When a ritual fire, or fire built specifically for the purpose of divination (see **Anthracomancy** and **Pyromancy**), had died down, any remaining wood or coal was removed and the state of the ashes was considered. The various ridges—their mounds and valleys—were interpreted with regard to high points and low points, intersections, dead ends, and so on.

Central Premonitions Registry

This bureau was started in New York in 1968 as a direct result of the large numbers of **prophetic dreams** experienced by people around Great Britain prior to the **Aberfan** tragedy, which took place October 20, 1966. On that date, in the little Welsh village of Aberfan, a half-million-ton mountain of coal waste, saturated by days of unrelenting rain, slid down over the village and buried dozens of houses and the village school. Sixteen adults and 128 schoolchildren died.

There were so many reports of detailed dreams prior to the tragedy that a London psychiatrist, Dr. J. C. Barker, suggested a survey be conducted. Many of the reported premonitions were rejected for lack of authenticating evidence or because they were too vague. At least thirty-six prophetic dreams could be fully documented and confirmed, together with twenty-four non-dream premonitions. Consequently, the **British Premonitions Bureau** was established in 1967 and the New York Central Premonitions Registry the following year.

Sources:
Buckland, Raymond. *Gypsy Dream Dictionary*. St. Paul, MN: Llewellyn, 1999.
Holroyd, Stuart. *The Supernatural: Dream Worlds*. London: Aldus Books, 1976.
http://mainportals.com/precog.shtml.
Mysteries of the Unknown: Psychic Powers. Alexandria, VA: Time-Life Books, 1987.

Cephalomancy; Cephalonomancy; Kephalonomancy

Divination by studying an ass's head after it has been boiled. This was also done with a goat's head or a donkey's head. Sir Thomas Urquhart, in *The Third Book of the Works of Mr. Francis Rabelais* (London, 1693), mentions "Cephalomancy, often practiced amongst the High Germans, in their boiling of an Asses Head upon burning coals."

The head was boiled until all flesh fell from it. It was then carefully studied both for its shape and its condition. Much as the cracks in the shoulder blades of animals are interpreted in **scapulomancy,** so are any cracks or breaks found in the ass's or goat's head in cephalomancy. Unusual shape was also noted, in an art akin to the later **phrenology.** The interpretation of the features found in the animal, were applied to the animal's owner. Thus might be found his past, present, and future.

Sources:
Oxford English Dictionary. Oxford: Clarendon Press, 1989.
Spence, Lewis. *The Magic Arts in Celtic Britain*. London: Rider, 1945.

Ceraunomancy; Ceraunoscopy

This is divination by thunder and lightning or by thunderbolt (meteoric iron). The augurs of ancient **Rome** searched the skies for signs of the will of the gods. Along with the flights of birds (known as **orniscopy**), the major class of **augury** was by such sky signs as thunder, lightning, falling stars, and comets. Lightning from left to right was considered favorable but from right to left a presage of ill omen. On the appearance of lightning, whatever its form and whatever its direction, all business in the public assemblies was halted for the rest of the day. Since the official augur could not be questioned as to whether or not he actually saw lightning, this gave him tremendous power. By stating that he saw lightning, he could stop any public assembly and bring a halt to any meetings. He rapidly became a tool of the political scene of that time. In later republican times, however, this power was considerably curtailed. But when a new consul, prætor, or quæstor was installed and began his first day in office, it was usual for the augur to report seeing lightning, flashing from left to right, so that all might have the day free to welcome the newcomer.

Ceraunomancy is a term also applied to divination from thunderbolts; that is, from examination of lumps of meteoric iron. The shapes of such meteorites were studied and interpreted much as were the shapes assumed by lumps of wax allowed to drop into water in **ceromancy.**

Sources:

Adkins, Lesley and Roy A. Adkins. *Dictionary of Roman Religion*. New York: Facts on File, 1996.
Encyclopedia Britannica. Chicago: William Benton, 1964.

CERAUNOSCOPY ***see*** **Ceraunomancy**

Ceremonial Magic

Ceremonial magic—also known as High Magic or Ritual Magic—is the practice of conjuring spirits (termed variously entities, demons, devils) to do your bidding. Alphonsus de Spina, in 1459, stated that there were 133,306,668 of these entities. This was "corrected" by Johann Weyer, in 1577, to 7,405,926 demons and seventy-two princes. Others tried to count them also, but came up with widely differing totals. Certainly there was a belief in a whole host of entities, all named and in a regular hierarchy, and each was thought to be an expert in a particular field. Depending upon what you wished for, the pertinent entity should be conjured. For example, to be able to speak in tongues, Agares must be summoned. To learn secrets and gain marital love, Furfur must be reached. To discover the whereabouts of buried treasure, Purson is the one.

A number of spirits can help with divining the past, present, and future. One to conjure in order to learn about the future is Amon. He is described as a wolf with a serpent's head and is a marquis in the hierarchy. He can see into both the past and the future. Aina—a duke with three heads: a man's, a cat's, and a snake's—knows all things. Amy specializes in science and can teach **astrology.** The mighty Astaroth, who rides a dragon, knows all of the past, the present, and the future. Aymon is a count who rides on a wolf. He teaches divination. Caim, who appears as a thrush, claims to know secrets of the future. Curson, a king, can tell all of the past, present, and future. Furcus, a duke who appears as an old man riding on a pale horse, teaches astronomy and **cheiromancy.** Gaap is a prince who can tell of the past and the future. Marchosias, a mighty marquis, will truthfully answer all questions. Solas, who appears first as a black raven, is a prince who will teach astrology. Among the thousands of other entities, there are many more who deal with various aspects of divination.

These entities were very unwilling to appear and obey, so they had to be threatened; the magician had to show that he was more powerful than the spirit. Once the spirit acknowledged that superiority, it was forced to obey, albeit reluctantly. To

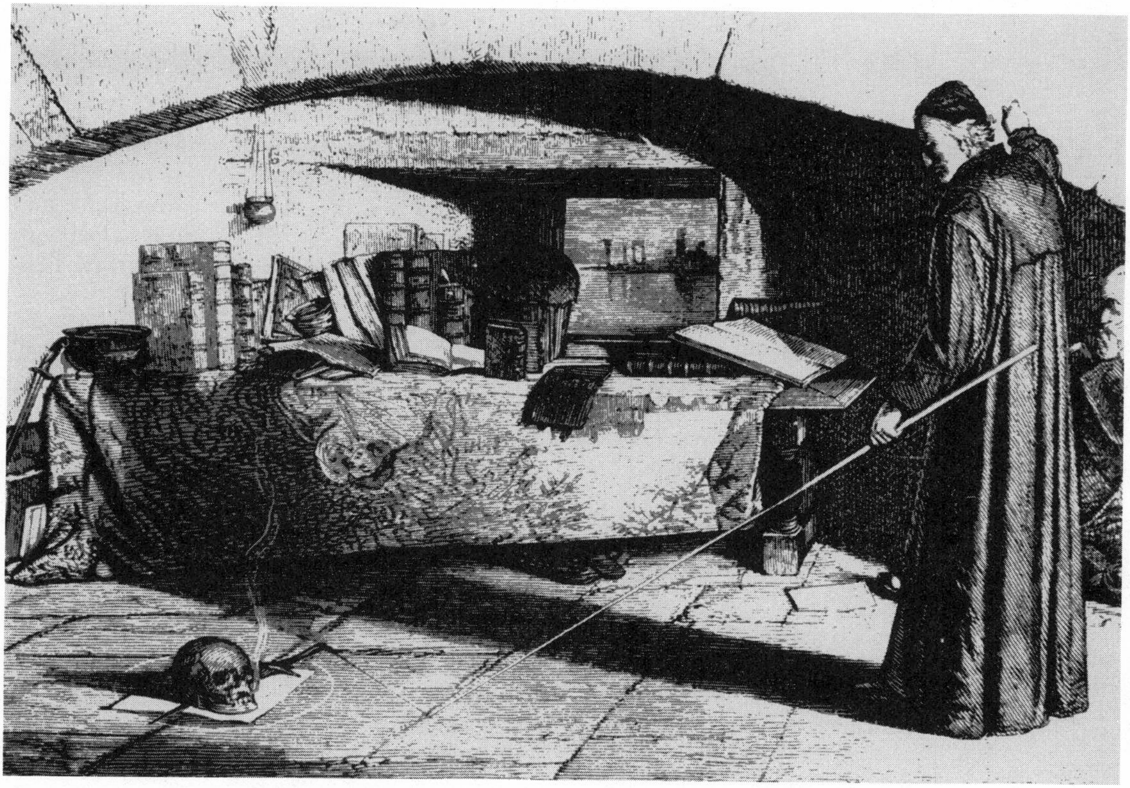

A magician performing a spell-casting ceremony. Engraving by Stephen Miller after a painting by William Douglas. *Fortean Picture Library.*

demonstrate his superiority, the magician would conjure with "words of power," usually using the names of God and of the angels and archangels.

A book containing the details of such rituals of the "art magic" was known as a *grimoire*, from the Old French for "grammar." There are a number of these grimoires extant in the libraries and private collections of Europe and America, although many seem to be no more than copies of copies. Some of the most notable grimoires are *The Key of Solomon the King, The Lesser Key of Solomon, The Arbatel, The Heptameron, The Grimoire of Honorius, The Black Pullet, The Pansophy of Rudolph the Magus*, and *The Book of Sacred Magic of Abra-Melin the Mage*.

For the magician there is a great deal of preparatory work to be done before he can start the conjuration. All the instruments used in the work must be made by the magician and constructed to an exacting formula. For example, wood for wands and the handles of knives, etc., must be cut from certain trees on specific days in the hours of specified planets. Everything has to be purified to the utmost, including the magician himself, through fasting, bathing, and prayer. The temple where the conjuration will take place must be carefully prepared and purified.

The Abra-Melin suggests that the magician's "age ought not to be less than twenty-five years nor more than fifty; he should have no hereditary disease, such as virulent leprosy; whether he be free or married importeth little." He must be dressed in special robes, prepared as carefully as the various instruments. He wears a crown of parchment and from his belt and around his neck hang amulets and pentacles. He operates within a large magic circle, carefully constructed and written around with the names of power. Outside the circle is a small triangle, also surrounded with names and words of power. Into this triangle the entity is conjured. Since the spirit is so loathe to appear, he can be very dangerous. Everything done—the tools, robes, circle—is, then, there to protect the magician.

The actual rituals to conjure the spirit are long and demanding, frequently in Latin or Greek. Exhortation after exhortation is made. If the magician is successful, the entity will finally appear in the triangle. Many times he appears "in terrible form," hoping to scare the magician out of his circle of protection. But if he does appear, no matter his form, then he must obey the magician.

Unfortunately it does not end there. When the conjurer has got what he wants, he then has to dismiss the entity. The spirit is not always willing to leave, having been brought there. Again there are many exhortations and threats by the magician. Only when he is absolutely sure that the spirit has gone does the ceremonial magician dare leave his circle of protection.

Sources:

Buckland, Raymond. *The Witch Book: The Encyclopedia of Witchcraft, Wicca, and Neo-paganism*. Detroit: Visible Ink Press, 2002.

Buckland, Raymond. *The Anatomy of the Occult*. New York: Samuel Weiser, 1977.

Barrett, Francis. *The Magus, or Celestial Intelligencer; being a complete system of occult philosophy*. London: Lackington, Allen & Co., 1802.

Mathers, S. L. Macgregor. *The Book of Sacred Magic of Abra-Melin the Mage*. De Laurence, 1932.

Ceromancy; Ceroscopy

Divination from the figures produced by dropping melted wax into water. Fine wax shavings were placed in a brass bowl, which was set over a flame. The wax was melted until it was a liquid of uniform consistency. Another large vessel was filled with cold water. Drops of liquid wax were then allowed to fall onto the surface of the water. They would harden into numbers of irregularly shaped discs. The disks would then be interpreted by the **seer.** He or she would interpret based on suggested shapes (as in **tasseography**) together with the proximity of those shapes to one another.

In Sir Thomas Urquhart's *Third Book of the Works of* Mr. *Francis Rabelais* (London, 1693), it says: "By ceromancy, where, by means of wax dissolved into water, thou shalt see the lively representation of thy future wife."

Sources:

Oxford English Dictionary. Oxford: Clarendon Press, 1989.

Shepard, Leslie A. (ed.). *Encyclopedia of Occultism & Parapsychology*. New York: Avon, 1978.

CEROSCOPY ***see*** **Ceromancy**

Chair Test

This was a test carried out at the University of Utrecht by Professor Willem H. C. Tenhaeff, the Dutch parapsychologist, during his years of testing the famous psychic **Gérard Croiset** of the Netherlands. Professor Tenhaeff had set up an Institute of Parapsychology at the university, similar to the well-known one founded by **Dr. J. B. Rhine** at Duke University. Among Professor Tenhaeff's many tests for Croiset, he devised one where the number of a chair in a lecture hall was chosen at random, days or even weeks ahead of time. The seats could not be reserved and sometimes even the actual venue was not determined till close to the date of the lecture.

Anywhere from a few hours to several days before the lecture, Croiset would describe, and give a number of personal details of, the person who would occupy the chair on the date in question. These were never vague or in any way general, but could include hair and eye color, height, physique, age, dress, even marks on the body. Croiset's **predictions** would be recorded, and the recording would be placed in a sealed bag and locked away in a safe. At the lecture, the recording would be played back and the occupant of the chair asked to stand up and comment on Croiset's observations. Croiset showed incredible accuracy with this test, and with many others.

Occasionally Croiset would seem unable to get any information. On those occasions it turned out that the seat remained empty for the lecture. Sometimes he got very confusing images, which were later explained by the fact that more than one person used the chair.

The first such test was given in Amsterdam in October 1947 in front of the Dutch Society of Psychical Research. By 1951 experts from around the world had been invited to participate and to monitor the conditions, gradually improving the test to make it more severe. In 1961 Professor Tenhaeff published a scholarly collection of records of the tests in a 300-page book titled *De Voorschouw* (**Precognition**).

One of the cases is quoted by Jack Harrison Pollack in his book on Croiset. He calls it "Last Minute Ticket":

> On the afternoon of March 6, 1950, when nosing around for a story, Amsterdam journalist E.K. telephoned Gérard Croiset in Enschede asking for some concrete evidence of his powers, the news of which was then spreading over the Netherlands.
>
> "Well, in two days," replied Croiset, "I am giving a chair test before the Utrecht chapter of the Society for Psychical Research. Please pick a chair number for then. Name any number you want."
>
> "Row 7, third chair from the right," volunteered the Dutch journalist.
>
> "All right," replied Croiset. "Please make a note of these impressions that I am now giving you. I see on this chair will sit a lady with gray hair. She has a slim figure and is a lean type. She likes to help people, but calls everything she does 'Christian social work'."

> When these facts were checked under Dr. Tenhaeff's supervision on the evening of March 8, this particular chair was found to be occupied by a Protestant Sister of Mercy, Sister L.B., who, indeed, did Christian social work. Croiset's description of her was a direct hit. It couldn't possibly have fitted anyone else present.
>
> Sister L.B. acknowledged the paragnost's description of her as being accurate. She said that she had almost stayed at home, and her choice of the seat was unpremeditated. . . . Investigator Tenhaeff's later check-up revealed: "Sister L.B. was *not* a member of the Dutch Society for Psychical Research. It was purely accidental that she received an admission ticket as late as 5:40 p.m. on March 8. Croiset gave his information to journalist E. K. when the participants of the test had not yet received their invitations. Moreover, the person who gave Sister L.B. her ticket did not know any of the facts furnished by the paragnost."

Sources:

Pollack, Jack Harrison. *Croiset the Clairvoyant*. New York: Doubleday, 1964.
Wilson, Colin (ed.). *The Supernatural: Mysterious Powers*. London: Aldus Books, 1975.

CHANCE REMARKS ***see*** **Cledonomancy**

Channeling; Mediumship

Although mediums are channeling information, they are not "channels" in the nomenclature of the New Age. Similarly, channels are not mediums. The differences are, perhaps, subtle, but there are differences. Looking first at mediums, these are part of the world of spiritualism. They are the intermediaries between this world of the living and the "other" world of the dead. They bridge the gap between those who are still alive and their deceased relatives and loved ones who have "crossed over." Usually, though not always, there is a direct relationship between the two personalities connected through the agencies of the medium. The medium may or may not go into a **trance.** He or she may use **clairvoyance, clairaudience, clairsentience,** direct voice, or any of a number of different ways to bring through the messages from the other side. The messages can, and usually do, come from a wide range of **spirits**—many different people who have lived before. The living receivers are often able to ask questions of the deceased and receive answers, advice, and confirmation of a continued existence.

Channels, on the other hand, are bringing information from "entities" that may or may not have ever lived on this earth and are generally not related in any way to the receivers of the information. Each channel usually produces information from only one particular source, which is frequently delivered as a lecture. Some of these sources claim to be from such origins as ancient Atlantis; some from other planets, other worlds, other universes. This information is imparted using the vocal cords of the channel, who is usually in trance and completely unaware of what is going on. The channel is the direct voice conduit for the entity, who preaches to the audience. A medium usually works with a small, intimate group while a channel may speak in a large auditorium.

There are examples still extant of some of the paraphernalia used by ancient **Egyptian** priests when claiming to channel messages from the Egyptian gods themselves (for example, the mask worn when representing Anubis, the jackal-headed god). In the **Mayan** temples the priests played the part of their gods, giving and relaying instructions, messages, and advice to the people. In **Voodoo,** a possessed worshiper will channel the deity, known as a *loa*. In modern Panchmuda, northwest of Calcutta, India, at the Temple of Manasa during the Snake Festival, the Serpent Mother will take possession of a worshiper, much as in Voodoo, and speak through him or her.

Writers, musicians, and artists have long composed through a process of channeling. Wolfgang Mozart heard music in his head and simply wrote down what he heard verbatim. Many visual artists claim they work the same way, simply putting onto canvas what is processed through them.

"Seth" was an entity channeled by Jane Roberts (1929–1984). Seth defined itself as "an energy personality essence" that was no longer in physical form. It claimed various lifetimes on Earth, though stating that such lifetimes are actually occurring simultaneously because past, present, and future all exist at the same time. Judy "Zebra" Knight, another channeler, claimed to be the instrument for a character she called "Ramtha." He was supposed to have lived 35,000 years ago on the now lost continent of Lemuria. His speech patterns and mannerisms were remarkably like those of Judy Knight herself. Jessica Lansing channeled "Michael," who said he was "of the mid-causal plane" and made up of 1,000 fragments of an entity like himself. Jach Pursel's "Lazaris" says that he has never been in human form; he is a "group form" living in another dimension. Elizabeth Clare Prophet channeled what she described as "ascended masters" no longer living on the physical plane. Darryl Anka's "Bashar" says he is from the planet Essassani, 500 light years away. Interestingly, regardless of the sex of the channel, the entity that comes through always seems to be masculine.

Many of the channels bring "doom and gloom" prophesies, some claiming that the world will end in a certain period of time. Some, such as "Ramtha," appear extremely egotistical and strangely materialistic. Some have urged their followers to give away all their worldly goods or to sell them and donate the proceeds to the organization supporting the channel.

Although there are the charlatans and suspects among the channelers, most of the lectures that come through are positive, leading to a better standard of life. The listener should be prepared to listen and decide for him- or herself what is right, rather than being told what to do.

In the same way, there are many charlatans and those who are self-deceived among the mediums. From the very beginning of spiritualism in the middle of the nineteenth century, there have been frauds who found it easy to prey on those who were bereaved. But—again as with channelers—just because there are fakes does not mean that all are fakes. There have been, and still are, excellent mediums who are above reproach. John Edward is probably the prime example today, doing a regular television program where he contacts the dead relatives of members of his studio audience.

Sources:

Bentine, Michael. *The Door Marked Summer.* London: Granada, 1981.

Bentine, Michael. *Doors of the Mind*. London: Granada, 1984.
Buckland, Raymond. *Doors to Other Worlds*. St. Paul, MN: Llewellyn, 1993.
Cook, Mrs. Cecil. *How I Discovered My Mediumship*. Chicago: Lormar, 1919.
Guiley, Rosemary Ellen. *Harper's Encyclopedia of Mystical & Paranormal Experience*. San Francisco: HarperSanFrancisco, 1991.
Klimo, Jon. *Channeling: Investigations on Receiving Information from Paranormal Source*. Los Angeles: Jeremy P. Tarcher, 1987.

Chaomancy

The word chaomancy is from the Greek *chaos*, which, in Paracelsian language, means "the atmosphere." According to Thomas Blount's *Glossographia* of 1681, it is "a kind of divination by the air."

It is a variation on ceraunoscopy, which deals specifically with thunder and lightning. Chaomancy includes lightning but deals with any and all variations of the air, such as changes in wind direction, force and intensity, squalls, tornadoes, and dust devils.

CHEESE ***see*** **Tiromancy**

CHEIRO ***see*** **Hamon, Count Louis**

Cheiromancy; Chiromancy; Cheirosophy; Chirognomy

(See also Palmistry)

Cheiromancy, or Chiromancy, is the same thing as palmistry: the reading and interpretation of the hand and the lines and markings on it. It has been subdivided into three parts: cheirognomy—recognizing a person's intelligence from the general shape of the hands; cheirosophy—the study of the comparative value of manual formations; and cheiromancy—the art of divination from the form of the hand and fingers, and the lines and markings on them.

There have been many references to the art over the centuries. John Skelton's *Poetical Works* of 1528 refers to "some pseudo **prophets** with chiromancy." *Overmatched II*, volume 66 (London) of 1876 says: "The cheiromant of old was an artist, as the augur and **astrologer** were." In the *Pall Mall Gazette* of September 10, 1883, it says, "He had better betake himself to a regular Chiromant and make himself miserable." One of the most famous palmists was **Count Louis de Hamon** (1866–1936), who adopted the professional name of Cheiro.

Cheiromancy, or palmistry, was known to exist in ancient **Greece** and **Rome.** Even in **Celtic** Europe there is evidence to show that the hand was seen as a reflection of the whole person. There is also evidence that it was known in ancient **China** and in **Egypt,** Babylonia, and Chaldea from at least 4000 BCE. Cheiromancy was popular in medieval times and throughout recent history.

The *Encyclopedia Britannica* describes palmistry as "a predictive system whereby the various irregularities and flexion folds of the skin of the hand are interpreted as being associated with mental or moral dispositions and powers as well as with the current of future events in the life of the individual." Tradition has it that when Siddhartha Gautama (Buddha) was born, around 563 BCE, his feet bore marks that indicated to the sages of the time that he would achieve greatness. Similarly, Krishna had markings on both hands and feet that foretold coming events. Even today talismans are made and sold that are in the shape of the Buddha's feet, marked with signs and symbols. Both hands and feet can be read but, today at least, the hands are generally more accessible.

Early **Indian palmistry** was closely linked to astrology, and such links are still recognized in all palm reading. The fingers, for example, are linked to planets: the thumb to Venus, forefinger to Jupiter, middle finger to Saturn, ring finger to Apollo, and the little finger to Mercury. The overall shape and size of the hand is significant, as are the respective lengths of the fingers. There has developed a fixed set of meanings for interpreting the map of the hand, but there is still room for personal intuition when reading it.

The hand changes throughout your life. The lines observed today are vastly different from the lines as they appeared some years ago. However, this is less so in the left hand, for it is said that the left hand retains what you were born with while the right hand shows what you have made of your latent abilities. (With left-handed people this is reversed.) Like much of divination, cheiromancy is a diagnostic reading. It can point out the forces that operate within yourself or another, and it can pinpoint the logical result(s) of these forces, but it is up to you whether or not you choose to accept them.

As with all forms of divination, when reading the palms of others it is well to give careful consideration to how you present what you see. Do not blurt out that the person is going to die, for example! Give cautions, especially in the area of health, and recommendations rather than stating that such-and-such an event is definitely going to happen. With divination comes responsibility. The diviner becomes an authority figure whose words carry power to the listener.

It can be a good idea to collect prints of a variety of hands for study and practice. It used to be that the best way to do this was to ink the hand and then press it down on a sheet of white paper. These days, however, a good impression can be obtained by pressing the hand on the glass of a copy machine and making a photocopy. Working this way, you can write comments and make notes on the prints of the various palms.

First Observation

Many palmists will consider the shape of the hands first. Generally a person with long, articulate hands and fingers will tend toward the contemplative and artistic, while one with short, broad hands and fingers will tend to enjoy doing things and making things without necessarily considering deeper meanings. These are, as mentioned, generalities, and the detailed examination of the palm and fingers help elaborate on them.

If all of the fingers are close together, it is an indication of caution and of being conventional. If the fingers are wide apart, it shows a quick and flexible mind. If the other fingers seem to lean toward the little finger, the subject's life will be ruled by emotions and instinct. If the fingers seem to lean toward the index finger and thumb, then

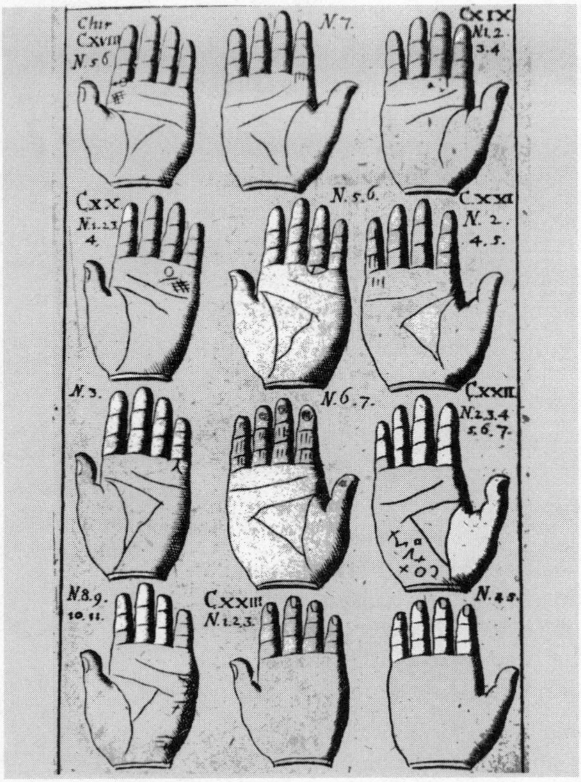

Cheiromancy engraving from the seventeenth century. ***Fortean Picture Library.***

this is a sign of potential leadership and of conscious effort in all that is done. A balanced personality has the outer fingers leaning in toward the middle finger.

If the thumb seems widely separated from the fingers, then it indicates a very open mind. If the thumb is held in close to the fingers, there is a tendency to be timid. High mounts at the bases of the fingers indicate a lively mind. If the person can bend back the fingers almost at right angles to the hand, it shows extreme versatility.

For a right-handed person, the left hand shows what the person was born with—the traits and habits that will develop along with the course the life will probably take. The right hand shows what that person has actually done with his or her life, and whether they have lived up to their potential. Very light lines on the right hand would seem to indicate that full potential has not been met. Someone who has constantly tried to improve their lot and avoided leaning on others is likely to have quite a difference between the two palms with strong, deep lines on the right.

If there seem to be a great many lines on the palm, it shows a very complex person—the sort of person who becomes more and more frustrated the more they learn, because they then realize how much more there *is* to learn! A line in the form of a "chain" indicates a weakness in that which the line symbolizes. The person must pay special attention to that area. In the few cases where a line branches and/or seems to have a parallel of itself, it is a rare condition where the subject has alternate courses available. Care needs to be taken in deciding which is the better course.

In studying the hands, it is best to begin with the left hand, or the "one that shows with what you were born." If the lines of the hand are clear and deep, they indicate a person who experiences and understands much of the pain and joy that will inevitably be encountered in life. But if the lines are light and faint, it indicates a superficial outlook and somewhat colorless personality. The person would gain by getting out and enjoying him- or herself.

Hand Types

What is known as the ELEMENTARY HAND is very basic, with little shape to the fingers. It has an almost primitive appearance and indicates a somewhat primitive mind. This type of hand usually has hard skin, stiffness, and lines that are few in number and seem more like creases in the hand than actual lines.

The SQUARE HAND is broad, with firm muscles and fingers that are rectangular in shape. They may have rounded tips, of course, but basically there is not a lot of shape to them. This is the hand of the pragmatist: one who is not interested in new ideas or theories but wants to know the basic, established truths. When the fingertips are almost square, there is a love of form such as may be found in builders and, sometimes, architects and sculptors. The person can be very literal-minded.

The CONIC HAND shows versatility and impulsiveness. There is a need in this person to try to make everything touched as attractive as possible. This person has infectious enthusiasm and makes a good companion. Most conic hands have small thumbs, and the fingers have cone-shaped tips.

The SPATULATE HAND has fingertips that are spatulated together with a wide, high, firm Mount of Venus. Either the top or the bottom of the palm is broad to the point of seeming out of proportion to the rest of the hand. The person with such a hand is a lover of action and usually has an original way of thinking.

A long and bony hand, with knots at the joints of the fingers, is a PHILOSOPHICAL HAND. This is a person who likes to examine all angles when pondering a question. This person usually understands other people very well and can be extremely tactful when necessary. Quiet, a need for occasional solitude, reading time, and enjoyment of the country rather than the city are traits of this person.

The PSYCHIC HAND is long, narrow, and delicate, and usually extremely flexible. The skin is very fine and sometimes appears glossy. This is the hand of the poet and the psychic.

The Line of Life

The Life line is the major line of the hand. It indicates, in general terms, something of the course your life is likely to take. The line curves about the base of the thumb. At the very beginning it is usually joined with the line of the Head. The point at which these two lines separate indicates the relative time at which the person becomes emotionally independent of the parents. If the two lines are never in contact at the beginning, it shows a person who was very independent from the earliest age.

The Life line is the only one on the hand that can be divided up into an approximate scale of years. Doing so, it is possible to foretell major events to within a year or so of their happening. If (with a soft lead pencil) you divide the Life line into four equal parts, they will represent approximately twenty years each. A deep, clear line, running smoothly around its full length, suggests a rich, full life with good health throughout. A line that is in the form of a chain, however, shows continual poor health. If the line is chained only in its lower length, the subject should beware of bad health in later years.

The pad at the base of the thumb, between the Life line and the thumb itself, is known as the Mount of Venus and will be looked at below. If there is a line that runs parallel to the Life line, on the side of the Mount of Venus, it is a good sign showing natural vitality and useful luck.

On most palms there are a number of tiny lines that run from the Head line to the Life line. Each of these indicates a goal of some kind that will be attained. Looking at the time scale marked on the Life line, it is often possible to see, within a year or so, when a major event is going to take place.

About two-thirds of the way down the Life line there may be a triangle formed by two short, minor lines with part of the Life line itself being the third line of the triangle. Its size varies, and it is not always present. But if it is present, then a talent of some sort is possessed from which the person will derive a great deal of satisfaction. An angle or sudden change of direction in the Life line shows a definite change of direction in the course of life. Again, the approximate time of this can be noted. If this is present, then care should be taken around this time since the manner of living could change radically.

Similarly, a branch in the Life line indicates that, at that point or time of life, there will be a choice of two possible courses to follow. This would be a time for careful consideration and planning. A break in the Life line means trouble. If that break is shown on both hands, then it could indicate fatality. But if a new line begins outside the break, or is parallel to the Life line and continues unbroken across the Mount of Venus, then the trouble will not be drastic.

The Lines of the Head and the Heart

Note the relative lengths of the Head and the Heart lines, for this will tell whether the subject tends more toward things intellectual or whether there is more of a leaning toward the emotions and intuition. For many people these two lines are more or less equal in length, but for others there is an obvious difference. These two lines should always be considered together.

By its length and depth, the line of the Head shows the intellectual capability of the person. The Heart line shows the strength of the emotional and intuitive capabilities. A long, deep, clear Head line shows a clear intellect that can be of great value. If the line is very long but slants downward, rather than straight across, this is a case of having a high intelligence but using it for the wrong goals; in occult terms, being drawn along the "left hand path." Such a person can become very powerful.

There are rare occasions when the Head and the Heart lines join to form a single deep line cutting directly across the palm. There are few barriers that can stand up to such a person; they may well be a genius . . . and very aware of it! However, tight control is called for since there is so slight a distance between the strong, controlled mind and the uncontrolled chaos of mental unbalance.

Someone with a deep and long Heart line is likely to feel, very deeply, both the bad and the good, the joy and sorrow, of his or her life. Emotions will be important to this person and both judgment and hunches will give amazing results.

Interestingly in this modern day, most people have a stronger Heart line on the left, or unconscious, hand than on the right, or conscious, one. Similarly, the Head line will be stronger on the right hand. The reason is that modern civilization, for better or worse, seems to emphasize the intellect over the feelings of the heart.

The Line of Fate

Sometimes called the line of Luck, the line of Fate does not show up in everybody's hand. Its length and depth will show just how much good fortune you may have. For some the line will run strong and deep from the wrist up to the middle finger. For this person luck will come readily and freely, seemingly with little effort. But for the majority, the line of Luck will be weak or nonexistent. Any "luck" will come only through careful planning and hard work!

If it exists, this line of Fate can give valuable insights into personality flaws that may exist and are not readily apparent. For example, the line of Fate may be deep and unbroken up to the line of the Heart, then break and disappear entirely at that point. A person with such a line would let emotions obstruct much of the good fortune that would normally come their way. Without realizing it, through worry, temper, or similar, they would limit themselves.

Similarly, a line of Fate breaking or terminating at the line of the Head shows a person who gets in their own way by being overly cautious and thinking over things too much. When he or she has finally made up their mind, the opportunity has come and gone. Someone whose line of Fate starts on the Mount of the Moon (the fleshy pad on the outside of the hand, under the little finger) should have a pleasing and peaceful life, finding happiness without trying. If the line starts down at the wristlets, there will be an inheritance of wealth or a rewarding career. If the line of Fate branches near the bottom, with one branch running into the Mount of the Moon, then good fortune will come in the form of a marriage or other attachment.

The Marriage Line(S)

The Marriage lines start, appropriately enough, above the beginning of the Heart line. The subject may well have more than one such line with possibly as many as four or five. Although called the Marriage lines, they do not necessarily indicate marriages *per se*. Rather, they are great loves felt and experienced throughout the lifetime—encounters that deeply stir the heart. Just how deeply the person concerned has stirred the heart may be gauged by the depth and length of the line. A rough time scale may be derived by noting whether the Marriage line in question is near the Heart line (early in life) or near the joint of the finger (later in life).

The Wristlets

These are the lines across the front of the wrist at the base of the hand. They can be a general indication of how long a life to expect (and may be compared to the time scale on the line of Life). Each complete, well-formed wristlet shows a complete and full twenty-five years. However, the wristlets will change considerably throughout life and be determined by lifestyle, diet, exercise, and the like.

The Mount Of Venus

Both the thumb and the large area at its base are under the influence of Venus. The Mount of Venus can give a good picture of the warmth, kindness, and affection in the person. If the mount is rounded, full, warm, and firm, the person is pleasing as a friend, delightful in love, and one whose kindness to others brings a warm response. However, if the mount is thin, dry, and leathery, the person is cold, probably thin-lipped, tolerating little warmth toward others and receiving little or nothing in return.

It can often be seen that Venus's mount is crossed with many vertical and horizontal lines. This indicates a person who, for all else that the palm says, is not as serene as appears on the surface. Underneath there are cross-currents of emotion that are felt deeply but are kept hidden.

The Mount of the Moon

The Moon has been linked with the psychic world from ancient times. It is so linked with cheiromancy. The Mount of the Moon is the pad on the outside of the hand, below the little finger. A triangle on this mount indicates some natural talent in one or more fields of the occult. Any lines that arise here will have in them a hint of unconscious magic and of its close relation, love between man and woman. Lines reaching toward the Mount of the Moon from around the edge of the hand will be a prediction of journeys to be made by sea or air.

Finally, the firmness and fullness of this mount gives a general indication of just how well the subject can combine practicality with imagination.

The Fingers

Square fingers are indicated by the parallel lines of the outside edge of the little finger and the outside edge of the index finger. These would be the two sides of a rectangle. This indicates a practical, methodical person with a love of the functional and utilitarian.

Short fingers are found on people who think quickly and tend to be impatient with details. Long fingers are on those who think in an abstract or analytical manner.

Each finger is associated with an astrological sign and is an indicator of the good and/or bad aspects of that sign. Thumb—Venus; Index finger—Jupiter; Middle finger—Saturn; Ring finger—Apollo; Little finger—Mercury. At the base of each finger is the mount associated with the planetary sign of the finger. The fullness or thinness of the mount shows how strongly that particular sign affects the individual.

Each finger is, in turn, divided into three sections to show the person's relative spiritual, intellectual, and material development, as associated with the particular planet. The lowest section is the material; the middle is the intellectual; the top section is the spiritual. For example, if the lowest segment of a person's little finger (Mercury) is notably larger and more developed than the other two segments of that finger, then there would be action and strength, especially in management and salesmanship (which are associated with Mercury), over and above any interest in spirituality or intellectual pursuits. Similar traits can be derived for each of the other signs, using judgment and intuition with the astrological characteristics given below.

Venus—thumb: The thumb can show more about a person than any of the other fingers or any other part of the hand. It shows whether or not the person can deliberately make the best of their talents and abilities or whether they will simply rely on chance. A short thumb shows lack of strong will power. It is a person ruled by instinct and emotion. A large thumb shows strong will and belongs to someone who works out a plan and sticks to it. Set low on the hand, the thumb is a sign of love of independence. With a waisted phalanx, it indicates great tact. If the tip of the thumb bends backward, there is a tendency toward extravagance.

Jupiter—index finger: The "father/mother image," showing drive, leadership, the executive. Principal traits of this sign are pride, ambition, and confidence. It should, ideally, be about the same length as the ring finger. If longer, it shows ambition though can also indicate egotism. If shorter, there is a lack of confidence, especially early in life. If very short, it shows a person who is timid and somewhat afraid of life.

Saturn—middle finger: The wise old man or woman, often a personification of old age and the very end of life. It is tied in with restrictions, restraint, and common sense. Principle traits are wisdom, solitude, shyness, melancholy, and solitary bleakness. Usually the longest finger on the hand, if it is exceptionally long the person will have trouble fitting in with others. If short, there will be carelessness and a lack of responsibility.

Apollo—ring finger: Associated with the sun and all things bright and good, also with the arts and medicine. It is the finger of beauty and creativity. Principle trait is the love of beauty. Ideally it should be straight. If it should curve toward the little finger, it shows a person who underrates their own creative ability. If it curves toward the middle finger, it shows a person who has sacrificed their own creativity for the mundane.

Mercury—little finger: This is known as the finger of communication, since it is named after Mercury, the messenger of the gods. It also relates to activity and to sex, sharpness and quickness of mind, cleverness, and shrewdness. Principle traits are buoyancy, friendliness, skill in management, and commerce. If the finger is straight, it shows the person to be basically honest. If it has a slight curve to it, toward the ring finger, it suggests that the person will suppress their own ambitions in order to further someone else's. Such a finger is often found on caregivers of various sorts.

Sources:

Buckland, Raymond. *A Pocket Guide to the Supernatural.* New York: Ace Books, 1969.
Cheiro (Louis Hamon). *Cheiro's Language of the Hand,* Chicago: Rand, McNally, 1897.
Encyclopedia Britannica. Chicago: William Benton, 1964.
Spence, Lewis. *An Encyclopedia of the Occult.* London: George Routledge & Sons, 1920.
Squire, Elizabeth Daniels. *The New Fortune in Your Hand.*New York: Fleet Press, 1960.
Webster, Richard. *Revealing Hands.* St. Paul: Llewellyn, 1994.

Chien Tung

Produced commercially, this is a very basic form of fortune-telling from China that utilizes a number of bamboo sticks in a container. It would seem to have been inspired by the I Ching. To use the Chien Tung for a general reading, the diviner shakes the container of sticks until one of them falls out. The sticks are numbered so the number

Chinese fortune teller. *Fortean Picture Library.*

on the fallen stick is consulted in an accompanying book and the fortune read. The fortunes generally seem to be on a par with those obtained from fortune cookies.

China

There are many forms of divination that—at least according to tradition—started in China. Examples include **astragalomancy, cartomancy,** and **cheiromancy.** The best-known form that is still most strongly associated with China is the **I Ching,** or Book of Changes. This has been revered for centuries as a source of wisdom and as a cryptic form of the epitome of a truly ancient philosophy.

Of the three historic religions found in China—Confucianism, Taoism, and Buddhism—it was Taoism that most promoted magic and divination. The ancient Chinese system of meditation is best exemplified in the Taoist teachings.

The Chinese call fate *Ming*, meaning "destiny" or "mandate." It is believed that humans are more elevated than animals, receiving the decrees of Heaven. Any who do not understand these decrees cannot become Superior Man, which, according to Confucius, means becoming a Sage. Good fortune or disaster depends upon fate. To investigate what fate might have in store calls for use of the I Ching or some other form of divination.

Chinese Astrology

The main classification in Chinese astrology is not by the sun sign but by the year of birth. From the earliest stages of Chinese civilization, in the Shang or Yin period (c. 1766–1123 BCE), the calendar was important. Each of twelve years is named for an animal, starting with the rat and ending with the pig: Rat, Ox, Tiger, Rabbit, Dragon, Snake, Horse, Goat or Ram, Monkey, Rooster, Dog, Pig, or Boar. This is commonly known as the Chinese zodiac. At the end of the twelve-year cycle the list starts over again.This represents a cyclical concept of time, rather than the Western linear concept of time.

The Chinese zodiac from 1900 to 2007 is as follows:

Rat: 1900, 1912, 1924, 1936, 1948, 1960, 1972, 1984, 1996
Ox: 1901, 1913, 1925, 1937, 1949, 1961, 1973, 1985, 1997
Tiger: 1902, 1914, 1926, 1938, 1950, 1962, 1974, 1986, 1998
Rabbit: 1903, 1915, 1927, 1939, 1951, 1963, 1975, 1987, 1999
Dragon: 1904, 1916, 1928, 1940, 1952, 1964, 1976, 1988, 2000
Snake: 1905, 1917, 1929, 1941, 1953, 1965, 1977, 1989, 2001
Horse: 1906, 1918, 1930, 1942, 1954, 1966, 1978, 1990, 2002
Goat: 1907, 1919, 1931, 1943, 1955, 1967, 1979, 1991, 2003
Monkey: 1908, 1920, 1932, 1944, 1956, 1968, 1980, 1992, 2004
Rooster: 1909, 1921, 1933, 1945, 1957, 1969, 1981, 1993, 2005
Dog: 1910, 1922, 1934, 1946, 1958, 1970, 1982, 1994, 2006
Pig: 1911, 1923, 1935, 1947, 1959, 1971, 1983, 1995, 2007

Each year is also designated as one of the five elements: fire, earth, metal, water, and wood. With twelve animals and five elements there is a different combination each year, which would then not repeat for sixty years. For example, 1905 was the year of the Wood Snake, but 1917 (the next Snake year) was the year of the Fire Snake. Then 1929 was the year of the Earth Snake, 1941 the Metal Snake, and so on.

The month, day, and hour of birth are also considered in Chinese astrology, along with the year. There are twenty-eight constellations considered, plus the five elements already mentioned, five planets (Mercury, Venus, Mars, Jupiter, Saturn), five directions (north, east, south, west, center), five seasons (spring, summer, fall, winter, and the dog days), and the influence of specific stars. The five elements correspond to colors and planets as follows:

Element	**Color**	**Planet**
Fire	Red	Mars
Earth	Yellow	Saturn
Metal	White	Venus
Water	Black	Mercury
Wood	Green	Jupiter

The twelve animals on the Chinese zodiac are different from those on the Western zodiac. *Fortean Picture Library.*

Chinese astrology is based on the lunar cycle. Each year begins with the new moon in what is Aquarius on the Western astrological setup, somewhere between late January and early February. This date, of course, will vary slightly from year to year. Next in importance, therefore, is the lunar calendar, though the Chinese lunisolar calendar is very different from the Western calendar. The Chinese adopted the Western calendar in 1911, but the lunar calendar is still used for festive occasions such as the Chinese New Year. Many Chinese calendars will print both the solar dates and the Chinese lunar dates.

Chinese astrology is concerned with the relationships of the seven main stars together with twenty-eight major constellations called lodges, or star-spirits. Each has its own auspicious or ominous meaning in terms of the yin-yang balance and the five elements. The lodges move in and out of palaces ruled by the seven main stars. In turn, each palace is associated with one of the twelve moons of the lunar calendar, the twelve earthly branches, and the twelve zodiac animals. Everyone has a main star, according to their year of birth. As the various lodges pass through that star's palace, the person will experience good or bad fortune.

The twelve earthly branches are important, with a tremendously complex set of meanings. They are used to number things that come in series of twelve and are often referred to as the horary cycle since their original function was to divide the day into twelve 120-minute "hours." The branches also designate the months of the year.

THE TWELVE EARTHLY BRANCHES

Order	Sign	Direction	Branch	Element
1	Mouse	N	Zi	Water
2	Ox	NNE	Chou	Earth
3	Tiger	ENE	Yin	Wood
4	Rabbit	E	Mao	Wood
5	Dragon	ESE	Chen	Earth
6	Snake	SSE	Si	Fire
7	Horse	S	Wu	Fire
8	Goat	SSW	Wei	Earth
9	Monkey	WWS	Shen	Metal
10	Rooster	W	You	Metal
11	Dog	WNW	Xu	Earth
12	Pig	NNW	Hai	Water

Much as the **Sun Signs** are generally studied in Western astrology, so are the Year Signs in Chinese astrology:

Year of the Rat: People born under this sign are noted for their charm and attraction to the opposite sex. Although easily angered, they are hardworking, like to acquire possessions, and try to achieve their goals. They are basically thrifty. They also love to gossip. They are likely to be perfectionists and have big ambitions, frequently becoming very successful. Compatibility: Dragon, Monkey, Ox.

Year of the Ox: These people inspire confidence in others, though they themselves speak little. However, when they do speak, they can be very eloquent. They have great patience. Like Rat people, they anger easily. They also have very bad tempers. They can be eccentric and can also be bigoted. Mentally and physically alert, they are easygoing but can be stubborn. They hate to fail and hate to be opposed. Compatibility: Snake, Rooster, Rat.

Year of the Tiger: Capable of great sympathy, Tigers are very sensitive. They are given to deep thinking and earn the respect of others, though they can come into conflict with their elders and with authority. They can be short-tempered. Tigers have difficulty making up their minds. This can result in missing opportunities or in making quick and therefore bad decisions. Courageous and powerful, they are nonetheless suspicious of others. Compatibility: Horses, Dragons, Dogs.

Year of the Rabbit: Ambitious, articulate, and talented, Rabbits are also virtuous and very reserved. They have excellent taste in most things, are admired and trusted. Rabbits are clever in business and frequently do very well financially. They always honor a contract made. Although fond of gossip, they are kind and tactful and don't often lose their temper. They seldom gamble, but if they did they would be very successful, always being able to make the correct choice. They are wise and conservative. Compatibility: Sheep, Pig, Dog.

Year of the Dragon: Short-tempered and stubborn, Dragons are excitable, energetic, and generally very healthy. They can be brave and are honest and sensitive, inspiring confidence. Dragons are the most eccentric of all the signs. They may be taken advantage of since they are very soft hearted. They do not borrow money themselves. Compatibility: Rats, Snakes, Monkeys, Roosters.

Year of the Snake: Possessing great wisdom, enigmatic Snakes say very little but are frequently selfish and vain. They never have financial problems and can be overly thrifty. They try to help those less fortunate than themselves and can show tremendous sympathy. They prefer to do things themselves, having reservations about relying on others through doubting others' judgment. They tend to overdo things, being very determined in their actions and hating to fail. Outwardly calm and serene, inwardly they are intense and passionate. Snakes are usually good-looking but, being fickle, can suffer marital problems. Compatibility: Ox and Rooster.

Year of the Horse: One of the most popular signs, Horses are cheerful, perceptive, and good with money. They do tend to talk too much, however. They are independent and rarely listen to advice. Talented and good with their hands, Horses can be very wise. They have a weakness for the opposite sex and are hot-blooded and impatient about most things. They enjoy crowds and entertainment. Compatibility: Tigers, Dogs, Goats.

Year of the Goat/Ram: Accomplished in the arts, these people are usually very elegant, giving the appearance of being far better off than other signs. But they are frequently shy and pessimistic, also puzzled about life in general. They can be deeply religious and passionate about what they believe in. They are gentle and compassionate. Their abilities bring financial rewards so they never have to worry about not having the creature comforts they enjoy so much. They are not good speakers and are timid by nature. Compatibility: Rabbits, Pigs, Horses.

Year of the Monkey: Clever, skillful, and flexible, these are the erratic geniuses of the zodiac. They can be incredibly original and inventive, solving problems with ease and having great common sense. They like to get things done immediately, and if that's not possible they get discouraged and walk away. Monkeys have good memories and a yearning for knowledge. They are strong willed and are good at making decisions. They very quickly get over their anger but tend to look down on others. Compatibility: Dragon, Rat.

Year of the Rooster: Roosters are very capable and talented deep thinkers. Often eccentric, Roosters can have a hard time relating to other people. They like to keep busy and think themselves more capable than they actually are. Consequently, they often get frustrated when things don't work out as they had hoped. They are usually right about things but, even if they're not, they *think* they are! Outwardly adventurous, frequently brave, they can actually be inwardly timid. They are frequently loners, can be selfish and too outspoken. Their emotions, and their fortunes, go up and down. Compatibility: Ox, Snake, Dragon.

Year of the Dog: Dogs possess the very best traits of human nature. They have a deep sense of loyalty; they are honest; they inspire others. Dogs can be cold and distant emotionally, seeming very standoffish at parties. But they know how to keep secrets. They can be eccentric, very stubborn, and somewhat selfish. They always seem to have money though they care little for wealth. Dogs have sharp tongues and can find fault with many things. They make very good leaders. Compatibility: Horse, Tiger, Rabbit.

Year of the Pig/Boar: This is the chivalrous, gallant sign of the zodiac. Pigs are extremely loyal and kind. They will move forward at top speed, looking neither to left nor right, but intent on what they are doing. Also, they will not retreat. They are extremely honest and have tremendous fortitude. Pigs don't make a lot of friends, but those they do make are close and loyal and friends for life. Pigs have a thirst for knowledge. They don't talk much but study a great deal, keeping very well informed. They can be quick tempered yet they hate arguments. Whatever problems arise, Pigs try their hardest to work them out. Compatibility: Rabbits, Sheep.

Sources:

http://www.c-c-c.org/chineseculture/zodiac/zodiac.html.
http://www.solsticemoon.com/spiritual.
Lau, Kwan. *Secrets of Chinese Astrology*. New York: Tengu Books, 1994.
Orion, Rae. *Astrology for Dummies*. Foster City, CA: IDG Books, 1999.
White, Suzanne. *The New Chinese Astrology*.

CHINESE BUDDHIST DIVINATION

(See also Tibet)

Divination in **China** and in **Tibet** is used within the sphere of Buddhist concepts. It functions in accordance with Buddhist principles such as karma. By looking into someone's future, it is believed that the **seer** may assess the particular situation and recommend how to deal with it. It is recognized that rituals alone will not bring about change, but it is known that the performance of ritual can induce latent positive potential to cause change.

Sources:

Tseten, Dorjee. *Tibetan Art of Divination*. Tibetan Bulletin, March-April 1995.

CHINESE PALMISTRY

In the Chinese system of **palmistry,** the palm is divided into eight areas known as "palaces." Each palace is associated with one of the eight trigrams that form the backbone of the **I Ching.** There is no regard given to the fingers, wrists, etc., the focus being entirely on the palm. It is said that the art is at least 2,000 years old.

Sources:

Headon, Deirdre (ed.) *Quest for the Unknown—Charting the Future*. Pleasantville, NY: Reader's Digest, 1992.

CHIROGNOMY *see* Cheiromancy

CHIROGRAPHY *see* Graphology

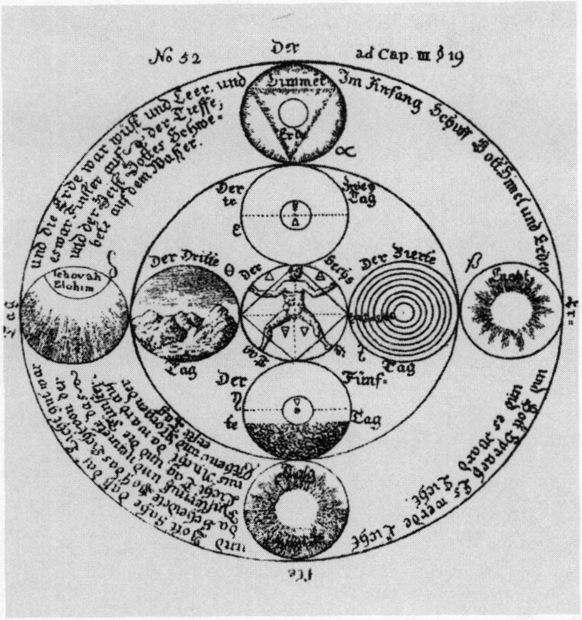

Model of the microcosmic man according to the Christian qabbalistic system. ***Fortean Picture Library.***

CHIROMANCY ***see*** **Cheiromancy**

CHRISTIAN QABBALAH

The **Qabbalah** as utilized in medieval times had absorbed a lot of **ceremonial magical** tradition. Some of this had specifically Jewish traits, but much of it came from international sources. In magic, the sacred names of god and with various sacred letters of those names were considered containers of special knowledge. This preoccupation developed into using those letters and names as sources of power in themselves. Christian occultists quickly became attracted to the paraphernalia of ritual magic and to the Qabbalah. Magical amulets, incantations, seals, and magical squares all seemed fascinating. Beginning in the late fifteenth century, a Christian form of the Qabbalah was constructed that was supposed to prove the divinity of Jesus. Even alchemical symbols were incorporated into it.

It was Jews who taught the first generations of Christian Qabbalists. Consequently these early practitioners had a reasonably sound knowledge of the subject. But from the seventeenth century on, enthusiasts became more and more ignorant of the true meanings until eventually the word *Qabbalah* became simply a euphemism for any mixture of alchemy, hermeticism, occultism, Rosicrucianism, and general occult lore. Writers such as Robert Fludd and Thomas Vaughan presented a Qabbalah that combined what Fludd called "theosophical and philosophical truths." Henry More claimed that the Platonists had "more of that Cabala than the Jews themselves have at this day."

Qabbalistic magic became a matter of combining and permuting Hebrew letters and their numerical values throught the use of anagrams, magical squares, and such. By the nineteenth century such non-Jewish occultists as Francis Barrett and **Gérard Encausse** (Papus) had taken an interest in the Qabbalah, linking it to such things as the **tarot** and **astrology.** Dion Fortune referred to it as the "Yoga of the West."

Sources:

Fortune, Dion. *The Mystical Qabalah*. London: Ernest Benn, 1935.

Guiley, Rosemary Ellen. *Harper's Encyclopedia of Mystical & Paranormal Experience*. San Francisco: HarperSanFrancisco, 1991.

Scholem, Gershom. *Kabbalah*. New York: New American Library, 1974.

Werblowsky, R.J. Zwi. *Man, Myth & Magic: Cabala*. London: BPC Publishing, 1970.

CHRONOMANCY

Divination utilizing the passing of time. This is most often used in conjunction with other forms of divination such as **ornithomancy.** For example, where the flight of a

bird is significant based upon its direction, it can also have further significance based on the amount of time it takes for the bird to complete its flight.

Cicero, Marcus Tullius (106–43 BCE)

Educated in **Rome** and in **Greece,** Marcus Tullius Cicero was a Roman statesman, scholar, lawyer, and writer. He tried to uphold the republican principles at a time when the civil struggles were destroying Rome.

In his book *De divinatione (On Divination)*, Cicero stated that divination was a religious matter since it depended upon a belief in the divine. He said it would be unwise to neglect the Providence that designed a destiny for humankind. According to both Cicero and Plato, there were two kinds of **prophecy,** one of art and the other of nature. He spoke of *entechnos*, or that which could be taught, and *atechnos*, which is not taught. Entechnos was based on the observation of phenomena, while atechnos was a form of madness because it presupposed that a familiar of some kind could enter the diviner and thrown him or her into a trance, thus enabling the foretelling of the future. Cicero had himself been an **augur** and, since augury was state approved, he said nothing against that in his book. However, he did speak out against all other forms of divination.

In 59 BCE Cicero declined Caesar's invitation to join the political alliance of Caesar, Crassus, and Pompey. The following year he also declined Caesar's offer of a place on his staff in Gaul. In 58 BCE Cicero was forced to flee Rome in fear of his life when P. Clodius became tribune. Cicero had derided all paranormal explanations of **dreams** in his book, making fun of those who looked to dreams for prophetic knowledge. Then, while in exile, he himself had a dream of a noble-looking youth who descended from the sky on a chain of gold and stood at the door to a temple. The next day the man he saw in his dream—who turned out to be Octavius, great nephew of Caesar—came to visit him. Cicero was recalled to Rome on August 4, 57 BCE.

Sources:

Encyclopedia Britannica. Chicago: William Benton, 1964.

Headon, Deirdre (ed.). *Quest for the Unknown—Charting the Future*. Pleasantville, NY: Reader's Digest, 1992.

Holroyd, Stuart. *The Supernatural: Dream Worlds*. London: Aldus Books, 1976.

Clairaudience

Clairaudience is, literally, "clear hearing." It is homologous to **clairvoyance** and **clairsentience.** Clairaudience is the ability to hear sounds and voices from other dimensions, usually from spirits of the dead, at **séances.** Most clairvoyants seem also to be occasionally clairaudient. A spiritualist medium can receive messages from the spirits in various ways. He may hear, in his head, what the spirits are saying; he may see them and describe what he sees, interpreting actions almost as is done in the game of charades; or he may simply sense what is being passed on to him. There are other forms of communication, but these are probably the three main ones.

Hearing what is communicated can be just like hearing someone whispering in your ear, though no one else physically present will hear any sound. It can also be similar to sensing in that you hear, in your head, the voice and the words themselves yet are not aware of the sound originating externally alongside your ear. Clairaudience can include hearing music, songs, and other sounds.

Clairaudience can also sometimes be experienced when in the hypnagogic and hypnapompic states—those states that occur just as you are falling asleep and just as you are awakening. It can even occur during meditation.

A classic example of clairaudience was in the case of Joan of Arc (see **Jeanne d'Arc**), in the fifteenth century, who heard voices she attributed to God and various angels. In her father's garden, at age thirteen, she first heard a voice she believed came from God. During the next five years she heard voices two or three times a week and was able to distinguish these as being (so she said) Saints Catherine, Margaret, and Michael. Her voices directed her to lead the French army against that of the English in an attempt to restore the Dauphin to his throne.

Throughout history people have been guided by voices they have heard, either internally or externally. Examples are Samuel, Moses, Solomon, and other characters in the **Bible,** who believed they heard God speaking. In the same way, the ancient **Greeks** heard whispered advice from *daimones*, or *genii*, regarded more or less as guardian spirits (Socrates claimed to be advised by a specific daimon). The English poet William Cowper, in the eighteenth century, was advised of upcoming events in his life by voices he heard in his ear. Wolfgang Mozart heard music in his head and simply wrote down what he heard, note for note. Aura May Hollen, in the late 1920s, began to write her many books of poetry and song from what was dictated to her in her head.

Clairaudience is sometimes confused with "direct voice," which is actually quite different. This is when the medium him- or herself speaks with the voice of a deceased spirit or, more accurately, a spirit speaks through the medium, using the medium's vocal cords.

Holding a seashell up to the ear and hearing what seems to be the sounds of the sea is a fascinating child's pastime. Such a **shell** is often used as a tool by beginning mediums as the basis for initiating clairaudience. Listening with a seashell can gradually lead the listener to distinguish human voices, perhaps initially vague and far off. Over a period of time these voices become louder and clearer, until distinctive speech is heard and individual voices are recognized. Another tool for development is a telephone, albeit one that is not connected. Even an imaginary telephone will serve the purpose. The medium takes up the receiver (or imagines holding it) and will hear a voice speaking on the end of the line. Some mediums will use this as their way of "turning on" the mediumistic gift. They will imagine a telephone beside them and know that when it rings (in their head), there will be a spirit waiting to speak to them.

A word of warning to those who experiment with mediumship. If, after working with such exercises over a period of time, you continue to hear "voices" in your head even after you have stopped the experiment, then you need to take a break. The secret—if secret there is—is to not try too hard. Concentrate but do not strain to hear. If voices are to come, they will come. Not everyone can be a good medium, though we do all have the potential. It may be that clairaudience is not to be your forte, so be prepared to try other mediumistic forms.

Sources:

Buckland, Raymond. *Doors to Other Worlds*. St. Paul, MN: Llewellyn, 1993.
Cowan, Tom. *The Book of Séance*. Chicago: Contemporary Books, 1994.
Hollen, Henry. *Clairaudient Transmissions*. Hollywood, CA: Keats Publications, 1931.
Klimo, Jon. *Channeling: Investigations on Receiving Information from Paranormal Sources*. Los Angeles: Jeremy P. Tarcher, 1987.
Owens, Elizabeth. *How to Communicate with Spirits*. St. Paul, MN: Llewellyn, 2002.
Shepard, Leslie A. (ed.). *Encyclopedia of Occultism & Parapsychology*. New York: Avon, 1978.

Clairgustance

Similar in many ways to **clairaudience, clairvoyance** and **clairsentience,** clairgustance is the smelling of scents coming from other dimensions. It is frequently lumped under the general heading of clairvoyance but is a separate, distinct form of psychic cognizance.

Many times, at a **séance,** not only the medium but all present will be aware of the perfume of a particular flower of significance to someone at the sitting. Specific pipe tobacco might similarly be smelled. Any odor that is significant to someone at the séance may be detected by any or all present. Not all smells received are pleasant but all are meaningful, frequently tied into some memory of a past event.

Sources:

Owens, Elizabeth. *How to Communicate with Spirits*. St. Paul, MN: Llewellyn, 2002.

Clairsentience

Many mediums receive all their information by means of psychically sensing it. They may sense that words are said, rather than actually hearing them. They may sense that a deceased person is tall and elderly, for example, rather than actually "seeing" them **clairvoyantly.** They may sense the spirit's previous occupation, likes, and dislikes. All of these things and more are sensed, or "picked up," by the medium and relayed to the sitter(s). Clairsentience involves the psychic perception of sights, sounds, smells, tastes, emotions, and physical sensations.

Many people experience clairsentience without realizing that they do. Many people have had a sense, or sense perception, of something about to happen. They might think they have had a "flash," or fleeting impression, of some scene or sound. This is actually clairsentience. Many more people have had a clairsentient moment on meeting someone for the first time; they have felt that they do not like a particular person yet are unable to find any logical reason for the dislike. They just "feel" or "know" that they do not like the person. This sometimes extends to a feeling that the person they dislike is in some way evil. They sense this, and sometimes later investigation brings to light good reasons for the feeling.

Many **psychics,** as opposed to mediums, use clairsentience. They may get initial impressions directly from the person they are reading but then supplement this information with other material they get through clairsentience.

Sources:

Buckland, Raymond. *Doors to Other Worlds*. St. Paul, MN: Llewellyn, 1993.

Guiley, Rosemary Ellen. *Harper's Encyclopedia of Mystical & Paranormal Experience*. San Francisco: HarperSanFrancisco, 1991.

Owens, Elizabeth. *How to Communicate with Spirits*. St. Paul, MN: Llewellyn, 2002.

Clairvoyance

Clairvoyance is from the French "clear seeing," applied to **psychic** awareness. It is the ability to see—in the mind's eye—people and things in another dimension. Many spiritualist mediums are clairvoyants,actually seeing and describing the spirits of the deceased. In the **Bible** there is reference to the **woman of Endor,** visited by Saul (1 Samuel 28). She is described as "a woman that hath a familiar spirit." In other words, a spirit guide or guardian angel. She is a spiritualist medium (not a witch, as is the common misconception). When Saul meets with her—despite the fact that he tried to get rid of all such mediums—she describes exactly what she sees clairvoyantly: "I *saw* gods ascending out of the earth. An old man cometh up and he is covered with a mantle." This turns out to be Samuel, and Saul is able to speak with him through the agencies of the medium. Similarly, Isaiah had a clairvoyant vision of "the Lord . . . high and lifted up" attended by seraphim (Isaiah 6).

William E. Butler divides clairvoyance into his own divisions of psychological clairvoyance, spatial clairvoyance, astral clairvoyance, and true spiritual clairvoyance, though he tends to combine clairvoyance with clairsentience in many instances. Nandor Fodor divides it into X-ray clairvoyance, medical clairvoyance, traveling clairvoyance, and platform clairvoyance. X-ray clairvoyance is the ability to see what is inside closed objects, from inside sealed envelopes to behind brick walls. Medical clairvoyance is self-explanatory, seeing illnesses and reading auras to diagnose disease. The term is also used to cover medical **clairsentience.** Traveling clairvoyance is also sometimes termed remote viewing and refers to seeing actual people and events at a great distance. Platform clairvoyance is the demonstration of the facility literally on a platform before an audience or in the séance room. Other people have given other breakdowns of the gift.

Lewis Spence makes the distinction of being able to see people and events not only in the present but also from the past. This is certainly valid. One of the most striking examples of this was the case that has become known as the Versailles adventure.

On August 10, 1901, two young Englishwomen traveling in France, Annie E. Moberly and Eleanor M. Jourdain, visited the Petit Trianon at Versailles. Annie Moberly was the daughter of the bishop of Salisbury, and her friend was the daughter of a Derbyshire vicar. As Eleanor Jourdain put it:

> We went on in the direction of the Petit Trianon, but just before reaching what we knew afterwards to be the main entrance I saw a gate lead-

> ing to a path cut deep below the level of the ground above, and as the way was open and had the look of an entrance that was used, I said "Shall we try this path? It must lead to the house," and we followed it. . . . I began to feel as if I were walking in my sleep; the heavy dreaminess was oppressive. At last we came upon a path crossing ours, and saw in front of us a building consisting of some columns roofed in, and set back in the trees. Seated on the steps was a man with a heavy black cloak round his shoulders, and wearing a slouch hat. At that moment the eerie feeling which had begun in the garden culminated in a definite impression of something uncanny and fear inspiring. The man slowly turned his face, which was marked by smallpox, his complexion was very dark. The expression was very evil and though I did not feel he was looking particularly at us, I felt a repugnance to going past him.

The two women went on to describe points of architecture and landscape that seemed to pinpoint the date of the building and its surrounds to around 1770, since alterations were later made to parts of the Petit Trianon. In their perambulations, the ladies saw men in three-cornered hats, a woman with a large white hat, and others in the dress of the eighteenth century. The Petit Trianon was built by Louis XV for his mistress, the Marquise de Pompadour, who was later succeeded by Madame Dubarry. Later, Louis XVI gave the house to Marie Antoinette. This seems to be a fine case of clairvoyance where the mediums were able to see, and later describe in detail, events in a past century.

There is also a well-known case of a Captain Youatt who, in a dream, saw a group of emigrants trapped on a mountain in the snow. Especially obvious was a white cliff-face and other landmarks. He saw this dream repeatedly and related it to a friend who recognized some of the features and believed it to be the Carson Valley Pass, about 150 miles from where they were. A company of men, with mules, blankets, food, and other supplies, set off and actually found the stranded group just as Youatt had described them. This was related in the 1875 volume of *Sunday at Home* magazine. Clairvoyance, then, may manifest in internal or external visions.

Most examples of clairvoyance are connected to the here and now. It can be brought about by mechanical means, using drugs, incense, hypnosis, crystal-gazing, drumming, or any one of a number of methods. It can also be a part of ritual dance and song. Bringing about *ekstasis*, or ecstasy—getting out of oneself—has been a part of ritual for thousands of years, frequently leading to clairvoyant visions. Virtually anyone can develop clairvoyance with suitable training.

Sources:

Buckland, Raymond. *Doors to Other Worlds*. St. Paul, MN: Llewellyn, 1993.
Butler, William E. *How to Develop Clairvoyance*. New York: Samuel Weiser, 1971.
Cowan, Tom. *The Book of Séance*. Chicago: Contemporary Books, 1994.
Holroyd, Stuart. *The Supernatural: Minds Without Boundaries*. London: Aldus Books, 1976.
Iremonger, Lucille: *The Ghosts of Versailles* London: Faber & Faber, 1957.
Owens, Elizabeth. *How to Communicate with Spirits*. St. Paul, MN: Llewellyn, 2002.
Shepard, Leslie A. (ed.) *Encyclopedia of Occultism &amp Parapsychology*. New York: Avon, 1978.

Cleidomancy, divination by means of a key, is sometimes called dactylomancy because the key is dangled from the third (ring) finger. *Fortean Picture Library.*

CLAMANCY

From the Latin *clamare*, to cry out. Clamancy is interpreting the unexpected cries that people make under various circumstances. The intensity, length, pitch, unexpectedness, and so on, are all considered by the **diviner.**

CLEDONOMANCY; CLEDONISMANCY

Cledonomancy is **divining** by any chance remarks that are heard by the diviner. For example, in a crowd a number of brief comments may be heard from several different people, none of them complete in themselves. By putting those remarks together, the diviner can see words and phrases pertinent to the person seeking to learn of their future.

Simply hearing a brief remark or small part of a conversation may be seen as meaningful. There is a certain similarity to **apantomancy** (chance objects at hand) and **bibliomancy** (random passages in a book). It is believed that the remarks heard are not really heard "by chance" but are meant to come through at that particular time.

CLEIDOMANCY; CLIDOMANCY

Cleidomancy involves the use of a key, usually suspended on a thread, for divining. One version says that for a question to be answered, the key should be suspended by a thread from the nail of the third finger of a young virgin. The virgin should then repeat the verse from the Psalms: "*Exurge, Domine, adjuva nos, et redime nos propter nomen sanctum tuum.*" If the answer to the question asked is positive, the key will revolve. Some say only that the key will revolve; others say it will revolve clockwise for a positive answer and counterclockwise for a negative answer.

Another method is to hold the key suspended so that it hangs inside the bowl of a wine glass. Questions asked will then be answered by the key swinging and ringing against the side of the glass, once for Yes and twice for No. Longer messages may be obtained by asking a question and then slowly reciting the letters of the alphabet. The key will ring against the side of the glass as each pertinent letter is called out, thus spelling a word or words.

Yet another method, which is used to determine who is a thief, is to place a street door key on the fiftieth psalm and close the book on it. The **Bible** is held tightly closed by fastening a woman's garter about it. The book is then suspended from a nail. It is claimed that it will rotate when the name of the thief is said.

According to Edward Smedley's *The Occult Sciences* (1855): "Clidomancy should be exercised when the sun or moon is in Virgo, the name should be written upon a key, the key should be tied to a Bible."

Sources:

De Givry, Grillot. A *Pictorial Anthology of Witchcraft, Magic & Alchemy*. London: Spottiswoode, Ballantyne, 1931.

Oxford English Dictionary. Oxford: Clarendon Press, 1989.

Cleromancy

Cleromancy is a form of drawing—or, more specifically, throwing—**lots.** Black and white beans are used, as are small bones, dice, and stones. Methods vary and are detailed under **sortilege.** When dice are used it is more specifically **cubomancy.**

CLIDOMANCY *see* Cleidomancy

CLOUDS *see* Aeromancy

COAL *see* Anthracomancy

COCKEREL *see* Alectromancy

Coffee Grounds

Coffee was being cultivated in southern Arabia about 500 years ago and was introduced into Europe in the sixteenth and seventeenth centuries. The first London coffeehouse was established in 1652. A form of divination using coffee grounds is connected with both **tasseography** and **geomancy** and was in existence as a divinatory practice in the eighteenth century. Tomaso Tomponelli published what was probably the first treatise on divination with coffee grounds in the eighteenth century, thus suggesting that the practice first appeared in Italy.

The usual method of working is to pour some coffee dregs onto a white, unglazed plate and allow them to settle. The liquid is then carefully poured off, leaving the coffee grounds in a multitude of patterns. The diviner then interprets these patterns much as the tea leaves are interpreted in tasseography.

Tomponelli did specify that a certain ritual be followed when preparing to read the coffee grounds. The coffee should be prepared by the diviner him- or herself. When the water is first added to the coffee in the coffee pot, the diviner should say, "*Aqua boraxit venias carjôs.*" When the mixture is stirred with a spoon, the words "*Fixatur et patricam explinabit tortare*" must be said. And finally, while pouring the dregs onto the plate, *Hax verticaline, pax Fantas marobum, max destinatus, veida porol.*" As with tea- leaf reading, the person being read should take at least three sips of the liquid before the rest is poured away, leaving the dregs.

Sources:

De Givry, Grillot. A *Pictorial Anthology of Witchcraft, Magic & Alchemy*. London: Spottiswoode, Ballantyne, 1931.

Coins

It has been said that the very first example of divination using coins was the first time that someone flipped a coin to choose heads or tails. That choice was made on the assumption that the turn of the coin indicated which would be the more fortunate selection. Using a number of coins, it would follow that a wide variety of choices or decisions could be made on a wide variety of subjects.

Using coins for divination is extremely convenient, for it is seldom that someone doesn't have a few coins in their pocket that can be used. There is no need to seek out and purchase special equipment of any sort. Coins of any type can be used: any denomination, any currency, any metal. Different numbers of coins together can be used for different divinations.

Many people who use coins frequently for divination will keep certain coins for that special application. They will consecrate the coins before use by ritually cleansing them in saltwater and in the smoke of **incense.** The coins will then be kept wrapped in a cloth or special bag for use only in divination. Although any coins can be used, just one example of those that might be of special significance is the ten singold coins of Singapore. These are small gold coins, each bearing an image of one of the twelve animals of the Chinese **zodiac.** People who specialize in coin divination find such special sets to be very attractive and suitable.

Yes-and-no answers are the simplest to obtain and can be got with just a single coin. Traditionally, heads is the equivalent for yes and tails for no. For more than yes/no answers, the coin can be tossed into marked concentric circles, each circle assigned one of a variety of possible answers. Two coins will give four variables: head and tail, tail and head, head and head, tail and tail. Similarly, three coins give eight possibilities, and so on. Each of these combinations can have a separate, different meaning.

A version of **numerology** can be done using five coins. The basis of all numbers and calculations are the numbers one through nine, with any higher number reduced to these primaries. For example, 36 would be 3 + 6 = 9; 387 would be 3 + 8 + 7 = 18 = 1 + 8 = 9. Giving the value of 1 to the heads of the coins and 2 to the tails, five coins can be thrown down and, as an example, might give tail, tail, head, tail, head. This would be the equivalent of 2 + 2 + 1 + 2 + 1 = 8. To further diversify the possible combinations, the five coins are thrown into a marked circle and any falling outside the circle are discounted. From the result obtained, interpretations are given (shown below) that can be answers to questions, analyses of personalities, or suggestions of various sorts, applied to the questioner or to the person about whom the question is being asked:

1: Associated with the Sun. A driving life force; a leader. Ambitious; extroverted; opinionated.

2: **Moon** association. Domestic and sensitive. Can be emotional. Easily influenced. Likes to live near water. Patriotic. Often possesses musical talents.

3: Jupiter. Scientific inclinations. Investigator; seeker. Material rather than spiritual. Good sense of humor. Little interest in money.

4: Uranus. Eccentric. Frequently ahead of his or her time. Drawn to anything out of the ordinary. Good intuition. Can be sarcastic.

5: Mercury. Physically and mentally active. An inquiring mind; a researcher. Fond of reading and writing. Good teacher. Methodical.

6: Venus. Sociable, friendly, gentle, and refined. A peacemaker. Has difficulties with finances. Very good host or hostess.

7: Neptune. Frequently very psychic. An introvert; can appear mysterious. Often knowledgeable in **astrology,** science, and all aspects of the occult.

8: Saturn. Little sense of humor. Appears cold and unfeeling. Usually pessimistic. Good with money and often connected with real estate and the law. Believes in hard work. Fascinated by the past.

9: Mars. Very emotional. Can be jealous and ruled by the emotions. Impulsive. Loyal and family-oriented. Suspicious of strangers. Afraid of the unknown.

As mentioned, different denominations and different numbers of coins can lead to a wide variety of interpretations. Using ten coins to represent the different planets (Sun, Moon, Mercury, Venus, Mars, Jupiter, Saturn, Uranus, Neptune, and Pluto), a form of astrological reading can be obtained by tossing the coins onto a drawn chart of the zodiacal houses (see **astrology**).

House 1 is associated with self-image, and the role adopted in formative years. It is also associated with the head.

House 2 is the house of material possessions, and associated with the neck.

House 3 deals with siblings, short journeys and communications. Body parts are the shoulders, arms, and lungs.

House 4 is the home, roots, and childhood. Also deals with one's mother and one's age. The chest is the body part.

House 5 is creativity, children, love, and entertainment. Heart and circulatory system.

House 6 is health and capacity to work. Upper abdomen.

House 7 deals with partnerships, love and marriage, and business. Lower abdomen and digestive system.

House 8 is birth, death, regeneration. Also, the occult and other people's resources. The generative organs.

House 9 deals with religion, education, philosophy, and travel—especially long journeys. The thighs.

House 10 is of career and social achievement. It also deals with the underworld. The knees.

House 11 is ideals and aspirations, also groups and societies. It also deals with friends, hopes, and wishes. Calves and ankles.

House 12 is the house of things "locked away" in the unconscious mind. Karma and secret enemies are also in this House. Body part: the feet.

By throwing coins you can obtain positions for the planets in the houses. Coins landing heads-up are considered well aspected, while those tail-up are under affliction. Different planets will give different results depending upon the house in which it falls. Again, see astrology for full details of planets in the Houses.

There are many different forms of divination that can be adapted to working with coins: **tarot, dice,** and **dominoes,** for example. One that was very early adapted was the Chinese **I Ching** (pronounce *yee jing*). Traditionally devised by a legendary Chinese sage named Fu Shi more than 4,500 years ago, it has now become popular around the world. It was originally done with yarrow stalks, but Chinese coins, and later any coins, were quickly substituted.

Throwing down three coins would give either three heads or three tails, indicating an unbroken line, or a mixture of one and two (one head plus two tails or one tail plus two heads), indicating a broken line. Originally it was simply that an unbroken line indicated yes and a broken line indicated no, but it soon became obvious that the majority of questions needed more meaning than this. By throwing the three coins three times, it was possible to obtain what was known as a trigram, or set of three lines. These would be made up of three broken and/or unbroken lines, signified by the heads and tails of the three throws. Doing this a second time would give another set of three lines. Putting the two together (Upper Trigram and Lower Trigram) would give what was known as a Hexagram, which could come in as many as sixty-four different combinations. These Hexagrams were used for giving answers to questions.

Whatever form of divination is performed using coins, anyone who does it regularly usually likes to utilize coins that have been personalized. Some will keep a store of coins of various sizes, or of those from many different countries. Some will adopt and adapt medals, tokens, or the like. Some will even make their own, using blank discs of brass, copper, steel, iron, aluminum, and so on. Electric engravers, or hand engravers, can be used to put personal markings on the coins. Or you can paint the pieces either a variety of colors or with a variety of signs and symbols.

Sources:

Blofeld, John. *I Ching: the Book of Change*. New York: Dutton, 1968.

Buckland, Raymond. *Coin Divination: Pocket Fortuneteller*. St. Paul, MN: Llewellyn, 2000.

Da Liu. *I Ching Coin Prediction*. New York: Harper & Row, 1975.

González-Wippler, Migene. *The Complete Book of Amulets and Talismans*. St. Paul, MN: Llewellyn, 1991.

Colorology

In 1867 Francis Francis, in *A Book on Angling*, said, "The colorologists argue that it is not necessary to trouble your head . . . with considerations of what is on the water." The colorologists are those who divine by studying color.

Pythagoras used color for healing. The ancient Egyptians used it in their temples of healing. The Chinese and the Chaldeans used it, as did the mystics of India who associated color with the seven chakras, as follows: Base chakra (perineum gland)—red; second (supernal)—orange; third (solar plexus)—yellow; fourth (heart)—green; fifth (throat)—blue; sixth (pineal)—indigo; crown chakra (pituitary)—violet.

The apparent color of an object is dependant upon the wavelength of light that it reflects. Light is, in fact, radiant energy traveling in the form of waves. The rate of vibration is measured in units known as Ångstrom units, measuring one ten-millionth of a millimeter. Colors exert a vibratory influence over human affairs. This is confirmed by physical science.

In astrology, the planets are equated with colors: the Sun with gold, Moon with silver, Mercury with Purple, Mars with red, Venus with green, Jupiter with blue, Saturn with brown or black. The Sun signs are also associated with colors, as follow:

Astrological Sign	Primary Color	Secondary Color
Aquarius	Blue	Green
Pisces	White	Green
Aries	White	Pink
Taurus	Red	Yellow
Gemini	Red	Blue
Cancer	Green	Brown
Leo	Red	Green
Virgo	Gold	Black
Libra	Black	Blue
Scorpio	Brown	Black
Sagittarius	Gold	Red
Capricorn	Red	Brown

In such things as candle-burning magic, the colors have symbolism as follows:

Red: Courage, health, sexual love, strength, vigor.
Pink: Honor, love, morality.
Orange: Adaptability, attraction, encouragement, stimulation, inspiration.
Gold/Yellow: Attraction, charm, confidence, persuasion, protection.
Greenish-Yellow: Anger, cowardice, discord, jealousy, sickness.
Green: Fertility, finance, healing, luck.
Brown: Hesitation, neutrality, uncertainty.
Light Blue: Health, patience, tranquility, understanding.
Dark Blue: Changeability, depression, impulsiveness.
Violet: Healing, peace, spirituality.
Purple: Ambition, business progress, power, tension.
Silver/Gray: Cancellation, neutrality, stalemate.
Black: Confusion, discord, evil, loss, nothingness.
White: Purity, sincerity, truth.

The human aura is seen as color(s), and from this it is possible to divine a person's health, mood, spiritual state, and so on. In 1858 Baron Karl von Reichenbach, an industrial chemist, discovered that radiations emanate from magnets, crystals, plants, animals, and humans. In 1911, Dr. Walter Kilner of St. Thomas's Hospital, London, devised ways of seeing these radiations. But many psychics can see them without the use of artificial aids, and by studying them can not only read a person's character but can often foretell future actions.

RED is the most forcible of colors, with a constantly active urge. A red aura does not necessarily indicate a headstrong nature, however, for it can be cool and calculating as well as vigorous.

PINK is, of course, a very light shade of red and is more inclined to show the gentleness of love rather than the pure passion of lust. It also indicates a person who is easily hurt.

ORANGE is a color of inspiration. There is a certain lack of warmth, though orange people tend to get what they want. They should, however, learn to recognize their own limitations.

YELLOW is the color of the sun. Wisdom is restrained by caution, though a vivid yellow indicates someone who will always take a chance. A pale yellow embraces timidity.

GREEN shows a very easygoing nature, though a definite firmness when necessary. There is usually a sympathetic ear to be found and there may be a tendency to sentimentality. An olive shade of green shows a weakness and a dullness that can be shaken off if the person is made aware of it.

BLUE shows calmness and someone not likely to panic in any situation. It is a color of devotion and faithfulness. Different shades of blue will produce variations on the basic character. Darker blues will bring in moodiness and coldness, while lighter blues will show a person who tends to be self-centered.

INDIGO shows deep devotion and often a strong religious element. There can be moodiness and mood swings that are frequently downward, tending to pessimism.

VIOLET is a color of grandeur and importance. These are people with high ideals and, frequently, high positions. There is a religious element found here also, with strong views of right and wrong.

There are many variations of colors and combinations of colors, which can be interpreted by a seer who has studied colorology. Another use of color, as applied to the human or animal aura, is to project the colors for healing purposes. There are many who specialize in this field. Color projection through light gels can also be applied to healing.

Sources:

Buckland, Raymond, *Color Magic—Unleash Your Inner Powers*. St. Paul, MN: Llewellyn, 2002.

Gibson, Walter B. & Litzka R. *The Complete Illustrated Book of the Psychic Sciences*. New York: Doubleday, 1966.

Combe, George (1788–1858)

George Combe came from a large family of thirteen children. His father was a brewer in Edinburgh, and his family lived at the base of the rock on which Edinburgh Castle stands. Despite the number of brothers, sisters, and servants in the household, as a child George felt he did not get the attention he deserved. This feeling remained with him for many years. At sixteen he took elocution classes so that he might achieve "a higher sphere of intellectual life," as he later wrote in an autobiographical article.

The Combes insisted their children learn their Calvinist religious studies by rote, though they were not actually deeply religious. Later, George rejected the religion. In 1802, Combe began attending classes at Edinburgh University and studied there for two years before becoming an apprentice to a firm of lawyers in 1804. It was as he advanced in the business world that Combe felt the need to be, and to give the appearance of being, a gentleman. He avidly read all current literature, the *Edinburgh Review,* and began to keep a diary. In a later biographical work, he said: "When yet a child I was animated by the strongest ambition to do some great and good service to my fellowmen, which should render me an object of their love and respect . . . I owe to **Phrenology,** presented to me by mere accident, a field in which it has been possible for me to pursue this object."

In 1810 Combe joined a small weekly debating society known as the Forum, where the issues of the day were discussed. There he quickly became a leading speaker, known as one who liked to do all the talking. In 1815 the phrenology pioneer Johann Gaspar Spurzheim (1776–1832) visited Edinburgh and spoke on the subject of phrenology. Although Combe first mocked Spurzheim and his subject, he did attend a course of his lectures, met the man, and became fascinated by the subject. Combe ordered plaster casts from London to study. Quickly he became the local expert on the subject. In 1815, Thomas Foster called the work of Spurzheim "phrenology" (*phrenos* is Greek for "mind") and the name stuck.

Combe visited Spurzheim in Paris and even encouraged his younger brother Andrew, a doctor, to study medicine there. Both brothers became firm phrenologists. Back in Edinburgh they met others who had found a similar fascination with this new science, among them Sir George Stewart Mackenzie and David Welsh. At the suggestion of Welsh, in February 1820 they founded the Edinburgh Phrenological Society. It was the first such body ever created and by 1826 had 120 members.

Combe purchased a hall for the society and its ever-growing collection of skulls and casts. He started traveling extensively about Britain and Germany and also visited the United States, speaking on phrenology. His book, *The Constitution of Man* (London, 1836), became one of the best-selling books of the nineteenth century, selling over 350,000 copies between 1838 and 1900. In contrast, Darwin's *Origin of the Species* (1859) sold only 50,000 copies between 1859 and 1900. Combe's work is basically a book of natural philosophy. The first steps of life, it said, were to study and obey the distinct natural laws. The Bible and its teachings were noticeably omitted from the book. This led to much controversy, with Evangelicals founding societies just to oppose the volume and even burning copies of it. This, of course, only drew more attention to the work.

Combe dedicated his life to promulgating the cause of phrenology and to promoting a philosophy of natural laws and a secular society. He died in 1858.

Sources:

Combe, George. *A System of Phrenology*. New York: S.R. Wells, 1876.
http://pages.britishlibrary.net/phrenology/combes.html.

Conchomancy

(See also African Divination)

The Afro-Cuban religion of Santeria (known to its adherents as *Las Reglas de Ocha de Los Lucumi*) makes use of seashell **divination,** or *Diloggun*. It utilizes the cowry shells used for trading on the coast of Guinea, in areas of the Pacific, and elsewhere. This is the *Cypræa moneta* shell, a variety of the gastropodous. For followers of Lucumi/Santeria, seashell divination is a sacred ritual making contact with the spirit world and with the gods, or *orishas*, themselves.

Migene González-Wippler says:

> During the consultation with the Diloggun, the santero (**seer**-priest) searches into the life of his consultant, seeking to discover the source of that person's problems and the best way to solve them. The Diloggun acts in two ways:
>
> 1. It gives a general reading of the consultant's life and special circumstances, focusing on any specific problems faced by the individual.
> 2. It suggests possible solutions to the consultant's problems. Most of the time these solutions necessitate the aid of one or more of the orishas.
>
> The Diloggun is used during all the major ceremonies and all the initiations of Santeria.

The Yoruba are **African** farmers who inhabit a coastal area extending across the southern edges of Ghana, Togo, Benin, and into Nigeria. They make use of a form of divination known as *Ifa,* which also utilizes the cowry shell. The practice has now been adopted by many other areas of Africa. Ifa was actually a man-god who came to earth to put the world right, say the Yoruba. His **oracle** was to be used in helping humankind in sickness and in childbearing and to give guidance in the occult. Yoruba tribes include the Yoruba, Oyo, and Ibadan. Some seven million people speak their language. The Yoruba have an amazing array of deities known as orishas who, as in most of Africa's religio-magical systems, are rooted in nature and could be compared to the **Greek** deities in their pantheon. The system represents division into light versus dark, or good versus evil. Both the white orishas and the dark orishas are anthropomorphic. All may be used in the seashell divination system. There are more than four hundred myths and legends about their lives, and the high priest of Ifa has to know all the stories in order to use them in that system, relating the stories to the patterns obtained from the throw of the shells.

The shells are further related to certain marks that the priest makes on the divination board, or table, known as the "Table of Ifa." This is covered with white sand, grain, or very fine powder. Cowry shells, or sometimes nuts, are used for the casting. When cast, the shells may land on their faces, with the smooth, rounded side uppermost, or on their backs with the smoothly serrated, vulva-like openings (known as the "mouth") upward. To make it easier for the shell to lay flat on its back, many diviners will break an "eye" there.

Combinations of four and sixteen shells are used. They are shaken in the hands and cast into the circle. The number of "mouths" is counted. The original casting was tied in with the myth of Fa, who had sixteen eyes. Fa lived on a palm tree in the sky, from the height of which he was able to see all that went on in the world. Every morning God's son, Legba, climbed the tree to open Fa's eyes. Fa didn't want to speak out loud of what he had seen so he placed nuts in Legba's hands to indicate how many of his eyes should be opened. If men use the nuts (now shells) correctly, they may open all of Fa's eyes to see the future.

A simple form of Ifa divination, using sixteen shells, is as follows. The prepared shells are shaken in the hands and cast onto the board—or they may be cast into a circle drawn on the ground, or on a piece of cloth or paper. As the shells are shaken, the question to be asked is concentrated upon. From the shells that fall within the circle or onto the table, the number of mouths facing upward is counted. If necessary, the digits of this number are totaled to give a single digit (e.g. 15 = 1 + 5 = 6). The answer to the question may now be obtained by referring to the below list:

Number	First Answer	Second Answer
1	Yes	Freedom, spirit, creation, take charge
2	No	Partnership, unity, uncontrolled energy, need for diplomacy
3	Yes	Frustration, caution, learning for happiness, hard work
4	Not yet	Opportunities, talents, expansion, be with others
5	Yes, but use power to create or destroy, think before acting caution	
6	Not yet	Sacrifices, compromises, caring, inner strength
7	Yes, but use intuition	Victory, love, women, uneasy relationships, caution
8	Not yet	Learn to plan and communicate, think carefully
9	Yes	Very emotional, stressed out, need time to think, births
10	No	Delay necessary, absolutely no

As can be seen, numbers 4 and 8 are not as simple as Yes or No. Also, all of these answers are actually indicators, or prompts, for the diviner to use his or her intuition and expand on them. First the Yes/No answer is given and then the appropriate advice. It should be borne in mind that if dealing with a reduced number (e.g. 16 reduced to 7), then that is considered a "stronger" form than the simple single number. In other words, 16 is stronger than 7. It therefore gives more of a challenge, or is more positive or negative. As an example, with a question about love life, 7 would indicate victory in love, with somewhat uneasy relationships, but 16 would indicate that the victory might well be hard fought with challenges along the way yet with a very positive outcome. In either case, the person involved should listen carefully to his or her own inner voice.

Sources:

González-Wippler, Migene. *Introduction to Seashell Divination*. New York: Original Publications, 1985.

Lele, Ocha'ni. *The Secrets of Afro-Cuban Divination: How to Cast the Diloggun, the Oracle of the Orishas* New York: Inner Traditions, 2002.

CONVULSIVE TWITCHINGS *see* Spasmatomancy

Copernican System

In the third century BCE a **Greek** grammarian named Aristarchus of Samos (c. 220–143 BCE) developed the concept of the heliocentric universe, but no one believed him. It wasn't until 1543 that Nicolaus Copernicus, or Mikolaj Kopernik (1473–1543), an astronomer and Polish church official, put forward his theory that the sun, rather than the earth, lay in the center of the solar system. Aristarchus's idea had been known to Renaissance scholars but had not been taken seriously.

In Ptolemaic or geocentric astronomy, the term "planet" was applied to the seven heavenly bodies that were seen to change their places as projected against the so-called fixed stars. In the modern or heliocentric astronomy, it is applied to all dark and opaque bodies in revolution around the sun.

In 1530 Copernicus circulated a manuscript, the *Commentariolus*, which was a summary of his ideas on the universe being centered by the sun rather than by the earth. However, the manuscript did not contain any calculations, diagrams, or illustrations. In 1543 he finally published *De revolutionibus orbium cœlestium*—written in six sections—which slowly came to exert a vital influence on astronomy and **astrology.** The final part of the book was published when Copernicus was on his deathbed; he died at Frauenburg on May 24, 1543. He had waited that long to publish the work because he feared the wrath of the Church. His fears were well founded, for as the implications of Copernicus's work became clearer over the next fifty years, the church became very hostile. Giordano Bruno, a supporter of Copernicus, was burned at the stake in 1600, and in 1663 the great Galileo was forced to recant.

Sources:

Anderton, Bill. *Fortune Telling*. North Dighton, MA: JG Press, 1996.
Encyclopedia Britannica. Chicago: William Benton, 1964.
Parker, Derek and Julia. *The Compleat Astrologer*. New York: McGraw-Hill, 1971.

COSCINOMANCY; COSQUINOMANCY

A form of divination practiced with a pair of tongs and a sieve. It has been popular from the earliest part of the Middle Ages to the present day. An erstwhile name for it was "spinning the *sas*." Sas was an old word for sieve or strainer.

According to Jean Baptiste Belot in part one of his *Œuvres diverses* (1640), the tongs were supported either on the thumbnails or on the nails of the middle fingers of two people while they gazed into each other's eyes. Of the practice, Curé Belot said, "Since **lots** were permitted in antiquity and when the Church was at her beginning, let it be permitted me also by our masters to give without scandal, following the ancients, the lots of the sieve as our ancestors used from the reign of Charlemagne."

John Potter, in *Archæologiæ Græcæ, or The Antiquities of Greece* (1697–1699), said:

> It was generally used to discover thieves, or others suspected of any crime, in this manner; they tied a thread to the sieve by which it was upheld, or else placed a pair of shears, which they held up by two fingers, then prayed to the gods to direct and assist them; after that they repeated the names of the persons under suspicion, and he, at whose name the sieve whirled round or moved, was thought guilty." In volume two of Cornelius Agrippa's *Opera Omnia* (sixteenth century), there is an

illustration of the manner in which the shears are held to support the sieve.

Coscinomancy was also used to discover love secrets. It is said that Agrippa, at the end of his works, gives certain mystic words to be pronounced before the sieve will turn. In 1653 Henry More, in *An Antidote Against Atheisme*, mentions "Coskinomancy, or finding who stole this or that thing by the Sieve and Shears." Francis Grose, editor of the *Antiquarian Repository* (1775), says a chapter in the **Bible** should be read and the appeal made to St. Peter or St. Paul. In 1871 Edward B. Tylor, in *Primitive Culture*, mentions "the so-called coscinomancy, or, as it is described in Hudibras, 'th'oracle of sieve and shears.'"

Leland's *Etruscan Magic & Remedies* quotes the *St. James's Gazette* (without giving a date) as saying that, to find a thief:

> a sieve was suspended from a pair of scissors held by two assistants. The operator, having pronounced the name of the suspected person, repeated a shibboleth consisting of six words—*dies, mies, jesquet, benedoe, fet, dowina*—which neither he nor his assistants understood. If the person whose name was mentioned were guilty, the six magical words "compelled the demon to make the sieve spin round."

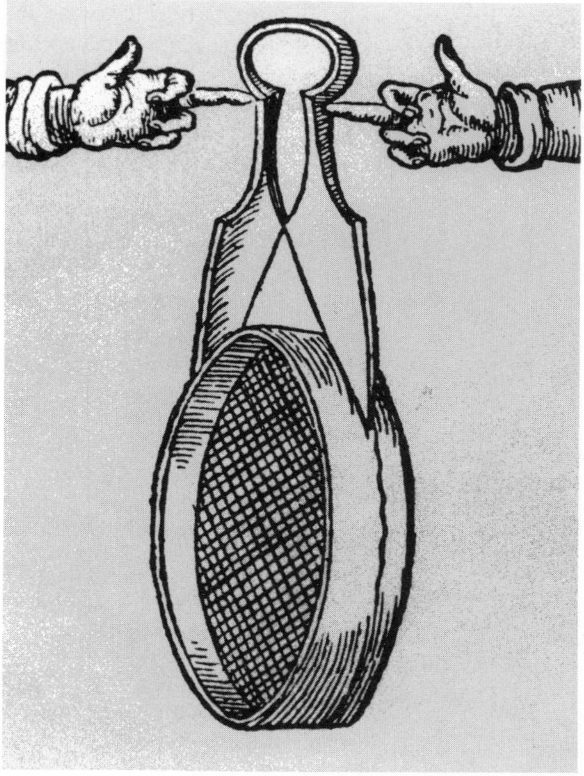

Coscinomancy refers to divination by means of a sieve that turns when an important name is mentioned. *Fortean Picture Library.*

Sources:

De Givry, Grillot. *A Pictorial Anthology of Witchcraft, Magic & Alchemy*. London: Spottiswoode, Ballantyne, 1931.

Oxford English Dictionary. Oxford: Clarendon Press, 1989.

COUNTING ***see*** **Mathemancy**

CRATIPPUS (FIRST CENTURY BCE)

A **Greek** peripatetic philosopher who was chosen by **Cicero** (106–43 BCE) as his son Marcus's instructor. Cratippus's views on divination are outlined in Cicero's *De Divinatione (On Divination)*, showing that Cratippus argued that the failure of some **predictions** does not mean that **prophesy** is not proven, especially if it is matched by even a few successes that cannot be explained by chance.

Cratippus rejected what he thought of as artificial methods of divination, such as **astrology** and **augury,** accepting only precognition from **dreams** or through divine inspiration.

Sources:

Encyclopedia Britannica. Chicago: William Benton, 1964.

CRITHOMANCY; CRITOMANCY

Divination by meal strewn over sacrificed animals. The meal was interpreted much as in other forms of divination, where the shapes it has assumed are seen and interpreted by the seer. Sometimes cakes and other articles of food were used. Critomancy also applied to cakes themselves offered in sacrifice. With these, the cakes were later broken apart and the condition of the flour was observed and interpreted.

CROESUS (SIXTH CENTURY BCE)

Croesus of the Mermnad dynasty was the last king of Lydia, reigning from 560 to 540 BCE. His wealth was proverbial. Herodotus reported on seeing many expensive gifts that Croesus gave to the **Delphic** oracle, which Croesus consulted on a regular basis.

There is a story that Croesus consulted the **oracle** to find out whether it would be advantageous to attack Cyrus the Great of Persia. He was told that he would destroy a mighty empire if he did so. He then asked how long his kingdom would last and was told, "Until a mule is monarch of Media." Croesus's last question at that time was to ask if his mute son would ever speak. The oracle replied that it would be a very bad day for Croesus when he did.

Croesus did invade Persia but was driven back and finally defeated by Cyrus at Sardis. When an enemy soldier came upon him unexpectedly and was about to slay him, Croesus's son cried out in alarm. All of this, supposedly, explained the oracle's predictions. When Croesus attacked Persia a mighty empire was indeed destroyed . . . his own. When his son finally spoke, it was certainly a "very bad day for Croesus." Finally, he was defeated by Cyrus, who was of mixed parentage, which would make him a metaphorical "mule."

Sources:

Encyclopedia Britannica. Chicago: William Benton, 1964.
Headon, Deirdre (ed.) *Quest for the Unknown—Charting the Future*. Pleasantville, NY: Reader's Digest, 1992.

CROISET, GÉRARD (1909–1980)

Gérard Croiset was born at Laren, the Netherlands, on March 10, 1909. He had an unhappy childhood, being neglected by his parents who were in show business. His father, Hyman, was a prominent actor, and his mother was a wardrobe mistress. The parents separated (never having been officially married) when Gérard was eight, leaving him to move through a series of orphanages and foster homes.

From the age of six, Gérard had visions and over his early years was frequently punished by his elders when he spoke of them. He dropped out of school when he was thirteen and took a variety of unskilled jobs, none of which he held for very long. He finally got a job as a grocery helper at one of the stores in the Albert Heyn chain. This he managed to keep for several years.

At twenty-five Gérard married Gerda ter Morsche, an Enschede carpenter's daughter, and the following year he opened a grocery store with money loaned by his in-laws. Unfortunately it didn't last long, and Gérard went bankrupt very quickly. But about that time he came into contact with some local **spiritualists** and was finally able to work on developing his **clairvoyant** talents. These developed quickly, and his reputation as a **psychometrist** and **psychic** blossomed. He was instrumental in locating lost children and animals. He found that he also had an inherent healing ability. With the start of World War II he was able to do healing on injured soldiers. He saw a number of scenes from the war before the actual outbreak of hostilities, and he predicted the war at least four years before it began.

During the war, Gérard spent time in a concentration camp but was released in 1943. He was able to aid the Dutch resistance with his clairvoyant powers but was arrested again, by the Gestapo, in October of 1943.

After the war, in December 1945, Gérard attended a lecture on parapsychology given by Professor Tenhaeff. The two men spoke together after the lecture, and Tenhaeff went on to run tests on Gérard. Croiset accompanied the professor to the University of Utrecht, where he was subjected to such tests as the Rorschach personality (ink blots), the Murray Thematic Apperception (storytelling), the Pfister-Heisz (color pyramid), the Luscher color selection (German), and the Szondi (Swiss). One of the most amazing tests, in terms of startling results, was the **chair test.** Professor Tenhaeff reported: "In early 1946 I made many psychoscopic tests with him. I realized fairly soon that he was very gifted. The more I tested him, the more I became persuaded that Croiset was a remarkable subject for parapsychological research." Tenhaeff went on to introduce Gérard to the Dutch Society for Psychical Research. They came to admire his abilities and to look upon him as a talented artist with rare paranormal gifts. Soon nearly all of Holland began to accept this view of Gérard Croiset.

The Croiset cases have been meticulously documented over the years. He worked with the police, private individuals, and with institutions, tracing lost people and objects, tracking down thieves and murderers, and solving numerous puzzles and problems in many countries. He was tested by parapsychologists all over the world and all reached the same conclusions.

Gérard specialized in cases dealing with young children, especially when they were missing. Many of the cases he dealt with over the telephone. He accepted no payment for any of the things he did, though he did accept donations to his healing clinic. At the clinic, it was not unusual for him to deal with more than 100 cases a day. Much like **Edgar Cayce,** Gérard Croiset could sense the condition of a patient, what was wrong and how to correct it, but unlike Cayce he did not have to go into

Cromnyomancy is divination using onions or onion sprouts. *Janet and Colin Bord*/Fortean Picture Library.*Fortean Picture Library.*

trance to do so. Gérard Croiset died on July 20, 1980. His son took over the running of the clinic.

Gérard Croiset Jr., second oldest of five children, seems to have inherited his father's talents. From Holland he directed South Carolina police in a search for two missing girls. He drew a detailed map of the area where he saw them to be, at a place called Folly Beach, near Charleston. The bodies of the girls were found in shallow graves in the sand.

Sources:

Guiley, Rosemary Ellen. *Harper's Encyclopedia of Mystical & Paranormal Experience*. San Francisco: HarperSanFrancisco, 1991.

Pollack, J. *Croiset the Clairvoyant*. New York: Doubleday, 1964.

Wilson, Colin (ed.). *The Supernatural: Mysterious Powers*. London: Aldus Books, 1975.

Cromnyomancy

Divination by using onions and onion sprouts. Names are written on a number of onions and they are laid on the altar on Christmas day. On Twelfth Night they are taken out and planted. Whichever one first sprouts is the looked-for individual. This could be used for a number of purposes. For example, if a young woman had a number of suitors, she could do this to find which one she would marry. Or, if there was suspicion that one of a number of people was a thief, this would show the guilty party. Obviously, since it could only be done at this one particular time of year, it had its limits. However, laying the onions on the altar for a period of time at any time of year would probably still give results.

Another version of cromnyomancy says that if the onions are laid out on a table on Christmas Eve, each marked with a name, then the one that most speedily sprouts indicates the person who is in the best of health.

Sources:

De Givry, Grillot. *A Pictorial Anthology of Witchcraft, Magic & Alchemy*. London: Spottiswoode, Ballantyne, 1931.

Grand Orient (A. E. Waite). *The Complete Manual of Occult Divination: Volume 1—Manual of Cartomancy*. London: William Rider, 1912.

Crookes, Sir William (1832–1919)

William Crookes was born in London on June 17, 1832. His father was a tailor. As one of sixteen children, Crookes was largely self-taught. At sixteen he enrolled in the Royal College of Chemistry, graduating in 1854. From there Crookes went to Radcliffe Observatory, Oxford, in the position of superintendent of the Meteorological Department. In 1855 he moved on to become professor of chemistry at Chester Training College.

Crookes married Ellen Humphrey in 1856. They had eight children. Five years after marrying, Crookes discovered the element thallium and the correct measurement of atomic weight. He was then elected fellow of the Royal Society, at the age of thirty-one.

Keenly interested in **spiritualism** and **mediums,** William Crookes was president of the Society for Psychical Research from 1896 to 1899. As a scientist, Crookes made many important discoveries in addition to thallium. He also invented the radiometer and edited the prestigious *Quarterly Journal of Science*. At different times he was president of the Royal Society, the Chemical Society, the Institute of Electrical Engineers, and the British Association. He was knighted in 1897 and was the recipient of any number of medals of distinction. Crookes is considered one of the greatest physicists of the nineteenth century.

Crookes first came into contact with **psychic** phenomena in July 1869 at a **séance** with Mrs. Marshall. He attended this after the death of his youngest brother, Philip. From there he took an interest in J. J. Morse, Henry Slade, and others, and announced his intention of starting a thorough investigation of psychic phenomena. The newspapers and journals of the time were delighted to hear this, presuming that Crookes would do an exposé of spiritualism. They were extremely disappointed, for Crookes did intensive investigations of many mediums and psychics only to endorse them and to endorse most psychic phenomena. After intensive examination of Daniel

Sir William Crookes. *Fortean Picture Library.*

Dunglas Home (1833–1886), the sensational British physical medium, Crooke stated: "Of all the persons endowed with a powerful development of this Psychic Force, Mr. Daniel Dunglas Home is the most remarkable and it is mainly owing to the many opportunities I have had of carrying on my investigation in his presence that I am enabled to affirm so conclusively the existence of this force."

Many years later, in 1917, Crookes told the *International Psychic Gazette*: "I have never had any occasion to change my mind on the subject. I am perfectly satisfied with what I have said in earlier days. It is quite true that a connection has been set up between this world and the next."

Sources:

Fishley, Margaret. *The Supernatural*. London: Aldus, 1976.

Fournier, D'Albe. *The Life of Sir William Crookes*. London: T. Fisher Unwin, 1923.

Guiley, Rosemary Ellen. *The Encyclopedia of Ghosts and Spirits*. New York: Facts on File, 1992.

Crowley, Aleister (1875–1947)

Born Edward Alexander Crowley in Leamington Spa, Warwickshire, England, on October 12, 1875, Crowley grew up to become a most prolific writer and the best-known occultist in the world. His parents were strict Plymouth Brethren, his father traveling about the country trying to convert others to his religious beliefs. The Crowley family was the manufacturer of Crowley's Ales, which was a major English brand. Detesting his parents, the younger Crowley changed his name to Aleister so that he wouldn't share the same name as his father. Edward Sr. died when Aleister was eleven.

There were daily **Bible** readings with the family, which Crowley came to despise. But through these readings he became familiar with such characters as the Great Beast of the Book of Revelation, the Scarlet Woman, and the False **Prophet.** All of these were to play parts in his later life. It was actually his mother, Emily Bertha (née Bishop), who, despairing of his rebelliousness, first called him "Beast 666," thus drawing his attention to the Book of Revelation.

Crowley was educated privately, and then at Malvern and Tonbridge schools before going on to Trinity College, Cambridge. At college he read assiduously and thought of entering the Diplomatic Service, though later abandoned the idea. He published his first poetic works while still at Trinity (*White Stains* and *Aceldama*), followed by *The Tale of Archais*, *Songs of the Spirit*, and *Jephthah*, all privately published in

1898. He also became interested in, and extremely accomplished at, mountain climbing. During 1900–1902 he made a trip around the world by way of New York, **Mexico,** San Francisco, Honolulu, **Japan, China,** and Ceylon. Included in the trip was a six-month expedition to the Himalayas where, in 1902, he scaled the Chogo Ri (K2). He spent sixty-five days on the Baltoro Glacier and attained a height of 22,000 feet.

At age fourteen Crowley had his first sexual experience with a maid in the family house. By seventeen he had contracted gonorrhea from a prostitute. While at college he experimented with sex with both females and males.

On November 18, 1898, Crowley joined the London chapter of the Hermetic Order of the Golden Dawn and took the magical name Frater Perdurabo (meaning "I will endure"). Other members at that time were William Butler Yeats, the actress Florence Farr, Oscar Wilde's wife Constance, Allan Bennett, Dr. William Westcott (one of the founders of the British branch of the order), **Arthur Edward Waite,** and Samuel Liddell "MacGregor" Mathers. The Golden Dawn's contribution to the Western Magical Tradition brought about the synthesis of alchemy, **astrology, divination,** the Kabbalah, **numerology,** ritual magic, and **tarot** into one coherent system. Innumerable magical groups and societies have since sprung from this.

Many of the senior members of the Order looked upon Crowley as something of a juvenile delinquent, so they were not pleased when, in 1899, he demanded to be moved up to a higher magical grade. When this was refused, Crowley went to Paris and talked Mathers into doing the rite. By the following year Crowley had departed the Golden Dawn, leaving chaos behind him.

In 1899 Crowley bought a Scottish estate named Boleskine, on the southern shore of Loch Ness in Invernesshire, where he privately practiced the magic of Abra-Melin, as originally taught to him by Mathers. He also developed his own versions of Golden Dawn rituals. In 1902 he married Rose Kelly, sister of the artist Gerald Kelly, later Sir Gerald Kelly President of the Royal Academy.

In 1905 Crowley scaled Kangchenjunga, third highest mountain in the world, to a height of 23,000 feet. He walked across China and visited Morocco. The previous year, he and Rose had visited Cairo. There they had a most important experience that was to help shape Crowley's future life. On March 16, 1904, they took an apartment near to the Boulak Museum (now the National Museum). Two days later, almost as though entranced, Rose suddenly came out with the statement that "He who was waiting was Horus." She had, a day or so earlier, made the mysterious statement to Crowley that "they are waiting for you." She went on to say that Crowley had offended Horus and needed to invoke him and beg his pardon. When Crowley asked his wife who Horus was (knowing she knew nothing of Egyptology), she led him across to the museum and, passing a number of images of the deity, took him to one particular display case. It contained an image of Horus in the form of Ra-Hoor-Khuit, painted on a wooden stele of the twenty-sixth dynasty. This was known as the "Stele of Revealing." Rose said, "There he is!" Crowley saw that the number of the exhibit was 666, the number of the Great Beast of the Book of Revelation.

Back at the apartment, at Rose's behest, Crowley went through an elaborate ceremony honoring Horus, which she directed. Crowley's Holy Guardian Angel, named Aiwass, then came through and stated that "the Equinox of the Gods has come." Crowley was to formulate a link between the solar-spiritual force and humankind. Exactly at noon on April 9, 1904, Aiwass started to dictate to him. Crowley had long been trying to conjure Aiwass and now the **spirit** made itself felt, first speaking through Rose (whom Crowley dubbed Ouarda the Seer). For three days Crowley wrote down what was dictated to him. This produced what became known as the *Liber AL vel Legis* or *The Book of the Law;* a book that was to become the central theme of Crowley's philosophy. It was a series of dithyrambic verses that can be broken down into three principles:

1: There is no law beyond do what thou wilt.
2: Every man and every woman is a star.
3: The only sin is restriction.

The meaning of the first (sometimes rendered as "Do what thou wilt shall be the whole of the law") is along the lines of doing what the Higher Self dictates, rather than just whatever you want to do. The meaning of the last is that everything that inhibits the true will is bad.

Rose gave birth to a daughter whom Crowley wanted to name Nuit Ma Ahathoor Hecate Sappho Jezebel Lilith. Unfortunately she died of typhus in Rangoon in 1906. The following year Rose gave birth to a second child, named Lola Zaza. Also in 1907 Crowley formed the *Argenteum Astrum* (Order of the Silver Star), a magical organization centered around the *Liber AL vel Legis*. Two years later he started publishing what became a ten-volume set of books called *The Equinox*, a biannual publication, largely commenting on the Book of the Law. In 1910, a year after divorcing Rose and abandoning her and Lola Zaza, he was contacted by the head of a German magical order, the *Ordo Templi Orientis* or "Order of the Templars of the East," which had been founded in 1902. They accused Crowley of publishing the secrets of their ninth degree, which featured sex magic. Ultimately Crowley became the head of the English-speaking branch of the O.T.O.

With the outbreak of the World War I Crowley went to America. He stayed at 40 West 36th Street in New York, and later at One University Place, on the corner of Washington Square in Greenwich Village. He met with William Seabrook (for whom he developed a great affection) and traveled to Vancouver, San Diego, New Orleans, and other cities. He spent his own fortune and also those of various women who became attracted to him, as he developed a string of mistresses. Of three of the women Crowley knew while in New Orleans, he described them: "I.S., extremely voluptuous and of the greatest possible skill and goodwill; E.J. claims to be 'pure American' but is, I think, a mixture of negro and Japanese; and A.G., big fat negress, very passionate." One woman he met in Greenwich Village was Leah Faesi, who immediately became his Scarlet Woman. She remained with Crowley for many years. She later had a son whom Crowley named Dionysus; they then had a daughter named Anne Leah, also known as Poupée.

In 1916, Crowley gave himself the magical grade of Magus. After the war, deeply in debt, he returned to England where, for a while, he acquired another mistress, the Australian violinist Leila Waddell (dubbed Sister Cybele).

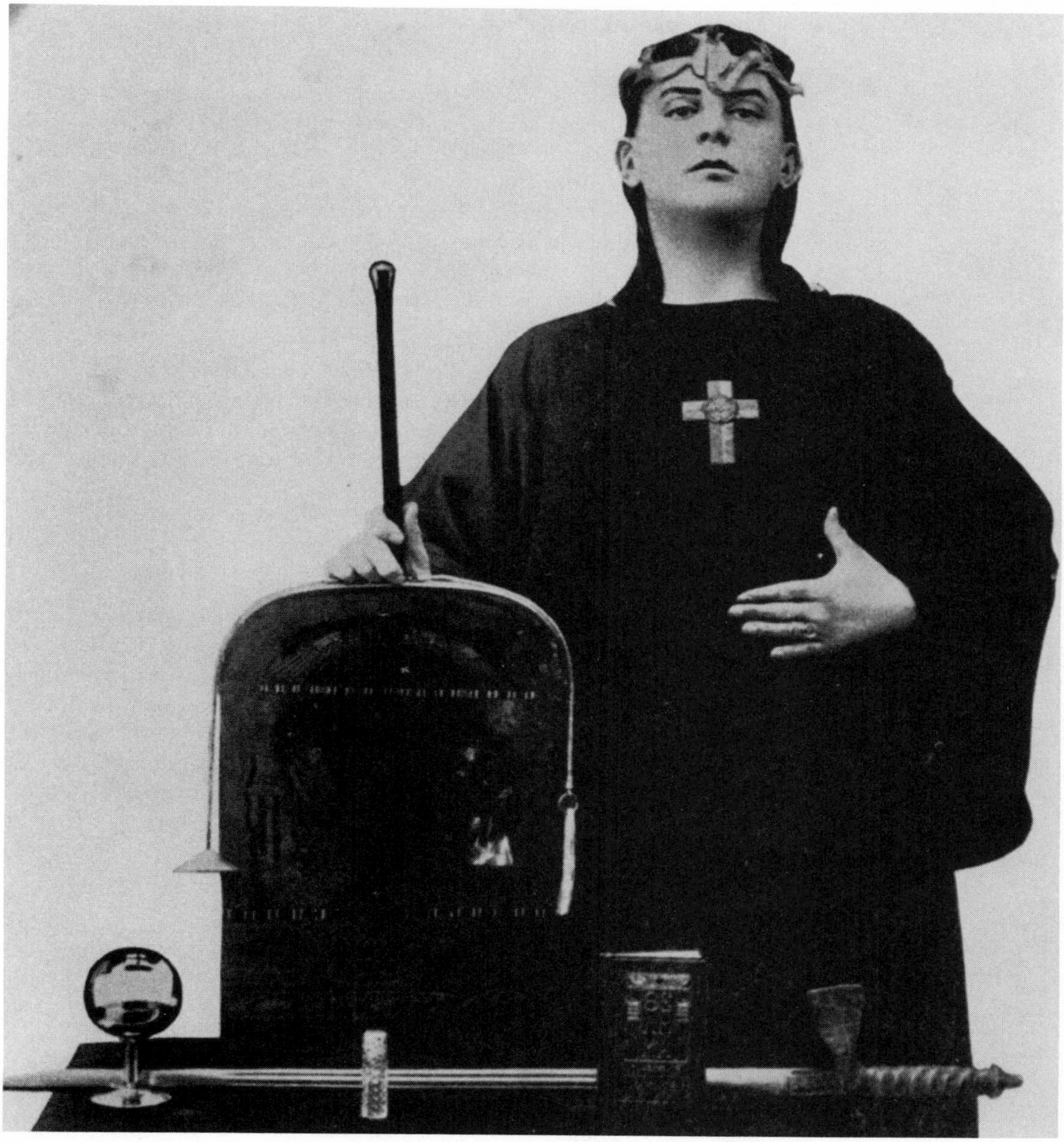

Aleister Crowley wearing Uraeus serpent crown and with wand, cup, sword, bell, phial of holy oil, the *Book of the Law* and the *Stele of Revealing*. *Fortean Picture Library.*

In 1920, suffering from asthma, Crowley went to Sicily accompanied by Leah and Ninette Shumway and her son. Ninette had been taken on as a governess for Dionysus, but quickly became known by a magical name, Cypris, and also became, in effect, a second wife to Crowley. The two women were extremely jealous of one another and got into many fights. In April of 1920 Poupée became very ill; she died on October 14. Crowley was heartbroken, having truly loved the little girl.

At Cefalù, Crowley rented an old abandoned farmhouse with the aid of a legacy of twelve thousand dollars. He named it the Abbey of Thelema and it became his *Collegium ad Spiritum Sanctum,* the center for his new religion of Thelema. He wanted it to become a world center for the study of occultism. It was primitive, with no plumbing. Crowley, who had become addicted to both heroin and cocaine, was able to provide almost limitless drugs to his followers and practiced a lot of sex magic, much of it with his disciple Victor Neuberg. While at the abbey, he wrote what he termed his hagiography (the biography of a saint), titled *The Diary of a Drug Fiend.* This was published by Collins, in London, in 1922.

One of Crowley's most loyal followers was Frederick Charles "Raoul" Loveday, an Oxford undergraduate. He later died at the abbey as a result of drinking impure water, though it was rumored he had also been forced to drink the blood of a sacrificed cat. His wife, Betty May, who had always hated Crowley, went back to England and sold a story to a tabloid newspaper, the *Sunday Express,* about the scandalous proceedings at the Cefalù abbey. It was a tale of black magic and sex practices. This was at a time when Benito Mussolini was coming to power in Italy. As a result, Crowley and his entourage were expelled from Sicily in 1923. He was dubbed "the wickedest man in the world," an epithet that has ever after been applied to him.

By the outbreak of the World War II Crowley was taking as much heroin as would kill a dozen men, and had also become an alcoholic. He abandoned his followers and managed to find enough new, rich disciples to support himself. He finally retired to rented rooms in Hastings, on the south coast of England, and there died from myocardial degeneration on December 1, 1947, at the age of seventy-two. His cremation caused another sensation in the press when the novelist Louis Wilkinson (Louis Marlow) read Crowley's *Hymn to Pan,* extracts from *The Book of the Law,* and the Anthem from his *Gnostic Mass.*

Apart from his other material, one of the finest things Crowley left was his ***Thoth*** *Tarot* (pronounced "Toath," the **Egyptian** god of writing and patron deity of knowledge). It was created in London during the early days of World War II. The artwork was done by Lady **Frieda Harris,** an enigmatic figure in the occult world.

Sources:

Crowley, Aleister. *The Book of the Law.* Tunis, 1925.
Crowley, Aleister. *The Confessions of Aleister Crowley.* New York: & Wang, 1970.
Crowley, Aleister. *Magick in Theory and Practice.* New York: Castle Books, nd.
Crowley, Aleister. *Diary of a Drug Fiend.* London: W. Collins, 1922.
Crowley, Aleister. *Oeth_____: The Holy Books of Thelema.* York Beach, ME: Samuel Weiser, 1983.
Skinner, Stephen (ed.). *The Magical Diaries of Aleister Crowley.* York Beach, ME: Samuel Weiser, 1979.
Stephensen, P.R. *The Legend of Aleister Crowley.* St. Paul, MN: Llewellyn, 1970.
Symonds, John. *The Great Beast.* New York: Roy Publishers, 1952.
http://www.supertarot.co.uk/adept/friedaharris.htm.

CROWS *see* Ravens

CRYSTAL *see* Crystallomancy; Spheromancy

Crystallomancy

Divining using crystal has a number of names, depending upon the method used. **Spheromancy** is specifically using a crystal ball. **Scrying,** although also referring to working with a crystal ball, is a term that covers using virtually any reflective surface. Crystallomancy is the general term referring to any and all of the various methods of working with crystals, be they balls or rough minerals.

It has long been held that crystals of all types possess energies that can be beneficial to humankind. This has been described as electromagnetic energy. Crystals are used for healing, as synthesizers in meditation and prayer, for chakra purification, programming, treating plants and animals, and a host of other things. Crystals of particular minerals—amethyst, jade, obsidian, or tourmaline—are used for specific purposes, but the quartz crystal is the one most generally used and seems to be the panacea.

Since crystals appear to stimulate the senses, they can help bring about awareness of the past, present, and future, contributing as a tool for divination.There can be a noticeable improvement in **mediumistic** abilities when working with a crystal. Here is one method based on that suggested by Dale Walker, an author and lecturer on crystals and their properties. It is used to make contact with the greater consciousness or tap into the universal knowledge.

Sit comfortably in a chair or on the floor. You should be dressed in loose clothing so that there are no restrictions, no tightness to draw your mind away from what you are doing. Hold the crystal in one hand, or cupped in both hands, over your abdomen. Close your eyes and breathe deeply. Picture the crystal in front of you. See it slowly growing in size with each breath. See it growing and growing until it fills the room. Then see it continuing to grow to the size of a house. In your mind, approach the giant crystal and picture a door or entranceway in the side of the crystal. Going through that door, you will find yourself at the end of a corridor leading to a huge room. Enter the room and you will discover that it is like a library of incredible size but instead of books, there are crystals. They are lined up on the shelves, and many of them glow and flicker. If you think of a particular subject, one of the crystals will shine brightly. Going to that crystal, you can pick it up and look into it. You will see something like a computer screen, which will give you any information you desire on that subject. You can then return the crystal to its place and seek out others. When you are finished, return through the corridor to the outside and then find yourself back in your room, holding your crystal.

This is one method that has been used successfully to get information about the past, present, and future. Another is to place four crystals around you, at east, south, west, and north, and to use a crystal ball or other scrying tool in the center of this setup. The crystals at the four cardinal points will act as amplifiers for the energies at work and considerably enhance the scrying.

A number of Scottish families possess amulets and talismans that have been passed down through their families for generations. The Stone of Ardvorlich is pos-

Crystallomancy refers to divination using crystals. *Fortean Picture Library.*

sessed by the Stewarts of that name. It is an egg-shaped rock crystal set in four silver hoops. Legend has it that it was the badge of office of an ancient Arch-Druid. The Stone of the Standard, or *Clach na Bratach*, is also a crystal. It adhered to a clod of earth that stuck to the standard of the Chiefs of Clan Donnachaidh when it was drawn out of the ground at Bannockburn. Other famous stones include the Glenorchy Charm stone (rock crystal), Keppoch Charm rock (rock crystal), the Auchmeddan Stone (a black ball of flint mounted in silver), the *Clach-Bhuai* of the Campbells of Glenlyon, and the *Leug*, or Charm Stone, of the Macleans. With all of these, it is believed that so long as they remain in the possession of the various clans, the families will survive and prosper.

Sources:

Besterman, T. *Crystal-Gazing*. London: Rider, 1924.

Buckland, Raymond. *Scottish Witchcraft*. St. Paul, MN: Llewellyn, 1992.

DaEl (Dale Walker). *The Crystal Book*. Sunol, CA: The Crystal Company, 1983.

Grand Orient (A.E. Waite). *The Complete Manual of Occult Divination: Volume 1—Manual of Cartomancy*. London: William Rider, 1912.

Harold, Edmund. *Focus on Crystals*. New York: Ballantine Books, 1986.

CUBOMANCY

Cubomancy is divination using dice. Dice, along with **dominoes,** have long been used as a tool for reading the future. There are various ways of using them. One is simply to draw or mark a large circle on the ground and then to throw three dice into the circle, three being long considered a "lucky" number. It is said that the **prophetic** answer will come to pass within nine days: three times three.

The circle should be about twelve inches in diameter. Hold the dice in the right hand (or the left, if left-handed) and concentrate on your question. Then cup both hands and shake the dice before throwing them down into the circle. Disregard any die or dice that roll out of the circle. If all of them roll out, it means there will be an argument in the immediate future. You are allowed to throw them again. If all roll out a second time, you must wait at least twenty-four hours to try again.

Of the die or dice that remain in the circle, add together the number of dots. They then have the following meanings:

ONE: Loss; loneliness.
TWO: Love or infatuation.
THREE: A pleasant surprise is on its way.
FOUR: An unpleasant surprise is on its way.
FIVE: You will be influenced by a stranger you will meet.
SIX: You will lose something of value.
SEVEN: You will be involved in a scandal.
EIGHT: A wrong that you did in the past will catch up with you.
NINE: There is a wedding in the near future.
TEN: Business advancement.
ELEVEN: Death of a friend or acquaintance.
TWELVE: A letter of some importance is on its way to you.
THIRTEEN: There will be cause for you to weep.
FOURTEEN: You have a new admirer.
FIFTEEN: Trouble is in the offing; be especially cautious.
SIXTEEN: You will have a happy journey.
SEVENTEEN: Profitable business is coming to you from across the water.
EIGHTEEN: Some very great good is on its way to you.

Another popular method matches up basic questions and set answers. There are thirty-two possible questions from which to choose. The use of just two dice gives a choice of 672 possible answers. No matter which question is chosen, the answer that comes up usually seems appropriate. The two dice are held in the right hand, as in the above working, while the question (chosen from the thirty-two possibilities) is concentrated upon. Then the dice are cupped in both hands, shaken, and thrown down. There is no circle for them to be thrown into. The upturned faces are noted and the answers found from the list, looking for the same number answer as the question.

Questions

1: Does the one I love often think of me?
2: Will anyone soon date me?

3: What must I do to please my love?
4: Shall I answer?
5: Shall I agree to what is asked of me?
6: How many admirers will I have?
7: How many times will I be married?
8: What sort of person will my spouse be?
9: What does he (or she) think of me?
10: May I trust him/her?
11: Does he/she love me?
12: Does he/she think the love is returned?
13: Will my heart remain free for long?
14: Will I soon get married?
15: Will I have many adventures?
16: Will I be rich?
17: Will my secret be discovered?
18: Am I considered good looking?
19: Am I thought to be discreet, witty, and interesting?
20: Will I marry the person I'm thinking of?
21: Shall I do it?
22: Shall I soon see my love again?
23: Shall I soon receive a letter?
24: Which of the two shall I choose?
25: Shall I soon receive a gift?
26: Shall I soon make a journey?
27: Will my condition shortly be changed?
28: Will my wish be fulfilled?
29: What is he/she doing at the moment?
30: What will my spouse be?
31: Will it prove a blessing to me?
32: Shall I soon receive the news I'm waiting for?

Answers to 1–1 Combination

1: They think of you as much as you think of them.
2: Tomorrow morning, about eleven o'clock.
3: Whatever you do, do it gracefully and especially always treat them with respect.
4: Yes, but word your reply discreetly.
5: No. You must not.
6: A dozen at least.
7: One.
8: Young, slender, and fair complexioned.
9: That you are a very special person.
10: No, you may not, for they are not good at heart.
11: They cannot help themselves.
12: You have shown it plainly enough.
13: You know very well that it has not been free for a long time.

14: In a week.
15: Your life will be as peaceful as a quiet lake.
16: You will always have all you need.
17: It would be a good thing if it were discovered.
18: All except your nose.
19: Discreet indeed, but not witty, and only interesting at times!
20: No.
21: Why not?
22: Tomorrow.
23: Not as soon as you would wish.
24: The one who has the longest nose.
25: Very soon, and it will be a kiss.
26: Yes. A very long one.
27: Yes, to your joy and happiness.
28: It will.
29: Busy attending to his or her own affairs.
30: Very rich.
31: It will lead to the greatest happiness.
32: Sooner than you expect.

Answers to 1–2 Combination

1: Not in the least.
2: Much too soon, as it will turn out.
3: Always dress well. Never have bare arms unless absolutely necessary.
4: It is hazardous.
5: Yes, without the slightest fear.
6: As many admirers as you will have spouses.
7: Twice.
8: Fat and round as a ball. But of a very sweet disposition.
9: That you have stolen their heart.
10: Haven't you already had enough proof of this?
11: They are yours, heart and soul.
12: There are doubts.
13: Tomorrow, when you first go out, you'll meet someone who will become very special to you.
14: In two years.
15: Your life will move along like a foaming torrent.
16: As rich as you are at present.
17: No, but it would be good to disclose it as soon as possible.
18: When you are pleasant and friendly, but not when you're ill-tempered.
19: To one person at least, very interesting.
20: If you really want them.
21: If you wish; it will do no harm.
22: Within three weeks.
23: Yes, but not the one you had hoped for.
24: The darker one.

25: Yes.
26: You will soon be seeing cities you never expected to see.
27: When you shall wish it changed.
28: If it is really your wish.
29: Looking through books and papers.
30: An engineer.
31: No, that's impossible.
32: Not for quite a while.

Answers to 1–3 Combination

1: Are you not fascinating?
2: Yes, but be careful. It is a rogue who will be next.
3: Show a little more kindness to other human beings.
4: Frankly and without affection.
5: It would be too cruel to refuse.
6: Only one. But that one will admire you more than all others put together.
7: Once.
8: Very homely, but in your eyes very handsome.
9: That it would be dangerous to trust you.
10: Oh, yes. With all your heart.
11: Haven't you noticed how they blush when looking at you?
12: Without a doubt.
13: At the next social event you attend, your heart will be touched.
14: Never.
15: Too many by far.
16: You'll have so much wealth you won't know what to do with it.
17: It is discovered already.
18: Not greatly so, but somewhat.
19: Mischievous.
20: Yes, and others.
21: Do what you can't help doing.
22: Very soon.
23: The one you would like to receive, you will never receive.
24: The one with the long hair.
25: Very soon.
26: Yes. One that you are looking forward to.
27: It will depend entirely on you.
28: It will. Certainly.
29: Dining with someone else.
30: A lawyer.
31: It will bring you joy and happiness.
32: Perhaps within the year.

Answers to 1–4 Combination

1: They would like to but dare not.
2: When you stop worrying about it.
3: Show your appreciation of their friendship.

4: It would never do to keep silent.
5: You can't do otherwise.
6: Four; possibly five.
7: Once, and it will be the joy of your life. Name begins with a "G."
8: Very tall with a light complexion. Wears spectacles and is very friendly to everyone.
9: That they can understand neither your actions nor your words.
10: You can believe what they say and discount the gossip.
11: You can find that out next time you pass them a drink. If, in taking it, they touch your hand, then there is love.
12: Yes, and is flattered by it.
13: At the moment your heart is *not* free. Examine it.
14: Within a year.
15: Very many. Mostly with rogues and robbers.
16: Rich in love and friendship but not in money.
17: You think that it's a secret but it never has been one.
18: Passably so.
19: You are thought to be capricious.
20: It's very doubtful.
21: It will do no harm, and no good either.
22: If you send an invitation; otherwise, no.
23: Very soon, a very tender one.
24: The one who first reaches out to touch you.
25: Yes, a living one.
26: Yes, but not the one you're presently thinking of.
27: Not so very soon.
28: Yes, but not as soon as you'd like.
29: Sleeping.
30: A doctor.
31: Only so long as you keep your heart pure and true.
32: Yes, in a few hours.

Answers to 1–5 Combination

1: As often as circumstances permit.
2: You will have wrinkles before that happens to you.
3: Don't be so terribly affected. Try to be more natural.
4: Yes, just as your heart prompts you.
5: Be very careful. You might be laughed at.
6: Seven, at least.
7: Once, to a dear, good, and amiable friend.
8: Friendly and cheerful, of a romantic turn, somewhat poetical, but just a trifle weak.
9: That you are the guiding star of their existence.
10: You can tell by looking into those honest eyes.
11: Only as a brother or sister would.
12: If you keep giving those tender glances, they can hardly doubt it.

13: At the moment you love one, but you will soon love another.
14: Within four years.
15: Your life will be a very weary one.
16: If you are careful and watch your money.
17: There is one person who knows it but will not tell it.
18: Some think so . . . others do not.
19: You are generally thought to be heartless and soulless.
20: You know yourself that is impossible.
21: Think what your family would say.
22: Yes, in the not too far distant future.
23: Yes, but it will bring sad news.
24: The one who blushes most often.
25: You must be patient for a while.
26: Not as soon as you hope.
27: Very soon, and in a particular way.
28: It will be fulfilled, but not completely and not quite as you had hoped.
29: Spending time with an older person of the opposite sex.
30: A merchant.
31: If you take it as it is meant.
32: Probably within a month.

Answers to 1–6 Combination

1: Yes, and regrets it.
2: Congratulate yourself if you don't, for there are few worth having.
3: Don't get so sentimental, don't talk so much, and try to use a little more common sense.
4: What is spoken, vanishes; what is written, remains.
5: You may grant all that is asked, for nothing unworthy will be requested.
6: Over 20; five of whom are already in love with you.
7: Three times.
8: A large person in love with him- or herself.
9: That you would like to bring them to despair.
10: Consult your best female friend about this.
11: Their heart has long belonged to another and they would never be unfaithful.
12: No, but they think how pleasant it would be if you did.
13: Your heart is free at present but won't be for much longer.
14: Not until you love a certain person more tenderly than you do at present.
15: Yes, and they will prove too exciting for you.
16: So long as you make good use of the money.
17: No, it will not.
18: If you wear more subdued clothing and improve your complexion.
19: Discreet, but very vain and proud.
20: Yes, if you are not already engaged.
21: Of course. You would be a fool not to.
22: Not very soon.

23: Yes, and the paper will be wet with tears.
24: The one with the larger ears.
25: Someone will offer you one but you would do well to reject it.
26: An important and joyful occurrence will prevent it.
27: Not very soon.
28: That will depend on you. Act prudently.
29: Hurrying to see you.
30: A government worker.
31: If you keep your presence of mind.
32: Not for some time.

Answers to 2–2 Combination

1: Always.
2: Aren't you always surrounded by admirers?
3: Treat them with frankness and honesty.
4: It would be better if you didn't.
5: Yes, but do it prudently.
6: Five.
7: Once, to a very jealous person.
8: Loving and tender.
9: That you are very hard-hearted.
10: You don't need to be so mistrustful.
11: Can't you tell from their face?
12: Hope so, but has many doubts.
13: At five o'clock tomorrow afternoon love's arrow will strike!
14: In six weeks.
15: Many thrilling adventures.
16: Quite wealthy.
17: It will unless you are always on your guard.
18: Quite attractive.
19: Reasonably so.
20: Yes.
21: If it will give you pleasure.
22: No, you are separated for ever.
23: There is one on the way right now.
24: The one who always gazes upon you with such a shrewd expression.
25: Yes, but from someone other than the one you thought.
26: A short, sentimental one.
27: Yes, but you won't benefit from it.
28: It you do everything you can to bring it about.
29: Reading a book.
30: Very spiritual.
31: It will bring you both joy and sorrow.
32: Never.

Answers to 2–3 Combination

1: They are far too busy with other things to keep thinking of you!

2: If you would treat a certain person with a little more regard, they would be happy to do so.
3: Don't pay so much attention to others.
4: Answer as it deserves to be answered.
5: Follow your heart.
6: Many, but most of them you'll find boring.
7: Once, to a very unromantic person whose name begins with a "B."
8: Very tall and of dark complexion; somewhat quarrelsome, jealous, but with the best of intentions.
9: That it would be very dangerous to see you often.
10: Inquire what others say about them. There's a lot of truth on what's said.
11: With heart and soul.
12: Since the last time you were together, they are sure of it.
13: You know very well that right now you are in love.
14: In five months.
15: No. Very few.
16: You will have money, which is not necessarily the same as being rich.
17: If you tell no one . . . no.
18: If you could be a little less self-conscious you would be thought so.
19: Many people think you are a genius but, because of that, think you have many faults.
20: Yes, you will.
21: Certainly not.
22: At a time when you least expect it.
23: Yes, and it will make you very happy.
24: The one with the largest hands.
25: Not soon.
26: Yes, the one you are thinking of.
27: Not in the way you wish.
28: Yes, and sooner than you expect.
29: Arguing with someone.
30: Connected with science.
31: Yes, though it won't appear so at first.
32: Within three days . . . or never.

Answers to 2–4 Combination

1: Yes, as well you know.
2: Yes, but you won't be serious about it.
3: Do not be over-sweet.
4: It would be best if you would.
5: Yes, if you can do it without blushing.
6: Two; one dark and one fair.
7: More than once, and none of them good.
8: A small person, full of conceit and vanity.
9: That you are as near perfect as possible.
10: It is well to be prudent.

11: Yes, but they also love many others.
12: Not exactly, but they think it would be easy to win your heart.
13: For a year yet, but no longer.
14: In six years. No sooner, no matter how hard you try.
15: Many, but none especially interesting.
16: You will have plenty of money, but if you or your spouse should gamble you will lose it all.
17: You will betray yourself.
18: A lot of people think you are homely, some few think you are pretty, and one or two think you beautiful.
19: You are thought to be quick at repartee but not really witty.
20: Yes, if you succeed in winning their heart within two weeks.
21: Do it, even though there's someone it will greatly displease.
22: You will have to wait awhile.
23: Yes, a very long one.
24: The more modest of the two.
25: Very soon, and one that will delight you.
26: Yes, but one that will cost you many tears.
27: Soon, and by an unexpected occurrence.
28: Yes, and more fully than you have reason to expect.
29: Preparing witticisms to speak in your presence.
30: A broker.
31: It will cost you many tears at first, but will turn out well.
32: Very soon.

Answers to 2–5 Combination

1: All the time.
2: Yes, but it won't bring you happiness.
3: Just enjoy life; relax and be yourself.
4: Without hesitation.
5: Go to your mother for advice.
6: Two. The initial of one of them is "L."
7: Only once.
8: Young and handsome, with rosy cheeks.
9: That you have been deceitful.
10: Yes, but not too far.
11: From the moment you first met.
12: They think that at least you would like to love them.
13: The next journey you take, you will fall in love.
14: Within two years.
15: Some pleasant ones; and kind friends will protect you from the unpleasant ones.
16: No, never.
17: No one even thinks of asking about it.
18: Yes.
19: You are thought to be thoroughly charming.

20: You would, if it were not for a false friend.
21: Certainly. You can't do better.
22: They are working on how to bring that about.
23: A very foolish one quite soon.
24: The one with the large mouth.
25: A splendid one, very soon.
26: You will have the opportunity, though you may not take it.
27: Yes, in the way you expect.
28: It will be your own fault if it's not.
29: Practicing what to say to you.
30: A professional person.
31: It will be the prelude to the fulfillment of your warmest wishes.
32: You will soon receive it and shed tears of joy.

Answers to 2–6 Combination

1: Frequently.
2: Yes, a plain looking person with a good sense of humor.
3: Pay a little more attention to them.
4: Answer what your heart dictates.
5: No.
6: About a dozen.
7: Once, or possibly not at all.
8: A great favorite, especially of the opposite sex.
9: That you don't like him, or her.
10: Have they ever done anything to make you distrust them?
11: With great longing.
12: Did so once but no longer.
13: In about six weeks, by starlight, your heart will be softened.
14: In a year or two.
15: A reasonable number.
16: Labor always to be rich in contentment of mind.
17: It is half discovered already.
18: Absolutely beautiful.
19: In every respect.
20: No, so don't expect to.
21: If you don't, you're lost.
22: In a few weeks.
23 Yes, in eight days.
24: The one who gives you a gift.
25: One that you will soon wish you never got.
26: Yes, in the company of someone of the opposite sex.
27: In a very agreeable manner.
28: An unexpected accident will prevent it.
29: Contemplating a change of job or lifestyle.
30: A business person.
31: If you are strong enough to suppress all vanity.

32: Not as soon as you'd like; there will be a wait.

Answers to 3–3 Combination

1: Thinking of you now and very tenderly.
2: Quite a number.
3: Work on your hair.
4: Place a poppy under your pillow tonight and you will dream of what you should.
5: Ask advice of your closest friend.
6: One older man, whom you won't care for.
7: Twice.
8: A person of strong character; high-minded and energetic, with wit and humor also.
9: That you have broken many hearts.
10: No one better deserves confidence.
11: They are a true friend to you; that is all.
12: They have never thought about it at all.
13: It will always be free enough.
14: Very soon.
15: Many, and most of them interesting.
16: If you keep from speculating.
17: If you can refrain from babbling!
18: If you didn't wrinkle your nose when you laugh you would be better looking.
19: Some people think you peculiar, but there are a few who really understand you.
20: If you truly love them.
21: Yes, it will give you both great pleasure.
22: Not until you both have gray hair!
23 Not soon, but when you do it will be a very tender one.
24: The least pretentious one.
25: At the moment no one is thinking of giving you anything.
26: One that will give you much pleasure.
27: Soon, and in a way you would never have dreamt of.
28: Sooner than you expect.
29: Sighing over the low state of their finances.
30: A farmer.
31: If you can always stay cheerful and optimistic.
32: You should know when you may expect it.

Answers to 3–4 Combination

1: Yes, but not in the way you would like.
2: You will soon have more than you can accept.
3: Get a good sun tan.
4: Yes, but make it clear you are not happy about it.
5: Only in part.
6: Many, but few of them attractive.
7: If you accept all that offered, it would be twenty-five times at least!

8: Tall and thin as a beanpole.
9: "You do not deserve my love."
10: Fully and frankly.
11: Yes, but resist it thinking you do not return the love.
12: Not that you truly love, just that you are a little smitten.
13: It will be a long time before you give away your heart.
14: Within the year.
15: No.
16: Gold will rain upon you.
17: You had better be on your guard or it will leak out.
18: Don't think about it.
19: Good natured enough but rather vain.
20: If you flirted less with others, they would be a lot more interested in you.
21: People will laugh at you but don't let them stop you.
22: It will only happen by accident.
23 Yes, but you won't understand it.
24: The one who agrees with you.
25: Yes, one with which you will be delighted.
26: A sad occurrence will prevent it.
27: Yes, but not in the way that you expect.
28: Wicked people will prevent it.
29: Thinking how boring life can be.
30: A literary person.
31: It will give you initial pleasure but later tears.
32: Yes, and you know who it will be from.

Answers to 3–5 Combination

1: More than you think of them.
2: No one worthy of having.
3: Not eat so heartily.
4: There's no danger in it.
5: If you do, you will bring joy to one heart and break another.
6: Two, both good looking.
7: Once, and that will be one too many.
8: A drunkard and a gambler.
9: "They have caused me so much suffering I can never forgive them."
10: Yes, but keep your wits about you.
11: As much as possible, but that may not be much.
12: No. They think your feelings are those of a brother or sister.
13: Is your heart really your own now?
14: Within three years.
15: Only a few.
16: You will have gold by the bushel.
17: Not if you are discreet.
18: You roll your eyes too much, your ears are not well shaped, but your hands are well formed.

19: More or less so.
20: You don't really wish it.
21: If you are prudent it can do no harm.
22: By the end of next summer.
23 Not the one you wish. That will be delayed.
24: The one who is polite and well mannered.
25: Yes, over which you will shed tears of joy.
26: Very soon, and in pleasant company.
27: Yes, and exactly to your wishes.
28: It will, and it will bring you great happiness.
29: Counting the hours till seeing you again.
30: A mechanic.
31: Everything is a blessing. Sometimes we misinterpret.
32: Not soon. Don't be impatient.

Answers to 3–6 Combination

1: Only as one thinks of a small, insignificant creature.
2: Yes, a sailor. But this sailor is heir to a fortune.
3: Do what is asked of you.
4: No! It would turn out very badly.
5: Better not to, though it would do no real harm.
6: Three; one rich and two poor.
7: Once, to someone who will remain completely under your thumb.
8: A wearying person, with little energy.
9: That you are fairly attractive and that if they could love anyone, it would be you.
10: Although a flirt, toward you the intentions are honorable.
11: You are their first and only love.
12: At times they imagine it's possible, because they desperately want it to be so.
13: For at least two more years.
14: Within five years.
15: When you are traveling; not any other time.
16: If you always watch the pennies.
17: Nothing is so carefully hidden that it doesn't eventually come to light.
18: You are considered near perfect in looks.
19: Somewhat thoughtless but good at heart.
20: Yes, and you will live happily ever after.
21: There is certainly danger in it but, if you are careful, there's no real reason why you should not.
22: This very day.
23 Not before you have written one.
24: The first to confess love to you.
25: Yes, from someone you can't stand.
26: You will certainly have the opportunity.
27: Not for a very long time.
28: Yes, but it will break someone's heart.

29: Writing a letter, but not to you.
30: A wealthy person.
31: Yes.
32: This very day.

Answers to 4–4 Combination

1: Don't expect too much.
2: The first person you meet tomorrow.
3: Argue with them a little, but not too much.
4: Yes, but choose your words carefully.
5: Ask the advice of a close relative.
6: One. A slow, fair-haired person with a large mouth.
7: As many times as you have already had lovers.
8: Attractive and in the prime of life.
9: That you are amusing.
10: Trust no one blindly in this world.
11: Yes, and hopes that it is returned.
12: They think that you are dying of love for them.
13: You have already been in love a dozen times. You may be another dozen.
14: In three to four years.
15: Storms and calms by the score.
16: You will never want, so long as you remain industrious.
17: No, but by keeping it secret you will bring upon yourself many disagreeable consequences.
18: You would look better if you smiled more often.
19: Witty and amusing.
20: If not it will be through no fault of your own.
21: Yes, but as quietly as possible.
22: At the next party you attend.
23 Not for a long time.
24: The one with the soft eyes.
25: Very soon, from the one you love.
26: Yes, and it will have a decisive effect on your life.
27: If you act prudently in a critical moment that is at hand, it will.
28: Yes, and you'll wish it hadn't been.
29: Writing a love letter.
30: A politician.
31: If it happens without our interference, it will bring much happiness to you.
32: It will come one day, but not yet.

Answers to 4–5 Combination

1: You are in their thoughts by day and dreams by night.
2: Not for a very long time.
3: Be gentle and patient and do not contradict.
4: It's now immaterial—tears will flow whether you do or not.
5: If you do you will later regret it.
6: One tall, slender, handsome person with dark eyes.

7: Once, to a real tyrant.
8: Congenial but apt to overeat.
9: That you are still quite childish in many ways.
10: You would deeply hurt them if you didn't.
11: You cannot imagine just how much.
12: Yes . . . you along with all the rest!
13: You will fall in love very soon, after some unhappiness.
14: Within six years.
15: Yes, many.
16: Not very.
17: Not for a while.
18: Your face is considered your greatest asset.
19: Possibly.
20: If it were not for a very bitter enemy of theirs.
21: If you do, there will be many tears . . . both of sorrow and of joy.
22: Only if you make the first move.
23: No, the people you want to hear from are all preoccupied.
24: The one who will stumble when next with you.
25: Yes, but an insignificant one.
26: You will certainly not want for invitations.
27: Not in any matter of importance.
28: Yes, but it will make many enemies.
29: Buying new clothes.
30: A military person.
31: No.
32: Tomorrow possibly, if not then by next week.

Answers to 4–6 Combination

1: Yes, and affectionately.
2: Why do you ask? They are already on their knees before you!
3: Try not to make a joke out of everything. Some things need to be treated seriously.
4: Reflect on what that might lead to.
5: Do so as though it's unimportant and you'll come to no harm.
6: At least three.
7: One short, one tall, and one medium.
8: Short, with a large nose.
9: You were always thought to be an angel but now it appears there's a bit of a devil in you!
10: Try for as long as you feel you honestly can.
11: Without you all would be darkness.
12: Yes, but it is thought that you also love others.
13: Very soon you will fall in love with someone you thought you couldn't stand.
14: Not for seven years.
15: Many, and when you least expect to.
16: For a short time, but your foolishness will impoverish you.

17: No.
18: At times, with certain expressions, you are captivating.
19: No one would dispute it.
20: Yes, but you won't be as happy as you thought possible.
21: It really doesn't matter one way or the other.
22: There has been a misunderstanding that will take time to heal.
23: Very soon. A very nice letter.
24: The stoutest.
25: Not for some time.
26: A very long one.
27: When you decide it should be.
28: Yes, but it will cause envy and that will bring you sorrow.
29: Making plans that do not include you.
30: Someone connected with the sea.
31: A blessing to you and a delight to your friends.
32: Not the wished for, but very different news.

Answers to 5–5 Combination

1: Not yet.
2: Someone desperately wants to, and hopes to.
3: Whatever you do, you won't be able to do enough.
4: Meditate on whether it would be right.
5: If it will give you pleasure, yes.
6: Three, one whose name starts with a "W."
7: Once, to someone you already know; whose name starts with a "J."
8: A very funny person, full of tricks and jokes.
9: "If I only knew what to do to gain favor."
10: Test carefully first before trusting completely.
11: In secret, but may never say so aloud.
12: Yes, but is afraid you may not.
13: It's not free at the moment, but will be free again very soon.
14: This year.
15: One big one very soon.
16: Yes, but you must handle money carefully or you will lose it.
17: Very soon.
18: You look better in the evening than you do earlier in the day.
19: You can sometimes be very silly but people generally overlook that, knowing you will grow out of it.
20: No, for they will never marry.
21: Do it and enjoy it.
22: It's possible that you may never meet again.
23: In a few days.
24: The one who laughs most easily.
25: Possibly tomorrow, though there may be a delay.
26: Yes, across the ocean.
27: Somewhat, and agreeably.

28: That will depend upon your behavior.
29: Thinking of you and longing to be with you.
30: A medical person.
31: It will, at least, cause you many happy hours.
32: Unless you work toward it, no, never.

Answers to 5–6 Combination

1: Yes, but with some bitterness.
2: Someone you will meet within the next three days.
3: Whatever you like, for there's really no pleasing them.
4: At least wait for a letter to arrive before answering.
5: If you do, the person who asked will then laugh at you.
6: Two; one distantly related.
7: Once, to the person you now consider the least likely.
8: A good-for-nothing who will bring you nothing but trouble.
9: That you are an enigma.
10: Not too much. Be cautious.
11: Truly and faithfully.
12: They are too jealous to be certain.
13: No, it will shortly be stolen.
14: Before next winter.
15: Not soon, but in due course.
16: You could become so if you put your mind to it.
17: You have nothing to fear.
18: Only by your lover.
19: Your heart is pure and your mind is clear.
20: Of course!
21: First consider whether or not anyone would get harmed.
22: Yes, very unexpectedly.
23: Tomorrow.
24: The one with the snub nose.
25: Yes, very soon.
26: A delightful journey westward.
27: Not as soon as you expect nor in the way that you expect.
28: If you really wish it, yes.
29: Reading one of your letters.
30: A tradesperson.
31: It is extremely doubtful.
32: Very soon, but not all your expectations will be gratified.

Answers to 6–6 Combination

1: Yes, though they are afraid of getting carried away with such thoughts.
2: An older person.
3: Let your love see that you return the love.
4: Yes, but in a cheerful, laughing way.
5: It will be a step with important consequences.
6: Many, but none of them serious.

7: However many times, it would be better if it were none.
8: Handsome and brilliant. You will be made for each other.
9: That you are overly sentimental.
10: Who else if not?
11: As much as you love them.
12: They think it's impossible, yet hope it isn't.
13: Not for more than a year.
14: When acts lay eggs!
15: You are too cautious.
16: You will always have as much as you have at present.
17: There is someone among your friends who will betray you.
18: As a beautiful flower.
19: You are thought to be thoughtless.
20: Don't let go. In the end there will be surrender.
21: If you can without being embarrassed.
22: Before the spring.
23: In a few weeks, a long one.
24: The one you met by chance.
25: Someone is considering giving you one, but is undecided.
26: Yes, to Europe.
27: Very soon and drastically.
28: Not entirely.
29: Longing to be with you.
30: An artist.
31: Decidedly. You will be very happy because of it.
32: The tidings are close at hand and will be more agreeable than you could hope.

Sources:

Buckland, Raymond. *Secrets of Gypsy Fortunetelling*. St. Paul, MN: Llewellyn, 1988.

Gibson, Walter B. & Litzka R. *The Complete Illustrated Book of the Psychic Sciences*. New York: Doubleday, 1966.

Gypsy Queen, A. *Zingara Fortune Teller*. Philadelphia: David McKay, 1901.

Line, David and Julia. *Fortune Telling by Dice: Uncovering the Future through the Ancient System of Casting Lots*. London: Aquarian Press, 1984.

CURAN, PEARL *see* Automatic Writing

CYCLOMANCY

Divining from a turning wheel. This was performed much like television's *Wheel of Fortune*. A wheel would have possible answers to questions, or names, written around its rim. A marker would be placed alongside the rim. The wheel would then be spun and whichever item stopped alongside the marker was deemed the pertinent one.

A variation was to mark the wheel of a wagon, with a mark on the side of the vehicle alongside the rim of the wheel. The horse or ox pulling the wagon would be urged forward and then left to stop when it would. When it did stop, the information next to the marker was read.

Cylicomancy

Divining using cups of **water,** in much the same way as is done with a crystal ball for **scrying.** A silver cup or clear glass is filled to the brim with fresh water taken from a well or spring. The **seer** relaxes and gazes into the water. It is important to have the right attitude of mind and to be in the right mood. A comfortable seat will help, as may the burning of incense, which seems to help establish the right atmosphere for the practice.

There should be absolute silence, if possible, so that the seer is not distracted by sounds. A series of deep-breathing exercises before starting, to help calm body and mind, is a help. Then the seer relaxes and gazes into the cup of water without straining.

If some particular information is sought from the scrying—where a person is at that time, or what is happening in some area—then the question is concentrated upon for a few moments before starting the scrying. Then it is put out of the mind and the scrying done allowing anything to come into the picture that may.

Pictures of people and events are seen in the water, which can magnify them. These pictures may be colored or monochrome, still or moving. Sometimes what is seen is purely symbolic and needs to be interpreted. Sometimes only signs and symbols are seen, these too needing interpretation.

Sources:

Besterman, T. *Crystal-Gazing*. London: Rider, 1924.
Buckland, Raymond. *Doors to Other Worlds*. St. Paul, MN: Llewellyn, 1993.
Hill, Douglas. *Man, Myth & Magic: Scrying*. London: BPC Publishing, 1970.

D

Dactyliomancy

This is a form of divination performed by means of rings. There are a number of variations of it; one is with the rings placed on the fingernails. These were rings of gold, silver, copper, iron and lead; one on each fingernail starting with the gold on the thumb. There is little detail to be found on this, though Samuel Purchas mentions it in his *Pilgrimage* (1613), saying only, "Dactyliomancie was a divination with Rings." Similarly, Edward B. Tylor, in his *Primitive Culture* (1871), says, "These mystic arts . . . are rude forms of the classical dactyliomancy." Apparently this divination was done according to certain conjunctions of the planets.

One form was to set up a circular table with the letters of the alphabet arranged around the edge. A ring is then suspended over the center and it will swing out, as a pendulum, over the letters, spelling out answers to questions. This is basically a form of **radiesthesia.**

Another form of dactyliomancy—which, again, is a type of radiesthesia and of **cleidomancy**—is to suspend a ring so that it hangs inside the bowl of a wine glass. Questions asked will then be answered by the ring swinging and ringing against the side of the glass, once for Yes and twice for No. Longer messages may be obtained by asking a question and then slowly reciting the letters of the alphabet. The ring will tap against the side of the glass as each pertinent letter is called out, thus spelling a word or words.

Sources:

De Givry, Grillot. A *Pictorial Anthology of Witchcraft, Magic & Alchemy*. London: Spottiswoode, Ballantyne, 1931.

Spence, Lewis. *An Encyclopedia of the Occult*. London: George Routledge & Sons, 1920.

DACTYLOMANCY ***see*** **Dactyliomancy**

Dactyls

There was a Herakles who was a wizard, and was also known as Dactyl (literally, "finger"). The *Encyclopedia Britannica* states that it was he who founded the Olympic Games, but gives no further details. There was also a group of sorcerers in Phrygian Ida who were known as the Dactyls. Originally there were three of them: Celmis, Damnameneus, and Acmon, though later their number increased. Acmon was the most powerful. In the caves of the mountains they practiced the "art of Hephæstus," which was metalworking. From Phrygia they went to Crete, where they taught the inhabitants to work with metals.

The Dactyls have been described as conjurers, exorcists, magicians, **soothsayers,** and sorcerers. Pausanias says there were five of them; Perecydes says fifty-two; Orpheus the Argonaut just mentions "a large number." They have been credited with many things including discovery of musical notes, the introduction of musical instruments into Greece, the discovery of minerals, and the introduction of fire into Crete. They were said to be good runners, **seers,** excellent dancers, and skilled in science.

Sources:
Encyclopedia Britannica. Chicago: William Benton, 1964.
Larousse Encyclopedia of Mythology. London: Paul Hamlyn, 1965.
Spence, Lewis. *An Encyclopedia of the Occult*. London: George Routledge & Sons, 1920.

Daphnomancy

Divination by means of a branch of laurel. If the branch was placed in a fire, the way in which it burned could be interpreted. It is mentioned by Thomas Blount in his *Glossographia* (1681). By crackling as it burned, it signified good fortune. If it burned silently, it was a bad **omen.** The time it took for it to crackle was also significant (see **Chronomancy**).

DEAD SPIRITS ***see*** **Necromancy; Psychomancy**

Dee, Dr. John (1527–1608)

English mathematician and **astrologer** to Queen Elizabeth I, Dee made many contributions to the scientific knowledge of his time. He claimed that he was descended from Roderick the Great, Prince of Wales, and also that his family was from the old Welsh noble house of Nant y Groes of Radnorshire. John Dee was born in London on July 13, 1527, and at fifteen attended St. John's College, Cambridge. After two years there he received his bachelor of arts degree. Dee was made a Foundation Fellow of Trinity College in 1546. He later studied in Brussels and Paris, where he lectured on the principles of geometry.

On his return to England, Dee received a pension from the young Edward VI in 1551, being granted the rectory of Upton-upon-Severn, in Worcestershire. But in 1553 he was accused of attempting to take the life of the new Queen Mary by magical means and was imprisoned at Hampton Court. He remained there until 1555. Mary's successor, Queen Elizabeth (whose astrological chart Dee had done when she was still a princess), released him and asked him to name the most propitious day for her coronation. Dee later spent some time giving lessons in metaphysics to the monarch.

John Dee, seventeenth-century engraving. *Fortean Picture Library.*

Dee spent thirty years of his life giving advice and instructions to mariners regarding navigation and piloting, and he developed a large scientific and mathematical library. He took a great interest in alchemy and also in **scrying,** or **crystal gazing.** His *Diary* records that he first saw "**spirits**" in his crystal on May 25, 1581. His experiments with the crystal had been preceded by his preoccupation with **dreams,** both his own and those of his wife, Jane Fromond. One day, in November 1582, Dee was on his knees in prayer when he became aware of a brilliant light in the west window of his laboratory. In the middle of the light he saw the angel Uriel (or so he claimed). Dee was rendered speechless. Uriel smiled at him and presented him with a convex piece of crystal, telling him that when he wished to communicate with the beings of another world, he had only to gaze into it and they would immediately appear and reveal to him the mysteries of the future. Uriel then vanished. Dee called the glass his "shew stone" or "angelical stone."

Despite his excitement and his interest in scrying, Dee was not adept at the practice himself. He found that he could not keep in his head what it was the spirits told and showed him; he therefore decided to employ other crystal gazers to scry for him. Unfortunately Dee was not a good judge of character and at least two turned out to be charlatans. The first of these was Barnabas Saul, and the second was Edward Talbott, who later changed his name to **Edward Kelley.** Kelley was supposed to see angels in the crystal and report to Dee on what they instructed. Kelley claimed that they communicated in their own language, called *Enochian*.

In 1583 Dee was introduced to Count Albert Laski, a representative of the King of Poland, who was visiting Queen Elizabeth. Laski was interested in all that Dee did and especially in the prognostications revealed, by way of Kelley, in the shew stone. Among other things, Kelley implied that Laski would become the head of a vast European monarchy governing the world. Subsequently Dee and Kelley moved to Poland as guests of Laski, and Dee did not return to England until 1589. During that time Dee and Kelley traveled extensively and were everywhere entertained both royally and by royalty.

There have been many stories of Dee spying for Elizabeth, of using scrying to obtain money from various rulers and aristocrats, and of conducting alchemical and necromantic experiments. To the Church, at that time, there was a difference between what they considered "natural" or white magic and black magic, which was essentially of the devil. The view was that natural magic was permissible. Yet on May 6, 1586, the Papal Nuncio submitted a document to the Emperor Rudolph II, with whom Dee and Kelley were staying, accusing Dee of necromancy. This resulted in the pair being expelled from Prague.

Kelley was subject to fits of temper and sometimes refused to scry for Dee. Kelley also lusted after Dee's young, attractive wife. Eventually, on one occasion in 1587, Kelley did scry and reported that the angels had ordered that he and Dee should share their wives in common. Dee and Jane were not willing initially, but eventually they gave in and did so rather than lose the services of the scryer. Shortly thereafter, however, Kelley left the employ of John Dee.

After Dee's return to England in 1589, he was given the post of warden to Christ's College, Manchester, in 1595. He had been a member of the "School of Light," a group that met secretly at the home of Sir Walter Raleigh, to discuss occult subjects. He held the post for ten years. But Dee did not fare well under James I, who had succeeded Elizabeth in 1603. In 1608 Dee died, penniless, at his home in Mortlake.

Sources:

Buckland, Raymond. *The Witch Book: The Encyclopedia of Witchcraft, Wicca, and Neo-paganism*. Detroit: Visible Ink Press, 2002.

Deacon, Richard. *John Dee*. Muller, 1968.

Encyclopedia Britannica. Chicago: William Benton, 1964.

Spence, Lewis. *An Encyclopedia of the Occult*. London: George Routledge & Sons, 1920.

Delphi

(See also Pythia)

Delphi was the site of the most celebrated of all **oracles** in ancient **Greece.** It was located at the Temple of **Apollo** in Phocis, on the southern slope of Mount Parnassus. Its history is complicated and little is known about the early period of its existence. It seems certain that the shrine was not originally Apollo's. The site was formerly known as Crisa. There was an ancient oracle to Gæa already at that place, guarded by a female dragon/serpent named Python. Apollo slew the dragon and built his own shrine there, making this the Oracle of Delphi, with the **diviners** known as **Pythia.** In looking for someone to administer his new temple, Apollo spied some Cretan sailors passing in their ship. He appeared to them in the form of a dolphin and conjured great winds to drive their ship ashore at the site of the temple. There he revealed himself to them. Since he had first appeared as a dolphin, they called him Apollo Delphinius (the Greek word for dolphin) and the site of the oracular temple became known as Delphi.

According to Æschylus (*Eumenides*), the original giver of oracles at this site was Earth. Earth was succeeded by her daughter Themis, and Themis later succeeded by Phœbe, who gave the shrine to Apollo as a birthday gift. This ties in with the idea that the oracles come from the earth-goddess herself. Delphi is ancient and the worship of goddesses was prominent in pre-Hellenic cults.

The most sacred object at Delphi was the omphalus, or navel of the earth; the very center of the earth (which was conceived of as flat). No less sacred than the omphalus was the **tripod** on which the Delphic priestess sat while giving her divine utterances. The tripod was, as its name implies, a three-legged seat and was formed with a circular slab on which a laurel branch would be laid when the priestess was not present.

It has been said that Pythia gave her answers to questions in a state of trance, induced by intoxicating fumes. According to Justinian (Flavius Anicus Iustinianus, 483–565 CE): "In a dark and narrow recess of a cliff at Delphi there was a little open glade and in this a hole, or cleft in the earth, out of which blew a strong draft of air straight up and as if impelled by a wind, which filled the minds of poets with madness." In fact, geologically and architecturally this is impossible. There is no crack or cleft and the local strata have never been capable of producing any kind of gas. However, that the Oracle went into a trance is more than likely.

Consulting the oracle at Delphi*, painting by Knapp. *Fortean Picture Library.

Sources:

Encyclopedia Britannica. Chicago: William Benton, 1964.
Spence, Lewis. *An Encyclopedia of the Occult*. London: George Routledge & Sons, 1920.

Dement, William Charles (b. 1928)

Born in Wenatchee, Wisconsin, William Charles Dement qualified as a doctor at the University of Chicago. He rapidly developed an interest in **dream** research, and by 1960, when he was working at Mount Sinai Hospital in New York, he began to seriously experiment with dreams.

In 1963 Dement became director of the Sleep Laboratory at Stanford University Medical School and, seven years later, director of the Sleep Disorders Clinic. In his research, Dement discovered that dreams are essential to psychological and physical health. He found the correspondence between a sleeper's eye movements and the images in dreams.

Sources:

Fishley, Margaret. *The Supernatural*. London: Aldus, 1976.

DEMONS *see* **Demonomancy; Emonomancy**

DEMONOMANCY

Demonomancy is based in **ceremonial magic,** where spirits or demons are conjured and made to appear. This was a practice popular in the Middle Ages, requiring a great deal of knowledge (especially of Greek and Latin), lots of time, and a good financial backing. The people who had all three of these things, usually in some abundance, were the ecclesiastics. Many bishops, archbishops, even some of the popes, indulged in ceremonial magic.

Also known as high magic, this is the practice of conjuring spirits (termed variously entities, demons, devils) to do your bidding. Alphonsus de Spina stated in 1459 that there were 133,306,668 of these demons. This was "corrected" by Johann Weyer (1577) to 7,405,926 demons together with seventy-two princes. Others tried to count them also, but came up with widely differing totals. Certainly there was a belief in a whole host of entities, all named and in a regular hierarchy, and each was thought to be an expert in a particular field. Depending upon what was wished for, the pertinent entity should be conjured. For example, to be able to speak in tongues, Agares must be summoned. To learn astronomy, **astrology** and philosophy, Furcus must be reached. To destroy cities and prominent people, Raym is the one. With the right demon, the past, the present, and the future all could be probed, making the magician a **seer** of sorts.

These demons were very unwilling to appear and obey, so they had to be threatened; the magician had to show that he was more powerful than the spirit. Once the demon acknowledged that superiority he was forced to obey, albeit reluctantly. He would then have to answer any questions, including foretelling the future and divining situations and answers to problems. To demonstrate his superiority, the magician would conjure with "words of power," usually using the names of god and of the angels and archangels.

A book containing the details of such rituals of the "art magic" was known as a *grimoire*, from the Old French for "grammar." There are a number of these grimoires extant in the libraries and private collections of Europe and America, though many seem to be no more than copies of copies. Some of the most notable grimoires are *The Key of Solomon the King*, *The Lesser Key of Solomon*, *The Arbatel*, *The Heptameron*, *The Grimoire of Honorius*, *The Black Pullet*, *The Pansophy of Rudolph the Magus*, and *The Book of Sacred Magic of Abra-Melin the Mage*.

Sources:

Barrett, Francis. *The Magus, or Celestial Intelligencer; being a complete system of occult philosophy*, London: Lackington, Allen & Co., 1802.

Buckland, Raymond. *The Anatomy of the Occult*. New York: Samuel Weiser, 1977.

Macgregor Mathers, S. L. *The Book of Sacred Magic of Abra-Melin the Mage*. De Laurence, 1932.

DENDROMANCY

Dendromancy is foretelling the future with **trees.** Because it is specifically connected to oaks and mistletoe, there would seem to be a further connection to the Druids.

Druidic temples were outdoors, frequently in a grove of oak trees. They were usually circular or oval in form, sometimes enclosed by a palisade or bank and ditch.

In the center was a large stone representing deity. W. B. Crow thinks that Druidism was a tree cult, since Europe was, at that time, mainly covered with extensive forests; the predominant tree being the oak. It is certainly known that an object of their veneration was mistletoe; a semi-parasitic plant growing on trees and particularly prevalent on the oak tree. Mistletoe was also held sacred by the Teutons. The Druids would cut the mistletoe from the tree with a golden sickle, allowing it to fall into a cloth held out below to catch it, since it was not allowed to touch the ground. The only detailed account we have of this ceremony comes from Pliny, who stated that the mistletoe was cut on the sixth day of the **moon.** He also said that two white bulls were sacrificed after the cutting, and a feast was held.

Whether or not the mistletoe was plentiful indicated the probable state of the coming year. If the mistletoe was scarce then the gods needed to be either appeased or supplicated to ensure good harvests.

Sources:

Crow, W. B. *A History of Magic, Witchcraft, & Occultism*. London: Aquarian Press, 1968.
Piggott, Stuart. *The Druids*. London: Thames & Hudson, 1968.
Spence, Lewis. *The Magic Arts in Celtic Britain*. London: Rider, 1945.

DESTINY *see* Fate

Deunov, Peter (1864–1944)

Also known as Beinsa Douno, Peter Deunov was a Bulgarian **prophet** who liked to be known as "the Master." He was born near the Black Sea on July 12, 1864. His father was a Bulgarian Orthodox priest. Deunov studied theology and medicine in the United States from 1888 to 1895, making a very favorable impression those with whom he came into contact. When he returned to Bulgaria, he retired into the mountains to prepare himself for what he felt was his mission.

He began his teaching work in 1897. The following year he issued a "Call to My People." He claimed to have descended to Earth from "Alfeola, the Star of Stars," and said that he was here to pave the way for the coming "Age of the Slavs." In 1900 he set up the "Fellowship of Light," based on divine love, goodness, truth, justice, and wisdom. He traveled the country before setting up his headquarters in Sofia. He died December 27, 1944.

Sources:

Cavendish, Richard (ed.). *Encyclopedia of the Unexplained*. London: Routledge & Kegan Paul, 1974.
Webb, James. *The Occult Liberation*. London: Alcove Press, 1973.
http://www.esotericpublishing.com/pr/deunov.html.

Dice

(See also Astragalomancy; Cleromancy; Cubomancy)

Divination by the throwing of dice is called **cubomancy.** It is a form of sortilege but specifically using dice. The dice are thrown down after being mixed or shaken togeth-

Divination by the throwing of dice is called cubomancy. ***Adam Hart-Davis/Fortean Picture Library.***

er. Their relationship on landing is interpreted, as may be the area where they land, which may be subdivided into pertinent sections. The face of the dice is significant.

Divination

Divination is so called because it is considered a gift of the divine—a gift from the gods. It is the art of foretelling the future—of obtaining knowledge of the unknown—using **omens, portents,** visions, and divinatory tools. It is an art that many have perfected over the years, in its various forms. Most **Gypsies,** for example, are experts at one or more branches of divination, favorites including **cartomancy** (card reading), **cheiromancy** (palm reading), casting runes or dice, crystal gazing (**scrying**), and more. They recognize what is important in what they see and present it to the person questioning. But divination was originally a tool of royalty, used to determine disasters, wars, plagues, and lines of succession. The Babylonians and the Chaldeans had priests who spent their whole time in divination. The **Chinese** had court diviners who threw the yarrow stalks (**I Ching**). The ancient **Egyptians** had priests who did nothing but attempt to dream the future for the pharaohs.

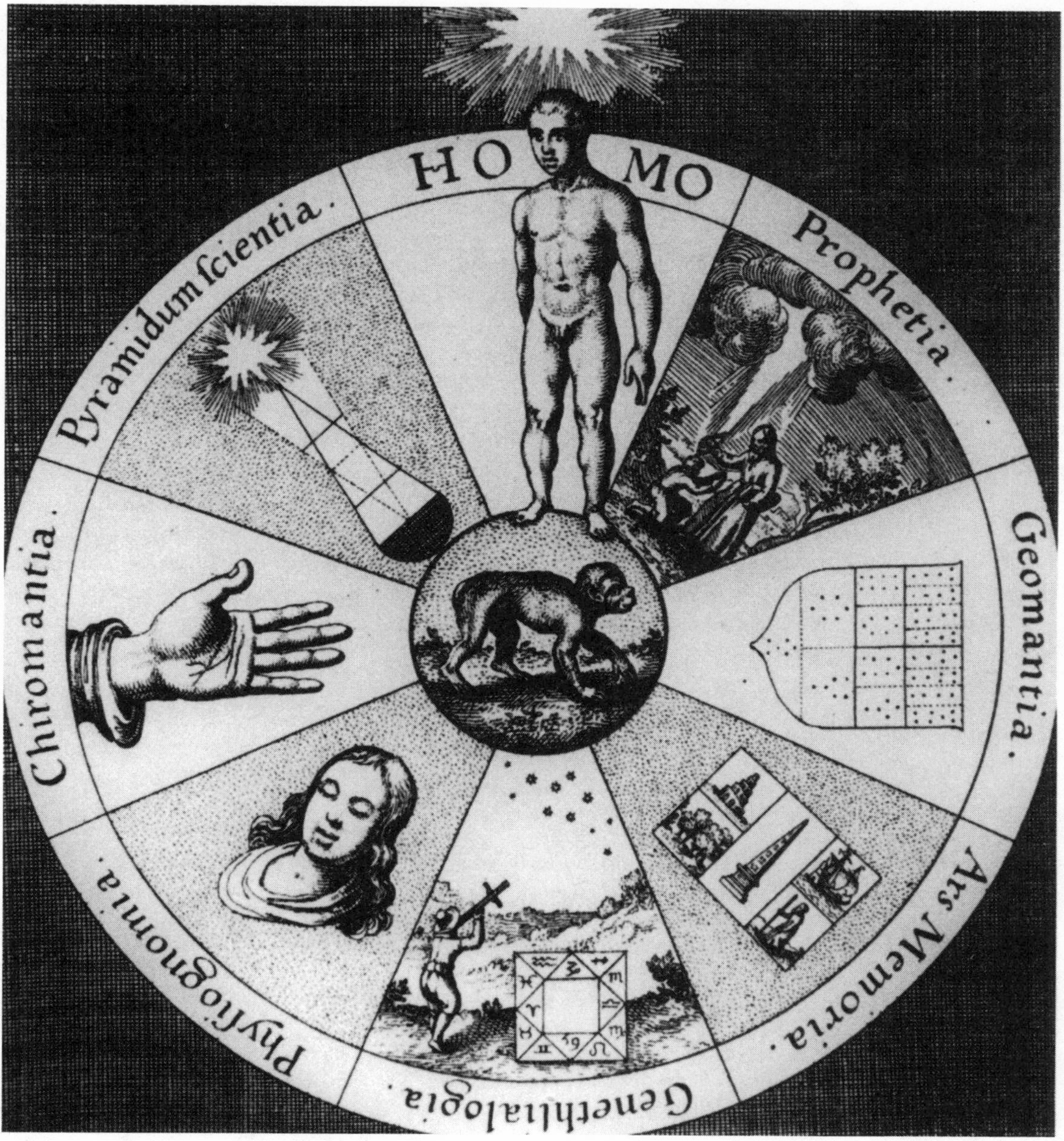

The eight divinatory arts, according to Robert Fludd (1574–1637), from *Utriusque Cosmi Maioris*, 1617. *Fortean Picture Library.*

There are possibly hundreds of methods of divining, ranging from observing dust (**abacomancy**) to observing the behavior of animals (**zoomancy**). **Pyromancy,** or gazing into the flames of a **fire** and "seeing" pictures, is something that many people have done, probably without realizing that they were indulging in divination. But whatever tools are used, they are only that—tools. They serve as a focal point for the psychic senses. It is the interpretation of what is seen that is important. The diviner must see and then interpret the signs, awakening in him or herself the psychic ability to do so and to recognize what is important to the person for whom the reading is being done. There may be warnings of danger, illness, or even death. In the case of the latter, it is up to the reader to determine how best to present what is seen so as not to alarm the querier.

Divination has, for thousands of years, been a tool of priests, **seers, shamans, astrologers,** medicine men, Gypsies, and wise men and women. It is frequently referred to in the **Bible.** Even when divination extended beyond strictly royal use, in many civilizations it was still only a special class of people who were allowed to divine. The ancient **Greeks** had the **oracles** and **sibyls;** the **Romans** had **augurers,** a special priest class. The ancient Egyptians also had special priests. The **Celts** had the Druids. Divination was done both for the individual and for a group, often being used to determine the fate of kingdoms and countries.

In its simplest form, divination can be gauging what the future may hold judging by the flight of a bird or birds. A complex form might be throwing down yarrow stalks to form hexagrams for the ancient Chinese practice of I Ching, or mathematically working through **numerology.** There are enough types of divination, ranging from very basic to very complex, that most people can achieve some sort of results with practice.

It has been said that divination falls into three categories: interpretation of natural phenomena, interpretation of artificial phenomena (such as the casting of lots), and direct communication with deity through such means as dreams, visions, or trance.

Sources:

Anderton, Bill. *Fortune Telling*. North Dighton North Dighton, MA: JG Press, 1996.

Buckland, Raymond. *A Pocket Guide to the Supernatural*. New York: Ace, 1969.

Foli, Prof. P. R. S. *Fortune-Telling by Cards*. Philadelphia: David McKay, 1902.

Gibson, Walter B. & Litzka R.*The Complete Illustrated Book of the Psychic Sciences*. New York: Doubleday, 1966.

Grand Orient (A. E. Waite). *The Complete Manual of Occult Divination*. London: William Rider, 1912.

Gray, Magda (ed.). *Fortune Telling*. London: Marshall Cavendish, 1974.

Guiley, Rosemary Ellen. *Harper's Encyclopedia of Mystical & Paranormal Experience*. San Francisco: HarperSanFrancisco, 1991.

DIVINING ROD *see* Dowsing; Rhabdomancy

Dixon, Jeane (1918–1997)

Jeane Dixon was one of the best-known, if controversial, **psychics** of recent times. It was her possible **prediction** of the death of President John F. Kennedy that catapulted her into the limelight.

She was born Jean Pinkert on January 3, 1918, in Medford, Wisconsin, to a wealthy lumber family. When she was still young, the family moved to California. At the age of eight she had her fortune told by a **Gypsy,** who said that she would become a famous seer. Jeane attended high school in Los Angeles and took some training toward being an actress and singer. In 1939, at twenty-one, she married James L. Dixon, an automobile dealer. They moved to Detroit and started a real estate business.

American psychic Jeane Dixon. *Fortean Picture Library.*

During World War II, Dixon entertained servicemen by making predictions. This she did through the Home Hospitality Committee, organized by Washington socialites. When the couple moved to Washington, D.C., they continued in real estate, and Dixon herself continued with her predictions.

A devout Roman Catholic, Dixon saw no problem with giving predictions, saying that "a revelation is something special. Sometimes two, three, or even four years go by without God granting me a revelation, and then some mornings I wake up and feel inspired and know that something great is going to happen." She goes on to say: "Another but a less certain way through which I receive knowledge of future events is what I call the 'psychic way.' Often when I meet people and shake their hands, I feel vibrations. But sensing and interpreting these vibrations, I can tell many things about that person. I 'see' even more if I have a chance to *touch* their hands with the tip of my right hand. My fingers are supersensitive, and many times a gentle touch enables me to pick up an individual channel of communication with eternity." She claimed she could see the past, present, and future.

It was **Ruth Montgomery**'s trumpeting of Jeane Dixon's claimed prediction of the assassination of President Kennedy that brought her most firmly to public attention. Ruth Montgomery was a newspaper political columnist who wrote the book *A Gift of* ***Prophesy:*** *The Phenomenal Jean Dixon,* published in 1965. The book sold more than three million copies and launched Dixon on the lecture circuit. But the basis of the book left many in doubt. In a 1956 article in *Parade* magazine, it was stated: "As for the 1960 election, Mrs. Dixon thinks it will be dominated by labor and won by a Democrat. But he will be assassinated or die in office." However, Dixon also said that the occurrence would "not necessarily [be] in his first term." At another time she made the statement: "During the 1960 election, I saw Richard Nixon as the winner." At that time, she went on to add that "John F. Kennedy would fail to win the presidency." She also predicted that World War III would start in 1958, that there would be a cure for

Sacred oak growing out of remains of the Temple of Zeus in Dodona, Greece. *Kristan Lawson/Fortean Picture Library.*

cancer found in 1967, and that the Russians would put the first man on the moon. In 1956 she said that Indian Prime Minister Nehru would be ousted from office, yet he served until his death in 1964. She also said that Fidel Castro would be overthrown.

However, Dixon did make some very dramatic, and accurate, predictions. She warned Carole Lombard not to travel by air just a few days before the actress died in a plane crash. She similarly predicted the death of Dag Hammarskjöld, also in a plane crash. But most of her predictions were couched in such a way that she could claim to have been right no matter what happened.

Sources:

Bringle, Mary. *Jeane Dixon: Prophet or Fraud?* New York: Tower Books, 1970.

Dixon, Jeane. *My Life and Prophesies*. New York: Bantam, 1970.

Montgomery, Ruth. *A Gift of Prophesy*. New York: Morrow, 1965.

http://www.cnn.com/SHOWBIZ/9701/26/dixon/.

http://www.news-journalonline.com/2002/Jun/10/NOTE1.htm.

DIZZINESS *see* Gyromancy

Dodona

The first prophetic center in **Greece** was at Dodona, in Epirus, Greece, where a shrine to Zeus was established. Contact was kept between this **oracle** center and that of the **Egyptian** god Amon's, in the Libyan desert, by using doves. The earliest mention of Dodona is by Homer in the *Odyssey*.

There was a **tree** at Dodona that was reputed to give oracles. This was done by interpreting the rustling of its leaves. Herodotus mentions priestesses there who gave the oracles. Plato classes them with the Delphic **prophetesses,** speaking of them prophesying while in ecstasy.

Thanks to excavations at the spot, it is known that questions were written on lead tablets and in such a form that a simple Yes or No would answer them. However, longer answers were sometimes given by the oracle.

Sources:

Encyclopedia Britannica. Chicago: William Benton, 1964.

Headon, Deirdre (ed.). *Quest for the Unknown—Charting the Future*. Pleasantville, NY: Reader's Digest, 1992.

Dog

(See also Ololygmancy)

In ancient **Mesopotamia,** it was believed that if a white dog lifted his leg against a man it indicated that hard times were coming. However, if it was a brown dog then the man would receive great happiness. In the Ozark region of Missouri and Arkansas there are many old superstitions still alive. One of these is to do with dogs and their ability to foresee events. It is believed that after a dog rolls on the ground in front of the main door to a house, when it gets up its nose will point in the direction from which a stranger is approaching. It is also believed that a person who does not make friends with a dog is a suspicious person. A dog chasing its tail and running around in circles signifies that that there is a storm brewing, either a wind storm or a storm of words.

Sources:

Randolph, Vance. *Ozark Superstitions*. New York: Dover, 1964.
Sagges, H. W. F. *Man, Myth & Magic: Mesopotamia*. London: BPC Publishing, 1970.

Dominoes

Many **Gypsies** have a superstition that they should not touch the "dotted ivories" on a Monday or a Friday. Also, they believe that the dominoes should not be consulted more than once in a **moon**'s span (once a month). They do, however, believe that the tiles are very **prophetic.** In some ways they are read in a similar way to **dice.** One thing that is unique about dominoes is that they can be used to tell the fortune of more than one person at a time.

Generally speaking, all sixes are connected with good luck. Fives generally refer to jobs and careers. Fours deal with financial matters. Threes are connected to love. Twos refer to family and close friends. Ones indicate journeys to be taken. All blanks refer directly to the querier.

One way to give a very quick reading is for the dominoes to be spread out face down and thoroughly mixed. Up to three people may each draw three dominoes, which they place face up in a line, horizontally, in front of them. The tile on the left represents the past; that in the center, the present; and that on the right, the future. With just the broad meanings given above, a general reading can be given. For example, if the drawn dominoes are Two/Three, One/Five, and Four/Blank, then it could be said that in the past the querier had a number of very close friends and family, with much love around. At present, there is some travel to be undertaken, connected with his or her employment. And in the future, there are going to be some financial matters that will affect the querier personally.

More detailed meanings need to be considered, however. These are shown in the "doubles":

Double Six: The marriage of the querier. If already married, then there will be good fortune coming as a result of that marriage.
Double Five: A job promotion to a better-paid, higher position.
Double Four: Unexpected money coming in a dramatic way.

Double Three: The querier will unexpectedly fall in love.

Double Two: There will be new friends who will become close and dear.

Double One: A wonderful, and very enjoyable, vacation journey is on its way.

Double Blank: Extreme caution needs to be exercised. This domino can be a serious warning.

Apart from these short meanings, much longer interpretations can be read from just one of the dominoes. Many diviners will therefore have the querier pick only one. (Again, in this way, many people can pick a tile from the full deck at the same time.) The upturned dominoes have the following meanings, for this more in-depth **divination:**

Double Six: A happy marriage, with children. Riches by speculation. This is not a good tile for farmers so far as crops are concerned, but it does indicate a rise in land values.

Six/Five: If you're looking for a job, persevering will bring you to a good one. Similarly, if you are looking for love, don't be discouraged by rebuffs; success awaits you. This tile indicates luck in purchasing real estate but the possibility of being cheated buying jewelry, silverware, or a watch. If you are waiting on a possible inheritance, there's a good chance you will get it.

Six/Four: Early marriage followed by much happiness. Children will be equally divided between boys and girls. When grown, they will all leave home early—the girls to get married and the boys to jobs. Neither wealth nor poverty is indicated with this tile.

Six/Three: A domino for constancy and affection. It shows an early marriage with much happiness and no troubles to mar it. There will also be honors and riches. There is a slight possibility of death in middle age but, if you survive that, you will live to a ripe old age.

Six/Two: Excellent domino for lovers, foretelling a happy marriage. Those looking for luck in business will find more profits than they expected. However, if there are any dishonest schemes, they will be "rewarded" with disaster.

Six/One: To young married people, this tile indicates that they will be better off in later life than they are now. It can also indicate that there will be a second marriage that will be better than the first.

Six/Blank: This tile is an indicator of death to someone near to you, be it a close friend or an acquaintance. It may also indicate the death of an animal.

Double Five: This is lucky in all ways: finances, job, marriage. It does not mean you will become rich, but it does signify good luck.

Five/Four: This is not a good tile where money is concerned. If you have money, you may lose it or you may find that you owe more than you realized.

Five/Three: You will never be poor, but you may never be rich. You will always have sufficient. If you already have money, you will not gain much more. It indicates much the same where love and sex is concerned—status quo.

Five/Two: This is a reasonably fair card for women but not so for men. If in love, or married, the woman may turn out to have a short temper. A marriage may turn out to appear happy and successful on the outside but will deteriorate and be unhappy in the end. Financial speculation for a man will not be successful.

Five/One: For those fond of excitement, this is a good tile. There is the possibility of an invitation to an event that will thrill you. If money is expected, there will be disappointment. A young woman may find an admirer who is rich but rough. She will discard him and marry another.

Five/Blank: To a man, this tile implies that there is a certain amount of dishonesty present, with a tendency to gambling or sex. To a woman, this indicates an unhappy love affair.

Double Four: A good, smooth sign for lovers, farmers, and all laborers. But for professional people this indicates hard times to come. There is also a wedding in the near future.

Four/Three: Those who turn this tile will marry young, live happily, and will not have more than one child. There is neither poverty nor riches here. Married persons who have children already will face the possibility of a long separation and even a second marriage.

Four/Two: There will be a change in your circumstances, which could be for the better or for the worse. It may be something slight or something that will be very traumatic. If you have offended anyone dear to you, this tile shows that you will soon make up with them.

Four/One: Referring to married couples, the more children in the marriage, the more the financial position will deteriorate. Those who are unmarried may soon get married, with the same results. If there are no children, the bank account will grow.

Four/Blank: This is an unfortunate tile for lovers. It foretells arguments and quarrels; possibly separations. If you should trust a friend with a secret, the secret will not be kept. There is also an indication that your partner is a believer in the occult.

Double Three: Nothing to do with love or matrimony but does indicate the accumulation of riches. There is no indication of any unhappiness associated with the buildup of wealth.

Three/Two: This is a good tile for the following: love-making, marriage, recovery of stolen property, travel, speculation, collecting on a debt, planting a crop. It is, however, a bad tile for gamblers.

Three/One: A young woman turning this tile will be likely to lose her virginity. A married woman will be approached by a man with a view to having an affair. For a man, this foretells the loss of money through illicit sex. It is not a favorable domino for anyone.

Three/Blank: Your sweetheart is artful and deceitful. If you are married, the wife will be shrewish and vain; the husband will be dull, slow, and not very bright. This tile may also indicate that you will be invited to a party where you will be attracted to someone, but it will end with a violent quarrel.

Double Two: Success in love matters and much happiness. Success in any undertaking. No great riches but there will be comfort.

Two/One: A woman will marry young and her husband will die young, leaving her wealth and property. She will later remarry. A man will have a life of luxury, will never marry, but will be a favorite of the ladies. Not a good tile for business people, since it foretells losses by failures.

Two/Blank: Poverty and bad luck. This is a tile of good luck for thieves and dishonest people, indicating success in shady dealings. In reference to any possible journey, it indicates a safe passage.

Double One: Affectionate constancy and happiness in the married state. This is an excellent tile to turn, both for lovers and for married people.

Double Blank: The worst tile of the whole set. Bad luck to everyone except the dishonest and unscrupulous, for whom it means rewards. Unfavorable for love and business.

The first record of dominoes comes from twelfth-century **China.** They were probably used there for divination rather than for gaming. One theory is that they were designed to reflect all the possible throws of two dice (Chinese dominoes have no blanks). They are still widely used in Korea and **India** today. It is possible, though not certain, that they made their way to the West from China. Dominoes were certainly found in France, Italy, and England by the middle of the eighteenth century.

Sources:
Buckland, Raymond. *Secrets of Gypsy Fortunetelling*. St. Paul, MN: Llewellyn, 1988.
Encyclopedia Britannica. Chicago: William Benton, 1964.
Gibson, Walter B. & Litzka R. *The Complete Illustrated Book of the Psychic Sciences*. New York: Doubleday, 1966.
Gypsy Queen, A. *Zingara Fortune Teller*. Philadelphia: David McKay, 1901.

DONKEY ***see*** **Cephalomancy**

DOTS ***see*** **Geomancy**

Dowsing

Dowsing is a branch of **rhabdomancy.** It primarily involves using a largely unconscious human response in order to make contact with **water,** oil, metal, minerals, cables, pipes, and other underground materials. The term "dowsing" is usually only applied to searching for non-living materials. It is distinct from **radiesthesia,** which, although also used for dowsing, can be applied to finding lost people and objects, health diagnosis, and many other applications. Dowsers use rods, sticks, and **pendula,** though the traditional tool is a Y-shaped wooden stick. Radiesthetists favor the pendulum.

Divining rods were used by the Greeks, Romans, Persians, and Scythians. In the **Bible** Moses dowsed for water in the desert, using his staff as a divining rod (Exodus 17; Numbers 20). Marco Polo found rods in use throughout the orient in the late thirteenth century. Georg Agricola gave the first printed description of a dowsing, or divining, rod in his book *De re metallica* (Basel, 1556). His interest was primarily with mining and in locating minerals, but the techniques he describes are the same as those used for water divining or water witching. A well-known illustration from his book

Hamish Miller dowsing in Cornwall. ***Paul Broadhurst/Fortean Picture Library.***

shows a variety of men both digging and walking about with Y-shaped rods in their hands. One man is in the act of cutting a forked branch from a tree. In Sebastian Münster's *Cosmographia universalis* (Basel, 1544) is another illustration of a man divining with a forked stick and showing a cross-section of the ground beneath him, where miners are at work. There is a bas relief in the Shantung Province of **China** showing Yu, a "master of the science of the earth and in those matters concerning water veins and springs." He is shown holding a forked instrument.

The hazel twig seems to have been the favorite, especially for water, but for finding metals popular woods were: hazel for silver, iron and steel for gold, ash for copper, and pitch pine for lead and tin. Other popular general purpose sticks are of ash, rowan or willow. The method is for the operator to hold the two ends in his or her hands and walk over the area thought to be the probable source for the water or mineral. As the operator crosses the underground source, the twig twists in the hands, often with such force that any bark may be stripped from the wood.

Modern dowsers have developed such sensitivity and skill that they are able to measure the actual depth at which the substance will be found and, in the case of water, the rate of flow. According to the **British Society of Dowsers,** although no thorough scientific explanations for dowsing have yet been found, it is generally acknowledged that there is some correlation between the dowsing reaction and changes in the magnetic flux of the site being dowsed. German scientist Baron Karl von Reichenbach, in 1910, said that the movement of the rod was due to earth force fields sending out radiations and vibrations that are picked up by the dowser.

As well as branches, many dowsers today use tools as varied as bent wire coat-hangers, pendula (with cavities for a "witness"—samples of what is being sought), and commercially produced, swinging rods especially designed for the job. Many modern well-drilling companies employ a dowser on their force. Some even guarantee that if they can't find water, there will be no charge.

Some dowsers will work with a map before going out to the actual site. A finely pointed pendulum is used for this type of dowsing. The map may be a commercial one or a rough sketch map drawn by the dowser or the person wanting the water. Dowsers have been widely employed around the world. The Government of India had an official water diviner who, between 1925 and 1930, traveled thousands of miles and located numerous wells and bore holes. In more recent years, the British Society of Dowsers had one of their experts go to India where, in southern India, he sited boreholes for more than 1,800 previously dry villages.

As with any form of psychic skill, everyone has within them the inherent ability to dowse. But, again as with any other psychic skill, it is by practice and constant use that that skill is developed. As with so much in the field of psychic development, young children seem to be able to draw upon the skill very easily and naturally. To try dowsing, cut two lengths from a wire coat-hanger and bend each of them into an L-shape. Hold the short legs of the L, with the longer legs pointing away from you at an angle parallel with the ground and parallel to each other. Hold the wires with just sufficient pressure to keep them pointing straight ahead and not waving about uncontrollably. If you find it difficult to keep the ends from swinging wildly, angle down the ends just a little, so that they stabilize. Then walk forward slowly over the ground, concentrating on water (or whatever is being sought; it is probably best to start out with water). As you reach the point where there is water, the two ends will swing in toward one another, finally crossing. If you back up, they will gradually uncross. Mark the ground where they cross and then repeat the procedure from a different direction—perhaps from opposite where you were. You will find that the pointers will again swing together when you reach that point. If there is a water line running along underground, you will find that if you are walking parallel with it, but to (for example) the right of it, the two pointers will both swing toward the left, to point to the water pipe source.

One rough method for judging the depth of the water is to walk away from the target point to where the pointers fully uncross. That distance, from the target to the uncrossing point, is equal to the depth of the water. There is an individualism to the dowsing process, so you may find certain idiosyncrasies regarding how the pointers react. Over a period of time these will become apparent and will remain constant.

Sources:

De Givry, Grillot. *A Pictorial Anthology of Witchcraft, Magic & Alchemy.* London: Spottiswoode, Ballantyne, 1931.

Guiley, Rosemary Ellen. *Harper's Encyclopedia of Mystical & Paranormal Experience*. San Francisco: HarperSanFrancisco 1991.
http://www.britishdowsers.org/.
Maury, Marguerite. *How to Dowse, Experimental and Practical Radiesthesia*. London: Bell, 1953.
Mermet, Abbé. *Principles and Practice of Radiesthesia*. London: Watkins, 1975.
Pike, S. N. *Water-Divining*. London: Research Publications, 1945.
Shepard, Leslie A. (ed.). *Encyclopedia of Occultism & Parapsychology*. New York: Avon, 1978.

DREAMS *see* **Oneiromancy**

DRESS, MANNER OF *see* **Stolisomancy**

Dririmancy; Drymimancy

When there was a ritual sacrifice of an animal (or of a human), the way in which the blood dripped from the altar was often considered by the priest/**soothsayer.** Divining in this way was known as dririmancy. This form of divination might also be employed on the battle field. Dririmancy was a form of **hæmatomancy.**

DRUIDS *see* **Celts**

DRYMOMANCY *see* **Dririmancy**

DUNG, SEEDS EMBEDDED IN *see* **Stercomancy**

Dunne, John William (1875–1949)

John William Dunne put forward a theory about the nature of **dreams** and the possibility of being able to see past, present, and future through experiencing time on different levels.

Dunne was the son of General Sir John Hart Dunne. He served in the Boer War and, in World War I, designed Britain's first military aircraft. He was a fellow designer of S. F. Cody and believed that the best way to achieve stability in flight was with a V-wing tailless configuration. With official support, he built an airplane designated D1. It flew, as a glider, in 1907. Two years later it was flown as a powered biplane and was so successful that he could fly it "hands off" while he sat back and wrote his report!

Dunne had been interested in dreams from as early as 1899, at which time he started recording his own dreams. In late 1916 he had a dream so strange and moving that he recorded it in great detail. It was of an explosion in a London bomb factory. In January 1917 there was just such an explosion, killing seventy-three workers and injuring more than one thousand others. Dunne worked out a theory that human beings experience time on several different levels. One of those levels allows the individual to see backward to the past and forward to the future. He wrote of this theory in a book called *Experiment with Time* (London, 1927). After its publication Dunne started receiving hundreds of letters from people who had also had **prophetic** dreams. In 1934 he followed up with another book, *The Serial Universe*, and in 1938 with *The New Immortality*. He referred to his first book as "the first scientific argument for human immortality." His theories influenced such writers as J. B. Priestley and W. Somerset Maugham.

Sources:

Fishley, Margaret. *The Supernatural*. London: Aldus, 1976.

Taylor, John W. R. A *Picture History of Flight*. London: Hulton Press, 1955.

E

EGGS ***see*** **Oomancy; Ovomancy**

EGYPTIANS, ANCIENT

In ancient Egypt there were various orders of priests, ranked according to their particular office. The priest who offered sacrifice and libation in the temple was the highest of the priests and was generally called the **prophet.** He dressed in a leopard skin fitted over his linen robes. He was a very eminent personage and sometimes carried a special name. For example, the high Theban pontiff was "First Prophet of Amon in Thebes," while the one in Heliopolis was "He who is able to see the Great God" (later changed to "The great one with visions of the god Re"). The duty of the prophet was to be well versed in all religious matters, the laws, the worship of the gods, and the discipline of the whole order of the priesthood. He presided over the temple and the sacred rites.

Other priests were known as *horologues* (priest-timekeepers) and **astrologers.** The astrologers had to know the mythological calendar and to be able to explain all the important dates. Each day of the year was labeled as either good, neutral, or bad, according to events of the past that had occurred on those days. In magical papyri there can be found instructions not to perform certain ceremonies on particular days, since hostile powers would be present and prevent the sought-after outcome. In the last epochs of the Egyptian civilization, the astrologer-priests tied in the **destiny** of every person to the cosmic circumstances of his or her birth, drawing a **horoscope** to show the astral influences. However, in Egypt astrology did not hold the place that it did in Babylonia. References made to its use were few and meager.

Priests known as *pastophores* were bearers of sacred objects and slayers of sacrificial beasts. Then there were those the Greeks called the *oneirocrites*, who interpreted **dreams.** For a period there was a custom of spending a night in the temple in order to receive guidance from the gods. This guidance came in the guise of dreams, which had

In ancient Egypt there were various orders of priests and prophets. ***Fortean Picture Library.***

to be interpreted by the oneirocrites. But the Egyptians believed that even without sleeping in a temple, people could learn the will of the gods through dreams, and great importance was attached to dreams that included figures of the gods. The skill to interpret dreams was cherished. There are many examples, in the Egyptian texts, of important dreams that were interpreted by the priests. Those of Thothmes IV, king of Egypt c. 1450 BCE, and of Nut-Amen, king of the Eastern Sudan and Egypt c.670 BCE, are especially notable.

Since prophetic dreams were desired, the priests devised methods to encourage them. This included the drawing of magical pictures and the reciting of magical words. Papyrus No. 122, in the British Museum, contains the lines:

> To obtain a vision from Bes. Make a drawing of Bes, as shown below, on your left hand, and envelope your hand in a strip of black cloth that has been consecrated to Isis and lie down to sleep without speaking a word, even in answer to a question. Wind the remainder of the cloth round your neck. The ink with which you write must be composed of the blood of a cow, the blood of a white dove, fresh frankincense, myrrh, black writing ink, cinnabar, mulberry juice, rain water, and the juice of wormwood and vetch. With this write your petition before the setting sun, saying: "Send the truthful seer out of the holy shrine, I beseech thee, Lampsuer, Sumarta, Baribas, Dardalam, Iorlex: O Lord send the sacred deity Anuth, Antuh, Salbana, Chambré, Breïth, now, now, quickly, quickly. Come in this very night."

Here is another example, from the same papyrus:

> To procure dreams: Take a clean linen bag and write upon it the name given below. Fold it up and make it into a lamp wick, and set it alight, pouring pure oil over it. The word to be written is this: "Armiuth, Lailamchoüch, Arsenophrephren, Phtha, Archentechtha." Then in the evening, when you are going to bed, which you must do without touching food, do thus. Approach the lamp and repeat seven times the formula given below: then extinguish it and lie down to sleep. The formula is this: "Sachmu . . . epaëma Ligotereënch: the Æon, the Thunderer, Thou that hast swallowed the snake and dost exhaust the **moon,** and dost raise up the orb of the sun in his season, Chthetho is thy name; I require, O lord of the gods, Seth, Chreps, give me the information that I desire."

Sources:

Budge, Sir E. A. Wallis. *Egyptian Magic*. New York: Bell Publishing, 1991.
Rawlinson, George. *History of Ancient Egypt*. New York: Dodd, Mead & Company, 1881.
Sauneron, Serge. *The Priests of Ancient Egypt*. New York: Grove Press, 1960.
Wilkinson, Sir J. Gardner. *The Ancient Egyptians: Their Life and Customs*. New York: Crescent Books, 1988.

EMANATIONS *see* Aura

EMONOMANCY *see* Demonomancy

EMPYROMANCY

Divination using objects placed in a sacrificial fire. After burning, they would be inspected to see what shapes they had assumed and how the form had changed.

This name is also sometimes applied to divining from the smoke that comes from burning laurel and other sacred leaves (a form of **capnomancy**). The smoke would be interpreted according to its volume, density, and the way in which it ascended. The direction it moved would be important, as would the consistency of it: whether it was continuous or sporadic, for example. Broiling, swirling, thick smoke might indicate troubles and problems, while thin, wispy smoke could indicate slight activity of an inconsequential nature. If the smoke assumed unusual shapes, this too would be significant. Empyromancy was favored by the Pythagoreans, who would not practice **haruspicy** because of their dislike of bloodshed.

Sources:

Rakoczi, Basil Ivan. *Man, Myth & Magic*. London: BPC Publishing, 1970.

Encausse, Gérard Anaclet Vincent—"Papus" (1865–1916)

Encausse was born at La Coruña in Spain on July 13, 1865. His mother was Spanish but his father, Louis, was a French pharmacist. When Gérard was four, the family moved to France and he was educated in Paris. As he grew up, Encausse spent a lot of time at the Bibliothèque Nationale, where he studied alchemy, **tarot,** the **Qabbalah,** and magic. He was particularly intrigued by the writings of Eliphas Lévi. Completing his education, Encausse became a physician. He received his doctor of medicine degree from the University of Paris in 1894.

Encausse joined the French Theosophical Society but later left it because of its emphasis on Far Eastern material. In 1888 he published his first work, *Traité élémentaire de science occulte* (*Elementary Treatise on Occult Science*), which he wrote under the name "Papus." He took the name from Eliphas Lévi's *Nuctemeron of Apollonius of Tyana* (a supplement to his *Dogme et Rituel de la Haute Magie*). The name meant "physician."

That same year Encausse and his friend Lucien Chamuel founded the Librarie du Merveilleux, and started its monthly journal *L'Initiation*, which continued for twenty-six years. The year 1888 proved eventful for Encausse. In that year he also joined the Marquis Stanislas de Guaita, de Guaita's secretary Oswald Wirth (a disciple of Lévi), Joséphin Péladan, and the Marquis Joseph Alexandre Saint-Yves d'Alveydre (1842–1910); together they founded the Kabbalistic Order of the Rose-Croix. Encausse also founded the Independent Group for Esoteric Studies.

In May of 1891, in the midst of the "magical wars" between de Guita and his rival the Abbé Boullan, Encausse was involved in a saber duel with Jules Bois, a writer who had attacked de Guaita in print. Both Encausse and Bois were injured in the duel, neither of them badly. Later in the year Encausse founded yet another organization, this one called *l'Ordre des Supérieurs Inconmnus*, commonly known as the Order of the Martinists, which was based on the teachings of Louis Claude de Saint-Martin (1743–1803). This organization became a primary focus for Encausse and is still in operation today.

In 1897, after the death of de Guaita, Encausse became the head of the Kabbalistic Order of the Rose-Croix. Four years earlier he had also been consecrated as a bishop of *l'Église Gnostique de France* and in 1895 was one of the synod of three bishops who took over control of this French Gnostic Church. In March of 1895 he also joined the Ahathoor Temple of the Golden Dawn, in Paris.

Encausse is probably best known for his works on the tarot. In 1889 his *Le tarot des bohemians* (*The Tarot of the Gypsies*) appeared, and in 1909 his *Le tarot divinatoire* (*The **Divinatory** Tarot*). His other works were *Traité méthodique de science occulte* (1891), *Traité méthodique de magie pratique* (1932) and *Le science des nombres* (1934). He died of tuberculosis while serving in a military hospital in World War I, on October 25, 1916. Three of his later books were edited by his son, Philippe Encausse.

Sources:

Cavendish, Richard (ed.). *Encyclopedia of the Unexplained*. London: Routledge & Kegan Paul, 1974.

Crow, W. B. *A History of Magic, Witchcraft and Occultism*. London: Aquarian Press, 1968.

Papus. *The Tarot of the Bohemians: Absolute Key to Occult Science*. New York: Arcanum Books, 1958.

Shepard, Leslie A. (ed.). *Encyclopedia of Occultism & Parapsychology*. New York: Avon, 1978.

http://www.hermetic.com/sabazius/papus.htm.

Endor, Woman of

(See also Sciomancy)

In the **Bible** there is reference to "the woman of Endor" (Samuel 1:28), described as "A woman that hath a familiar spirit at Endor." Endor is a small hamlet on the northern slope of a hill, four miles south of Mount Tabor. Saul, despite the fact that he had tried to purge the land of her sort, went to consult her on the eve of the battle of Bilboa because he was afraid of the massed armies of the Philistines. She immediately recognized him despite his disguise, but Saul assured her he would cause her no harm. The woman of Endor—who was actually no more than a **spiritualist medium**—was able to connect Saul with the spirit of Samuel. She described to Saul, in detail, what she saw **clairvoyantly.**

In the King James translation of the Bible, James headed the chapter: "Saul, having destroyed all the witches, and now in his fear forsaken of God, seeketh to a witch," yet nowhere in the actual passages is the word "witch" used. The woman is simply described as having a "familiar spirit," and there is no physical description of her, of her age, or of her house. Yet later writers continue to refer to her as a witch and depict her as an old hag living in a hovel. Indeed, Montague Summers, a supposed "authority" on witchcraft, says, "In a paroxysm of rage and fear the haggard crone turned to him (Saul) and shrieked out: 'Why hast thou deceived me?'" Where he gets this from we do not know. Reginald Scott, as early as 1584, doubted the existence of witches and suggested that Saul actually saw nothing but "an illusion or cozenage."

Sources:

Buckland, Raymond. *The Witch Book: The Encyclopedia of Witchcraft, Wicca, and Neo-paganism*. Detroit: Visible Ink Press, 2002.

Scot, Reginald. *Discoverie of Witchcraft*. London, 1584.

Summers, Montague. *The History of Witchcraft and Demonology*. University Books, 1956.

ENOPTRMANCY ***see*** **Catoptromacy**

Saul consults the Woman of Endor, who raised Samuel's ghost. ***Fortean Picture Library.***

ENTRAILS *see* **Anthropomancy (human); Extispicy; Haruspication (animal)**

EROMANCY; EROMANTY *see* **Aeromancy**

ETRUSCANS

Like the Maya of **Mexico,** the Etruscans of ancient Italy held sacred the role of diviner-priest, whose prognostications were considered to represent the destiny of the people.

The diviners of the Etruscan civilization used **haruspication** to foretell the future. There is an extant bronze, dating from about the fifth century BCE, decorated with the scene of an Etruscan priest examining the entrails of a sacrificed animal. Generally it was the liver that was examined, though other organs might also be studied.

Dropping hot lead or tin into water was another method occasionally employed by the Etruscans in a version of **molybdomancy,** much like **ceromancy.** Charles Godfrey Leland gives details of how the Etruscan method proceeded: "The ceremony consisted of melting the lead (wax was also used), dropping it into water, and inferring future events from its shapes. Then these were taken to bed by the person for whom the **oracle** was destined, when, by the influence of the image, a **dream** would confirm what its appearance predicted." As Leland points out, many other people make use of varieties of ceromancy, but few go on to take the figure to bed in order to invoke dreams. This seems to be a peculiarly Etruscan practice.

Akin to dropping the molten metal into **water** is the Etruscan practice of dropping an egg into water, again described by Leland: "Take a glass of water at midnight exactly. Let fall into it the white of an egg, and say:

> *Faccio quest' uovo,*
> Perche che tu maladetta strega
> La fortuna tu possa darmi
> Un spiegazione
> Sopra questo uovo,
> Te lo lascio fuori di finestra
> Venti Quattro ore
> Chet u abbia il tempo
> Di farmi vedere
> La mia fortuna!
> I show this egg, curst witch, to thee,
> That I in turn my fate may see.
> For a day at thy command,
> On the window it shall stand,
> That my fortune I may know.
>
> "After twenty-four hours consider it closely. If it shall have taken the form of a burying-ground, it means a death in the family; if it shows a church and a priest giving the benediction, it means a wedding. Stars presage happiness. And if the lineaments of any person can be traced, it means good fortune from that particular person."

The Etruscans also practiced divination by oil. Three small drops of oil were allowed to drop into a glass of water. If they combined immediately, it was a good omen or an affirmative answer to a question. If the three drops remained apart, it was a negative sign. If the negative was received, then there was a chance to change it by dropping a teaspoonful of salt into the glass. If the oil then turned a whitish color, all would go well.

Sources:

Leland, Charles Godfrey. *Etruscan Magic & Occult Remedies*. New York: University Books, 1963.
Spence, Lewis. *An Encyclopedia of the Occult*. London: George Routledge & Sons, 1920.

EXTISPICY; EXTISPEX

(See also Haruspication)

Akin to **haruspicy,** extispicy is the act of studying the entrails of sacrificed animals and humans for the purposes of **augury.** The extispex (*pl.* extispices) was the one whose duty it was to do the inspection. *Chambers's Cyclopædia of English Literature* of 1751 states the following: "extispex: In Italy the first extispices were the Etrurians." In Sir Thomas Urquhart's *The Third Book of the Works of Mr. Francis Rabelais* (London, 1693) it says: "Will you have a trial of your fortune by the art of aruspiciny? By augury? Or by extispicine?"

Sources:

Oxford English Dictionary. Oxford: Clarendon Press, 1989.

EXTRASENSORY PERCEPTION

Extrasensory Perception, **PSI,** paragnosis, or ESP as it is more generally known, is accepted by many as fact. This is mainly due to the work of Dr. **Joseph Banks Rhine,** one of the pioneers of parapsychology. Thanks should also go to Dr. **Samuel George Soal,** who for many years conducted parapsychological studies in **mediumship** in its many forms and statistical experiments in telepathy, in England. In later years Soal was found guilty of fraud in some of his telepathic experiments, be it conscious or unconscious. This certainly tarnished his image, yet he had done outstanding work in the field for decades.

Serious investigation of possible "thought transference" dates from the late nineteenth century, when a number of experiments were conducted in England by Mrs. A. Verrall and C. P. Sanger. By the late 1920s, in similar experiments, Miss I. Jephson and R. A. Fisher had found that the everyday playing cards previously relied upon were not ideal for testing purposes. This led to the introduction of the **Zener** deck consisting of twenty-five cards—five each of five different designs. The black-and-white designs were very basic: circle, square, cross, star, and wavy lines. Today these cards are used almost exclusively for testing ESP.

The point of ESP testing is to ascertain whether or not a person can know what is in another person's mind a greater number of times than could be explained purely by chance. With one person looking at the twenty-five Zener cards, it is known that a second person would guess correctly which card was being looked at five times out of the twenty-five, if it was simply by chance. Going through the deck a number of times, the *average* correct guesses would be five per twenty-five cards. Scores above that would, then, be notable. As an example of what has been achieved in such tests, a Hubert E. Pearce Jr., when tested at Duke University guessed correctly 3,746 cards out of 10,300. In London, B. Shackleton guessed correctly 1,101 cards out of 3,789. Shackleton guessed not the actual card being looked at, but the card that was going to be looked at next! Such scores, carried out in laboratory conditions, would seem to prove beyond doubt that extrasensory perception is a fact.

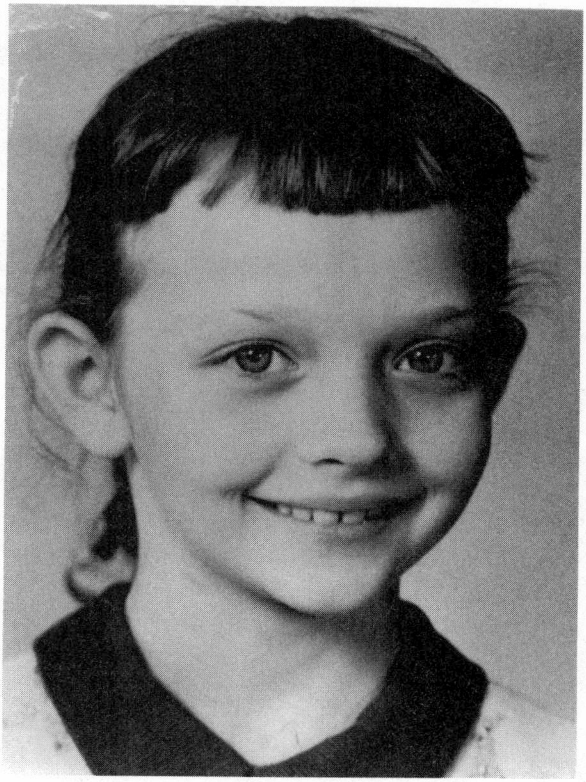

In one reported case of ESP, Joicey Hurth, five years old in 1955, followed her father and brother to the movies in Cedarburg, Wisconsin. Her mother suddenly felt Joicey had had an accident, rang the theater, and was told that Joicey had been hit by a car. *Fortean Picture Library.*

If two people sit down facing one another at opposite sides of a room, with one holding the cards in front while the other tries to guess which card is being looked at, this would not be "laboratory conditions." No matter how impressive the scores, they would not be considered seriously. Many minor factors could contribute to the guesser's choices. The cards may have odd marks, such as spots, specks, scratches, or other visual clues, on their backs. If only unconsciously, these could help the guesser differentiate one card from another. Another factor might be the face of the sender. Again, an unconscious facial movement might trigger the choices. For the results to be truly under laboratory conditions, many precautions must be taken. The two participants must not be in the same room. Moving on from one card to the next should be signaled by a flashing light or a buzzer. Even the cards should not be picked by the sender; they should be shuffled by a machine and put into truly random order. Every possible precaution should be taken, and even then, if your mind is set against it, you can discount the results. If a person guesses, for example, 8,000 correct cards out of 10,000 (astronomical odds against chance), who is to say that if they went on to try another 10,000 they might not be so far off that the overall score would be no more than chance? Just where is the line drawn?

Without going to such lengths, there are simple experiments, described below, that can be done at home to test your ESP. For these you can use Zener cards, ordinary playing cards, or just plain pencil and paper.

In the laboratory, the two people are termed the "agent" and "percipient"; at home we'll call them simply "sender" and "receiver." It should be remembered, by the way, that the person concentrating to send the image has just as important a role as the person trying to pick up the image.

Start with the two people in the same room, on opposite sides, with their backs to one another. A curtain or screen can be placed between the two. In front of the receiver should be a picture of each of the cards: circle, square, cross, star, and wavy lines. In addition to the sender and receiver, there should be a supervisor. Records are all important in any aspect of parapsychology and especially so in testing ESP. The supervisor takes a deck of Zener cards, shuffles them, and then makes note of the order of the cards (on a sheet of paper that is folded and put away) before passing them, face down, to the sender. At the word "start" from the supervisor, the sender turns up the top card and concentrates on it, thinking hard about the design. The receiver points, without speaking, to the design he thinks it is. The supervisor records the guess and calls for the next card. (An alternate method, without supervisor, is for the receiver to write down his or her guess at each card and to signal, with a ring of a bell, to move on to the next card.) This is continued through all twenty-five cards. The supervisor will then reshuffle, note the order, and pass them back to the sender for another run through. The deck is gone through a number of times in this way before checking any scores. The fact that the record of the cards' order is kept in the pocket of the supervisor ensures that the receiver is not "picking up" from anyone other than the sender.

Checking the score for one run might give results similar to this:

Card	**Guess**
Square	Square
Wavy lines	Star
Circle	Cross
Circle	Wavy lines
Cross	Circle
Square	Star
Star	Star
Wavy lines	Cross
Star	Square
Square	Wavy Lines
Star	Star
Circle	Circle
Square	Circle
Cross	Square
Circle	Cross
Wavy lines	Wavy lines
Star	Square
Circle	Circle
Cross	Cross
Cross	Wavy lines
Wavy lines	Star
Square	Square
Star	Circle
Wavy lines	Cross
Cross	Wavy lines

This shows a total of eight correct guesses out of twenty-five. Although above what would be expected by chance, it doesn't mean much at the moment. The next run might produce only three correct out of twenty-five. This is why it is important to do as many runs as possible. The more that are done; the truer the picture.

But suppose that on checking it was found that there was a result like this:

Card	**Guess**
Square	Wavy lines
Wavy line	Circle
Cross	Wavy lines
Circle	Cross
Circle	Star
Square	Circle
Star	Square
Wavy lines	Star
Star	Wavy lines
Square	Cross
Star	Square
Circle	Square
Square	Circle
Cross	Star
Circle	Cross
Wavy lines	Circle
Star	Wavy lines
Circle	Cross
Cross	Star
Cross	Cross
Wavy lines	Wavy lines
Square	Square
Star	Square
Wavy lines	Star
Cross	Circle

This gives a total of only three correct guesses out of twenty-five. On the face of it this is not at all impressive. But look at the results again. The second card looked at was Wavy lines. The receiver incorrectly guessed a Circle. But when the next card, a Cross, was studied, the receiver came up with the Wavy lines. The guess was one card behind. Similarly, the sixth card was a Square against the seventh guess of a Square; the seventh card was a Star, against the eighth guess of a Star. *Each guess was one card behind*. Looking at the full run again, and comparing "second" to the drawn cards, there is a score of twelve correct out of twenty-five . . . very much more impressive. Similarly, as in the above-quoted example of B. Shackleton's guesses, the receiver may guess *ahead* of the sender, knowing what is going to be turned up next. Or it could be two behind or two ahead. Or even in completely reverse order! But again, these results should not be studied alone but should be part of a large number of runs through the deck, with the results studied in total.

Actually, getting very low scores consistently is significant. A theory is that the unconscious is trying to avoid revealing the possession of E.S.P. and in so doing is purposefully giving incorrect guesses.

The above home experiment could—in fact should—be tried again but with stricter limitations. The sender and receiver should be in separate rooms, with the advance of cards signaled by bell or by running a line of wire with a small bulb that can be flashed. An even greater challenge and precaution would have the two participants in different houses with the contact by telephone or similar object.

A further, and often significant, aspect of the receiver's guesses is how strongly they are felt. For this reason it may be a good idea to have a notetaker/secretary beside the receiver, who can record the guesses and also note whether the "signal" is strong, average, or weak. A "chance" score of five out of twenty-five would be more impressive if all of those five were very strong feelings, rather than just average. Recording would then look like: 1: Circle—weak. 2: Star—weak. 3: Star—strong. 4: Wavy lines—strong. 5: Square—average. And so on.

If you cannot get Zener cards, there is no reason why you should not start off with regular playing cards. In fact, there are many ways of working that will make the whole experiment more interesting. With a deck of **tarot** cards, for example, there are seventy-eight cards in the deck, so you would not need to go through them anywhere near as many times.

Other possibilities for testing are numbers (perhaps using **dominoes**), words from a dictionary opened at random, sketches done by both sender and receiver, clipped-out advertisements, etc. If a number of people in a group are interested, there is no reason why the above experiments should not be carried out using two small groups. One group would act as senders and the other group as receivers. Later, the positions could be reversed.

Sources:

Buckland, Raymond. A *Pocket Guide to the Supernatural*. New York: Ace Books, 1969.
Ebon, Martin. *True Experiences in Telepathy*. New York: Signet, 1967.
Rhine, Joseph Banks. *New Frontiers of the Mind*. New York: Farrar & Rinehart, 1937.
Spraggett, Alan. *The Unexplained*. New York: New American Library, 1967.

EYE *see* Oculomancy

F

FACE *see* **Anthroposcopy; Metopomancy; Physiognomancy**

Fate; Destiny

In Greek mythology, the three Fates (otherwise known as the Mœræ; to the Romans, Parcæ) are Clotho, the spinner of destiny who personifies the thread of life; Lachesis, the weaver of chance and the element of luck that humankind feels it has a right to expect; and Antropos, the inescapable Fate who cuts the thread of life. They are the ones who apportion to each mortal his or her share of good and evil. The Fates sat in the assemblies of the gods and possessed the gift of **prophesy.** In the Germanic and **Scandinavian** traditions, the Fates were known as the Norns. They were seen as wise women who sat at the foot of the **Tree** of Life, **Yggdrasil.**

Although many view fate as inescapable, as something preordained, there is still a fascination with it; hence the perennial enthrallment with **divination.** Whether or not one's destiny can be changed is a question that has been asked for thousands of years. Many do believe that the future can be changed; that there is free will. Others think in terms of **karma;** that what lies ahead is predestined based on actions in past lives. Some have a strong feeling of personal destiny; that they were created to fulfill a particular task and that nothing can change that.

Most modern-day **fortune-tellers** will advise that all they do is show what is most *likely* to happen if things continue as they are. They will emphasize that things *can* be changed. **Tarot** card readers, **palmists,** and **astrologers** all seem to share that belief. The **Chinese I Ching** is known as the "Book of Changes" because it reflects that all life does change. But the question remains: does it change because of a predetermined pattern or because we are constantly changing it?

Sources:

Guirand, Félix. *Greek Mythology*. Paul London, 1963.

Rakoczi, Basil Ivan. *Man, Myth & Magic*. London: BPC Publishing, 1970.

The Wheel of Fortune as a symbol of destiny, 1490. The wheel is turned by an angel, and the persons on the wheel are personifications of the planets. *Fortean Picture Library.*

FATIDICENCY

Foretelling the future; any method of divination. Sir Thomas Urquhart's *The Third Book of the Works of Mr. Francis Rabelais* (London, 1693) says: "Let us make trial of this kind of Fatidicency." The word is from "fate" and means simply to test fate. It can therefore be applied to any form of divination.

FECES *see* Scatomancy; Spatilomancy

FEET *see* Podomancy

FIGS; FIG LEAVES *see* Sycomancy

FINGERNAILS *see* Onychomancy

FIRE *see* Causimancy; Empyromancy; Pyromancy

FISH *see* Ichthyomancy

FLAME *see* Lampadomancy

FLIGHT OF BIRDS *see* Orniscopy

FLOROMANCY

This is divination by flowers. Plucking the petals from a flower while saying the words "She (or he) loves me; she loves me not," until the last petal, is a form of floromancy. Finding the first flower of spring has relevance also. To find it on a Monday means good fortune for the rest of the season. Finding it on a Tuesday means your greatest efforts will be rewarded. On a Wednesday: there is a coming marriage. A Thursday: be cautious; this is a warning. A Friday: wealth is on its way. A Saturday: there will be misfortune. A Sunday: nothing but good luck for the whole of the spring.

If the first flower found is a wildflower, then someone with the same initial as the flower will be attracted to you. For example, if you find a daisy, it will be someone whose name starts with a D. If you find a buttercup, it will be someone whose name starts with B.

The term floromancy is also applied to the belief that flowers have feelings and emotions. They are living, breathing, communicating creatures. In experiments, a plant attached to a lie detector showed violent reaction when threatened with having one of its leaves burned. Similar reactions have been found showing responses to anger, love, affection, cruelty, and so on.

Sources:
Telesco, Patricia. *A Victorian Grimoire*. St. Paul, MN: Llewellyn, 1992.
Tompkins, Peter and Christopher Bird. *The Secret Life of Plants*. New York: Avon, 1973.

FLOUR *see* **Aleuromancy**

FLOWERS *see* **Anthomancy; Floromancy**

Fodor, Nandor (1895–1964)

Nandor Fodor was born in Beregszasz, Hungary, on May 13, 1895. He studied law at the Royal Hungarian University of Science in Budapest, where he received his doctorate in 1917. Four years later he went to New York, getting a job as a journalist. After reading **Hereward Carrington**'s book *Modern* ***Psychic*** *Phenomena* (1919), Fodor contacted Carrington and quickly became friends with him. Carrington introduced him to Sir Arthur Conan Doyle. Some years later Fodor and Carrington coauthored *Haunted People* (in Britain titled *Story of the Poltergeist down the Ages*). While in New York, Fodor interviewed Sandor Ferenczi, an associate of Sigmund Freud's. Fodor believed that psychoanalysis could throw light on psychic phenomena. Freud later came to support Fodor and his work.

Fodor moved to England in 1929, working for newspaper tycoon Lord Rothermere. Five years later he became an editor of *Light*, the oldest British journal of **spiritualism.** Fodor had become seriously interested in spiritualism while in New York, having been to a **séance** given by direct voice **medium** William Cartheuser. In England, Fodor started to investigate seriously all forms of psychic phenomena, visiting sites of hauntings, poltergeist activity, levitations, and materializations. In 1934 he wrote his most important book, *Encyclopedia of Psychic Science*. Sir Oliver Lodge was sufficiently impressed with Fodor's work that he contributed a preface to the book. In 1935 Fodor became London correspondent for the **American Society for Psychical Research.** In 1939 he resigned that position but returned to the United States to live in New York.

For many years Fodor was on the teaching staff of the Training Institute of the National Psychological Association for Psychoanalysis and one of the editors of the *Psychoanalytic Review*. He was a member of the New York Academy of Science. He was also an honorary member of the Danish Society for Psychical Research and the Hungarian Metaphysical Society. Other Fodor books include *On the Trail of the Poltergeist* (1958), *The Haunted Mind* (1959), *Mind over Space* (1962), and *Between Two Worlds* (1964).

Sources:
Fishley, Margaret. *The Supernatural*. London: Aldus, 1976.
Guiley, Rosemary Ellen. *The Encyclopedia of Ghosts and Spirits*. New York: Facts on File, 1992.
Shepard, Leslie A. (ed.). *Encyclopedia of Occultism & Parapsychology*. New York: Avon, 1978.

FOOTPRINT *see* **Pedomancy**

FOOTSTEPS *see* **Ichnomancy**

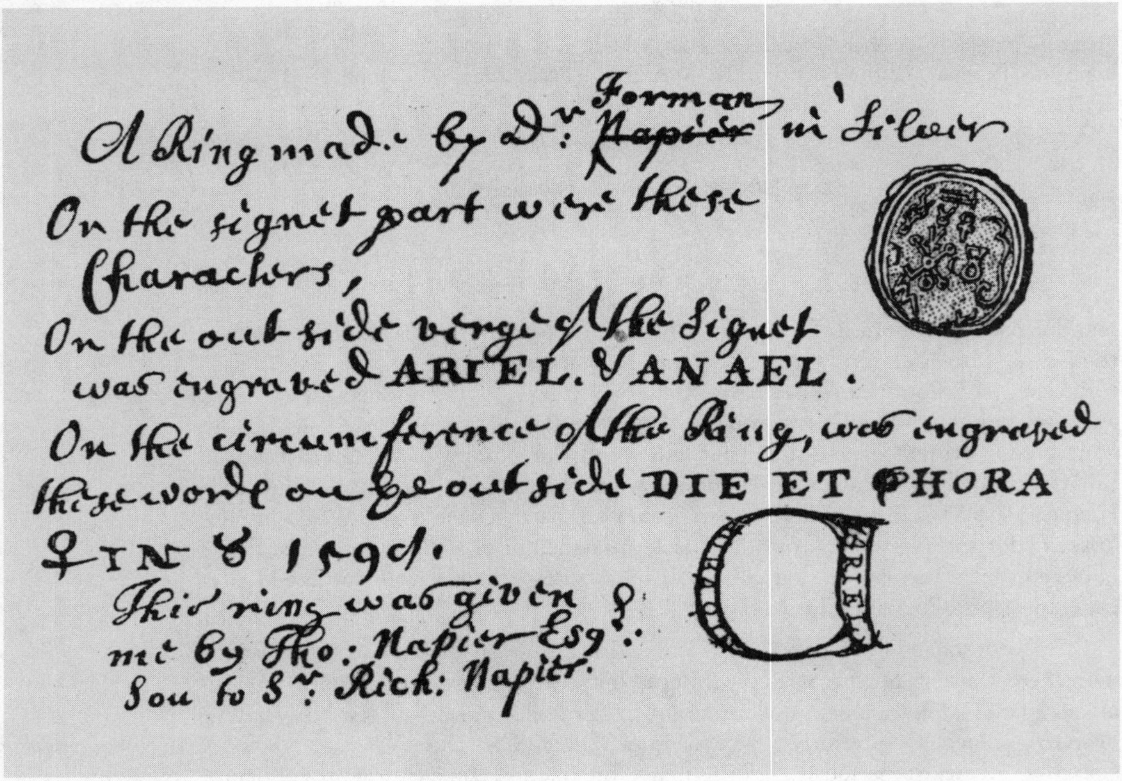

A Ring made by Dr: ~~Napier~~ Forman in Silver
On the signet part were these
Characters,
On the out side verge of the signet
was engraved ARIEL. VANAEL.
On the circumference of the Ring, was engraved
these words on the out side DIE ET ♀HORA
♀ IN ♉ 1590.
This ring was given
me by Tho: Napier Esq:
Son to Sr: Rich: Napier.

Magical ring of astrologer Simon Forman, from a sixteenth-century manuscript. ***Fortean Picture Library.***

FOREHEAD ***see*** **Metopomancy**

FORMAN, SIMON (1552–1611)

Simon Forman, **astrologer** and **diviner,** was born December 30, 1552, in Quidhampton, England. He received some small education at a school in the Salisbury area but left there on the death of his father in December 1563. For ten years Forman was an apprentice to Matthew Commin, a merchant who dealt in herbal medicines, salt and cloth. Forman moved to Oxford in 1574, where he spent an unhappy year at Magdalene College. By 1579, after a number of jobs including that of schoolteacher, he decided to focus his mind on the occult.

At age forty Forman moved to London and set up an alternative medical center in Billingsgate. He based his diagnoses and prescriptions on astrology. He had an ongoing battle with the Royal College of Physicians, who did not want him practicing, but eventually, in 1603, he received his license to practice from Cambridge University.

Forman was a good example of a **seer** who kept detailed records of all his **predictions,** thus enabling historians to determine his accuracy. He recorded his successes—of which there were many—and his failures. Forman used both astrology and **geomancy.** His casebooks can be seen at the Bodleian Library at Oxford University, England.

One example of his predictions is the case of a military exercise ordered by Queen Elizabeth I. The queen sent the Earl of Essex to Ireland to put down the rebels there. It was presumed that this would be undertaken without much difficulty. However, Forman wrote in his diary that the exercise would result in "treason, hunger, sickness, and death." Of the Earl of Essex, Forman said specifically, "The end will be evil to himself, for he shall be imprisoned . . . He shall find many enemies on his return and have great loss of goods and honour." Forman wrote this in his diary on March 19, 1599. It wasn't until a month later that the expedition left for Ireland.

Ignoring the queen's orders, Essex made a bad truce with the rebels. When he returned to England, despite having been the queen's favorite, Essex was stripped of his office and all his property was confiscated. He was imprisoned and eventually beheaded for high treason.

Forman foretold his own death a week before it transpired, which was in September 1611. He was crossing the river Thames at the time and collapsed in his boat. His death was documented by the famous astrologer **William Lilly.**

Sources:

Headon, Deirdre (ed.). *Quest for the Unknown—Charting the Future*. Pleasantville, NY: Reader's Digest, 1992.

http://www.mysteriousbritain.co.uk/occult/drforman.html

FORTUNA

An Italian goddess who later became identified with the Greek Tyche, daughter of Oceanus and Tethys and divinity of chance, or **lot.** The original Italian deity was the bearer of increase and prosperity so was, in effect, a fertility deity. Called Fors, then Fors Fortuna, she represented **fate** with all its unknown factors. Her symbols are the cornucopia and the rudder, and she is usually depicted standing on a ball. The cornucopia represents the giving of abundance. The rudder shows that she is the controller of destinies. The ball on which she stands indicates the uncertainty of fortune.

Fortuna was worshiped in Italy from earliest times. There was a temple to her outside Rome, on the right bank of the Tiber, set up in 204 BCE. There were also numerous shrines to her throughout the city. Of those beyond Rome, the most famous was at Præneste, in Latinum. There her shrine was an oracular one. A man named Numerius Suffustus, digging in a cliff, discovered some oak tablets inscribed with mysterious formulas. By means of these tablets, **oracles** could be delivered. When someone came to Fortuna with a problem, a child would randomly draw one of the ancient wooden tiles. The message on it would always relate to the problem presented.

The shrine at Antium (detailed in Horace's *Odes,* i:35) had two Fortunæ who gave responses by mysterious movements of their statues.

Anyone who had especially good, or bad, luck would have a statuette of Fortuna in the home. A gold statuette of her was always kept in the sleeping quarters of Roman emperors.

Fortuna, engraving by John Spilsbury, c. 1781. ***Fortean Picture Library.***

Sources:

Encyclopedia Britannica. Chicago: William Benton, 1964.

Larousse Encyclopedia of Mythology. London: Paul Hamlyn, 1965.

Fortune Cookies

The origin of the fortune cookies served in most Chinese restaurants has long been argued. They were most likely invented in 1914 by Makoto Hagiwara, a Japanese American. At his Japanese Tea Garden in Golden Gate Park, San Francisco, Hagiwara introduced cookies containing thank-you notes. He also served them at the 1915 Panama-Pacific Exhibition, which was San Francisco's world's fair of that time. However, David Jung, founder of the Hong Kong Noodle Company in Los Angeles, also claims to have invented them in 1918. He offered them as a treat for the post–World War I unemployed who gathered in the streets.

Whoever did invent the fortune cookies—and they could have been introduced by both men quite independently—the Chinese restaurant owners on the West Coast quickly saw them as a way of satisfying American customers who looked for dessert with their meal. Desserts were an alien concept to the Chinese.

Fortune cookies themselves were unknown in **China** until 1993, when the Wonton Food Company opened a factory for them. They were advertised there as "Genuine American Fortune Cookies." The project was short-lived, since the cookies did not catch on with the Chinese.

Some believe, however, that fortune cookies dates back much further: to the thirteenth and fourteenth centuries, when China was occupied by the Mongols. At that time, traditional moon cakes made of lotus nut paste were used to hide secret messages regarding a plot to rise up against the invaders. It is said that a patriotic revolutionary, Chu Yuan Chang, disguised himself as a Taoist priest and distributed the cakes, thus spreading the word that led to the successful uprising.

It was in the days of the California gold rush and the railroad boom that the cakes made their transition to today's fortune cookies. When the Chinese '69ers were building the great American railroads through the Sierra Nevada to California, they put happy messages inside biscuits, rather than cakes, to exchange at their Moon Festival. There is also a Chinese custom that when a child is born, the family will send out cake rolls with a birth announcement inside.

Fortune cookies were made by hand until 1964, when the first automated production began, thanks to a machine invented by Edward Louie. The world's largest fortune cookie factory is today located in New York. It is the Wonton Food Company, based in Long Island City. They produce 2.5 million fortune cookies a day.

Sources:
http://www.jrn.columbia.edu/studentwork/cns/2002-04-03/320.asp

FORTUNE-TELLING IN POPULAR CULTURE

It seems certain that divination was a part of human existence from earliest times; humankind having a desire to know what the future might hold and to develop methods that might indicate that future. There is evidence that some form of fortune-telling was practiced in ancient Babylonia, Chaldea, **China,** and **Egypt** at least six thousand years ago. Fortune-telling has often been an integral part of religion and medicine, and was frequently a prerogative of the priesthood.

During the Middle Ages important people had their own personal **soothsayers,** who often also practiced alchemy and/or **ceremonial magic. Astrologer** Michael Scot (1175–1232) was tutor and adviser to the emperor Frederick II, and Nostradamus (1503–1566) was adviser to Catherine de Medicis. Dr. John Dee (1527–1608) worked for England's Queen Elizabeth I, as astrologer, alchemist, **scryer,** and necromancer.

When the **Gypsies** descended on Central Europe in the fourteen and fifteenth centuries, they sparked a tremendous interest in fortune-telling. As nomads, they had to fend for themselves and find ways to make a living. They found that wherever they went, people were interested in fortune-telling, so the Gypsies gave the people what they wanted. It is most likely that they were responsible for introducing the **tarot** cards into Europe. They certainly popularized **cartomancy, palmistry,** and **crystal-gazing.** Even today, 1,000 years after they first came out of the northern part of India, they are found telling fortunes around the world.

From the turn of the twentieth century through the 1930s, fortune-telling booths at vacation resorts were very popular. They were usually manned by Gypsies or by those who passed themselves off as Gypsies. They offered everything from **cheiromancy** to **tasseography,** crystal-gazing to astrology. Newspaper and magazine horoscope columns became popular and remain so. Few readers seemed to stop to think that not everyone born in the same month, all across the country, could possibly have the same horoscope! In the 1960s and 1970s a number of specialty horoscope magazines were produced and sold well.

In the 1930s, coin-operated fortune-telling machines began to appear in amusement arcades. They remained popular until well after the World War II. There was something of a revival of interest in them in the 1970s and, in fact, the occasional one can still be found. These machines varied from very simple to elaborate and artistic. There were "palm-reading" machines where the player placed his or her hand on a grid of metal studs that, on insertion of the coin, moved up and down under the palm. A card finally dropped out of the machine with the cheiromantic fortune on it. There were **zodiac** machines, where the player turned a dial or heavy metal arrow to point to

The prevalence of fortune-telling in popular culture is evidenced in this 1991 Festival of Mind, Body and Spirit. ***Guy Lyon Playfair/Fortean Picture Library.***

his or her date of birth. A card with a horoscope printed on it dropped out. Frequently the card also offered "lucky numbers"and "lucky days."

A machine known as the "Mystic Pen" wrote out a special fortune for the player. Exhibit Supply's "An Answer from Beyond" had players select questions and then gave answers from an ancient Egyptian mummy named "Ramasees." There were Magic 8 Balls, Gypsy Fortune-Tellers, and Grandmother Fortune-Tellers. These last were elaborately produced, life-size figures, shown from the waist up, inside mahogany and glass cases. They would hold cards or gaze into crystal balls. There were also beturbaned mystics. Some of these in later years, such as the Zoltan figures of the 1970s, offered a telephone headset for the player to listen in and hear the fortune. One of the most memorable machines in the 1970s was Bacchus's "Madame Morgana." This was a mannequin-type figure with a blank face. A woman's face was then projected onto it by movie projector inside the case, giving the illusion that the figure actually looked at the player and spoke with lips moving.

By the 1960s the "occult explosion" found a vast number of people taking an interest in tarot cards, astrology, numerology, and similar, not just as recipients of the information but as dispensers. The term "New Age" came into popular use, albeit applied to ancient wisdom. However, it did serve to calm those previously frightened by the term "occult." With this great interest in the field, many people found that there was no special "gift" to divination; anyone could do it, with a little practice. Today there is such an interest in tarot, for example, that as many as 2,000 different decks are available, with more being produced all the time. Books on all aspects of divination and fortune-telling are readily available, as are classes in the different disciplines.

In England the Vagrancy Act had been passed in 1824 (extended to **Scotland** and Ireland in 1871), providing that anyone pretending to tell fortunes with intent to deceive was liable to imprisonment "as a rogue and a vagabond." In 1951 this was replaced by the Fraudulent **Mediums** Act, which extended to embrace fraudulent mediums, **spiritualists,** telepathists, and **clairvoyants.** In America many cities and states still have laws against fortune-telling.

Fortune-telling falls into two categories. It is divining the future, but it is also reading a person's character and determining how that character has been shaped by events of the past. Fortune-telling takes two basic forms: *natural* and *operational*. Natural divination consists of observing occurrences in the natural world, such as cloud formations, lightning, and **bird**'s flight. Operational divination involves the use of tools, such as cards, **dice,** smoke, and **water.**

Fortune-tellers often provide outlets for people with overburdened minds. Where it might be difficult for a person to confide his or her problems to a family member or close friend, it is often possible to tell a complete stranger (in the guise of a fortune-teller) what has become a major problem. The astute diviner will then reassure and reinforce where necessary. **Telepathy,** whether conscious or unconscious, can be very much a tool of the fortune-teller's trade, allowing a close rapport with the client. It is significant that fortune-telling flourishes in times of national and international insecurity.

Sources:

Cunningham, Scott. *Pocket Guide to Fortune Telling*. Crossing Press, Freedom 1997.
Encyclopedia Britannica. Chicago: William Benton, 1964.
http://www.yesterdayland.com/popopedia/shows/arcade/ag1256.php.
http://www.geocities.com/wolfreader/FunPage.html.

FOSSILS ***see*** **Oryctomancy**

FOUNTAINS ***see*** **Pegomancy**

Fox, Oliver (1885–1949)

"Oliver Fox" was a pseudonym of Hugh G. Callaway, a British pioneer exponent of **astral projection.** He was born in Southampton on November 30, 1885. He studied science and electrical engineering at Harley Institute in Southampton. He experienced his first astral projection at the age of seventeen.

In 1907 Callaway/Fox married Bertha Knight. He briefly joined a theatrical touring company then invested in two unsuccessful business ventures. In 1910 Fox inherited a small legacy and started writing poetry and short stories, with some success. In 1919 the couple moved to London and Fox's writing took an occult emphasis. After publishing a number of articles in the *Occult Review,* he finally had his book *Astral Projection: A Record of Out-of-Body Experiences* published. It was the first major British publication on the subject. He died April 28, 1949.

Sources:

Fox, Oliver. *Astral Projection: A Record of Out-of-Body Experiences*. London: Rider, 1939.
Shepard, Leslie A. (ed.). *Encyclopedia of Occultism & Parapsychology*. New York: Avon, 1978.

FROGS *see* Batrachomancy

G

Galgal

The word *galgal* (plural: *galgalim*) is from the Hebrew meaning "whirling." It refers to the Sephiroth, which are the western equivalent of the eastern chakras, as they exist within the human aura.

Galgal, as a system of divination, was first published in 1972. It is a set of divination cards related to the tarot and astrology. It is loosely based on the Qabbalah and, as such, works with organizing the Hebrew letters through a complex system of the Tree of Life.

Gall, Franz Joseph (1758–1828)

Franz Joseph Gall was born in Tiefenbrunn, Germany, in 1758. As a boy, he made the observation that many of the brighter students in his school seemed to have very distinctive head shapes, often with prominent eyes. From this he formulated a theory that the noticeable lumps on their heads had to be related to the brain power they possessed.

Gall practiced medicine in Vienna but spent some years visiting lunatic asylums, prisons, and schools, measuring heads with calipers and recording what he found. He also examined and measured innumerable skulls. As a physician, he had a detailed knowledge of the brain and the nervous system.

Gall lectured on his findings in Vienna and then, between 1805 and 1807, traveled and lectured on the anatomy of the brain and the elements of **phrenology.** His theories were mostly greeted with derision. In 1807 he settled in Paris, dying there in 1828. His pupil, J. K. Spurzheim, continued Gall's work in both England and America.

Sources:

Chambers, Howard V. *Phrenology*. Los Angeles: Sherbourne Press, 1968.

Eileen Jeanette Garrett, trance medium. *Fortean Picture Library.*

Shepard, Leslie A. (ed.). *Encyclopedia of Occultism & Parapsychology*. New York: Avon, 1978.

Garrett, Eileen Jeanette (1893–1970)

In his introduction to Eileen Garrett's autobiography, Allan Angoff says: "Eileen Garrett holds no professional degrees and has no license to practice any of the healing arts, but she has helped and apparently cured hundreds of physicians, scientists, writers, editors, secretaries, psychiatrists, psychologists, bereaved parents and children, and the prime minister of a very large country."

Born on March 17, 1893, in County Meath, Ireland, Eileen Jeanette Vancho Lyttle showed **psychic** abilities from a very early age. Suffering from tuberculosis and bronchial asthma, she spent many long weeks confined to her bed. As a young child, she claimed that she was able to speak with the dead. Her **mediumship** started in earnest following the end of World War II. She came to be considered one of the greatest mediums the world has ever known.

During the war, and after a failed marriage to a young architect named Clive Barry, Eileen ran a hostel for wounded soldiers. She had precognitive visions of many of the men with whom she came into contact, often seeing them killed on returning to action. One of the soldiers she saw die in this way was a man who, as she nursed him, she agreed to marry.

At the end of the war, in 1918, she married James William Garrett, another wounded soldier. Like her two previous marriages, this one did not last long. After it ended in divorce, Garrett did not marry again.

One day Garrett joined a group of women who were doing **table tipping.** In the middle of the session, she went into a trance and started speaking of seeing dead relatives of the women around the table. The women were so surprised that they shook her awake. Garret was persuaded to consult with a man who would help her understand this aspect of herself. When the man put her into a light hypnotic trance, a spirit "control" named Uvani came through and stated that Garrett would be active as a trance medium for the next several years. This turned out to be true. It took a while for her to come to terms with this new role, but eventually—through the agencies of people like James Hewat McKenzie and the British College of Psychic Science—she accepted her gift.

Garrett came to work with people like **Hereward Carrington, Nandor Fodor,** Sir Arthur Conan Doyle, and Sir Oliver Lodge. In 1931 she was invited to visit the **American Society for Psychical Research.** While in America she also worked with other notable mediums, including Dr. **J. B. Rhine,** and Dr. Anita Muhl. In 1938 she wrote a book titled *My Life as a Search for the Meaning of Mediumship* (London: Rider, 1939) that was published and successful. Shortly after its appearance, she traveled to Juan-les-Pins, France. At the beginning of the World War II she tried to remain in France to help orphaned children but eventually had to leave.

On March 8, 1941, back in New York, Garrett was inspired by the name of the Life Extension Building to start a publishing company at its location on East 44th Street. On impulse she rented two rooms on the eighteenth floor and planned to launch a magazine, to be called *Tomorrow,* which would deal with serious investigation of the paranormal. The proceeds, she decided, would go to the starving children of France. She actually started by publishing two books, one on **Nostradamus** by Lee McCann, and one of her own called *Telepathy*. These were under the banner of her publishing company, Creative Age Press, though this name was later changed to Helix Press. The first issue of *Tomorrow* appeared on September 1, 1941. In 1947 Garrett became a U.S. citizen.

In 1951 Garrett founded the Parapsychology Foundation to promote organized scientific research into parapsychology. The foundation published the *International Journal of Parapsychology*. Garrett was always somewhat uncertain about psychism generally, and her own in particular, and she allowed herself to be subjected to numerous tests at such institutions as Johns Hopkins University and the New York Psychiatric Institute.

Eileen Garret died on September 15, 1970, in Nice, France, following a long illness. She has been acclaimed as one of the world's greatest mediums.

Sources:
Angoff, Allan. *Eileen Garrett and the World beyond the Senses*. New York: William Morrow, 1974.
Garrett, Eileen J. *Many Voices: The Autobiography of a Medium*. New York: G. P. Putnam's, 1968.

GASTROMANCY

Gastromancy is defined as "divination by the belly." It seems there were two types of this form of divination. The first was aligned with ventriloquism, indicating that in some way rumblings coming from the belly might be taken for words. Low sounds, even words, might be heard coming from the source. Edward Smedley, in *The Occult Sciences* (1836), says, "Gastromancy, or divination from the belly, is now generally explained by ventriloquism." However, John Gaule's *The Magastromancer, or the magicall-astrologicall-diviner posed and puzzled* (1651) says: "Gastromancy; divining by the sound of, or signes upon the belly," indicating that marks on a person's belly (see **moleosophy**) might also be interpreted by the diviner.

The second type of gastromancy deals with the "" of a glass vessel. It seems to be a type of **scrying,** for John Healey, in *St. Augustine of the citie of God* (1610) says: "Hydromancy . . . done in a glass bottle full of water, wherein a Childe must looke (and this is called Gastromancy of the glasses belly)." Samuel Purchas agreed, in *Pilgrimage* (1614): "Gastromancie procured answers by pictures, or representations in glasse-vessels of water, after the due Rites." There was, then, a particular ritual that was performed leading up to this scrying. The bottle holding the water was probably stood in a circle, or semi-circle, of lit candles. Incense would burn, and the **seer** would be a young child. For scrying, young boys seemed to be favored over young girls, though both could do the duty. The diviner would ask questions and the child would say what was seen in the glass belly of the bottle.

Arthur Edward Waite, writing as "Grand Orient," put it this way:

> It is performed in the following manner. Place some globular vases, filled to the brim with clear water, between a number of lighted waxen tapers. Make an invocation of the angelical or planetary intelligences—such as Israfel, Gabriel, or Metron, the spirit of the north—and direct the natural magician, who should be a boy or a girl of absolute and assured virginity, to gaze intently into the vases, when they will behold upon the surface of the water, amidst the reflected light of the tapers, a pictorial reply to the questions proposed by the consulters of the "**oracle.**"

Sources:

Grand Orient (A. E. Waite). *The Complete Manual of Occult Divination: Volume 1—Manual of Cartomancy*. London: William Rider, 1912.

Oxford English Dictionary. Oxford: Clarendon Press, 1989.

Spence, Lewis. *An Encyclopedia of the Occult*. London: George Routledge & Sons, 1920.

Geloscopy; Gelotoscopy

This was a way of **divining,** or discovering, the character of a person based on the way in which they laughed. It was an offshoot of **phrenology, physiognomy,** and similar methods.

Sources:

Headon, Deirdre (ed.). *Quest for the Unknown—Charting the Future*. Pleasantville, NY: Reader's Digest, 1992.

Gematria

Based on **numerology,** this is a cabbalistic method of interpreting the **Qabbalah** and Hebrew scriptures by interchanging words whose letters have the same numerical values when added. There is a related cabbalistic system known as *notarikon*, where new words are made up from letters taken from the beginning, middle, or end of the words in a sentence and then combining them to make a new word.

Gemology

Stones, both precious and semi-precious, have at times served as **divining** agents among various peoples. Beliefs in the magical power of gems sprang from the **color** affinities.

An early cuneiform tablet gives a list of precious stones that supposedly facilitate conception and birth and can also induce love and hate. Belief in the power of stones continued from earliest time through to the nineteenth century; even today there are those who swear by their efficacy. In 315 BCE Theophrastus suggested that gems could be either male or female and would reproduce if placed in the ground. The Hindus believe that it is only the most perfect gems that have any virtues, with lesser ones inducing bad luck and misfortune. In **India,** gems are viewed as most effective when used in traditional combinations, such as the five-gem *pa'charatna,* which is amethyst, diamond, emerald, gold and pearl.

Occult uses of precious and semi-precious stones are as follows:

Agate (chalcedony variety): grounding, healing, discovering the truth.
Amazonite (feldspar): creativity, joy, **psychic** expander.
Amber (burmite, pimetite, puccinite, ruminite): harmonizing, soothing, awakens the kundalini.
Amethyst (quartz): dispels illusion, healing, meditation, promotes psychic abilities especially **channeling,** protective.
Beryl: discipline, humor, patience.
Bloodstone (heliotrope): reduces emotional and mental stress, stimulates the kundalini, is a psychic healer.
Carnelian (chalcedony): aligns and grounds.
Chrysolite (peridot, olivine): purifies, prevents nightmares, increases psychic awareness.
Coral (calcium carbonate): positiveness, stabilizer.
Diamond: Panacea; covers everything in psychic and spiritual matters.
Emerald (beryl): **dreams,** meditation, tranquility, contact with the higher self.
Garnet: compassion, grounding, general stimulant.
Jade: courage, protection, wisdom, dispels negativity.
Lapis Lazuli (lazurite): promotes psychic abilities, contact with higher self.
Lapis Linguis (azurite): meditation, promotes psychic abilities.
Lapis Lingurius *(malachite)*: protection from the "evil eye."
Moonstone (adularia variety of orthoclase): compassion, relieves stress, governs the affections.
Opal: enhances intuition, amplifies the chakras, protects.
Pearl: meditation, soothing.
Quartz Crystal: amplifier, purity, spiritual protector, assists channeling.
Rose Quartz: creativity, self-confidence, eases tensions.
Ruby (corundum): integrity, regeneration, spiritual devotion.
Sardonyx (cryptocrystalline quartz): soothes emotions.
Topaz (alumino-fluoro-silicate): inspiration, soothing, calming, tranquility, emotional balance, stops nightmares.
Tourmaline (black): protection, imagination, intuition, **clairvoyance,** overcomes fear.
Tourmaline (pink/green): regeneration, balance, harmony, compassion, rejuvenation.

Turquoise (copper-and-aluminum phosphate): calming, loyalty, communication, peace of mind.

Zircon (hyacinth): self-esteem, strength, storage of psychic power.

Sources:

Buckland, Raymond. *Advanced Candle Magick*. St. Paul, MN: Llewellyn, 1996.

Leach, Maria (ed.). *Funk & Wagnalls Standard Dictionary of Folklore, Mythology, and Legend*. San Francisco: Harper & Row, 1972.

Genethlialogy

Genethlialogy is the science or art of casting an astrological birth chart showing the position of the stars at the moment of birth. Traditionally **astrology** is divided into *natural* astrology, which is basically astronomy since it deals with the movements of the heavenly bodies, and *judicial* astrology, which interprets those movements in terms of terrestrial life. There are many subdivisions within judicial astrology, one of which is genethliacal or natal astrology—the erecting and interpreting of individuals' horoscopes. (*See* **astrology**)

Sources:

MacNeice, Louis. *Astrology*. Garden City, NY: Doubleday, 1964.

Geomancy

Also known as gemensye, geomesye, and geomanty, this is divination by means of signs derived from the earth, such as by studying the figure(s) assumed when a handful of earth is thrown down on a hard surface. An extension of this is to jab a stick into the ground a number of times at random (or jot down, with pencil and paper, a series of random dots). In fact geomancy was also known as the "art of the little dots." In Madagascar, geomancy is known as *sikidi*. On the west coast of Africa it is *djabe* or *fa*.

As the frontispiece to the second volume of Robert Fludd's *Utriusque cosmi historia* (1619), there is a schematic figure showing various forms of divination including geomancy. This is represented by a shield-shaped figure divided into fifteen segments, with numbers of dots in each segment. In his 1533 book *De occulta philosophia*, Agrippa gives an interpretation of three of these, as follows:

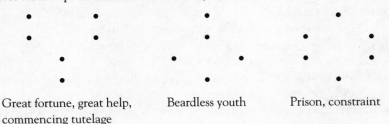

Great fortune, great help, commencing tutelage

Beardless youth

Prison, constraint

At that time there were sixteen basic shapes recognized for geomancy. This came from a formalization of the art. Whereas originally the dots—whether produced

Girl practicing geomancy, Arabic style, using shells and pebbles. ***Fortean Picture Library.***

by thrown earth or by conscious pencil marking—were interpreted in much the same way that tea leaves would be interpreted in **tasseography,** the formalization was based on the dotting-by-pencil method. Rather than having the inspirational uttering of a diviner inspired by his study of shapes and near-shapes, cut-and-dried meanings were catalogued to be read from a standard list. As explained by John Michael Greer in his book *Earth Divination Earth Magic*, if you make four lines of dots across a piece of paper, you will end with either an odd number of dots in any one line or an even number. To construct the figures of geomancy, these four lines are reduced with lines containing an odd number of dots being represented by a single dot in the final figure and lines containing even number of dots represented by two dots. There are sixteen possible combinations that can come from this, and these are the figures used in formal geomancy:

Number of Dots	Meaning
1	Boy—destruction; energy; rashness; violence.
1	
2	Generally unfavorable except in love and war.
1	

1 Loss—of short duration; loss; outside one's grasp.
2
1 Favorable for love but not for material things.
2

2 White—purity; peace; wisdom; favorable but weak.
2
1 Good for beginnings and for business ventures.
2

2 People—a gathering of people; a multitude.
2
2 Neutral—good with good and/or evil with evil; neither favorable nor unfavorable.
2

2 Greater Fortune—great good fortune and inner strength.
2
1 Figure of power and success; favorable for any competition.
1

2 Conjunction—recovery of things lost; combination of people or things.
1
1
2 Neutral; neither favorable nor unfavorable.

1 Girl—harmony; happiness.
2
1
1 Favorable in nearly all things.

2 Red—fierceness; passion; power; vice.
1
2 Evil in all that is good; good in all that is evil.
2

2 Gain—success; gain; profit; things within one's grasp.
1
2
1 Favorable in nearly all things.

1 Prison—delay; limitation; restriction; imprisonment.
2
2
1 An unfavorable figure.

2 Sorrow—illness; pain; suffering; sorrow.
2
2 An unfavorable figure except in questions relating to building and the earth.
1

1 2 2 2	Joy—health; happiness. A favorable figure.
1 1 1 2	Dragon's Tail—an exit; doorway out. Brings good with evil and evil with good. Favorable for endings and losses but unfavorable in most questions.
2 1 1 1	Dragon's Head—an entrance; doorway in. Brings good with evil and evil with good. Favorable for beginnings and gain; neutral in other questions.
1 1 2 2	Lesser Fortune—outward strength; help from others. Good for anything where a person wishes to proceed quickly.
1 1 1 1	Way—movement; change; change of fortune. Favorable for journeys and voyages.

In modern times, geomancy can be practiced easily by using a **coin,** which can be tossed to produce a Head or a Tail. If a Head is designated One and a Tail is designated Two, then four tosses will give a geomancy figure. However, this does rather defeat the spirit of geomancy, which is working with the earth. In various parts of the world, different methods are used to obtain the four lines from which the geomantic figures are derived. Straight lines may be randomly scratched in the dirt with a stick, giving long or short lines that are assigned One or Two. Straight lines and wavy lines may be done the same way, and distinguished to give the necessary figures. Or a large number of dots may be made and then counted, to get odds and evens. In the African *fa,* a number of palm kernels are passed from the left hand to the right. From the original total of eighteen, the number remaining in the left hand is counted to see if it is an even or odd number.

For a fuller reading, the dots of geomancy may be placed to form a **horoscope.** This is done using the more ancient square-and-triangles form of chart. In this there are twelve triangles spread around a central square. They represent the twelve houses: the first house is the middle triangle on the left; the triangle immediately below it is the second house; the third is next to that, and so on counterclockwise around the square. The houses have slightly different meanings from the regular **astrological** houses, according to medieval and Renaissance handbooks on geomancy:

First House is the querier him- or herself.

Second House is material wealth, business transactions, material desires, stolen property.

Third House is siblings, close neighbors and environment, short journeys, communications, rumors.

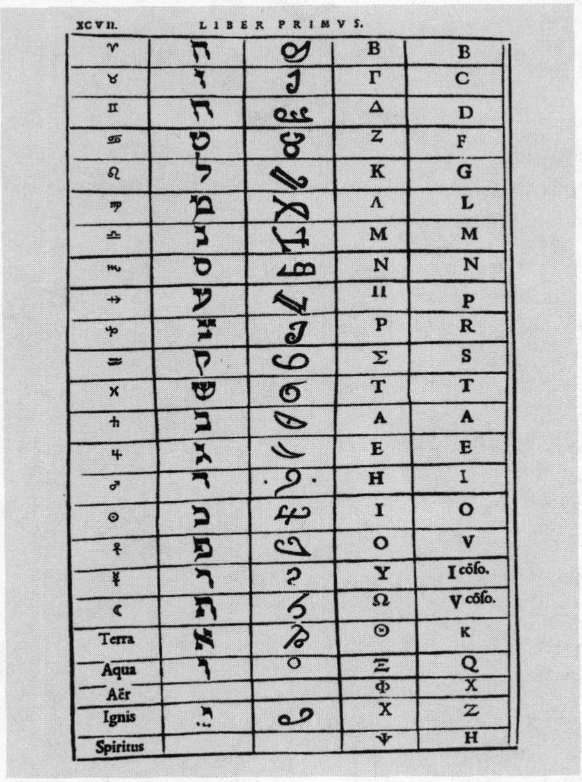

Table of geomantic characters, with the equivalent zodiacal, Hebraic, Roman, Greek, and English letters, 1534. *Fortean Picture Library.*

Fourth House is parents, inheritances from parents, land, agriculture, buildings, treasures, anything underground or hidden, ancient places and things.

Fifth House is children, pregnancy, entertainment, bodies of **water,** and rain.

Sixth House is employees, small animals, injuries, and illness.

Seventh House is spouse or lover, love relationships, partnerships, quarrels, any unidentified person.

Eighth House is suffering, danger, death, inheritances other than from parents (which are in Fourth House).

Ninth House is religion, philosophy, education, the arts, wisdom, long journeys, divination.

Tenth House is employment, position in society, people in authority, courts, judges, the **weather.**

Eleventh House is friends, sources of help, good fortune, hopes and desires.

Twelfth House is enemies, suffering, difficulties, imprisonment, secret matters, large animals, fears.

According to James Sanford's 1569 translation of Cornelius Agrippa's *Of the vanitie and uncertaintie of arts and sciences*, "There is also another kind of Geomancie the which doth divine by certaine conjectures taken of similitudes of the cracking of the earth." So in addition to studying the images formed from thrown earth, the science or art could also be applied to study of the natural fissures and cracks in a particular area of earth. **Arthur Edward Waite,** writing as "Grand Orient," says of this:

> Bituminous exhalations, which issue from the bowels of the earth and are fraught with the tenebrous mysteries of the "concentrated centre of Nature," are, however, comparatively uncommon, but there is yet another method of geomantic magic, which may be performed by tracing lines and circles on the ground, and then exercising the clairvoyant faculty upon their various combinations.

Henry Cornelius Agrippa (1486–1535) wrote about geomancy in his *Three Books of Occult Philosophy* (Graphæus, Antwerp, 1531–1533). There was also a spurious *Fourth Book of Occult Philosophy* (London, 1655) attributed to him that included some geomantic material.

Sources:

Buckland, Raymond. *Coin Divination: Pocket Fortuneteller.* St. Paul, MN: Llewellyn, 2000.

Greer, John Michael. *Earth Divination Earth Magic: A Practical Guide to Geomancy*. St. Paul, MN: Llewellyn, 1999.
Innes, Brian. *Mysteries of Mind Space & Time: The Unexplained*. Westport, CT: H. S. Stuttman, 1992.
Oxford English Dictionary. Oxford: Clarendon Press, 1989.
Tyson, Donald (ed.). *Three Books of Occult Philosophy written by Henry Cornelius Agrippa of Nettesheim*. St. Paul, MN: Llewellyn, 1993.

GHOSTS *see* **Sciomancy**

GOAT *see* **Cephalomancy**

GRAND ORIENT *see* **Arthur Edward Waite**

GRAPHOLOGY; GRAPTOMANCY

Graphology, or graptomancy, is the interpretation of character and personality traits by means of handwriting. Empirical interpretation of handwriting goes back to ancient times. Gaius Suetonius Tranquillus, the **Roman** biographer and antiquarian (c. 70–122), noted that the Emperor Octavius Augustus ran all his words together, without separating them. From this he concluded that the emperor was "showing himself neglectful of detail in forming a picture of a whole situation." Aristotle said that he could define the soul of a person by their way of writing. As early as the eleventh century, the **Chinese** drew attention to the relationship between personality and handwriting. The first recognition of graphology in print was in 1622 when an Italian physician and college professor, Camillo Baldi, wrote a treatise on the subject titled *De Signis ex Epistolis*. Baldi categorized the analysis of handwriting into its elements, which later gave impetus to the French school of Abbé Hippolyte Michon and Crepieux-Jamin. Michon was the one who originated the term "graphology." But it was not until the nineteenth century that graphology started to emerge as a science or pseudo-science. In France, Abbé Flandrin (1809–1864) began a study of people's autographs. In 1872 Adolphe Desbarolles published his book on the subject, *Les mystères de l'écriture; art de juger les homes sur leurs autographes*. Further books and much study followed in France, England, and other parts of Europe.

The slope of the writing, the size and formation of the letters, how letters are joined or not joined, and the degree of ornamentation gives indications of the personality. Yet many graphologists admit that there is far more to it than the cold clinical analysis of the letters; there is a **psychic** element involved. Although writing is a learned activity, it has been found that the preschool scribblings of a young child can show enough individual characteristics to identify that child with its writing at a later age.

Although it is not always possible to tell sex, age, and/or intelligence from examination of writing, such estimates have been made by experts with results far better than chance. Today, some businesses have job applicants' writing analyzed by a graphologist to determine suitability for a particular job. For example, unusually large handwriting is said to characterize the ambitious, imaginative person while very small handwriting shows a pedantic personality.

Some of the basics of graphology are as follows: If the lines of writing go "uphill," sloping up from lower left to upper right, then the person is usually optimistic. If the writing slopes "downhill," from upper left to lower right, then the person tends to be pessimistic. If the lines seem to be very exact and rigid, wandering neither up nor down, then there may be a tendency to be too strict and dogmatic. This could also indicate a domineering, perhaps even unreasonable person. The opposite would be lines that wander up and down, never really becoming level for any great length. This would be a person who needs some balance in their life, a changeable person with a weak disposition.

If there is wide spacing between the lines, proportionately larger than the size of the letter formations, then the person is generous in attitude. If the lines are close together, with little space between the words or the lines, then the person is cautious in spending money and has a cautious view toward other people. If there are many breaks, not only between words but also between letters, it shows an intuitive mind and a person who gets spontaneous reactions to new people and ideas. If the letters are all connected, then the writer is not apt to rely on intuition but prefers to work more logically.

Margins can also be important: left, right, top, and bottom. Basically, a wide margin indicates generosity while a narrow one shows thriftiness. If the writer leaves a wide margin on the left hand side of the paper, with a relatively narrow one on the right, it is a sign of conflict between generosity and thrift. They start out wanting to be generous but the basic need to be thrifty takes over. Similarly, if there is a narrow left-hand margin and a wide right-hand one, they start out trying to be thrifty but their inherent generosity gets the better of them. These attributes are also reflected in a writer who starts out with a wide left margin, for example, which gradually gets narrower as the writing moves down the page. The right margin stays consistently close on the right hand sign. Conversely, they might start with a narrow left margin that progressively gets wider as they move down the page, again with the right margin remaining consistent.

A line of writing may appear, at first glance, to be straight across the page. But if you draw a line across the paper, underneath the words, you may find that they are written either in a concave curve (dipping down in the center) across the page, or in a convex curve (rising up in the center). The concave writing shows a person who starts out in a pessimistic, hesitant way but then gains confidence as they go, becoming more and more optimistic. The convex example is the reverse: the person starts out with an attitude of optimism, but can quickly revert back to pessimism if results are not soon forthcoming.

Most people's writing slopes forward, to the right. Some have their writing slope back, to the left, while still others have theirs upright. There are found, of course, many degrees of slope, and the slope is not dependent upon whether or not the person is left-handed. Vertical writing, without a slope, shows an individual who is well controlled and who strikes an even balance between heart and head. This person may not be very demonstrative where love is concerned but is very loyal and devoted.

Handwriting that leans forward slightly from the vertical is one of the most common. It shows friendliness and affection and looks for that in return. When the slope becomes a little more pronounced, the person is more ardent and extroverted.

An extreme forward slant shows a very emotional person, someone who doesn't like to be tied down.

Handwriting that slopes backward slightly from the vertical is a sign of the introvert—someone who is very reserved, perhaps shy. With the backward slope a little more pronounced, the person is inclined to pull back from other people and does not show emotions, keeping them instead under strict control. A very strong backward slope is a person who, although they may be as ardent and emotional as someone with a strong forward slant, keeps those emotions very tightly bottled up. Extreme slants, backward or forward, indicate someone not necessarily easy to understand, whose emotions or inhibitions may be carried to the extreme.

When just one or two letters slope the opposite way to the rest of the writing, and do so consistently, it indicates a person who is unsure of him or herself and who permits small things to grow out of proportion to more important things. Such a person may become very stubborn over minor details.

Sometimes a person will use a lot of underlining, multiple exclamation marks, dashes, and so on. This is the sign of a person who loves to dramatize and to exaggerate. It may be a good idea to take everything such a person says with a grain of salt. This person is frequently also a compulsive talker.

One of the notable signs in handwriting analysis is the way the writer crosses the letter "t." If the basic cross stroke is placed proportionately to the upright, and extends for equal lengths on either side, this shows a person who is careful with details and who likes to have everything in its allotted place. This person is not a risk taker and will not start something that may not get finished. If the cross stroke is all behind the upright, not crossing it at all, then this is a sign of a procrastinator. If that same cross stroke is sloping downward, toward the upright stem, then the person is not only a procrastinator, but also extremely stubborn. When the downward-sloping cross stroke does go across the upright, equally on each side of it, the person is not only stubborn but also skeptical and cautious of other people's ideas.

When you see hooks on the end of the cross stroke of the "t," the person can be extremely persistent but cautious and will not proceed with any plan unless certain that it is the right time to carry it out. Graceful curves at the end of the stroke show a romantic individual, though conventional and respectful of tradition. The very long cross stroke, usually going off to the right, shows an assertive person and someone who can be very enthusiastic about new ideas. When this long stroke goes upward, from low left to high right, is shows that there are aspirations that may start on a practical level but quickly gain momentum, reaching toward spiritual satisfaction.

The stroke that crosses above, and not connected to, the main upright of the "t" is a sign of a wild imagination, with enthusiasm for the unattainable. This writer does not like to be tied down to routine. When this stroke is in the form of a curve, making the letter like a little umbrella, it shows a sensitive person who has difficulty showing feelings and emotions. This person is a serious thinker and can often be very inventive. When the cross stroke is curved upward, in an arc," the person may easily be influenced by stronger personalities. When one long stroke is used to cross through several "t's" in one word, it indicates a quick mind that can be very resourceful.

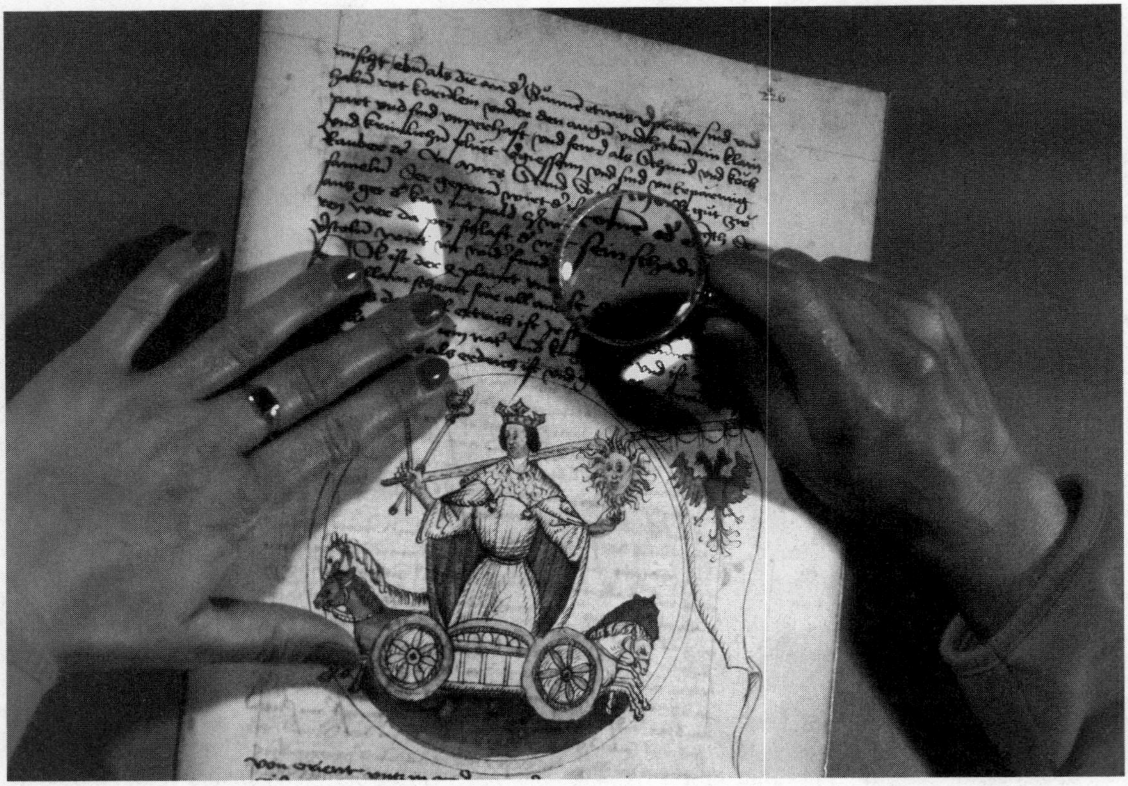

A graphologist examining a fourteenth-century astrological manuscript. ***Fortean Picture Library.***

Another notable indicator is the way of dotting the "i" (this also applies to "j"). If the dot is omitted, at least most of the time, it indicates a person who has little concentration and may even be absent-minded. A regular dot placed over the letter in good alignment shows a person good with details, who is not impulsive and is in good control of his or her emotions. It also shows a cautious approach to life. A small circle in place of a dot can mean an artistic flair, good taste in fashion and decorating, and a desire to be surrounded by beauty. It can also, or alternatively, mean a desire for attention, with the writer trying to obtain admiration from others. Some people also use a small circle instead of a period at the end of a sentence for the same reasons.

Loops—as in b's, h's, and l's—that rise well above the rest of the letters show someone trying to reach upward and away from the material side of life. They frequently have high aspirations for spiritual and intellectual satisfaction. If the loop is also very wide and rounded, there is a need for attention and recognition. Very small upper loops indicate someone who is very reserved and is neither fickle nor frivolous. They do not let their ambitions get out of hand. This person can be very loyal.

Lower loops—which fall well below the other letters as in y's, f's, and g's—show someone who has materialistic aspirations. It can also indicate physical activity and an enjoyment of active surroundings. A very small lower loop is a sign of hesitancy to proceed on the person's own initiative. The writer has modest ambitions.

Very tiny, neat writing is a sign of an artistic personality, or someone with a literary talent who gives great attention to detail. There is great economy of time and energy. Small, rather than tiny, writing shows a scholar or person of keen observation who will usually do very well in his or her chosen field. Very large writing shows an active, often restless, nature, with a desire to accomplish bigger things in life. These are also frequently big-hearted people. Huge writing, however, belongs to the person who is full of him- or herself, egotistical, and unable or unwilling to accept any criticism.

Sources:

Encyclopedia Britannica. Chicago: William Benton, 1964.

Gibson, Walter B. & Litzka R. *The Complete Illustrated Book of the Psychic Sciences*. New York: Doubleday, 1966.

Martello, Leo. *Your Pen Personality*. New York: Hero Press, 1961.

Sara, Dorothy. *Personality & Penmanship: A Guide to Handwriting Analysis*. New York: HC Publishers, 1969.

Shepard, Leslie A. (ed.). *Encyclopedia of Occultism & Parapsychology* New York: Avon, 1978.

Gray, Eden (1902–1999)

Born Priscilla Partridge (changing her name for the stage), Eden Gray was born in 1902 to Florence (Mimi) and Albert Partridge. Her father was son and heir to a Chicago real-estate mogul. They had homes in Florida, the Bahamas, the Hamptons, and Switzerland. Gray did not do at all well in school, failing to graduate. At eighteen she eloped to New York City to marry Lester Cohen, a bohemian poet from a respectable Jewish family. Gray's parents disowned her because of the marriage

Cohen became a writer and Gray turned to the stage, breaking into Broadway. The two traveled extensively, with Cohen eventually making it big as a screenwriter. Gray got some walk-on parts in Hollywood and acted with Frederic March, Brian Aherne, and Katharine Cornell, among others.

During World War II Gray put her acting career on hold to become a lab technician with the Women's Army Corps and, later, earned a doctorate of divinity degree from the First Church of Religious Science in New York.

During the 1950s, Gray owned a bookstore and publishing house—Inspiration House—in New York City. These she had for ten years, publishing books and later also teaching classes on the **tarot.** For three years she had her own radio program.

Gray had not always had an interest in the tarot. It was through ordering tarot books for her customers that she developed an interest. At her country home in Mount Kisco, New York, she taught herself to use the cards. She quickly learned that what few books were available on the subject, such as those of **A. E. Waite** and **Papus,** were written in esoteric, veiled terms. They were hard to read and comprehend, which made the acquiring of knowledge of the subject a hard task. Her customers echoed this criticism. Finding there were no books on the tarot that were easy to use, Gray decided to write her own. The result was three of the best books on the subject, which probably did more than any others to make the cards popular. The books were *The Tarot Revealed* (1960), *Mastering the Tarot* (1970) and *The Complete Guide to the Tarot* (1971).

Gray also started teaching classes on card reading. She later branched out and taught "Science of the Mind" at New York's First Church of Religious Science. It has been said that Gray started a tarot revolution, "moving the cards out of the cloistered salons of metaphysical scholars and into everyday use." She moved to Vero Beach, Florida, in 1971, where she became a member of the Vero Beach Art Club and Riverside Theater and Theater Guild. She died January 14, 1999, in Vero Beach, at age ninety-seven.

Sources:

Gray, Eden. *The Tarot Revealed*. New York: Inspiration House, 1960.
Gray, Eden. A *Complete Guide to the Tarot*. New York: Crown, 1970.
http://www.denelder.com/tarot/tarot013b.html.
http://www.tarotsociety.org.

GREECE

(See also Delphi and Pythia)

The **Oracles** of Greece were of great antiquity. They featured divination and **prophesy** inspired by various means. The Oracles of **Delphi,** Dodona, Epidaurus, and Trophonius were most famous, though there were many others.

At Epidaurus the temple was dedicated to Æsculapius the Healer and Dream-sender. There people would go to sleep in the temple and have **dreams** that would tell them how to heal their sickness. At Trophonius there were a great many caverns. In them it was reported that the sounds of underground waters could be heard, while vapors rose up from them. Seekers would sleep in these caverns for several days and nights. When they were awakened by the priests, they would be questioned. Most of them woke feeling they had terrible sorrow and melancholy.

The Oracle at Dodona, which was dedicated to Pelasgic Zeus, was the oldest of the Oracles and lasted for 2,000 years. There divination was done by interpreting the rustling of leaves in the sacred groves, the sound of wind-blown chimes, and the sound of **water** rushing and falling over rocks. The three priestesses there were known as *Peliades*, meaning "doves." Their titles signified "Diviner of the Future," "Friend of Man," and "Virgin Ruler of Man."

Delphi is probably the best known of all the Oracles. It was located in Phocis on the southern slope of Mount Parnassus. Although dedicated to **Apollo,** it seems certain that the shrine was not originally Apollo's. The site was formerly known as Crisa. It has been said that the Oracle was built above a volcanic chasm and that the **Pythia** gave her answers to questions in a state of trance, induced by intoxicating fumes. According to Justinian (Flavius Anicus Iustinianus 483–565): "In a dark and narrow recess of a cliff at Delphi there was a little open glade and in this a hole, or cleft in the earth, out of which blew a strong draft of air straight up and as if impelled by a wind, which filled the minds of poets with madness." However, both geologically and architecturally this is impossible. There is no crack or cleft, and the local strata have never been capable of producing any kind of gas.

Apart from the **seers** and **sibyls** of the Oracles and the various temples, there was a class of diviners known as interpreters who would divine by the flights of **birds,** and by entrails, thunder, lightning, dreams, and the various other methods common to the area. They would accompany armed forces, if necessary, so that they could advise the commanders before battle. They also advised the government, to prevent uprisings or revolts of any kind.

Æschylus (c. 525–456 BCE), the earliest and perhaps greatest Greek tragic poet, in a passage in his work *Prometheus Vinctus*, has Prometheus tell of the subjects in which he first instructed humankind. He lists dreams and their interpretation, chance words overheard, chance meetings on the road, **auspices,** observation of the flight of birds, **augury** from entrails and from visions seen in the fire. To these, "Suidas" (compiler of the *Suda Lexicon* of c. 1000 CE) adds what he terms "domestic divination"—the interpretation of various trivial incidents of domestic life. He also lists **palmistry** and divination from the twitching of any part of the body. Within his domestic divination were such events as the appearance of a weasel on a roof (bad omen), a snake (good omen), or the spilling of oil (bad—poverty to come), honey, wine (good—success to come), water, or ashes (both indications of misfortune to come). The crackling of logs on a family fire could also be pertinent. Generally it meant that a good friend or good news was coming; but if accompanied by sparks jumping out into the room, it meant that trouble and anxiety were on the way.

In ancient Greece divination from hearing chance words (**cledonomancy**) was a well-established, popular religious form of divination. Lawson relates how an enquirer at the temple of Hermes Agoæus would burn incense before the statue of the god, fill bronze lamps with oil and light them, place a certain bronze **coin** on the altar, then whisper his question in the ear of the statue. The petitioner would then immediately put his hands over his ears and leave the temple. Once outside he would remove his hands and the first words he heard spoken he would accept as the god's answer to his question. At Thebes, Apollo Spodios gave his answers in the same way.

Similar to that is **xenomancy:** divining by the actions of strangers met by chance on the road. For example, it was always unlucky to meet a priest; this more unlucky for men than for women. Worse still is if the priest is riding on a donkey. Meeting a cripple is also a presage of bad luck to come. But to meet someone obviously insane was thought to be lucky, as was meeting a woman and child. This latter indicated that the future would bear fruit.

One of the major forms of divination in ancient Greece was **haruspicy** and **extispy,** the inspection of the entrails of animals. Along with this went **capnomancy,** the study of the smoke when certain parts of the sacrifice were burned.

Sources:

Halliday, W. R. *Greek Divination*. London: William Rider, 1913.

Lawson, John Cuthbert. *Modern Greek Folklore and Ancient Greek Religion*. New York: University Books, 1964.

Lissner, Ivar. *The Living Past*. New York: Capricorn Books, 1961.

Spence, Lewis. *An Encyclopedia of the Occult*. London: George Routledge & Sons, 1920.

Groundhog

One of the old pagan festivals was Imbolc, also known as Oimlec, Candelaria, and Lupercus. It was celebrated on February 2. As with so many pagan festivals, this was later claimed by Christianity, who renamed it Candlemas. Originally being marked with the lighting of bale fires on hilltops across Europe, it was a celebration of the movement through the winter months toward the spring. The festival is still celebrated around the world, as in Sweden with the Lucia Queen and her crown of candles.

There is an old English song that says:

If Candlemas be fair and bright,
Come, Winter, have another flight.
If Candlemas brings clouds and rain,
Go Winter and come not again.
A similar Scottish song goes:

If Candlemas Day be dry and fair,
The half o' winter to come and mair (more).
If Candlemas Day be wet and foul,
The half of Winter's gone at Yule.

This was a time of year when animals were starting to emerge from their hibernation. In Europe the hedgehog was especially noticed. It is said that if the animal came out of hibernation and saw its shadow, indicating that the sun was shining, it would take this as an indication that there would be more weeks of winter to come. If it emerged to find the day overcast, giving no shadow, this would indicate that winter was almost over. You may well think that this is a complete reversal of what might be expected: that sunshine would be an indication of the end of winter and an overcast indicate continuing winter. But such are the vicissitudes of folklore! Tradition held that if the weather was fair at Imbolc, the second half of winter would be stormy and cold.

In America, the animal most noticed in this context of emergence was the groundhog, or woodchuck. According to a Punxsutawney Web site:

> In 1723 the Delaware Indians settled Punxsutawney, Pennsylvania, as a campsite halfway between the Allegheny and the Susquehanna Rivers. . . . The Delawares considered groundhogs (their) honored ancestors. According to the original creation beliefs of the Delaware Indians, their forebears began life as animals in "Mother Earth" and emerged centuries after to hunt and live as men.

By the late 1700s the Germans had settled in Pennsylvania, bringing with them their tradition of Candlemas. An old German couplet went this way:

For as the sun shines on Candlemas Day
So far will the snow swirl until the May.

The earliest reference to Groundhog Day as such is found in the diary of a Morgantown, Pennsylvania, storekeeper named James Morris. For February 4, 1841, his entry reads: "Last Tuesday, the 2nd, was Candlemas day, the day on which, according to the Germans, the groundhog peeps out of his winter quarters and if he sees his shadow he pops back for another six weeks."

Groundhog Day as a time for divining the coming weather was not exclusive to Pennsylvania. An amusing article in Missouri's *Springfield Leader* for February 4, 1936, stated: "Groundhog saw no shadow here and a large faction says it makes no difference whether the hog saw a shadow or not on February 2, as the correct date for such an observation is February 14. The second-of-February faction claim that those who stand by the fourteenth have mixed the date up with Valentine's Day. A great many people are neutral on the subject, or pretend to be in order to avoid making enemies." Interestingly—at that time at least—the majority of the Missourians seemed to believe February 14 to be the correct date.

Since records began to be kept in the early 1800s, it seems that the "official" groundhog, Punxsutawney Phil, has been accurate only 39 percent of the time.

Sources:

Randolph, Vance. *Ozark Superstitions*. New York: Dover, 1964.
http://www.groundhog.org/.

GYPSIES

The Gypsies are a nomadic population who originated in northern India. A mass exodus from that area began about the middle of the ninth century as large groups departed their homeland and moved westward, driven out by successive armies of invaders: Greeks, Scythians, Kushites, Huns, and Mohammedans. The Gypsies passed through Pakistan, Afghanistan, and Persia, eventually reaching the Caspian Sea, north of the Persian Gulf. There they split into two distinct groups, one going northward through Turkey and, by way of Byzantium, into Bulgaria; the other, smaller band, going southward, sweeping down through Jordan into Egypt. By 1348 the nomads were in Serbia with others heading north, through Walachia and into Moldavia. By the turn of that century they were to be found as widely spread as in Peloponnesus and Corfu in the south; Bosnia, Transylvania, Hungary, Bohemia; and, in the early 1400s, in Central Europe. They were in Germany by 1417 and England and Wales by 1430.

As they spread across Europe and other areas, the local populations wondered where these travelers had come from. With their dark, swarthy skin and colorful dress, many people believed that they were descendants of the ancient **Egyptians.** The idea caught on and they were referred to as "Egyptians." This was sometimes shortened to "Gyptians" and eventually to "Gypsies." The Gypsies themselves played up to this idea, claiming to have originated in "Little Egypt."

Gypsies—more correctly Romanies, or Roma—were in many places equated with witches and sorcerers. They were wrongly accused of engaging in black magic and dealing with the devil. In many countries they were banished. But they managed to hang on, tenaciously. They had to do whatever they could in order to survive. Along with making metal and wooden objects, weaving baskets, and mending pots and pans, they trained animals to dance and to do tricks. They also told fortunes. Everybody was interested in trying to learn what the future held, so **fortune-telling**

A Gypsy fortune teller reads the hand of the wife of the Dutch artist, Teniers, early eighteenth century.
Fortean Picture Library.

was a big attraction. Not being great mathematicians, the Gypsies seldom got into astrology or numerology, but they did do a great deal of **cheiromancy, tasseography, phrenology** and **cartomancy.** People treated them as mystics, and the Gypsies filled that role. They carried with them **tarot** cards, and they would work magic, do spells, and perform divination. The author known as **Papus** (Gérard Encausse) said that the Gypsy "has given us the key which enables us to explain all the symbolism of the ages. . . . In it, where a man of the people sees only the key to an obscure tradition, [are] discovered the mysterious links which unite God, the Universe, and Man."

The Gypsies were probably most responsible for the spread of tarot cards across Europe, since they traveled and took the cards with them wherever they went. They have their own ways of reading the cards (see *The Buckland Romani Tarot*), which is extremely effective and accurate. In the days when it was difficult to get tarot cards, they would work with regular playing cards as the minor arcana and add their own handmade cards for the major arcana.

Charles Godfrey Leland (1824—1903), the scholar and litterateur who was founder and first president of the Gypsy Lore Society, wrote that "next to the **Bible** and the Almanac there is no *one* book which is so much disseminated among the millions, as the fortune-teller in some form or other." Leland also says that "Gypsies have done more than any other race or class on the face of the earth to disseminate among the multitude a belief in fortune-telling, magical or sympathetic cures, amulets and such small sorceries as now find a place in Folklore. . . . By the exercise of their wits they have actually acquired a certain art of reading character or even thought, which, however it be allied to deceit, is in a way true in itself, and well worth careful examination."

Sources:

Buckland, Raymond. *The Buckland Romani Tarot: The Gypsy Book of Wisdom*, St. Paul, MN: Llewellyn, 2001.
Buckland, Raymond. *Gypsy Dream Dictionary*. St. Paul, MN: Llewellyn, 1999.
Buckland, Raymond. *Gypsy Witchcraft and Magic*. St. Paul, MN: Llewellyn, 1998.
Buckland, Raymond. *Secrets of Gypsy Fortunetelling*. St. Paul, MN: Llewellyn, 1988.
Clébert, Jean-Paul. *The Gypsies*. Penguin, 1967.
Fraser, Angus. *The Gypsies*. Oxford: Blackwell, 1992.
Leland, Charles Godfrey. *Gypsy Sorcery & Fortune Telling*. Fisher-Unwin, 1891.

Gyromancy

A form of divination where a person walks, or whirls, continually around in a circle until he or she becomes dizzy and falls down. The circle would be marked around its perimeter with letters, possible answers to questions, or even marked as the **houses** of an **astrological** chart. **Omens** were read depending upon the area of the circle where the person fell. Often the person would get up and go on around, to fall time and again, and so give a number of letters or other responses. The object was to ensure that the places where the person fell were pure chance and not premeditated.

Another form of gyromancy was simply to induce a state of **prophetic** delirium. As part of religious rites, the participants sometimes spun around repeatedly, on one or both feet, with arms outstretched. There is a similarity here to the Whirling Dervishes, the sect of Islam that originated in Konya on the Anatolian plateau of Turkey. The sect was founded by Jalal al-din Rumi in the thirteenth century. The object of the Whirling Dervishes was to pass into an ecstatic trance, part of the sacred ceremony known as *sema*.

In Sir Thomas Urquhart's *Third Book of the Works of Mr. Francis Rabelais* (London, 1693) he mentions gyromancy when he says: "Have you a mind to have the truth of the matter more fully and amply disclosed unto you . . . by giromancy, if thou shouldst turn round circles thou mightest assure thyself from me, that they would fall always on the wrong side."

Edward Smedley, author of *The Occult Sciences* (1855), says: "Gyromancy was performed by going round continually in a circle, the circumference of which was marked by letters."

Sources:

Oxford English Dictionary. Oxford: Clarendon Press, 1989.
Spence, Lewis. *An Encyclopedia of the Occult*. London: George Routledge & Sons, 1920.

H

Hæmatomancy

Divination using blood. This was an adjunct of **householdririmancy,** or interpreting signs read from the dripping of blood from a sacrifice or even from a casualty wounded or killed in battle. The quantity of blood, direction of flow, and shape it assumed as it congealed were all things taken into account.

Halomancy

From the Greek *halo*, meaning "salt," and *manteia*, meaning "divination," this is divination using salt. It is done by interpreting random patterns in the salt when it is poured or spread over a surface. Ridges indicate problems and obstacles while depressions and valleys show delays and frustrations.

The idea of spilled salt bringing bad luck comes from the association of salt with life. Salt symbolizes semen, so to spill it is to spill life itself. Consecrated water, such as that used for baptism, is simply water with salt in it.

Sources:

Jones, Ernest. *The Symbolic Significance of Salt*. New York: Spring Publications, 1995.

Hamon, Count Louis—"Cheiro" (1866–1936)

Described as one of the most famous and colorful figures of the early twentieth century, Count Louis Hamon was actually born William John Warner in Bray, south of Dublin, Ireland, on November 1, 1866. Little seems to be known about his early life except that he took the name Louis Hamon and assumed the title of Count. When he got into **palmistry,** he also added the name "Cheiro" (from **cheiromancy**).

Count Louis Hamon, who worked as a palmist under the pseudonym of Cheiro. *Fortean Picture Library.*

Hamon did not confine himself to palmistry; he was also proficient in **numerology, astrology,** and other fields of the occult. During his life he was a lecturer, war correspondent, newspaper editor, and author. One of his books, *World Prediction* (1928), was a best seller despite the fact that it contained few **predictions** that came true.

Cheiro had many famous clients, including Oscar Wilde, Lord Kitchener, Lord Charles Russell, and King Edward VII. He seemed to have been much more successful and accurate predicting the fate of individuals rather than world events. Cheiro predicted the exact date of Queen Victoria's death and the month of Edward VII's death. He also accurately predicted the execution of the czar of Russia.

Cheiro based most of his work on that of medieval writers and modeled his hand classifications on those of Count Casimir D'Arpentigny, a nineteenth-century French palmist. He died October 8, 1936, in Hollywood, California, having predicted the day and time.

Sources:

http://www.solsticepoint.com/astrologersmemorial/cheiro.htm

HANDLING OBJECTS *see* Psychometry

HANDS *see* Cheiromancy

HANDWRITING *see* Graphology; Graptomancy

Harris, Frieda (1877–1962)

Frieda Harris was born Frieda Bloxam in 1877. Little is known of her life other than for the few years surrounding her association with **Aleister Crowley.** She learned metaphysics from him, worked with him on producing the acclaimed **Thoth tarot** deck, and became one of the executors of his will. She moved to India after the death of her husband, where she died in Srinagar in 1962.

As a young woman, Frieda Harris had something of a reputation as a "party girl," vivacious, outgoing, and living life to its fullest. In apparent contradiction to this lifestyle, she married the very staid Sir Percy Harris, Britain's parliamentary chief whip of the Liberal party. He knew, and sternly disapproved of, Aleister Crowley, who had been labeled "the wickedest man in the world" by the media. But as he had with so many women, Crowley seemed to attract Frieda Harris. She knew of him through mutual friend Greta Valentine. Crowley had a large number of affairs with a wide variety of women over the course of his life (though apparently not with Valentine). There is no concrete evidence that he had an affair with Harris, but it would seem completely out of character if he did not, having worked with her for so long.

Harris was interested in metaphysics. She was a member of Co-Masonry, an offshoot of the Theosophical Society. Unlike regular Freemasonry, in Co-Masonry women have equal status with men. As an artist of some talent, Harris painted a number of esoteric "floor cloths" or "tracing boards," also sometimes known as the "carpet." This is a framework of board or canvas on which the emblems of any particular Masonic degree are inscribed for the assistance of a master giving a lecture. It is so called because it was originally the custom to draw these designs on the floor with chalk, which could then be wiped clean when the Lodge was closed. The designs, as Frieda rendered them, were intricate and colorful.

Lady Freida Harris was introduced to Crowley in 1937, fourteen years after he had been expelled from Sicily by Mussolini because of his infamous abbey at Cefalù. Sir Percy was well acquainted with Crowley's reputation—especially his reputation as a womanizer—but was not able to keep his very independent wife from becoming a student of the "great beast." She was formally introduced to Crowley by Clifford Bax, the author and playwright. Bax knew that Crowley was looking for an artist and had originally intended to introduce Meum Stewart and Leslie Blanche to him, but when they missed an appointment he took Frieda along to Crowley's lodging at 93 Jermyn Street, Picadilly. Crowley had been looking for an artist to work on his concept of a tarot deck. Harris seemed an ideal candidate. He envisioned it as a three-month project. It lasted five years.

Beginning officially on May 11, 1938, Crowley started teaching Harris occultism, though she had already been studying anthroposophy at Rudolf Steiner's school. Crowley also led her through his own books. She was no stranger to ritual from her Co-Masonry work, and it wasn't long before Crowley initiated her into his own magical order of the A.A.(*Argentum Astrum*). She took the magical name Tzaba, meaning "Hosts." According to Olive Whicher, who gave Harris some art lessons, she dyed her hair bright red at about this time. This was interesting in that Crowley always referred to his mistresses as "scarlet women."

Harris started sending Crowley money on a regular basis, since he was always desperate for funds. He sometimes asked for more, to the point where, in one of her letters to him (written from Morton House, Chiswick, on May 10, 1939), she had to say: "I am sorry to have to write plainly to you, because I enjoy our friendship & your instruction very much, but it is entirely spoilt by your attempts to use me as your bank & financial adviser. I have frequently told you that I have nothing but a weekly allowance, & that out of it I have given you all I can spare." She went on to say: "If you are expecting the Tarot to be a means of getting money, or my position as useful for pushing it—I am sorry I am not the right vehicle for such an enterprise as I intent to remain anonymous when the cards are shown as I dislike any notoriety."

She worked diligently on the cards, reworking some of them as many as eight times, according to Crowley. Her comments on the work included the following observations: "I have done the 10 of Swords & promptly Russia takes up arms. Where are we going!" She also wrote:

> I do not find the names of the Cards in the Index you have sent me at all illuminating in fact it took me hours to sort which was which. They are much too flamboyant, & I prefer the old names don't you. I hate all those rushing words & feel I've alighted in Taliesom. What am I to print in the surrounds, because I won't do them wrong; it is very hard work. . . . Have you seen that all the Sephiroths in the Index are spelled wrong, at least nearly all

Later Harris makes the remark:

> Do you think there was ever "a woman satisfied"? With what a smirk she would greet the dawn. But, all the same, I want to finish all the experimental work first, tho Mercury is yelling to re-enter the Womb & Incarnate with his Companions. . . . I have acted, however, on the indications afforded by your sketches. Freud would deduce a great deal from your preference.

Crowley, writing from 57 Petersham Road, Richmond, Surrey, responded with:

> "My experience of satisfied women is that they do greet the dawn with a smirk; if not the dawn, any time up to five o'clock in the afternoon, and only when it wears off does one have to start all over again."

Sources:

Crowley, Aleister. *The Book of Thoth*. London: The O.T.O., 1944. http://www.geocities.com/Athens/Acropolis/1896/crowhar.html.

Hartlieb, Johann (c. 1400–1468)

Johann Hartlieb was born about 1400, in Bavaria, on the Danube. His father William was cellar master to Duke Ludwig VII of Bavaria. At age twenty-three, Johann made a pilgrimage to Rome and on his return took up a position with Duke Ludwig as his representative in a lawsuit against Heinrich von Valbert. In 1432, sponsored by the duke, Hartlieb got his degree then went to Vienna. Between 1433 and 1435 he wrote a book on **geomancy.** By 1440 he had a doctorate and, disillusioned with Vienna, went back to Bavaria where he went into the service of Duke Albrecht III of Munich. As adviser and physician, he gained a lot of influence, even in religious affairs. Hartlieb continued his writing on a variety of subjects, including an herbal book. In 1444 he married Sibilla, daughter of Albrecht and Albrecht's first wife Agnes Bernauer of Augsburg. Agnes had been executed in 1435 as a witch.

Shortly after his marriage, Hartlieb opened a pharmacy and did international business. In 1448 he published his work *Chiromantie;* the first book on the subject of **palmistry.** He wrote many books during his lifetime, among them his *Book of All Forbidden Arts* (1456), in which he detailed the arts forbidden by the Church. In 1465 he was appointed physician to Duke Sigmunds. In the next two years he translated an anonymous work on gynecology titled *Of the Secrets of Women*. He was taken ill in 1467, made a temporary recovery, but died on May 18, 1468. The Catholic Church honored his memory as a "fighter against paganism."

Sources:

Headon, Deirdre (ed.). *Quest for the Unknown—Charting the Future*. Pleasantville, NY: Reader's Digest, 1992.

http://www.esonet.at/groups/hartlieb.html.

Haruspication; Haruspicy; Haruspex

(See also Extispicy and Hepatoscopy)

In Sir Thomas Urquhart's *The Third Book of the Works of Mr. Francis Rabelais* (London, 1693) it says: "Will you have a trial of your fortune by the art of aruspiciny? By **augury**? Or by extispicine?"

Aruspiciny, or haruspication, is divining from the entrails of animals, especially from the liver. (The inspection of entrails from *human* victims of sacrifice is **anthropomancy.**) An extant **Etruscan** bronze of the fifth century BCE shows a priest examining an animal's entrails. There is another **Roman** relief from Ostia, dating from the third century CE, that shows a haruspex (*pl.* haruspices)—a specialist in haruspicy—standing with the entrails of an animal. Haruspicy goes back far beyond **Biblical** times. In Ezekiel 21:21 it says: "For the king of Babylon stood at the parting of the way, at the head of the two ways, to use divination: he made his **arrows** bright, he consulted with images, he looked in the liver."

Palmist Johann Hartleib examining his own hand, 1885. *Fortean Picture Library.*

The overall shape of a liver was examined, as were any discolorations or deformities. A swollen gallbladder indicated an increase in power. A depression in the liver-gate (the *porta hepatic*) was a lessening of power. Vein markings and colorings were interpreted according to their resemblance to symbols and to weapons.

In both Babylon and Hittite there have been found clay models of livers that were probably used for training purposes. The oldest of these dates from around 2000 BCE. They are divided into sections and bear markings and inscriptions. One, a representation of a sheep's liver, is divided into fifty-five different sections, reflecting the divisions of the heavens. Another, an Etruscan bronze from Piacenza, is of a liver divided into forty sections, each aligned with a different deity or one of the elements. Etruscan augurers were supposed to be especially adept at interpreting from entrails and were employed in both **Greece** and Rome.

It is not known precisely why so much credence was put into the divination of entrails. One theory states that the anatomical construction of the victim was directly affected by the prayers and religious rites to which it had been subjected. Another held that when an animal is sacrificed to a god it is, in a sense, absorbed by that god. Therefore, to examine the animal is to examine the god, which is a means of ascertaining the divine will and the course of future events. Another theory held that the internal symptoms were so inexorable that only divine agency could fill the diviner's mind in his choice of animal and the interpretation of its entrails. Plato offered yet another view: that the liver was like a divine **mirror** on which the visions contemplated by the soul were left recorded.

Gregory of Tours (538–594), in his *Historia Francorum*, reports an occasion when an emissary of King Guntchramnus consulted the haruspices "in a barbarous manner." Hepatoscopy and **extispicy** (another name for examination of all the entrails) were used by the Romans from about 200 BCE through until the fifth century CE. By the end of the first century BCE, a haruspex was an established permanent member of the staff of a commander-in-chief and was consulted on campaigning tactics and policies.

Haruspication continued in various areas to the eleventh century. The **Incas** practiced it using the viscera of llamas; white llamas were favored for this. In relatively recent times haruspication has been practiced in areas of Africa, Borneo, and Southeast Asia.

Sources:

de Givry, Grillot. *A Pictorial Anthology of Witchcraft, Magic & Alchemy*. London: Spottiswoode, Ballantyne, 1931.

Headon, Deirdre (ed.). *Quest for the Unknown—Charting the Future*. Pleasantville, NY: Reader's Digest, 1992.

Lawson, John Cuthbert. *Modern Greek Folklore and Ancient Greek Religion*. New York: University Books, 1964.

McIntyre, Loren. *Incas and Their Timeless Land*. Washington, DC: National Geographic Society, 1975.

Oxford English Dictionary. Oxford: Clarendon Press, 1989.

HEAD *see* Phrenology

HEARING *see* Clairaudience

HEBREW

The origins of Jewish mysticism are obscure. Although many of the visionary and prophetic passages in the Old Testament played a considerable role in subsequent mystical lore, they were not a part of a continuous esoteric tradition. Some Jewish writings not in the Old Testament suggest the existence of groups that cultivated mystical disciplines. The Qumran sect, for example, had a secret lore of magic. The Zohar, or "Book of Splendor," was written in the late thirteenth century. In due course it became the classical main text of the **Qabbalah.**

The idea that the Hebrew alphabet enshrines the secrets of the universe is one basis of modern **numerology.** In the Old Testament, One is the number of god. Two is a female, and evil, number; the exact opposite of One. In the **tarot,** the twenty-two cards of the major arcana are frequently linked with the twenty-two letters of the

Hebrew alphabet. The cards are also often laid out for a reading in the pattern of the Hebrew Tree of Life, as depicted in the Qabbalah.

The Old Testament of the **Bible** is full of miraculous events and examples of **prophesy, divination, dowsing, precognition,** and **dreams.** Examples are Moses's dowsing for water in the desert, Saul's meeting with the **Woman of Endor,** and the dreams experienced by Joseph and by Jacob.

In the series *Mysteries of Mind Space & Time: The Unexplained*, David Christie-Murray says: "The prophets aimed not so much at foretelling the future as at describing what they saw as the will of God in the circumstances of their time. But in doing so, their prophesies *were* fulfilled, often in ways more profound and long-lasting than they ever imagined."

Sources:

Cave, Janet, Laura Foreman, and Jim Hicks (eds.). *Mysteries of the Unknown: Ancient Wisdom and Secret Sects*. Alexandria, VA: Time-Life Books, 1989.

Christie-Murray, David. *Mysteries of Mind Space & Time: The Unexplained*. Westport, CT: H. S. Stuttman, 1992.

Werblowsky, R. J. Zwi. *Man, Myth & Magic: Cabala*. London: BPC Publishing, 1970.

Hepatoscopy

(See also Extispicy and Haruspication)

Practiced by the Babylonians in the fifth century BCE, this was the art of divining by interpretation of signs and symbols seen in the liver from a sacrificed animal, usually a sheep. To the Babylonians, the liver, rather than the heart, was the center of life and as such was a sacred organ.

The liver is divided into four lobes, which could be interpreted or associated with the four elements or any other significant quadrisection. The surface was then divided into fifty squares. There were also significant layers within the body of the liver, each with its own esoteric interpretation.

Hepatoscopy was essentially the same thing as haruspicy, though the latter might be applied to divination from any of the entrails while hepatoscopy applied only to divination from the liver. Hepatoscopy was also sometimes known as liver-gazing, and involved gazing at the shiny surface of the liver to perform a type of **scrying.** The Babylonian priests known as the baru were experts at this form of divination.

Sources:

Cavendish, Richard (ed.). *Man, Myth & Magic*. London: BPC Publishing, 1970.

HERBS ***see*** **Botanomancy**

HEXAGRAM ***see*** **I Ching**

Hieromancy

Hieromancy is divination from the observation of objects offered in religious sacrifices, or from sacred things. This could be observing the movements of sacrificed animals or humans (**spasmatomancy**), examining their entrails (**anthropomancy, extispicy, haruspicy, hepatoscopy**), and divining from their blood (**hæmatomancy, dririmancy**). In the case of inanimate things, it would cover anything used in a religious context, be it candles, arrows, lots, or anything else.

Hieroscopy

Hieroscopy is divining by observing the movements of victims—be they animal or human—as they are in the process of being led to sacrifice. Fear, anger, horror, despair, frustration—all would be considered and interpreted. Ephraim Chambers's *Cyclopædia; or an universal dictionary of arts and sciences* of 1728 defines it as "a kind of divination, performed by considering the victim and observing every thing that occurs during the course of the sacrifice."

Hippomancy

Observing the actions of a horse, and interpreting them as **omens** of the future, is known as hippomancy. This was a practice of the **Celts,** who had a horse goddess named Epona. They kept white horses in a consecrated, sacred grove for the express purpose of foretelling future events. The toss of the horse's head, the spontaneous prancing, and leading with left or right foreleg were all significant. The Germans similarly kept sacred horses—not necessarily white—for the same purpose. They were kept in a consecrated circle and, when released, it was noted whether the horse crossed the line of the circle with left or right leg first. The right leg was regarded as propitious; the left leg as foretelling inauspicious events.

There is nothing religious about the hippomancy found still existing in the Ozark regions of Missouri and Arkansas. Here various events are looked for following actions observed with horses. One long-held belief is that to see a red-haired woman or girl riding on a white horse is a very good omen. To see such a rider on a mule presages the utmost in good fortune to come. When horses are observed running about their pasture and neighing for no obvious cause, it means that someone in the immediate vicinity is dying. When horses' tails suddenly appear to be very large and bushy, it means that rain is on the way. This is especially so if there has been a drought.

Sources:

Randolph, Vance. *Ozark Superstitions*. New York: Dover, 1964.

Spence, Lewis. *The Magic Arts in Celtic Britain*. London: Rider, 1945.

Horoscope; Horoscopy

(See also Astrology)

Horoscopy is the art of casting a horoscope. A horoscope is an **astrological** natal chart, or birth chart. In effect, it is a map of the configuration of the planets at the very moment of birth of the individual for whom it is drawn. That individual is referred to as the "native." Its accuracy depends on knowing the time of birth—year, month, day,

Astrologer casting a horoscope. *Fortean Picture Library.*

hour, minute—and the place of birth. From this information, the positions of the planets can be placed in the twelve houses of the chart, each of which governs certain events and characteristics, which are drawn in the circle of the horoscope.

To astrologers, the natal chart is a cosmic mirror showing the native's personality, physical features, natural abilities, hopes, fears, worries, and potential for the future.

Sources:

Anderton, Bill. *Fortune Telling*. North Dighton, MA: JG Press, 1996.

HORSE *see* Hippomancy

HOWLING (DOGS) *see* Ololygmancy

Hurkos, Peter (b. 1911)

Peter Hurkos was born Pieter van der Hurk in Dordrecht, the Netherlands, in 1911. He was a member of the Dutch underground movement in occupied Holland during World War II. Prior to the war he was a merchant seaman.

In 1943 Hurkos fell off a ladder while painting an army barracks. He landed on his shoulders and on his head and was unconscious for three days, in a hospital in the Hague. When he finally recovered, he claimed that he had developed **psychic** abilities, including **psychometry.**

Hurkos has told many stories of his own heroic exploits during the war but, unfortunately, none of them can be documented. In fact, some of them seem totally fictitious because of errors in supposed facts he gives. After the war he and his showman brother started giving stage performances of "clairvoyance." From reports it seems that it was pure illusion. When Hurkos was investigated by Professor Albert Bessemans, an investigator of the paranormal and also an expert in stage conjuring, Hurkos failed miserably. Undeterred, Hurkos visited Britain in 1950 but again researchers, including the notable Dr. Eric John Dingwall, found no evidence of paranormal powers.

Various of Hurkos's later claims turned out to be untrue, including one impressive one that he had received a written commendation from the Pope for helping solve the murder of a priest in Amsterdam—a murder that never happened. Others of Hurkos's claimed solving of police cases have also proven untrue.

Hurkos emigrated to the United States where he became a citizen in the 1950s. There his showmanship impressed people in Hollywood, and soon he had a following of credulous celebrities. However, with the exception of Dr. Andrija Puharich, not a single recognized psychic investigator has been impressed with Hurkos's performances.

Sources:

Hoebens, Piet Hein. *Mysteries of Mind, Space & Time: The Unexplained*. Westport, CT: H. S. Stuttman, 1992.

Hydatoscopy

(See also Pegomancy)

Hydatoscopy is **Hydromancy** using rainwater. Many considered rainwater to be more "divine," since it fell from the heavens.

Hydromancy

Divination by means of signs derived from **water,** of which there were many forms. It could be done with water from various sources. Done with rainwater it was termed **hydatoscopy** and with water from a spring, **pegomancy. Scrying** using water was common in ancient times. Any basin of rock filled by rain or by running water would serve as a reflective surface, as would any small pool, pond, or lake.

A common method of working hydromancy was to fill a bowl with water and to suspend a ring on a thread or a fine chain and hold it so that it hung, like a **pendulum,** beside the bowl. It would then be swung so that it struck the side of the bowl. This would cause ripples to move across the surface of the water, and these would be interpreted. This is described by Martin Antoine Del Rio in his *Disquisitionum Magicarum* of 1599. He also mentions another form, which was for three pebbles to be thrown into standing water and observations drawn from the circles that formed.

Nineteenth-century print showing the divination of the future from light cast on a bowl of liquid. ***Fortean Picture Library.***

According to Rimual in *Consilia in causis gravissimis* (1845), one method of finding a thief was to light a consecrated white candle and place it on an altar next to a basin filled with water. A virgin then had to say: "Angelo bianco, Angelo santo, per la tua santità e per la mia virginità, mostrami che ha tolto questa cosa." This meant: "White angel, holy angel, by thy holiness and by my virginity show me who has stolen this thing." Immediately the water would reflect a picture of the thief, as though it were a mirror with the thief standing in front of it.

One method was to study the actions of the sea and interpret by its agitation and color. There was also divination of fountains; the fountains of Palicorus in Sicily were some of the most famous for consultation.

Allowing a single drop of oil to fall on the surface of water contained in a silver or glass cup allowed scrying of the reflective spot it gave. Clemens Alexandinus (fifth century CE) claimed that the women of Germany gave prophetic interpretation based on the sources, whirls, and courses of rivers. This was also commented upon by Juan Luis Vives (1492–1540) in his commentary of St. Augustine's *De Civitate Dei* (Basel 1522). He also stated that diviners in Italy would write the names of three suspected thieves on each of three small balls and toss them into a pond of blessed water. Whichever one first floated back to the bank was the guilty party.

Sources:

de Givry, Grillot. *A Pictorial Anthology of Witchcraft, Magic & Alchemy*. London: Spottiswoode, Ballantyne, 1931.

Grand Orient (A. E. Waite). *The Complete Manual of Occult Divination: Volume 1—Manual of Cartomancy*. London: Rider, 1912.

Spence, Lewis. *An Encyclopedia of the Occult*. London: George Routledge & Sons, 1920.

Hypnomancy

Hypnomancy is described as divination by means of sleep. In this it would cover **dreams** and their interpretation. Also under this general heading could come **spasmatomancy,** which is specifically interpretation of the twitching of the limbs. This, however, could be applied to any twitching that a sleeping person might make while being observed by a diviner.

I

I Ching

I Ching (pronounced Yee Jing), Yi King, or Yik-Kim–also known as the "Book of Changes"—was devised as a form of divination more than 4,500 years ago, by a legendary **Chinese** sage named Fu Shui (or Fu Hsi). China's oldest history book, the *Shu Ching,* states that the I Ching was consulted by ancient governments, its judgment superceding that of the emperor. The I Ching expounds a classical Chinese philosophy based on the dual cosmic principles of **Yin and Yang.** It has been consulted since long before the days of Confucius (540–480 BCE), who claimed to have used it so much that he wore out three sets of leather thongs that held together his copy of the book.

The ancient Chinese philosophers did not believe in a motionless universe; they felt it was constantly changing, hence the name the "Book of Changes" for this oracular method. Changes happen constantly in life, depending upon the operation of **fate.** However, if the future may be viewed, then fate may be influenced. The I Ching allows that to happen. As with the seasons of the year, the changes are cyclical: joy—sorrow—joy—sorrow; wealth—poverty—wealth—poverty; success—failure—success—failure; and so on. The I Ching can tell where you are in the cycle so that it is possible to see ahead and plan accordingly.

The main body of the book consists of sixty-four sections, each headed by a diagram of a hexagram. A hexagram is a figure made up of six lines. These are of two types: broken and unbroken. In earliest times the oracle worked with great simplicity—an unbroken line signified Yes and a broken line signified No—but it eventually became obvious that more than Yes/No answers were needed. The broken and unbroken lines were therefore joined in combinations of three, which gave eight possible arrangements, or *trigrams*. A meaning was given to each of these:

A woman consults the I Ching with the aid of sticks. *Fortean Picture Library.*

Trigram	Name	Meaning
——— ——— ———	Chi'en	Heaven. Male. Creative. Active.
— — — — — —	K'un	Earth. Female. Passive. Receptive.
— — — — ———	Chên	Thunder. Peril. Movement.
— — ——— — —	K'an	Unstable Water. Pit. Danger.
——— — — — —	Kên	Mountain. Arresting progress.

——— ——— — —	Sun	Wood. Wind. Gentle penetration.
——— — — ———	Li	Fire. Beauty. Brightness.
— — ——— ———	Tui	Lake. Marsh. Satisfaction.

If two of the trigrams are placed one above the other (upper trigram and lower trigram), it forms a hexagram. This will give a total of sixty-four possible combinations, and these are what are used for answering divination questions.

Traditionalists throw fifty yarrow stalks to arrive at the necessary hexagrams of interpretation, building them up line by line. More recently **coins** have also been used, which is understandable when the intricacies of using the yarrow stalks are considered. For example, using the yarrow stalks, they are first passed through the smoke of burning **incense** then one is returned to the container in which they are kept. This leaves forty-nine, which are laid down on the ground, or on one of two trays. With his right hand, the diviner quickly separates the sticks into two piles; one now on each side of the first tray. Taking one stick from the right side, the diviner places it between the last two fingers of the left hand. Then the left pile is diminished by pushing away four sticks at a time until only one, two or three remain. This remaining number is placed between the next two fingers of the left hand. Now the right pile is diminished by fours until there is a remainder which goes into the left hand. There will now be, in the left hand, a total of either five or nine sticks. These are laid down in a heap on the second tray. The remaining sticks on the first tray are then bunched together and the whole process is repeated, this time giving a total of four or eight sticks. These are also placed in the second tray, though separate from the first ones. Again the process is repeated with all the remaining sticks on the first tray. This time the result will again be either four or eight. From these three processes, the second tray will contain one of the following combinations: 5 or 9, plus 4 or 8, plus 4 or 8. That will determine whether the bottom line of the hexagram (they are built from the bottom upward) is unbroken or broken, hence a yin or yang line. It will also indicate whether the line is "moving" or not (see below). From here the forty-nine sticks are again bunched all together to begin working on the second line. It can be seen that to work with three coins can be much simpler.

Any three coins of equal size can be used, though three of the traditional Chinese ones—round with a square hole in the center, to allow them to be carried on a square stick—are preferred by many people. The hexagram is built by throwing down the coins. Heads score 3 and tails score 2. A throw might give three tails for the following equation: 2+2+2 = 6. Sixes and nines are what are known as a "moving" line, which is shown as __X__ or ______. If the coins give two heads and one tail, that is 3+3+2 = 8. Eight is a broken line: ___ ___. Even totals are Yin and the odd totals are Yang. Here, then, are the possibilities:

Coins	**Score**	**Representation**
3 tails	6	__X__ (yin, moving line)
2 tails, 1 head	7	_____ (yang)
1 tail, 2 heads	8	__ __ (yin)
3 heads	9	_____ (yang, moving line)

A moving line is said to be in the process of change, with the change being to its opposite. For example, a 9 moving line, although a yang (all heads), is in the process of changing to a yin; from 9 to 8. Similarly, a 6 moving line is a yin in the process of changing to a yang; from 6 to 7. This all means that although the coins (or stalks) have been thrown to obtain a hexagram (and therefore an answer to a question) then if there are one or more moving lines in that hexagram, that question is actually unsettled; it is in the process of change. If the moving lines are then changed to their opposites (to the next progression, up or down . . . 6 to 7 or 9 to 8), then a different hexagram is obtained. The interpretation for this one is read, which will give indications of changes that will be coming up in the future.

The coins, like the yarrow stalks, should be held in the smoke of incense before starting the ritual. They should then be shaken up in the hands rather than in a container, since the vibrations of the questioner will then be absorbed. When thrown, the result should be written down. The first throw is the bottom line of the hexagram, and the other lines are worked upward from there. Each of the hexagrams has a number, which is then looked up in the Book of Changes. That will give the answer to the question.

Here is a chart for finding the number of a particular hexagram. Look along the top for the upper trigram and down the left side for the lower trigram. Where they meet on the chart is the number of the hexagram. For example, K'un (on the top line) and Sun (left column) give the hexagram 46.

HEXAGRAM CHART

	Ch'ien	*Chên*	*K'an*	*Kên*	*K'un*	*Sun*	*Li*	*Tui*
Ch'ien	*1*	*34*	*5*	*26*	*11*	*9*	*14*	*43*
Chên	25	51	3	27	24	42	21	17
K'an	6	40	29	4	7	59	64	47
Kên	33	62	39	52	15	53	56	31
K'un	12	16	8	23	2	20	35	45
Sun	44	32	48	18	46	57	50	28
Li	13	55	63	22	36	37	30	49
Tui	10	54	60	41	19	61	38	58

Hexagrams

1: *Ch'ien*—the creative principle; Grandfather—double creativity, activity, heaven

____
_______ *Ch'ien*
____
____

——— *Ch'ien*

———

A complete set of unbroken lines shows that the "superior person" is capable of benefiting from any endeavor, as long as they are firm in that endeavor. You are powerful enough not to have to call on anyone else's aid. However, it is important that you remain on the straight and narrow path, and that you are correct in all dealings and true in all friendships. This is the best indication of success, no matter what you are trying to achieve. Health, wealth, luck, and good fortune are indicated.

2: *K'un*—the passive principle; Grandmother—double earth, devotion, receptivity

— —

— — *K'un*

— —

— —

— — K'un

— —

The full set of broken lines indicates harmony, but *passivity* is the keyword. You may go astray at the start of projects but will get your bearings and return to the true path. It is necessary to submit to recognized authority, so initiative should be kept at a low ebb. You should be cautious in relations with youngest sons, yet strive to cultivate relations with oldest daughters. Open up your mind and embrace all things.

3: *Chun*—initial difficulty; Oldest son/second son—thunder, movement; unstable water, a pit, danger

— —

——— K'an

— —

— —

— — Chên

— —

Caution is the watchword. Progress and success will be gained by being firm. Nothing should be undertaken lightly. Be wary and you will be able to see the danger ahead and avoid it. Exercise patience. Don't hesitate to seek advice, from any and every quarter. This may be the time to reexamine your priorities and your plan of action. Try to come up with a better plan for the future.

4: *Mêng*—youthful inexperience or immaturity; second son/youngest son—unstable water, a pit, danger; mountains, delay

———

— — Kên

— —

— —

——— K'an

— —

Be resolute in your conduct. New projects need to be carefully nourished. Be wary of ignorance, stubbornness, youthful pride and arrogance, inexperience, and scorn of knowledge. Do not seek out youth to teach, but if youth approaches you, then give advice. However, do so only once; don't waste time and effort in repetition. With the right attitude, you will be assured of success.

5: *Hsü*—waiting; father/second son—creativity, activity, heaven; unstable water, a pit

— —
——— K'an
— —
———
——— Ch'ien

There will be great success if you are sincere in what you do, but you need to be patient and to wait, even though you may feel you need to act right away. Changes are in the process and are all about you. Shifting forces will generate new ideas and fresh opportunities. Good fortune comes with firmness and persistence. Advancement brings achievement. Look at the present situation and procedure as a learning process.

6: *Sung*—conflict; second son/father—unstable water, a pit, danger; creative, active

———
——— Ch'ien
———
— —
——— K'an
— —

Caution; your present path could lead you to conflict. It will not be advantageous to "cross the great stream," be it a stream of thought, consciousness, or tradition. Good intentions alone are not enough. It could help to visit a "great man," someone with power and influence. You need an inner adjustment; a new outlook on life. In your personal life, try to stay away from open confrontation at this time.

7: *Shih*—the army (battle; competition); second son/mother—unstable water, a pit, danger; earth, receptivity

— —
— — K'un
— —
— —
——— K'an
— —

There is some optimism. Weakness is in the lines, but harmony is also there. A seasoned leader is needed; someone who is firm and exact. Nourishment and feeding of the people is the best way to have an army of good soldiers in readiness. In other words, prepare well in advance for future contingencies. Be aware of others' needs and thoughts. Be firm in your resolve and know that what you are doing is right.

8: *Pi*— mother/second son—earth, receptivity, devotion; unstable water, a pit, danger

— —
——— K'an
— —
— —
— — K'un
— —

Reexamine your values and intentions. If you are on the true path, and your resolve is firm, then you will succeed. If you are hesitant, success will be slow in coming. If you are too slow in acting, failure will be the result. There is a chance that you have been chosen to be a special leader and to take people forward on a positive course. If this is so, you must be absolutely certain of your own feelings and desires and must be sure that you are working for the common good.

9:*Hsiao Ch'u*—restraint from lesser powers; father/eldest son—creative, active, heaven; wind, wood, gentleness

———
——— Sun
— —
———
——— Ch'ien
———

It will seem as though your best efforts are thwarted and you are making no progress. There will eventually be progress leading to success, though not quite as you had envisioned it. Although there are indications of possible further problems, they will not manifest. When you do attain success, it will be advantageous not to proclaim it loudly. Relations with eldest sons can be helpful.

10: *Lü*—treading carefully; youngest daughter/father—lake, marsh, joy; creativity, activity, heaven

———
——— Ch'ien
———
— —
———
———

You may accidentally "tread on the tiger's tail," but you will be lucky in that it will not bite. A hazardous position, but no failure as a result. You may, then, be cautiously optimistic. Success awaits you. This can be a very inspiring time for you if you conduct yourself well. Beware of chaos and disorder.

11: *T'ai*—peace; father/mother —creativity, activity, heaven; earth, receptivity, devotion

```
—— ——
—— ——      K'un
—— ——
——————
——————     Ch'ien
——————
```

Good fortune and success. The small and bad are gone; the good and the great have come. The hexagram is enigmatic. The active and bright principles of yang lie within while the dark, passive forces of yin are without: there is strength within and acceptance without. Expectation of slow but steady progress is indicated. At the moment, ideal conditions exist for new awakenings. Tread carefully and plan well. A good time for the start of new projects.

12: *P'I*—stagnation; mother/father—earth, receptivity, devotion; creativity, activity

```
——————
——————     Ch'ien
——————
—— ——
—— ——      K'un
—— ——
```

There is a negative omen, though it is more of an impasse than an outright failure. There is little expectation of good luck, but nothing is set in concrete. A great deal of patience and obedience is necessary at this time. There are strong counterforces present. The "superior person" must not slacken from righteous persistence.

13: *T'ung Jên*—fellowship with humankind; second daughter/father—fire, brightness, beauty; creativity, activity

```
——————
——————     Ch'ien
——————
——————
—— ——      Li
——————
```

A harmonious union is to come. If your goal is pursued with no taint of selfishness, then it will be achieved. The results will be long-lasting. It will be favorable to make a journey of some sort, though one involving the crossing of water will be especially efficacious. Do not slacken your righteous persistence.

14: *Ta Yü*—abundance; father/second daughter—creativity, activity, heaven; fire, brightness, beauty

```
——————
—— ——      Li
```

———
———
——— Ch'ien
———

Great progress and absolute success. The "superior person" suppresses what is evil and gives distinction to what is good. Prosperity and abundance are indicated, for families as well as for individuals. This is undreamed of. The only possible downfall could come from excessive pride, but this is extremely unlikely.

15: *Ch'ien*—humility; youngest son/mother—mountain, delays; earth, receptivity, devotion

— —
— — K'un
— —
———
— — Kên
— —

Modesty and humility bring success especially with new projects, which show great promise. Make modesty and moderation your special goals. Forces at work around you are in the process of balancing out, so extremes of any sort are not in evidence. Moderation should therefore be your keyword. Watch your reactions to people and events, and try not to overreact.

16: *Yü*—enthusiasm; Mother/oldest son—earth, receptivity, devotion; thunder, movement

— —
— — Chên
———
— —
— — K'un
— —

Happiness and preparation, plus enthusiasm. This is a condition of harmony, pleasure, and satisfaction; there is much optimism here. This is a time to install helpers and to start armies marching; however, beware of showing too much enthusiasm when starting new projects. This is a good sign for musicians and entertainers of all sorts.

17: *Sui*—following; oldest son/youngest daughter—thunder, movement; lake, marsh, joy

— —
——— Tui
———
— —
— — Chên
———

The balance in the lines of this hexagram indicate long-range goals. If there are long, verbose discussions, it is essential that decisions are made shortly after these discussions. Firm and consistently correct behavior is equally essential. There is no possibility of error. Plan ahead for the distant future, laying in stores in case of any future shortages.

18: *Ku*—stop decay; oldest daughter/youngest son—wind, wood, gentleness; mountain, delay

Kên

Sun

It is important to proceed with plans and, if necessary, to make a journey in connection with those plans. Conditions may not be good now, but they will improve. Some duties will be viewed as annoying, even painful, but they must be completed and brought to a satisfactory conclusion. Try to learn lessons from any such problems.

19: *Lin*—approach; youngest daughter/mother—lake, marsh, joy; earth, receptivity, devotion

K'un

Tui

Righteous persistence brings rewards. Cautious optimism may be allowed. Favorable results through the proper use of authority. Inspect, comfort, then rule. You are in a wonderful position to successfully carry out your plans and to help others carry out theirs. Watch for misfortune in the eighth month.

20: *Kuan*—contemplation and observation; mother/oldest daughter—earth, receptivity, heaven; wind, wood, gentleness

Sun

K'un

The ablution has been made but the offering has not yet been given. Inspire trust and respect through sincerity and dignity. There is a division between those in authority and those under them. If you are the one in authority, put yourself in the other's place before acting. There is room for instruction. Remember that others are watching you as you watch those below you.

21: *Shih Hô*—biting through; first son/second daughter—thunder, movement; fire, brightness, beauty

———
— — Li
———
— —
— — Chên
———

A favorable time for legal proceedings. There are natural antagonisms between inferiors and superiors. There may be some small regret but there is no error. Stick to the letter of the law. Optimism is more prevalent than pessimism; there is good progress in the endeavor. This is a good time to reform. Seek out the barriers to your progress and help change them and remove them.

22: *P'I*—elegance; grace; father/first daughter—fire, brightness, beauty; mountain, delay

———
— — Kên
— —
———
— — Li
———

Ornamentation is found in nature and is appropriate in society but it should be secondary to that which is substantial. Don't be carried away by outward appearances. Don't spend so much time in beautifying that you do not prepare for coming problems. The sun shines on the mountains in beauty, but the darkness of night is not far behind. You may be flamboyant in your working, but there should be a hidden strength behind the outward display.

23: *Po*—disintegration; mother/youngest son—earth, receptivity, devotion; mountain, delay

———
— — Kên
— —
— —
— — K'un
— —

Extreme caution is called for. You are not at a stalemate; do not proceed in any direction at the moment. Force will not help. Delay any and all decisions. Carefully examine those who would undermine your position. Great patience is needed. Watch carefully the opposition and competition. Be kind and benevolent to others. This is a time for submissive action.

24: *Fu*—return; eldest son/mother—thunder, movement; earth, receptivity, devotion

```
— —
— —      K'un
— —
— —
— —      Chên
———
```

Within seven days you will be back in an advantageous position; you will then be able to proceed in any direction you wish. There will be no opposition. Friends will come to you, to join you and lend their forces. Projects initiated on the heels of old failures will gain immediate success. You need to continually keep reassessing your position and your goals.

25: *Wu Wang*—the unexpected; eldest son/father—thunder, movement; creativity, activity, heaven

```
———
———      Ch'ien
———
— —
— —      Chên
———
```

Simply do what you feel should be done, without detailed planning and goaling. The farmer plows in the spring even though he cannot predict what will happen in the fall. When he encounters difficulties, he must adapt to them. So let it be with you. Righteous persistence will bring its reward. Those opposed to righteousness will meet with injury.

26: *Ta Ch'u*—the great taming force; father/youngest son—creativity, activity, heaven; mountain, delay

```
———
— —      Kên
— —
———
———      Ch'ien
———
```

There is much work to be done. There will be difficulties but you must struggle onward and not despair. Try to develop a friendship with problem people, for they may be of help to you at a later date. This is a good time for travel. You are in possession of valuable information, whether or not you realize it; this is potential advancement for you. Now is the time to undertake new projects, carefully planning ahead for all contingencies.

27: *I*—nourishment; oldest son/youngest son—thunder, movement; mountain, delay

———
— —　Kên
— —
— —
— —　Chên
———

With firm correctness there will be good fortune. An important advance will be made in one project. Beneficial gains require careful consideration of all aspects of the situation. You must look hard at what you plan to do and ensure that all efforts are directed to its completion. Trust your own judgment. Benefit from lessons learned in the past.

28: *Ta Kuo*—excess; oldest daughter/youngest daughter—wind, wood, gentleness; lake, marsh, joy

— —
———　Tui
———
———
———　Sun
— —

The present situation is becoming weighted with a large number of considerations. A decision must be made immediately, for it could quickly become an explosive situation. Look for a way out, an avenue of escape. Success is for those who remain resolute, firm, and strong. You cannot ignore the situation.

29: *K'an*—the abyss; second son—doubly unstable water, a pit, danger

— —
———　K'an
— —
— —
———　K'an
— —

There is grave danger! Action is important, but think carefully before you act. An advance will be followed by achievement. The knowledge and experience you are about to gain will be invaluable in the future. Beware of trickery and deceit; watch out for theft. You could be injured or become involved in a serious dispute.

30: *Li*—fire; the clinging; second daughter—double fire, brightness, beauty

———
— —　Li

Li

The energy of the total far exceeds the energies of the separate parts. Make the best use of energy; don't fight it but use it. External conditions are constantly changing. You must be ready to change with them. Be flexible—do not try to stick to predetermined plans. Cling to that which is available at the moment.

31: *Hsien*—influence; youngest son/youngest daughter—mountain, delay; lake, marsh, joy

Tui

Kên

You must be open and receptive to whatever may present itself at the moment. A quiet openness allows you to be influenced and also to influence. Both must be experienced to allow change. It will be to your advantage to seek advice from your superiors. The "superior person" keeps his mind free from preoccupation and open to receive the advice of others.

32: *Hêng*—duration; oldest daughter/oldest son—wind, wood, gentleness; thunder, movement

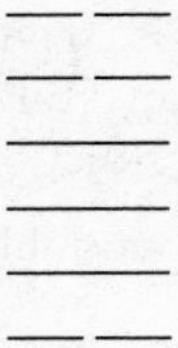

Chên

Sun

Remain firm and do not change your plans. However, do have a long-term goal in mind. Righteous persistence brings rewards. Continuity and unity are important. Avoid undisciplined actions. Listen to your inner voice. There will be successful progress and no errors.

33: *Tun*—withdrawal; youngest son/father—mountain, delay; creativity, activity, heaven

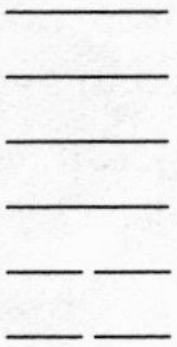

Ch'ien

Kên

Caution is needed. Do not try to contest an opponent directly but compromise, if necessary, and be prepared to retreat immediately if you have to. Keep "small men" at a distance and in their place. Do not abandon your principles, but now may be a good time to take a sabbatical, review the past and plan the future.

34: *Ta Chuang*—the power of the great; father/oldest son—creativity, activity, heaven; thunder, movement

```
— —
— —     Chên
———
———
———     Ch'ien
———
```

Advantage will come to the one who judiciously employs power and authority, yet strength should only be employed to do that which is right. This is a good time to advance. Exercise your power, but do not abuse it. You will find that you have unusual power, especially in personal relationships. Be responsible in all that you do; responsibility is the keynote.

35: *Chin*—progress; mother/second daughter—earth, receptivity, devotion; fire, brightness

```
———
— —     Li
———
— —
— —     K'un
— —
```

This is a very positive hexagram. Gratitude will be shown by a superior; gifts are possible. There are good things in the immediate future: progress, rewards, advantages. This is also a wonderful opportunity for good communication with family and in business; with family, unity is a blessing. This is a good time to examine your relationship with others: your equals, those above you, and those below you.

36: *Ming I*—darkening the light; second daughter/mother—fire, brightness, beauty; earth, receptivity

```
— —
— —     K'un
— —
———
— —     Li
———
```

You need to be patient and understanding. There will be benefits if you are able to stand up to your superior's inadequacies, but do not flaunt your knowledge. Be patient and await the right time. To act now would cause jealousy and difficulties.

Time is an excellent teacher and now is a time to draw on past experiences. Expand your knowledge by study and research.

37: *Chia Jên*—the family; second daughter/oldest daughter—fire, brightness, beauty; wind, wood, gentleness

———

——— Sun

— —

———

— — Li

———

When everything is in its proper order, all is well. The family is headed by father and mother, then come the children in the order of their seniority. If everyone knows their place, then things run smoothly and progress is made. It will be advantageous to assist those who have the greatest responsibility. One of the best ways to do this is to see that you attend to your own responsibilities.

38: *K'uei*—opposition/contradiction; youngest daughter/second daughter—lake, marsh, joy; fire, brightness, beauty

———

— — Li

———

— —

——— Tui

———

There is a sense of contradiction and of opposition, yet there can still be progress in small matters. This is a time to examine both sides of every question. Others may see you as indecisive or even contradictory, but take the time to examine. Strongly avoid discord. Watch out for distrust and suspicion among family members and business associates.

39: *Chien*—obstruction; youngest son/second son—mountain, delay; unstable water, a pit, danger

— —

——— K'an

— —

———

— — Kên

— —

It will be advantageous to meet with a "great person." Don't be afraid to seek advice. Persistence is important. Obstacles in your path are part of the normal course of events and must be overcome in order for you to progress. If necessary, pause and build your strength before tackling the obstacle. Within yourself, these are inhibitions that, again, must be overcome.

40: *Hsieh*—liberation; second son/oldest son—unstable water, a pit, danger; thunder, movement

— —
— — Chên
———
— —
——— K'an
— —

This hexagram follows from the previous one in that it shows relief of the tension and removal of the obstruction. Tension and anxiety are passing, both in business and in personal relationships. This is a time for a fresh new start. Put the past behind you and look to the future. In business, this is a good time for expansion. In your personal life, it is a good time to make a fresh start with loved ones.

41: *Sun*—decrease; youngest daughter/youngest son—lake, marsh, joy; mountain, delay

———
— — Kên
— —
— —
——— Tui
———

Take control of your emotions. Use whatever you have in hand to promote your interests. You could lose some income or property, though this may be through giving to others. Lack of profits from investments now means increased profits later. Remember that the pendulum swings and, though it may swing backward now, it will swing forward again later. Be totally involved and totally sincere in all that you do.

42: *I*—increase; oldest son/oldest daughter—thunder, movement; wind, wood, gentleness

———
——— Sun
— —
— —
— — Chên
———

Much optimism. A good time to start new projects. An active time in business, with prosperity ahead. There is a great deal of energy coming into your situation so make the most of it; work on new projects immediately, getting them off the ground. By showing your commitment constantly and consistently, you will meet with success.

43: *Kuai*—resolution; father/youngest daughter—creativity, activity, heaven; lake, marsh, joy

— —

——— Tui
———
———
——— Ch'ien
———

Beware of speaking too frankly and do not flaunt, or even show, your strength. Advance with caution. Defeat your enemies by making a firm, public resolution to advance as you wish to advance. Undermine them without doing battle with them. Change will only come with determination and steady, open progress.

44: *Kou*—encountering; youngest daughter/father—wind, wood, gentleness; creativity, activity, heaven

———
——— Ch'ien
———
———
——— Sun
— —

Not a good time to marry or join in partnership. If you are not careful, problems could escalate. Women hold the power at this time. There is negativity here, but negativity from which you can learn. New situations can arise suddenly and unexpectedly. You will encounter a person or situation that you cannot avoid. This is a time of temptation, so be on your guard.

45: *Ts'ui*—assembling; mother/youngest daughter—earth, receptivity, devotion; lake, marsh, joy

— —
———
———
— —
— — K'un
— —

There is a celebration, party, or convention; a gathering together of many people. Whether you are the leader of this group or simply one of those involved, you should give all your energies to the good of the group and its advancement. You may be called upon to contribute or make a sacrifice. It will benefit you in the future if you do this. Prepare your forces for any unforeseen circumstances. A good time for marriage.

46: *Shêng*—ascending; oldest daughter/mother—wind, wood, gentleness; earth, receptivity, devotion

— —
— — K'un
— —
———

——— Sun

— —

You will be recognized from an unexpected source, gaining public praise. Don't let this praise go to your head. This recognition could be in the form of a promotion, an increase in income, or merely an announcement of your worth. Business will prosper; blooming like flowers in the spring. As your business and personal life prosper, do not become prideful or arrogant; in addition, do not become lazy and careless.

47: *K'un*—adversity; second son/youngest daughter—unstable water, a pit, danger; lake, marsh, joy

— —

——— Tui

———

— —

——— K'an

— —

Cautious pessimism is here. Many outside forces are restricting progress and success. Don't allow the negative forces to destroy your character. Persistence in a righteous cause will eventually lead to success. You will feel exhausted and tired of battling the odds. There will be empty promises made; do not rely on the spoken word. Not a good time for marriage.

48: *Ching*—the well; oldest daughter/second son—wind, wood, gentleness; unstable water, a pit, danger

— —

——— K'an

— —

———

——— Sun

— —

It may take the cooperation of several others to accomplish what you want. If you do not have success, you need to work at improving your career, your image, and your way of doing things. Togetherness is important. Knowledge is there for the taking; it is never-changing. All you have to do is reach out for it.

49: *Kô*—revolution; second daughter/youngest daughter—fire, brightness, beauty; lake, marsh, joy

— —

——— Tui

———

———

— — Li

———

What may, on reflection, seem like an unwise alteration to your original plans will actually turn out for the best. This change will come after careful reflection and recognition of circumstances. You will see what went wrong and how you should have planned for it in the first place. Learn by this experience. Do not be afraid of change, but be prepared for it.

50: *Ting*— the cauldron; oldest daughter/second daughter—wind, wood, gentleness; fire, brightness, beauty

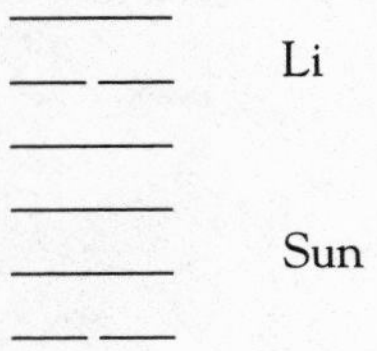

This is a time when you can confidently express your opinion, but do not say anything vicious or contrary. You, and all those with whom you are associated, will attain success. Everything around you is developing positively at this time. Share knowledge, so that it may be meaningful—knowledge kept to yourself is of little use.

51: *Chên*—thunder/shock; oldest son—double thunder, movement

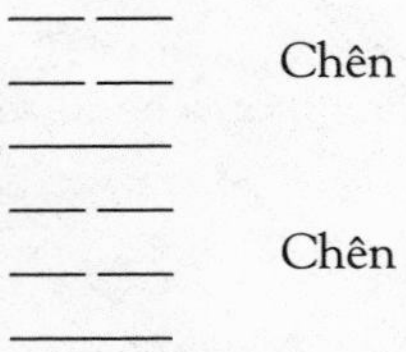

There will be a favorable advance into a good position. It will startle others like a crash of thunder. It is time to shock a few people! This is a good time to examine your business and personal relationships. Unfinished business can cause trouble at this time; tie up all those loose ends as quickly as possible. You will find that you have a sudden burst of energy to get things done. Once the immediate shock is over, you will be able to look back and laugh.

52: *Kên*—stillness; youngest son—double mountain, delay

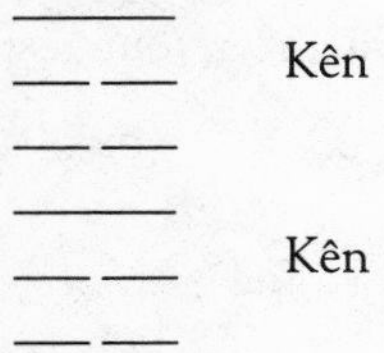

Rest when it is time to rest—as it is now—and act when it is time to act. In this way your progress will be even and constant. The truth is found in balance and harmony. This is a good time for meditation. Practice it; it will refresh body, mind, and

spirit. Meditate on your goals and your plans for reaching them. This is a quiet time, not a time for action.

53: *Chien*—gradual progress; growth; youngest son/oldest daughter—mountain, delay; wind, wood, gentleness

———
——— Sun
— —
———
— — Kên
— —

Reward and advancement will soon be here. You should be aware of the true nature of daily life; it is neither positive nor negative. Be aware of all that is good in life. In order to reach your objective, you must take the slow, traditional path, which may seem too long for you. Be patient; there are no shortcuts.

54: *Kuei Mei*—the marriageable maiden; youngest daughter/oldest son—lake, marsh, joy; thunder, movement

— —
— — Chên
———
— —
——— Tui
———

This is not a good time for business. You are completely at the mercy of circumstance. Try to stay flexible. You are not in control of anything and must be ready to jump in any direction. Be frugal; this is not the time for spending. Marital disputes cannot be resolved at this time; it is well to remember that strife is as much a part of marriage as is bliss! Try to avoid any great arguments.

55: *Fêng*—abundance; second daughter/oldest son—fire, brightness, beauty; thunder, movement

— —
— — Chên
———
———
— — Li

This is no time for sadness; you should be celebrating. There is development and progress. You may feel a sense of satisfaction at what you have achieved. Greatness, prosperity, and brilliance are suggested in this hexagram. However, you must make some judgments about where you are and where you wish to be. Get rid of excess baggage.

56: *Lü*—the wanderer; youngest son/second daughter—mountain, delay; fire, brightness, beauty

———

— — Li
———
———
— — Kên
— —

Success in small things. A stranger, or exile, is shown in this hexagram. Sometimes he finds friends and shelter, but many times he must simply rough it and survive as best he can. If you are able to make the best of things, you will progress, step by step. Recognize when you have exhausted your resources and know when to move on. When it is time to move, it is time—so don't delay! All of this applies as much to "inner journeys"—to thoughts and imagination—as it does to physicality.

57: *Sun*—willing submission/gentle penetration; oldest daughter—double wind, wood, gentleness

———
——— Sun
— —
———
——— Sun
— —

You must allow the other person to influence you. Willingly submit in order to gain advancement in small things. Try to understand the thinking of your superiors. From this you will be able to recognize what is possible for you and what is not. At all times keep your long-term goals in mind. Be prepared for a long, slow move forward to achieve your goals.

58: *Tui*—joyfulness; youngest daughter—double lake, marsh, joy

— —
——— Tui
———
— —
——— Tui
———

Caution brings success. Progress and attainment are shown. You will find encouragement. True joy depends upon strength within and firmness of purpose, manifested outwardly as gentle yielding. Keep the atmosphere around you one of gentleness and good will. Your success will be continuing.

59: *Huan*—dispersion; second son/oldest daughter—unstable water, a pit, danger; wind, wood, gentleness

———
——— Sun
— —
— —

——— K'an

— —

Progress and success. Travel, especially over water, is advantageous at this time. This is a good time to relocate and to change careers. Business travel would be advantageous. Persistence will pay off if the course is righteous. Marriage plans may be delayed due to pressures of work for both parties. On all things, take time to look within; try to see the whole picture before making any decisions.

60: *Chieh—limitation; youngest daughter/second son—lake, marsh, joy; unstable water, a pit, danger*

— —

——— K'an

— —

— —

——— Tui

———

There are limitations throughout nature, from the changing time of the year to the weather conditions. It is necessary to adapt to these changes in order to move ahead. Consider the limitations being presented to you and how they are preventing your attainment of goals. Evaluate the situation so you can bypass any hindrances and move ahead. Where there are limitations that you cannot change, accept them rather than needlessly fighting against them.

61: *Chung Fu*—insight; youngest daughter/oldest daughter—lake, marsh, joy; wind, wood, gentleness

———

——— Sun

— —

— —

——— Tui

———

Inward confidence and sincerity. Highly favorable circumstances. This is an excellent time to cross the waters and to make use of an unloaded boat (or carrier of some kind). Don't be deceived into thinking that brute force and physical strength have any lasting impact. The advantage here is in selflessness; there is good fortune for those who appreciate its advantages.

62: *Hsiao Kuo* —conscientiousness; youngest son/oldest son—mountain, delay; thunder, movement

— —

— — Chên

———

———

— — Kên

— —

Progress and attainment. It is advantageous to be firm and correct. Action is called for in small projects, but hold off and show patience where large projects are concerned. Listen to any ideas or suggestions from those beneath you, whom you might normally consider inferiors. There might even be advantages in making small deviations from what would be considered normal. Maintenance is important at this time, as is restraint.

63: *Chi Chi*—after completion; second daughter/second son—fire, brightness, beauty; unstable water, a pit, danger

```
___ ___
_______     K'an
___ ___
_______
___ ___     Li
_______
```

Progress and success in small matters. You've been very lucky to start with, but there may be some problems ahead. Plan for the future and guard against any negative eventuality. Persistence in a righteous cause will pay dividends. A major project could be completed ahead of schedule, but in order to hold on to any gains you need to be on top of things constantly. This is also a good time to start new projects.

64: *Wei Chi*—before completion; second son/second daughter—unstable water, a pit, danger; fire, brightness, beauty

```
_______
___ ___     Li
_______
___ ___
_______     K'an
___ ___
```

Progress and apparent success. The goal is within sight; within grasp. However, there is some humiliation due to being overconfident. Beware of showing off. This is the moment just before what seems like certain victory, but do not assume that by achieving this goal you will be home and free. Good judgment will still be called for and order must prevail. There are still many things that need to be done after the moment of victory.

Note that in the full translations of the I Ching, far more detailed interpretations are given and they are followed by additional line-by-line interpretations.

Sources:

Blofeld, John. *I Ching: the Book of Change*. Allen & Unwin, London 1968.

Buckland, Raymond. *Coin Divination: Pocket Fortuneteller*. St. Paul, MN: Llewellyn, 2000.

Da Liu. *I Ching Coin Prediction*. New York: Harper & Row, 1975.

Wilhelm, Richard (Cary F. Baynes, tr.). *The I Ching*. Princeton, NJ: Princeton University Press, 1967.

Wing, R. L. *The I Ching Workbook*. New York: Doubleday, 1979.

Ichnomancy

According to Edward Smedley's *The Occult Sciences* (1855), "Ichnomancy is the art of finding out the figure, peculiarities, occupations, etc., of men or beasts by the traces of their posture, position and footsteps." This would seem to mean that it was a form of divination by interpreting body language, though for animals as well as humans.

Ichthyomancy

This was the ancient art of examining the heads and the entrails of fish and interpreting them for divination purposes. It was a branch of **haruspication.**

Iconomancy

Iconomancy is divination using icons. An icon is, for example, a likeness, image, picture, or portrait. An icon used in divination is invariably a religious image. It may be an image painted on a flat surface or a sculpted figure (**idolomancy**).

The word "divination" is so called because it is considered a gift of the divine—a gift from the gods. By sitting quietly, possibly meditating and focusing on the icon, the seer makes contact with the deity and receives that gift directly. It may come in the form of a vision (**clairvoyantly**), by hearing a voice (**clairaudiently**), whether audible to others or not, or in some other way. The act may or may not be accompanied by some type of ritual.

Idolomancy

(See also Teraphim)

A variation on **Iconomancy,** where a sculpted figure is used rather than a painting.

IDOLS *see* Idolomancy; Teraphim

IFA *see* Conchomancy

INCA *see* Mexico and Central America

INCENSE *see* Knissomancy

Incubation

(See also Palmistry: Indian and Vedic Astrology)

In **Egypt** through the Greco-Roman period, and in **Greece** and **Rome** themselves, there was a practice known as incubation, where a priest or priestess would sleep in a temple for the express purpose of receiving divine knowledge through **dreaming.** In ancient Greece and Rome, dreams were regarded as tools by which the gods let humankind know what was to happen in the future. To interpret these sleep-thoughts, there came into being a class of interpreters known as the *oneirokritai* or *oneiromantists*.

They were professional interpreters and the art they practiced was **oneiromancy.** One of the books they used, in which they tabled their interpretations, was the *Oneirokritika* of Artemidorus, produced in the second century CE and still in existence.

India

The ritual focus of the Aryan cult, which entered northwest India somewhere between 1700 and 1200 BCE, was animal sacrifice. **Haruspicy,** and its attendant forms of divination, then came to the fore. In the *Rig-Veda* mention is made of great sacrifices. Later records speak of smaller sacrifices, many of them domestic in nature. The diviner of the period was the *Brahmana,* or priest-magician of the Vedic tribe. But although in the past many of the forms of divination outlined throughout this volume have been practiced, in India today the emphasis is on **palmistry, numerology,** *Jyotish* or Vedic **astrology,** and the **I Ching.**

Indian palm readers term their art *Samudrika,* named after king Samudra of prehistoric times. It is said that Shiva, the third deity in the Trimurti of the gods, taught palmistry to Sarasvati, the wife of Brahma, who is the senior member of the triad. Sarasvati is the goddess of music, wisdom, and knowledge. Although many of the Indian palmists claim that theirs is an ancient art and that in ancient times there were many texts on the subject, in fact they all follow the traditions of Western **cheiromancy** of the Victorian period.

There are about twelve palm leaf libraries, containing **oracle** texts, still in existence in India. The palm leaves in the libraries were written in an ancient form of Tamil, a Dravidian language of Madras state. These libraries may be consulted in a Nadi-reading, which concern the lifelines and life expectancies for each man and woman, and are designed to help manage their present incarnations.

In India a board known as the Sungka Board is used for divination. It may once have been a form of the abacus. It is described as having two large wells, one at each end. These then have a row of seven smaller wells extending from them. The two rows of seven are parallel, giving the board a total of sixteen wells: two large and fourteen small. Apparently these wells were once filled with such items as cowrie **shells,** nuts, and pebbles. It was mostly used for such mundane things as finding when a person would get married or what was the most auspicious day for travel.

Sources:
http://www.brihaspatinet.atfreeweb.com/.
http://www.vedalink.com/.
Wheeler, Sir Mortimer. *Man, Myth & Magic: India*. London: BPC Publishing, 1970.
Wheeler, Sir Mortimer. *Early India and Pakistan*. London: Praeger, 1968.

Internet Fortune-Telling

There are numerous Internet sites on the World Wide Web that offer to tell fortunes. There are **astrology** sites, **palmistry** sites, **I Ching, conchomancy, tarot,** and even sites that delve into lesser-known, esoteric methods of divination. They are far too numerous—and tenuous—to attempt to include them all in this volume, though some of the better, more stable ones are to be found in the Resources section at the end of this book.

Internet fortune-telling has become big business, with people paying (mainly by credit card) to have their fortunes told. By going to any search engine and entering the type of divination sought, innumerable sites may be found.

J

Japan

There is no single dominant religion in Japan; several religious and quasi-religious systems exist side by side. In connection with some of the Shinto sects, various occult rites are practiced, the aim of which is to bring about possession by spirits of the gods. Both priests and lay persons practice this, undergoing a period of purification to promote it. They use *gohei,* the Shinto symbols of consecration, together with the *shintai,* or god-body. **Prophesy,** divination, and the curing of disease are the objects of these rites.

At many Japanese Shinto shrines, slips of paper containing fortunes are for sale. If the fortune written on the paper is not favorable, the recipient will loosely tie the piece of paper to a neighboring tree, hoping that the wind will blow away the bad fortune. In the *Nihongi,* the Japanese cosmological "bible," there is the story of certain discontented princes with treasonous plans who, in 658 CE, sought to divine their future. They made offerings to appropriate spirits and did incantations. They then drew **lots** in the form of slips of paper covered with magical inscriptions.

Many Japanese customs have a magical significance. At the Festival of the New Year, houses are thoroughly cleansed, physically and spiritually. Gateways are decorated with straw ropes made to represent the lucky numbers of three, five, and seven. Mirror cakes, associated with the Sun Goddess, are eaten along with lobsters.

Divination is performed by various methods. **Divining rods** are used, and **scapulomancy** and **omoplatoscopy**—using the shoulder blade of a deer—are also performed. The I Ching is also a favorite in Japan. The celebrated medieval Japanese seer, Taka Shima Kaemon, made prognostications with very accurate and far-reaching results, based on the I Ching. He is still held in high regard in Japan. Many modern diviners,who use I Ching claim to carry on a tradition transmitted from him, through is successors. Modern businessmen and politicians consult them frequently.

A divination method popular among women who have lost their lover by death, is to put a hundred rush-lights into a paper lantern and repeat an incantation one hundred times. One rush-light is removed at the end of each repetition. When there is only one light left, that is taken out into the darkness and blown out, at which time the ghost of the lost lover is supposed to appear.

The Association of Friends of the Spirit—*Reiyuka*—came into being in Japan in the early 1920s, founded by Kakutaro Kubo and Kotani Kimi. It was a new movement focused on the mandala and Lotus Sutra of the thirteenth-century Buddhist monk Nichiren. Reiyuka emphasized the transfer of merit to ancestors by reading the Sutra. An offshoot of Reiyuka developed in 1938, called *Rissho Koseikai*—The Society for Righteousness and Friendship. This was founded by Niwano Nikkyo and Mrs. Naganuma Myoko, a **spiritualist medium.** The organization practiced two types of divination: **astrology** and **numerology.**

Another method found in Japan (which probably came from China) is turtle divination. This was the method used by the official diviners, attached to the Emperor's court, from the middle of the seventh century until 1868. Heat is applied to a turtle shell and the cracks that develop are then interpreted. The Shinto god Saniwa-no-kami had to be summoned when the divination was performed. The shell itself was prepared by being cut into a pentagonal shape and had the figure known as *machi* incised on the back, using a chisel *katahori*. A twig of cherry wood, about the thickness of a finger and known as *hahaka*, was lit and drawn down the grooves of the shell. It was first moved down the vertical line and then along the horizontal ones. This was continued until there was a loud report and the shell cracked. It was then sprinkled with water, using bamboo stalks, and the lines of the cracks were highlighted with India ink.

Sources:

Davis, F. *Myths and Legends of Japan*. London: Hadland, 1917.
Loewe, Michael and Carmen Blacker. *Oracles and Divination*. London: Allen & Unwin, 1981.
Offner, C. B. and H. van Straelen. *Modern Japanese Religions*. London: Twayne, 1963.
Spence, Lewis. *An Encyclopedia of the Occult*. London: George Routledge & Sons, 1920.

JUNG, CARL GUSTAV (1875–1961)

Carl Gustav Jung was born July 26, 1875, at Kesswil Thurgau, Switzerland. He studied medicine at the University of Basel from 1895 to 1900, receiving his doctorate in 1902 from the University of Zurich. He read a number of books on the occult while he was still a student, and he attended **spiritualist séances.** The material he gathered while studying alchemy, spiritualism, and **clairvoyance** became the basis of his doctoral thesis. As a physician, he assisted Eugene Bleuler at the Burghölzli Mental Hospital in Zurich.

At age twenty-eight, Jung married Emma Rauschenbach. They had one son and four daughters. Between 1907 and 1912 Jung became a disciple of Sigmund Freud, though Jung later went his own way because of Freud's emphasis on sexual theories and disregard of occult ideas. He marked his break with Freud with a paper titled "Symbols of the Libido" (1913) .

Jung's psychology is based on the theory that the mind is in three parts: the conscious, the personal unconscious, and the collective conscious. This last contains archetypes derived from distilled memories of the whole human species. He believed that **dreams** gave "expression to ineluctable truths, to philosophical pronouncements, illusions, wild fantasies . . . and heaven knows what besides!"

Carl Gustav Jung. ***Fortean Picture Library.***

In order to better understand the value of predictions arrived at by casting **lots** and similar, it is necessary to consider Jung's theory of what he termed *synchronicity*. Cause and effect express the evolutionary aspect of physical and psychological phenomena, but synchronicity looks at the random and the unique. Synchronicity is an attitude toward nature that is diametrically opposed to that of causality. Separate things occurring simultaneously, if studied by a **seer,** can be used for predicting the future.

Jung used the **I Ching** with some of his patients, finding parallels between the **oracles** and the patient's dreams or psychological states. In 1959 he published a book on flying saucers: *Flying Saucers: A Modern Myth of Things Seen in the Sky*. Notable works of Jung's (in English translation) include *The Theory of Psychoanalysis* (1912), *Psychology of the Unconscious* (1916), *Psychology and Religion* (1938), and *Psychology and Alchemy* (1953). Both he and his wife died in 1961.

Sources:

Burt, Cyril. *Man, Myth & Magic: Jung*. London: BPC Publishing, 1970.
Fishley, Margaret. *The Supernatural*. London: Aldus, 1976.
Rakoczi, Basil Ivan. *Man, Myth & Magic*. London: BPC Publishing, 1970.
Spence, Lewis. *An Encyclopedia of the Occult*. London: George Routledge & Sons, 1920.

JYOTISH *see*Vedic Astrology@chapter break:

K

KAPLAN, STUART R.

Stuart R. Kaplan became interested in **tarot** cards while vacationing at the Nuremberg Toy Fair in February 1968. There he purchased his first deck: the Swiss 1JJ Tarot deck. He actually bought the deck for his children, but after finding how well tarot decks sold, he gave up his job on Wall Street and concentrated on cards, eventually starting his own publishing company. At the urging of Brentano's, a New York bookstore, Kaplan wrote his first book on the subject in 1970: *Tarot Cards for Fun and* ***Fortune Telling.***

Kaplan began to collect decks of interest, gradually building one of the largest and best collections in the world. He quickly became the recognized expert on the subject of the cards. When speaking of Italian decks recently, Kaplan said, "There exist today several fifteenth-century Visconti-Sforza *tarocchi* decks which comprise the earliest known tarot cards. . . . Italy holds the honor of having produced several of the earliest known *tarocchi* packs that contain the mystical and allegorical trump cards."

Today Kaplan is president of U.S. Games Systems, Inc., one of the largest distributors of cards, games and tarot-oriented items in the world. With his wife, Marilyn R. Kaplan, they have the world's largest collection of more than 800 tarot decks.

Kaplan's other books include *The Tarot Classic* (1972), *Encyclopedia of Tarot, Volume 1* (1978) and *Volume 2* (1988), and *Tarot of the Witches Book* (1989). The Kaplans live in Connecticut with their five children: Mark, Peter, Michael, Christopher, and Jennifer.

KARMA

The word means "action" but, according to the doctrine of Brahmanism, Hinduism and Buddhism, amounts to "as you sow, so shall you reap." It is tied into the concept of

reincarnation, in which everyone goes through a number of lives and in each life atones for the errors of the previous one. What actually occurs after death varies a little with different theologians. According to Hindu and Buddhist doctrines, a system of rewards and punishments starts immediately following death. Those who have led an exemplary life will enjoy a brief period of joy in paradise. Those who have been wicked will suffer any of a number of hells of varying torment, depending upon the transgressions, though these serve only as reminders of what has been done and foretastes of what is to come. Eventually all are reborn to again be either rewarded or punished in the new life, dependent upon what was done in the previous life. There is a succession of lives until the slate has been wiped clean.

The concept of karma in Wicca is somewhat different. There is a belief in the "Threefold Law," or the law of threefold return. Do good, and good will be returned, either three times or at three times the intensity. But do evil, and that too will return threefold. But these returns are thought to be within the current lifetime. There is no "putting off" of rewards or punishments; they come about in the present life.

In the Hindu and Buddhist doctrines, the point of reincarnation is to return, in other incarnations, in order to expiate one's transgressions. It is not until the slate has been totally wiped clean that there will be no further incarnations. In Wicca, however, the purpose of reincarnation is for experience. A number of lives on Earth are gone through in order to learn and to experience all things. Only when everything has been learned and experienced does the cycle cease. Each individual life is not dependent upon the previous life, as it is in the Hindu and Buddhist doctrines.

Sources:

Buckland, Raymond. *The Witch Book: The Encyclopedia of Witchcraft, Wicca, and Neo-paganism.* Detroit: Visible Ink Press, 2002.

Spence, Lewis. *An Encyclopedia of the Occult.* London: George Routledge & Sons, 1920.

Kelley, Edward (1555–1593)

Edward Kelley made a name for himself as assistant to Queen Elizabeth I's **astrologer,** Dr. **John Dee.** A native of Lancashire, England, Kelley—who sometimes used the name Talbott—was born in 1555. Little is known of his early years other than the fact that he lost his ears after being convicted of the offense of "coining," at Lancaster. He then affected the wearing of a black cap to cover his loss. He subsequently moved to Worcester and established himself as a druggist.

Kelley was a lover of luxury and turned to alchemy and searching for the Philosopher's Stone, in the hopes of striking it rich. It was said that as a necromancer he could get the dead to speak and tell the secrets of what the future held. He gained a reputation for **scrying.** This reputation reached the ears of Dr. John Dee, whose own scryer, Barnabas Saul, had recently left his employ. Kelley took over the position, allowing his powerful imagination to describe incredible sights he said he received from the "great crystalline globe" that Dee possessed. By his enthusiasm—and fertile

Edward Kelley raising a corpse. *Fortean Picture Library.*

imagination—he quickly won Dee's confidence and established himself as a needed associate to Dee.

Dee carefully recorded all the conferences he held with the **spirits,** courtesy of Kelley's **crystal ball** gazing. In 1659 Méric Casaubon published *A True and Faithful*

Relation of what passed between Dr. John Dee and some Spirits. Soon the reputation of the duo extended across Europe, and Kelley found himself traveling with Dee and both their families.

First was a visit to Poland in the company of Albert Laski, Count Palatine of Siradz. They lived sumptuously for a while with the count, ostensibly trying to create gold using the count's own gold as part of the experiment. When they had drained him of his fortune, they continued on to Prague and the Emperor Rudolph II. The emperor was aware of Dee and his reputation but wary of Kelley. After a short stay they had to rapidly move on, due to a Papal Nuncio complaining of them being heretical magicians.

Stephen, king of Poland, was next to greet them but soon tired of their demands for gold. Count Rosenberg was the next in line and they stayed two years living off his hospitality at Trebona, in Bohemia. Kelley, on a number of occasions, proclaimed to Dee that he did not like what the "spirits" were telling him to do and that he would quit. Each time Dee would increase his salary, and Kelley stayed. Eventually Kelley claimed that the spirits were demanding that the two men exchange their wives. Dee and his wife, Jane Fromond, were virulently opposed to this but, when Kelley left and later returned, Dee was so glad to have him back that he acquiesced and the four signed an agreement to share everything in common.

Dr. John Dee eventually grew restless to go back to England and, obtaining permission from Queen Elizabeth to return, finally did so, leaving Kelley in Bohemia. Kelley tried to go back to Prague, but on his arrival there he was arrested by order of the emperor and thrown into prison. He managed to get release and wandered about Germany telling fortunes and scraping a living. Arrested a second time, as a heretic and sorcerer, he tried to escape and fell from the dungeon wall, breaking both his legs and two ribs. He died of his injuries in February 1593.

Sources:

Buckland, Raymond. *The Witch Book: The Encyclopedia of Witchcraft, Wicca, and Neo-paganism*. Detroit: Visible Ink Press, 2002.

Shepard, Leslie, A. (ed.). *Encyclopedia of Occultism and Parapsychology*. Detroit: Gale Research, 1978.

KEPHALONOMANCY *see* Cephalomancy

KEY *see* Cleidomancy

KERAUNOSCOPIA *see* Ceraunomancy

King, Bruce—"Zolar" (1897–1976)

Bruce King was born into a poor family on Chicago's north side on July 22, 1897. When he was about five years old he received a hit on the side of his face from a baseball bat, which gave him a crossed right eye. As a result he became the butt of other kids' jokes for the early part of his school life. Eventually, of his own volition, King went to a free eye clinic where he was operated on. He returned home to find his parents frantic, not knowing where he had been.

His parents, devout Roman Catholics, wanted King to be a priest, but he dropped out of his freshman year of high school to study drama. Although he wrote and acted in his own play at age sixteen, King ended up selling men's hats. From that job he went on the road with a salesman for a line of men's wholesale clothing. King was the "packer-model" for the line. From there he went out again as a salesman for himself and, by the age of nineteen, was making $20,000 a year and driving a red Roamer. (Manufactured by the Barley Motor Company, the Roamer slogan was "America's smartest car.") King enjoyed this success for a year before going into the army during the last few months of World War I.

Bruce King. ***T.H.O.T.H.***

Once out of the army, King headed for California, where he went from men's wear to the securities business, and quickly became a successful broker. At the crash of 1929, having survived it himself, King went to Mexico City intent on opening Mexico's first stock exchange. The Mexican government had other ideas, however, and he was sent back to the United States. By 1931 the Depression had passed and King, returning to California, bought a radio station in Los Angeles. There he found that the only person who made any real money was an **astrologer** known as "Kobar." Kobar would give readings over the air and then sell **horoscopes** at one dollar each. King found that Kobar was selling over 4,000 horoscopes a week. King made Kobar station manager, though later both of them decided to quit. King went to New York but, not finding what he wanted there, decided to go back to his hometown, Chicago. When he got there he found several letters from Kobar waiting for him.

King went to the local radio station and purchased seven-and-a-half hours a week of air time and wired for Kobar to join him. They became partners, with Kobar doing the show and King managing the business. After only a month they were making $5,000 a week, selling horoscopes at a dollar each. Within a few months they had the third-highest-rated radio show in Chicago. This inspired them to expand to Detroit, St. Louis, Wheeling, Columbus, Pittsburgh, and Fort Worth. In each city King would hire an actor, give him a mystical name such as "Ramar" or "Yogar," and have him read Kobar's old scripts. They had to hire thirty women in a large room in Chicago to ship the horoscope orders.

One day, quite unexpectedly, Kobar decided he was quitting and left the partnership. King did the only thing possible—he took over as "astrologer." He armed himself with Kobar's old scripts and starting reading up on astrology. After only one show he knew he had found his niche. From national radio stations, King expanded into theater lobbies with a machine called the *Astrolograph*, which dispensed ten-cent horoscopes. The first one, placed in the Paramount Theater in New York, sold 1,800 horoscopes the first day. About this time King dubbed himself "Zolar," which was a combination of "zodiac" and "solar." He trademarked the name.

The machines proved unreliable, with frequent breakdowns, so King next expanded into retail stores, selling horoscopes first in Kresge and later in Woolworth department stores. Full counter and window displays ensured initial sales as high as 700 a day. King later published the *Official Astrology Magazine* and started writing books on astrology, **dreams,** and other aspects of the occult.

In 1972 King met **R. Donald Papon,** who was at that time editing ***Sybil Leek***'s *Astrology* magazine. Papon was also teaching astrology courses at New York City's New School University. King didn't usually let anyone cast his chart, but he made an exception and let Papon do his horoscope. He was sufficiently impressed that he asked Papon to edit his own astrology magazine, which Papon agreed to do. They worked together for a number of years on astrological and other projects. In 1975 King's health deteriorated from bone cancer. One evening he called Papon to his apartment, at 25 Central Park West, and asked him if he would take over Zolar Publishing, a going concern, saying "Don, you're the next Zolar." Papon, however, declined. King seemed not surprised. On January 15, 1976, King died.

In February 1979 King's widow, Billie, also died, leaving the Zolar Publishing Company and all rights to the Zolar name to Donald Papon. Papon picked up the banner and has been writing "Zolar" books ever since.

Sources:

http://www.zolar-thoth.org/.
R. Donald Papon: personal papers.

KLĒDŌN

The klēdōn was a recognized **omen,** or utterance, received at a **Greek** oracle. At the **oracle** of Hermes, at Achæa, there was a large statue of the god in the market place. In front of the statue was a stone hearth that had bronze lamps attached. The petitioner would burn **incense** on the hearth, fill the lamps with oil and light them, place a **coin** in the right hand of the statue, and whisper his or her question into the statue's ear. The petitioner would then cover his or her own ears and leave the market place. When the ears were uncovered, the first words or sound heard signified the answer to the question. This was the klēdōn, an omen or utterance that meant more than the person realized.

Sources:

Encyclopedia Britannica. Chicago: William Benton, 1964.

KNISSOMANCY; LIBANOMANCY; LIVANOMANCY

The majority of magical, religious, and **divinatory** rites are accompanied by the burning of incense. There was an old belief that the smoke of incense carried prayers up to the gods. In addition to this, the burning of incense very much added to the ambience, or "vibes," of a ritual area. The **Etruscans** used incense on burning coals to ascertain who, if anyone, had bewitched them. It was only a small step from there to noticing and studying the smoke of the incense as a sign of forthcoming events—a form of **capnomancy.** Grains of sesame or black poppy were thrown on hot coals and, from the smoke that rose from it, omens were drawn.

It seems probable that incense smoke would be interpreted according to its volume, density, and the way in which it ascended. The direction it moved would be important, as would the consistency of it: whether it was continuous or sporadic, for example. Broiling, swirling, thick smoke might indicate troubles and problems, while thin, wispy smoke could indicate slight activity of an inconsequential nature. If the smoke assumed unusual shapes this, too, would be significant.

Sources:

Leland, Charles Godfrey. *Etruscan Magic & Occult Remedies*. New York: University Books, 1963.

KNOTS *see* Omphalomancy

KUMULAK

Kumulak, as a form of divination, is from the steppes of Kazakhstan, in Central Asia. The word means "sheep droppings" and is a form of **scatomancy.** It was also known as *Bhal* and "the mirror of destiny." Kumalak was practiced by the *bhalcha*, or **shamans,** of the area. In modern times, and beyond Kazakhstan, it is practiced using such items as coffee beans, small broad beans, and other types of bean rather than actual sheep "beans." A Kazakhstan **soothsayer** is known as a *shakerjan*. He would dry sheep droppings in the sun before using them for divination.

The method, as refined, is to use forty-one beans. These are laid out in a preordained order, on a grid drawn on a cloth. The simple grid represents a Kazakh horseman of the steppes, with each square corresponding to a part of the body:

3 EYE *Köz*	2 HEAD *Bas*	1 EYE *Köz*
6 HAND *Qol*	5 HEART *Jürek*	4 HAND *Qol*
9 FOOT *Ayaq*	8 HORSE *At*	7 FOOT *Ayaq*

The first row describes the past. The second row describes the present. The third row describes the future.

The forty-one beans are placed in a pile below the grid, then roughly divided into three smaller piles. One pile is placed on the left, one in the center, and one on the right. Beginning with the pile on the right, four beans are removed at a time until there are left only one, two, three, or four beans. These leftover beans are placed in square one on the grid. The same thing is then done with the middle pile, taking away in fours until there is only one group left, which is placed in square two. Repeat with the third (left-hand) pile and place the remaining beans in square three.

All the remaining beans are now gathered together and once again randomly divided into three piles. Again beginning with the pile on the right, the same process is gone through, placing the leftover beans in squares four, five, and six. For the third time the steps are repeated, putting beans into squares seven, eight and nine. Any remaining beans are discarded. Each group of beans on the grid will contain one, two, three or four beans. The traditional names for the combinations of beans describe the elements, such as "water in the head," "wind in the eyes," "sand in the heart" and "fire in the hands." The best combination is known as "Mother Earth" and consists of four beans in each square of the bottom row. This indicates that nothing can go wrong.

The actual interpretation is based on numerology, numbers being of great importance in the Kazakh tradition. See **numerology** for the meanings associated with numbers. These meanings may then be applied to the configuration of the grid.

Sources:

Blau, Didier. *Kumalak Mirror of Destiny*. Australia: Simon & Schuster, 1999.
http://www.serenapowers.com/.

L

LABIOMANCY

From the Latin *labium*, meaning "lips," this is a form of divination involving lip reading. It is similar to **cledonomancy** in that it is a combining of different people's lip movements, taken at random. Even if the actual words uttered are not heard or recognized, the movement of the lips and the suggestion of words leads the diviner to his or her conclusions.

LAKE, LISSANNE (B. 1956)

Lissanne Lake is an award-winning professional artist and illustrator who works primarily in the science-fiction/fantasy and New Age fields. She was born in Jersey City on August 30, 1956. She obtained a bachelor of arts degree in illustration from Jersey City State College and went to work in advertising, in New York. She later turned to freelance illustration.

Lake has done more than seventy book covers plus numerous paintings for magazines, advertisements, games, **cards** and other products. She has done work for Doubleday, Harper Prism, Upper Deck, TSR, *Dragon* magazine, Middle Earth, Mythos, Galactic Empire, Supernova, Gridiron, Redemption and more. She has done covers for books by Terry Pratchett, Thomas Disch, **Raymond Buckland,** and Scott Cunningham, among others. Her work has been prominently featured at many gallery shows, including the prestigious Olympia and York Show in New York. She has collected a number of awards including at Worldcon.

One of the book covers Lake did for Llewellyn Publications was *Secrets of Gypsy Fortune-Telling* by Raymond Buckland. Buckland liked the cover so much he asked Lake if she would be the artist for a **tarot** deck he was working on. This became the acclaimed *Buckland Romani Tarot,* published in 2001.

In her spare time, Lake studies Italian rapier fencing, using full weight weapons. She has a sixteen-year-old cat named Sebastian and is a lifetime gamer, playing (and winning) a variety of card games. As a collectible-card artist, Lake has done well over three-hundred cards for various games, including Doomtown, Legend of the 5 Rings, Age of Empires, Shadowfist, Mythos, Middle Earth, and Warhammer 40K.

Sources:

Buckland, Raymond. *The Buckland Romani Tarot: The Gypsy Book of Wisdom*. St. Paul, MN: Llewellyn, 2001.

LAMPADOMANCY

While John Gaule, in *The Magastromancer: or the magicall-astrologicall-diviner posed and puzzled* (1652), says simply: "Lampadomancy (divining) by candles or lamps," *Sydenham (New) Society Publications: Lexicon of medicine and allied sciences* (1888) calls it "a mode of divination by the observation of substances burned in a lamp."

Lampadomancy is divination from the form, color, and various movements in the light of a lamp, all of which might vary dependant upon the fuel used. Some burned cleanly, with little flicker, while others burned with much spluttering and even smoke. Sparks from the wick meant news. Other interpretations depended upon the individual **seer.**

Sources:

Grand Orient (A. E. Waite). *The Complete Manual of Occult Divination: Volume 1—Manual of Cartomancy*. London: Rider, 1912.

Oxford English Dictionary. Oxford: Clarendon Press, 1989.

LANDFORMS *see* Topomancy

LAPP *see* Siberia

LARGE OBJECTS *see* Macromancy

LAUGHING *see* Geloscopy

LAUREL TREE *see* Daphnomancy

LAVATER, JOHANN KASPAR (1741–1801)

Johann Kaspar Lavater was a Swiss clergyman, born in 1741 at Zurich. Lavater noticed that everyone's hands seemed to be unique. He said that "the hands of man are equally diverse and dissimilar as their faces . . . just as it is impossible to find two faces perfectly alike, so it is impossible to find two people whose hands resemble each other perfectly." It has been said that in this he anticipated the forensic art of fingerprinting.

Lavater went on to become a proficient **palmist** and also founded the art of **physiognomy,** or reading character from faces. He wrote a book titled *Physiognomical Fragments for the Promotion of a Knowledge of Man and of Love of Man*. This included his drawings of faces and how to interpret them in terms of character. The book was published in 1775. The German playwright and poet Goethe contributed a chapter to the book, about the skulls of animals. Lavater's book contained comments of his such as: "The eyes and nose in particular tell of sincerity, frankness, and sensibility. A benevolent person," and, "A face of noble character, including sincerity, fortitude, humor, perseverance, harmony." He included a sketch of his own face, with the words "the commentary is before the world—in this book."

Lavater was very exact in his interpretation of faces. Of one example he said, "The man with this face is a heavy drinker, and this is seen in every one of its features. The nose, the lips, the wrinkles—all suggest an 'unquenchable thirst.' There is a lack of energy in the look, and the whole face has been altered. It is puffy, wrinkled, and very ruddy."

Sources:

Fishley, Margaret. *The Supernatural*. London: Aldus, 1976.
Wilson, Colin (ed.). *The Supernatural: Signs of Things to Come*. London: Aldus, 1975.

LEAD *see* Molybdomancy

Leadbeater, Charles Webster (1847–1934)

Born February 17, 1847, in Hampshire, England, Charles Webster Leadbeater early in life was a curate in the Church of England. At age thirty-seven he went to Adyar, Madras, India, to visit the headquarters of the Theosophical Society and to meet its co-founders, **Helena Blavatsky** and Henry Steel Olcott. He quickly became enamored of the society and devoted himself to the cause of theosophy, which was dedicated to the foundation of a universal brotherhood without distinction of race or creed, the study of comparative religion, and the investigation of unexplained faculties in humans.

Leadbeater spent some time traveling through India and to Ceylon, accompanying Colonel Olcott, and publicly professed himself a Buddhist. He developed various **psychic** abilities and began to gain a reputation as a **seer** and as an expert at **crystallomancy.** Leadbeater became a leading member of the Theosophical Society. He returned to England in 1890, where he became a private tutor. The following year, on the death of Madame Blavatsky, Leadbeater started working closely with Annie Besant, who grew to fill Blavatsky's place as leader of the society, eventually becoming its president in 1907.

In 1906, while Leadbeater was in the United States, a number of mothers brought charges against him for sexual misconduct with their sons. Leadbeater was homosexual and had unusual views on the tutoring of young men. Annie Besant couldn't accept these charges so Colonel Olcott was appealed to. But a judicial committee of the society summoned Leadbeater to appear before them. In the face of clear evidence, he was asked to resign.

In 1907, on Colonel Olcott's death, the General Secretary of the Society, Dr. Weller van Hook, sent an open letter championing Leadbeater's theories on the sexual upbringing of young boys, even claiming that the defense was dictated to him by one of the Mahatmas. The following year the British convention of the society requested of the general council that Leadbeater and his practices be repudiated. The council disagreed, and Leadbeater was restored to membership. As a result of the controversy, seven-hundred members resigned. But Leadbeater went on to exert a powerful influence with his clairvoyant teachings and theories on **reincarnation.** He was especially influential in India.

In 1908 Leadbeater and Annie Besant jointly sponsored a young Brahmin boy named Jiddu Krishnamurti, whom they believed to be a Messiah. They founded the Order of the Star of the East to propagate his mission, but in 1929 the young man renounced his role and dissolved the order. He did, however, go on to become a notable spiritual teacher.

Late in life Leadbeater moved to Australia and became a bishop of the Liberal Catholic Church there. He died in 1934. During his lifetime he wrote a number of books that have since become minor classics in their field. They include *Man: Visible and Invisible* (1902), *The* ***Astral*** *Plane* (1905), *A Textbook of Theosophy* (1912), *The Hidden Side of Things* (1913), ***Clairvoyance*** (1918), and *Man: Whence, How and Whither* (1913). This last was in two volumes and written with Annie Besant. In *Man: Visible and Invisible* Leadbeater included illustrations of **auras,** which he claimed to see clearly. He said that auras and halos were emanations of astral bodies.

Sources:

Shepard, Leslie A. (ed.). *Encyclopedia of Occultism & Parapsychology*. New York: Avon, 1978.

LEAVES *see* Phyllomancy

Lecanomancy

Lecanomancy is divination by the inspection of **water** in a basin. Author Grillot de Givry states that it was performed by allowing precious stones to drop into water. He said that a mysterious whistling sound resulted, which then announced the thing desired. Samuel Purchas, in his *Pilgrimage* (1614), says: "They had also their Lecanomancie, which was observed in a Bason (*sic*) of Water, wherein certaine plates of golde and silver were put with Jewels, marked with their jugling characters." Their "juggling characters" were, presumably, magical sigils inscribed to promote the divinatory process. Thomas Blount, in *Glossographia* (1656), refers to a Lecanomancer as "a diviner by water in a bason."

The fact that the water was in a basin, or vessel with a large surface area, would seem to have been important, since it was stressed repeatedly. What the "whistling sound" mentioned by de Givry might have been, we do not know. It might have been solely in the mind of the seer. The action of adding gold, silver, and jewels probably contributed colors and sparkle to the water, which were triggers for the process of divination.

Arthur Edward Waite, writing as "Grand Orient," says: "This is another method of divination by water, which must be placed in a silver vase on a clear moonlight night. The light of a candle is reflected from the blade of a knife on to the water, on which the gazer must fix his concentrated attention. Should he possess any faculty of **clairvoyance,** he will read an answer to his questions either pictorially or literally represented upon the smooth and shimmering surface."

Sources:

de Givry, Grillot. *A Pictorial Anthology of Witchcraft, Magic & Alchemy*. London: Spottiswoode, Ballantyne, 1931.

Grand Orient (A.E. Waite). *The Complete Manual of Occult Divination: Volume 1—Manual of Cartomancy*. London: Rider, 1912.

Oxford English Dictionary. Oxford: Clarendon Press, 1989.

Leconomancy

Leconomancy is similar to **lecanomancy** in that it utilizes **water** in a basin, but it is described as divination using oil poured onto water in basins. The **seer** studies the shapes assumed by the oil and is also influenced by the colors seen in the oil, much as the colors of the jewels are seen in lecanomancy.

Sources:

Hill, Douglas. *Man, Myth & Magic: Scrying*. London: BPC Publishing, 1970.

Leek, Sybil (1923–1983)

Sybil Leek was an **astrologer** who emigrated from England to America in the mid-1960s. In her books and through various newspaper and other interviews, Leek created a confused and frequently contradictory background to her life, with few verifiable details. She was born Angela Carter (though in one of her books she gives her family name as Falk) in Staffordshire, England, in 1923. Her father was a civil engineer who, in his earlier years, had been an actor. He went walking and climbing with his children and taught his daughter Yoga exercises. Leek came from a large, close family. Her maternal grandmother was an astrologer who taught some of that art to Leek. She had home schooling, with very little time in public schools until she was eleven.

Leek said that in late 1939, at sixteen, she married a famous pianist who died two years later, though she gives no details of the man, not even his name. She also said that following the marriage they toured Europe for two years before his death, though Europe was in the throes of World War II at that time. Leek claims to have been initiated into the Craft in the south of France, in the hills above Nice, after the death of her husband, making no mention of the German occupation of France. Back in England she lived for a year with some **Gypsies** before opening an antique shop in the New Forest.

In addition to running her antique store, Leek worked as a roving reporter for Southern Television, providing material for documentaries about life in the south of England. She also claims she joined a coven of witches in the New Forest area and became its high priestess. At some point she married a man named Brian and with him had two sons, Stephen and Julian.

By the early 1960s Leek was claiming a mainly witchcraft background. Unfortunately her publicity drew unwelcome attention to her antique shop, and her landlord terminated the lease. She had meanwhile written *A Shop in the High Street,* about her experiences in the antique business. The book mentioned her life in the New Forest and her encounters with Gypsies. Nowhere was there any mention of witches or witchcraft, since it was written prior to her initial claims of witchcraft association. It had moderate success and was published in the United States in 1964. To help promote the book there, Leek came to the U.S. for a self-publicity tour presenting herself as a practicing witch. At that time her claims were many and varied. The *New York Times* of April 26, 1964, said that she was "the only practicing witch in England today," while *Fate* magazine of June 1964 called Leek the "Chief Witch of England." On a number of occasions Leek claimed that she was "Chief Witch" or "Queen of all the Witches," having been voted into that position "by the witches of the world in 1947"—even though Wicca was fragmented and still underground at that time, and also despite the fact that there is no such position as "Queen of all the Witches." In October of 1964 Leek was selling Halloween candy at the New York World's Fair and claiming that she was "one of 80 professional witches in Great Britain." She said that she communicated "with the more than 300 ghosts she keeps around her old beamed cottage" (*New York Daily News,* October 13, 1964) .

Leek was fascinated with figures, as was evident by her claims to have starred in "some 926 television shows" (*Boston Herald,* September 16, 1964) and commanded "800 full-fledged, initiated witches in addition to some 8,000 followers of witchcraft" (*New York Sunday News,* December 6, 1964). The latter report said Leek "boasts that she can trace her witch lineage back some 500 years." On a WNEW-TV show, June 11, 1966, she claimed to be 450 years old. Other claims of that period were that, in addition to being an antique dealer, she was "an anthropologist" (Reuters, 1965), "a journalist by trade" (*Houston Post,* November 28, 1966), "self-proclaimed Queen of England's witches and a spiritualist" (*Staten Island Sunday Advance,* March 20, 1966), and "a British writer and medium" (*New York Sunday News,* July 3, 1966) .

By the end of 1966 Leek had taken to using the title "Dame." A dame of the British Empire is the female equivalent of a knight. Sybil Leek's name does not appear on the honor rolls of that period; the Queen did not bestow the title on her, and it is certainly not a witchcraft title.

Leek lived with a series of people in New York for a number of years. In fact this author became friends with her at that time and we even appeared on a television show together. She was a colorful character, invariably dressed in floor-length purple dresses and capes. She later moved to California, then Texas, and finally to Florida. She continued her work as an astrologer and for several years and published a popular astrology magazine, *Sybil Leek's Astrology.* Although in her early American years she gave out much misinformation about Wicca, over the years she did educate herself on its true workings and for the last few years of her life did a lot of good work in helping straighten the misconceptions, despite her earlier stumbling. The rituals of her tradition owed much to Gerald Gardner. She died in Melbourne, Florida, in 1983.

Sources:

Buckland, Raymond. *Witchcraft from the Inside*. St. Paul, MN: Llewellyn, 1971.

Buckland, Raymond. *The Witch Book: The Encyclopedia of Witchcraft, Wicca, and Neo-paganism*. Detroit: Visible Ink Press, 2002.
Jordan, Michael. *Witches: An Encyclopedia of Witches and Witchcraft*. London: Kyle Cathie, 1996.
Leek, Sybil. *A Shop in the High Street*. London: McKay, 1964.
Leek, Sybil. *My Life in Astrology*. Englewood Cliffs, NJ: Prentice-Hall, 1972.
Leek, Sybil. *The Complete Art of Witchcraft*. New York: Signet, 1973.

Leftwich, Robert

Robert Leftwich is a very successful modern British **dowser.** He uses a dowsing rod that will twist violently in his hands when he passes over whatever he is looking for. Leftwich has demonstrated his abilities while blindfolded. He is also able to tell when someone else, walking ahead of him, passes over water. Leftwich is a member of the **British Society of Dowsers.**

Lenormand, Marie-Anne Adélaide (1768–1843)

Marie-Anne Adélaide Lenormand was born in Alençon, France. Although some biographies put her date of birth as May 27, 1772, others put it as 1778. However, according to Louis du Bois (1773–1855), in *De Mlle Le Normand et de ses deux biographies récemment publiées*, she was born September 16, 1768.

Whatever the date, she was one of three children, a boy and two girls. Her father was a respected tailor, who died when Marie-Anne was still young. Her mother remarried but never got over losing Marie-Anne's father. It is said that when Marie-Anne was young, a **Gypsy** read her palm and foretold a future of greatness for her. While still young, she started reading the palms of her schoolmates, which did not sit well with her Mother Superior headmistress. Marie-Anne became preoccupied with **predictions.** Her favorite **tarot** deck was the Ètteilla deck, which she used all the time.

By age fourteen Marie-Anne had moved with her family to Paris. While there she became involved with a young man who taught her **numerology** and **astrology.** Her first job after leaving the convent school was in a laundry. She encountered a Dr. Gall and, together with the young man, they came up with the winning number for a lottery. With the money, Marie-Anne left home and traveled to England, arriving there in 1787. Despite the fact that she could not speak the language, she rapidly developed a following and within the space of three years was **fortune-telling** for the British royal family.

Growing bored with England, Marie-Anne returned to Paris. There, together with a Mme. Gilbert (*see note below*), she opened a salon on the rue de Tournon. At the time it was against the law to advertise as a **clairvoyant,** so the sign outside the door said: "Mademoiselle Lenormand; Bookseller." As it was, she was imprisoned for a week, but this just seemed to enhance her reputation.

She entertained upper-class society using **cheiromancy,** tarot cards, and astrology, predicting the future of her clients. Quickly she attained a great reputation as a clairvoyant and was known as the "**Sybil** of Faubourg Saint Germain." She produced a deck of divinatory cards that is still used today. Her clients included Marat, Robespierre and Saint-Just. At that time Joséphine of Beauharnais married Napoleon Bonaparte. One of Marie-Anne's predictions was that Napoleon would one day ascend the throne of France, a prediction at which Napoleon himself laughed when he heard it. She amassed a considerable fortune before she died in Paris on June 25, 1843.

Marie-Anne Lenormand's cards have thirty-six in the deck, each numbered and with a picture and title. On some decks there were four languages on the cards: German, Hungarian, Russian and Serbo-Croatian. The meanings of the cards are as follows:

1: Cavalier—News from a distance (9 Hearts)
2: Cloverleaf—Good luck; hope; wealth (6 Diamonds)
3: Ship—Travel; opportunities (10 Spades)
4: House—Home; fruitful projects (King of Hearts)
5: Tree—Health; energy (7 Hearts)
6: Clouds—Obstacles; unpleasant events (King of Clubs)
7: Snake—Jealousy; betrayal (Queen of Clubs)
8: Coffin—Completion; financial loss; serious illness (9 Diamonds)
9: Flowers—Contentment; Abundance; love (Queen of Spades)
10: Scythe—Danger; accident; separation (Jack of Diamonds)
11: Birch Rod—Arguments; conflict; strife (Jack of Clubs)
12: Bird—Short journeys; thoughts; problems (7 Diamonds)
13: Child—Trust; friends; children (Jack of Spades)
14: Fox—Treachery; hidden traps (9 Clubs)
15: Bear—Power; need for strength; care needed (10 Clubs)
16: Star—Success (6 Hearts)
17: Stork—Change; relocation (Queen of Hearts)
18: Dog—True friendship (10 Hearts)
19: Tower—Your lifetime; events from the past; protection (6 Spades)
20: Garden—Creativity; meeting; party (8 Spades)
21: Mountain—Strong enemies; overseas connection (8 Clubs)
22: Road—Decisions (Queen of Diamonds)
23: Mouse—Theft; losses (7 Clubs)
24: Heart—Love; happiness (Jack of Hearts)
25: Ring—Marriage; partnership (Ace of Clubs)
26: Book—Secrets; mysteries (10 Diamonds)
27: Letter—News (7 Spades)
28: Man—Male querier (Ace of Hearts)
29: Woman—Female querier (Ace of Spades)
30: Lily—Support; life attitude; business (King of Spades)
31: Sun—Success; optimism; happiness (Ace of Diamonds)
32: Moon—Honors; respect; recognition (8 Hearts)
33: Key—Solutions; new beginnings (8 Diamonds)
34: Fish—Excess; wealth; luxury (King of Diamonds)
35: Anchor—Stability; security; success (9 Spades)
36: Cross—Misfortune; suffering; destiny (6 Clubs)

Note: Although most biographies of Mlle. Lenormand mention that she opened her Paris salon with a Mme. Gilbert, no further mention is ever made of this partner. It has been suggested that the reason for this is that Marie-Anne's own real name was Gilbert and that she changed it to Lenormand at the time she opened the salon.

Sources:

Anderton, Bill. *Fortune Telling*. North Dighton, MA: JG Press, 1996.
Hargrave, Catherine Perry. *A History of Playing Cards*. New York: Houghton Mifflin, 1930.
http://www.bmlisieux.com/normandie/sybille.htm.
http://www.serenapowers.com/.

Leo, Alan (1860–1917)

Alan Leo was the pseudonym of British **astrologer** William Frederick Allen. He was possibly the most important of modern astrologers and has been described as "this century's major astrological publicist and, furthermore, the first astrologer of all time to practice his art on a large and well-organized professional scale" (Ellic Howe, *Urania's Children*, London, 1967).

Allen was born in London on August 7, 1860. His father, a soldier in a Scottish regiment, abandoned the family when William was still a child. After leaving school, Allen became apprenticed to a draper. He didn't stay there long and moved on to work for a pharmacist and then a grocer. None of the jobs lasted any length of time. By sixteen he was living in Liverpool, in the north of England, and was destitute.

Allen became a sewing-machine salesman and rapidly prospered. While selling, he became ill and was recommended to an old herbalist. As well as curing him, the herbalist taught Allen about astrology. Allen also met and became friends with astrologer Walter Richard Old, also known as Walter "Gorn" Old, who wrote under the pseudonym of **Sepharial.**

In 1890, at the age of thirty, Allen joined the Theosophical Society and also started doing astrological charts by mail order. As both an astrologer and a theosophist, Allen was considered an occultist; some thought his astrology was had a strong esoteric component. He started writing books, and these were often written in "obscure and confusing occult jargon," according to Francis King. Five years later, in 1895, he married Bessie Phillips, a professional **palm-reader** and **phrenologist.** On Bessie's insistence, the marriage was purely platonic. In fact they only got married after discovering that his Moon and her Sun were both in the same degree of Aries.

Together with another astrologer, F. W. Lacey (known as Aphorel), as co-editor, Allen launched *The Astrologer's Magazine*. In 1895 it was renamed *Modern Astrologer*. The magazine was aimed at the general public and featured Allen's style of simplifying what had, until then, been a very complex art. His many books also served to make astrology available to virtually anyone. Rather than the detailed training and advanced mathematics previously needed, Allen showed how to become an astrologer with relatively little effort. Not surprisingly, his books became extremely popular in Britain and America and, in translation, throughout Europe.

Cover of Alan Leo's *Modern Astrology* quarterly, 1897. *Fortean Picture Library.*

In both 1914 and 1917 Allen was arrested for **"fortune-telling;"** specifically for "pretending and professing to tell fortunes." The first time he was acquitted and the second time fined.

Allen's books remain popular today. The most important were *The Horoscope and How to Read It* (1902), *Astrology for All* (two volumes, 1904), and *How to Judge a Nativity* (two volumes, 1908). His wife, as Bessie Leo, wrote his biography, *The Life and Work of Alan Leo* (1919), and other books. For many years after his death she received letters from people who claimed that her dead husband was still teaching them astrology and theosophy from the astral plane.

Sources:

Howe, Ellic. *Urania's Children*. London: Kimber, 1967.

King, Francis. *Man, Myth & Magic*. London: BPC Publishing, 1970.

MacNeice, Louis. *Astrology*. Garden City, NY: Doubleday, 1964.

Shepard, Leslie A. (ed.). *Encyclopedia of Occultism & Parapsychology*. New York: Avon, 1978.

LeShan, Lawrence (b. 1920)

Dr. Lawrence LeShan was, for ten years, head of the Department of Psychology at New York's Trafalgar Hospital and Institute of Applied Biology. He is known as one of the pioneers of parapsychological research in the United States. He served as practicing psychologist in the U.S. Army before joining the Trafalgar Hospital.

LeShan started to explore **psychic** healing, hoping to expand the parameters of orthodox psychotherapy. This led him to further explore relationships between mysticism, modern physics, and psychic phenomena. LeShan worked with the famous **medium Eileen Garrett,** spending more than five hundred hours with her, and was extremely impressed with her powers of psychometry.

Since 1970 LeShan has been teaching psychic healing in New York. In 1974 he published his book *The Medium, the Mystic and the Physicist* (New York: Viking). He feels that there are different types of reality, such as what he calls **"clairvoyant** reality," "sensory reality," and "trans-psychic reality." All of these he describes in his book.

Sources:

Fishley, Margaret. *The Supernatural*. London: Aldus, 1976.

Shepard, Leslie A. (ed.). *Encyclopedia of Occultism & Parapsychology*. New York: Avon, 1978.

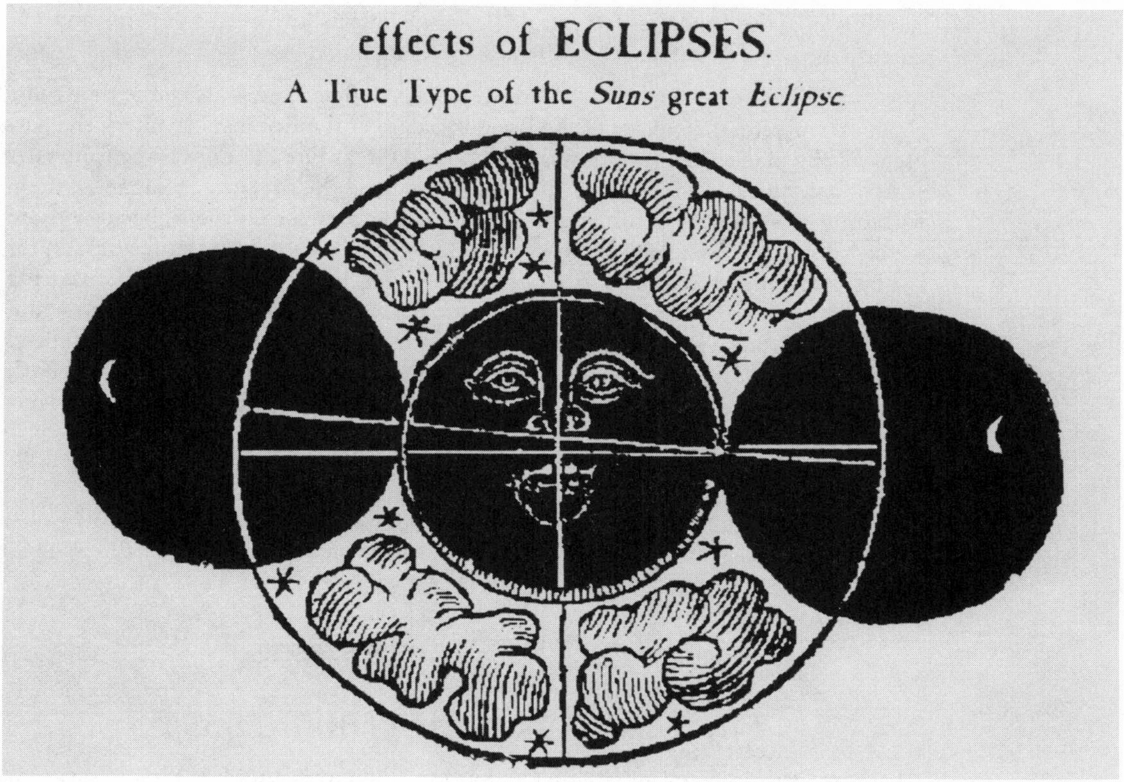

Illustration from William Lilly's *Annus Tenebrosus, or The Dark Year,* 1652. *Fortean Picture Library.*

LETTERS OF A NAME *see* Onomancy

LIBANOMANCY *see* Knissomancy

LIBATIONS *see* Œnomancy

LIGHTNING *see* Ceraunomancy

Lilly, William (1602–1681)

The English **astrologer** immortalized as "Sidrophel," in Samuel Butler's satirical poem *Hudibras* (1663). Lilly was born on May 1, 1602, at Diseworth, Leicestershire, England, and was educated at Ashby-de-la-Zouch.

It wasn't until Lilly was thirty that he started practicing astrology, having been taught by a hard-drinking Welsh clergyman. He said later that he only started looking into the science out of curiosity, to see if there was any truth in it. Lilly began publishing astrological almanacs in April of 1644. These received serious attention from some of the prominent members of the Long Parliament for, like all successful astrologers of the time, he tied astrological indications into current events and frequently showed that the stars endorsed the political mood.

Lilly's most accurate predictions were made ten or more years before they came about. They were: the victory of the Roundheads over the Royalist Cavaliers, the outbreak of the plague in London in 1665, and the Great Fire of London the following year. When he made his predictions of the plague and the fire, he accompanied them with drawings showing innumerable corpses being buried in shrouds, because there weren't enough coffins, and he showed London (symbolized by Gemini, the sign for the city) consumed in flames. Because of this latter, he was later accused of starting the fire and had to explain to Parliament how it was that the stars could show him what was to come about. However, despite these successes he completely misjudged the scientific revolution that spread rapidly through England during the seventeenth century, and consequently lost his popularity after the Restoration. He died at Hersham, Surrey, on June 9, 1681.

Sources:

Encyclopedia Britannica. Chicago: William Benton, 1964.
King, Francis. *The Supernatural: The Cosmic Influence*. London: Aldus, 1975.
MacNeice, Louis. *Astrology*. Garden City, NY: Doubleday, 1964.

LIMBS, MOVEMENT OF *see* Spasmatomancy

Lincoln, Abraham (1809–1865)

Abraham Lincoln was a **spiritualist** and attended many **séances,** having some at his own home. Colonel Simon F. Kase told of one notable one, which both he and the president attended in the home of Mrs. Laurie. The Laurie's daughter, a Mrs. Miller, was the **medium,** playing piano while in a trance. As she played, two legs of the instrument levitated several inches off the floor then repeatedly banged back to the floor to beat time to the music. As it kept rising up, Kase, a judge, and two soldiers who were present all climbed on the piano together but were unable to make it settle down again until the medium stopped playing. The legs rose as high as four inches off the floor.

Abraham Lincoln had many **prophetic dreams,** including one of his own death. In early April 1865, he dreamed he was lying in bed when he heard the sound of sobbing. Getting up and leaving his bedroom, he went into the East Room of the White House where he saw a line of people filing past a catafalque. They were all paying their respects to the figure lying in state, guarded by four soldiers. The face of the figure was covered so, in the dream, Lincoln asked one of the soldiers who had died. The soldier replied, "The President. He was killed by an assassin." Lincoln later told his wife, Mary, and several friends about the dream. It was later that same month that he was shot and killed by John Wilkes Booth.

Another of Lincoln's prophetic dreams was of a damaged ship sailing away with a Union ship in hot pursuit. Lincoln had this dream on a number of occasions, each time just before an important Union victory.

Sources:
Headon, Deirdre (ed.). *Quest for the Unknown—Charting the Future*. Pleasantville, NY: Reader's Digest, 1992.
Shepard, Leslie A. (ed.). *Encyclopedia of Occultism & Parapsychology*. New York: Avon, 1978.
Stemman, Roy. *The Supernatural: Spirits and Spirit Worlds*. London: Aldus, London 1975.

LINES (ON FACE) ***see*** **Metopomancy**

LIPS ***see*** **Labiomancy**

LITHOMANCY

(See also Psephomancy)

Divination by signs derived from stones. Sir Thomas Browne, in *Pseudodoxia epidemica* (1646), mentioned the "Lithomancy, or divination, from this stone, whereby Helenus the **Prophet** foretold the destruction of Troy." He is here probably referring to the Byzantine poet Joannes Tzetzes's twelfth-century Greek hexameter poem that says that Helenus divined Troy's downfall using a lodestone, or magnet, washed with spring **water** and passed through an elaborate ritual. When interrogated, at the end of the rites, the stone spoke with the voice of a child. The lodestone is well described as "rough, hard, black, and heavy, graven everywhere with veins like wrinkles." It is also described as "the true and vocal sideritis, which others call the animated ophites." Sideritis, or siderite, is another name for blue quartz (or chalybite). It is quite different from lodestone, which is iron-bearing rock with magnetic properties.

Frederick T. Elworthy, in *The Evil Eye* (1895), also refers to the blue quartz when he describes "Lithomancy, divination with a precious stone called siderites." However, Thomas Blount, in *Glossographia* (1656) speaks of "lithomancy, divination by casting Pibble stones, or by the Load-stone."

From the above it would seem that there were two possible ways of working lithomancy. The major method was with a magnetic loadstone. Magically, it was said to produce a voice that would answer questions. There is no indication of how the siderite was used, other than the reference to pebbles. This second method may employ a semiprecious stone such as blue quartz, probably in small pieces like pebbles, and used in a manner similar to **geomancy.**

Photius (820–891 CE), the patriarch of Constantinople, spoke of an oracular stone called the bætulum, and referred to it as a tool for lithomancy. This was probably the bætyl (Latin: bætulus), which was a sacred meteoric stone and would therefore seem to endorse the lodestone idea.

Sources:
Encyclopedia Britannica. Chicago: William Benton, 1964.
Oxford English Dictionary. Oxford: Clarendon Press, 1989.
Schumann, Walter. *Gemstones of the World*. New York: Sterling, 1977.
Spence, Lewis. *An Encyclopedia of the Occult*. London: George Routledge & Sons, 1920.

LIVANOMANCY ***see*** **Knissomancy**

LIVER *see* Hepatoscopy

Logomancy

Logos is the Greek for word, speech, discourse, reason. Logomancy, as divination by word or words, could cover a number of different forms of fortune-telling. Considering the written word, it would cover such methods as bibliomancy (reading random passages in books). Considering the spoken word, it would cover such things as cledonomancy (chance hearing of random words and phrases). It would also cover psychography (spontaneous writing of a divine nature) and onomancy (using the letters of a name). Unfortunately the exact method does not seem to have been recorded.

LOT DRAWING *see* Bible; Lots of Præneste; Sortilege

Lots of Præneste, The

The *Lots of Præneste* were connected with the worship of Fortuna. Fortuna was an ancient fertility goddess, hence the connection with good fortune. She later became identified with the Greek Tyche.

Questions put to the goddess were answered by drawing **lots** from a case made of ancient wood. A young boy would draw the oaken lots. A second method was to use an urn with a very narrow neck, filled with **water.** Because of the narrowness of the neck, only one lot at a time could rise to the surface.

Sources:

Kaster, Joseph. *Putnam's Concise Mythological Dictionary*. New York: G.P. Putnam's, 1963.
Shepard, Leslie A. (ed.). *Encyclopedia of Occultism & Parapsychology*. New York: Avon, 1978.

Lottery

A lottery is a system for the distribution of prizes as determined by chance. Lotteries have been held for centuries, reputedly having been invented by the **Romans.** In its usual form, tickets bearing numbers are sold and distributed. Duplicates are placed in a container, often a rotating drum, and winners are drawn after these have been thoroughly mixed.

The Roman emperors Nero and Augustus gave away slaves, ships, and even houses through lotteries, the tickets for which were free. Lotteries as enjoyed today originated in Italy during the Middle Ages. They spread in popularity to France, Germany and Austria, and were used there to raise revenue for the rulers. The first English lottery was held in 1569. (In Shakespeare's *Merchant of Venice* of 1596, there is reference to "The lottery that he hath devised, in these three chests of gold, silver, and lead." Act I, sc ii.)

American colleges such as Harvard, Dartmouth, and Columbia were originally financed through lotteries patterned after the British ones, though in 1762 they were denounced by the Pennsylvania Provincial assembly as being injurious to trade and encouraging vice and idleness. Lotteries flourished after the Civil War but, over a period of time, came to be outlawed by many states at different times. Today, state-run lotteries provide vast amounts of money for such things as education.

Beginning in 1758 there was a royal lottery in France. Author Grillot de Givry states that when it was finally suppressed by Louis Philippe, all the secret methods of winning it were lost. It had been believed that winning numbers could be found in **dreams.** There was an intricate interpretation involved, however. For example, if an ostrich was dreamt of, that represented the number seventy-three. A barometer indicated the numbers thirteen, seventeen, and forty-nine. To dream of a Negro meant the numbers eighteen or sixty-eight. If there seemed little chance of dreaming, then there was a specific prayer prescribed that had to be said, then written on virgin parchment and placed under the pillow. An intricate geometric figure known as the Pentagonal Figure was also a favorite for determining which numbers would be winners.

Many of the various forms of divination mentioned in this volume can be, and have been, directed toward the finding of the winning numbers in lotteries. Some people have been very successful at it. Harold Horwood, an electrical engineer in London, had many of his dreams documented by the *Sunday Pictorial* newspaper during the 1940s and 1950s. He mostly dreamed of winning racehorses but could also apply his dreams to lotteries.

Sources:

Buckland, Raymond. *Gypsy Dream Dictionary*. St. Paul, MN: Llewellyn, 1999.
Encyclopedia Britannica. Chicago: William Benton, 1964.
de Givry, Grillot. *A Pictorial Anthology of Witchcraft, Magic & Alchemy*. London: Spottiswoode, Ballantyne, 1931.

Lunomancy

Lunomancy is divining by the shadows cast on a person's face in moonlight. A full **moon** is best for this but any moon that gives a reasonable amount of light may be utilized.

The shadows must be observed randomly, without the **seer** trying to position the person's head for special emphasis. The depth of shadow, length, and observed shape are all taken into consideration.

An old superstition is that it is bad luck to have a child born in moonlight. It was also believed that anyone sleeping in moonlight for any length of time ran the risk of going either blind or crazy. If a girl looked at a new moon over her right shoulder, she would dream of her future husband if she repeated the words:

New moon, new moon, do tell me
Who my true lover will be.
The color of his hair,
The clothes that he will wear,
And the happy day that he will wed me.

Sources:

Randolph, Vance. *Ozark Superstitions*. New York: Dover, 1964.

M

Macromancy

(See also Micromancy)

Macromancy is divination by studying the largest object in the area. Whether a rock, a tree, or a house, the object is studied and the **seer** interprets. Size, general shape, and color all have their place in the interpretation. With trees (see **dendromancy**), there are specific qualities associated, as also with colors (see **colorology**). The closeness of the object to others, or the distance from them, may also be significant.

Maculomancy

Maculomancy is divination using spots. These are randomly espied spots, and so may be the markings on an animal (such as a dalmatian **dog** or a leopard), stains on a cloth, marks on the ground, spots left by rain or **water** from washing, or virtually any spots that have a haphazard pattern.

The interpretation depends upon the **seer,** but generally follows the same characteristics of **tasseography, geomancy,** and similar methods. If the diviner has a knowledge of astronomy and constellation shapes, then **astrology** might also be employed

Mah-Jongg

Originating in China, each province of that country originally had its own variation of the name for this game. The name signifies "sparrow" and has been variously transliterated as *ma tsiang, ma chiang, ma cheuk,* and *ma ch'iau,* as well as mah-jongg. Mah-jongg was coined and copyrighted by Joseph P. Babcock, an American resident of Shanghai who introduced the game to the west after World War I.

The tiles, or *p'ais*, are about the size of dominoes and made of bone, ivory, wood or plastic. In most forms of the game there are either 136 or 144 of them, depending upon whether or not certain ones are included. One American version uses 152. The 136-tile galme is made up as follows:

Bamboos, numbered 1 to 9; four of each	=	36 tiles
Circles, numbered 1 to 9; four of each	=	36
Characters, numbered 1 to 9; four of each	=	36
Honors: 4 red, 4 green, 4 white dragons	=	12
Winds: 4 east, 4 south, 4 west, 4 north	=	16
		136 tiles

The 144-tile game adds four each of flowers and seasons. On the American 152-tile version, all of the suit tiles, flowers, winds, and jokers are marked with Roman letters and Arabic numerals. The red and green dragon tiles depict dragons, while the white dragon tile uses a rectangular design. Eight of the tiles are jokers. The one bamboos of this set depict cranes.

One form of divination with Mah-jongg tiles is to draw thirteen of them and place them in the following order:

	North 10, 11, 12	
West 7, 8, 9	Center 13	East 1, 2, 3
	South 4, 5, 6	

The center tile refers to the question being asked. The eastern tiles (on the right) are the present situation. The western tiles (left) represent any obstacles standing in the way. The south tiles are the near, or immediate, future, while the north tiles are the more distant future.

A variation on this is to put down the tiles one at a time, starting in the east, and going around clockwise:

	North 4, 8, 12	
West 3, 7, 11	Center 13	East 1, 5, 9
	South 2, 6, 10	

As the tiles are turned, it may be that a flower or a season has been drawn. If this is the case, draw an extra tile and place it next to that flower or season tile.

Meanings of the Tiles

Circles

1 (Pearl—*Chu*): Luxury, wealth, honor, refinement. An older woman is important in your life.

2 (Pine—*Sung*): Success comes through firmness and strength. Diplomacy is preferable to aggression. Older woman or younger man.
3 (Phoenix—*Feng*): Happiness, joy, and splendor. Good news to come.
4 (Jade—*Yü*): Hard work brings rewards. Justice. Build and maintain friendships.
5 (Dragon—*Lung*): Sudden and unexpected good fortune.
6 (Peach—*Tao*): Fine arts. Aim for beauty without extravagance. A young woman is important in your life.
7 (Insect—*Ch'ung*): Industry, craft, skill. Manual work. Business over a short period brings short-term rewards.
8 (Tiger—*Hu*): Authority. Superiors. Issues with an older man. Bravery and assertiveness necessary.
9 (Unicorn—*Ch'I*): Ability to see ahead. Beat rivals by seeing through them.

Bamboo
1 (Peacock—*K'ung*): Success comes from changing direction. Beware of pride and vanity.
2 (Duck—*Ya*): Enduring partnership, devotion, and fidelity.
3 (Toad—*Min*): Sickness and medication. Recovery from sickness. Beware of overambition, overextension.
4 (Carp—*Li*): Peace and contentment leading to longevity.
5 (Lotus—*Lien*): Awakening to new life. A need to begin again.
6 (Water—*Shui*): Short journeys. Correspondence.
7 (Tortoise—*Kuei*): Gradual progress, together with learning, bring success. Possible issues of illegitimacy. Success after a delay.
8 (Fungus—*Chün*): Unexpected event. Issues of virtue may be important.
9 (Willow—*Liu*): Diplomacy and tact necessary. Strength through flexibility.

Characters (*Wan*)
1 (Open Door—*Ju*): New opportunities. Obstacles removed.
2 (Sword—*Chien*): A decision is needed for progress to be made. Twins.
3 (Earth—*Ti*): Stability. Issues involving relocation, real estate, countryside.
4 (Lute—*Ch'in*): Time to relax. Music, leisure, performing arts.
5 (House—*Fang*): Issues regarding a house or property.
6 (Fire—*Huo*): Possibility of loss; danger. Beware of depleting your resources: mentally, physically, and financially. Intelligence and inspiration also threatened.
7 (Seven Stars—*Tuo*): Dreams and ambitions are important. Encourage writing, literature.
8 (Knot—*Chieh*): A state of flux. Tying/untying.
9 (Heaven—*Tien*): End of one cycle; start of another. Achievement, fulfillment. A ceremony. Spiritual matters.

Winds
East Wind (*Tung*): Associated with spring, the color green, the element wood and the dragon constellation. New beginnings. Concerned with issues to do with the self.

South Wind (*Nan*): Associated with summer, the color red, the element of fire, and the phoenix constellation. Good fortune, growth, and progress.

West Wind (*MHsi*): Associated with autumn, the color white, the element of metal, and the tiger constellation. Issues to do with your goals and objectives, or to do with your partner.

North Wind (*Pei*): Associated with winter, the color black, the element of water, and the tortoise constellation. There are difficulties. Patience is called for. There is a lack of what is needed at this time.

Dragons

Red Dragon (*Chung*): This tile represents the arrow striking the target. Success in all you desire.

Green Dragon (*Fa*): The arrow about to be shot from the bow. Now is the time to start. Do not delay.

White Dragon (*Pai*): The arrow in flight. The mysterious unknown. Ghosts. Documents are important.

Seasons

Spring (*Yu*): Associated with the Fisherman, the east wind, the color green, the element of wood, and the plum blossom flower. Strive for commonsense, together with good management skills and good working relationships.

Summer (*Ch'iao*): Associated with the wood-cutter, the south wind, the color red, the element of fire, and the orchid flower. Activity brings success.

Autumn (*Keng*): Associated with the farmer, the west wind, the color white, the element of metal, and the chrysanthemum flower. Hard labor brings its own rewards.

Winter (*Du*): Associated with the scholar, the north wind, the color black, the element of water, and the bamboo flower. Exercise caution and concentrate on paperwork, whether literary or administrative.

Flowers

Plum Blossom (*Li*): East wind and spring. A sign of renewed vitality and luck. Innocence and inexperience are assets.

Orchid (*Lan*): South wind and summer. Seek refinement; the rare and the precious.

Chrysanthemum (*Chü*): West wind and autumn. Enjoy leisure, entertainment, and social activities.

Bamboo (*Chu*): North wind and winter. Planning, research, writing, learning.

Sources:

Babcock, Joseph P. *Babcok's Rules for Mah-Jongg*, 1923.
Encyclopedia Britannica. Chicago: William Benton, 1964.
http://www.serenapowers.com/mahjongg.html.

MARGARITOMANCY

Margaritomancy is divination by pearls. Pierre de l'Ancre, in his *L'Incrédulité et mescréance du sortilège* (1622), said: "The pearl is to be enchanted, and shut in a pot; then if it chance that the name of a thief be pronounced the pearl will leap, striking against the pot." As described by Lewis Spence, "A pearl was covered with a vase, and placed near the fire, and the names of suspected persons pronounced. When the name of the guilty one was uttered the pearl was supposed to bound upwards and pierce the bottom of the vase." The mention of its being placed "near the fire" would seem to give a clue that there was some natural effect of heat on a pearl that might cause it to jump.

Sources:

de Givry, Grillot. *A Pictorial Anthology of Witchcraft, Magic & Alchemy*. London: Spottiswoode, Ballantyne, 1931.

Spence, Lewis. *An Encyclopedia of the Occult*. London: George Routledge & Sons, 1920.

Mathemancy

Children's nursery rhymes, songs, and stories are rich depositories of ancient folklore. This has been elaborated upon by such writers as Katharine Briggs, Lewis Spence, and, more recently, Iona and Peter Opie. The "counting-out games" of children are especially interesting in that they contain remnants of mathemancy. Mathemancy is divination by counting.

Charles Godfrey Leland, in his book on the Etruscans, says: "A vast amount of ancient erudition on the subject of divining by **numbers** and similar matters, may be found in a very rare work . . . *Tractus Philologicus de Sortitione Veterum, Hebræorum inprimis ex S. Scriptura Talmude, &c* by Martin Mauritius (Basel, 1692)." He notes that the Sortes Virgilianæ were in the nature of, or allied to, counting-out rhymes.

Sources:

Briggs, Katharine. *The Anatomy of Puck*. London: Hillary House, 1959.

Leland, Charles Godfrey. *Etruscan Magic & Occult Remedies*. New York: University Books, 1963.

Opie, Iona and Peter. *The Lore and Language of Schoolchildren*. Oxford: Oxford University Press, 1959.

Spence, Lewis. *Myth and Ritual in Dance, Game, and Rhyme*. London: Watts, 1942.

MAYA *see* Mexico and Central America

Meconomancy

Meconomancy is generally referred to as divination by sleep. The root word *mecon*, however, relates to the poppy and to opium (for example, meconium is the thickened juice of the poppy; meconic acid is a white crystalline acid obtained from the opium). It seems certain, therefore, that this is divination from dreams/hallucinations experienced while under the influence of opium. It differs from **oneiromancy** in that in the latter the divination comes from dreams obtained in natural sleep.

The diviners of ancient **Mexico** used meconomancy, working with such hallucinogenic plants as morning glory, jimsonweed, and peyote.

Sources:

Miller, Mary and Karl Taube. *The Gods and Symbols of Ancient Mexico and the Maya*. London: Thames & Hudson, 1993

Oxford English Dictionary. Oxford: Clarendon Press, 1989

Nicola Cutolo, an Italian psychic, works with a pendulum to diagnose the illnesses of the woman in the photograph, 1984. *Dr. Elmar R. Gruber/Fortean Picture Library.*

MEDICAL RADIESTHESIA

The use of **radiesthesia** for diagnosing and prescribing for disease. Radiesthesia is the use of a **pendulum** or rod. Medical radiesthesia grew out of the discovery by **Abbé Bouly,** Curé of Hardelot, that it was possible to estimate the percentage of salts in any specimen of **water** by holding a sample in the hand and testing with the pendulum. From there it was possible to go on to test the bodies of animals and of humans, looking for infections. The next step was to use the diagnostic tool for finding remedies.

Everything in nature generates a radiation that can be detected by a pendulum or a **radionic** instrument. Working solely with a sample of blood or saliva, it is possible to tune into this radiation and to work with it to the point of diagnosing and prescribing treatment or medicine for disease. The precise nature of the radiation or influence operating in radiesthesia has not yet been detailed in the field of scientific investigation but is generally referred to as the "Life Force."

Sources:

Mermet, Abbé Alexis. *Principles and Practice of Radiesthesia*. London: Watkins, 1975.

Wethered, Vernon D. *An Introduction to Medical Radiesthesia & Radionics*. London: C.W. Daniel, 1962.
Wethered, Vernon D. *The Practice of Medical Radiesthesia*. London: C.W. Daniel, 1967.

MEDIUM; MEDIUMSHIP *see* Channeling

MERMET, ABBÉ ALEXIS (1866–1937)

Alexis Mermet was born in 1866, in Savoy, France. He grew up to become a country priest. He learned to **dowse** from his father and grandfather, both famous for their abilities in France and in Switzerland. Mermet studied and developed a natural sensitivity to radiations and forcefields, applying his knowledge to the discovery of **water,** gold, disease, and missing persons and property. During his lifetime the Abbé Mermet was acclaimed the "King of Dowsers," not only in France but all across Europe. He caused even the Pope to take an interest in dowsing and **radiesthesia.**

By distant projection, Mermet discovered fields of petroleum in Africa, Galicia, and other parts of the world. He was consulted by the Vatican authorities for important archaeological researches in Rome, all of which were very successful and are recorded in the Archives of the Vatican Library.

Mermet came to the conclusion that if what lay hidden in the earth and in inanimate objects, could be studied with a **pendulum,** then why couldn't that same pendulum detect hidden conditions in animals and human beings? His hypothesis was threefold: 1: Everything emits radiation; 2: Some kind of "current" flows through human hands; and 3: Holding appropriate tools renders them diagnostic instruments. These instruments, he found, could be used not only for locating objects in the ground, lost and stolen objects, and missing persons, but also for diagnosing and prescribing for disease.

Mermet died in 1937. His book, *Principles and Practice of Radiesthesia*, has sold nearly 100,000 copies.

Sources:

Mermet, Abbé Alexis. *Principles and Practice of Radiesthesia*. London: Watkins, 1975.

MESOPOTAMIA

Ancient Mesopotamia was the cultural area located, c. 5000 BCE, approximately where Iraq exists today. The southern part of the region was known as Babylonia, the northern part, Assyria.

The Mesopotamian gods were thought to determine the future—of humans, of cities, of the nation. But by using suitable means, it was possible to obtain glimpses of the future. Many forms of divination were developed for this. Some were available to all but many were restricted to the use of the king. **Astrology, exstispicy, oneiromancy, augury, ophiomancy,** and **zoomancy** were all employed. In later Assyria, a "dream book" gave the interpretation of hundreds of dreams.

A famous example of metagnomy, or divination by vision, in which Constantine sees the sign of the cross marked with the words, "By This Sign You Will Conquer." ***Fortean Picture Library.***

Sources:

Oppenheim, A .L.. *Ancient Mesopotamia: Portrait of a Dead Civilization*. Chicago: Chicago University Press, 1964.

METAGNOME; METAGNOMY

Metagnomy is divination by visions obtained when in a trance state; knowledge acquired through cryptesthesia (without the aid of the five senses). In other words, the divination of **seers, mediums, sibyls,** the **Pythia, shamans,** and all who go into trance or who receive their knowledge in some psychic manner. All such would be termed metagnomes. Emile Boirac's *The Psychology of the Future* (1918) says: "**Clairvoyance,** or 'metagnomy' . . . it is especially in the somnambulistic state, natural or provoked, that metagnomic manifestations occur."

Sources:

Oxford English Dictionary. Oxford: Clarendon Press, 1989.

METAGRAPHOLOGY

This is psychometric power on the basis of scripts. **Psychometry** is the ability to handle an object and to be able to tell the history of that object, receiving the information psychically. Metagraphology is similar in that the information is obtained from handling an example of handwriting, rather than a ring, a piece of jewelry, or some other object. From this handwriting, the **diviner** can describe the person who wrote the sample, and in some cases even give their state of health, state of mind at the time of writing, and other details. Joseph R. Buchanan, in *Outlines of lectures on the neurological system of anthropology* (1854), mentions that "old manuscripts requiring an antiquary to decipher their strange old penmanship, were easily interpreted by the psychometric power."

Sources:

Oxford English Dictionary. Oxford: Clarendon Press, 1989.

METEORS ***see*** **Meteoromancy**

METEOROMANCY

In the *Encyclopædia Metropolitana* of 1845, Edward Smedley states: "In Etruria, the frequency of sacrifice and the temperament of the air, gave popularity to **extispicy** and meteoromancy." The former is the inspection of the entrails of sacrificed animals. The latter is divination by the observation of meteors.

Sources:

Oxford English Dictionary. Oxford: Clarendon Press, 1989.

METOPOMANCY; METOPOSCOPY

Mathematician and **astrologer** Jerome Cardan (1501–1576) was the first to suggest that the wrinkles on a person's forehead might represent a compilation of indicators as to a person's character, and that no two people would have the same wrinkes. In 1658 his work *Metoposcopia* was published in Latin by Thomas Jolly in Paris. Later the same year a French translation, by C. M. de Laurendière, appeared.

Cardan suggested that the lines on the forehead of a person can be used for divination and pointed out that they are easier to read than the lines of the hand, in **cheiromancy,** since the latter needs the cooperation of the person being read. The art or science of metopomancy would come under the general heading of **physiognomancy.**

Thomas Blount mentions it in *Glossographia* (1656), as does Sir Thomas Urquhart in *The Third Book of the Works of Mr. Francis Rabelais* (1693), where he says: "Ye know how by the Arts of Astrology . . . Chiromancy, Metopomancy . . . he foretelleth all things to come." In James Sanford's translation of *Agrippa's Of the vanitie and uncertaintie of artes and sciences* (1569) it says: "Metoposcopie doth avaunte that she can foretell all mens beginninges, proceedinges, and endinges by the onely beholding of the foreheade." In the **Bible,** Revelation 14:9, there is reference to it: "If any man worship the beast and his image, and receive his mark in his forehead, or in his hand."

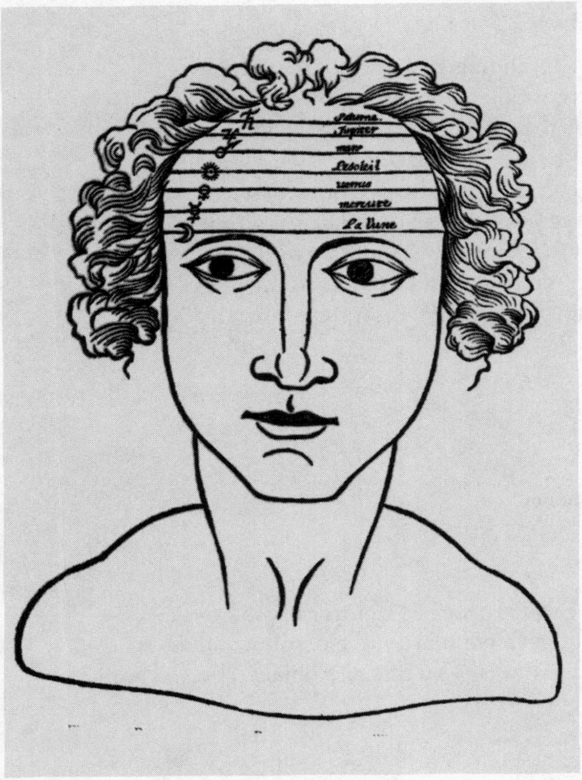

Illustration of the rulerships of the seven planets over the seven main frontal lines, in descending order from Saturn, according to ancient planetary spheres, 1658. *Fortean Picture Library.*

Cardan concluded that there could be up to seven lines across a forehead. These he equated with the seven planets of astrology (from bottom to top of the forehead): **moon,** Mercury, Venus, Sun, Mars, Jupiter, Saturn. No one is likely to have all seven lines but a person might have, for example, the lines of Mars and Jupiter, or the lines of Mercury, the Sun, and Saturn. Long and perfectly straight lines indicated "a simplicity of the soul" and a sense of justice, regardless of the planets with which they were associated. Wavy lines, curving lines, and broken lines would have other interpretations, as would vertical lines, crosses, angled lines, cross lines, and so on.

Cardan also noted various combinations of facial spots, **moles,** and other blemishes. These spots and blemishes he equated with the twelve signs of the **zodiac.** Taurus, Aries, and Gemini were on the upper part of the forehead; Cancer, Leo, and Virgo lower down. Libra was at the top of the nose, Scorpio near the ear, Sagittarius at the top of the cheek, Capricorn below it, Aquarius below that, and Pisces at the bottom of the cheek by the chin.

Sources:

de Givry, Grillot. *A Pictorial Anthology of Witchcraft, Magic & Alchemy*. London: Spottiswoode, Ballantyne, 1931.

Headon, Deirdre (ed.). *Quest for the Unknown—Charting the Future*. Pleasantville, NY: Reader's Digest, 1992.

Oxford English Dictionary. Oxford: Clarendon Press, 1989.

Mexico and Central America

Divination was an important part of all Mesoamerican religious life, as was the 260-day calendar that served as a divinatory almanac. The calendar was often used in conjunction with **sortilege,** which was done using seeds. The seeds were randomly cast and then counted for the divination.

Using pools of **water** and polished surfaces for **scrying** was another common form of divination in Mesoamerica. The visions seen by **seers** using scrying were accepted as evidence in court cases among the Tarascans of Michoacán. Reading muscle-twitching (**spasmatomancy**) and the pulsing of blood (a form of **dririmancy**) were also divination methods. **Meconomancy** was employed using such common hallucinogenic plants as jimsonweed, morning glory, and peyote.

Aztec

The Aztecs had a college of diviners known as the *calmecac*. This was similar to the **augurs** college of ancient **Rome,** though the Aztec diviners worked solely on the flight and song of birds. If a young Aztec boy showed mystical leanings, he would be sent to the calmecac to become a priest. The Spaniards compared the school to a monastery. This was also the place where the ruler-aspirants were trained. The name calmecac means "house of the large corridors." According to Victor von Hagen, a student at the school would learn to read glyph writing and learn about the calendar, **astrology,** rituals, and the interpretation of phenomena. The *Codex Florentino*, written in Spanish and translated directly from the ideographic Nahuatl speech, speaks of how boys at the calmecac religious schools "must learn artfully all the songs, the songs of the gods . . . which are written in the books."

The Mexican (Aztec) Calendar can be read in terms of cycles covering thousands of years. *Fortean Picture Library.*

The remains of the calmecac portion of the site are to be seen at the ruined complex of Calixtlahuaca, famous for its Temple of Quetzalcoatl.

A major Aztec goddess—the mother of all the people and the "Mother of the Gods"—was Toci. She was patroness of midwives and healers and also goddess of diviners.

Inca

Apu-Rimac was the main **Oracle** of the Inca Empire, said to dwell in the Apurimac River Gorge west of Cuzco. The oracle was attended by an Inca priestess. Long before the Spaniards appeared in the area, Apu-Rima **prophesied** that bearded men would come and subvert the Inca Empire. The Jesuit priest Father Bernabé Cobo, in his four-volume *Historia del Nuevo Mundo* of 1890–93, stated that the oracle's effigy was a tree trunk the size of a human body. It was splashed with human blood, he said. He also said that it had "a golden belt one palm wide, with two women's breasts of solid gold . . . Next to this idol were other smaller ones . . . bathed with blood and dressed like women." He said that the priestess was an old woman who kept in the shadows while incanting her prophesies. When the Spaniards came, she threw herself over the cliff.

There were sacrificial Inca ceremonies carried out on Lake Titicaca's Island of the Sun, legendary birthplace of the first Inca. While a young white llama was prepared for sacrifice, the Aymara Indian women **soothsayers** sat with piles of coca leaves (*Erythroxy-*

The Kukulkan pyramid at Chichen Itza, Mexico, built by the Mayas, photographed during the spring equinox in 1994. *Klaus Aarsleff/Fortean Picture Library.*

lum coca), which they used to determine the most propitious site on the island for performing the sacrifice. This they did by chewing the coca, something done only by soothsayers and nobles. The coca was known as the "divine plant." When the llama was sacrificed, the priests would inspect the viscera. This **haruspicy** ritual was known as *calpa*.

Oracles were consulted regularly by the Inca rulers. The third Inca, Lloque Yupanqui, was extremely ugly. He was also unable to produce a son and heir. Consulting the oracle, toward the end of his reign, he was told to try once more with his *coya*, or principal wife. It was also suggested that he might try a younger coya. This he did, and a son was born—Mayta Capac, who became something of an Inca Hercules.

Every important decision and war fought was first investigated through the oracles. Favorable augury was looked for among the soothsayers. Pachacamac was the most famous shrine in South America. Located about fifteen miles south of present-day Lima, pilgrims had traveled to the oracle there long before Inca times. Votaries would fast for a period and would then approach the oracle walking backward. Prophesies were heard issuing from the mouths of many carved figures in the walls and recesses, and were usually delivered with a sibilant hiss. After Tupa Inca adopted the site following his conquest of Chan Chan, Pachacamac became the empire's greatest oracle.

Maya

Divination was an important part of Mayan religion. Scribes recorded the texts of history and divination in the most complex writing system ever developed in the New World. In the sixteenth- century Codex Magliabechiano there is a picture of women performing divination to determine the outcome of a disease. This was performed at night and involved the casting of coca leaves onto a board or blanket.

The primordeal ancestral couple, Cipactonal and Oxomoco, was believed to possess great powers of divination. They are referred to as diviners and shown casting lots in Codex Borbonicus. They are associated with the origin of the 260-day calendar, because of its importance in divination. By divining with cast *tzite* seeds, the couple instructed the creator gods on how to create humankind. Much like the Aztec's Toci, the Mayan Goddess O (of the Schellhas System) was a creator goddess and a diviner.

Mary Miller and Karl Taube state: "Not only do Mayan diviners play a role in creation accounts, but the actual practitioners frequently compare their ritual acts to that of creation. Thus the diviner commonly describes and invokes the images and forces present at the time of creation."

Sources:

McIntyre, Loren. *Incas and Their Timeless Land*. Washington, DC: National Geographic Society, 1975.
Miller, Mary and Karl Taube. *The Gods and Symbols of Ancient Mexico and the Maya*. London: Thames & Hudson, 1993.
Spence, Lewis. *An Encyclopedia of the Occult*. London: George Routledge & Sons, 1920.
Stuart, George E. and Gene S. Stuart. *The Mysterious Maya*. Washington, DC: National Geographic Society, 1977.
Von Hagen, Victor Wolfgang. *The Aztec: Man and Tribe*. New York: New American Library, 1961.
Von Hagen, Victor Wolfgang. *World of the Maya*. New York: New American Library, 1960.
Von Hagen, Victor Wolfgang. *Realm of the Incas*. New York: New American Library, New York, 1957.

MICE *see* Myomancy

MICROMANCY

(See also Macromancy)

Micromancy is divination by studying the smallest object in the area. Whether a rock, a tree or a house, the object is studied and the **seer** interprets. Size, general shape, and color all have their place in the interpretation. With trees (see **dendromancy**), there are specific qualities associated, as also with colors (see **colorology**). The closeness of the object to others, or the distance from them, may also be significant.

MIKHAILOVA, NELYA (B. 1927)

Born in 1927, when only fourteen years old Nelya Mikhailova served in the Red Army's Tank Regiment, fighting the Germans in World War II. Recovering from war injuries in hospital at the end of the war, she discovered that she had developed psychokinetic powers; she was able to make objects move without physically touching them. The first time it happened was when Mikhailova was angry about something and a small pitcher moved off a shelf and smashed on the floor. She found that she could control this energy.

A number of scientists at Moscow State University tested, and confirmed, Mikhailova's powers. At the Utomski Institute in Leningrad, Dr. Gerady Sergeyev set up tests and found there was a magnetic field surrounding her body that was only ten times less than that of the earth itself. Mikhailova's brain waves could generate fifty times more voltage from the back of her head than from the front, while the average person generates only four times as much. During PK (psychokinesis), her pulse rate climbed to 240 per minute. Some forty top scientists, including two Nobel Prize winners, tested Mikhailova.

An Associated Press release from Moscow stated: "Nelya has astounded Soviet scientists with her ability to move such things as match sticks or wine glasses without touching them." One of the PK demonstrations Mikhailova was able to do was to separate the yolk from the white of an egg by mind power alone. In the 1960s, at a time she was in a hospital for a period, she discovered that she could "see" the colors of her embroidery threads through the tips of her fingers. This **psychic** sight was later tested and confirmed by Dr. Leonid Vasiliav, a notable pioneer in Russian psychic research.

Sources:

Fishley, Margaret. *The Supernatural*. London: Aldus, 1976.

Ostrander, Sheila and Lynn Schroeder. *Psychic Discoveries behind the Iron Curtain*. Englewood Cliffs, NJ: Prentice-Hall, 1970.

MIRRORS *see* Catoptromancy; Enoptromancy

Mirror-Gazing

(See also Catoptromancy; Scrying)

Mirror-gazing is one of the many forms of **scrying:** divining by looking into a reflective surface. The mirror is used much like a crystal ball, being gazed into with the diviner seeing scenes from the past, present, or future. The **Roman** god Vulcan had a magic mirror in which he was able to see all things. England's Merlin had one that warned him of treason. In Geoffrey Chaucer's *Canterbury Tales*, the mirror of Cambuscan told of misfortunes to come. In Oliver Goldsmith's *Citizen of the World*, Lao's mirror reflected pure thought. In the *Arabian Nights*, there is the all-seeing mirror of Al-Asnam, and in *Snow White and the Seven Dwarfs* there is the magic mirror of the wicked Queen, in which she can see Snow White.

In Étienne Pasquier's *Recherches de la France* (1560), he speaks of a magic mirror owned and used by Catherine de Médicis (1519–1589). In this, she supposedly could see the future of France, especially as it pertained to the de Médicis family. According to Grillot de Givry, Père Cotton used that same mirror to show Henri IV all the plots that were being hatched against him.

A drawing by Leonardo da Vinci (now in the Library of Christ Church, Oxford, England) shows a woman holding up a mirror to a seeress, as part of a ritual. In the mirror can be seen the face of an old man.

All types of mirrors have been used, including those with polished metal faces, glass, **crystal** and obsidian. The mirror may or may not be enclosed in a frame. If it is, the frame is usually engraved, or marked in some way, with sigils to help generate and amplify the images seen. In Francis Barrett's book *The Magus* (1801), there is shown a mirror set in a frame of "pure gold" with the sacred names Michael, Gabriel, Uriel, and Raphael inscribed around it, inside a double circle. These are the angels ruling over the sun, **moon,** Venus, and Mercury. Above the name Michael is drawn a six-pointed star. On the other side of the frame there is also a circle engraved, inside which (next to the glass) is a six-pointed star together with a five-pointed star and a Maltese-style cross. These are followed by the word "Tetragrammaton." The glass, Barrett says, should be "of a lapidary good clear pellucid crystal . . . about one inch and a half in diameter." There are also instructions for the preparation and inscribing of the table on which the glass should stand. Other authorities give other instructions and suggestions as to what would be appropriate to mark around the frame, though some leave the frame unmarked.

Many diviners say that a black mirror is far superior to any other. Similarly, a concave mirror is an advantage. One way to make a mirror that follows both these suggestions is to obtain one of the old framed pictures, from around the turn of the previous century, which has an oval, convex glass. Reversing the glass and painting what then becomes the back of it with black paint produces a convex black mirror that is perfect for mirror-gazing. Old books of magic state that the glass should be painted three times with asphaltum. To make the asphaltum stick to the glass, it first needs to be cleaned with turpentine. The asphalt should be laid on with a camel-hair brush. However, using modern black enamel from a spray can seems to work just as well. As with all magical practices, while making the object you should be concentrating on its purpose—on it being good for projecting scenes from past, present, and future.

The *Revue Archéologique* of 1846 contains an illustration and description of a magic mirror that belonged to a Spanish family at Saragossa in the seventeenth century. It was a metal, convex mirror decorated with figures and with the words "Muerte, Etam, Teteceme, and Zaps." It was said that images appeared on the surface of any liquid reflected in the mirror's surface.

Sources:

Barrett, Francis.*The Magus, or Celestial Intelligencer; being a complete system of occult philosophy.* London: Lackington, Allen & Co., 1802.

Buckland, Raymond. *Buckland's Complete Book of Witchcraft.* St. Paul, MN: Llewellyn, 1986.

Encyclopedia Britannica. Chicago: William Benton, 1964.

de Givry, Grillot. *A Pictorial Anthology of Witchcraft, Magic & Alchemy.* London: Spottiswoode, Ballantyne, 1931.

MISTLETOE *see* Dendromancy

MOLES *see* Moleosophy

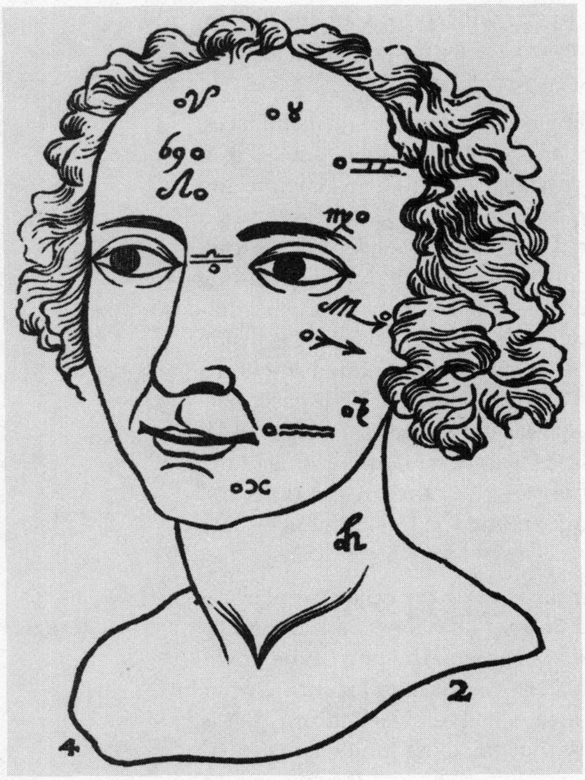

Fifteenth-century engraving showing a correspondence between facial moles and zodiacal signs. *Fortean Picture Library.*

Moleosophy

(See also Phallomancy)

Moleosophy is divining according to the size, shape, color, and location of moles on the human body. Large moles are more significant than small ones.

Shape and Color

Round moles indicate a good nature and a good sense of humor, a person able to get along with virtually anyone. The more round, the greater the good fortune to come.

Angular moles show good and bad characteristics. The person may be very changeable, moody, or easily influenced. If the mole has two or more points, it indicates great misfortune to come.

Oblong moles show some wealth; material well-being. Money may flow in but it flows out just as fast.

If there is any suggested shape to the mole, reminding the seer of an animal or object, then that is interpreted.

If the mole is large and raised, it is a sign of great potential.

If the mole is hairy, it is an extremely negative sign.

Light-colored moles show good luck.

Dark-colored moles show that there will be difficulties to overcome.

The postion of the moles is interpreted as follows:

Position

Head, above the eyebrows: On the right—great intelligence, with the potential for fame and fortune. On the left—extravagance and irresponsibility. In the center—honors, wealth, and love are predicted.

Eyebrows: Right—happiness; possibly an early marriage; perseverance. Left—Unhappy marriage unless much effort is put into it.

Eyelid: Thriftiness. On the outer corners of the eyelid—honesty, reliability, forthrightness.

Cheek: A serious and studious person. Right cheek—happiness, with a good marriage. Left cheek—struggles and problems throughout life.

Nose: Sexuality; good fortune; travel. Sincere friendships.

Mouth: Sensuality; happiness.

Chin: Good luck, good fortune and prosperity. A loving disposition. Accepts responsibilities.
Jaw: Continuous ill health.
Ears: Left—recklessness. Right—bravery.
Throat: Ambition. Wealthy marriage.
Neck: A hard life, with setbacks equaling opportunities. On the front of the neck—unexpected fortune late in life.
Shoulders: A difficult life with much hard work. Right—discretion; a faithful marriage and/or business partner. Left—Lack of ambition.
Arms: Right—success. Left—financial problems.
Hands: Right—natural abilities. Left—ability to learn easily.
Chest: Right side—many changes in fortune throughout life, ending in good fortune. Left side—ever-changing fortune with barely sufficient wealth.
Ribs: Right side—cowardice and insensitivity. Left side—a slow developer and a slow healer.
Abdomen: Greed, self indulgence, laziness. A tendency to excess in eating and drinking.
Back: Upper—generosity, but inclined to arrogance. Lower—sensuous and loving.
Hips: Strong, healthy children.
Buttocks: A good sense of humor. Accepting of life and all that it brings.
Thighs: Right—happiness in marriage; health and wealth. Left—loss, loneliness, poverty, but remaining optimism.
Knees: Right—good at handling finances. Left—rash and frivolous.
Lower legs: Right—refined, with good dress sense. Left—casual but elegant.
Ankles: Hard worker and good provider.
Feet: Right—love of travel. Left—fear of travel.

Sources:

Buckland, Raymond. *Gypsy Witchcraft and Magic*. St. Paul, MN: Llewellyn, 1998.
Gibson, Walter B. and Litzka R. *The Complete Illustrated Book of the Psychic Sciences*. New York: Doubleday, 1966.

MOLTEN LEAD *see* Molybdomancy

MOLYBDOMANCY

Molybdomancy is divination by molten lead. Drops of lead were allowed to fall into a vessel of **water.** The resulting hissing and bubbling noises were listened to and interpreted. Lead is traditionally the metal of death and is associated with Saturn.

Frederick T. Elworthy's *The Evil Eye* of 1895 notes: "Molybdomancy, (divination) by noting motions and figures in molten lead." This would seem to indicate that it was not only the sounds of the lead hitting the water that were significant, but also the shapes assumed by the lead as it cooled. This later was much like the wax in **ceromancy.**

Sources:

Oxford English Dictionary. Oxford: Clarendon Press, 1989.

Monroe, Robert Allan (1915–1995)

Robert Monroe was born in Indiana in 1915. From 1937 to 1949 he worked for an Ohio radio station, writing and producing programs. He rose to become the president of several radio and electronic corporations.

As a child, Monroe experienced what he later came to realize were out-of-body experiences (OOBEs), or **astral projections.** These became more and more frequent as he got older. In 1956 Monroe started a small research and development program in his New York–based company, RAM Enterprises. This was designed to determine the feasibility of learning during sleep. He registered three patents for methods and techniques for inducing and controlling various states of awareness.

From 1965 to 1966 Monroe took part in experiments at the Brain Wave Laboratory of the University of Virginia Medical School. There it was noted that while astrally projecting, his blood pressure fell though there was no change in his heart rate. His brain-wave pattern was as normal for dreaming sleep.

In 1971 Monroe opened the Mind Research Institute at his farm in Virginia at the base of the Blue Ridge Mountains. That same year he authored the book *Journeys out of the Body.* Three years later the MRI became the Monroe Institute, which is still functioning today. More than 8,000 people have now attended its programs, and an estimated two million worldwide have used its Hemi-Sync® learning exercises in audio cassettes and CDs.

On one of his projections, Monroe went to an unknown destination and saw a young woman he knew talking to two young girls. He projected a pinch to the woman and she reacted as though she felt it. Later, when he saw her, he asked what she was doing at the time he projected. She said she had been talking with the girls. He asked her if she had felt a pinch. Surprised, the woman said she had, and attributed it to her young brother. She was even able to show Monroe the still-red mark on her body where he had pinched her. This is most unusual, since normally an astral body cannot affect the physical plane.

An interesting feature of Monroe's astral projections was that many times he felt that he was someone else, while projecting. Robert Monroe died at the age of seventy-nine, on March 17, 1995, of complications of pneumonia.

Sources:

Fishley, Margaret. *The Supernatural*. London: Aldus, 1976.
Monroe, Robert A. *Journeys out of the Body*. New York: Doubleday, 1971.
Mysteries of Mind, Space & Time: The Unexplained. Westport, CT: H. S. Stuttman, 1992.
http://www.monroeinstitute.org/.

Montgomery, Ruth (1912–2001)

Born Ruth Schick on June 11, 1912, in Princeton, Indiana, she attended both Baylor and Purdue universities though she never obtained a degree. Despite an early desire to be a missionary, Ruth went into journalism and eventually got a job with the International News Service in Washington, DC. She married Robert H. Montgomery, a management consultant whom she met in Detroit.

In St. Petersburg, Florida, in 1956, Montgomery attended her first **spiritualist** séance with direct-voice **medium** Malcolm Pantin. She later attended other **séances** in Washington, including those given by Hugh Gordon Burroughs. She wrote a newspaper series about séances for the INS, and started using a **Ouija® board.** Through it, Montgomery believed that she contacted her dead father and also Burroughs's control, Father Murphy. In an interview, Montgomery said:

> That initial story led to an assignment to go to a Spiritualist camp in Silver Bell, Michigan, to produce an eight-part series. In it, I pointed out the obviously phony things, such as materialization séances, but I honestly reported what I couldn't understand that did seem authentic. I did a straight reporting job that was carried in just about every city in America.

After receiving encouragement from medium Arthur Ford, Montgomery started doing **automatic writing** and producing material that she published. From automatic writing she moved on to do automatic typing. In 1965 she wrote a book about medium **Jeane Dixon,** titled *A Gift of* ***Prophesy.*** It became a national bestseller. The following year she wrote *A Search for the Truth*, which dealt with her personal spiritual explorations. In 1970 she gave up her syndicated column and, with her husband, moved to Mexico.

By the late 1970s Montgomery was writing about aliens and UFOs, with *Strangers among Us* (1979) and *Aliens among Us* (1985). Her last book, *The Worlds to Come: The Guide's Long-Awaited* ***Predictions*** *for a Dawning Age*, was released in 1999 by Harmony Books of New York. In it Montgomery gave her predictions for the future of planet Earth. These included the view that the planet would shift on its axis and that "in a lot of areas the waters will be where the land is, and vice versa. Lands will rise from the sea."

Sources:

Guiley, Rosemary Ellen. *Harper's Encyclopedia of Mystical & Paranormal Experience*. San Francisco: HarperSanFrancisco, 1991.

Montgomery, Ruth. *A Search for the Truth*. New York: Bantam Books, 1968.

http://www.geocities.com/HotSprings/Spa/2366/montgomery.html.

MOON ***see*** **Selenomancy**

Moon Phases

Many **seers, diviners,** and others believe that it is important to work according to the phases of the moon. Witches, Wiccans, and various magicians work this way. Basically, they do constructive work during the waxing phase and eliminating work during the waning phase. It is an extension of sympathetic magic. Working to bring about something constructive, to bring increase, the person works as the moon is growing and increasing. Working to get rid of (for example) bad habits, they work as the moon

Many seers believe it is important to work according to the phases of the Moon. This fifteenth-century print shows the Moon and its influence over daily events. *Fortean Picture Library.*

is decreasing. Some divination is done at the full moon. It is seldom that any is done specifically at the new moon.

A guide to the phases of the moon can be found in the times of its rising. The new moon always rises at sunrise. The first quarter always rises at noon. The full moon always rises at sunset. The last quarter always rises at midnight. For each day following the above, the moon will rise about fifty minutes later than the previous day.

Sources:

Buckland, Raymond. *Wicca for Life*. New York: Citadel, 2002.

MOSES, WILLIAM STAINTON (1839–1892) ***see*** **Automatic Writing**

Myers, Frederick William Henry (1843–1901)

Frederick William Henry Myers was born at Keswick, Cumberland, England, on February 6, 1843. His parents were Rev. Frederick Myers and Myers's second wife Susan Harriet Marshall. Young Frederick had two younger brothers. When his father died in 1851 the family moved to Cheltenham and Myers was sent to school at Cheltenham College. There Myers showed outstanding classical and literary ability and in 1860 moved on to Trinity College, Cambridge.

Myers graduated from Trinity College in October 1864 and early the next year traveled in Europe, spending time in Greece and Italy. Later that year he visited the United States and Canada. He was then offered a fellowship in classics at Trinity College, which he accepted. He remained at Trinity for four years before resigning and turning to the higher education of women. In 1873 he became an inspector of schools in Cambridge, a position he maintained for nearly thirty years.

Myers's personal life was checkered. As a young man he was homosexual but later led a heterosexual life. He fell in love with Annie Eliza, the wife of his cousin Walter James Marshall. She returned the love, though it was never consummated. Annie committed suicide in September 1876, but both she and Myers believed they would be together in the afterlife. On March 13, 1880, Myers married Eveleen Tennant and they had three children. By 1900 Myers had become seriously ill and went for unorthodox medical treatment in Rome, where he died on January 17, 1901.

While a fellow at Trinity College during the 1870s, Myers became close with Henry Sidgwick and Edmund Gurney. Sidgwick became a mentor of Myers's, and Gurney became Myers's student. In 1874, after a sitting with the medium **William Stainton Moses,** the three formed a loose group to study **mediumship.** In 1882, at the urging of Sir William Barrett, the three men formed the **Society for Psychical Research,** with Sidgwick as president and Gurney as secretary. In 1888, after Gurney's unexpected death, Myers became secretary and, in 1900, president.

Myers co-wrote, with Gurney and Frank Podmore, *Phantasms of the Living*, published by the Society for Psychical Research in 1886. In 1903 Myers's classic two-volume work *Human Personality and Its Survival of Bodily Death* was published posthumously. The first volume of this work deals with various phenomena such as **dreams** and dissociation of the personality, while the second volume examines and reports on the communications of **spiritualist** mediums, apparitions of the dead and other phenomena of the paranormal.

Frederick William Henry Myers. *Fortean Picture Library.*

One of the major contributions made by Myers to the field of **psychic** research was the introduction of cross-correspondences as proof that mediums are not transmitting anything from their own unconscious nor indulging in telepathy (a word coined by Myers) from the sitter. Cross-correspondences are a series of messages that come through a number of different mediums, often spread around the world; each message is incomplete in itself but fits together with the others to give a whole. The received messages are sent to a central control—in the early experiments this was the Society for Psychical Research—where they are examined and correlated. The early experiments revolved around obscure classical subjects that made no sense at all to the mediums channeling them, but indicated that they came from the then recently deceased Myers, Sidgwick, and Gurney.

Sources:

Broad, C. D. *Man, Myth & Magic: F. W. H. Myers*. London: BPC Publishing, 1970.

Myers, Frederick W. H. *Human Personality and Its Survival of Bodily Death*. New York: University Books, 1961.

Myomancy

Myomancy is divination by rats and mice. It is not only dependant upon their movements, but also upon any cries or noises they may make and the destruction of property caused by their gnawing. All of these signs were taken to foretell evil. Ephraim Chambers's *Cyclopædia; or, an universal dictionary of arts and sciences* of 1728 says: “Some authors hold myomancy to be one of the most ancient forms of divination; and think it is on this account that Isaiah lxvi, 17 reckons mice among the abominable things of the idolater.”

The Roman emperor Quintus Fabius Maximus is said to have resigned his dictatorship of Rome because of the perceived warnings of rats and mice. Marcus Terentius Varro (116–27 BCE), the prolific Latin writer, spoke of Cassius Flaminius retiring for the same reason from his command of the cavalry fighting Hannibal.

Sources:

Oxford English Dictionary. Oxford: Clarendon Press, 1989.

Spence, Lewis. *An Encyclopedia of the Occult*. London: George Routledge & Sons, 1920.

N

NABHI

Meaning a "called" person, a nabhi was a **prophet** as found in the **Old Testament.** According to Geoffrey Ashe, in the early period (c. 1050–1015 BCE) the nabhi appeared little more than a **fortune-teller.** However, if true to the calling, the nabhi made him or herself receptive to whatever messages or prophecies might come from deity, rather than claiming to employ techniques that would draw such information.

Sources:

Ashe, Geoffrey. *Man, Myth & Magic: Prophecy*. London: BPC Publishing, 1970.

NAMES *see* **Numerology; Onomancy**

NARCOMANCY

A branch of **metagnomy,** narcomancy is visions obtained when in a sleep state. It is very much like **meconomancy** in that it is drug-induced sleep. But where meconomancy is induced by opium, narcomancy may be induced by other narcotics. It is divination from dreams or hallucinations experienced while under the influence of narcotics. It also differs from **oneiromancy** in that in the latter, the divination comes from dreams obtained in natural sleep.

NATIVE AMERICAN

It is the **shamans** of the Native American tribes who interpret **dreams** and visions and practice various types of divination. Other terms, beside "shaman," are also used: "medicine man" and "angakok" (Inuit), for example. It is interesting that most of the various types of divination found among the native peoples of North America were, and are, the same as those found in ancient times across Europe and Asia.

The practice of shamanism differs from one area and tribe to another. In many groups he is greatly respected for his ability to communicate with the supernatural powers, yet he is also feared. In some areas he is a political leader as well as shaman. Among the Klamath of Oregon, he occupies an important place where he may be more highly regarded than the chief, and where he may have more wealth and a larger house than anyone else. With the Cherokee, he is not only shaman but is also doctor, counselor, historian, educator, philosopher, and politician.

Probably the most common form of divination is through dreams and visions. This is found almost universally among the many tribes. **Belomancy** is also practiced. Many shamans bring about such divinatory tools by fasting, and some use narcotics and stimulants such as jimsonweed or the slices of cactus known as peyote. With the Mohave, all dreams have a meaning and all are **omens.** However, they feel that the omen does not necessarily show what *will* happen, but what *could* happen. Also, the dream may indicate potential; it may show what will be only if the dreamer actualizes it. The most crucial factor in what the Mohave call "power dreams" is the role of myths, especially the Creation Myth. However, each Mohave shaman may dream his own individual version of an aspect of the Creation Myth. Because of this, he will not tell or perform his dream experience in the presence of another shaman, in case it should lead to anger between the two of them over differences.

The Navajo is the largest group of Native Americans, occupying a reservation of some fifteen million acres mostly in northeastern Arizona and northwestern New Mexico. The Navaho medicine man is called a "singer," since all the rituals, divinations, and magics are sung. He knows all the long prayers and rituals and the sequences in which they must be sung. He learns his trade over many years of study. There are also diviners who are not necessarily singers as well. They specialize in divination and may be called upon to help individual families. Although women seldom become singers, they do often practice divination. These diviners receive their power as a gift, rather than through years of study. They may be employed to find lost or stolen property, locate **water,** diagnose illness, and recommend treatment.

The Ojibwa is the second most numerous group, after the Navaho. They are related to the Algonkian groups. They employ **clairvoyance, telepathy,** apparitions, dreams, spirit communication, telekinesis, and many other forms. This is because the Ojibwa have no clear boundaries between the natural and the supernatural, or the material and the spiritual. Magic is as real as an axe and projected thought as real as an **arrow** shot from a bow. It is through a traditional vision quest that the Ojibwa shaman receives his clairvoyant and curative powers. He may use the greatest variety of divination tools. In 1709 Antoine Raudot, writing from Quebec, related that the shaman "tells them things that they ask him; to invoke they place themselves in a cabin of bark or skin where they give frightful yells; the devil appears to them and sometimes beats them badly; this cabin while they are there trembles with so much force that one would think it was going to turn over." The "shaking tent" ceremony is performed when requested and paid for. It is done to find out about the future. It may also be used to discover lost or stolen property, or the course that an illness will follow. The "tent" itself is extremely substantial, making the shaking of it notable. One description, from 1764, said:

> The Ojibwa braves built an extra large wigwam, and inside it a smaller tent made of moose-skins hung over a framework of wood. The frame consisted of five poles, of five different kinds of lumber. Each pole was about ten feet long and eight inches in diameter. The diameter of the tent was four feet, and the poles were set two feet deep in the earth. They were tied together at the top with a hoop or girder. The moose-skin covering was fastened tightly to the poles with thongs of hide, but a loose flap was left on one side, to admit the medicine man.

In the pueblos of Arizona and New Mexico, the **seers** use crystals to do **scrying.** Scrying was also a practice in the northern plains, where the seer would gaze into a mixture of badger and buffalo blood. In a so-called "hand-trembling" ceremony with the Navaho, the shaman's hand begins to tremble uncontrollably. It is said that the Gila Monster Spirit controls it. Once this starts, the man passes into a trance from which he can diagnose disease and look into the future. With the Huachuca Mountain Apaches, the shaman is possessed by bear spirits. The Yuma, the Havasupai and the Walapai are all possessed by spirits. Sioux shamans in the Dakotas are believed to have mysterious beings living inside them, which give them certain powers. Inspirational possession also takes place with the Iroquois of New York.

Within the Hopi Indians of northeastern Arizona, the Kachina Dancers represent the legendary Kachinas, believed to have lived on Earth at one time. These Kachinas are now in a spirit world and cannot be seen by mortals. There are a lot of them; more than 350 have been catalogued. They are not worshiped as gods but are considered benign spirits who can visit with mortals. When these visits take place, the Kachinas are welcomed, for they are helpful to humankind. Dreams play an important role in the Kachina cult, just as dreams and visions do in so many Native American groups.

In Iroquois ritualism, there is no constant association between a rite and the spirit being honored. What rites are performed to cure the sick depend upon the dreams of the patient. If he or she has not had a dream, then the shaman is consulted. These days the shaman uses **cards, tea leaves,** or some similar method to ascertain which ritual to perform.

Sources:

Lambert, R. S. *Exploring the Supernatural: The Weird in Canadian Folklore*. Toronto: McClelland & Stewart, 1955.

Tooker, Elisabeth. *The Iroquois Ceremonial of Midwinter*. New York: Syracuse University Press, 1970.

Waters, Frank. *Book of the Hopi*. New York: Ballantine, 1969.

Waters, Frank. *Masked Gods: Navaho and Pueblo Ceremonialism*. New York: Ballantine, 1970.

NECROMANCY; NIGROMANTIA

Necromancy is the art of revealing future events by means of communication with the dead. Although any form of **spiritualism,** such as using a **Ouija® board,** technically would be classed as a branch of necromancy, true necromancy is generally regarded as communicating by means of a corpse. That is, by obtaining a corpse and, by magical ritual, giving back to it the power of speech so that it might be interrogated about the future.

The word "necromancy" comes from the Greek *nekros*, meaning "dead body," and *manteia*, meaning "divination." The Greeks themselves believed that it was necessary to descend to Hades in order to consult with the dead, rather than bringing back the dead to this plane. The word was corrupted by Latin writers to Nigromantia, giving the practice the subtitle of "the black art."

In medieval times it was believed that the dead, unrestricted by human limitations, were able to see into the future and, if questioned, could tell what lies ahead. Some people also regarded the dead as omniscient and were more interested in learning of the location of buried treasures. For nine days before the ritual, the necromancer and his assistants would fast and abstain from the sight of women. Some would dress in clothes taken from corpses, the better to attune themselves to the vibrations. Some felt it necessary to eat dog's flesh and black bread, and to drink unfermented grape juice.

In order to conjure the spirits that had already departed this earthly plane, it was necessary to employ powerful magic of the ceremonial kind. This involved drawing a consecrated circle of protection, for the magician-operator and his assistant. It was an elaborate design with the names of powerful angels and archangels written around it, together with various forceful magical sigils worked into the design.

There were many different techniques recorded. One involved going to a graveyard and, as the hour of midnight struck, scattering graveyard earth about and loudly declaiming, "*Ego sum te peto et videre queto*. The dead rise and come to me." In **Robert Cross Smith**'s weekly magazine *The* **Astrologer** *of the Nineteenth Century* (1825) there is a painting by W. Raphael of **Dr. John Dee** (1527–1608) and either his assistant **Edward Kelley** or a man named Waring. The two men stand inside an elaborate ritual circle, Dee holding a book and a wand and the other man holding high a torch. Outside the circle stands a shroud-wrapped corpse, newly taken from its grave. The scene is supposedly in the churchyard at Walton Le Dale in Lancashire, England.

Necromancy was supposedly employed in Haiti in order to make a zombie. The word "zombie" comes from the Congolese *nvumbi*, meaning "a body deprived of its soul." Traditionally a zombie is made by a Boko—the black magician of the world of Voudoun. He will go to a graveyard as soon as possible after a burial and his assistants will dig up the coffin and pry off the lid. The Boko will then perform a ceremony of necromancy. He will take a handful of meal, flour, or grain, and draw the vévé of the god of the dead, Guédé, on the freshly turned earth. A **candle** is lit at each of the four directions and the Boko pours rum to the *loa*, or gods. One of the assistants beats out a rhythm called "Petro Dance" on a drum. It is said that the corpse will only respond to its own name, so the Boko will repeatedly call it by name until it answers. When it does answer—as it invariably does—it is then obliged to climb out of the coffin and follow the Boko.

According to Eric Maple, *The Catholic Encyclopedia* states: "The Church does not deny that, with a special permission of God, the souls of the departed may appear to the living, and even manifest things unknown to the latter. But, understood as the art or science of evoking the dead, necromancy is held by the theologians to be due to the agency of evil spirits."

Sources:

Buckland, Raymond. *The Anatomy of the Occult*. New York: Samuel Weiser, 1977.
Catholic Encyclopedia. New York: Encyclopedia Press, 1914.
Cavendish, Richard. *The Black Arts*. New York: G. P. Putnam's, 1967.
Maple, Eric. *Man, Myth & Magic: Necromancy*. London: BPC Publishing, 1970.
Spence, Lewis. *An Encyclopedia of the Occult*. London: George Routledge & Sons, 1920.

Necyomancy

According to Henry Cockeram, in *The English dictionarie, or an interpreter of hard English words* (1623), necyomancy is "divination by calling up damned spirits." It is, therefore, akin to **necromancy.** With necromancy, the spirits called up are not necessarily "damned"; they may be the spirits of recently dead relatives, for example. But with necyomancy, the spirits summoned are of dubious extraction; some or all of them having had no previous life on this earth. As in **Ceremonial Magic,** they may be termed demons, devils, shades, wraiths or similar. And, again as in Ceremonial Magic, they are very much averse to being summoned into this dimension and will harm the would-be diviner if possible. It is, therefore, necessary to work within a consecrated ritual circle when practicing necyomancy.

Sources:

Buckland, Raymond. *The Anatomy of the Occult*. New York: Samuel Weiser, 1977.
Oxford English Dictionary. Oxford: Clarendon Press, 1989.

NEEDLES *see* Acultomancy

NEWTS *see* Batrachomancy

NIGROMANTIA *see* Necromancy

NOMANCY *see* Onomancy

Nostradamus (Michel de Nostredame) (1503–1566)

Nostradamus was a French **astrologer** of Jewish descent, though his family converted to Christianity. His real name was Michel de Notre Dame, or Nostredame. He was born at St. Rémy, in Provence, on December 14, 1503. His father was a notary and ancestors on both his father's and his mother's sides were mathematicians and men of medicine. Nostradamus studied philosophy at Avignon and then read medicine at the university of Montpellier, graduating from there in 1529. He first practiced at Agen, where he married. His wife and two small children later died. On their deaths he retired to Provence. From there he was invited to Aix by the Parliament of Provence. He established himself at Salon, near Aix, in 1544 and became famous for his medical

Nostradamus portrayed with the great men of history concerning whom he has supposedly written in his prophecies. *Fortean Picture Library.*

work during the plagues at Aix and Lyons. The town of Aix voted him a pension for his services during the contagion.

Nostradamus moved to Salon de Craux, between Avignon and Marseilles. There he remarried, to Anne Ponce Gemelle, and the couple had three sons and a daughter (some records say three sons and three daughters). He could read **Hebrew, Greek,** and Latin, and spoke several foreign languages. In 1540 he published an almanac of **weather** predictions, based on his astrological research. It was in 1547 that Nostradamus started giving his major **prophesies.** These he collected together and, in 1555, published them at Lyons, in a book titled *Centuries*. The first of them he dedicated to his oldest son, Cæsar. An enlarged second edition, dedicated to the king, was published three years later. The book consisted of quatrains (four-line verses) grouped in hundreds. Each group was called a century. Nostradamus claimed that he derived his gift of prophecy from the tribe of Issachar, one of the 10 lost tribes of Israel.

Astrology was at a peak at this time and many of Nostradamus's prophesies were fulfilled. Consequently he was appointed physician-in-ordinary by Charles IX, and given the title of counsellor. He received the duke of Savoy at his salon and was invited to visit Queen Catherine de Médicis.

It is said that Nostradamus slept only three or four hours a night. He denied that he was a prophet, though he did feel that he had a gift of divine origin: "an infusion of supernatural light . . . inspired revelation . . . participation in divine eternity." He suffered from severe gout and other ailments. Nostradamus died at dawn on July 2, 1566, having foretold the exact day and even hour of his death. His widow set up a marble stone with a Latin inscription, which said:

> Here lie the bones of the illustrious Michel Nostradamus, whose almost divine pen alone, in the judgment of all mortals, was worthy to record, under the influx of stars, the future events of the whole world. He lived 62 years, 6 months, 17 days. He died at Salon in the year 1566. Posterity, disturb not his sweet rest! Anne Ponce Gemelle hopes for her husband true felicity.

For almost five-hundred years people around the world have read Nostradamus's prophesies and tried to see how they might apply to the immediate future. They have been hailed as genuine prophetic messages, no matter how obscure the contents of the quatrains. Many have seemed to prove exceptionally accurate in the past, yet the possible meanings of most are perpetually disputed. All are written in such a convoluted manner that they could be applied to any one of a large number of possible historic events. It is possible, of course, that Nostradamus composed them all with his tongue firmly in his cheek. Apparently they were written in this veiled manner so as not to offend the Church of the time.

Enthusiasts claim that Nostradamus foretold the death of Charles I, the rise of Napoleon, the rise of Hitler, the atomic bombing of Japan, the abdication of Edward VIII, and the deaths of John and Robert Kennedy.

Sources:

MacHovec, Frank J. *Nostradamus: His Prophecies for the Future*. Mount Vernon, NY: Peter Pauper Press, 1972.

Ward, Charles A. *Oracles of Nostradamus*. New York: Charles Scribner's Sons, 1940.

NOTARIKON ***see*** **Gematria**

NUMBERS *see* Arithmancy; Mathemancy; Numerology

NUMEROLOGY

The numerals 1 through 9 give the basis of all numbers and calculations. Numerology is divination through the occult significance of numbers. Pythagorus said, "The world is built upon the power of numbers." He was the one who reduced all to the power of the nine primaries. This is done by adding anything above 9. For example, 26 = 2+6 = 8. No matter the size of the number, it can be reduced in the same way, e.g. 7,548,327 would become 7+5+4+8+3+2+7 = 36 = 3+6 = 9.

Working in Numerology, the same reduction can take place with words and letters, based on the following:

1	2	3	4	5	6	7	8	9
A	B	C	D	E	F	G	H	I
J	K	L	M	N	O	P	Q	R
S	T	U	V	W	X	Y	Z	

The word "castle," for example, would have the values C=3, A=1, S=1, T=2, L=3, E=5; 3+1+1+2+3+5 = 15 = 1+5 = 6.

In Numerology, dates, and names are reduced to their primary numbers and then interpreted according to the values attributed to those numbers. Working with this, it can be determined everything from where best to live and what job would be best for you, to what sort of person to marry. To do this, it is necessary to find your birth number and your name number.

Birth Number

Someone born on August 27, 1986, would reduce that date to a single digit: 8+2+7+1+9+8+6 = 41 = 4+1 = 5. That person's birth number is then 5. This number represents the influences at the time of birth. In many ways it corresponds to the palm of the left hand (see **Cheiromancy**), which shows the qualities a person is born with. It also ties in with natal **astrology.** This birth number is the number to consider for all important events. Since it is the number of your birth, it cannot be altered, unlike a name number. In this example, any important business, such as the signing of contracts, should be done on a date that also reduces to 5.

Name Number

The name number is taken from the above chart. For example, Elvis Presley had a name number that was 5+3+4+9+1+7+9+5+1+3+5+7 = 59 = 14 = 5. Notice how many fives occur. "Five" people are physically and mentally active, make friends easily and get along well with almost any other number. They are usually leaders of one sort or another. Another even more striking example of 5 was John F. Kennedy:1+6+8+5+6+2+5+5+5+5+4+7 = 59 = 14 = 5. Here there is a tremendous preponderance of 5's, ending with the name number itself. Any recurring numeral is considered to affect the personality.

The name you reduce in this way should be the name most generally used. Hence, "John F. Kennedy" rather than just "John Kennedy" or "John Fitzgerald Kennedy." Based on this, Elvis's stronger name number would be simply Elvis = 5+3+4+9+1 = 24 = 6; the 5 would be a secondary name number, contributing some qualities but not the major ones.

An excellent example of marriage compatibility can be seen with Napoleon and Josephine, who shared the throne of France from 1804 to 1809. Both names first reduce to 11 and subsequently to 2.

Number Values

The following values are attached to the nine primary numbers:

1: Sun
Letters A, J, S.
Element—fire
A leader and driving force who automatically assumes control. An explorer, with lots of ambition. Very much the extrovert. There is a tendency to be impatient, and there are usually strong feelings either for or against; seldom in the middle. Often plays the role of "big brother or sister" to others. Does not realize own strength yet would not knowingly hurt another. Can stand praise, which may spur to further achievements.

2: Moon
Letters B, K, T.
Element—water
Can be emotional and easily influenced to tears. Sensitive and domestic; very fond of the home but can easily accept changes in surroundings. Has a fertile imagination. Patriotic. Preference for living near water. May have musical talents and great psychic ability.

3: Jupiter
Letters—C, L, U.
Element—fire
Interested in the material rather than the spiritual, this is the scientist and investigator; the seeker; wanting to know "how" and "why." Possesses a very good sense of humor, and is not greatly interested in money. Religious ideas are flexible. Very trusting.

4: Uranus
letters—D, M, V.
Element—air
Has strong, intuitive tendencies. Very interested in the occult and psychic research. Usually ahead of his or her time and because of this is often regarded as strange or eccentric. Drawn to anything out of the ordinary. Believes in liberty and equality but can be bitingly sarcastic if crossed. Very good at predicting things.

5: Mercury
Letters—E, N, W.
Element—air
Active, both physically and mentally. Fond of reading, research; inquiring and exploring. Makes friends easily. Good at languages and at simplifying systems. Would make a good teacher or writer. Usually methodical and orderly.

6: Venus
Letters—F, O, X.
Element—earth
Usually good looking, Venus is gentle and refined, pleasant and sociable, friendly and agreeable. A natural peacemaker who is able to soothe ruffled feelings. Would make an excellent diplomat. Excellent as a host or hostess but can experience difficulties with finances.

7: Neptune
Letters—G, P, Y.
Element—water
Extremely psychic, usually possessing E.S.P. An introvert who, although not saying much, thinks and knows a great deal. Can appear mysterious. Often interested in botany, chemistry, psychology, and psychiatry. Knowledgeable in astrology and most occult fields. Enjoys fishing and tends to take from the "haves" to give to the "have nots."

8: Saturn
Letters—H, Q, Z.
Element—earth
Little sense of humor, inclining to be cold and pessimistic. Believes that hard work never killed anyone. Although frequently slow off the mark, usually ends up ahead of everyone else. Good at finances. Frequently connected with real estate, mining, and the law. Often prepossessed with thoughts of the past. Interested in cemeteries and pawn shops.

9: Mars
Letters—I, R.
Element—fire
Can be very jealous and gets overly emotional. Active and frequently ruled by the emotions. Tied to family background and extremely loyal. Can be impulsive and afraid of the unknown. Often associated with surgery and with illnesses, both physical and mental.

From the above it is possible to look at anyone from the numerology point of view. As an example, examine someone named John Doe (better known to his friends as Johnny), born on July 18, 1974, who is considering moving to an apartment in Trenton, New Jersey. He can make the move any time but would prefer to do it in the summer rather than the winter. Should he take a roommate and, if so, what type? How should he decorate the apartment? All this and more can be examined with numerology.

First of all, work out the name number and birth number for Johnny Doe.

Johnny Doe **July 18, 1974**

168557 465 = 47 = 11 = 2 7+1+8+1+9+7+4 = 37 = 10 = 1

The name number is 2 and birth number is 1. As a 2, Johnny can easily accept a change in his surroundings. Wherever he happens to be moving from, therefore, he will be comfortable making the shift to New Jersey, and he probably did not have to do a lot of soul-searching before deciding to make the move. His preference is to live near water, so Trenton should be fine, situated as it is on the Delaware River. Additionally, he is patriotic, so the history of the area should suit him. Numerologically, "Trenton New Jersey" equals a 5 and "Trenton NJ" equals a 4. Both 4 and 5 are air signs, which are not really in conflict with Johnny's water sign. But a town with a water sign or, better yet, with a number value of 1 would have been the ideal choice.

Since Johnny is fond of the home and very domestic, he will almost certainly turn his new apartment into a comfortable abode. He may have musical talents and also psychic ability. Should he decide to have a roommate, Johnny should choose one whose name number is also a water sign (a 2 or a 7) or an earth sign (a 6 or an 8), which is compatible. The 8 should be the last choice, since it goes with Saturn, a cold and pessimistic person. The others are all much closer to the sensitivity of Johnny.

Although he would prefer to move in the summer, rather than the winter, January (the first month) would be the best choice, agreeing with his birth number of one. Second choice would be October, a 10 that again equals 1. The exact day of the month should be determined, depending on the year. As for decorating the apartment, there is an affinity of colors to numbers:

1—yellow, brown, gold
2—cream, green, white
3—lilac, mauve, violet
4—blue, gray
5—*light* shades of any color; pastels
6—all shades of blue
7—light shades of yellow and green
8—dark gray, blue, purple, black
9—pink, red, crimson

Colors or combinations of cream, green, or white would be best for Johnny to decorate. It is possible to go on with musical tastes and so on, but this gives an idea of the scope of numerology. It is used in a wide variety of situations.

There are also other systems of numerology. All seem workable, but it is not wise to mix different systems. They should certainly be tried, however, to see which seems most suitable. The above system is the most commonly used, and is referred to as the "modern" system or the "Pythagorean" system. The Hebrew system does not use the number nine, and does not follow the normal arrangement of letters. The Hebrew equivalents of English letters have been used, except where there is no exact parallel:

1	2	3	4	5	6	7	8
A	B	C	D	E	U	O	F

I	K	G	M	H	V	Z	P
Q	R	L	T	N	W		
J		S			X		
Y							

Another system is the one devised and used by Samuel Liddell MacGregor Mathers of the Order of the Golden Dawn (nineteenth century):

	1	2	3	4	5	6	7	8
	A	B	G	D	E	U	O	F
I	C	L	M	H	V	Z	P	
	J	K	S	T	N	W		
	Q	R			X			
	Y							

Sources:

Cavendish, Marshall. *The Book of Fate & Fortune*. London: Cavendish House, 1981.
Cavendish, Richard. *The Black Arts*. New York: G. P. Putnam's, 1967.
Cheasley, Clifford W. *Numerology*. Boston: Triangle, 1916.
Cheiro (Louis Hamon). *Cheiro's Book of Numbers*. New York: Arc, 1964.
Leek, Sybil. *Numerology: The Magic of Numbers*. New York: Collier, 1969.
Lopez, Vincent. *Numerology*. New York: Citadel, 1961.

O

OAK ***see*** **Dendromancy**

OATMEAL ***see*** **Aleuromancy**

Oculomancy

Oculomancy is divining from a person's eye. It was said that a thief could be identified by "the turn of his eye" when this was accompanied by a certain ritual. Generally, however, it seems to be the act of gazing deep into someone's eye and "seeing" the future there. Basically this is using the reflective surface of an eye for scrying purposes.

Sources:
Grand Orient (A. E. Waite). *The Complete Manual of Occult Divination: Volume 1—Manual of Cartomancy*. London: Rider, 1912.

Odontomancy

Odontomancy is divining using the teeth. The **seer** will by guided by the color, size, regularity, and spacing, plus whether or not any are missing and, if so, which ones.

In the Ozarks there is a belief in the timeliness of tooth extraction. Although not odontomancy, it is in some ways related. It is said that a tooth should not be pulled when the **moon** is in Capricorn (associated with the head). It is far better, it is said, to wait until the moon is in Aquarius or Pisces, even if there is a lot of pain.

Œnomancy; Oinomancy; Olinomancy

This is divination based on the appearance of wine that is poured as a libation. Grillot de Givry refers to an eighteenth-century manuscript in the Bibliothèque de l'Arsenal, titled *L'Art magique d'Artephius et de Mihinius, divisée en huit propositions*. In it there is an illustration and details of a procedure called "The Three Vases of Artephius." The vases in question each hold oil, wine, and **water.** They are used to show the past, present, and future. The details of the ritual, as given, are quite complicated but basically it comes down to **scrying** the surfaces of the liquids. Although de Givry refers to the wine section of this ritual as oinomancy, it is not truly that, since oinomancy is connected to the wine of libations.

At religious rituals connected with deities, there is invariably a drinking of wine in honor of the gods. Before drinking or even pouring the wine into a goblet, a little is spilled on the ground or into a libation dish to be later poured onto the ground as an offering "to the gods." This is termed a libation. The diviner will study the wine as it is poured at this time. The way in which it flows, the color(s) it reflects, the amount poured, and the manner in which it hits the ground or the libation dish; all these are considered by the diviner in order to obtain details of the receptivity of the gods to any requests to be put forward in the ritual.

Sources:

de Givry, Grillot. A *Pictorial Anthology of Witchcraft, Magic & Alchemy*. London: Spottiswoode, Ballantyne, 1931

OIL ***see*** **Leconomancy**

OINOMANCY ***see*** **Œnomancy**

Old Testament

(See also Bible; Hebrew; Oneiromancy)

The Old Testament is replete with examples of fortune-telling and divination. It is full of miraculous events and examples of **prophesy, dowsing, precognition,** and **dreams.** Examples are Moses's dowsing for **water** in the desert, Saul's meeting with the **Woman of Endor,** and the dreams experienced by Joseph and Jacob.

A prophet was a *nabhi*, or a "called" person. According to Geoffrey Ashe, in the early period (c. 1050–1015 BCE) the nabhi appeared to be little more than a fortune-teller. However, if true to their calling, the nabhi made him or herself receptive to whatever messages or prophecies might come from deity, rather than claiming to employ techniques that would draw such information. In the series *Mysteries of Mind Space & Time: The Unexplained*, David Christie-Murray says:

> The prophets aimed not so much at foretelling the future as at describing what they saw as the will of God in the circumstances of their time. But in doing so, their prophesies *were* fulfilled, often in ways more profound and long-lasting than they ever imagined.

The references to the casting of lots (**astragalomancy; sortilege**) are numerous, in the Old Testament. In Leviticus 16:7–9, Aaron casts lots: "And he shall take the two goats, and present them before the Lord at the door of the tabernacle of the congregation. And Aaron shall cast lots upon the two goats; one lot for the Lord, and the other lot for the scapegoat. And Aaron shall bring the goat upon which the Lord's lot fell, and offer him for a sin offering." In Proverbs 16:33 it says: "The lot is cast into the lap; but the whole disposing thereof is of the lord."

Daniel's vision of the destruction of the temple is illustrative of the prophecy that is found in the Old Testament. Men or women could prophesy. While the prophets' main objectives were to warn, encourage, and teach, they did foreshadow events and so prophecy was tied in with prediction.

Sources:

Ashe, Geoffrey. *Man, Myth & Magic: Prophecy*. London: BPC Publishing, 1970.

Cave, Janet, Laura Foreman and Jim Hicks (eds.). *Mysteries of the Unknown: Ancient Wisdom and Secret Sects*. Alexandria, VA: Time-Life Books, 1989.

Christie-Murray, David. *Mysteries of Mind Space & Time: The Unexplained*. Westport, CT: H. S. Stuttman, 1992.

Werblowsky, R. J. Zwi. *Man, Myth & Magic: Cabala*. London: BPC Publishing, 1970.

Old, Walter Richard "Gorn"—"Sepharial" (1864–1929)

Born on March 20, 1864, at Harndsworth, Birmingham, England, Walter Richard Old grew up to write under the name of Walter Gorn Old and "Sepharial." Old was educated at King Edward's School, Birmingham. At an early age he became interested in **astrology** and read the books of **Alan Leo,** whom he met and befriended. He also took an interest in the **Qabbalah.** As a young man, Old studied ancient languages, the Orient, and medical dispensing. At thirty-five he moved to London where he joined the Theosophical Society. He rapidly became a member of the "inner circle" around **Helena Blavatsky,** the cofounder, and introduced Alan Leo to the society.

Old discovered that he had a talent for **astral projection** and also had strong psychic abilities. On the death of Madame Blavatsky, Old left the Theosophical Society and spent time developing his own system of astrological **prediction** for the stock market, though his first big win came from a similar horse-racing astrological system. He contributed a number of columns to the *Occult Review* but died, on December 23, 1929, before the newspaper astrological column had become popular. Among his many books were *Book of the Crystal and the Seer* (1897), *Prognostic Astronomy* (1901), *Second Sight* (1911), *Cosmic Symbolism* (1912), *The Kabala of Numbers*, (two volumes, 1913), *New Dictionary of Astrology* (1914), *A Manual of Occultism* (1914), *Astrology: How to Make and Read Your Own Horoscope* (1920), and *The Book of Charms and Talismans* (1923).

Sources:

Hyre, K.M. and Eli Goodman. *Price Guide to the Occult and Related Subjects*. Los Angeles: Reference Guides, 1967.

Shepard, Leslie A. (ed.). *Encyclopedia of Occultism & Parapsychology*. New York: Avon, 1978.

OLINOMANCY *see* **Œnomancy**

Ololygmancy

(See also Dog.)

Although there are methods of divining by the *actions* of dogs, ololygmancy is divination by the *howling* of dogs. It is interpreted by the pitch, length of the howl, and the distance from the observer. At the time of Theocritus (310–250 BCE), the Greek poet spoke of a dog howling at night near a house, which foretold a death to come in that house. He said (or had his character Simætha say): "Hark! The dogs are barking through the town. Hecate is at the crossways. Haste, clash the brazen cymbals." The clashing of the cymbals was to drown out the sound of the dog howling and so, hopefully, to prevent the **omen** from coming into eventuality.

Sources:

Lawson, John Cuthbert. *Modern Greek Folklore and Ancient Greek Religion*. New York: University Books, 1964.

Omen

Many of the entries found in this book refer to omens. Omens are presages or prognostications; indications of something that is to happen in the near or even the far-distant future. They came about in a variety of ways, most of them probably following some unusual occurrence that was closely followed by a remarkable happening, good or bad. If there was a repetition of that combination, then the omen became established. Omens vary from the sighting of a particular bird in flight to the observation of a comet. The movement of cats (**ailuromancy**), behavior of horses (**hippomancy**), the way a person laughs (**geloscopy**), and the howling of a dog (**ololygmancy**) can all be taken as omens and, from them, the possible trend of future events may be gauged.

Thomas Carlyle, in *Mrs. C's Letter* (1871), mentions "good or ill luck for the whole year being omened by your liking or otherwise of the first person that accosts you on New Year's morning." Also Sir Walter Scott, in *Peveril of the Peak* (1822), says: "These evil omenings do but point out conclusions . . . most unlikely to come to pass." Yet many people do feel that the things omened *will* come to pass. One definition of the word is "some phenomenon or unusual event taken as a prognostication either of good or evil."

The sightings of comets (**meteoromancy**) and the experience of eclipses have been taken as signs that the world is coming to an end. At the trial of England's King Charles I in 1649, the head of his staff fell off. This many saw as an ill omen. Charles was executed on January 30, 1649.

Shakespeare referred to many omens throughout his plays. In *Julius Caesar*, for example, a **soothsayer** warns Caesar about the Ides of March, presumably based on omens he has observed. There is also a scene where Casca meets with Cicero in a street late at night in a raging storm. Casca comments on the many strange omens that are occurring:

> Against the Capitol I met a lion, who glared upon me and went surly by, without annoying me. And there were drawn upon a heap a hun-

dred ghastly women, transformed with their fear; who swore they saw men, all in fire, walk up and down the streets. And yesterday the bird of night did sit, even at noon-day, upon the market place, hooting and shrieking. When these prodigies do so conjointly meet, let not men say, "These are their reasons; they are natural." For I believe they are portentous things unto the climate that they point upon.

There are many more omen and portents, including dreams (**oneiromancy**) and examination of the entrails of sacrificed animals (**haruspicy**), before Caesar is assassinated. As Calpurnia says in the play, "When beggars die there are no comets seen; the heavens themselves blaze forth the death of princes."

In **Greece** there are many traditional portents of good and evil. For a potential bride to see a weasel is the worst omen. The weasel, it is said, was once a young girl about to be married (the name means "little bride"). In some way she was robbed of her happiness and transformed into an animal. To see a snake, however, is a very good omen. The spilling of oil is an evil omen but the spilling of wine is good. The upsetting of **water** is also good, especially if it happens while on a journey. If the logs of the fire crackle it means that good news is coming. But if sparks should fly, then trouble may be expected. The spluttering of a candle flame or lamp flame is also unlucky.

Sources:

Lawson, John Cuthbert. *Modern Greek Folklore and Ancient Greek Religion*. New York: University Books, 1964.
Oxford English Dictionary. Oxford: Clarendon Press, 1989.
Shakespeare, William. *The Complete Works*. London: Odhams Press, 1938.

Omoplatoscopy

In 1871 Edward B. Tylor, in *Primitive Culture*, mentions "divination by a shoulder blade, technically called scapulimancy or omoplatoscopy." The Sydenham (New) Society's *Lexicon of medicine and allied sciences* of 1892 defines it: "Omoplatoscopy, the name given to a mode of divination formerly practiced by some tribes of **(Native) American** Indians, founded on the direction of the cracks which appeared on a blade bone when placed on a fire."

It is a division of **scapulomancy,** divination by studying the cracks found on the shoulder blades of animals, sacrificial or otherwise. The shoulder blades are placed on a fire, and the heat is what causes the cracks to appear. Exactly where on the blade the cracks appear and the direction in which they run indicate to the **seer** the events that are forthcoming.

Sources:

Oxford English Dictionary. Oxford: Clarendon Press, 1989.

O'Morgair, Malachy (eleventh century)

Canonized as St. Malachy, according to Anderton Malachy O'Morgair **prophesied** the succession of popes from his own time through to the end of the twentieth century.

With many of them he seems to have had a degree of accuracy. For example, in the descriptions he gives of the popes he refers to the nineteenth-century pope Leo XIII as *Lumen in Cælo*, meaning "Light in Heaven." This agrees with Leo's coat of arms, which depicts a comet. For Pope Paul VI, Malachy describes him as *Flors Florum*, meaning "Flower of Flowers." Paul's coat of arms bears the fleur-de-lys. For John Paul I the description is *De Medietate Lunæ*, meaning "of the half **moon.**" John Paul's reign lasted only thirty-three days, with him dying in the middle of the lunar month. Pope John Paul II was described as "Labor of the Sun," or *De Labore Solis*. Two more popes are listed after John Paul II, though Malachy's timing would indicate that they were to have occupied the papal throne before the end of the twentieth century.

"Malachi" is listed as one of the twelve minor prophets lumped together in one book in the books of the prophets in the Jewish scriptures.

Sources:
Anderton, Bill. *Fortune Telling*. North Dighton, MA: JG Press, 1996.
Encyclopedia Britannica. Chicago: William Benton, 1964.

Omphalomancy

"Omphalic" pertains to the navel. Omphalomancy is divining by the number of knots on the umbilical cord at the birth of a child. These knots indicate the number of children that the mother will have after that one.

Since the umbilical cord is part of the newborn child, it was believed to be intimately linked to that child's life and **fate.** Magically, the cord was regarded as a cure for barrenness. It was also regarded as the seat of the soul that wanders in **dreams** and that finally separates at death.

Sources:
Oxford English Dictionary. Oxford: Clarendon Press, 1989.
Sharpe, Eric. *Man, Myth & Magic: Birth*. London: BPC Publishing, 1970.

Oneiromancy

Oneiromancy is the name for seeing the future in dreams. In ancient Mesopotamian literature are found many warnings of impending doom so discovered. The hero Ziusudra, in a Sumerian legend, learns of a coming flood through a dream. In the *Epic of Gilgamesh* (which is filled with dreams, dream imagery, and interpretation), Enkidu advises his friend Gilgamesh of a coming cataclysm, which he saw in a dream. The ancient Egyptians believed in oneiromancy, as did the Sumerians, Babylonians, and Mesopotamians. In Egypt through the Greco-Roman period, and in **Greece** and **Rome** themselves, there was a practice known as **incubation,** where a priest or priestess would sleep in a temple for the express purpose of receiving divine knowledge through dreaming. In ancient Greek and Rome, dreams were regarded as tools by which the gods let humankind know of what was to happen in the future. To interpret these sleep-thoughts, there came into being a class of interpreters known as the *oneirokritai*. They were professional interpreters. One of the books they used, in which they tabled their interpretations, was the *Oneirokritika* of Artemidorus, produced in the second century CE and still in existence.

In 650 BCE King Assurbanipal of Assyria filled his library with clay tablets giving the meanings of dreams. In the fifth century BCE, Aeschylus the dramatist credited oneiromancy among the chief benefits conferred on humankind by Prometheus. Homer included **prophetic** dreams in his epics, naming Zeus as the sender of dreams. Plato, in the *Republic*, represents Socrates as declaring that dreams are pure and prophetic. Xenophon, talking about divination through dreams, maintained that in sleep the human soul reveals its divine nature and, being freed from the shackles of the human body, is able to gaze into the future.

One of the best-known examples of oneiromancy is found in Genesis 41:14–36. There Joseph foretold of seven years of plenty coming to **Egypt,** to be followed by seven years of famine. This was based on the Pharaoh's dream of seven fat cows emerging from a stream and going to graze in a meadow. These were followed by seven thin cows that devoured the fat ones, though the second seven remained thin after the feasting. A second dream of the Pharaoh's was of seven fat ears of corn, growing on a stalk, that were devoured by seven thin ears of corn. This confirmed Joseph's interpretation of plenty followed by famine. (See the **Bible** entry for further description of Joseph's dream interpretation.)

Ancient **Hebrew** literature has a number of examples of portentous dreams. For example, when Jacob was fleeing from the wrath of his brother Esau, he had a dream at Bethel (possibly an ancient Canaanite sanctuary) of a ladder stretching from Earth up to heaven. At the top of the ladder the God of Abraham informed Jacob that he and his descendants would be given the surrounding land in the future. Daniel interpreted the dreams of Nebuchadnezzar and had dreams and visions himself. In Judges 7:13–14 there is a man "that told a dream [about a cake of barley bread tumbled into the host of Midian] unto his fellow," which is then interpreted for him by the "fellow."

St. Thomas Aquinas, in his *Summa Theologica* (1266–1273), stated that "divination by dreams is not unlawful (in the eyes of the Church). It is the experience of all men that a dream contains some indication of the future. Therefore, it is vain to deny that dreams have efficacy in divination."

There are numerous well-documented cases of foreknowledge through dreams. Napoleon dreamed of his defeat at Waterloo before it happened. Adolf Hitler, when a corporal in the Bavarian Infantry in World War I, had a dream that saved his life by its forewarning. **Abraham Lincoln** had many prophetic dreams, including one of his own death. In that, he dreamed he was lying in bed when he heard the sound of sobbing. Getting up and leaving his bedroom, he went into the East Room of the White House where he saw his own body laid out, the victim of an assassin's bullet.

But perhaps one of the most fascinating accounts of oneiromancy was the case of John Chapman in fifteenth-century England. Chapman was a peddler who lived in the village of Swaffham, in Norfolk country. One night he had a dream of going to London and standing on London Bridge. There he met with a man who gave him news of a great fortune that could be his. Chapman told his neighbors of the dream but they just laughed at him. However, he was so moved by it that he journeyed on foot to London—over one hundred miles away—and proceeded to London Bridge. In those days London Bridge was covered across its span with houses and shops. Chapman stood in the center of the bridge and waited. He waited for three days, but nothing happened. Just as he was about to give up, a shopkeeper came out of one of the buildings and asked him what he was doing there all that time. Chapman told the story of his dream. The shopkeeper laughed at him and called Chapman a fool. "I had a strange dream myself a few nights ago," he said. "But I didn't go chasing across the country because of it. I dreamed of a little village in Norfolk called Swaffham and of a man named John Chapman, who lived there. In the dream he had a pear tree in his back garden and buried underneath it was a great store of treasure. Now, you don't suppose I'm going all the way to Norfolk to dig under some man's tree? What a fool I'd be!" The shopkeeper laughed some more and returned to his store. John Chapman hurried home. Digging under the pear tree in his back garden, he unearthed a great treasure of silver and gold. In gratitude, Chapman gave a lot of money to the village church where, today, there is a carving of him on one of the pews and stained glass windows showing his story.

In the Welsh village of **Aberfan** on the night of October 20, 1966, a nine-year-old girl named Eryl Mai Jones had a dream that there was no school the following day. She didn't just dream that there would be no classes, but that there would be no school in existence. The next morning she told her mother that "something black came down all over it." But she went to school anyway. Shortly after nine o'clock that morning a half-million-ton mountain of coal waste, saturated by days of unrelenting rain, slid down over the village, burying houses and the entire school. Nearly 150 people, most of them schoolchildren including Eryl Jones, were buried and died. Many other people all over Great Britain had experienced similar dreams before the tragedy. Some saw an actual mountain of coal slag pour down the mountainside onto the village. One man who had never heard of the village dreamed the word "Aberfan." There were so many reported dreams of the tragedy that a survey was conducted. At least thirty-six prophetic dreams were definitely confirmed. As a result of this, the **British Premonitions Bureau** and the (New York) **Central Premonitions Registry** were established.

The London *Sunday Pictorial* of January 11, 1959, featured a story about Harold Horwood of Slough Lane, London, who consistently not only dreamed of racehorse winners but placed bets on them and made money. As the article says: "In 1946 he won £775 on the November Handicap race, and £200 on the winner of the Cambridgeshire. [In 1945] he dreamed of more than 20 winners, including the Queen's horse Pall Mall, the Two Thousand Guineas winner." It went on to say that Horwood "believes that his dreams are inspired and he has given much to charity."

A remarkable example of oneiromancy occurred in Ohio, coming to a climax on May 26, 1979. Starting ten days before that, David Booth, a twenty-three-year-old office manager in Cincinnati, started to have a vivid dream about an airplane crash. In the dream he saw a three-engined American Airlines jet roll over in the air and fall to the ground with a horrendous explosion of smoke and flame. Booth said that the dream was so real he could feel the searing heat of the flames. He had the dream for several nights in a row and became so concerned that he telephoned

American Airlines and reported it to them. He also called the Federal Aviation Authority and a psychiatrist at the University of Cincinnati. They all treated his calls with the greatest interest and concern, but there was nothing anyone could do on the basis of what he was able to tell them. Four days later an American Airlines DC-10, taking off from Chicago's O'Hare International Airport, turned on its back and smashed into the ground, killing 273 people. It had been the worst aviation disaster in U.S. history to date. The previously reached authorities were amazed at the accuracy of Booth's dream but admitted there was nothing anyone could have done to prevent the disaster.

In modern-day Greece there is a traditional custom used by many a young woman to discover her matrimonial destiny. On the eve of St. Catharine's day (November 26) the young woman must bake special cakes that have salt as the main ingredient. That night she must eat a large number of these cakes, slaking the resultant thirst with generous quantities of wine. This results in her falling asleep to dream of her destined husband. A variation of this is found in some areas of Greece, where only a small piece of the cake is eaten and the rest is divided into three portions and tied respectively with red, black, and blue ribbons. These three sections are placed under the pillow that night and, in the morning, one is drawn out by chance. The red ribbon denotes that the future husband will be a bachelor; the black ribbon a widower; the blue ribbon a stranger. This is followed by an example of **cledonomancy,** overhearing chance remarks made by people passing by. The first name, occupation, or other reamark that is heard is regarded as applying to the future husband.

Sources:

Buckland, Raymond. *Gypsy Dream Dictionary*. St. Paul, MN: Llewellyn, 1999.

Garfield, Patricia L. *Creative Dreaming*. New York: Simon & Schuster, 1974.

Hall, Angus. *The Supernatural: Signs of Things to Come*. London: Danbury Press, 1975.

Headon, Deirdre (ed.). *Quest for the Unknown—Charting the Future*. Pleasantville, NY: Reader's Digest, 1992.

Holroyd, Stuart. *The Supernatural: Dream Worlds*. London: Aldus Books, 1976.

Horwood, Harold. *The Conquest of Time*. London: Fowler, 1959.

Lawson, John Cuthbert. *Modern Greek Folklore and Ancient Greek Religion*. New York: University Books, 1964.

Onimancy

(See also Onymancy; Onychomany)

Onimancy is also known as "observation of the archangel Uriel," who rules the north in white magic. It is, in effect, a form of the divination known as **onychomancy.**

Some olive oil or walnut oil is painted on the fingernails of the right hand of a virginal boy or girl. The oil should be mixed with tallow or some kind of blackening agent. Alternatively it may be painted in the palm of the hand. If money or buried treasure is being sought, then the child must face toward the east. If knowledge of a person is desired, for purposes of love or affection, then the child must face south. South-facing is also recommended for all inquiries into crimes. If robbery is being investigated, then the child must face west. For murder, he or she must face north.

Onimancy is divination by observing the archangel Uriel, portrayed here with the falling Satan. *Fortean Picture Library.*

Instructions now become somewhat vague. According to Spence, the child must repeat the seventy-two verses of the Psalms, "as found in the third book of Reuclin on the **Qabbalistic** art; also found in *de verbo mirifico*." In each of the verses, says Spence, there is to be found "the venerable name of four letters (presumably YHWH), and the three-lettered name of the seventy-two angels. These are referred to the inquisitive name Schemhammaphoras, which was hidden in the folds of the lining of the tippet of the high priest." It is said that when this is all done, the child shall "see wonders."

It seems likely that all of the above is actually a lead-in to simple **scrying.** The reflective surfaces of the nails, or the oil in the palm of the hand, would certainly suit that purpose. When the child has said the Psalms, he or she then gazes at the nails, or into the blackened and oiled palm of the hand, and "sees wonders."

Sources:

Spence, Lewis. *An Encyclopedia of the Occult*. London: George Routledge & Sons, 1920.

ONION *see* Cromnyomancy

Onomancy

Onomancy is divination by using the letters of a name. This, as in **numerology,** would depend upon given numerical values to the letters. Ephraim Chambers's *Cyclopædia; or an universal dictionary of arts and sciences* (1728) defines it as: "Onomancy, or rather, Onomamancy, the art of divining the good or evil fortune which shall befall a man from the letters of his name." Chambers goes on to say "In strictness onomancy should rather signify divination by asses. To signify divination by names it should be onomatomancy." Certainly, according to the Oxford English Dictionary, *onolatry* means "Worship of the ass," and *onology* means "foolish talking; braying," but it seems Chambers is playing with semantics.

William Camden, in *Remaines of a greater worke concerning Britaine* (1605), says: "The superstitious kinde of Divination called Onomantia, condemned by the last General Counsell, by which the Pythagoreans judged the even number of vowels in a name to signifie imperfections in the left sides of men, and the odde number in the right."

With two competitors, onomancy may be used to determine the better—the one with the higher value to his name using numerology. Supposedly this was what determined that Achilles would triumph over Hector in the Trojan Wars.

Sources:

Cavendish, Marshall. *The Book of Fate & Fortune*. London: Cavendish House, 1981.
Oxford English Dictionary. Oxford: Clarendon Press, 1989.
Shepard, Leslie A. (ed.). *Encyclopedia of Occultism & Parapsychology* New York. Avon, 1978.

Onymancy; Onychomancy

(See also Onimany)

Richard Sanders, in ***Physiognomie and chiromancie, metoposcopie,*** *the symmetrical proportions and signal moles of the body, fully and accurately handled* (1653), says: "Onymancy is commonly called the science of the nails." Sir Thomas Urquhart's *The Third Book of the Works of Mr. Francis Rabelais* (1693) refers to it when he says: "by Onumancy; for that we have Oyl and Wax."

Some olive oil or walnut oil, mixed with tallow or some other blackening agent, is painted on the fingernails of the right hand of a virginal boy or girl. The child then stares at the nails while reciting certain words, such as from the Psalms. It seems likely that this is actually a form of **scrying.** The reflective surfaces of the nails would reflect the sun's rays and create the equivalent of a **crystal** ball's shining surface. On that surface the child, as scryer, would see visions.

It is said that if money or buried treasure is being sought, then the child must face toward the east. If knowledge of a person is desired for purposes of love or affection, then the child must face south. South-facing is also recommended for all inquiries into crimes. If robbery is being investigated, then the child must face west. For murder, he or she must face north.

There is another branch of onychomancy that is purely the study of the nails themselves. It is akin to **palm-reading.** The shape and condition of the nails are considered: smoothness, roughness, whether or not there are ridges, blemishes, the hardness, brittleness, and so on. All of these things have meaning to one adept at onychomancy and can be interpreted. *Cheiro's Language of the Hand,* by **Louis Hamon,** contains a section on how to determine the health of the person from the shape and condition of their nails.

Sources:

Cheiro (Louis Hamon). *Cheiro's Language of the Hand.* Chicago: Rand, McNally, 1897.

de Givry, Grillot. *A Pictorial Anthology of Witchcraft, Magic & Alchemy.* London: Spottiswoode, Ballantyne, 1931.

Grand Orient (A. E. Waite). *The Complete Manual of Occult Divination: Volume 1—Manual of Cartomancy.* London: Rider, 1912.

Oxford English Dictionary. Oxford: Clarendon Press, 1989.

Rakoczi, Basil Ivan. *Man, Myth & Magic: Palmistry.* London: BPC Publishing, 1970.

Spence, Lewis. *An Encyclopedia of the Occult.* London: George Routledge & Sons, 1920.

OOBE (Out-of-Body Experience) ***see*** **Astral Projection**

Oomancy; Oomantia; Ooscopy

(See also Ovomancy)

The art of divining by using an egg. The word comes from the **Greek** for egg or ovum. The favorite method was to break an egg and allow the inside to fall slowly into a glass of **water.** The shapes assumed by the white of the egg could then be interpreted. This was also a method popular in Victorian times to see the future. It had to be done either at Halloween or on New Year's Eve, though some said it could be done at any full **moon.**

Sources:

Grand Orient (A. E. Waite). *The Complete Manual of Occult Divination: Volume 1—Manual of Cartomancy.* London: Rider, 1912.

Newall, Venetia. *Man, Myth & Magic: Eggs.* London: BPC Publishing, 1970.

OOMANTIA ***see*** **Oomancy**

OOSCOPY *see* Oomancy

Ophidiomancy; Ophiomancy

Ophidiomancy is divination by snakes and other reptiles. To the early **Egyptian,** to **dream** of a snake was lucky, symbolizing that a dispute would be favorably resolved. However, to the **Greeks** to dream of a snake was a warning of either enemies or impending sickness. If a **Hebrew** dreamed of a snake, it meant there would be a lost livelihood.

In Greece, to actually see a snake is to know that good fortune is coming, for the snake is the guardian genius who looks after its own. The **Etruscans** would paint a serpent on the wall to keep away the evil eye and to bring good luck. The head of the snake had to be down and intertwined with the body, and the tail uppermost.

Sources:

Headon, Deirdre (ed.). *Quest for the Unknown—Charting the Future*. Pleasantville, NY: Reader's Digest, 1992.

Lawson, John Cuthbert. *Modern Greek Folklore and Ancient Greek Religion*. New York: University Books, 1964.

OPHIOMANCY *see* Ophidiomancy

Oracles

(See also Theomancy)

An oracle is a shrine to a deity, at which questions may be asked. It is also the term for the answers to those questions. The word comes from the Latin *oraculum*, meaning "to speak."

Oracles were numerous in antiquity. Among the most celebrated were the Oracle of **Delphi,** the one of Dodona, of Amphiaraus in Bœotia; and of Trophonius at Lebadea. In Italy the best-known oracle was that of Fortuna at Præneste.

Various methods of presenting the oracles—the answers to questions—were employed, differing from one site to another. The commonest method was known as "incubation." This meant that the enquirer slept in the sacred area until he or she received an answer in a **dream.** The main oracle for this was at the temple of Asclepius at Epidaurus, though many other oracles also provided it. Also common was divination by lot (**sortilege**), as at Præneste and sometimes at Delphi, and direct voice from the priestess (**metagnomy**).

The only kind of oracle that was native to Italy was that which divined by sortilege. **Cicero** described the sortilege performed at Præneste, saying that there were various pieces of wood inscribed with antique lettering. They were mixed together and then one was pulled out by a young boy. This would have on it the answer to the question.

The Delphic oracle was located at the Temple of **Apollo** in Phocis, on the southern slope of Mount Parnassus. The site was formerly known as Crisa. There was an ancient oracle to Gæa already at that place, guarded by a female dragon/serpent named Python. Apollo slew the dragon and built his own shrine there, making this the Oracle of Delphi with the diviners there known as **Pythia.** The most sacred object at Delphi was the omphalus, or navel of the earth— the very center of the earth (conceived of as flat). No less sacred than the omphalus was the **tripod** on which the Delphic priestess sat while giving her divine utterances. The tripod was, as its name implies, a three-legged seat formed with a circular slab on which a laurel branch would be laid when the priestess was not present.

While Delphi was the best-known Apolline oracle, there were many others. A celebrated one was Claros in Asia Minor. There was also a mystery cult there, which was unusual in that Apollo usually had nothing to do with mysteries. There was an oracle to Hermes at Pharæ, in Achæa, which was located in the marketplace in front of a huge statue of Hermes.

The oracle of Trophonius at Lebadea was unusual. The supplicant had to spend several days there undergoing certain restrictions, such as abstaining from bathing except in the local river. Animal sacrifices had to be made to a number of deities, and the priests would inspect the entrails (**haruspicy**). Finally a nocturnal sacrifice of a black ram was made, its blood being run into a ritual trench and Agamedes, associate of Trophonius, was invoked. The entrails of the black ram indicated whether or not the oracle might be consulted. If the answer was favorable, then the supplicant was bathed and anointed by two boys called *Hermai*. He or she then had to drink from two springs, called Lethe and Mnemosyne (Forgetfulness and Memory), so that all but what was revealed would be forgotten. Finally, the petitioner descended into the shrine and thrust his or her feet through a hole in the wall. Being mysteriously sucked down, the revelation was received—which was sometimes by sight and sometimes by sound—then the person was returned by the same opening. He or she was then seated on the "Throne of Memory" and questioned by the priests. A written record of the experiences was also required.

The expression "to work the oracle" meant to influence the message given by bringing pressure to bear to obtain an utterance in your favor.

Sources:

Encyclopedia Britannica. Chicago: William Benton, 1964.

Parke, H. W. *Sibyls and Sibylline Prophecy in Classical Antiquity*. New York: Routledge, 1988.

Potter, D. *Sibyls in the Greek and Roman World*. Rhode Island: Journal of Roman Archæology 3, 1990.

Rose, H. J. *Religion in Greece and Rome*. New York: Harper & Row, 1959.

Orniscopy; Ornithomancy

Divination by the flight, songs, and cries of birds was a common form found in many areas. Ephraim Chambers's *Cyclopædia; or an universal dictionary of arts and sciences* of 1728 said: "Ornithomancy, among the **Greeks,** was the same as **augury** among the **Romans.**" The term augury has come to be applied to divination in general, but originally it was specifically to do with birds. In addition to Greece and Rome, it was also practiced in **India, Africa,** South America, and New Guinea.

Plutarch, the Greek biographer (c. 46—120 CE), said that "birds, by their quickness and intelligence and their alertness in acting upon every thought, are a ready instrument for the use of God, who can prompt their movements, their cries and songs, their pauses and wind-like flights, thus bidding some men check, and others pursue to the end, their course of action or ambitions."

In Greece the observation was mainly based on the actions of large predatory birds: "The largest, the strongest, the most intelligent, and at the same time those whose solitary habits gave them more individual character," according to French writer Bouché Leclarcq (*Histoire de la Divination*). Eagles, vultures, **ravens,** crows, hawks, and herons (although these quickly fell out of favor as birds of augury in Greece), wrens, owls, and woodpeckers were all used for divination. The raven was regarded as the favorite and companion of **Apollo,** so that some people came to specialize in raven **prophesies,** disregarding all other birds.

Positive identification of bird species was necessary for accurate **predictions,** since different species had different characteristics. For example, if a raven cried out behind you, it meant anxiety and difficulties to come. For a crow, the same meaning came from hearing the bird in front of you. Similarly, if a raven flew past your right side, crying out, it presaged hope and good fortune to come, while from a crow that message came from seeing it fly by and caw on your left side. To hear a cawing on the roof of your house could mean either a death, if it was the sound of a crow, or a coming letter, if the sound was from a jackdaw. Distinction had to be made between, for example, a barn owl and a tawny owl.

Along with distinguishing the species, the action of the bird had to be carefully observed. There were meanings given to the bird's flight, its cry, its posture when landed and settled, and any movements it made after settling. Numbers were also important, as in the number of cries or the number of times a bird circled before landing.

Easier than interpreting from the majority of birds was observing the actions of domesticated birds, such as chickens. Their movements on the ground such as pluming, dust-bathing, scratching holes, or standing on one leg all had meaning, though many of the meanings were associated with the coming weather.

As John Cuthbert Lawson says, "The special aptitude of birds to carry divine messages to man was never questioned in ancient Greece; it was the very axiom of religion, without which the whole science of auspices would have been a baseless fabrication."

Sources:

Encyclopedia Britannica. Chicago: William Benton, 1964.

Lawson, John Cuthbert. *Modern Greek Folklore and Ancient Greek Religion*. New York: University Books, 1964.

ORNITHOMANCY *see* Orniscopy

OROMANCY *see* Urimancy

Oryctomancy

Oryctomancy is divining by fossils, minerals, and excavated objects. The diviner interprets by the images he or she observes in the rock. If the interpretation is done in situ, then the location, time of day, and any and all aspects of the excavation are taken into account and may play a part in the interpretation.

Ossomancy; Osteomancy

Ossomancy, also known as osteomancy, is divination by bones. In Virgil's *Ænid* (Book Seven), he speaks of a priestess sleeping on fleeces in order to converse with deity. This points up the **oracular** significance of sheep. It would be natural, then, that sheep bones might be used for divination purposes. The shoulder bones were used in **scapulomancy** and **omoplatoscopy,** as were the shoulder bones of other animals.This was done not only in ancient Greece and Rome, but also by the Bedouin, English, Icelanders, Mongolians, Slavs, and Scots.

Bones were used by Bushmen of South Africa in **astragalomancy;** they also marked them with special signs and symbols, casting them and interpreting them based on their positions and conjunctions. Bones were also used in the Congo by the *Mganga* or *Mufumu*, the combination **soothsayer,** herbalist, and psychologist. There, they are invariably the leg bones of goats that have been highly polished and shaped to resemble the heads of different animals. In a self-induced trance, the Mganga casts the bones. Witnesses have claimed that some of the bones actually stand up on end and remain standing until he has finished with them.

Sources:

Adkins, Lesley and Roy A. Adkins. *Dictionary of Roman Religion*. New York: Facts on File, 1996.
Armstrong, Edward A. *Man, Myth & Magic: Sheep*. London: BPC Publishing, 1970.

Ouija® and Other Talking Boards

The name is taken from the French (*oui*) and the German (*ja*) words for "yes." The board is a tool used to communicate with **spirits** of the dead to ascertain answers to questions about the past, present, and future. Various examples of this divination tool have been used for centuries, one of the earliest forms being **alectromancy,** where a cockerel picks up pieces of corn or wheat placed alongside letters of the alphabet arranged in a circle, thereby spelling out words in answer to questions asked by the diviner. In ancient **Greece** and in **Rome,** a small table on wheels moved about, to point to answers to questions, while in **China,** c. 550 BCE, similar tools were used to communicate with the dead. The Ouija is not unlike the *squdilatc* boards used by various **Native American** tribes, to obtain spiritual information and to locate lost people and objects.

The Ouija board itself is a flat, smooth-surfaced board that has the letters of the alphabet marked on it. A small platform, or **planchette,** usually heart shaped, slides over the board. The diviner sits with fingertips placed on the planchette and asks questions. The answers are given by the platform sliding about the board and stopping at a series of letters, to spell out words. On most boards, along with the letters of the alphabet are found the numbers from one to nine, the words "Yes" and "No," and sometimes "Goodbye" and/or other greetings. Although the diviner's fingers rest

A medium using a talking board. ***Fortean Picture Library.***

on the planchette, there is no conscious propelling of it. Supposedly, the platform moves as directed by spirits of the dead.

A number of different boards are commercially produced today. The first was patented in the late 1800s by Elijah J. Bond, who sold the patent to William Fuld in 1892. Fuld founded the Southern Novelty Company in Maryland, which later became known as the Baltimore Talking Board Company. They produced the "Oriole Talking Boards," later labeled "Ouija, the Mystifying Oracle." In 1966 Parker Brothers, the big toy and game manufacturer, bought the rights to the board and marketed it to the point where it outsold their famous Monopoly game. In its first year with Parker, more than two million Ouija boards were sold. Understandably, many other companies started producing similar boards, though they were not allowed to use the name "Ouija."

The Parker Brothers' recommended way of using the board is for two people to sit facing one another, with the board resting on their knees between them. At the outset the planchette is in the center of the board and the two people have their fingers resting lightly on it. To avoid confusion, just one person acts as spokesperson. They enquire, "Is there anybody there?" This is repeated until the planchette starts to move. It should move across to "Yes" and then return to the center. In fact, it is possible to work the board with a number of participants sitting around a table. The more people there are, the more energy there is available to move the planchette. Also, just one person can have success by working alone.

The first time someone experiences the planchette moving, the feeling is that someone present is pushing it. This can quickly be discounted when messages are spelled out that give information not known to anyone present, such as names, places, or documents that need to be researched after the session. If the information received is known to any one person there, it cannot be assumed that the message is coming from the spirit world. Although no one may be pushing the pointer consciously, they may be doing so unconsciously. They may also be picking up the information through **Extrasensory perception.**

Although no one present is *directing* the planchette, the participants are, in fact, pushing it in the sense that their muscles are being used to cause it to slide across the surface of the board. The spirits are making use of their muscles to produce the physical movement.

It is difficult to keep a finger on the planchette, observe to which letters it points, and at the same time write down everything. It is therefore a good idea to have a secretary for any extended Ouija board sessions. The spokesperson, as well as being the one to call out the questions, also calls out the letters so that they can be recorded.

Many times what is recorded seems to make little sense at first. It appears that this is not an easy method of communicating from the next world back to this one. There is often confusion between similar-looking letters: N, M, and H; O and Q; P and R; I and J, and so on. Careful study of the written results should make it possible to correct any such substitutions. Another problem can be that words run into one another. This can easily be solved by requesting that the planchette make a quick circle of the board between each word to indicate the break. Other possible problems might be receiving anagrams, or finding letters arranged as though by a person with dyslexia. All in all, it is frequently necessary to study a received message very carefully in order to make sense of it.

Still, many messages do come through "loud and clear," perfectly spelled and making absolute sense. An explanation is that the spirit responsible may or may not have had previous experience with this form of communication. If the planchette sits still without moving, it may be that the question asked is ambiguous. Thought should be given to the phrasing of questions.

Record keeping is an important aspect of Ouija board use if it is done seriously. Although many people use a Ouija board for fun, acknowledging that someone *is* pushing the planchette for laughs, this should not be tolerated among serious **psychic** investigators. A list of questions to be asked may be prepared ahead of time, which will save time when actually dealing with the spirit. It is also a good idea to choose as many questions as possible that can be answered with a yes or no. This saves time and also avoids any misunderstanding of received information. But obviously not everything can be covered this way, so spelled-out answers are definitely part of the looked-for result.

A fear among novice Ouija board users is that they may become "possessed" through using the board. (There are innumerable urban legends about people who have been so afflicted.) Certainly the board can become addictive, but if handled sensibly it is no more a vehicle for possession than is the telephone. There are stories of young teenagers who have (foolishly?) asked the board when they are going to die, and been told that it will happen the next week, month, or year. Needless to say, this can be a self-fulfilling prophesy with a terrible psychological effect on the person concerned. But this only points up the fact that the Ouija board is a serious tool, not a toy.

There are certain precautions that beginners should take. First, if you start getting a lot of negative messages—especially messages directing you to do certain things that go against your grain and that you would not normally do—then don't do them and stop using the board. It's as simple as that. If the board (or a particular "spirit" coming through the board) tells you to give away all your worldly possessions, stop and think about it. Exactly who is telling you to do this and why? It may be a spirit calling itself Jesus, or describing itself as an angel—but what are the chances? And why, if they are who they say they are, would they tell you to do something that would harm you? Many overly religious people claim it is the devil who speaks through the board. If this is what you believe, then "hang up the phone"! Don't quit your job on the advice of, say, a long-dead relative. What do they know about today's labor market? Don't jump off a rooftop on the direction of an unknown spirit. Why should you do so? In other words, use your head. Don't run to the board looking for answers to all of life's questions. Don't expect it to solve every little problem you have. The board is not an **oracle;** it cannot tell you the absolute future. Use it with common sense and don't abuse it. Enjoy it. If you don't enjoy it, don't use it.

Some extremely interesting information has been obtained through the Ouija board. The prime example is probably that of **Patience Worth.** On July 8, 1913, **Pearl Curran,** a St. Louis homemaker, was persuaded by her friend Emily Hutchinson to try a Ouija board. She did so and received the words: "Many moons ago I lived. Again I come; Patience Worth my name." This turned out to be the start of an avalanche of information that kept coming over a period of five years. Eventually moving on from the Ouija board to **automatic writing,** Mrs. Curran produced 2,500 poems, short stories, plays, and allegories, plus six full-length novels, all authored by Patience Worth, who claimed to be an Englishwoman from the seventeenth century. In all over four million words were produced. What is interesting is that, of all those millions of words, not a single anachronism has been found by experts; the vocabulary is consistent with that of the claimed time period.

Sources:

Buckland, Raymond. *Doors to Other Worlds*. St. Paul, MN: Llewellyn, 1993.

Covina, Gina. *The Ouija Book*. New York: Simon & Schuster, 1979.

Guiley, Rosemary Ellen. *Harper's Encyclopedia of Mystical & Paranormal Experience*. San Francisco: HarperSanFrancisco, 1991.

Hunt, Stoker. *Ouija: The Most Dangerous Game*. New York: Harper & Row, 1985.

Owens, Elizabeth. *How to Communicate With Spirits*. St. Paul, MN: Llewellyn, 2002.

OURANOMANCY; URANOMANCY

Since ouranomancy is divination by the stars, then **astrology** is a facet of it. However, while astrology is a formalized system of mapping the heavens as they were at the moment of birth, ouranomancy is divining by the stars and planets themselves, noting such elements as their movements or seeming movements, brilliance, and relationships. In the same way that figures such as Orion can be seen in the relative positions of the stars, so the seers would look up at the night sky and see other forms that were pertinent to the question being asked, and from these deduce an answer.

Ovomancy

Ovomancy is divination by eggs. **Oomancy** would come under the general heading of ovomancy.

Gaius Suetonius Tranquillus, the **Roman** biographer (c. 70–122 CE), said that when the Roman empress Livia Drusilla (55 BCE–29 CE) was pregnant she was anxious to divine whether her child would be a boy or a girl. She did this by taking a freshly laid chicken's egg and carrying it in her bosom, to keep it at the appropriate temperature. When it hatched, it produced a chick with a beautiful cockscomb. Sure enough, Livia gave birth to a boy.

Divining was also done based, for example, on the number of eggs laid by a group of chickens, where they were found, or how many of them were together.

Sources:

Newall, Venetia. *Man, Myth & Magic: Eggs*. London: BPC Publishing, 1970.
Spence, Lewis. *An Encyclopedia of the Occult*. London: George Routledge & Sons, 1920.

P

Palmistry

(See also Cheiromancy)

Aristotle Palmistry

Palmistry is said to have been known to Aristotle (384–322 BCE) who, legend has it, discovered an Arabic treatise on the subject written in letters of gold and lying on an altar dedicated to Hermes. This he presented to Alexander the Great. It seems more probable that Aristotle wrote it himself, to give to Alexander. It was later translated into Latin by Hispanus. Palmistry was certainly known in the reign of Alexander (fourth century BCE). Apparently, great as he was, Alexander was concerned enough about his future that he took much interest in anything that might predict it.

Although most of what Aristotle wrote on the subject of palmistry has been lost, his work on **physiognomy** is still in existence and contains a section on palmistry. Most early works deal more with the shape and form of the hand than with the lines on it, but Aristotle's *De Historia Animalium* does talk about short lines on the hand indicating short lives and long lines indicating long lives. Unfortunately, if Aristotle wrote extensively on the lines of the hand, it is no longer extant. Later writers did attribute some of what they wrote to Aristotle, to lend some credulity to what they had to say.

Chinese Palmistry

Chinese palmistry (known as *wu hsiang* or *shou wen xue*) has two different systems. One is called the Five Element or Five Phase System and the other is the Eight Trigram System. The former is similar to Western palmistry, or **cheiromancy,** while the latter is based on the *bagua* figure of Feng-Shui.

A palmist reads the hand of a young woman. *Fortean Picture Library.*

FIVE ELEMENT SYSTEM This is so called because it is based on the five elements of **water,** air, fire, earth, and ether. In this system a man's left hand and a woman's right hand are looked upon as indicators of actions, fortune, hopes, and thoughts, showing how their life has changed through actions, personality and thoughts. A man's right hand and a woman's left hand show inherited characteristics and the influences of family. This is the hand that shows how life was started. For the man it is the opposite of Western palmistry, where the left hand for both sexes shows what they were born with and the right hand what they have made of life.

Hand shapes determine character types. When a palm is square and the fingers extend at the top and are the same length as the palm, then that is an Earth hand. Earth people tend to be very practical, very grounded. They are usually in control of their emotions. Although they may not speak of love, they show love by their actions. They are good at practical work with no great desire for high office.

Hands that are long and thin, with the fingers a little longer than the palm, are Water hands. Such people are very sensitive and impressionable. The hands are usually pale and fine-boned. These people have refined tastes in most things. Women with such hands make good wives and mothers. Men with such hands are prone to poor health. They do well in jobs where they can interact with others. Both men and women Water types need romance in their lives.

Fire hands reflect that element, with palms that are red and blotchy. The fingers are shorter than the palm, which is rectangular. This is an active, passionate person. He or she can be a leader. They are full of energy and can motivate others. They need to keep active and should be careful never to become idle.

Short, thin fingers that are shorter than the square palm belong to the Air hand. These people are communicators, connecting best on a mental level. They are always looking for new horizons, hating to be stifled in marriage or other commitments. They are inventors and explorers.

The Ether hand is the hand of the highly intellectual person. The fingers are gently tapered, with knots at every phalange. The fingers rise from triangular, lotus-pad palms. These people are teachers, guides, and counselors. They can become doctors and diplomats. They are "old souls."

There are eight divisions of the hand, in the Five Element system. These correspond to the Western system as follows:

Position	**Chinese Star**	**Western Equivalent**
Under Index Finger	Wood Star	Mount of Jupiter
Under Middle Finger	Earth Star	Mount of Saturn
Under Ring Finger	Sun Star	Mount of Apollo/Sun
Under Little Finger	Water Star	Mount of Mercury
Under Wood Star	First Fire Star	Active Mars
Under Water Star	Second Fire Star	Passive Mars
Middle of Palm	Five Stars Field	Plain of Mars
At base of Thumb	Metal Star	Mount of Venus
Lower Palm area, opposite to Thumb	Moon Star	Lunar Mount

The lines of the hand are as follows:

Chinese Line	**Alternative Name**	**Western Equivalent**
Earth Line	Major Earth Line	Life Line
Line of Man	Major Wood line or Brain Line	Head Line
Heaven Line	Major Water Line	Heart Line
Jade Column	Minor Earth Line	Fate Line
Sun Line	Minor Fire Line	Sun Line/Success
Line/Line of Apollo		
Health Line	Line of Mercury/Line of Business/Health Line	
Indulgence Line	Via Lasciva	
Sex Lines	Marriage Lines	
Inspiration Line	Line or Bow of Intuition	

As in western palmistry, the fingers have correspondences: Thumb—energy/ether; Index Finger—water; Middle Finger—Earth; Ring Finger—Fire; Little Finger—

Air. Also as with Western palmistry, the relative sizes of the phalanges have meaning, as do the setting of the thumb and the types of thumb.

Eight Trigram System In this system the diviner will imagine a bagua placed on the palm, or the back, of the hand and will interpret according to the traditional divisions and their meanings. This system is used a lot where health is a concern.

Trigram	Position on Palm	Health, etc.
Chên (Thunder)	Upper Metal Star	Nervous system; education
Sun (Wind/Wood)	Wood Star	Liver and gallbladder; wealth
Li (Fire)	Earth Star	Heart; blood circulation; eyesight; fame
Kswun (Earth)	Water star	Abdominal area; father & elder daughter
Tui (Marsh)	Second Fire Star	Lungs; large intestine; wife; mistress; children
Ch'ien (Heaven)	Moon Star	Lungs; psychological condition; father & elder son
K'an (Water)	Soil Mount	Kidney; bladder; reproductive system; inheritance
Kên (Mountain)	Lower Metal Star	Spleen; stomach; brothers

Indian Palmistry

Indian palm-readers term their art *Samudrika sastra,* named after King Samudra of prehistoric times. It is said that Shiva, the third deity in the Trimurti of the gods, taught palmistry to Sarasvati, the wife of Brahma, who is the senior member of the triad. Sarasvati is the goddess of music, wisdom, and knowledge. In the south of India there is a popular school known as *sariraka sastra,* based on the writings of Kartikeya. (This system is also known as the *skanda* system.) This system places great emphasis on the lines of the hand, recognizing up to 153 different lines.

Although many of the Indian palmists claim that theirs is an ancient art and that in ancient times there were many texts on the subject, in fact they all follow the traditions of Western cheiromancy of the Victorian period. There are early references to palm-reading within the Indian sub-continent in the Code of Manu and in the Vasishtha Rules (the *V_sish_ha-dharmas´_stra*), where there are prohibitions forbidding the ascetic from earning a living through "explaining prodigies and omens or by skill in astrology or palmistry." This is possibly the oldest written mention of palm-reading anywhere. The Code of Manu is a compilation of laws reflecting Hindu thought in the Buddhist period, preserved in a metrical recension, or survey, dating from c. 100 CE. The Brahmajal Sutta of the Buddhist Vinaya Pitaka (c. third century BCE) likewise prohibits monks from indulging in prognostication and divination through palm-reading.

Signs on the hand play an important part in Hindu palmistry. Old treatises discuss twenty-three different signs, including the following:

Yav: This is at the base of the thumb. Yav means "son." At the base of the left-hand thumb it means adopted son. When found on the Line of Fate it indicates loss of parents at an early age.

Fish: Wealth, prosperity, a comfortable life.

Conch: Money and fame (a rare mark).

Trident: A fortunate sign meaning wealth and fame.

Lotus (also called *Padma*): A rare sign meaning the same as the trident together with greatness. This sign was reputed to have been on the hands and feet of Lord Krishna.

Canopy: Power, wealth, and respect. Another rare mark reputed to have been on the feet of Lord Krishna.

Circle: A rare mark. On the Mount of the Sun this is an auspicious sign, though not so special elsewhere. On the Mount of the Moon it indicates death by drowning. One circle is cleverness, two means beauty, three for luxury, four for poverty, five for wisdom, six for intelligence, seven for love of solitude, eight for poverty, nine for a king, and ten for a government servant!

Shell or Whorl (also called *Shankha*): Found on the tips of the fingers. One shell indicates a king, two wealth, three spiritual power, four poverty, five wealth, six spirituality, seven poverty, eight wealth, nine spirituality, ten poverty.

Flag: Strength of character, renunciation, and purity; wealth and success.

Bow: A rare mark found on the hands of royalty, millionaires, and great people.

Tree: An indicator of success, especially if all the branches point upward.

Temple (also called *Shivalaya*): A mark of wealth and success, with a high position in society.

Triangle: On the Life Line indicates acquisition of property. On a rascette indicates accession to others' wealth and honor. On the great triangle, between the Line of Fate and the Line of Life, indicates military renown.

Serpent: Opposition from enemies.

Sword (also called *Kuther Rekha*): On the mount of the Sun indicates troubles in life.

Scales: Wealth and prosperity.

Moon and Sun: Honor, respect, and appreciation by others.

Swastika: Respect, wealth, and fame.

The Line of Renunciation, found under the Jupiter Finger (called Diksha Rekha): Intelligence, judgment, wealth, knowledge of the occult. A half Rekha indicates an unwillingness to work for material advancement.

Hanwant or *Kapi Rekha:* Triangles found on the upper end of the Line of Life, Fate Line, Head Line, and Sun Line, indicating a highly religious person with a clear vision of his or her deities.

Ring of Saturn encircles the base of the Saturn Finger: Magical and occult powers.

Sources:

Encyclopedia Britannica. Chicago: William Benton, 1964.

http://www.serenapowers.com/.

http://www.zorrapredictions.com/5elements/palmistry.

PAPON, ROBERT DONALD (B. 1940)

Robert Donald Papon was born into a Protestant family on November 29, 1940, in East Orange, New Jersey. His father, Charles King Papon, was a commodities reporter for Reuters News Agency. At age twelve, Papon claims, he was expelled from school

Robert Donald Papon. *T.H.O.T.H.*

for hypnotizing his classmates, even though he had never learned hypnosis. At fourteen he purchased a book titled *Fourteen Lessons in Yoga Philosophy*, by Yogi Ramacharaka (William Walker Atkinson), which he says changed his life. He took the book with him to Red Bank High School one day and showed it to a classmate. It happened that the classmate's father was Dr. John D'Amico, a Master in a secret order called the Spiritual Christian Crusaders. At eighteen Papon joined the Crusaders. He was also affiliated with the College and Church of Divine Metaphysics in Indianapolis, a year later was ordained a New Thought Minister. He went on to study with Paramahansa Yoganada's Self-Realization Fellowship and with the Rosicrucian Order AMORC, becoming an officer of the latter in their New York City lodge.

Papon entered New York University on a full scholarship but soon withdrew to seek other interests. He later entered Bard College, Columbia University, Monmouth College, and the New School for Social Research in New York City, where he eventually finished undergraduate and graduate studies in philosophy. It was as an undergraduate that Papon began to study **astrology.** He started out to disprove it but quickly realized his own talent for it. Constructing and reading **horoscope** charts, Papon rapidly built a large clientele. It was at this time that he began writing articles for various astrology magazines.

In the early 1970s, Papon was asked to take over a failing magazine: ***Sybil Leek****'s Astrology*. In a few short issues he had turned around the magazine's finances, making it highly successful. At this time he founded the Academy of Mystic Arts in New York, which taught various metaphysical courses through correspondence. It was also at this time that he met **Bruce King,** who ran a highly successful publishing company under the name of "Zolar." King was looking for help with his own magazine and Papon took on that as well as the Sybil Leek one. When King died in 1976, Papon carried on with the Zolar banner, writing books and articles under the pseudonym.

Papon later turned his interest to holistic health and, obtaining a doctor of science degree from Columbia Pacific University and a doctor of homeopatic medicine degree from the Institutum Internationale Homeopathiae in Mexico, he became a consultant in homeopathy. He authored the book *Homeopathy Made Simple*. In more recent years he accepted the position of Grand Master of **T.H.O.T.H.** (The Hermetic Order Temple Heliopolis), an order along the lines of the Order of the Golden Dawn. Papon resides in Ozona, Florida.

Sources:

http://www.zolar-thoth.org/.

PAPUS *see* Encausse, Gérard

PARAGNOSIS *see* Extrasensory Perception

PAST EVENTS *see* Retrocognition

PEARLS *see* Margaritomancy

PEBBLES *see* Pessomancy; Psephomancy

Pedomancy

(See also Podomancy)

Thomas Blount, in *Glossographia* (1656), refers to pedomancy as "a kind of divination by the lines of the sole of the feet." He obviously took seriously what Gabriel Harvey, sixty-three years earlier, had put forward as a joke. Harvey's *Pierces Supererogation, or a new prayse of the old asse* of 1593 contained the jocular comment: "Pedomancie (is) fitter for such Conjurers than either **Chiromancie,** or **Necromancie,** or any Familiar Spirite but contempt." The *North British Advertizer* of May 19, 1883, said: "Pedomancy, or divination by the soles of the feet, may also in these times become as interesting and useful a study (as **palmistry**)." It's uncertain whether or not that was stated seriously.

Serious or not, the idea of foot-reading has taken hold, sometimes under the name "Solistry." Certainly in Buddhism, the "Footprint of Buddha" is marked with 108 auspicious signs. In *Indian Palmistry* (1895), Mrs. J. B. Dale states:

> Broken and unclear lines signify problem areas according to the line. When both lines point towards the big toe, then you will be wealthy and give to charity. When only one line points to the big toe, your life will be difficult and hard. A line which curves to the big toe nail reveals that the owner is well respected, honest and generous. Shallow lines indicate a passionate nature and deep lines indicate a troubled life. For a woman, a line leading to the second toe (next to the big toe) reveals an early loving marriage.

Sources:

Cheiro (Louis Hamon). *Cheiro's Language of the Hand.* Chicago: Rand, McNally, 1897.
Oxford English Dictionary. Oxford: Clarendon Press, 1989.

Pegomancy

Pegomancy is **hydromancy** using spring **water.** Rainwater was thought by many to be more "divine," since it fell from the heavens, but hydromancy could certainly be done with spring water. One method was to drop small stones into a pool and to observe and interpret their movements as they fell to the bottom.

There was also divination of fountains; the fountains of Palicorus in Sicily were some of the most famous for consultation.

Sources:

de Givry, Grillot. *A Pictorial Anthology of Witchcraft, Magic & Alchemy*. London: Spottiswoode, Ballantyne, 1931.

Grand Orient (A. E. Waite). *The Complete Manual of Occult Divination: Volume 1—Manual of Cartomancy*. London: Rider, 1912.

PENDULUM *see* Radiesthesia

Pessomancy

(See also Psephomancy; Thrioboly)

Pessomancy is divination by means of pebbles. This could be done in a wide variety of ways. Throwing a number of pebbles onto the ground and then divining by their positions and relationships would be one way. This would be a form of **geomancy.** Another way would be to place a number of pebbles in a bag and then to draw out a random number. The number withdrawn would then be interpreted according to their **numerological** value and meaning. The random finding of pebbles would be another method, which would be a form of **apantomancy.**

Phallomancy

Serena Powers defines phallomancy as "the science and art of judging a man's character and lovemaking style and capability, by the shape of his penis." Forms of phallomancy have been practiced for centuries in **India, China,** and other areas. In India, a smooth, round stone rising out of another shaped like an elongated saucer represents the powerful deity Siva, for it has the form of a *lingam* (male sex organ) and *yoni* (female sex organ) in union. At weddings, the **Greeks** used to eat cakes shaped like the lingam and the yoni. Representations of the lingam and yoni were common all over Europe and, as late as the sixteenth century, lingam/yoni figures made of wax were offered to St. Foutin, at Varailles, in Provence, France. They were suspended from the ceiling of the chapel and when the wind disturbed them, there was the sound of lingams striking against yonis.

The **Tibetans** believe it is unlucky for a man to be overendowed. In order to be a good husband, the penis should be no longer than the width of six fingers. When squatting, if the penis hangs down to reach the heels then there will be a life of sorrow. The Hindus agree, saying that a large penis brings problems to all aspects of life.

On the subject of semen, the ancient Sanskrit astrological treatise, the *Brihat Samhita,* says that if it smells sweet like honey, the man will be rich. If it is like salt, he will be poor. If it smells like fish, he will have many children. Thin, transparent semen indicates daughters and a life of luxury.

Divining by the penis starts with study of the flaccid organ. Taking its natural length first, if less than three inches it is classed as "short"; longer than three inches is "long."

Long: This is the mark of the extrovert, the innovator. Anything new and original is of interest. This person is always looking for new experiences but should beware becoming over-confident. A long and fat penis, according to the Hindus, means the man will be poor and have no sons.

Short: This is the romantic and the **dreamer.** It may take a while to build confidence but there is always good performance. The man is a traditionalist but can exhibit a temper at times. The Hindus say that a small, sinewy penis foretells riches to come.

Thick: A sign of a good imagination, solid determination and fiery energy.

Thin: The sensitive, romantic, poetic lover. Talk comes easily but don't let it take over.

Smooth: A smooth penis indicates an intuitive lover, able to adapt easily to his partner's feelings.

Bumpy: A whole plan of action is usually mapped out in the head before the encounter begins. The man is cautious and logical, and tends to hold back until sure of himself.

Pointed tip: Both idealistic and artistic in relationships. This man has trouble relaxing. He values his independence and is rarely a submissive partner.

Blunt/Square tip: A practical lover who prefers to let his actions speak for him.

Wide/Bulbous tip: Strong sex drive. Active and original with a magnetic personality, but he delivers no more than is promised.

Curve to the left: In matters of love and sex, this is a taker, not a giver. He likes to keep his secrets. He is cautious until he is sure he will not get hurt. According to the Hindus, this left-hand curve also indicates poverty.

Curve to the right: A giver, not a taker, in love and sex. Sex is the favorite topic of conversation, and he is completely open in discussing it.

Sharp bend: A sharp bend rather than a curve indicates a lecherous person and a user. He will lie and cheat to get what he wants.

Long and bent: Not to be trusted in matters sexual.

Short and bent: Performance anxiety is his main problem. He must learn to relax.

Bent right at the base: He is plagued with the feeling that he doesn't fit in or belong anywhere. He tends to be very critical of others, and believes that all others have it easy compared to him.

Thick, bushy, pubic hair: A strong, physical lover who is very competitive. However, he is not very refined.

Thin, sparse, pubic hair: Very refined sexual tastes but the libido tends to fluctuate with the level of self-confidence. He needs reassurance.

Equal size testicles: These indicate the man will be a powerful person with command over others.

Odd size testicles: These indicate a fondness for sex.

There is an aspect of **moleosophy** that applies to phallomancy. Moles and other marks on or near the penis can be significant.

On the base: Beware taking risks with sexual health.

On the tip: A sincere lover who accepts responsibility.

On the right side: This man enjoys making love in the outdoors and in adventurous places.

On the left side: Can be changeable and unreliable.

To the right of the groin: A prosperous future is indicated, but the health needs to be watched.

To the left of the groin: Attention needs to be paid to matters of health. He should beware of becoming complacent.

On the buttocks: This is someone who needs to make an effort to do things for himself, instead of relying on others.

On the nipple: There is a tendency to be fickle and unfaithful.

Sources:

Goldberg, B. Z. *The Sacred Fire: The Story of Sex in Religion*. New York: University Books, 1958.

Holt, Peter. *Stars of India: Travels in Search of Astrologers and Fortune-tellers*. Edinburgh: Mainstream Publishing, 1998.

http://www.serenapowers.com/.

Phrenology

Phrenology was a pseudo-science invented by a German, **Franz Joseph Gall** (1758–1828), and first promoted by him in 1796. Gall was himself a student of **Johann Kaspar Lavater** (1741–1801), propounder of **physiognomy.** Gall's claim was that character and personality can be judged from the shape of a person's head and, especially, from the various lumps and bumps of the skull. It follows from the belief that character traits were reflected in physical appearances and associated with physiognomy, the study of all outward aspects of an individual.

In phrenology the skull was divided into three major regions, each in turn subdivided into smaller regions for a total of twenty-six areas. The main regions were:

1: The lower portion of the back of the head, dealing with instincts and propensities.

2: Most of the upper portion of the head, dealing with sentiments and moral faculties.

3: The front of the head, including the forehead, dealing with intellectual faculties and abilities.

Johann Gaspar Spurzheim (1776–1832), another student of Gall, increased the total number of sub-sections to thirty-two. Spurzheim, a Viennese physician, was lecturing on the subject in Scotland and impressed **George Combe** (1788–1858) who, in turn, took up the study and increased the number of areas to thirty-six. Finally Orson and Lorenzo Fowler, two brothers, increased the number yet again to a total of forty-two. Combe was instrumental in establishing phrenology in America. He wrote on the subject, as did the American Fowlers. Such notables as Edgar Allan Poe and Walt Whitman took an interest in it.

Orson and Lorenzo Fowler issued charts on the subject of phrenology, lectured extensively, and send out others to lecture (and promote their books). They started giving phrenological readings in New York in 1835. From the beginning, readings concentrated on the most noticeable bumps, interpreted to give the individual's outstanding

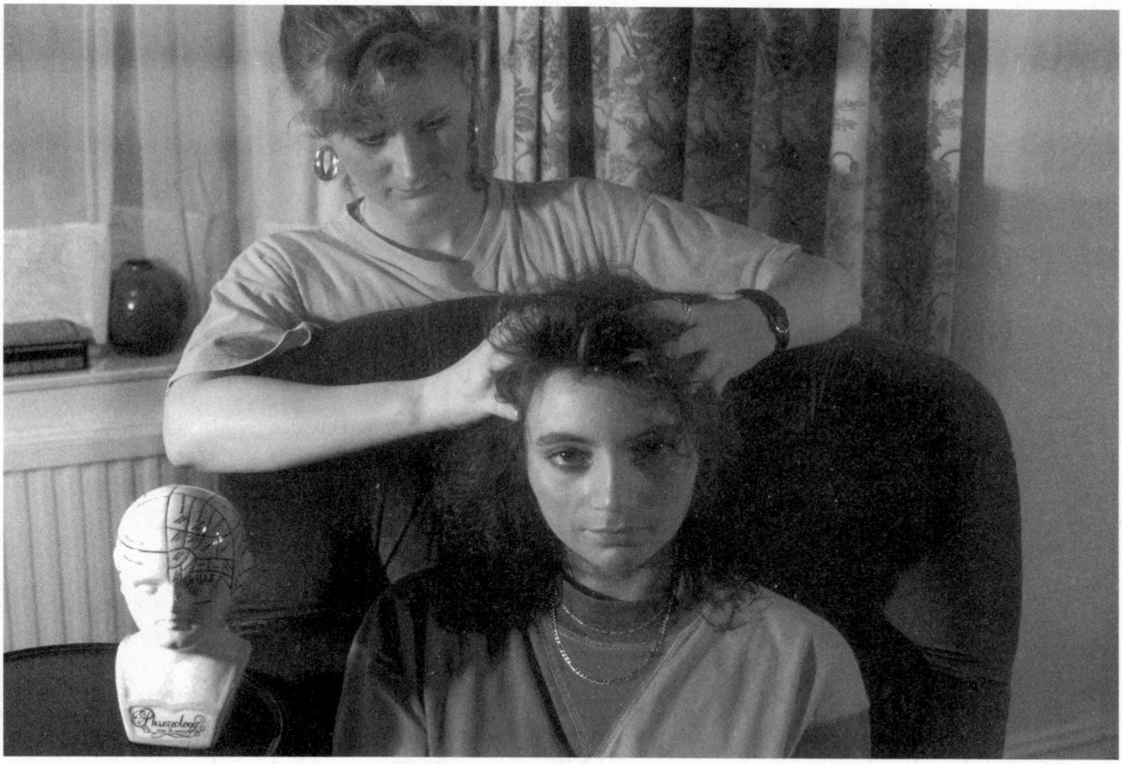

Phrenologists judge a person's character and personality from the shape of his or her head and, especially, from the various lumps and bumps of the skull. ***Fortean Picture Library.***

traits. As the number of readings rose into the thousands, the Fowlers and other professional phrenologists became aware of subtle differences between people and were able to fine-tune their interpretations. But many of the small areas of definition were close together and it wasn't always easy to tell where one area finished and another began. Many times adjacent areas dealt with similar themes so it wasn't too much of a problem. But some adjacent areas were not complementary; for instance, the areas of friendship and combativeness, and those of combativeness and cautiousness.

From the detailed descriptions given by the Fowlers, Combe, and others, it was obvious that professionals relied on more than just the feel of the bumps; they were guided by **psychic** impressions also. However, dealing with the average person who had no obviously excessive bulges and bumps, the basic examination involved measuring set distances. These were usually from the center of the ear and were used as a datum and taken as the axis of the brain. Comparative distances then were used to determine the development of the various faculties.

Unfortunately the popularity of phrenology inevitably drew to it large numbers of fraudulent practitioners, with no knowledge whatsoever of the areas and their interpretations. The true study of the brain and its areas of function advanced, but the phrenologists were left behind and people lost interest. The British Phrenological Society was founded in 1886 by Lorenzo J. Fowler, and struggled on in existence until as recently as 1967. Eventually, however, even that succumbed to the general public's loss of interest in the subject. In 1815, Thomas Foster had called the work of Gall and Spurzheim "phrenology" (*phrenos* is Greek for mind), and the name stuck.

Sources:

Boardman, D. *Defence of Phrenology: A Work for Doubters*. New York: Fowler & Wells, 1865.
Chambers, Howard V. *Phrenology*. Sherbourne, 1968.
Combe, George. *A System of Phrenology*. New York: S. R. Wells, 1876.
Fowler, Orson S. *Practical Phrenology*. New York: Fowler & Wells, 1866.
Fowler, Orson S. *The Practical Phrenologist; and Recorder and Delineator of the Character and Talents–A Compendium of Phreno-Organic Science*. Boston: Fowler, 1869.
Fowler, Orson S. *Self-Instructor in Phrenology and Physiology*. New York: Fowler & Wells, 1863.
Gibson, Walter B. and Litzka R. *The Complete Illustrated Book of the Psychic Sciences*. New York: Doubleday, 1966.

PHYLLOMANCY

(See also Phyllorhodomancy; Sycomancy)

Divination by leaves. Methods differed from one area to another. For some, the sound made by leaves as they were rustled by the wind would be significant. For others, it was the falling of leaves in the autumn: the number that fell, how and where they fell, and so on. When leaves fell and landed face up, it was a positive sign. If they landed face down, then it was a negative sign.

In Oxfordshire, England, if a girl placed an ivy leaf in her bosom, the first man who spoke to her would be the one she would marry, even if he was already married at the time he spoke to her. In **Scotland** the girl would place the ivy leaf in her bosom but would have to say the following as she did so:

Ivy, Ivy, I love you.
In my bosom I place you.
The first young man who speaks to me
My future husband he shall be.

To **dream** of ivy leaves was to foresee happiness and contentment. To dream of apple leaves was to foresee a coming marriage. To dream of falling leaves was to foresee bad news and troubles. If an ivy leaf was placed in water on New Year's Eve and was still fresh on Twelfth Night, it meant that the coming year would be a good one. If black spots formed on the leaf, there would be illness. If the whole leaf was covered in black spots, there would be death before the end of the year.

Sources:

Huxley, A. J. *Man, Myth & Magic: Holly and Ivy*. London: BPC Publishing, 1970.

PHYLLORHODOMANCY

A branch of **phyllomancy,** phyllorhodomancy is divination by rose leaves. One of the methods used by the Greeks was to place a rose leaf on the palm of one hand and then slap the palm of the other hand against it. The resulting sound signaled the coming success or failure of whatever was to be attempted.

The rose was associated with love and with celebrations of all sorts. It was also associated with death, since roses were both strewn and planted on graves. For these reasons, divination with rose leaves was usually done for matters concerning these subjects.

Sources:

Shepard, Leslie A. (ed.). *Encyclopedia of Occultism & Parapsychology*. New York: Avon, 1978.

Physiognomancy; Physiognomy; Anthroposcopy

Physiognomy, or physiognomancy, is divination by facial features—judging mental and moral characteristics by the features of the face. As de Givry says: "Rightly or wrongly, we have got into the way of looking on the face as the mirror of the soul . . . it is very difficult for us to shake off the bad impression which may be made by a face of a sinister or criminal cast."

Physiognomy was popular in ancient **Greece.** Aristotle (384–322 BCE) wrote the first systematic treatise on the subject (*History of Animals and a Treatise on Phsyiognomy*), and many Greeks were practitioners. In the twelfth century Michael Scot (1175–1234) translated Aristotle's work. **Johann Lavater** (1741–1801), a Swiss Protestant pastor, published a major work on physiognomy in 1775. An offshoot of physiognomancy is **metoposcopy,** which deals with the lines on the forehead.

The principles of physiognomy are somewhat vague. Faces are usually divided into seven planetary types. The Solar face is a round, jovial one framed in fair hair. The Venus face has perfect features, an engaging smile, and fair hair. The Mars face is rugged and square-cut with near-brutal features. The Mercurial face is beautiful, with muted coloring and black hair. The Lunar face tends to be pale, cold and melancholy. The Jupiter face is beautiful and noble, with bold, strongly marked features. The Saturn face has a mournful look, and may have a yellowish tinge and black hair.

The forehead is an important tool for physiognomists. David l'Agneau, in his *Traité de Métoposcopie et Physiognomonie* (Paris, 1635), said:

> Those with a high forehead are lazy and ignorant, and if it is fleshy and sleek they are wrathful, and if with this they have prick ears they are still more wrathful, according to Aristotle. Those who have little foreheads are bustling and foolish, as are they likewise who have them great and narrow. Those with long foreheads are docile and gentle and of good sense; those who have them as it were square and pleasant are magnanimous and strong.

According to Barthélemy Coclès, in his *Physiognomonia* (Strasbourg, 1533), foreheads with smooth, unwrinkled skin indicate "vain, salacious men" ready for trickery, while those with foreheads that are "meager in every part" are simple-minded and irascible people who are cruel and grasping. Coclès also speaks of eyes and includes illustrations of various types. Even the eyelashes are significant, according to him. As to noses, he claims that snub noses indicate people who are "vain, untruthful, luxurious, and unstable." He says they are also seducers and infidels. Hair is also of note, with close-cropped, coarse, bristling hair indicating strength, self-confidence, and pride, but also deceitfulness. Such a person is also somewhat simple-minded. But the person with long, flowing locks—straight, sleek hair, fine and soft–is "timid and weak, yet peaceful and gentle." A man whose hair covers the temples and part of the forehead is "simple, vain, luxurious, credulous, rustic in speech and manners, and thick-witted."

Michel Lescot, in his *Physionomie* (Paris, 1540), says of mouths:

> Mockery abounds in the mouths of fools and of those with great spleens. He, on the contrary, whose mouth laughs easily is a frank man, vain and inconstant; fickle in belief, of heavy understanding and well-liked; willing and not secret. Whose mouth laughs but seldom and briefly is a steadfast man; ingenious, of clear understanding; secret, faithful, and laborious.

Sources:

Encyclopedia Britannica. Chicago: William Benton, 1964.

Fowler, O. S. *Self-Instructor in Phrenology and Physiology*. New York: Fowler & Wells, 1863.

de Givry, Grillot. *A Pictorial Anthology of Witchcraft, Magic & Alchemy*. London: Spottiswoode, Ballantyne, 1931.

PHYSIOGNOMY ***see*** **Physiognomancy**

PINS ***see*** **Automanzia**

Piper, Leonore E. (1857–1950)

Born in Boston in 1859, Leonore Piper grew up to be one of the foremost trance **mediums** in the history of **spiritualism.** At the age of eight, when playing in the garden, she felt a blow to the side of the head and heard a long, sibilant "S" in her ear. This sound resolved into the word "Sara" and then the words: "Aunt Sara is not dead but with you still." She told her mother, who was wise enough to make a note of the day and time. Several days later it was found that Leonore's Aunt Sara had indeed died at that hour. Leonore had several other psychic experiences as she grew up.

At eighteen, she married William Piper. Shortly after this she consulted a Dr. J. R. Cocke, a blind, professional **clairvoyant** who was earning a reputation for his psychic diagnoses and cures. While there Lenore fell into a spontaneous trance. On her next attendance at Cocke's **séance,** when Cocke put his hand on her head she saw "a flood of light in which many strange faces appeared." Then, entranced, she picked up a piece of paper and a pencil and wrote some notes. Standing up, Piper moved across to a member of the circle, Judge Frost of Cambridge, and gave him what she had written. It turned out to be the most remarkable message he had ever received from his dead son.

Word spread quickly, and Piper was soon besieged with people wanting sittings with her. She refused and withdrew, seeing only close friends and family. Then she agreed to see Mrs. Gibbons, who happened to be the mother-in-law of Professor

William James, founding member of the **American Society for Psychical Research.** What Piper told Mrs. Gibbons was powerful enough to cause Professor James to spend the next eighteen months in deep investigation of her séances.

Leonore Piper was thoroughly examined by all the top psychic investigators of the time. In the *Psychological Review* of 1898 William James wrote:

> Dr. Hodgson (also of the ASPR) considers that the hypothesis of fraud cannot be seriously maintained. I agree with him absolutely. The medium has been under observation, much of the time under close observation, as to most of the conditions of her life, by a large number of persons, eager, many of them, to pounce upon any suspicious circumstance, for (nearly) fifteen years. During that time not only has there not been one single suspicious circumstance remarked, but not one suggestion has ever been made from any quarter which might tend positively to explain how the medium, living the apparent life she leads, could possibly collect information about so many sitters by natural means.

Piper also practiced **automatic writing,** and some of what she produced forms part of what is known as "cross correspondences," produced at the beginning of the last century by a number of different mediums. All of the material produced appears to come from the deceased F. W. H. Myers, who had been a leading member of the ASPR. The sections produced by the various individuals made sense only when they were all placed together.

Leonore Piper stopped practicing her trance mediumship in 1911, though she did continue to do some automatic writing. One significant message she received, on August 8, 1915, concerned the coming death of Sir Oliver Lodge's son Raymond in World War I.

Sources:

Piper, Alta L. *The Life and Work of Mrs. Piper*. London: Kegan Paul, Trench, Trubner, 1929.
Shepard, Leslie A. (ed.). *Encyclopedia of Occultism & Parapsychology*. New York: Avon, 1978.

Planchette

A planchette (French for a small plank or board) is an instrument used to communicate with spirits, in **spiritualism.** It is usually about three inches wide and four inches long, resting on three small legs. There are many different designs but an early, popular design was heart shaped, with the point of the heart working as a pointer. On a **Ouija®** board or similar, the planchette slides about the surface of the board, pointing at letters to spell out messages. In use, one or more people lightly rest their fingers on the top edges of the device, to channel into it the power to make it move.

The three legs either are covered in felt, so that they will slide easily on a polished surface, or have small castor-wheels on them. Sometimes, if automatic writing is to be done, one of the legs is replaced with a pencil, the point tracing letters onto a sheet of paper over which the planchette moves.

In this political cartoon from 1903, pundits use a planchette to determine the next leader of the Liberal Party. ***Fortean Picture Library.***

The moving platform was invented in 1853 by the well-known French spiritualist M. Planchette. It was named after its inventor, whose name was most appropriate for the "small plank." It was fifteen years after its original appearance that it became widely used, thanks to an American toy manufacturer who started producing them in quantity. It is said that a form of communicating board was in use in **Greece** at the time of Pythagoras, about 540 BCE. According to a French writer there was a "mystic table on wheels" that moved about indicating signs engraved on a stone slab.

There has been a wide variety of designs for planchettes, some of them connecting the platform to a clock-like dial with the letters of the alphabet on it, others allowing the platform to slide sideways in a track to do its pointing. The board produced commercially by Parker Brothers has a planchette on three legs, whose shape comes to a point under the single leg. In the middle of the device there is a plastic window with a pin in its center, pointing down. The instructions that come with the set say, "The mysterious message indicator will commence to move . . . as it passes over Ouija talking board each letter of a message is received as it appears through the transparent window covered by the message indicator." This is not strictly true. Sometimes a string of letters is received that make no sense whatsoever . . . until it is realized that the planchette is no longer showing the relevant letters through its plastic "window" on the one line, but is pointing to the letters on the line above with its tapered point.

A very simple, yet very effective, talking board can be made by writing the letters of the alphabet on pieces of paper and laying them down, in a circle, around the edge of a table. A wine glass can then be upturned and used as a planchette, the participants resting their fingers on the now-top edge of the glass. The glass will slide over the table surface to stop in front of appropriate letters. In this set-up, then, a wine glass acts as a planchette.

Sources:

Buckland, Raymond. *Doors to Other Worlds.*. St. Paul, MN: Llewellyn, 1993.
Covina, Gina. *The Ouija Book*. New York: Simon & Schuster, 1979.
Hunt, Stoker. *Ouija: the Most Dangerous Game*. New York: Harper & Row, 1985.
Shepard, Leslie A. (ed.). *Encyclopedia of Occultism & Parapsychology*. New York: Avon, 1978.

PLANETS *see* Astrology

Podomancy

Podomancy is divination from signs derived from examination of the feet. Where there is some question about **pedomancy** being a valid form of divination (dealing with lines and marks on the soles of the feet much as in **cheiromancy**), podomancy seems to have a history of sorts, at least in Persia. It deals with the shape of the feet and of the toes, though the latter seems to be a relatively modern development.

Feet

With feet, high arches are an indication of a high intellect, but also of being a **dreamer.** Low arches or flat feet are a sign that the person is a practical realist and perhaps should dream a little more. Swollen, puffy feet indicate unwillingness to express emotions and an introverted outlook on life.

According to *Indian Palmistry*, by J. B. Dale (1895):

> If a crescent or elongated horseshoe mark appears on the sole of the foot, and the toes are well separated from one another, the person will have a harsh temper and will remain poor. If a female's toes are well set together and close, and if she has a wheel or flower mark on either or both feet, she will become a lady of rank and position. If there be an ear-shaped figure in the foot, and without hair, the person may expect to be successful in the world.

Toes

The reading of toes was developed by Imre Somogyi, together with his wife Margriet. Researching on beaches, in saunas, and similar places, they came up with what they feel to be the true interpretation of personalities based on toe shapes and sizes. They say that each of the toes of the foot relate to a zone in the body and to one of the chakras. It is also important to note that the meanings of the toes on the left foot differ from those of the right foot.

Toe	Meaning: Right Foot	Meaning: Left Foot	Element	Chakra
Big Toe	Joy	Sorrow	Ether	Throat
Second Toe	Desires	Emotion	Air	Heart
Middle Toe	Aggression	Creativity	Fire	Solar Plexus
Fourth Toe	Attachment	Love	Water	Lower Abdomen
Little Toe	Fear	Trust & Sex	Earth	Groin

Toe Meanings

Large Toe: Abundant energies, often exaggerated.
Short Toe: Restrained and difficult to express feelings.
Rounded Toe: Sensitive and tactful.
Pointy Toe: Energy releases in sudden bursts.
Rectangular Toe: Energy expressed in plain, commonsense terms.
Spatula Toe: Lots of energy expressed powerfully.
Toe bent in toward big toe: Hangs onto the past.
Toe bent toward little toe: Rushes toward the future.
Vertical ridges on toe nails: A metabolic disorder linked with the energies of that toe.
Horizontal ridges on toe nails: Emotional instability.

Sources:

Dale, J. B. *Indian Palmistry*. London: Theosophical Publishing, 1895.
Somogyi, Imre. *Reading Toes*. Saffron Walden, UK: C. W. Daniels, 1997.
http://www.serenapowers.com/.

PORTENT *see* **Omen**

POSTURE *see* **Ichnomancy**

Power Spots

There are certain areas on the surface of the earth that are regarded as power spots. *Leys* (pronounced "lays") is the term used to indicate ancient straight lines connecting these natural points of power. Where two or more leys cross is a power point that has, in the past, naturally drawn people to assemble or build structures such as standing stones, barrows, temples, and churches.

One of the most famous **oracles** in ancient **Greece** was at **Delphi.** It was built on what was regarded as a power spot and was located at the Temple of **Apollo,** in Phocis, on the southern slope of Mount Parnassus. It seems certain that the shrine was not originally Apollo's. The site was formerly known as Crisa. There was an ancient oracle to Gæa already at that place, guarded by a female dragon/serpent named Python. According to Æschylus (*Eumenides*), the original giver of oracles at this site was Earth. Earth was succeeded by her daughter Themis, and Themis later succeeded by Phœbe, who gave the shrine to Apollo as a birthday gift. This ties in with the idea that the oracles come from the earth-goddess herself.

In his book *The Old Straight Track* (1925), Alfred Watkins (1855–1935), an early photographer and inventor of the pinhole camera, showed that there was a vast network of straight lines crisscrossing Britain, which aligned large numbers of ancient sites, earthworks, standing stones, and burial mounds. He also suggested there were such ley lines in other parts of the world. Many believe that it is at the crossing of these leys that there may be found subtle earth energies, or power spots. Today many people use dowsing rods to map out both the ley lines and the power spots themselves.

Serena Powers. ***Serena Powers.***

Janet and Colin Bord give examples of a number of leys in Britain, such as the Montgomery ley on the Welsh border. In just six miles it includes six sites: Offa's Dyke; Montgomery Church; Montgomery Castle; Hendomen, the motte and bailey castle predating the Norman castle; Forden Gaer, a Roman camp; and a half mile of straight road exactly along the ley. All are in an exact straight line. One major ley runs from Glastonbury Abbey through Stonehenge and on to Canterbury Cathedral—from Somerset to Kent, more then 150 miles.

The complex of the **Egyptian** pyramids was also believed to have been built on a power spot, as were the pyramids of Tenochtitlan and Teotihuacan in **Mexico.** France's Notre Dame Cathedral was also built on a power spot.

Sources:

Bord, Janet and Colin. *Ancient Mysteries of Britain*. London: Guild Publishing, 1986.

Buckland, Raymond. *The Witch Book: The Encyclopedia of Witchcraft, Wicca, and Neo-paganism*. Detroit: Visible Ink Press, 2002.

Watkins, Alfred. *The Old Straight Track*. London: Methuen, 1925.

POWERS, SERENA (B. 1966)

Serena Powers was born in Melbourne, Australia, in March 1966. After leaving university she had a variety of employment including public service, banking, and working as a flight attendant. But from a very early age Powers had been fascinated by divination and fortune-telling. She had looked at various methods of divination much like secret codes that needed to be interpreted. It was this interest that led to a further fascination with foreign languages, a subject she majored in at the university level.

As a child, Powers read Colin Wilson's book *The Occult* (1971), which she says was "all I needed to set me on the never-ending path for knowledge." She was given her first deck of **tarot** cards when in her teens and rapidly learned how to use them. They drew her on to investigate many other systems of divination, especially with regard to their practical application and integration into everyday life.

Powers says that she saw the development of the Internet as a boon, in that it gave her access to worldwide sources of information on divination and other aspects of the New Age field. By the year 2000 she had launched her own Web site, making it a focus for information on a wide variety of divination methods, from **cartomancy** and **podomancy** to **Kumalak** and **Vedic astrology.** Her philosophy is that "divination should not be treated as completely separate from practical life. Rather, it should be accessible to anyone who desires the knowledge." Through her site, Powers has introduced people around the world to ancient, modern, universal, and regional types and techniques; her Internet source has rapidly become one of the most highly rated and respected in the field of divination.

Sources:

http://www.serenapowers.com/.

Precognition

(See also Oneiromancy)

Precognition literally means "to know beforehand." It is paranormal knowledge of future events; an impression that something specific is going to happen. There are many examples of it, such as **Jeane Dixon**'s precognition of the assassination of John F. Kennedy. Another example, though without knowing all the details, was when Colin Macdonald, a thirty-four-year-old marine engineer, three times refused to sign on as the second engineer on the *Titanic*, because of precognition that there would be a terrible disaster connected with the ship. Laboratory examples of precognition are seen in the results of **ESP** tests, where a person knows beforehand what card will be drawn by the sender.

There is really a fine line between precognition and **premonition.** Precognition implies a more certain knowledge of coming events, while premonitions are vague feelings without the specifics.

Precognition happens most frequently in **dreams,** where the dreamer "sees" an event that later happens. Such scenes are also experienced in trance, **visions,** hallucinations, and even in the waking state. Precognition can be brought about through various forms of divination, such as **scrying,** and by **mediumship.**

The vast majority of precognitive experiences deal with death, dying, and other negative events. During wartimes, there have been innumerable examples of mothers, fathers, spouses, and others knowing when someone was about to be killed, even though that person was hundreds or even thousands of miles away. These impressions came strongly and, usually, within a matter of hours or even minutes of the actual event.

In the Welsh village of **Aberfan,** on the night of October 20, 1966, nine-year-old Eryl Jones had a dream that there was no school the following day. She didn't just dream that there would be no classes, but that there would be no school in existence. The next morning she told her mother that "something black came down all over it." But she went to school anyway. Shortly after nine o'clock that morning a half-million-ton mountain of coal waste, saturated by days of unrelenting rain, slid down over the village, burying houses and the entire school. Nearly 150 people, most of them schoolchildren (including Eryl Jones), were buried and died. Many other people all over Great Britain had similar dreams before the tragedy. Some saw an actual mountain of coal slag pour down the mountainside onto the village.

In his book *Foreknowledge*, H. F. Saltmarsh suggests that different kinds of time are accessible to different states of consciousness. At the level of general awareness our experience of time is not constant, since time can seem to fly or it can seem to drag. His conclusion: We are living in the "specious present," where the time we perceive is of short duration. For our subconscious, however, the "present" is stretched out so that it actually includes part of the future. In his book he talks about a case published in the *Journal* of the Society for Psychical Research that gave details of precognition exhibited by John H. Williams, an eighty-year-old Quaker. On May 31, 1933, Williams woke up at 8:55 a.m. with vivid memory of a dream in which he had heard the radio commentary on the Derby horse race, to be run at 2 o'clock that afternoon. In the dream he heard the names of four horses, including King Solomon and Hyperion, and certain details of the race. Williams told both a neighbor and a business acquaintance about this.

Although personally uninterested in horse racing and betting, Williams made a point of listening to the commentary when the race was run later that day. He heard the identical commentary, with mention of the same horses, that he had heard in his dream. The other two people he had confided in later confirmed all he had told them.

Stuart Holroyd, in *The Supernatural: Dreamworlds*, gives the details of a scientific experiment that seems to prove conclusively that effects can precede causes, thus upsetting one of the basic laws of science and of common sense. Drs. Montague Ullman and Stanley Krippner ran a series of closely controlled, and very complex, tests on British **psychic** Malcolm Bessent at the Maimonides Medical Center. The idea was to check on what Bessent dreamed and to see if it was the same as an incident that was *going to happen* to him. They did this by first using EEG to monitor his brain rhythms and REM (rapid eye movement, the indicator that a subject is having a dream) and then immediately waking him to record the dream. This was carried out by one team, who woke him after four separate dreams then filed away the details of those dreams. The following morning a second team decided on a target word. In this case it was "corridor," one out of 1,200 possible words. Around this word they were to construct an elaborate multisensory "happening" for Bessent. Krippner selected Vincent Van Gogh's painting *Hospital Corridor at St. Remy* as the target picture.

The "happening" was started when two men dressed in white hospital uniforms burst into Bessent's room and forced him into a straitjacket. They took him out and led him down a darkened corridor, while eerie music from the movie *Spellbound* played in the background. There was also the sound of distant hysterical laughter. The men took Bessent to an office where Krippner, seated at a desk and laughing wildly, forced him to swallow a pill and swabbed his face to "disinfect" him. Obvious, on the wall of the office, was the Van Gogh painting. Krippner then turned off the lights and showed Bessent slides of weird drawings done by mental patients.

When the dream records were opened up and studied they showed that Bessent had had recurring visions of a mental hospital, a large concrete building, doctors and psychologists in white coats, and the theme of a female patient disguised as a doctor trying to escape down a corridor toward an archway. The dreams were all characterized by a feeling of hostility. This was an amazingly accurate series of dreams, dreamed before the events took place and all done under strict laboratory conditions. It would seem to be conclusive proof of precognition in dreams.

Sources:
Buckland, Raymond. *Doors to Other Worlds*. St. Paul, MN: Llewellyn, 1993.
Guiley, Rosemary Ellen. *Harper's Encyclopedia of Mystical & Paranormal Experience*. San Francisco: San Francisco: HarperSanFrancisco, 1991.
Holroyd, Stuart. *The Supernatural: Dream Worlds*. London: Aldus, 1976.
Saltmarsh, H. F. *Foreknowledge*. London: G. Bell & Sons, 1938.

PREDICTION

A prediction is the action of foretelling future events; of **prophesying.** In his masterful *An Encyclopedia of the Occult* (1920), Lewis Spence refers to Andrew Jackson Davis's (1826–1910) amazing predictions of the automobile and the typewriter, both of which were given in 1856. The first practical automobile was the Benz of 1885 and the first practical typewriter was placed on the market by Remington in 1874. Davis said:

> Look out about these days for carriages and traveling saloons on country roads—without horses, without steam, without any visible motive power—moving with greater speed and far more safety than at present. Carriages will be moved by a strange and beautiful and simple admixture of aqueous and atmospheric gases—so easily condensed, so simply ignited, and so imparted by a machine somewhat resembling fire engines as to be entirely concealed and manageable between the forward wheels. These vehicles will prevent many embarrassments now experienced by persons living in thinly populated territories. The first requisite for these land-locomotives will be good roads, upon which, with your engine, without your horses, you may travel with great rapidity. These carriages seem to be of uncomplicated construction.

About the typewriter, he said:

> I am almost moved to invent an automatic psychographer—that is, an artificial soul-writer. It may be constructed something like a piano, one brace or scale of keys to represent the elementary sounds; another and lower tier to represent a combination, and still another for a rapid recombination so that a person, instead of playing a piece of music may touch off a sermon or a poem.

In February 1914, an Australian spiritualist medium, Mrs. Foster Turner, in front of an audience of nearly a thousand people, told Sir Arthur Conan Doyle:

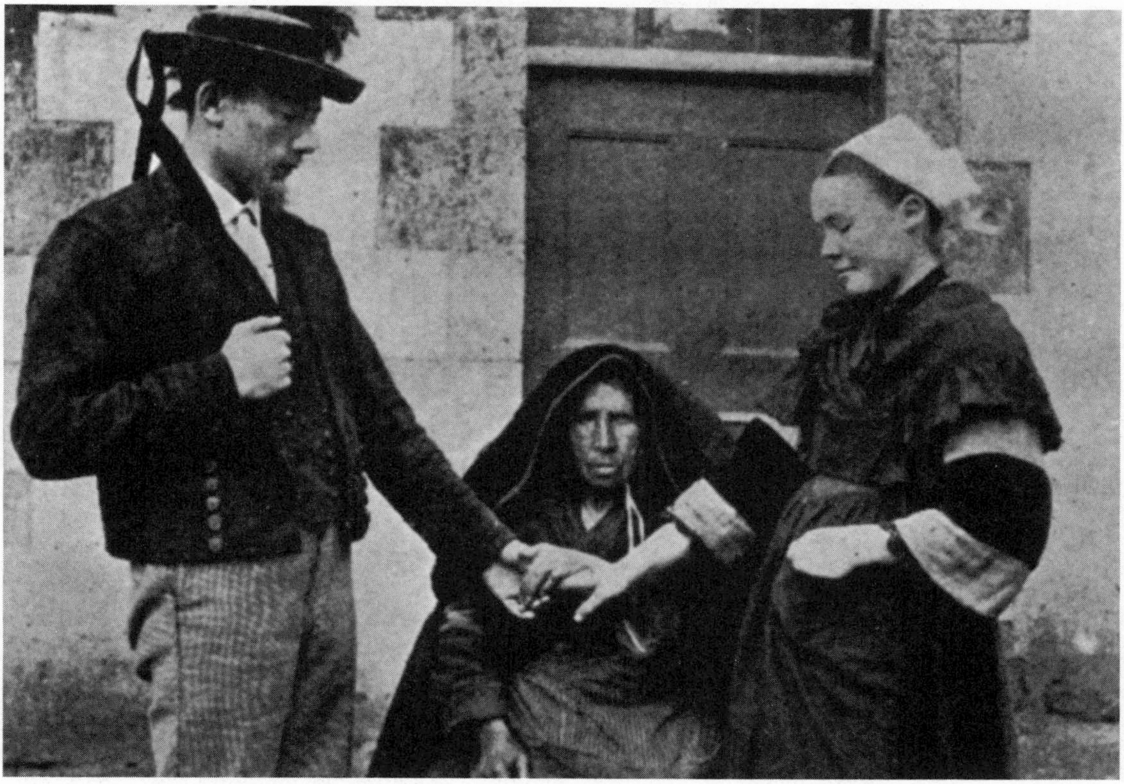

A witch in Brittany predicts the future of an engaged couple. ***Fortean Picture Library.***

> Although there is not at present a whisper of a great European war at hand, yet I want to warn you that before this year, 1914, has run its course, Europe will be deluged in blood. Great Britain, our beloved nation, will be drawn into the most awful war the world has ever known. Germany will be the great antagonist, and will draw other nations to her train. Austria will totter to its ruin. Kings and kingdoms will fall. Millions of precious lives will be slaughtered, but Britain will finally triumph and emerge victorious.

There have been tens of thousands of predictions made that have turned out to be accurate. Some are made as statements, some while in a trance, some have been seen in **dreams.** Predictions are given based on **astrological** charts, on the layout of **tarot** and other cards, based on **omens** such as the sighting of animals or birds, based on the actions of people or animals, and so on. Predictions are the utterances of those who **divine** the future.

Sources:

Spence, Lewis. *An Encyclopedia of the Occult.* George Routledge & Sons, London 1920.

Sixteenth-century prophet Joachim, Abbot of Fiore, writes his prophecies in his cave. *Fortean Picture Library.*

Premonition; Presentiment

A premonition, or presentiment, is a warning of a future event. Premonitions range from vague feelings to visions and auditory warnings. **Dreams** also may bring premonitions, which may be presented in a straightforward manner or purely symbolically. Premonitions differ from **predictions** in that the latter states that a certain thing will definitely come about, and may include minute details, while the former is simply a strong feeling that something is likely to happen.

Nandor Fodor (1895–1964), in *An Encyclopedia of Psychic Science* (1934), says that a premonition should have two fundamental conditions: "The fact announced must be absolutely independent of the person to whom the premonition has come," and "The announcement must be such that it cannot be ascribed to chance or sagacity."

In its early days, the **Society for Psychical Research** collected 668 cases of premonitions of death; 252 more were added in 1922 alone. Camille Flammarion (1842–1925) collected 1,824 cases.

Sources:

Fodor, Nandor. *An Encyclopedia of Psychic Science*. London, 1934.

Prophecy; Prophet

A prophet is one who speaks the will of a deity, quite often revealing future events. The ancient **Hebrews** called a prophet **nabhi.** In the early period (c. 1050–1015 BCE) a nabhi appeared to be little more than a **fortune-teller.** However, he made him or herself receptive to whatever messages or prophecies might come from deity, rather than claiming to use any special techniques that would draw such information. David Christie-Murray says: "The prophets aimed not so much at foretelling the future as at describing what they saw as the will of God in the circumstances of their time. But in doing so, their prophesies *were* fulfilled, often in ways more profound and long-lasting than they ever imagined."

The **Old Testament** used the term prophet very loosely, applying it to all those who were "friends" of God. For example, Abraham, Moses, Aaron, and Miriam were all named as prophets though Moses was the only true prophet of the four, as "the appointed mouthpiece of divine laws," according to Geoffrey Ashe. There were those who became known as the "Fanatical Prophets." In 1 Samuel: 10 there are bands of prophets who existed c. 1000 BCE, in Gibeah and Ramah. They were devotees of the national deity Jehovah (Yahweh). They were stimulated by rhythmic music, dancing, and chanting, building up into *ekstasis* (ecstasy) when their frenzied behavior exercised a hypnotic effect on the onlookers.

In ancient **Greece** the prophets were generally attached to the **oracles,** and in **Rome** they were represented by the **augurs.** In ancient **Egypt** the priests of Ra at Memphis acted as prophets. The Druids were frequently prophets to the **Celtic** people.

Sources:

Ashe, Geoffrey. *Man, Myth & Magic: Prophecy*. London: BPC Publishing, 1970.

Christie-Murray, David. *Mysteries of Mind Space & Time: The Unexplained*. Westport, CT: H. S. Stuttman, 1992.

Spence, Lewis. *An Encyclopedia of the Occult*. George Routledge & Sons, London 1920.

Psephomancy

(See also Pessomancy; Thrioboly)

Nathan Bailey's *An universal etymological English dictionary*, volume 2, of 1727, says: "Psephomancy . . . a Divination by Pebble-Stones, distinguished by certain Characters, and put as Lots into a Vessel; which, having made certain Supplications to the Gods to direct them, they drew out and, according to the Characters, conjectured what would happen to them." It is, then, a branch of **pessomancy.**

Each of the pebbles had a "character"—a sigil, letter, or number marked on it—then they were all placed in a container. They were probably shaken as prayers were made or a mantra chanted. Then the diviner would reach in and draw out one of the pebbles, interpreting according to the character marked on it. It was, as Bailey's definition says, like drawing lots in **sortilege.**

Sources:

Oxford English Dictionary. Oxford: Clarendon Press, 1989.

PSI *see* Extrasensory Perception

Psychics

A psychic is a sensitive; someone who is susceptible to spiritual influences. A psychic picks up knowledge **clairvoyantly, clairaudiently,** or **clairsentiently,** while fully conscious or in a trance. He or she differs from a **spiritualist medium** in that the latter receives the information from the spirit world while the psychic gets the information purely through his or her own sensitivity. The word comes from the **Greek** word for "soul."

Much of the information received by a psychic may be obtained through **extrasensory perception.** In other words, the psychic may attune to another person to the point where he or she is able to "read" that person's thoughts and get the information directly from them. However, many times the psychic will pick up information totally unknown to the person being read.

Psychics are also able to receive information from inanimate objects, such as letters, jewelry, even stones. This is termed **psychometry.** Many people claim to be psychic because they have occasional flashes of paranormal knowledge. Although no psychic seems to have a 100 percent success rate, many do have a very high percentage of successes—far more than experienced by the "occasional" psychic.

Often a psychic will need a "trigger" to spark the psychic knowledge. This may be in the form of **tarot** cards, a **pendulum** or a **crystal** ball, for example. Others need no more than a few moments of concentration. Most people have the latent ability, which can be brought out through a strict regimen of exercises and constant practice. Some people seem to be born with the facility and from childhood demonstrate their abilities. Some few seem to acquire an amazing degree of psychic ability after an illness or an accident of some sort—some physical trauma often involving a blow to the head.

Sources:

Buckland, Raymond. *Doors to Other Worlds*. St. Paul, MN: Llewellyn, 1993.
Guiley, Rosemary Ellen. *Harper's Encyclopedia of Mystical & Paranormal Experience*. San Francisco: HarperSanFrancisco, 1991.
Shepard, Leslie A. (ed.). *Encyclopedia of Occultism & Parapsychology*. New York: Avon, 1978.

Psychography

This was a term used by William Stainton Moses (1839–1892) for all forms of **automatic writing.** Moses was probably the greatest physical **medium** after D. D. Home, and produced a large number of automatic writings from various spirits.

Sources:

Buckland, Raymond. *Doors to Other Worlds*. St. Paul, MN: Llewellyn, 1993.
Moses, William Stainton. *Direct Spirit Writing*. London, 1878.

Psychomancy

Psychomancy is divination by spirits, usually spirits of the dead. It is similar to **necromancy** and encompasses necromancy, except that where the latter requires the presence of a corpse, in psychomancy such a device does not have to be present. The use of a **Ouija®** board, **automatic writing** or any form of **mediumship** would all come under the general heading of psychomancy, since they deal with information obtained from spirits. Psychomancy would also encompass practicing **ceremonial magic,** even though that is dealing with spirits that are not necessarily of this earthly plane.

Psychometry; Psychoscopy

(See also Metagraphology)

Psychometry is the ability to hold an object in the hands and to divine from it the history of that object. Spiritualist **mediums, psychics,** and others can take a ring, watch, or similar object that has been in close contact with a person and "read" the past and present of the object itself and of those who have been in close contact with it for any length of time. The name (derived from the Greek *psyche* meaning "soul" and *metron*, meaning "measure") was given by Dr. **Joseph Rhodes Buchanan** (1814–1899), a pioneer in psychometric research.

American psychic Peter Nelson performs a psychometry experiment, 1984. *Dr. Elmar R. Gruber/Fortean Picture Library.*

The theory is that everything that has ever existed has left its mark—some trace of its existence—on the ether. Lewis Spence suggests that haunted houses demonstrate this on a larger scale: events took place and left their impressions in the rooms, to be picked up by psychics.

Impressions received through psychometry may vary in intensity, depending upon the acuteness of the atmosphere that has affected the object. Everyone has the ability to psychometrize, though many need to practice in order to bring out what is latent. The steps are easy ones, and the following exercise can help develop the ability.

Take ten or so samples of different substances: cloth of various types, leather, fur, wood, metal, or stone. Sit quietly and, taking one object at a time in your hands, concentrate on it, feeling its texture. As you hold the sample, think of its origins seeing, in your mind's eye, the animal from which it came, the tree that was felled, the land or mountain of which the stone was a part. Some people hold the object in their cupped hands and rest the hands over their heart as they concentrate. Others hold it to their forehead or over the solar plexus. Experiment and see what seems the most natural for you. There is no one right way.

Hold the objects one at a time, taking plenty of time with each. Go through them in the same order each time you do this, and you should do this on a regular basis. Always go through the full set of ten, or however many you have settled on. After a few days or weeks of this initial exercise, place the samples in individual envelopes. The envelopes should all look the same so that, outwardly, there is no way of telling one from another. Number the envelopes from one to ten, or A to J.

Again go through the concentration regularly, this time trying to pick up a clue regarding what is in the envelope. It may be a good idea to lay the envelope on a table and simply hold your hands over it, or lay them on it; this way you won't get any clues from the weight or feel of the enclosed object. You may find that you get a clear impression of the object itself or you may get an impression of its origins—tree, animal, mountain, etc. In a notebook, write down what you receive. After a few days of this you may get results that look something like the following:

Content	**No.**	**#1**	**2**	**3**	**4**	**5**	**6**	**7**
Cotton	A	Silk	Cotton	Silk	Wool	Cotton	Cotton	Cotton
Silk	B	Cotton	Silk	Velvet	Silk	Silk	Cotton	Silk
Velvet	C	Wool	Feather	Bamboo	Velvet	Wool	Velvet	Oak
Snakeskin	D	Ivory	Feather	Snakeskin	Oak	Feather	Snakeskin	Feather
Seashell	E	Oak	Ivory	Shell	Ivory	Shell	Shell	Ivory
Wool	F	Shell	Oak	Velvet	Wool	Wool	Iron	Wool
Ivory	G	Feather	Shell	Ivory	Ivory	Ivory	Shell	Shell
Clay	H	Iron	Iron	Clay	Velvet	Feather	Clay	Clay
Iron	I	Velvet	Snakeskin	Ivory	Iron	Silk	Bamboo	Iron
Bamboo	J	Oak	Velvet	Bamboo	Oak	Bamboo	Oak	Oak
Oak	K	Oak	Wool	Oak	Oak	Oak	Bamboo	Bamboo
Feather	L	Clay	Wool	Cotton	Velvet	Snakeskin	Feather	Feather

It can be seen that, in this example, a pattern is emerging. By the seventh try, fifty percent are correct with others very close. For example, oak and bamboo are frequently confused, as are snakeskin and feather. Persevere with the envelopes, then gradually introduce new ones. When you feel you are keeping a good, consistent score, turn to actual objects and see how you do with them. Take a friend's ring, watch, or brooch. As you hold the object, first think of the thing itself. Then ask yourself, who has handled it most? Where did it come from? When and where was it made? Was it previously owned by someone else and, if so, for how long? See if you can get a picture of the previous owner, enough that you could describe him or her. Practice as much as you can, with a wide variety of objects from a number of different people. (Avoid coins, since they are handled so much by so many people.) Initially concentrate on personal objects. You can also do this with letters; hold a sealed letter to your heart or forehead and try to pick up what is in the letter and who wrote it. So far as you are able, check our results and keep a record of them.

There is a well-known story of Professor William Denton, a minerologist and researcher on psychometry, giving his wife and his mother meteoric fragments and other items, all carefully wrapped in paper so that they could not be seen. Denton's wife had done psychometry before. She held to her forehead a package containing carboniferous material, and immediately started describing swamps and trees with tufted heads and scaled trunks (palm trees). Denton then gave her lava from a Hawaiian volcanic eruption. She held it and described a "boiling ocean" of golden lava. Denton's mother, who did not believe in psychometry, was given a meteorite. She held it a moment then said, "I seem to be traveling away, away through nothing—I see what looks like stars and mist."

Spiritualist mediums say, "Spirit speaks first." What they mean is that you should go with your first impressions. If you think for too long about the object you are holding, your mind starts trying to think logically and, whether consciously or unconsciously, to reason. If you say what first comes into your head, no matter how outlandish it may seem at the time, it will invariably be the correct observation.

Psychics and sensitives have traced lost and stolen property and found missing people through the use of psychometry. **Gérard Croiset** is an example of one who frequently concentrated his energies on an object that had belonged to a person in order to find that person when they were missing.

Sources:

Buchanan, Joseph R. *Journal of Man*. Boston: Little, Brown, 1849.
Buchanan, Joseph R. *Manual of Psychometry*. Boston: Little, Brown, 1885.
Buckland, Raymond. *Doors to Other Worlds*. St. Paul, MN: Llewellyn, 1993.
Butler, William E. *How to Develop Psychometry*. New York: Samuel Weiser, 1971.
Carrington, Hereward. *Your Psychic Powers: And How to Develop Them*. New York: Dodd, Mead, 1920.
Spence, Lewis. *An Encyclopedia of the Occult*. London: George Routledge & Sons, 1920.

PSYCHOSCOPY ***see*** **Psychometry**

Pyramid, Great

The Great Pyramid of Cheops, at the Giza plateau in Egypt, is ten miles west of the modern city of Cairo, at the end of an avenue of acacia, eucalyptus, and tamarind trees. The base of the pyramid covers a little over thirteen acres, the ground being so level that it varies no more than one-half inch over the entire area. The pyramid itself is composed of four triangular sides once rising to a height of 485 feet though due to erosion it is now only 450 feet. Each side of the pyramid, at the base, is 755 feet, six inches across. The structure is made up of approximately two and a half million blocks of stone, each weighing from two tons to seventy tons, which are cut and set together so closely that something the size of a credit card could not be forced between them. The blocks were originally covered with slabs of highly polished limestone.

Many people see the Great Pyramid as a prophetic sign. Some Christians try to tie into the structure to passages in the Bible, such as Isaiah 19:19–20: "In that day shall there be an altar to the Lord in the midst of the land of Egypt, and a pillar at the border thereof to the Lord. And it shall be for a sign and a witness unto the Lord of hosts in the land of Egypt." To explain how the Great Pyramid can be "in the midst of the land" and yet "at the border" at the same time, some suggest that the word "Gizeh" is Arabic for "border." Others argue that the verses say that there will be an altar in the midst and *also* a pillar at the border: two separate things.

The reason for connecting Christianity with something built nearly 3,000 years before the coming of Jesus is not known. Yet the "prophesy" of the Great Pyramid is touted. A cross-section of the pyramid shows that there are "amazing correspondences of history with the symbolisms of [the] passage systems" (*The End Times Bible Report Quarterly*, summer 1999). It contains such correlations as the following: Air Passages: these "symbolize that life will be provided for all men on earth." Horizontal Passage: "This symbolizes 6,000 years of 'night of weeping' followed by a 1,000-year Sabbath rest and refreshing, which God promised." Queen's Chamber: "Symbolizes the everlasting home for all men upon the earth." King's Chamber: It is "symbolic of divine life—immortality—the condition of Christ's faithful followers in Heaven."

The Great Pyramid of Cheops and the Sphinx. ***Dr. Elmar R. Gruber/Fortean Picture Library.***

The Great Pyramid is so multidimensional that just about anyone can find some parallel, some "proof," to confirm their own beliefs and tie them in with the edifice. Many observers base their measurements on what they term the "pyramid inch" and the "pyramid cubit." The *Encyclopedia Britannica* says: "The theories that ascribe prophetic and esoteric meanings to the measurements, angles, and proportions of the Great Pyramid are wholly devoid of scientific foundation."

Sources:

Encyclopedia Britannica. Chicago: William Benton, 1964.
Tompkins, Peter. *Secrets of the Great Pyramid*. New York: Harper & Row, 1971.

Pyromancy

Pyromancy incorporates such other forms of divination as **anthracomancy** and **causimancy.** It is divination by fire or by signs derived from fire. Robert Green, in *The honorable historie of Frier Bacon and Frier Bongay* (1590), says, "Thou art read in Magick's mystery. In Piromancy, to divine by flames." Edward Smedley, in *The Occult Sciences*

A portrayal of pyromancy, or divination by fire or signs of fire. *Fortean Picture Library.*

(1855), described "Pyromancy, by which conjectures were made from the motions of the sacrificial flame."

The above quotations would indicate that this form of divination was done with the aid of the flames of a fire that was used for burning a sacrifice, as in **extispicy.** Unlike anthracomancy, where the burning coals are used, pyromancy is dependant upon the flames themselves. The color of them would be taken into account, as would the way they flickered, the height they attained, their rise and fall, and all other aspects of them. The presage was good when the flames quickly consumed the sacrifice, but evil if the fire was slow to start, was disturbed by the wind, and if it took a long time to consume the sacrifice. If there was little or no smoke, if the flames burned with no sound, or if they were bright red or orange, the prognostication was favorable. Not so if there was smoke, the fire crackled, and the flames were deep red in color.

Besides the flames of sacrificial fires, divination of the pyromantic variety was also done by the flames of torches. If the flame divided into two it was a bad omen, but if it was either a single point or three points then it was a very good sign. If the flames bent, then it was a sign of sickness, or even death, to come. If the flame was suddenly extinguished, it meant the coming of a great disaster.

Sources:
Grand Orient (A. E. Waite). *The Complete Manual of Occult Divination: Volume 1—Manual of Cartomancy*. London: Rider, 1912.
Oxford English Dictionary. Oxford: Clarendon Press, 1989.

PYROMANTIA

Similar to **pyromancy,** but the fire is not a sacrificial one. The flames are read after powdered resin or frankincense has been thrown onto them, causing them to blaze up. Such other substances as sugar, salt, and flour may also be thrown on. In *Trinum Magicum* (1611), in a reference to old Roman divination, the author says, "There is also Pyromantia, in which powdered resin was thrown into the flames. If the flame rose in one, it was a good sign; if lambent and divided, unfortunate; if in three points, a glorious *eventum* or result; if much dispersed, an ill death; if crackling or snapping, misfortune; if it was very suddenly extinguished, great danger."

Sources:
Leland, Charles Godfrey. *Etruscan Magic & Occult Remedies*. New York: University Books, 1963.

PYROSCOPY

Pyroscopy is the interpretation of scorch marks left on a piece of paper after it has been placed close to a flame. These marks may be from an accidental scorching or the scorching may be done deliberately, as a tool for the divination.

Sources:
de Givry, Grillot. *A Pictorial Anthology of Witchcraft, Magic & Alchemy*. London: Spottiswoode, Ballantyne, 1931.

PYTHIA

Apollo, with his twin sister Artemis, was born of Zeus and Leto. Barthell tells that Apollo was given over to Themis for nursing but, as soon as he had tasted the "divine ambrosia," he burst from his swaddling clothes a fully grown youth. He announced that from then on he would, through **oracles,** convey to the whole of humankind the will of his father.

After being accepted into Olympus, Apollo then set out to find a good location for his oracular shrine. He searched for some time before finding a wooded grove in Bœotia, where he laid out plans for his temple. Telphusa, a resident undine in a nearby stream, who claimed she did not want to be disturbed by a throng of pilgrims (but actually wanted the site for her own shrine), managed to talk Apollo into relocating. He went farther north to Crisa, below the glades of Mount Parnassus in Phocis. However, there was already an oracle there.

This was an ancient oracle of Gæa, and it was guarded by a female dragon named Python. Apollo slew this dragon and built his shrine there. The priestesses who became the oracles of Apollo's temple became known as Pythia, after Python, and

Aegeus of Athens consults the Pythia, portrayed in this fifth-century BCE artwork. *Fortean Picture Library.*

Apollo himself became Pythian Apollo. Celebrations were held quadrennially at Delphi, called the Pythian Games.

Sources:

Barthell, Edward E. Jr. *Gods and Goddesses of Ancient Greece*. Coral Gables, FL: University of Miami Press 1971.

Larousse Encyclopedia of Mythology. London: Paul Hamlyn, 1965.

Q

Qabbalah

(See also Christian Qabbalah)

Spelled variously Cabala, Kabbala, Qabbalah, and similar, this is a Jewish form of mysticism that originated in southern France and Spain in the twelfth century. The name has, in more recent times, come to be applied in reference to almost any mixture of occultism, Hermeticism, Gnosticism, Rosicrucianism, and exotic theosophy. Originally, however, it was a body of Jewish doctrines about the nature of man and his relationship to God. One fanciful story is that Moses received the Qabbalah at the same time that he received the Ten Commandments, but deemed it advisable to keep the Qabbalah secret and pass it on by word of mouth alone. It is said that he hid clues in the Pentateuch, the first five books of the **Bible.**

The *Sefer ha-Zohar,* or Book of Splendor, which came into being sometime in the thirteenth century (probably between 1280 and 1286), was written by a Spanish Jew named Moses de Leon. The idea of Moses receiving the Qabbalah along with the Ten Commandments may come from confusion with this Moses de Leon. The Zohar was a mystical commentary on the Pentateuch containing a mixture of stories, poems, commentaries, and **visions** based on Qabbalistic ideas and symbols.

The meaning of the word Qabbalah is "receiving" or "that which is received." It was originally a secret tradition handed down orally, from teacher to student. The Qabbalah was founded on a small book called the *Sepher Yesirah* or Book of Creation, dating from prior to the ninth century. It gives a discussion on cosmology and cosmogony, stating that the world was created by God using thirty-two secret paths of wisdom. These are made up of the *Sephiroth* or Sefirot (divine emanations), which are ten Sephirah plus the twenty-two letters of the Hebrew alphabet, the letters being the Paths connecting the Sephiroth. Together they make up the Tree of Life, or *Otz Chiim,* with every Sephirah being a level of attainment in knowledge.

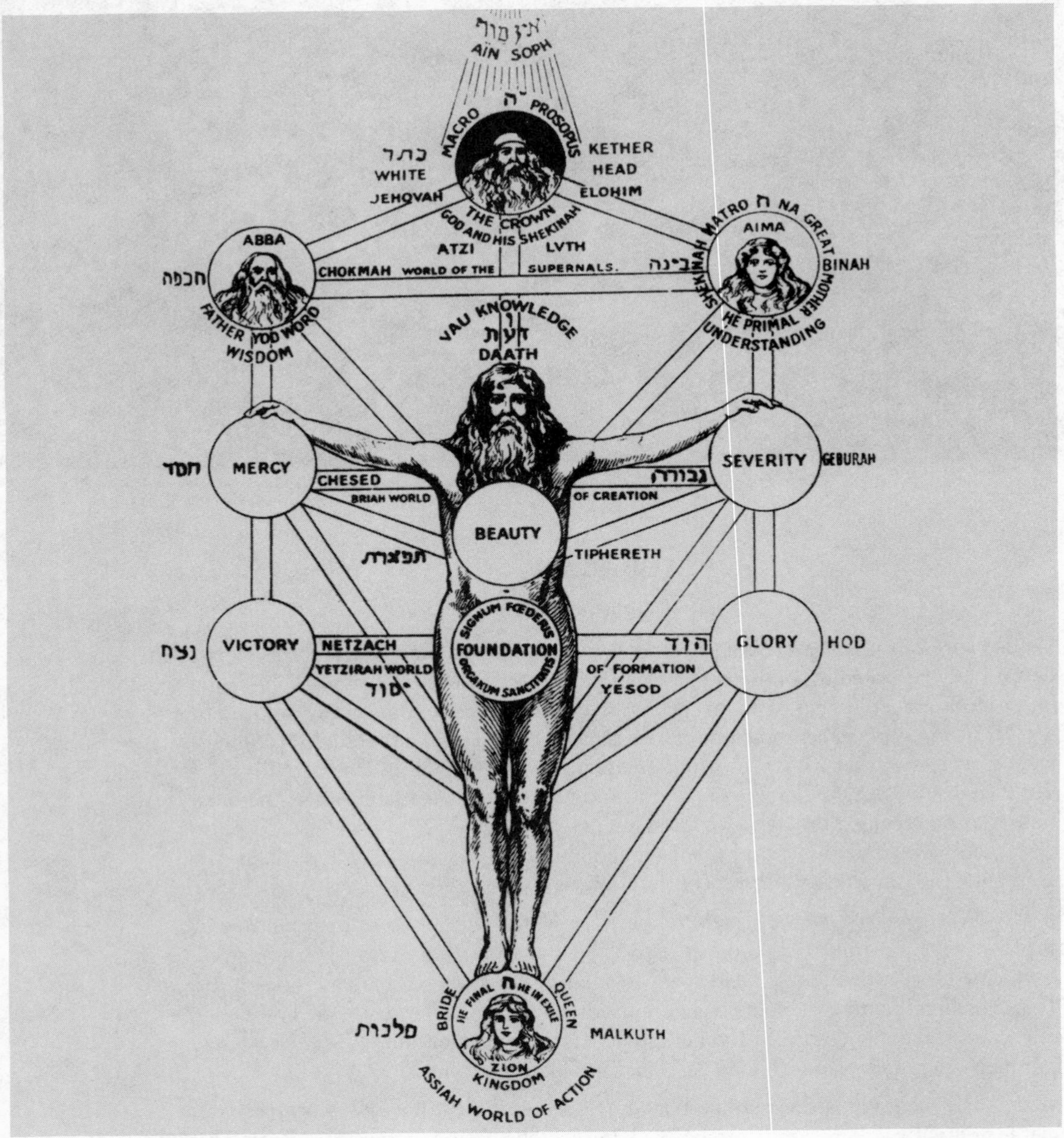

The Sacred Tree of the Sephiroth, from A. E. Waite's *The Holy Kabbalah*. *Fortean Picture Library.*

Each Sephirah emanates from the one above it, the top one being the first emanation, of the *Ein Soph Aur*, Kether. The centers are known as the Crown, or Supreme Crown (*Kether*); Wisdom (*Hokhmah*); Understanding (*Binah*); Love/Mercy (*Hesed*); Strength (*Din* or *Giburah*); Beauty (*Tifareth*); Endurance (*Netsah*); Splendor/Majesty (*Hod*); Foundation (*Yesod*); and Kingdom (*Malkuth*). The right-hand side of the Tree—Hokhmah, Hesed and Netsah—is regarded as male, while the left-hand side—Binah, Din and Hod—is female. The central section—Kether, Tifareth, Yesod, and Malkuth—balances and unifies the two sides.

Each of the triads symbolizes a portion of the human body: the first the head, the second the arms, and the third the legs. The first is the Celestial Triangle: Kether, Hokhmah, and Binah. The second is the Moral Triangle: Hesed, Tifareth, and Din (Giburah). The third is the Mundane Triangle: Netsah, Yesod, and Hod, with Malkuth below it.

In turn, every Sephirah is divided into four parts in which operate the Four Worlds. They are: *Atziluth*, the world of archetypes; *Briah* or *Khorsia*, the world of creation; *Yetzirah*, the world of formation; and *Assiah*, the world of the material. In Atziluth, the Sephiroth manifest through the ten Holy Names of God. In Briah, the manifestation is through the ten Mighty Archangels. In Yetzirah, the manifestation is through various orders of Angels. In Assiah, the manifestation is through the "Planetary Spheres." The ten Sephiroth exist on each of the Four Worlds, but on a different level.

According to R. J. Zwi Werblowsky in *Man, Myth and Magic*:

> The Mishna [a second-century rabbinic collection of religious law] attests the existence of two subjects that should not be taught in public and which, therefore, were considered as esoteric disciplines intended for initiates only. These subjects were "the work of creation" (based on Genesis, chapter 1) and the "work of the chariot" (the mysteries of the Divine Throne, based on Ezekiel, chapter 1). The precise nature and contents of these mystical disciplines is a matter for conjecture but it seems certain that some of the early rabbis practiced an ecstatic contemplation which culminated in the vision of the Throne of Glory, the Merkabah.

The Merkabah, or "Throne Mysticism," is the earliest detailed mystical system accessible to the historian of Judaism and predates the Qabbalah. The main characteristic of Merkabah is the emphasis on the supernatural, mysterious aspect of God. The initiate "rises through the spheres, worlds, heavens and celestial mansions or 'palaces' (*hekhaloth*) guarded by all sorts of terrifying angelic beings" to finally stand before the Divine Splendor.

The twenty-two Paths, which correspond to the letters of the Hebrew alphabet, each has both an occult meaning and a numerical value, and have been equated to the twenty-two cards of the **tarot** deck's major arcana, otherwise known as the trumps.

The path between any two Sephiroth must be considered in the light of those Sephiroth, each having its own significance. The **numerological** value of that path, together with the meaning of the equivalent tarot card, also needs to be carefully considered in order to have full understanding of that Path. The Four Worlds mentioned above must also be taken into account.

Sources:

Albertson, Edward. *Understanding the Kabbalah*. Los Angeles: Sherbourne Press, 1973.

Bardon, Franz. *The Key to the True Quabbalah*. Wuppertal, Germany: Dieter Rüggeberg, Wuppertal 1971.

Cavendish, Richard (ed.). *Man, Myth & Magic*. London: BPC Publishing, 1970.

Epstein, Perle. *Kabbalah: The Way of the Jewish Mystic*. Boston: Shambhala, 1988.

Fortune, Dion. *The Mystical Qabalah*. London: Ernest Benn, 1935.

Guiley, Rosemary Ellen. *Harper's Encyclopedia of Mystical & Paranormal Experience*. San Francisco: HarperSanFrancisco, 1991.

Kraig, Donald Michael. *Modern Magick: Eleven Lessons in the High Magickal Arts*. St. Paul, MN: Llewellyn, 1988.

Myer, Isaac. *Qabbalah: The Philosophical Writings of Avicebron*. New York: Samuel Weiser, 1970.

R

Radiesthesia

Radiesthesia may be defined as divination by utilizing human sensitivity to radiations, covering the whole field from any source, living or inert. It is a refinement of the art of **dowsing, rhabdomancy,** or **water** witching, and its history can be traced back over 5,000 years, being found in the ancient Orient. The principal instrument used in radiesthesia is the pendulum, though rods may also be used. The practice really came to the fore during the Middle Ages and remained popular through to the early nineteenth century. It then came to be regarded as a superstition without value. But radiesthesia saw a great resurgence of interest in the twentieth century.

The term radiesthesia was coined in France (as *radiesthésie*) by the Abbé Bouly, in 1930. That year *L'Association des Amis de la Radiesthésie* was formed, and three years later came the **British Society of Dowsers.**

A radiesthetist is a dowser sensitive to hidden information who uses an indicator, such as a pendulum or rod, to amplify that sensitivity. The pendulum is a weight of some sort suspended on a fine chain or length of thread. Some radiesthetists hold a short stick with the weighted chain or thread hanging off the end of it, but most modern-day diviners hold the end of the chain directly between their fingers. Virtually any small weight will work; some use a pendant necklace or a ring on the end of a length of silk ribbon. In the Middle Ages a key on the end of a chain was popular. Today there are commercially produced pendula made out of wood, brass, silver, gold, and plastic. A serviceable one can be fashioned from a fishing weight or plumb-bob. Some of the commercially produced ones are hollow, and unscrew to give access to an inside cavity. In this can be placed what is known as a "witness": a sample of what is being sought. For example, if the radiesthetist is looking for gold, then a small piece of gold would be placed inside the pendulum, to help make the connection. The pendulum is often used to diagnose and prescribe for dis-

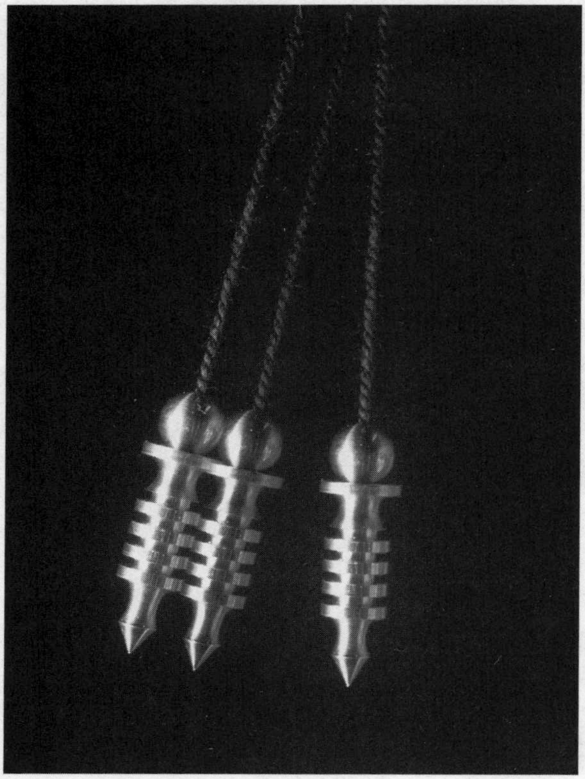

The principal instrument used in radiesthesia is the pendulum. ***Fortean Picture Library.***

ease (see **Medical Radiesthesia**). It can also be used to simply answer questions, in the manner of a **Ouija**® board.

Much radiesthesia is done seated at a table, working with charts, maps, or other simple accessories. The end of the chain or thread is held between thumb and first finger—right hand if right-handed; left hand if left-handed—allowing the pendulum weight to be suspended about an inch off the surface of the table. A square of paper, placed under the pendulum, is marked with a large cross and the words "yes" on the vertical axis and "no" on the horizontal axis.

Resting your elbow on the table, let the weight of the pendulum hang over the center of the cross and ask a "yes or no" question. Although you try to keep the pendulum still, it will start to swing along one of the lines of the cross, giving your answer. The paper or card is usually placed so that swinging toward you and away from you is the "yes" axis, and swinging across you is the "no" axis. An alternate method that does not employ any card or paper is simply to let the pendulum swing in a clockwise circle for "yes" and counterclockwise for "no."

Some practitioners suggest not having your elbow on the table, but this can make for fatigue and unsteadiness. It is essential that you do not consciously try to make the pendulum swing; it should swing of its own accord, much as the **planchette** of a Ouija board moves about without being directed. Although you do not *consciously* make the pendulum swing, it is almost certainly your muscles that are bringing it about. But as with the Ouija board, the question is, who or what is directing it to give the answers you get?

If the pendulum swings in a circle or doesn't swing at all, it may be because the question asked is ambiguous and needs rephrasing, or is one that cannot be answered with a simple yes or no. Think through the wording of the questions carefully. A question does not have to be asked out loud; you can just think of it. It is a good idea to draw up a list of questions before sitting down to use the pendulum.

To get more than yes-and-no answers, put the letters of the alphabet in a semicircle, drawn on a piece of paper and placed on the table. Starting with the weight of the pendulum hanging in the center, questions can be asked and answers obtained by observing to which letters the pendulum swings. This is not easy, however, since the swing of the pendulum does not seem to change direction very rapidly. A variation is to hold the pendulum so that it hangs down in the center of a water glass. It can then swing and "chink" against the side of the glass; one hit for A, two for B, three for C, and so on. This is a form of **dactyliomancy.**

The pendulum really comes into its own for dowsing. Out in the field, the radiesthetist walks over the land in a grid pattern, holding the pendulum. It will swing when water (or whatever is being sought) is passed over. Using the yes/no card, it can then be determined how deep it is necessary to dig, what the flow rate is, and any other pertinent information. Where the pendulum surpasses the forked hazel twig, however, is that it can be used away from the actual site that is being dowsed. It can be used while you sit at a table at home. For example, a map of the area (either a regular printed map or a hand-drawn sketch of the field) is placed on a table and the yes/no card set down alongside it. With the pendulum suspended over the card, the radiesthetist uses a finger of the other hand to indicate areas of the map, moving the finger along to follow the path that would have been walked in situ. When the sought-for area is found, the pendulum will swing on the "yes" line. Again, depth and rate of flow can be established.

This same mode of working can be used to find anything that is lost or stolen, be it human or non-human. If it is known approximately where the person or object was lost, then a rough sketch map can be drawn and used. To follow a trail on a map, it is also possible to move the pendulum itself along an indicated road. On coming to a crossroads, the pendulum will then swing to show which road to take. In this way it is easy to trace a route from one place to another.

Sources:

Lakhovsky, Georges (Mark Clement, tr.). *The Secret of Life: Cosmic Rays and Radiations of Living Beings*. London: True Health, 1963.

Maury, Marguerite. *How to Dowse, Experimental and Practical Radiesthesia*. London: Bell, 1953.

Mermet, Abbé Alexis. *Principles and Practice of Radiesthesia*. London: Watkins, 1975.

Wethered, Vernon D. *The Practice of Medical Radiesthesia*. London: C. W. Daniel, 1967.

Radionics

Originated by American physician **Albert Abrams** (1863–1924), radionics is a method of healing at a distance through the medium of an instrument or other means using the faculty of **ESP.** A trained practitioner can discover the cause of disease in any living system—human, animal, plant, or even the soil itself. Suitable therapeutic energies can then be made available to help restore optimum health. Abrams became aware of the electromagnetic waves emitted by the human body when studying spinal reflexes by means of percussion. He found that all tubercular patients, for example, gave off a dull sound when percussion was applied to their backs. This sound was present in all patients with tuberculosis. The dullness could then be transferred to a healthy person by connecting them in various ways. Abrams invented a way of measuring the various wavelengths for different diseases. He did this by way of an instrument dubbed the "oscilloclast."

As explained by *Radionics Quarterly*, the official journal of the British Radionics Association, the concept that humans and all life forms share a common ground in that they are submerged in the electromagnetic energy field of the Earth, is basic to radionic theory and practice. Each life form has its own electromagnetic field that, if sufficiently distorted, will ultimately result in disease of the organism. Accepting that "all is energy," radionics sees organs, diseases, and remedies as having their own particular frequencies or vibrations. These factors can be expressed in numerical values, known in radionics as "rates." Radionic instruments—the original oscilloclasts—are provided with calibrated dials on which such rates are set for diagnostic and treatment purposes.

In making an analysis, the radionic practitioner uses the principle of **dowsing** by applying the faculty of extrasensory perception to the problem of detecting disease, in much the same way that the dowser detects the location of water, oil, or mineral deposits. The particular form of ESP used in radionics is often referred to as "the radiesthetic faculty" through which the practitioner, by means of a series of mentally posed questions, obtains information about the health of the patient to which the conscious thinking mind has no direct access.

Radionics has become a major tool for some in the fields of horticulture and agriculture. For example, Enid Eden, daughter of a farmer and herself qualified in general agriculture, first tested the efficacy of radionics on her farm animals. Proving to herself that she could achieve significant results with radionic treatment, she gave up farming and took up radionics, rapidly becoming one of Britain's major figures in the field. She has said that "there is a vast potential for radionics in agriculture, as far as the healthy growth of crops is concerned, and for lessening the time and helping with the changeover to biological husbandry. On the animal side, radionics is helpful for healing, prophylaxis, working out rations, discovering the cause of low fertility eggs and their hatchability, and the solving of many other problems."

A radionics instrument is a box-like apparatus with a large number of calibrated dials on the front. There is often what is referred to as a "stick pad," a rubber membrane enabling the practitioner to become aware of otherwise unrecognizable changes in the behavior of the sweat glands in the finger using the pad. Some instruments incorporate a **pendulum** rather than a stick pad, since it is less liable to be influenced by changes in the practitioner's skin moisture or by fatigue. As a pendulum used in radiesthesia can use a **witness,** so can radionics. The person being diagnosed does not have to be present; the diagnosis can take place with a witness in the form of a spot of blood or urine on a piece of blotting paper. In the same way, treatment can be projected to the distant patient. The actual distance between the patient and the radionics operator seems to be immaterial.

Sources:

Tansley, David V. *Radionics & the Subtle Anatomy of Man*. Holsworthy, UK: Health Science Press, 1976.

Wethered, Vernon D. *An Introduction to Medical Radiesthesia & Radionics*. London: C. W. Daniel, 1962.

"RAPHAEL" ***see*** **Smith, Robert Cross**

RAPPING ***see*** **Typtology**

RATS ***see*** **Myomancy**

Ravens and Crows

Ravens are considered the most intelligent of birds, on a par with the smartest animals on earth, including dolphins and primates. John K. Terres suggests that corvids (*Corvidae*)—crows, ravens, magpies—have achieved "the highest degree of intelligence" to be found in any birds. Corvids are, in fact, tops among birds for overall brain size.

The raven was sacred to **Apollo** and regarded as a prophetic bird. In Norse mythology, Odin had two ravens, Hugin and Munin, who flew out over the world each day and reported back to the god all that they had seen. Odin was called *Hrafnagud*, or "God of the Raven." Alexander the Great supposedly was guided across the desert by two crows.

The crow features in **Native American** mythology. Roger Williams, writing in 1643, spoke of the reverence the Algonquins had for crows. In the Northwest, the Kwakiutl and Haida peoples have a leadership clan known as the Raven Clan, with Raven Priests. They speak of great leaders who were guided by crows and ravens. Among the Chipewyan of eastern Canada, crow is a trickster, while the Navaho refer to missionaries as crows because of their black robes. In France, many people believed that evil priests became crows and bad nuns became magpies.

In areas throughout Britain, to find a dead crow on the road is good luck, while to find one in a churchyard is bad luck. Similarly in Wales, if one crow crosses your path then it is bad luck, but if two crows cross your path it is good luck. Also in Wales, it was a common custom to doff one's hat at the sight of a crow to promote good luck. Two crows flying together from the observer's left were bad luck but if from the right were good luck. A single crow sitting on a roof is a sure sign of a coming death, according to the old adage: "A crow on the thatch, soon death lifts the latch." In **Scotland,** a raven circling a house predicts a coming death for someone in the house. A crow cawing while standing on a pile of rocks or near water is a sure sign of coming rain.

The **Greeks** and **Romans** considered the crow a weather **prophet,** though the Greeks had an expression: "Go to the crows!" that was the equivalent of "Go to hell!" The Romans had an expression, "to pierce a crow's eye," meaning that something was almost impossible to do. The Irish said, "You'll follow the crows for it," meaning that you would miss something after it was gone.

The raven was sometimes regarded by the Greeks as a "thunderbird" because of its ability to presage a storm or tempest. An old Irish saying is "to have raven's knowledge," meaning to have an **oracular** ability to see and know all things. In England, ravens are still kept "on the payroll" at the Tower of London. It is said that so long as they remain, England will never fall to her enemies. Crows and ravens are believed to have very long life, and in his *Metamorphoses*, Ovid (43 BCE—18 CE) speaks of the witch Medea injecting the veins of Jason, when he was an old man, with the blood of a crow that had outlived nine generations of men. In **Tibet,** the raven is the messenger of the Supreme Being.

Crow Augury

Counting the numbers of crows has been a popular way of foretelling the future in many countries for hundreds of years.

One: Bad luck; sorrow; a change for the worse; possible death.
Two: Good luck; a change for the better; joy; possibly finding something of value.
Three: A celebration; possible marriage; birth of a girl.
Four: Birth of a boy; a significant event to do with a son.
Five: Silver; a positive transaction.
Six: Gold; wealth; possibility of greed; a negative transaction.
Seven: A secret; a spiritual experience; sacred rites.
Eight: Something profound; a death or dying; a life-altering experience.
Nine: Passion; something sensual; forbidden delight; temptation.
Ten: Something overwhelming; extremes; something paid in full.
Eleven: Uncertainty; waiting; possibly to do with a spiritual matter.
Twelve: Fulfillment; riches; fruitful labor; completion.

Sources:

Buckland, Raymond. *The Witch Book: The Encyclopedia of Witchcraft, Wicca, and Neo-paganism*. Detroit: Visible Ink Press, 2002.
Feher-Elston, Catherine. *RavenSong*. Flagstaff, AZ: Northland Publishing, 1991.
Savage, Candace. *Bird Brains*. San Francisco: Sierra Club, 1997.
Terres, John K. *The Audubon Society Encyclopedia of North American Birds*. New York: Alfred A. Knopf, 1980.
http://www.shades-of-night.com/aviary.

Redcap, Old Mother

"Old Mother Redcap" was the name given to Granny Sarah Smith, a witch who lived in seventeenth-century Sussex, England. She was one of many who were known by that name. It is said that the witches in Ireland placed little red caps on their heads before flying off on their broomsticks. This probably gave rise to the dubbing of many old wise women "Mother Redcap." Granny Smith became well known for her foretelling of the future. None of her predictions survived, but in her lifetime she was visited by many titled people because of her reputation as a **seeress.**

Reincarnation

The general belief with reincarnation is that the spirit or soul goes through a number of lives on Earth, each in a separate body. This is a belief held by Buddhists, Hindus, Wiccans, **Spiritualists,** and many others. It was a doctrine adopted by the Essenes, Pharisees, Karaites, and other Jewish and semi-Jewish groups. According to **Roman** writers, both the Gauls and the Druids subscribed to it, as did the Orphics and Pythagoreans. It was also a part of early Christian teachings until condemned by the Second Council of Constantinople in 553 CE. The Orphics of ancient **Greece** held the doctrine from the Pythagoreans that a soul returned in a number of incarnations, each time gaining in purity by living a good life. This would continue until there was total purity, at which time divinity would be achieved. This is similar to the belief held in Wicca. Witches hold that the spirit goes through a number of incarnations, learning and experiencing in each until all things have been absorbed. At that time, the spirit becomes at one with the gods. The progression has been likened to passing through the grades in a school, where certain curricula have to be observed in order to "graduate." Since the psycho-physical experience of a male is dissimilar to that of a female, then lives as both sexes must be experienced by the spirit in order to gain the full knowledge.

Author Rosemary Ellen Guiley suggests that approximately two-thirds of today's population "accepts some form of reincarnation or rebirth as a fundamental belief." Most schools of thought believe that the spirit returns to earth in the next life as a human being, though whether male or female may vary. Yet some—certain Hindu sects, for example—believe that the spirit may be reborn as an animal or plant. Some believe that this depends upon the life that was led prior to the return, which will bring rewards or punishments for a good life or a life of crime. In the Hindu and Buddhist doctrines the point of reincarnation is to return in other incarnations in order to expiate one's transgressions. In Witchcraft each individual life is not dependant upon the previous incarnation, as it is in the Hindu and Buddhist doctrines; each life is a separate experience with its own agenda. The **Celts** were so sure that they would return in another life that they would lend money on the promise of repayment in a future life. Sixteenth-century Buddhists believed that enemies of the faith would not achieve rebirth. The entity Dharmapalas was ever watchful to sever the roots of a nonbeliever's life with his axe, if necessary.

There is a belief among many that the rebirth takes place immediately. Tibetans, for example, believe the Dalai Lama to be an embodiment of Avalokitesvara, whose soul enters a child's body at the very moment of the Dalai Lama's death. However, others believe that some time elapses between , in many cases a large number of years.

Some people have memories of past lives. Others are able to induce such memories through methods such as hypnosis. Although it may be interesting to discover who you were in a previous lifetime, it should not be dwelled upon. Regardless of the status of the individual in that past life, it is what you make of yourself in this present life that is important.

There have been some amazing cases of children who have displayed memories of previous lives. One of the best-known and best-documented was the case of Shanti Devi, born in Delhi, India, in 1926. When only a few years old, she insisted that she had lived before in a city some hundred miles from her present home—though neither she nor her parents had ever left their native village. They traveled with a researcher to the distant town, where Shanti was able to identify her former husband and relatives, and even point out secret places where she had hidden things. The husband agreed that his wife had died in 1926, the year Shanti was born.

A more recent case of past-life memory is that of Romy Crees of Des Moines, Iowa. In the early 1980s, as a toddler, Romy spoke of her life as Joe Williams in Charles City, 120 miles away. She gave details of the red brick house in which he had lived and of the motorcycle accident that took his life. She gave Joe's mother's name as Louise Williams and said that she had a pain in her right leg. The Crees family decided to check out what young Romy was saying and contacted a well-known researcher named Hemendra Banerjee. Banerjee and a group of journalists went with them to Charles City, where they found the house and family, including the mother with the bad leg whose son had died in a motorcycle accident. Romy was also able to look at family photographs and name all the people in them.

Sources:

Buckland, Raymond. *Wicca for Life*. New York; Citadel, 2002.

Buckland, Raymond. *Doors to Other Worlds*. St. Paul, MN: Llewellyn, 1996.

Buckland, Raymond. *Buckland's Complete Book of Witchcraft*. St. Paul, MN: Llewellyn, 1986.

Ducasse, C .J. *A Critical Examination of the Belief in Life after Death*. London: C. C. Thomas, 1961.

Dupont, Ellen and Nance Fyson (eds.). *Quest for the Unknown: Life beyond Death*. Pleasantville, NY: Reader's Digest, 1992

Guiley, Rosemary Ellen. *Harper's Encyclopedia of Mystical & Paranormal Experience*. San Francisco: HarperSanFrancisco, 1991.

Holzer, Hans. *Born Again—The Truth about Reincarnation*. New York: Doubleday, 1970.

Kelsey, Denys & Joan Grant. *Many Lifetimes*. New York: Doubleday, 1967.

Litvag, Irving. *Singer in the Shadows*. Macmillan, 1972.

Lutoslawski, W. *Pre-Existence and Reincarnation*. London: Allen & Unwin, 1926.

REPTILES *see* Ophidiomancy

Retrocognition; Retrodiction

A better-known term is ***pre*cognition,** knowledge of an event *before* it happens. *Retro*cognition is knowledge of a past event *after* it happens, albeit when the person has no natural knowledge of the event. (In the same way, retrodiction is the opposite of **prediction.**) J. M. Robertson, in *Buckle & His Critics* (1895), said: "Let us first put a little order in our conception of prediction and 'retrodiction' as they indisputably take place in the settled sciences." And in **Frederic W. H. Myers**'s 1901 work *Human Personality* he said: "Our retrocognitions seem often a recovery of isolated fragments of thought and feeling." Myers suggested that by combining retrocognition with his theory of psychorrhagic diathesis, there was an explanation of hauntings.

Most people who exhibit the ability to be retrocognitive are also precognitive. They have the ability to focus on people and events from either the past or the future. The information is frequently obtained through **clairvoyance, clairaudience,** or **clairsentience. Psychometry** is another one of the main ways of working with retrocognition. By handling an object, the **medium** is able to tell about the past connections with that object, such as people and events that have come into contact with it.

One of the most famous cases of retrocognition was that of two Englishwomen who, on August 10, 1901, visited the Petit Trianon at Versailles, France. Annie E. Moberly and Eleanor M. Jourdain went through a side gate, just before getting to the main gate, and found themselves on a path that they followed, thinking it must lead to the main house. Instead, they found themselves back in the year 1770. In their perambulations, the women saw men in three-cornered hats, a woman with a large white hat, and others in the dress of the eighteenth century.

Sources:
Buckland, Raymond. *Doors to Other Worlds*. St. Paul, MN: Llewellyn, 1993.
Holroyd, Stuart. *The Supernatural: Minds Without Boundaries*. London: Aldus 1976.
Myers, Frederick W. H. *Human Personality and Its Survival of Bodily Death*. New York: University Books, 1961.
Oxford English Dictionary. Oxford: Clarendon Press, 1989.

RETRODICTION *see* **Retrocognition**

RETROMANCY

Retromancy is divining by interpreting the things seen when turning to look back over your shoulder. To turn suddenly that way is to bring into perspective people and things that were not in sight when looking forward. The positions and actions observed are then interpreted. Many times these include animals and birds, bringing in such allied methods as **ailuromancy, augury, and hippomancy.**

RHABDOMANCY

Rhabdomancy is from the **Greek** word for "rod" and is divining by means of sticks. It is an ancient practice that de Givry equates with Moses and the twelve rods, in the Tabernacle of Witness (Numbers 17). He also suggests that Psalms 125:3 refers to rhabdomancy rods. But while de Givry sees the rhabdomancy rod in all magic wands, as instruments of divination they seem to be more directly associated with the divining rods of the Middle Ages. Divining rods were used by the Greeks, **Romans,** Persians, and Scythians. Marco Polo found them in use throughout the Orient in the late thirteenth century. There is a bas relief in the Shantung Province of **China** showing Yu holding a forked instrument. He is described as a "master of the science of the earth and in those matters concerning water veins and springs."

Georg Agricola gave the first printed description of a divining rod in his book *De re metallica* (Basel, 1556). His interest was primarily with mining and in locating minerals, but the techniques he describes are the same as those used for water divining or water witching. A well-known illustration from his book shows a variety of men both digging and walking about with Y-shaped rods in their hands. One man is in the act of cutting a forked branch from a tree. In Sebastian Münster's *Cosmographia universalis* (Basel, 1544) there is another illustration of a man divining with a forked stick and a cross-section of the ground beneath him is shown, where miners are at work. S.E. Löhneyss's *Bericht vom Bergkwerck* (Zellerfeldt, 1617) contains an illustration similar to Geog Agricola's. It also shows the exploration of a mining area, with some men walking about holding forked sticks and others busy digging at marked areas.

Despite this flurry of rhabdomancy in Germany in the sixteenth and early seventeenth century, it was not until the end of the seventeenth century that France discovered the art. The first to champion the forked stick was Jacques Aymar, a Dauphiné peasant, who used the rod to discover a large number of underground mines, water, and even buried treasure beginning in 1692. He went on to also trace robbers and murderers for the Procureur du Roi at Lyons, using his rhabdomancy skills. However, the Church saw this not as a skill but as the work of the Devil. In his *Lettres qui découvrent l'illusion des philosophes sur la baquette, et qui détruisent leurs systèmes* (Paris, 1693), Père Lebrun attributed the power to demon elementals, as did Père Malebranche and Père Ménestrier in their works published that same year and the following year. Yet by the early part of the eighteenth century the Abbé de Vallemont was not only speaking out against the possibility of diabolical intervention, but was promoting the use of the diving rod. In his work *La Physique occulte ou traité de la baquette divinatoire* (Paris, 1725) he not only endorses the divining rod but details how to use it. Illustrations in his book show various ways of holding the rods. Along with the traditional forked stick, there is a straight length of wood with only a very small fork at the very end; two straight lengths, with the end of one forced into the end of the other; and a very long stick that is slightly bent by the hands of the operator.

Sources:

de Givry, Grillot. *A Pictorial Anthology of Witchcraft, Magic & Alchemy*. London: Spottiswoode, Ballantyne, 1931.

Shepard, Leslie A. (ed.). *Encyclopedia of Occultism & Parapsychology*. New York: Avon, 1978.

Rhapsodomancy

According to Ephraim Chambers's *Cyclopædia; or an universal dictionary of arts and sciences* of 1728, "Rhapsodomancy is an ancient kind of divination performed by pitching on a passage of a poem at hazard and reckoning on it as a **prediction** of what was to come to pass." The usual method was to close one's eyes, say a short prayer, then open the book of poetry at random, placing a finger on the page before opening the eyes. The verse being touched would relate to any question being asked, and it would give some indication of what the future held or what action needed to be taken. Some diviners would stick the passage with a pin or the tip of a dagger, rather than just with the finger.

Rhapsodomancy, then, is a variation on **bibliomancy** but rather than just any book being opened, it is the work of a poet. The volume is opened at random and the first verse seen is read. It is believed that the verse will have some relevance to the question being asked. The **Greeks** preferred to take from Homer's works, while the **Romans** favored Virgil.

Sources:

Oxford English Dictionary. Oxford: Clarendon Press, 1989.

Spence, Lewis. *An Encyclopedia of the Occult*. London: George Routledge & Sons, 1920.

Rhine, Dr. Joseph Banks (1895–1980)

Joseph B. Rhine was one of the pioneers of parapsychology. He was the cofounder of the Parapsychology Laboratory at Duke University in Durham, North Carolina.

Rhine was born on September 29, 1895, in Juniata County, Pennsylvania. In 1920 he married Louisa Ella Weckesser. Rhine studied at the University of Chicago, obtaining his B.S. in 1922, M.S. in 1923, and Ph.D. in 1925. He became instructor in

Dr. Joseph B. and Louisa Rhine, 1978. ***Dr. Susan Blackmore/Fortean Picture Library.***

philosophy and psychology at Duke University in 1928 and advanced from instructor to professor of psychology from 1929 to 1949. He was the director of the Parapsychology Laboratory beginning in 1935.

His interest in parapsychology developed after Rhine investigated **spiritualist mediumship** with Dr. Walter Franklin Prince, at Harvard University in 1926. The following year he went on to Duke University and studied psychic phenomena with Dr. William McDougall. Encouraged by McDougall, Rhine set up a program for the statistical validation of **extrasensory perception** (ESP), with emphasis initially on **clairvoyance** and telepathy using the **Zener** deck of test cards. He later also investigated psychokinesis (PK), originally known as telekinesis (TK)

In 1934 Rhine's *Extrasensory Perception* was published by the Boston Society for Psychic Research. From 1937 onward he published the *Journal of Parapsychology* at Duke. In 1960 Rhine established the Psychical Research Foundation as an independent center to study phenomena relating to the survival of human personality after death. It was sponsored largely by Charles E. Ozanne. Chester F. Carlson, the inventor of xerography, sponsored the Foundation for Research on the Nature of Man, founded in 1962.

Among Rhine's notable books were *New Frontiers of the Mind* (1937), *The Reach of the Mind* (1947), *New World of the Mind* (1953), *Parapsychology, Frontier Science of the Mind* (with J. G. Pratt, 1957), *Parapsychology Today* (1968), and *Progress in Parapsychology* (1971).

Sources:

Cavendish, Richard (ed.). *Encyclopedia of the Unexplained.* London: Routledge & Kegan Paul, 1974.

Orbis Publishing. *Mysteries of Mind, Space & Time: The Unexplained.* Westport, CT: H. S. Stuttman, 1992.

Rhine, Joseph Banks. *New Frontiers of the Mind.* New York: Farrar & Rinehart, 1937.

Rhine, Joseph Banks. *New World of the Mind.* New York: William Sloane, 1953.

Rhine, Louisa. *E.S.P. in Life and Lab.* New York: Macmillan, 1967.

Shepard, Leslie A. (ed.). *Encyclopedia of Occultism & Parapsychology.* New York: Avon, 1978.

RING *see* Dactyliomancy

ROBERTSON, MORGAN ANDREW (1861–1915)

Morgan Robertson was a writer who authored a book titled *The Wreck of the Titan.* The story told how a huge, luxurious ocean liner—hailed as the safest in the world—set out on a voyage across the Atlantic between Southampton and New York. Partway across, the ship hit an iceberg, foundered, and sank with most of her 2,500 passengers lost. The *S.S. Titan* was a 66,000-ton ship but carried only twenty-four lifeboats, sufficient for fewer than half her passengers. The date of the *Titan's* departure from Southampton was April 1898.

Fourteen years later, on April 14, 1912, the 60,250-ton, supposedly unsinkable, White Star liner *R.M.S. Titanic,* traveling on her maiden voyage from Southampton to New York, hit an iceberg, foundered and sank with 1,513 lives lost. The *Titanic* carried only twenty lifeboats, sufficient for only half her passengers. Robertson's book has subsequently been referred to as "the most outstanding instance of **prophecy**" in the nineteenth or twentieth centuries.

Robertson was born in Oswego, New York, to Andrew and Ruth Amelia (*née* Glassford) Robertson. His father was a ship's captain on the Great Lakes. Morgan joined the Merchant Marine Service and, by 1886, had attained the rank of First Mate. He then left the service and became a jeweler in New York, though poor eyesight later forced him to give up that trade. Inspired by a Rudyard Kipling story, Robertson tried his hand at writing. He sold his first story two months after writing it, and he went on to write more than 200 more. He also authored fourteen books between 1896 and 1915.

One of his later books—*Beyond the Spectrum*—chronicles events leading up to and during World War II; even staging a war between the United States and Japan. Although written when airplanes were still frail, one-man craft, Robertson wrote of aircraft that carried "sun bombs" that were so powerful that with one brilliant flash of blinding light, one single bomb could destroy an entire city. The war in his story started in the month of December, when in 1941 the Japanese staged a sneak attack on Pearl Harbor, Hawaii.

SIMILARITIES BETWEEN ROBERTSON'S *TITAN* AND THE *TITANIC*

	TITAN	*TITANIC*
Registration:	British	British
Displacement:	66,000 tons	60,250 tons
Length:	800 feet	882 feet
Top speed:	24 knots	24 knots
Number of propellers:	3	3
Watertight bulkheads:	19	15
Capacity:	3,000	3,000
Passengers on board:	2,000	2,200
Number of lifeboats:	24	20
Damaged area:	Starboard, forward	Starboard, forward
Month of disaster:	April	April
Year of disaster:	1898	1912

Sources:

Hall, Angus. *The Supernatural: Signs of Things to Come*. London: Danbury Press, 1975.
Lord, Walter. *A Night to Remember*. New York: Henry Holt, 1956.
http://members.tripod.com/~rhazz/frobertson.html.

ROME

The ancient Romans were steeped in magical practice and superstition. They had many deities of their own but did not hesitate to adopt deities from other nations if they thought their powers would serve Rome. They incorporated into their own pantheon gods and goddesses of the **Egyptians, Greeks,** Persians, **Etruscans,** and Sabines, plus those of various indigenous tribes. Along with the gods, numerous **spirits** were honored with rites and rituals. Sacrifices were made, including human ones. Magical rites were innumerable; festivals and sacred banquets were packed into the calendar throughout the year.

A major part of Roman religious practice was divination. Circa 300 BCE a large priestly college was established by either Numa or Romulus, with three priest-**augurs.** By the time of Sulla the number had been increased to fifteen augurs and in the time of Julius Caesar there were sixteen. The augurs wore a uniform toga, known as the *trabea*, which had scarlet stripes and a purple border. Since their pronouncements were unchallengeable, the augurs developed great political power. An augur would travel with armies and fleets and would interpret the flight of **birds** to gain knowledge of coming events before battle was enjoined.

When doing a reading, the augur was accompanied by a magistrate who would verify the results. The magistrate was also the one who was officially entitled to ask the deities for signs. Rather than actually trying to see the future, the object was to ascertain whether or not the deities approved or disapproved of the course of action queried.

There was a book that contained augural ritual, together with a collection of answers to questions that had previously been given to the college of the senate. The augur always announced his finding with a specific set of words, which were duly recorded by the magistrate. The complexity of interpretation of phenomena grew by degrees until it finally became so complex it was unmanageable, and the Roman college had to be abandoned.

Chaldean astrologers were much sought after in ancient Rome, as were **numerologists** and **soothsayers.** Most noble houses had their own astrologers. **Dreams** and their interpretation were considered especially important. There are many instances on record of prophetic dreams. There was recognition of what is today termed **astral projection,** the Romans believing that dreams were the souls of individuals visiting one another during sleep. There was also a belief that the spirits of the dead could return to Earth through dreams.

Pliny the Elder wrote that "The art of magic . . . has brought in the arts of astrology and divination. For everyone desires to know what is to come to him and believes that certainty can be gained by consulting the stars."

Sources:

Encyclopedia Britannica. Chicago: William Benton, 1964.
Hamilton, Edith. *The Roman Way to Western Civilization*. New York: W. W. Norton, 1932.
Leach, Maria (ed.). *Funk & Wagnalls Standard Dictionary of Folklore, Mythology, and Legend*. San Francisco: Harper & Row, 1949.
Rose, H .J. *Religion in Greece and Rome*. New York: Harper & Row, 1959.

ROOSTER *see* Alectromancy

ROSE LEAVES *see* Phyllorhodomancy

Roses

To **dream** of red roses indicated coming success in love. To dream of white roses was unlucky. An old English custom was for a young woman to pick a rosebud on Midsummer Day and to wrap it in white tissue paper, keeping it safe till Christmas Day. Then she was to unwrap it and, if it was still fresh, she should wear it to church. There her husband-to-be would approach her and take the rosebud from her. If, when the bud had been unwrapped, it was withered, then that was a bad omen meaning that she would not marry during the coming year.

Runemal

The art of **rune** casting for divination purposes.

Runes

Runes are an ancient form of writing. The oldest extant decipherable runic writings, whose origins are not at all certain, were discovered at the bogs of southwestern Den-

Dreaming of white roses is considered unlucky. *Janet and Colin Bord/Fortean Picture Library.*

mark at Vi-mose in Fyn, dating from the middle of the third century. The word means "mystery" or "secret" in early English. It stems from the old Low German word *raunen*, "to cut" or "to carve," since runes were carved into wood and cut into stone.

Mythologically, runes were discovered by Odin (known to the Anglo-Saxons as Woden), the All-Father and leader of the Norse deities. Learning and wisdom were among his gifts. Once, as a sacrifice, he hung from the World Tree **Yggdrasil** for nine days and nights, pierced with a spear. At the end of that time he was able to bend down and lift up the magical runes, which brought secret knowledge to humankind. (This experience of Odin's was much like the visionary experiences of death and resurrection endured by **shamans** in various parts of the world as part of their initiation and preliminary to achieving powers of **prophecy.**) From the *Verse Edda* comes *Hávamál*, or "The Words of the High One (Odin)," which describes the event:

> I'm aware that I hung on the windy tree,
> Swung there nights all of nine;
> Gashed with a blade
> Bloodied for Odin,
> Myself an offering to myself:
> Knotted to that tree
> No man knows
> Whither the roots of it run.
> None gave me bread,
> None gave me drink.
> Down to the deepest depths I peered
> To snatch up Runes
> With a roaring screech,
> And fall in a dizzied faint!
> Well-being I won
> And wisdom too;
> I grew and took joy in my growth:
> From a word to a word
> I was led to a word,
> From a deed to another deed."

The *Verse Edda* was a collection of ancient poems by unknown authors. It is one of two literary works known as the *Eddas*. The other is the *Prose Edda*, which is a storybook of Norse myth together with a poet's handbook written by Icelander Snorri Sturluson (d. 1241 CE).

Runic was never a strictly utilitarian form of writing, and there are many variations of it to be found in different areas. Originally the runes consisted of twenty-four letters, though within Anglo-Saxon the runic characters vary in number from twenty-eight to thirty-three. Popular variations of Anglo-Saxon runes are *Ruthwell*, *Thames*, and *Vienna*. There are also Germanic runes (with variations), Danish runes, and Swedish-Norse runes. Runic writing was in use from the third century CE until relatively modern times, in remote areas of Sweden such as Dalarna and Härjedalen.

FUTHORC is the acronym for the first six characters of the Anglo-Saxon runic alphabet: feoh, ur, thorn, os, rad, cæn. The all-Germanic staves are known as "futhark" (again from the first six letters). By the third century runic writing had spread into Norway and was used to carve inscriptions onto stone monuments. By the fifth century the writing was found in England, where it flourished for five centuries, the entire Anglo-Saxon period. There it developed as a stave of twenty-eight letters, though by the ninth century these had increased to thirty-three. The best preserved example of runes in England is found on the whalebone-crafted Frank's Casket, which dates from about 650 CE. Runes, together with illustrations, cover the sides of the casket and the lid.

Runes were not simply a form of writing. The individual runes would be studied and interpreted for divination purposes. As Ralph Elliot said, "Communication . . . remained a secondary function of runic writing throughout its long history, much more common was the use of runes to invoke higher powers to affect and influence the lives and fortunes of men." In Teutonic times the main workers of magic and of divination were women. The Teutonic, or "Germanic," nations embraced the peoples of High and Low German speech, Dutch speech, Danes, and Scandinavians. There is a seventeenth-century illustration from *A Copendious History of the Goths, Swedes, and Vandals* (1658) by Olaus Magnus showing two women, one young man, and one old man holding large, elaborate, handled runesticks—long, flat sticks with various runic characters engraved along their length. There is no explanation given as to how these runesticks were used.

Individual runes, such as those on these stones, have been studied and interpreted for divination purposes. *Fortean Picture Library.*

The first runic character, *feoh*, is said to picture the head and horns of an ox and is named after that animal. The second letter, *ür*, is named after the bull; the third, *thorn*, after a **tree;** *ós*, a door; *rád*, a saddle; *cæn*, a torch; and so on. All are so named because, at some time, it was felt that the shape of the letter bore some small resemblances to these objects (or it may have been that they had evolved from some earlier purely pictorial system of writing). In modern times the runes have been adopted by a wide variety of occult groups and individuals, both as a form of ritual writing and also for divination purposes, with rune **cards** and rune tablets being produced commercially.

The runes themselves can be made from a wide variety of substances. One popular method is to cut small squares of wood and to burn the runes onto each one with a wood-burning tool. Similarly, a suitably sized tree branch can be sliced into a number of discs and the runes carved into them. Some people collect or buy flat pebbles and paint on the runes. Runes may be carved into clay tablets and fired in a kiln. They can also be etched or engraved into metal and mounted on small wooden tiles.

The number of runes produced depends on the method of divination to be followed. Most runes used for divination are based on the twenty-four original Teutonic runes. These were divided into three groups of eight runes, each group known as an *ætt* or *ættir* (Sandinavian meaning "number of eight"). They are comprised of Freyr's or Freya's Eight, Hagal's Eight, and Tiw's Eight. There is usually a blank rune added to these to give a total of twenty-five. Freya was the daughter of Njord and the sister of Frey. She was the goddess of love and beauty. Hagal was a minor deity about whom very little is known, though these eight runes are always attributed to Hagal. Tiw, Tyr, Tiuz, or Ziu was a sky god often identified with the Roman Mars.

The runes, their names (Anglo-Saxon names given), and meanings (various meanings are attributed to the runes, depending upon what book you consult), are as follows:

Freyr's Ættir

Name	Meanings
feh	money; goods; cattle; the price to pay; success and happiness
úr	auroch (European bison); obstacles; ox, strength, manhood; good fortune if no risks are taken
thorn	thorn; giant, great spirit; petty annoyances; take no risks
ós	god; something important to be said; be wary
rád	ride; saddle, a journey; long overdue change; be prudently adventurous
cán	torch; torch fire, a protection; listen to the inner voice; grasp available opportunities
geofu	gift; sacrifice; take others' advice
wynn	joy; happiness; separateness; be grateful for what you already have

Hagal's Ættir

hœgl	hail; natural forces that damage; someone else's battle; events are beyond your control
níed	need; constraint, necessity; needs may not be met; problems ahead
ís	ice; that which cools or impedes; no movement; no hasty actions
géar	year; harvest; time of natural change; be patient
éoh	yew tree; avertive powers, the hunting god; limitations; stay calm
peor_	elder tree; secret or hidden thing; roots of a mystery; take no chances and you may be lucky
eolhs	an elk, a sedge or rush, defense, protection; inspiration, health and safety; be decisive
sygil	sun; life force; good luck, time for a change; relax and be calm

Tiw's Ættir

tír	honor; time to get things moving; take action
beorc	birch; fertility growth; birch twig; formation of close relationships; take the long-term view
eoh	horse; transport, moving; assistance needed; be very prudent
man	human being; a man; strengths and weaknesses; avoid stress
lagu	water, sea; fluidity, conduction; trust feelings; things are not what they seem
Ing	a hero; the god of fertility; rune of withdrawal, fertility and marriage; be flexible
é_el	inheritance; property; practical issues to sort out; be patient, unselfish, and active
dœg	day; light, fruitfulness, prosperity; on the right path; make haste slowly

Most of the runes can have a different meaning if seen reversed (some few look the same whether upright or reversed). These are as follows:

Freyr's Ættir

Name	Reversed Meanings
feh	love frustrated; absence of initiative
úr	a chance missed; weakness
thorn	regret a hasty decision; disruptive opposition
ós	an elderly person who will prove to be a nuisance; ignorance or lack of inspiration
rád	traveling that will interfere with plans; error in judgment
cán	loss or misplacement of something valued or of a friendship; self-imposed ignorance
geofu	
wynn	be careful in business matters for three days; conflict and disharmony

Hagal's Ættir

hœgl	
níed	
ís	
géar	
éoh	
peor_	Too high expectation that will be disappointed; presence of negativity
eolhs	don't get involved with people who will use you; vulnerable and unprotected situation
sygil	

Tiw's Ættir

tír	don't trust him or her; they won't stay long; falsehood and double standards
beorc	worrying news concerning a relative; obstructions
eoh	journey by sea; disharmony, quarrels
man	an enemy - the next rune will tell how to handle it; alienation, underachievement
lagu	keep within your limits; insensitivity, lack of feeling
Ing	
é_el	beware mechanical devices; possible accident or damage; poverty, insecure circumstances

For divination purposes, to these twenty-four runes may be added a twenty-fifth that is blank on both sides. It can have various meanings, such as an indication that the question needs to be rephrased, that the forces at work are changing too quickly at present to give a definite answer, or that the answer is simply unknowable at the present time. It can also be used as a significator, in the manner of a **tarot** card, if you are throwing the runes for someone else. In the latter case it would be picked out and laid down ahead of any that were to be thrown.

No one knows exactly what each of the runes meant originally; those shamanistic meanings have been lost in time. For this reason the above meanings, and any others found in the many books on runes, are the meanings attributed by various authors. If you wish to work extensively with runes, it is a good idea to take each individual runic character and spend time meditating upon it in order to find what it means to you personally. Then stick with those interpretations.

The runes may be cast anywhere: onto the ground, a table, or a prepared surface. Some feel that it should be a prepared surface, since the runes may be viewed as sacred and as "voices of the gods." Such a prepared surface may be no more than a piece of cloth kept especially for the purpose, or it can be a richly tooled piece of leather or a decorated wooden board. The surface is traditionally referred to as the "field" for the runes. Some rune-casters will draw three concentric circles on the field, or in some other way divide it into three areas. Again, different specifications are found for these three areas. One possibility is: center—the inner self; second—influences; outer—future events. Another is: center—being; second—thinking; outer—doing. Other rune-casters do not draw anything but simply throw down the runes on the field.

The runes are usually kept in a drawstring bag. It is possible to shake up the runes inside and then to reach in and draw out any specific number for a random casting. Some of the popular castings are as follows:

Odin's Rune: Many people do this to start the day, or when they reach a point of needing an indicator of where or how to proceed. The method is simply to reach into the rune pouch and, while concentrating on any problem, to stir up the runes and then pull out just one. This is "Odin's Rune," and is an indicator of where your path lies. Another method is to spread all the runes on the field, face down, and then to pass your hands lightly over the backs of them until one in particular draws you. This one is turned over as "Odin's Rune." (A further suggestion is to again draw one rune at the end of the day, and to see how it compares to the first one drawn.)

Three-Rune Spread: Three has always been a "magical" number. It is associated with the three aspects of the Goddess, with the three Fates, the Three Graces, the **Egyptian** and Christian Trinity, and many other people and things. Tacitus, in his *Germania*, mentions that runes were removed three at a time and interpreted, in the divination practice known as **"Virgilian lots."** Drawing three runes from the bag (or turning over three from the full set laid face down), they can be interpreted in a variety of ways, such as: 1—past, 2—present, 3—future; 1—present situation, 2—suggested course of action, 3—new situation evolving; 1—you as you perceive yourself, 2—problem, whether recognized or not, 3—goal to aim for, to overcome problem.

Other Spreads: Five-rune spreads, seven-rune spreads, etc., can all be used. Any of the spreads used for tarot reading can be adapted for runes. So, also, can the layout of an **astrological** chart by placing a randomly selected rune in each of the twelve houses.

Sources:

Blum, Ralph H. *The Book of Runes*. New York: St. Martin's, 1982.
Branston, Brian. *The Lost Gods of England*. London: Thames & Hudson, 1957.
Branston, Brian. *Gods of the North*. London: Thames & Hudson, 1980.
Buckland, Raymond. *The Tree: The Complete Book of Saxon Witchcraft*. New York: Samuel Weiser, 1974.
Buckland, Raymond. *Signs, Symbols & Omens*. St. Paul, MN: Llewellyn, 2003.

Davidson, Hilda Roderick Ellis. *Scandinavian Mythology*. London: Paul Hamlyn, 1969.
Elliott, Ralph W. V. *Runes: An Introduction*. Manchester, UK: Manchester University Press 1959.
Encyclopedia Britannica. Chicago: William Benton, 1964.
Jackson, Nigel and Silver RavenWolf. *The Rune Mysteries*. St. Paul, MN: Llewellyn, 1996.

S

SACRIFICES *see* **Hieromancy**

SAINT MALACHY *see* **O'Morgair, Malachy**

SALT *see* **Halomancy**

Saxon Wands

A form of divination found in Saxon Witchcraft. It uses seven wands, or lengths of wood (these can be cut from doweling). Three of the wands are nine inches long, and four are twelve inches long. One of the twelve-inch wands is marked as the "Witan" wand. This can be done with **runes** or with any form of decoration.

To use the Saxon Wands, the diviner kneels and lays the Witan wand on the ground in front of him or her, laying it across pointing left and right. The remaining six wands are held out, between both hands, over the Witan wand. With eyes closed, and concentrating on the question to be asked, the wands are mixed together before being grasped in the right hand. The left hand now takes the tip of one of the wands and holds on to it as the right hand is opened and the wands are allowed to fall.

Upon opening the eyes, it will be seen how the wands have fallen. They are interpreted in this way:

1: If there are more long wands than short on the ground, then the answer to the question is in the affirmative.

2: If there are more short wands than long on the ground (excluding the Witan wand), then the answer is in the negative.

3: If any wand(s) touch the Witan wand, the answer to the question is a very definite one, with strong forces at work.

4: If any wand(s) are off the ground, resting on others, then circumstances are such (with forces still working) that no definite answer can be obtained at this time—regardless of (1) or (2) above.

5: If all of the wands point toward the Witan wand, then the person asking the question (or for whom the question is being asked) will have a definite role to play in the determination of the question and answer.

6: If none of the wands point toward the Witan wand, then the matter will be determined without the querier's interference.

In *Celtic Researches* (1804) Edward Davies describes how Druids use what were known as "omen sticks" or "omen wands" (*cœlbreni*) for casting lots. The future was divined by the way in which the wands fell to the ground and how they landed.

Sources:

Buckland, Raymond. *The Tree: Complete Book of Saxon Witchcraft*. New York: Samuel Weiser, 1974.
Davies, Edward. *Celtic Researches*. London: Davies, 1804.

SEA SHELLS *see* Conchomancy

Scandinavia

There was much divination and *prophecy* in Scandinavia. Prophetic utterance was usually induced by *ekstasis*, or ecstasy. There were professional diviners, known as *völva*, but there were also many ordinary people who were occasional **seers.** Anyone under stress, and particularly if near death, might become "fey" and start speaking of things they normally knew nothing about.

In Scandinavian mythology there is a trio of women known as the Norns, who appear as prophetesses at the birth of children. They are similar to the **Greek** *Moirai* and are named Urd (Fate), Verdandi (Being), and Skuld (Necessity). They were usually represented in the temples as three women seated together. They are said to spin or weave the destiny of men. They dwell beside the "Spring of Fate" alongside the World **Tree** of Life; the ash tree **Yggdrasil.** The Danish historian Saxo Grammaticus (twelfth century) tells a famous story of a king of the Danes who took his three-year-old son into a temple to pray to the three maidens, who prophesied about the boy's future.

The deities Freyr and Freyja were the twin children of Nörd, the god associated with fertility and with the sea. They belonged to a group known as the *Vanir*, the deities of fertility (distinguished from the *Aesir* group to which Odin and Thor belonged). People turned to the Vanir for help in divination. Freyja is especially linked to a particular divination rite; the rite of *seidr*. This was performed by a völva. She sat on a high platform, singing and chanting until she went into trance. She was then able to answer questions put to her about the future. The völva specialized in the destinies of children and questions about the coming season.

Sources:

Davidson, Hilda Roderick Ellis. *Scandinavian Mythology*. London: Paul Hamlyn, 1969.

Davidson, Hilda Roderick Ellis. *Man, Myth & Magic: Freyr, Freyja, Frigg*. London: BPC Publishing, 1970.
Spence, Lewis. *An Encyclopedia of the Occult*. London: George Routledge & Sons, 1920.

SCAPULIMANCY; SCAPULOMANCY

(See also Omoplatoscopy)

An ancient form of divination that was done by interpreting the cracks and marks found on an animal's shoulder blade. In the Highlands of **Scotland** it was known as *slinneineachd*. J. G. D. Clark, in *World Prehistory* (1961), said "It will be recalled that the practice of scapulomancy . . . can be traced back to the 'Neolithic' Lung-shan culture." William MacLeod, writing under the pseudonym of "Theophilus Insulanus," in his work *A Treatise on the* ***Second Sight, Dreams*** *and Apparitions* (1763), refers to scapulomancy as "another kind of divination, whereby, on looking into the shoulder-blade of a sheep, goat, etc., as in a book, some skilful in that occult science pretend to read future events." The practice was common in both England and Ireland in the twelfth century. Giraldus Cambrensis (1146–1223), archdeacon of Brecon, relates that it was also a common practice in Wales in the thirteenth century. He wrote that the bone usually used was the right shoulder blade of a ram, boiled not roasted.

Important events were foretold in the life of the owner of a slaughtered animal based on marks on the animal's shoulder blade bones. The right blade bone of a black pig or sheep was considered the most suitable for the purpose. It was thoroughly boiled so that it was completely clear of flesh, though great care was taken not to scratch it or mar it in any way. The bone was then divided into areas corresponding to the natural features of the geographical area where the divination was taking place. According to Spence: "The largest hole or indentation (in the bone) symbolized the grave of the beast's owner, and from its position the problem of whether he should survive the current year, or otherwise, was resolved. If it lay near the side of the bone, the omen was fatal, but if in its centre, prosperity was indicated."

On the night of the treacherous massacre of Glencoe, Scotland (February 12, 1692), some MacDonalds were examining the shoulder blade of a sheep that had been prepared for feeding the government troops who had been billeted with them. (These troops later suddenly attacked the MacDonalds, on the orders of Sir John Dalrymple, master of Stair.) One of those studying the shoulder blade said that there would be a great shedding of blood in the glen. Sensing some kind of treason, they hastily departed and so were saved from the great massacre that soon took place.

Sources:

Campbell, John Gregorson. *Witchcraft and Second Sight in the Highlands and Islands of Scotland*. Glasgow: James MacLehose, 1902.
Clark, John Grahame Douglas. *World Prehistory*. Cambridge, UK: Cambridge University Press, 1961.
MacLeod, William ("Theophilus Insulanus"). *A Treatise on the Second Sight, Dreams and Apparitions*. Edinburgh: Ruddimans, Auld and Co., 1763.
Spence, Lewis. *The Magic Arts in Celtic Britain*. London: Rider, 1945.

Scatomancy; Scatoscopy

(See also Stercomancy)

Divination based on the examination of feces. James Sanford, in *Agrippa's of the vanitie and uncertaintie of artes and sciences* of 1569, said: "For this cause Scatomancie, **Oromancie, Drymimancie,** be called the divinations or Prognostications of Physicians, gathered by odors and urines." The odor of feces certainly played a part in its interpretation; it was a pointer to its age, for example. Consistency also played a part, as did the location of the feces. The feces was also examined for its contents: seeds, nuts, etc., which might have significance.

Sources:

Oxford English Dictionary. Oxford: Clarendon Press, 1989.

Schematomancy

A form of divination whereby a person's history may be inferred from their form and appearance. The modern observances of "body language" could play a large part in this. The *Encyclopædia metropolitana* of 1826 says that schematomancy was a form of divination used among the Arabs.

Sources:

Oxford English Dictionary. Oxford: Clarendon Press, 1989.

Sciomancy

This form of divination is based on evoking **astral** bodies, or ghosts, to divine the future. Henry Cockeram, in his *The English dictionarie, or an interpreter of hard English words* of 1623, says sciomancy is "divination by shadows," using "shadows" in the sense of "ghosts." In Sir Thomas Urquhart's *The Third Book of the Works of Mr. Francis Rabelais* (London, 1693) he says: "If you be afraid of the Dead . . . I will make use of the Faculty of Sciomancy." It would seem, then, that sciomancy is related to **necromancy** but does not use actual dead bodies. In effect it is a form of **spiritualism,** with the **seer** working as a **medium** and causing departed spirits to materialize.

Sources:

Grand Orient (A. E. Waite). *The Complete Manual of Occult Divination: Volume 1—Manual of Cartomancy*. London: Rider, 1912.

Oxford English Dictionary. Oxford: Clarendon Press, 1989.

Scotland

Scotland has long been considered a home of people with "the **second sight"** (*an da shealladh*)—the ability to see the future. The shepherds of the Hebrides are those recognized as most gifted, though it is known all over the country. It is a gift looked upon with mixed feelings; some accept it, and even use it, while others wish they never had it. It is frequently, though not always, hereditary.

The most famous Scot with second sight was undoubtedly Kenneth Mackenzie, known as the "**Brahan Seer.**" He was born at the beginning of the seventeenth century on the Isle of Lewis, at Baile-na-Cille in the parish of Uig, and was a laborer on the Brahan estate. Kenneth came to be regarded as the greatest of all Highland **seers.**

The forms of visions seen by seers vary. The figures of living persons who are so seen are called *taibhs*. How the visionary person is dressed would give some indication of what fate might befall them: if dressed in everyday clothing then death will not be in the offing, but if dressed in funeral clothes than the person will die soon. If the death clothes cover the whole face then death is imminent. Also, when the feet are covered death is imminent.

The time of day at which a vision appears is also important; the later in the day, the sooner the death. If, however, the vision is seen in the early morning, then death is a long way off. If the person seen is destined to drown at sea, the figure would be seen surrounded by phosphorescent dots, as seen on summer nights in the Hebridean seas.

Not all visions are death related. Some are of future spouses, friends away from home, or of coming events (as in the case of the Brahan Seer). Several seers have reported seeing their future spouses, often sitting opposite them in front of a fireplace. Although not all had any intentions of marriage at the time of the sightings, invariably the eventual spouse turned out to be the one seen in the vision.

One traditional belief in the Scottish Highlands is that it is unlucky to hear the first cuckoo of the season before breakfast. Birds and their actions are carefully studied by all. "Raven knowledge" is the term used for wisdom of the **birds;** whether ravens and other varieties. John Toland, in his *A Critical History of the* ***Celtic*** *Religion and Learning: Containing an Account of the Druids* (Edinburgh, 1815), relates how he met two businessmen at the village of Finglass in 1697, who assured him their business would prosper because they had spotted a raven, with two white feathers in its plumage, on the road they were to travel. They had refused to move until they observed in which direction the bird flew. Since it flew southward, they felt assured of success.

A strange method of divination once practiced in the north of Scotland was the "swimming of names in water." It was used in cases of theft to find the culprit. The names of all the suspects were written on pieces of paper and dropped into a bowl of water. Whichever name sank was the guilty party. Classical Celtic accounts indicate that islands were considered gateways to the Otherworld, the world beyond ours that harbors the dead and all spiritual beings. Of the islands of Scotland, Iona is probably the most revered. It has many Celtic and Druidic connections. Legend has it that a witch lived on Iona in the second century, during the reign of Natholocus. The king was troubled by a rebellion and sent one of his captains to ask the witch of the outcome. The witch reported that the king would soon be killed, not by an enemy but by a trusted friend. When the captain asked for the name of the potential assassin, she gave his own name. After due reflection on what was likely to be the king's reaction to him bringing this news (perhaps kill him, to prevent any fulfillment of the witch's prophesy), the captain did indeed kill the king.

There were Druidic colleges on many of the western islands of Scotland and England. The island of Skye held a warrior college where the warrior queen Scathach taught her arts. The Fortunate Isles were ruled over by the priestess of the goddess Morgen, who held all arts and sciences in the control of herself and her Nine Sisters. In the churchyard at Trumpan, on the Isle of Skye, stands a stone with a hole in it. It is said that if a person closes their eyes and then successfully inserts a finger into the stone's hole at the first attempt, they will be blessed and die peacefully.

During Scotland's Middle Ages, a divination cake was baked when a person was sick. It was then left at a sacred place such as a well or fairy mound. If the cake disappeared during the night, the sick person would recover. But if the cake remained, untouched, the person would die. Seers were often wrapped up in the skin of a sacrificed bull and left lying beside a river all night. During the night various spirits would visit them from the Otherworld and could be questioned about the future.

Many people in both the Highlands and the Lowlands occasionally—perhaps only once or twice in their lifetime—"know" when someone is going to die. There have been innumerable instances of comments made about a coming death that have been later verified. Most of these people simply accept the gift of prophesy.

Sources:

Buckland, Raymond. *Scottish Witchcraft*. St. Paul, MN: Llewellyn, 1992.
Campbell, John Gregorson. *Witchcraft and Second Sight in the Highlands and Islands of Scotland*. Glasgow: James MacLehose, 1902.
Mackenzie, Alexander. *The Prophesies of the Brahan Seer*. Inverness, 1882.
Stewart, Bob, and John Matthews. *Legendary Britain*. London: Blandford, 1989.

Scrying; Skrying

(See also Crystallomancy; Cylicomancy)

The word scrying means "seeing"—in particular, seeing the future. Although many think of scrying in connection with crystal-gazing, it is a practice that can utilize any reflective surface. The Hindus and others use a blot of ink poured into the hand of a young boy (see below). Precious stones are occasionally employed, especially pale green beryl. The **Maya** of Central America used polished stones. Witches will utilize a highly polished copper disc.

Among the frescoes decorating the walls of the Villa of Mysteries at Pompeii, Italy, there is a scene of an initiate gazing into a concave polished copper or silver bowl. Behind her, a priest holds up a mask of Dionysus to trigger the series of scenes sparking a ritual palingenesis. Mirrors are popular for scrying, black mirrors in particular. The very first form of mirror was the reflection of a pool, pond, or small body of water. This is still good for scrying.

One of the most famous **seers** was **Dr. John Dee** (1527–1608), English mathematician, alchemist, and astrologer to England's Queen Elizabeth I. His assistant, **Edward Kelley,** was skilled at scrying and used either a perfect crystal or obsidian, the black volcanic glass. Known by Dee and Kelley as their "speculum," their scrying instrument is now preserved in the British Museum. A drawing by Leonardo da Vinci (now in the Library of Christ Church, Oxford, England) shows a woman holding up a mirror to a seeress so that she may scry as part of a ritual. In the mirror can be seen the face of an old man.

Seer using a scrying glass, or speculum, with a deep and dark reflective surface. *Fortean Picture Library.*

According to the ancient *grimoires*, or books of magic, it was necessary for the practitioner to fast for a period before using the scrying tool. This fast, the books say, should be for anywhere from twenty-four hours to three days. The magician should then make frequent ablutions and subject him- or herself to strict religious discipline. During the invocation before scrying, the operator should face the east and summon from the crystal or other gazing surface the spirit to whom he or she wished to speak. All this was done within the complicated ritual circle of **ceremonial magic.**

In fact none of the above is necessary. To successfully scry it is important to have the right attitude of mind and to be in the right mood, but elaborate ritual is unnecessary. You should have absolute silence, if possible, so that you are not distracted by sounds. You should do a series of deep-breathing exercises before starting to help calm your body and mind. Then you should relax and gaze into the scrying tool without straining. There is no need to try to remain unblinking; just blink as and when necessary. A comfortable seat will help as, for many, will the burning of incense. Incense seems to help establish the right atmosphere for the practice.

If some particular information is sought from the scrying—where a person is at that time, or what is happening in some area—then the question should be the object of concentration for a few moments before starting the scrying. Then put the question out of your mind and begin scrying with a completely open mind, allowing anything that may to come into the picture.

E. W. Lane, in his book *An Account of the Manners & Customs of the Modern Egyptians* (1856), gives a story of scrying he experienced in Egypt. He says that the "magician" burned incense and wrote invocations to his various familiar spirits on slips of paper. He then burned one of the slips with the incense. As he did so, he took hold of the right hand of a young boy who had not yet reached puberty. On the boy's palm he drew a square, with various mystical sigils inside it, and on its center poured a little black ink. The boy then looked into the blot of ink and described what he saw. As a test, Lane asked him to see Lord Horatio Nelson, of whom the boy had never heard. The boy described the admiral exactly, even to the empty sleeve of his tunic being fastened across his chest.

Sources:

Besterman, T. *Crystal-Gazing*. London: Rider, 1924.
Buckland, Raymond. *Buckland's Complete Book of Witchcraft*. St. Paul, MN: Llewellyn, 1986.
Lane, E. W. *An Account of the Manners & Customs of the Modern Egyptians*. London: C. Knight, 1856.
Melville, J. *Crystal Gazing*. New York: Samuel Weiser, 1970.
Spence, Lewis. *An Encyclopedia of the Occult*. London: George Routledge & Sons, 1920.

SÉANCES

The meaning of the word séance is "sitting." A séance is a sitting together of a group of people for an occult or metaphysical experiment. The people attending a séance are referred to as "sitters." Such a gathering can be of any size, though a group of six or eight people is most common. They usually sit with a **medium,** be it professional or amateur, who is the channel through which the spirits communicate. Two friends sitting with a **Ouija** board would be considered as having a séance.

People attend séances for a variety of reasons, but mostly the object is to make contact with spirits of the dead to get information from them. This may only be information that indeed the spirit continues to exist after death, or it may be more specific information concerning the quality of life in the afterworld, or to investigate some past, present, or future happening in this world.

Séances can be held at any time of the day or night, though the majority of such sittings seem, for whatever reasons, to be held in the late evening. Certainly at that time the "vibrations" are better for spirit communication. This may be something to do with the atmosphere; radio waves seem to travel further and with less interruption in the evening. There is also a certain stillness and clarity that is missing during the day. Additionally, of course, a private séance held in the late evening is less likely to be open to interruption from unexpected callers.

A séance can lift the veil between this world and the next, so that the living and the dead may temporarily reunite and communicate with one another. With physical mediums phenomena such as telekinesis (the moving of objects without

A séance, with people holding hands to raise spirits clairvoyantly. ***Fortean Picture Library.***

physical contact), levitation, or materialization may be experienced. With a trance medium there may be **automatic writing** or even direct voice communication—the speaking of a spirit through the medium's vocal cords. The spirits speaking, either through the medium or by way of the medium's guide, can impart knowledge of the past, present or even of the future. This might be viewed as a modern version of the ancient **sibyls, Pythia** and other guides.

The question of lighting at a séance is often debated. Some groups work in complete or near total darkness while others work in bright light. Some work in candlelight while others just dim the lights. A lowered level of light does seem preferable, if only to cut down on distractions and as being conducive to shifting consciousness and entry into trance. Most séances take place with the sitters around a table. It is usual to place the hands on the table initially, some groups spreading their arms so that little fingers touch with neighbor's fingers, forming an unbroken circle of energy. Feet should be flat on the floor with legs uncrossed.

Whether or not there is a medium present, the group should have a leader. This person is responsible for everyone, for the running of the evening, and for recognizing where talent is showing itself so that it may be encouraged. A brief meditation or the singing of a song is sometimes used as a relaxing and harmonizing tool, bringing everyone into accord. From there the séance can begin.

As stated, the purpose of the séance can vary, as can the method of operating. **Table tipping** is sometimes part of a sitting, as is automatic writing, clairvoyance, clairaudience, clairsentience, direct voice, telekinesis, levitation, and materialization. The aim may be to communicate with one or more specific spirits, perhaps related to sitters, or it may be to make contact with virtually any spirit.

Some sitters meet solely to hold "rescue séances." These are aimed to help those spirits who do not realize that they are dead. They may wander about their old neighborhoods literally haunting them and wondering what has happened. The rescue sitters can explain to them that they have crossed over and that they need to move on.

As well as group sittings there can be private séances. Someone with a strong desire to communicate with a deceased friend or relative may arrange a private sitting with an accomplished medium for this purpose. In this instance there is seldom input, in the form of energy, from the sitter; he or she is there to witness the phenomena produced by the medium and to acknowledge the material presented.

Sources:

Bentine, Michael. *The Door Marked Summer*. London: Granada, 1981.
Bentine, Michael. *Doors of the Mind*. London: Granada, 1984.
Buckland, Raymond. *Doors to Other Worlds*. St. Paul, MN: Llewellyn, 1993.
Cowan, Tom. *The Book of Séance*. Chicago: Contemporary Books, 1994.
Hollen, Henry. *Clairaudient Transmissions*. Hollywood: Keats Publications, 1931.
Moses, William Stainton. *Direct Spirit Writing*. London, 1878.
Mühl, Anita M. *Automatic Writing*. Dresden: Steinkopff, 1930.
Owens, Elizabeth. *How to Communicate with Spirits*. St. Paul, MN: Llewellyn, 2002.

SECOND SIGHT

In **Scotland,** second sight is known by the Gaelic name *da-dhealladh*, which literally means "the two sights." The vision of the world of sense, as possessed by all people, is one of those sights and the other is the vision of the world of spirits. It is the ability to see ghosts, phantoms, apparitions, doubles, and the many and various spirits of earth, air, fire, and **water.** It is said, in Scotland, that the shepherds of the Hebrides have the largest possession of the gift, but it is well known all over Scotland, and on the Isle of Man, in Ireland, in **Scandinavia,** and other parts of the world. Although not exclusive to the **Celtic** world, the second sight is more prevalent in Celtic countries than elsewhere.

J. G. Campbell said that "the Celtic priests had reduced the gift of seeing spectres to a system, a belief which formed part of their teaching." The idea of second sight is based on the idea that everyone has a *doppelganger*, or an **astral** double, which is visible to those with the gift of second sight. Spence says that the chief peculiarity of second sight is that the visions are often, though not always, of a symbolical nature, and so need to be interpreted. In second sight the percipient sees events happening at a distance, sees people never seen before with the naked eye, or foresees events that are coming but still a distance off.

Some believe that second sight is hereditary, but not all agree on that. In Lowland Fifeshire, it is said that a child born feet first would either be possessed of the gift of second sight or would be a wanderer in a foreign land. One of the earliest references to second sight is found in Ralph Higden's fourteenth-century *Polychronicon* where, speaking of the Isle of Man, he says, "There oft by day time, men of that island see men that hath died beforehand, beheaded, or whole, and what death they died."

Sources:

Campbell, John Gregorson. *Witchcraft and Second Sight in the Highlands and Islands of Scotland.* Glasgow: James MacLehose, 1902.

Spence, Lewis. *The Magic Arts in Celtic Britain.* London: Rider, 1945.

SEEDS, EMBEDDED IN DUNG *see* **Stercomancy**

SEEING/SIGHT *see* **Clairvoyance**

SEER/SEERESS

A seer is a "see-er," a **clairvoyant.** It is one who is able to see the future; one to whom divine revelations are made in visions. In the **Bible,** 1 Samuel 9:9, it says: "Beforehand in Israel, when a man went to enquire of God, thus he spake, Come, and let us go to the seer, for he that is now called a **Prophet** was beforetime called a Seer." In Israel a seer was called *iro'eh* (meaning "visionary") or *hozeh* ("gazer"), while a prophet was **nabhi.**

SELENOMANCY

Selenomancy is divination based on the appearance of the **moon.** Observation of the patterns on the surface of the moon, together with the phase of the moon and its visibility through cloud cover, are all interpreted in this form of divination.

There are also certain beliefs regarding the moon found in different areas of the world. A blue tinge to the moon is believed to be an indication that rain is on the way. A red tinge means there is wind to come. A white tinge signifies fine weather. In the south of England, it is said that fine days will follow if there is a fine Tuesday after a new moon. Moist days will come after a wet or humid Tuesday after a new moon. If the horns of the moon are obscured on the third or fourth day, this means rain is on the way.

If the circle of the moon is red, problems and hardships are coming. If it rains on the first Tuesday after the full moon, it will continue to do so for the rest of that moon period. Similarly, if it is dry on that first Tuesday, it will remain dry for that moon period. If the moon is clear on its rising, it means that in the summer there will be fine weather but in the winter there will be a severe cold spell. Clearness at the full moon promises a fair period, as does a halo that melts quickly. A double halo means there is going to be a storm.

Sources:
Grand Orient (A. E. Waite). *The Complete Manual of Occult Divination: Volume 1—Manual of Cartomancy*. London: Rider, 1912.

SENSING *see* Clairsentience

SEPHARIAL *see* Old, Walter Gorn

SHADOWS *see* Lunomancy; Sciomancy

SHAMAN

Shamanism is a religious phenomenon characteristic of Siberian and Ural-Altaic peoples, also found in North and South America, Oceana, Indonesia, and elsewhere. A shaman is a medicine man and a priest, curing sickness and, through techniques of ecstasy, accompanying the souls of the dead on their final journeys. The word shaman itself comes from the Siberian tribal language of Tungus (of the Ural-Altaic peoples of the Arctic and central Asian regions). There are also female shamans—more properly shamanesses—in many areas.

The shaman is an ecstatic who is a specialist in the sacred and succeeds in having mystical experiences. Shamans access information through spirit journeying. The shaman believes that there is a universal web of power that supports all life, all life forms being interconnected. They believe that all elements of the environment are alive and all have their source of power in the spirit world.

Although the primary function of the shaman is healing, he also performs divination. **Dreams** are one of the tools used for foreseeing the future. Interpretation of **omens** is another. A method popular with **Celtic** shamans was **aeromancy,** or observation of the clouds. They believed that the clouds, driven and shaped as they are by the winds, reflect the mysteries of life. Much as vague shapes formed by tea leaves (see **Tasseography**) can be indicators of coming events, so can the shapes formed by cumulus and other clouds. "Mares' tails," "mackerel" skies, and similar have specific meanings, but it is the ever-changing shapes of cumulus clouds that lend themselves more to prognostication. One method used by Celtic shamans was to find a hollowed stone or other depression that was filled with rainwater, and then to look into it—**scrying**—studying the section of sky reflected on its surface.

Shamans are often consulted to find animals that have gone astray and to recover lost objects. The Lapp shamans use their drums in divination. The Tungus of Turukhansk, Siberia, practice a form of divination involving throwing their drumsticks in the air and interpreting by the positions in which they fall. The Yukagir shaman of Central Asia employs **aurispicy** and **astragalomancy.** Eskimo shamans—the women especially—will seat a person on the ground and hold up their head with a belt. When the head becomes heavy, it is a sign that the spirits have arrived. Then questions are asked. If the head gets heavier still, it is an affirmative answer, while if the head gets lighter, it is negative.

A Huichol Indian shaman, performing a ritual in the desert of Wirikuta, Mexico, 1998. *Fortean Picture Library.*

Sources:

Eliade, Mircea. *Shamanism: Archaic Techniques of Ecstasy*. Princeton, NJ: Princeton University Press, Bollingen Series, 1972.

Harner, Michael. *The Way of the Shaman*. San Francisco: Harper & Row, 1980.

Matthews, John. *The Celtic Shaman*. Shaftesbury, UK: Element, 1991.

SHEARS *see* **Coscinomancy**

Shell Hearing

A branch of **conchomancy,** shell hearing is one way of promoting **clairaudience.** In **spiritualism,** a **medium** may hold a shell to his or her ear and listen. Through the "sounds of the sea" that are always associated with such listening, voices may be heard. These, in spiritualism, are recognized as voices of the dead, who may then be questioned. Some mediums hold one shell, such as a large conch, to one ear; others hold two shells, one to each ear.

Sources:

Buckland, Raymond. *Doors to Other Worlds*. St. Paul, MN: Llewellyn, 1993.

SHELLS *see* **Conchomancy**

"Shipton, Mother" (1488–1561)

Born in 1488 at Dropping Well, Knaresborough, Yorkshire, England, Ursula Sontheil (Southill, Sowthiel, or Southiel) became one of the most famous **prophets** of all time, known as "Mother Shipton." Her prophesies are said to rival those of **Nostradamus.**

Ursula was the daughter of a local witch, Agatha Sontheil (some records name her Emmatha). Her father was unknown though it was rumored he was the leader of a group of magicians who celebrated secret rituals in the forests of Knaresborough. Many of the stories claim that he was the Devil himself. One story goes that Agatha had from him the command of the winds and, when nosy neighbors crowded into her home to ply her with questions, she summoned up the wind that blew them all out of her house. Such stories multiplied until Agatha was eventually brought before the local justices on a charge of witchcraft. By revealing that the justice had been sleeping with his two female servants, Agatha got herself acquitted and was never again so charged.

Agatha's child was born in July 1488, and was named Ursula. It is said that Ursula was greatly deformed when she was born and that shortly after her birth, her mother retired into the convent of St. Bridget, near Nottingham, where she soon died. The orphaned Ursula was raised by the parish nurse, who sent her to school. Ursula did very well in school, though she was taunted unmercifully by the other children because of her deformities. She was extremely misshapen and generally referred to as "the Devil's child." Eventually she was sent away from the school; it is said because she magically punished her abusers.

At twenty-four Ursula married a carpenter named Toby Shipton, of Shipton, near York, and settled into her own home. There she built up a reputation as a prophetess and **seer.** Now known as Mother Shipton, Ursula found that people started to come from many miles away to ask her about their futures. Soon the ordinary folk were joined by the nobility.

One of the early **predictions** of note made by Ursula concerned Cardinal Wolsey. She said, "The Mitred Peacock shall now begin to plume himself, and his train shall make a great show in the world. He shall want to live at York, and shall see it, but shall never come thither—and finally after great misfortunes he shall finish with Kingston." The "Mitred Peacock" referred to Cardinal Wolsey, who had obtained the revenues of Bath, Worcester, Hereford, and St. Albans, among other churches. He had become extremely powerful. His train did make a big show, being comprised of some eight-hundred retainers. On his journey to York, which is where he had publicly stated he was going to live, he sent three men on ahead telling them to disguise themselves and consult Mother Shipton. They were taken there by a guide named Beasly. When they knocked at Mother Shipton's door she called out "Come in, Mr. Beasly, and those noble lords with you." After giving them cake and ale, she told them that Wolsey would never come to York. One of the lords said that when he did come, she would burn. Ursula took out her handkerchief and threw it into the fire, saying "If this burn, then I may burn." The handkerchief did not burn, despite lying in the fire for many minutes. Meanwhile, Cardinal Wolsey got as far as Cawood, just eight miles from York. As he paused there, within sight of the city, the Earl of Northumberland arrived and arrested him, taking him back to the Tower of London as a prisoner. The Tower, at that time, was in the charge of Sir William Kingston.

Prophet Mother Shipton. *Fortean Picture Library.*

Among Mother shipton's many other prophesies was:

Great London's triumphant Spire
Shall be consumed with flames of fire—
More wonders yet! A widowed Queen,
In England shall be headless seen.
The harp shall give a better sound,
An Earl without a head be found.

This referred to the fire that burned St. Paul's steeple, occurring in June 1561; to the beheading of Mary, Queen of Scots; to the prosperity of Ireland (the harp) under Elizabeth's reign; and to the beheading of the Earl of Essex, one-time governor of Ireland. Another example was:

The Crown then fits the white King's head,
Who with the Lilies soon shall wed:

Then shall a peasant's bloody knife
Deprive a great man of his life.

The "white King" was Charles I, who was dressed all in white for his coronation. He married Henrietta Maria, sister to Henri IV of France; the arms of France being lilies. The Duke of Buckingham became very unpopular and while embarking at Portsmouth for Rochelle, was stabbed to death by a soldier.

Many were the prophesies of Mother Shipton—for local people, for the nobility, and for the political times. She continued for many years and was held in great esteem. Even today her memory is honored in Yorkshire. Sometime before her death, she foretold the hour and the day that she would die. When that time came, she said goodbye to her friends, retired to bed, and died at the age of seventy-three, in 1571. On her tombstone it says:

Here lies she that never ly'd,
Whose skill so often has been try'd.
Her prophecies shall still survive,
And ever keep her name alive.

Sources:

Dropping Well Estate. *The Life and Prophesies of Ursula Sontheil better known as Mother Shipton*. Leeds, UK: Arthur Wigley, n.d.

Heywood, Abel. *Mother Shipton's Prophesies*. Manchester, UK: Abel Heywood, 1881.

Simpson, J. W. *Mother Shipton: Her Life and True Prophecies Those Fulfilled and Those Yet to Be*. Bath, UK: West Country Editions, 1976.

SHOULDER, LOOKING OVER *see* **Retromancy**

SHOULDERS *see* **Armomancy; Omoplatoscopy; Scapulomancy**

Siberian and Lapp

Siberian and Lapp **shamans** divine by beating on multicolored drums. They place small brass rings on the surface of the drums and divine the future through the vibrations of those rings—how they move and change their relationships as the drumhead is beaten.

The Lapps ornament their drums extensively with mythological figures and other images. Lapp drums represent the three cosmic zones, separated by boundary lines. Both the front and the back faces of the drumskins are decorated. There is usually a depiction of the World Tree, the sun and **moon,** stars, a rainbow, and more.

Sources:

Buckland, Raymond and Kathleen Binger. *The Book of African Divination*. Rochester, VT: Destiny Books, 1992.

Eliade, Mircea. *Shamanism: Archaic Techniques of Ecstasy*. Princeton, NJ: Princeton University Press, Bollingen Series 1972.

The Delphic Sibyl, a prophet of ancient Greece. ***Fortean Picture Library.***

SIBYL

Legend has it that the ancient sibyls could live for a thousand years. It seems likely, however, that it was their utterings that were so long lived. In fact Heraclitus, as quoted by Plutarch, said of them: "The Sibyl with raving mouth, uttering things without smiles, without graces and without myrrh, reaches over a thousand years because of the god."

The sibyls were the **prophets** of ancient **Greece** and **Rome.** They seem to have originated in Greek Asia Minor. They were always connected to Apollo, the god of prophecy, who also originated in Asia Minor. Where the **Pythia** of Delphi were controlled and protected by the priesthood, the Sibyls were in effect freelancers. The best-known sibyls were at **Delphi,** Erythræ, Marpessus, Phrygia, Sardis, and Thessaly. The majority of the prophecies uttered by the Sibyls dealt with war, famine, plague, and other disasters.

In Virgil's *Ænid* there is the story of the Sibyl of Cumæ, who predicts the wars that will follow Æneas's landing in Italy. Æneas had been told by the prophet Helenus to seek out the cave of the Sibyl of Cumæ as soon as he reached Italy. He was told that she was a woman of deep wisdom who could foretell the future and advise him what to do. This she did and, in fact, traveled with him to guide him, eventually leading him to meet his deceased father, Anchises.

Sources:

Hamilton, Edith. *Mythology*. New York: Little, Brown, 1942.

Kaster, Joseph. *Putnam's Concise Mythological Dictionary*. New York: G.P. Putnam's, 1963.

Parke, H. W. *Sibyls and Sibylline Prophecy in Classical Antiquity*. New York: Routledge, 1988.

Phillips, E. D. (ed.). *Man, Myth & Magic*. London: BPC Publishing, 1970.

Potter, D. *Sibyls in the Greek and Roman World*, Journal of Roman Archaeology 3, 1990.

SIBYLLINE BOOKS

(See also Sibylline Oracles)

The **sibyls** were the Roman oracles. According to Tacitus, their predictions and divinations were written in hexameter verses and collected into books, which were carefully preserved in the Capitol. They were kept under the guardianship of two Commissioners for Ritual (*duouiri sacris faciundis*), though that number was later increased to fifteen. These Commissioners were the only ones allowed to consult the books and the mysterious verses contained within. Although some Greeks came to look upon the predictions as nonsense, the Romans generally regarded them as sacred texts and referred to them when dealing with any abnormal and perilous situations.

When the Capitol was burned down during the civil wars between Marius and Sulla in 83 BCE, the books were removed to the temple of Apollo on the Palatine. The books were stored in the base of the great statue of Apollo. It is believed that they remained in existence until 339 CE, at which time they were destroyed by Stilikon. Three ambassadors—Paulus Gabinus, Marcus Otacillius, and Lucius Valerius—were sent by Augustus to collect whatever they could of the remaining records of the Sibylline Oracles, to replace the lost ones. The three traveled to Asia, Africa, and Italy, including to the Erythræan Sibyl.

In 293 BCE there was a pestilence in Rome—a not-uncommon occurrence with the city's poor sanitation—and one of the Sibylline oracles advised seeking the aid of **Æsculapius** (or Asklepios). A mission was sent to Epidaurus, one of the principal shrines of Æsculapius, and returned with a sacred serpent. As the boat carrying it came up the Tiber, the snake slipped overboard and swam ashore on a small island in midstream. A shrine was erected there in honor of Æsculapius, and it became a great healing center.

In 205 BCE Hannibal was still in possession of a corner of Italy and prolonging a twelve-year war. Showers of stones were experienced in Rome on several occasions (probably volcanic lapilli) and the Sibylline Books were consulted. According to Livy, the response was to the effect that "when a foreign foe had invaded Italy, he could be driven out and vanquished if the Idæan Mother were brought from Pessinus." Pessinus was a Phrygian city, one of the most famous seats of the cult of the Great Mother. An ambassador was duly sent to Asia and met with King Attalos of Pergamon. Through him they obtained a large, black stone said to be the representation of the Great Mother. This was brought back and placed in the Temple of Victory on the Palatine. Later a shrine was built for it, and games known as the Megalesia, or Festival of the Great Mother, were instituted in her honor.

Sources:

Phillips, E. D. (ed.). *Man, Myth & Magic*. London: BPC Publishing, 1970.
Rose, H.J. *Religion in Greece and Rome*. New York: Harper & Row, 1959.
Shepard, Leslie A. (ed.). *Encyclopedia of Occultism & Parapsychology*. New York: Avon, 1978.

Sibylline Oracles

The **Sibylline Books** were the records of the elder **sibyls** of earlier **Rome** and **Greece**—the **oracles** who predicted the future, albeit in mysterious and often symbolic language. The "Sibylline Oracles," or *Oracula Sibyllina*, were greatly falsified copies of these original books, disfigured with numerous interpolations. They were written originally by the Jews and later added to by the Christians, in their efforts to convert people from paganism. The hexameter verse form of the original predictions was copied, as was the Homeric language.

Book Three contains Jewish oracles relating to the Golden Age established by Roman supremacy in the east, about the middle of the second century BCE. Another Jewish oracle refers to the wars of the second Triumvirate of Rome. Book Four is mainly an attack on the pagan sibyls by the Jews and the Christians. Book Five has a form of the myth of *Nero redivivus*, brought up to date by Jewish or Christian writers, and eulogies of Hadrian, alongside the legend of the death of Titus after his destruction of Jerusalem. The other books appear to be mainly Christian, from the second and third centuries. It is said that these are still preserved in Rome.

Sources:

Encyclopedia Britannica. Chicago: William Benton, 1964.

Sideromancy

Sideromancy is divination based on the movement of straws placed on red-hot iron. According to Pierre de l'Ancre's *L'Incrédulité et mescréance du sortilège* (Paris, 1622), an odd number of straws were dropped onto red-hot iron, and "while they burned judg-

Henry Sidgwick. *Fortean Picture Library.*

ment was formed from the movement of the straws, from their twisting or bending, from the fiery figures of the sparkling of the flames, and from the flight and course of the smoke and otherwise."

Interestingly, while agreeing that it is divination by straws on red-hot iron, the *Oxford English Dictionary* offers a second definition for sideromancy, as "Forecasting the future by means of the stars." However, that would seem, more properly, to be termed **astromancy.** George Crabb's *Universal Technological Dictionary* of 1823 reinforces de l'Ancre's explanation with the statement that sideromancy is "a species of divination performed by burning straws, etc. on red-hot iron, in which operation conjectures were formed from the manner of their burning, etc."

Sources:

de Givry, Grillot. *A Pictorial Anthology of Witchcraft, Magic & Alchemy*. London: Spottiswoode, Ballantyne, 1931.

Oxford English Dictionary. Oxford: Clarendon Press, 1989.

SIDGWICK, HENRY (1838–1900)

Born May 31, 1838, Henry Sidgwick became the first president of the **Society for Psychical Research** in London, England. Sidgwick was Professor of Moral Philosophy at Cambridge University. He was once described as "the most incorrigibly and exasperatingly critical and skeptical brain in England." On becoming president of the SPR in 1882, he said: "It is a scandal that the dispute as to the reality of these [psychic] phenomena should still be going on, that so many competent witnesses have declared their belief in them . . . and yet the educated world, as a body, should still be simply in an attitude of incredulity." Sidgwick worked with the society for eighteen years, contributing many important studies to the *Proceedings*. He once wrote to a friend, a Mr. Dakyns, "I have actually heard the **raps** . . . however, I have no kind of evidence to come before a jury." He was initially most impressed with the phenomena of the **medium** Eusapia Paladino but took a leading part in the sittings with her, held at Cambridge in 1895, which resulted in her exposure as a fraud. He had a number of sittings with **Leonore Piper,** in 1889–1890, and retained the keenest interest in her trance phenomena.

After his death on August 28, 1900, a number of mediums purported to bring word from Sidgwick's spirit. When Mrs. Thompson channeled him on January 11, 1901, a Mr. Piddington who was present said that the diction, manner of speech, and the voice itself were all astonishingly lifelike, and he felt that he was indeed speaking with the man he had known.

Sources:

Fishley, Margaret. *The Supernatural*. London: Aldus, 1976.
Spence, Lewis. *An Encyclopedia of the Occult*. London: George Routledge & Sons, 1920.

SIEVE ***see*** **Coscinomancy**

SLEEP ***see*** **Hypnomancy; Meconomancy; Narcomancy**

SMALL OBJECTS ***see*** **Micromancy**

Smith, Pamela Colman (1878–1951)

Pamela Colman Smith was a British-born American who was a member of the Order of the Golden Dawn. She did the artwork for the best-known **tarot** deck of all time, the Rider-Waite deck (named after **Arthur Edward Waite** and his publisher Rider & Son, London). The deck was issued in 1909 and was the first to depict all the cards—Major and Minor Arcana—with full scenes and images.

Born on February 16, 1878, in Pimlico, London, England, Smith was the daughter of Charles Edward Smith, an American merchant, and Corinne Colman. The family lived in the greater London area and Manchester until 1893. During the last year or so there Smith traveled with Henry Irving and Ellen Terry as part of the Lyceum Theatre Group, working on set design and painting scenery.

By 1893 the family was back in the United States, in Brooklyn, where Smith enrolled in the Pratt Institute, studying art. She graduated at nineteen and started earning a living as an illustrator. She also did some wrote and illustrated stories based on Jamaican folk tales, having spent some time in the islands due to her father's business deals. Smith was known to her friends as "Pixie."

In 1899 Smith went back to England, with her father, where she met the poet William Butler Yeats who, in turn, introduced her to the magical Order of the Golden Dawn. This was headed, at the time, by MacGregor Mathers. The following year **Aleister Crowley** tried to take over the Order and many problems developed, leading to its eventual breakup. By 1903 Arthur Edward Waite, one of the leading members, broke away with his own faction, taking the name of the Golden Dawn with them. Smith followed Waite, and he saw in her some potential as an artist for a tarot deck he wanted to produce. They began work on it, with Waite directing. Smith was inspired by her own knowledge of the occult, and by psychic visions. However, Waite very much wanted to press his own views. Smith was only paid a small fee for her work; she did not share in royalties on the deck. The deck was finally released in December of 1909, published by Rider & Son. Despite the work that Smith put into the deck, it is generally referred to as the Rider-Waite deck, rather than the Waite-Smith deck.

Following World War I, Smith inherited some money and settled in Cornwall, England, at an artists' colony on The Lizard. She lived there with Nora Lake until

1939 and the outbreak of World War II. Pamela Colman "Pixie" Smith died on September 18, 1951, aged 73, in Bude, Cornwall.

Sources:

Kaplan, Stuart. *The Encyclopædia of the Tarot*. New York: U.S. Games, 1978.
http://allthingstarot.freeserve.co.uk/riderwaite.html.

Smith, Robert Cross—"Raphael" (1795–1832)

Robert Cross Smith was the first of a succession of **astrologers** who used the pseudonym "Raphael." He was born on March 19, 1795, in the village of Abbots Leigh, near Bristol, England. Smith maintained that he started studying astrology at an early age, in Bristol, though at that time there were few books available on the subject. By profession he was a carpenter. He moved to London in 1820 and married. He then took a job as a clerk with a builder in Upper Thames Street.

Smith was befriended by G. W. Graham, a balloonist who had an interest in astrology and in alchemy. He gave Smith financial assistance. With Graham's encouragement, Smith moved into a house off Oxford Street and set up as a professional astrologer—one of the first. In 1822 the two men collaborated on a book titled *The Philosophical Merlin*. They dedicated it to "the famous and renowned Mademoiselle **Le Normand,"** the French **cartomancer.**

In 1824 Smith was appointed editor of a new periodical, *The Straggling Astrologer of the Nineteenth Century*. It was in the twelfth issue of this magazine—on August 21, 1824—that Smith first wrote using the pen name "Raphael." Although the magazine did not last long, it was succeeded by *The* ***Prophetic*** *Messenger*, which started in 1826 and continued (after Smith's death) until 1858.

Smith gradually earned a reputation as an astrologer, though he also looked upon himself as an expert in magic and magical rituals. He wrote under the names Raphael, Royal Merlin, Medusa, Alfred the Inspired Penman, Extraordinary Genius, and Mercurius. He favored the Placidean system of astrology and produced almanacs and ephemerides of the time.

Smith studied Francis Barrett's book *The Magus*, published in 1801. This was a compendium of ritual magic and various aspects of the occult. Smith came to plagiarize much of Barrett's work. Many other astrologers attacked Smith, in writing.

When Smith started editing *The Prophetic Messenger*, he incorporated an almanac that caught on. It led many publishers to ask Smith to write for them. In quick succession he wrote and published the *Manual of Astrology* (1828), *Royal Book of Fate* (1829), *Royal Book of* ***Dreams*** (1830), and *Raphael's Witch* (1831). His last major work was the *Familiar Astrologer*. There is a story that Smith had an unknown client who would not give his birth date to the astrologer. The man was very well dressed and wore a large, expensive ring. Smith told him he would die within two years. It turned out to be King George IV, who did die on June 26, 1830, within the two years.

Smith wrote daily predictions, which became very popular. In 1827 he met William Blake and was "pouring over the fate of kings, emperors, and distinguished individuals." He was thinking of moving to a different publisher for *The Prophetic Messenger,* because he was paid a fixed sum and the magazine was increasing in sales dramatically, but he caught a violent cold and died of consumption on February 26, 1832.

Sources:

Cavendish, Richard (ed.). *Encyclopedia of the Unexplained*. London: Routledge & Kegan Paul, 1974.
http://www.stargazers.com/raphael.html.
http://www.urania.info/comments/2002/4/28/174740/593/0/post.

SMOKE *see* Capnomancy

SNAKE *see* Aspidomancy; Ophidiomancy; Ophiomancy

SNEEZE

Sneezing as an indication of future events, is a branch of **spasmatomancy.** In **Greece,** if anyone is interrupted in what they are saying by having to sneeze or by someone close by sneezing, then whatever was being said and was interrupted is regarded at being the absolute truth. If anyone is in doubt about how their comments will be received, they will somehow conjure up a sneeze to give emphasis to it.

In the American Ozarks, sneezing is carefully observed. If a woman sneezes before breakfast, it means that company will arrive before noon. If she sneezes during breakfast, then two or more people will leave the house before sundown. If she sneezes with food in her mouth, it means that within twenty-four hours she will hear of a death. A similarity to the Greek belief mentioned above is that if she sneezes while telling a story—whether or not she believes it to be true—then that story is the truth.

Sources:

Lawson, John Cuthbert. *Modern Greek Folklore and Ancient Greek Religion*. New York: University Books, 1964.
Randolph, Vance. *Ozark Superstitions*. New York: Dover, 1964.

SOAL, SAMUEL GEORGE (1889–19??)

An author, lecturer, and mathematician, Soal became a well-known figure in British parapsychology, though his image was later tarnished when it seemed evident that he had indulged in fraud with some of the results he obtained.

Soal was born in Kirby Moorside, Yorkshire, England, on April 29, 1889. He studied at London University where he obtained a B.Sc. with first-class honors mathematics (1910), an M.A. in mathematics (1914), and a D.Sc. in psychology (1945). Among a large number of prestigious teaching posts, he was president of the Nottingham University Society for Psychical Research in 1938, Perrott Student in Psychical Research at Cambridge from 1948 to 1949, and Fulbright Research Scholar in Parapsychology in 1951.

From 1919 on, Soal conducted parapsychology studies, collaborating in quantitative research with Mrs. K. M. Goldney, Frederick Bateman, and J. G. Pratt. He lectured widely both in England and the United States. He was able to duplicate many of the results obtained by **Dr. J. B. Rhine.** He wrote numerous articles and books, which included *Modern Experiments in Telepathy* (with F. Bateman, 1954) and *The Mind Readers* (with H. T. Bowden, 1959) .

Sources:

Shepard, Leslie A. (ed.). *Encyclopedia of Occultism & Parapsychology*. New York: Avon, 1978.

Society for Psychical Research

In 1882 a group of Cambridge University scholars, and other in and around London, got together to start a Society for Psychical Research. Its purpose was to thoroughly examine such things as **clairvoyance,** telepathy, **precognition,** and all other paranormal subjects, to see whether or not they really had a basis of fact. At the inaugural meeting Professor **Henry Sidgwick** was elected president, an office he held for nine years. The first council included Professors Barrett and Balfour Stewart, Edmund Gurney, Richard Hutton, F. W. H. Myers, Stainton Moses, E.T. Bennett, Dawson Rogers, Morell Theobald, and Dr. George Wyld.

Early activity was devoted to experimental investigation of **extrasensory perception,** which the society established as a fact. They also felt safe in confirming a connection existing between death and apparitions. The society collected and published a massive amount of research, finding a great deal of fraud among spiritualist **mediums** but also finding many instances of unexplainable phenomena.

In 1885 the **American Society for Psychical Research** was founded in Boston by Sir William Fletcher Barrett of the British society. Barrett was visiting the United States at the time. Originally independent, the American society affiliated with the British one in 1889.

For many years, Dr. Richard Hodgson led investigations of the trance **mediumship** of **Leonore Piper.** Eventually Hodgson was so impressed with her performances, and the evidence she produced, that he became converted to the cause of spiritualism himself. E. Dawson Rogers, President of the London Spiritualist Alliance, said of this that he (Hodgson) had been "a very Saul persecuting the Christians." His conversion, then, was an achievement for spiritualism.

The society seemed to build up a bias against physical phenomena, refusing to accept any evidence of it. Eventually the bias seemed so pronounced that, in 1930, Sir Arthur Conan Doyle and a number of other prominent members resigned from the society. Over the past fifty years the society has spent most of its time with mass experiments evaluated by statistical methods, with most of its interest in ESP and in psychokinesis.

Sources:

Guiley, Rosemary Ellen. *Harper's Encyclopedia of Mystical & Paranormal Experience*. San Francisco: HarperSanFrancisco, 1991.

Shepard, Leslie A. (ed.). *Encyclopedia of Occultism & Parapsychology*. New York: Avon, 1978.

SOLISTRY *see* **Pedomancy**

SONTHEIL, URSULA *see* **"Shipton, Mother"**

Soothsayer

A soothsayer is, literally, a "truth-sayer," one who speaks the truth. It is, by extension, a person who foretells future events. **Shamans, seers, astrologers, cheiromancers, Pythia,** and **sibyls** are all soothsayers in that sense, since they tell what they perceive to be the truth of coming events.

Sorcery

Sorcery is mainly concerned with the casting of spells and the making of charms, but it can also include divining the future. The word comes from the French *sors*, meaning "spell." Guiley points out that sorcery is "low magic," in other words akin to folk magic. There is no connection with worship of gods, although in Africa the sense of the two is reversed, with sorcery close to religion and "witchcraft" viewed as the evil working of magic.

Some anthropologists view sorcery as necessarily harmful magic, which is not the case. Within the western definition of the word, sorcery is magic by manipulation of natural forces and powers to achieve a desired end that is not necessarily negative. According to the **Bible**'s Acts 8: 9–11:

> But there was a certain man, called Simon, which beforetime in the same city used sorcery, and bewitched the people of Samaria, giving out that himself was some great one: To whom they all gave heed, from the least to the greatest, saying, This man is the great power of God. And to him they had regard, because that of long time he had bewitched them with sorceries.

Guiley mentions that by the late Middle Ages the term "sorcerer" was applied to men of higher learning, such as alchemists, physicians, and ceremonial magicians. These were the ones who would probably also be involved in trying to foretell future events; they would also be **seers, scryers, augurers** and **astrologers.**

In the year 1432, within a few days of each other, there were two records of arrest for sorcery in England. One was a Franciscan friar of Worcester named Thomas Northfield, who was seized with all his books and other materials of "conjuration," including astrological computations. The other was also a friar, named John Ashwell. This latter had two companions: a clerk named John Virley and a woman named Margery Jourdemayn. It was in this century that, in England, charges of sorcery were first raised against people of eminence; the charges invariably raised by their enemies for political reasons. One celebrated case was that of the Duchess of Gloucester in the reign of Henry VI. But there had been another case, that of Dame Alice Kyteler of Kilkenny, Ireland, a hundred years earlier. The Bishop of Ossory, Richard de Ledrede, became convinced that Dame Alice was not a poisoner of husbands (as had been claimed), but a sorceress. In 1324 he charged her with heretical sorcery and also charged ten accomplices with her. He indicted Dame Alice on seven counts.

Sources:
Buckland, Raymond. *The Witch Book: The Encyclopedia of Witchcraft, Wicca, and Neo-paganism*. Detroit: Visible Ink Press, 2002.
Guiley, Rosemary Ellen. *The Encyclopedia of Witches and Witchcraft*. New York: Facts on File, 1989.
Robbins, Rossell Hope. *The Encyclopedia of Witchcraft and Demonology*. New York: Crown, 1959.

SORTES

(See also Bibliomancy; Rhapsodomancy; Sortilege)

Divination by using passages taken at random from a book. The passage is believed to have some relevance to the person doing the divining. Some diviners will stick the passage with a pin or the tip of a dagger, rather than just with the finger. This practice was also known as *Sortes Biblicæ*. Often the **Bible** is used for this (*sortes sanctorum*) but also, at one time, the works of Homer (*sortes Homericæ*) and Virgil (*sortes Virgilianæ*) were very popular. Virgil's *Æneid* was a book commonly used in the Middle Ages. In **Greece** the preference was to take from Homer's *Iliad* and the *Odyssey*, while in **Rome** they favored Virgil. Mohammedans used the Koran.

The selected passages might also be written on discs that were strung together. (Rakoczi believes the word sortes comes from the Latin *serere*, meaning "to string," but the Oxford English Dictionary says that it comes from the plural of the Latin *sors*, meaning "chance.") The strung discs would be thrown down, in the manner of sortilege, and the revealed disc passages were then the significant ones.

G. E. Jewsbury in *A History of Ireland: Select Letters of G. E. Jewsbury to Jane Welsh Carlysle* (1892) quotes: "I send it you by way of a 'sortes,' and the Bible has as much virtue that way as Virgil."

Sources:
Grand Orient (A. E. Waite). *A Manual of Cartomancy*. London: Rider, 1912.
Oxford English Dictionary. Oxford: Clarendon Press, 1989.
Rakoczi, Basil Ivan. *Man, Myth & Magic: Lots*. London: BPC Publishing, 1970.

SORTILEGE

Sortilege is the casting of lots in order to divine the future. The word comes from the Anglo-Saxon *hlot* meaning "allotment"; *gehlot* meant "decision." This is one of the most ancient methods of divination. In the **Bible** there are several mentions of sortilege being used. For example, it was used by the sailors to determine whether Jonah was the cause of the tempest (Jonah 1:7): "And they said every one to his fellow, Come, and let us cast lots, that we may know for whose cause this evil is upon us. So they cast lots and the lot fell upon Jonah." It was used to determine who should take the place of Judas, in Acts 1:26: "And they gave forth their lots; and the lot fell upon Matthias; and he was numbered with the eleven apostles." Also, in Proverbs 16:33 it says: "The lot is cast into the lap; but the whole disposing thereof is of the Lord."

A form of sortilege is for verses taken from books to be written on discs, which are then strung together and thrown down (this is a variation on **sortes**). The revealed verses are then the pertinent ones. Rakoczi relates that at Præneste (Palestrina), Italy, the **oracle** of **Fortuna** had a number of oak tablets kept in a chest. Each was inscribed with signs and symbols. When the oracle was consulted, an acolyte would draw out one of the tablets at random from the chest. This would then be interpreted by the priest. Such drawing of lots could only be done at Præneste on certain days of the year. Fortuna (identified with the goddess Tyche in **Greece**) was in **Rome** the goddess of **fate,** chance, and luck.

The basic form of sortilege is for objects, such as stones, bones, **dice,** and **dominoes** to be thrown down after being mixed or shaken together. Their relationship on landing is interpreted, as may be the area where they land, which may be subdivided into pertinent sections. The face of the object, or the revealed color or symbol that lands uppermost, is also significant. Black and white beans are sometimes used, as are small bones, dice, and stones. When dice are used it is called **cubomancy.**

Methods vary. There are some classical forms of sortilege, such as *Sortes Thriæcæ*, a Greek form where pebbles or counters are thrown into an urn and then one is drawn out. They each have individual signs, letters, or symbols of some sort on them. This form of divination received its name from the Thriæ, three nymphs who nursed **Apollo** and were said to have invented this form of sortilege.

There is also *Sortes Viales*, or street lots. This was used in both Greece and Rome. In this, a person carried a number of marked lots and would walk about in a market place. A young boy, encountered by chance, would be asked to draw one of the lots, and that would be the infallible prophecy. According to Plutarch (46–120 CE), the Greek writer and biographer, this method came from **Egypt.** A variation on it was for a boy to set up in a marketplace, with a tablet covered in possible answers to questions. When consulted, the boy would cast dice on the tablet and read the verses on which they fell. Alternatively,various verses were written on pieces of paper and thrown into an urn. The verse drawn out was the significant one. Albius Tibullus (c. 19 BCE), the Roman poet, wrote of this when he said:

> Thrice in the streets the sacred lots she threw,
> And thrice the boy a happy **omen** drew.

Sortes Prenestinæ, or the Prenestine Lots, were used in Italy. Letters of the alphabet were written on individual tiles and placed in an urn. After being mixed, they were turned out on the ground and any words that were accidentally formed by the letters were taken as omens.

Sortes Homericæ and *Sortes Virgilianæ* have been mentioned in the article on sortes. They involved opening the works of either Homer (favored by the Greeks) or Virgil (favored by the Romans) and taking the first sighted verse as pertinent as an omen.

Variations of sortilege are **astragalomancy, coin** tossing, **cleromancy, geomancy, lithomancy, psephomancy, I Ching,** and many others.

Sources:

Adkins, Lesley and Roy A. Adkins. *Dictionary of Roman Religion*. New York: Facts on File, 1996.
Rakoczi, Basil Ivan. *Man, Myth & Magic: Lots*. London: BPC Publishing, 1970.
Rose, H. J. *Religion in Greece and Rome*. New York: Harper & Row, 1959.
Shepard, Leslie A. (ed.). *Encyclopedia of Occultism & Parapsychology*. New York: Avon, 1978.

SOUND *see* **Alveromancy**

Spasmatomancy

Spasmatomancy deals with convulsive twitching of the limbs—involuntary movements by which the future may be gauged. In **Greece,** both ancient and modern, the twitching of a person's eyebrows can be revealing. If it is the left eyebrow that throbs and/or twitches, then it means an enemy will soon be encountered. If it is the right eyebrow, then it will be a friend. Theocritus (310–250 BCE), the Greek poet, demonstrated this belief when he said "My eye throbs, my right eye; oh! Shall I see Amaryllis herself?" Similarly, a buzzing or singing in your ears is a sign that someone will soon be speaking to you; slander and ill words if the left ear and flattery and good wishes if the right. With the itching of the palms of the hands there is again evidence of what is to come. If the left palm itches then money is to be paid out. If it is the right palm, then money will be coming in. The feet, too, can indicate what is to be. The soles of the feet itching indicate a journey is soon to be undertaken. If it is the left sole that itches, then the journey will be unsuccessful; if it is the right foot, then it will be successful.

In Edward Smedley's *The Occult Sciences* (1855), he says: "Spasmatomancy is properly a part of medicine, for it is the art of foretelling from convulsive twitchings of the limbs diseases by which a man is about to be attacked."

Sneezing and hiccuping, or choking over food, indicate that there is a backbiter at work. The cure is to guess the name of the person. Sneezing may be interpreted in different ways. If anyone is interrupted in what they are saying by having to sneeze, or by someone close by sneezing, then whatever was being said and was interrupted is regarded at being the absolute truth.

Sources:

Lawson, John Cuthbert. *Modern Greek Folklore and Ancient Greek Religion*. New York: University Books, 1964.

Oxford English Dictionary. Oxford: Clarendon Press, 1989.

Randolph, Vance. *Ozark Superstitions*. New York: Dover, 1964.

Spatilomancy

(See also Stercomancy)

A branch of **scatomancy,** this is divination by means of feces, though in this case the emphasis is on animal feces. The odor of the droppings played a part in its interpretation; it was a pointer to its age, for example. Consistency also played a part, as did the location of the feces. The material was also examined for contents like seeds or nuts that might have significance.

Spheromancy

This is a form of **crystallomancy,** divining by a crystal ball or other sphere of glass. The basis of the divination is **scrying.** The actual ball used could be crystal, glass, or something like a garden ornament popularly known as a witch's ball.

Another form of spheromancy was not tied in to scrying. It involved the observation of a spherical ball (which could be wood, metal, or any substance) and its movement and stopping when rolled on a specific surface area, which might or might not be marked into areas representing aspects of the future.

SPIDER

(See also African Divination)

A spider seen running or spinning its web in the morning is a promise of money to come during the day. If the spider is active in the early evening, it means there will be news before nightfall. In England, very small spiders are called "money spiders." If one is seen on your clothing it means that money is coming. In Polynesia, a spider dropping down in front of you is a sign that you will receive a gift. Almost universally it is believed that to kill a spider will bring rain.

In the Ozark region it is considered very bad luck to kill a spider; such an act would bring great misfortune. It is also believed that if you should be able to see your initials in a spider's web near your front door, you will be happy and fortunate for as long as you live in that house.

The **Etruscans** believed that it was possible to learn the winning numbers of lotteries with the help of a spider. They would write numbers on tiny pieces of paper and then place them in the bottom of a small box. A large spider would be placed in the box and left to build its web. In building, the spider would move the numbered pieces of paper. Those pieces disturbed were the numbers that would be lucky for the lottery. The spider could similarly be used to pick lucky days, give yes/no answers, or turn up the names of friends from enemies.

A similar practice is found in **Africa** and is known as *Ngám* or Tikar spider divination. It is found in the northeastern section of the Bamenda Province in southwestern Cameroon and utilizes the actions of a relative of the trapdoor spider, the *Heteroscodra crassipes*. This is a very large, black, earth spider, four to six inches in total length with a three-inch-long body. It is sometimes confused with the tarantula, but although its bite is painful it is rarely fatal. The Kaka people believe that this spider, because it nests in the ground, possesses wisdom obtained from the earth deities. The spider is usually owned by the head man of a village, who uses it for daily divination to ascertain the will of the gods. All the villagers will gather at the head man's hut each morning to observe the daily ritual.

The rite and divination is actually performed by the *nkú-ngám*, or diviner. (Ngúm means "divination," while ngám means "spider".) He has a set of **cards** made from leaves of the African plum tree (*Pachylobus edulis*). There may be as many as two-hundred of them, each with different signs and symbols marked on them by cutting or burning. These cards have been placed in a large calabash pot. A lid is on the pot but the bottom of it is broken and placed over the home of the earth spider, the hole in the pot allowing the spider access to the leaves. When the lid is removed in the morning the diviner will see how the cards have been disturbed and rearranged by the spider. Interpreting these movements constitute the divination.

Sources:

Buckland, Raymond and Kathleen Binger. *The Book of African Divination*. Rochester, VT: Destiny Books, 1992.

Leach, Maria (ed.). *Funk & Wagnalls Standard Dictionary of Folklore, Mythology, and Legend*. San Francisco: Harper & Row, 1972.

Leland, Charles Godfrey. *Etruscan Magic & Occult Remedies*. New York: University Books, 1963.

SPIRITS ***see*** **Channeling; Necromancy; Necyomancy; Psychomancy; Spiritualism; Typtology**

SPIRITUALISM

The spiritualism movement started in the mid-eighteenth century, sparked by the episode of the Fox sisters in Hydesville, New York, in 1848. It focuses on communication with the world of spirits of the dead. Margaretta and Kate (later joined by Leah) Fox showed that such contact was possible and inspired thousands to try to renew communication with loved ones who had died. In its childhood, spiritualism became a breeding ground for fraudulent **mediums** and those seeking fame and fortune. However, despite the large number of fakes, there were many who showed that true contact was possible. In its heyday spiritualism commanded over two million followers on both sides of the Atlantic. Repeated exposés by scientists quickly reduced that number, but a hard core remains and is still active today. There have been some outstanding mediums never found to be fraudulent, such as **William Stainton Moses,** Daniel Dunglas Home, **Eileen Garrett,** Ena Twigg, Estelle Roberts, George Anderson, and Jean Cull.

Many enthusiasts made the movement into a religion, inspiring spiritualist churches of various types. The movement became especially big in South America, **Brazil** in particular. The focus of a lot of the spiritualist groups, whether religiously affiliated or not, is healing of the sick through the agencies of departed medical experts. The laying-on of hands and **auric** healing are very popular and effective.

Home circles, or **séances** (meaning "sittings"), allowed the movement to develop with groups of friends working together, with or without a professional medium, thus cutting out a controlling priesthood. From the use of **Ouija**® boards, **automatic writing, clairvoyance, clairaudience, clairsentience,** etc., a true grassroots movement gave spiritualism a foundation that it may never totally lose. Divination is something that has become a part of it. Today has seen something of a renaissance of spiritualism with outstanding mediums such as John Edward and Sylvia Browne appearing not in semi-darkened rooms but under the bright lights of television, before live audiences. A Gallup poll showed that, in 1996, 20 percent of those questioned expressed a belief that it was possible for the dead to communicate with the living. A further 22 percent believed it might be possible.

Sources:

Buckland, Raymond. *Doors to Other Worlds*. St. Paul, MN: Llewellyn, 1993.

Edward, John. *Crossing Over: The Stories behind the Stories*. New York: Princess Books, 2001.

Owens, Elizabeth. *How to Communicate With Spirits*. St. Paul, MN: Llewellyn, 2002.

SPLANCHOMANCY ***see*** **Anthropomancy**

The largest spiritualism assembly in the world, at Forest Temple, Lily Dale, New York. ***Fortean Picture Library.***

SPODANOMANCY; SPODOMANCY

(See also Tephramancy)

Spodomancy is divination using cinders that, in the original practice, were from sacrificial fires. According to **Arthur Edward Waite,** writing as "Grand Orient," this was still practiced in Germany during the first half of the nineteenth century, but with regular ashes. He says:

> It is performed by scattering ashes thickly in some place exposed to the air and writing therein with the end of the finger any question about which information is needed. The inscribed ashes are then left for the night, and on the following morning the letters that remain legible are used as **oracles,** for which purpose they may be placed in their natural order, when if they form an intelligible word, it may be considered to contain the mystic sense of the oracle and an answer to the question proposed. Otherwise, the insight of the contriver must be used to extract an appropriate answer from the assemblage of letters arranged after any fashion. As destiny is supposed to decide what letters should

> remain legible, and what should be effaced, this intervention of the operator does not interfere with the working of the oracle, but simply manifests its message. Should other characters than those inscribed originally appear upon the surface of the ashes, there is no need for apprehension, though such interferences, according to a time-honored custom, have been frequently ascribed to the devil.

Despite this final warning, it seems that taking the remaining legible letters, either in the order they appear or treating them as an anagram, gives the **seer** an answer to any question asked. Charles Kingsley, in *Two Years Ago* (1857), said: "[He] stared fiercely into the fire, as if to draw from thence omens of his love, by the spodomantic **augury** of the ancient **Greeks.**"

Sources:

Grand Orient (A. E. Waite). *The Complete Manual of Occult Divination: Volume 1—Manual of Cartomancy*. London: Rider, 1912.

Oxford English Dictionary. Oxford: Clarendon Press, 1989.

SPOTS *see* Maculomancy

STAINS, BURN *see* Pyroscopy

STARS *see* Astrology; Astromancy; Genethlialogy; Ouranomancy

Stercomancy

Stercomancy is a form of divination based on the finding of seeds in dung. It is a branch of **spatilomancy,** since it is worked with animal feces rather than with human excrement. The number of seeds contained in the droppings and their distrbution are significant to the **seer.** The types of seed can also have a bearing on the interpretation.

Stichomancy

This is a variety of **rhapsodomancy** and akin to **bibliomancy.** It is divination by lines of verse taken from a book at random. The works of Shakespeare, Byron, Keats, and Shelley have all been favorites for this form of divination. One method is to slide the point of a knife into a book between the pages, and then to open the book at that page. The knife point would then be touched down on a random verse. This verse, or the information in it, would be the answer to the question being posed.

STICKS *see* Xylomancy

Stoicheomancy

Like **stichomancy,** stoicheomancy is also a variation on **rhapsodomancy.** Rather than just any book of verse being opened, it is the work of either Homer or Virgil. The volume is opened at random and the first verse is read. It is believed that the verse will have some relevance to the question being asked. In **Greece** the preference was to take from Homer's works, while in **Rome** they favored Virgil.

Sources:

Spence, Lewis. *An Encyclopedia of the Occult*. George Routledge & Sons, London 1920.

Stolisomancy

Stolisomancy is divination by the manner in which a person dresses him- or herself. Gaius Octavius Augustus (63B CE–14 CE), emperor of **Rome,** believed that a military revolt was predicted on the morning of its occurrence by the fact that his valet had buckled his right sandal onto his left foot.

Sources:

Spence, Lewis. *An Encyclopedia of the Occult*. London: George Routledge & Sons, 1920.

STONES ***see*** **Lithomancy**

STONES, PRECIOUS AND SEMI-PRECIOUS ***see*** **Gemology**

STRANGERS ***see*** **Xenomancy**

STRAWS ***see*** **Sideromancy**

Sun Signs

(See also Astrology)

In astrology, the sun signs are the names given to the twelve main divisions of the zodiac: Aries, Taurus, Gemini, Cancer, Leo, Virgo, Libra, Scorpio, Sagittarius, Capricorn, Aquarius, and Pisces. The dates they govern are as follows:

Aries: March 21—April 19.
Taurus: April 20—May 19.
Gemini: May 20—June 20.
Cancer: June 21—July 22.
Leo: July 23—August 21.
Virgo: August 22—September 22.
Libra: September 23—October 22.
Scorpio: October 23—November 21.
Sagittarius: November 22—December 21.
Capricorn: December 22—January 20.
Aquarius: January 21—February 19.
Pisces: February 20—March 20.

However, if you are born between September 23 and October 22, for example, this does not mean that you were born under the actual group of stars known as Libra. The sun did appear to be among that group at one time, but due to what is known as the "precession of the equinoxes" it is no longer there. This precession is a very slow shift in the pattern of the sky, as seen from the earth, which takes 25,800 years to go full circle. Those names have been retained for the zodiacal divisions, however, as exactly 30° sections, regardless of the actual stars contained in each section.

The sun sign shows the personality, or image, the person presents to the world. It influences the conscious self, the active life, vitality, and self-expression. It is, however, greatly modified by the ascendant (that which rises on the eastern horizon at the time of birth) and by the position of the moon in regard to the planets of the zodiac. The ascendant more closely resembles the true self. The moon governs the instincts and emotions.

Each sun sign has traditional traits:

Aries: Positive traits are enterprising, courageous, energetic, a lover of freedom, with a pioneering spirit. Negative traits are selfishness, impulsiveness, quick temper, impatience, being unsubtle and not at all diplomatic. Aries people are usually very lively and generous, rapidly grasping situations, but they can be very aggressive to the point of giving offense. They can be quick-tempered and selfish but are also quick-witted and able to acknowledge their own selfishness. However, that quick-wittedness can lead to being erratic. The Aries person needs to express his or her sexuality, though in a positive manner. There is a liking for trying new things, exploring new areas, and taking new approaches. Sports connected with force and noise are favorites.

Taurus: Positive traits are reliability, patience and endurance, determination, trust, and affection. Negative traits are laziness and self-indulgence, stubbornness, greed, temper and obsession with routines. It is important for the Taurus person to feel secure at work and at home. There is a very bad temper that can easily be triggered. This can especially be brought on by jealousy, due to possessiveness. Taurus people have an excellent business sense, making money and holding on to it. There is also an artistic side, with an interest in sculpture and architecture. There is too much caution and fear of risk for there to be any chance of being rushed. There is great patience but also a tendency to bore others.

Gemini: Positive traits are versatility with adaptability and spontaneity. The Gemini can be witty and lively, an amusing conversationalist with a flair for languages and writing. Negative traits are changeability, restlessness, inconsistency and great inquisitiveness. They feel they are always right and there is an ability to bluff through complicated situations based on very little knowledge. Very easily bored, Gemini has a need to keep occupied and invariably does more than one thing at the same time. If not properly stimulated, the mind can turn to cunning and even to fraud. Tedium and boredom should be avoided, especially in the workplace. Languages can be appealing.

Cancer: Positive traits are a strong parental instinct, with a great love of the home. Kindness, sympathy and sensitivity are present, as are resourcefulness, shrewdness, protection, and caution. Negative traits are changeability, hyper-sensitivity, instability, and moodiness. There is a tendency to be overly emotional and also self-pitying. Although often willing to listen to other people's problems, Cancers are more often caught up in their own worries and cares. They can be moody and uncommunicative. Although prone to make unthinking comments about others, they can be overly sensitive to comments made about them. Excellent memory and highly intuitive.

Leo: Positive traits are generosity and enthusiasm, also broadmindedness and a sense of the dramatic. Negative traits are a tendency to bully, intolerance, conceit, and pomposity. The Leo person can be intolerant and interfering, pompous, and dogmatic, yet does have a warm-hearted charm that can be spontaneous when allowed. He or she can be easily hurt but would never show it. There can be extravagance, with little control over the spending of money. There is a definite flair for the dramatic and a tendency to "think big." There is also a closed mind, with things once learned retained for all time. There is a need to be able to admire the object of affection and Leo will then remain fiercely loyal at all times.

Virgo: Positive traits are a strong tendency to be analytical, meticulous, and tidy. Virgos are frequently modest. Negative traits are being hypercritical, fussy, and overly worried. The Virgo person does not find it easy to express him or herself, especially with regard to emotional relationships. A hard worker, Virgo pays great attention to detail and finds it difficult to slow down and relax. There is a tendency to intestinal problems, often brought on by worrying and nervousness. Hobbies can be enjoyed if they involve making and doing things. There are great analytical talents, making Virgos excellent at research.

Libra: Positive traits are romanticism and being very easygoing, idealistic, and diplomatic. Negative traits are indecision, frivolity, changeability, gullibility, and being easily influenced by others. The Libra person can be very flirtatious and can easily rush into a relationship that will be later regretted. There is an intense dislike of quarrels but, in order to avoid them, he or she may try to be all things to all people. There can be great indecision and there is a reputation for laziness. Once the mind *is* made up, then the Libran will usually get what is wanted. They are usually better working in partnership than alone. Libran is a cheerful, natural optimist, but hates to be lonely. There is a very strong sense of a need for justice.

Scorpio: Positive traits are persistence, determination, subtlety, imagination, powerful feelings, and emotions. Negative traits are jealousy, resentment, obstinacy, secretiveness, and suspicion. There is a need to find a positive outlet for sex, due to the powerful emotional level of a Scorpio. Love can be intense and passionate, but it can be accompanied by jealousy. There is also extreme passion in other aspects of life, with an intensity that pervades his or her life. Changes of direction in life are eagerly seized upon, with the person often destroying what has been built purely for the sake of change. There is a well-tuned intuition that can be relied upon, though there is a tendency to concentrate on analyzing reactions rather than working on the problem. Scorpios have a great personal magnetism, fascinating others with their force and energy.

Saggitarius: Positive traits are jovial optimism, versatility, adaptability, and open-mindedness. Negative traits are extremism, exaggeration, irresponsibility, tactlessness, carelessness, and blind optimism. Sagittarians have good judgment and are dependable, sincere, and scrupulous, but may overlook details. If tired, it is usually a sign of boredom. The Sagittarian needs freedom, whether physically or emotionally; he or she tends to be claustrophobic and does not like to be tied down in marriage or other close relationships. Versatile, the Sagittarian has a need for challenge and often works two different jobs. There is a love of challenge, though the fact of the challenge itself is of more interest than the problem or solution. Sagittarians do not waste time worrying but tend more toward blind optimism.

Capricorn: Positive traits are ambition, reliability, discipline, and determination. There is also a good sense of humor, patience, and perseverance. Negative traits are pessimism, miserliness, being too conventional, and having too rigid an outlook. There is a general difficulty managing human relationships, due either to shyness or lack of communication. The mind can be cool and calculating, with constructive thought patterns, and there is a need to study situations and work through them, which may take time. Depression comes easily, as does worry. There is, however, a great sense of humor with an oftentimes dry wit. The Capricorn person is conventional and usually good in business, able to advance up the ladder.

Aquarius: Positive traits are idealism, humanitarianism, independence, friendliness, and willingness. Also loyalty, originality and faithfulness. Negative traits are unpredictability, rebelliousness, perversity, eccentricity, and fixed opinions. There is a tendency to be stuck in his or her opinions; not easily persuaded if wrong. Personal independence is important, as is scope for inventiveness. The Aquarian is not concerned about what others think, ignoring their opinions. Family life does not come easily, the solitary life being preferred; if married, however, there is great loyalty and faithfulness. The Aquarian will readily help others, but with an air of detachment.

Pisces: Positive traits are compassion, humility, emotion, sensitivity, adaptability, kindness, and receptiveness. Negative traits are carelessness, vagueness, secretiveness, easy confusion, and indecisiveness. Pisces has great compassion and is always happy to ease the suffering of others. Always eager to escape from reality, of all the signs a Piscean is the most susceptible to outside influences. He or she cannot stand too much reality and will seek escape through prayer or meditation, for example. The arts are an attraction, also as an escape. Emotions can be deep and strong, sometimes to the point of confusing the person him or herself, allowing the Piscean to be carried away by seeing things in others that do not really exist. It is not easy to conform or to obey rules and orders. The natural charm of the Piscean can inspire friends and acquaintances.

Sources:
MacNeice, Louis. *Astrology*. Garden City, NY: Doubleday, 1964.
Parker, Derek and Julia. *The Compleat Astrologer*. New York: McGraw-Hill, 1971.

Svantovit; Svetovit

Svantovit, or Svetovit, was the god of the Baltic Slavs who was famous for his **prophesies,** especially those to do with the harvest. The best-known center of worship for the western Slavs was at Arkona, on the island of Rügen in the Baltic Sea, where a large wooden temple held an image of the god. This image had four heads: two facing to the front and two behind. Beside the statue hung a huge sword together with a saddle and bridle. Saxo Grammaticus, the twelfth-century Danish historian, described the statue as depicting a man who was clean shaven, with short hair, holding a bull's horn in his right hand and a bow in his left. The horn was filled with wine by the priests. Each year the priests would carefully examine the bull's horn. If much wine remained in it, that was a good **omen** for the coming year. But if the wine had considerably diminished, it was an omen of coming famine and other troubles.

A great festival was held in Svantovit's honor after each harvest. His temple was elaborately decorated and people came from all over the island to sacrifice cattle to him. Svantovit was well known for the victories his priests foretold, and he was especially accurate at divining the coming success or failure of the crops.

A beautiful white horse was housed in the temple. It was known as the White Horse of Svantovit and was venerated much as was the god himself. It was also used for divining. Several rows of spears would be fixed into the ground by the priests, and the horse would be driven through them. If it passed all the way through without injuring itself in any way on any of the spears, then the future was a bright one.

Along with the horse, an armed detachment of three-hundred soldiers was assigned to the temple, maintained by the temple. The temple received one-third of the spoils when they went to war. A war banner was also kept at the temple, which was shown by the priests before the men went to war.

Sources:

Larousse Encyclopedia of Mythology. London: Paul Hamlyn, 1965.
Wosien, Maria-Gabriele. *Man, Myth & Magic: Slavs*. London: BPC Publishing, 1970.

Swedenborg, Emanuel (1688–1722)

Emanuel Swedenborg was a Swedish engineer, philosopher, and mystic. He was born in Stockholm on January 29, 1688. He is regarded as one of the greatest and most learned men of his country. He assumed the name Swedenborg when he was elevated to the nobility by Queen Ulrica in 1719. Swedenborg was the second son of Jesper Swedberg, who was later appointed bishop of Skara.

Swedenborg was educated at Uppsala University. After graduating in 1710, he traveled Europe for five years, pursuing scientific and mechanical knowledge. In 1716, back home, he started the publication of a scientific periodical called *Dædalus hyperboreus*. Charles XII of Sweden, who was interested in the publication, appointed Swedenborg Assessor Extraordinary to the Royal College of Mines, a position to which Swedenborg devoted thirty years of his life. He finally resigned to devote the rest of his life to the spreading of the spiritual enlightenment for which he believed himself to have been especially chosen.

In 1734 Swedenborg published an important work, *Opera Philosophica et Mineralia*, about the formation of the planets. That same he he produced *Prodomus Philosophiæ Ratiocinantrio de Infinte* on the relationship between the finite and the infinite and between the soul and the body. Swedenborg followed these with other major works on anatomy, geology, and mineralogy.

Swedenborg believed he was in direct communication with heavenly spirits and recorded conversations he had with them in his books. He was an established **clairvoyant,** at one time describing a fire that was taking place 250 miles away from where he was. He had shown psychic ability as a child. The Swedenborg Church, also known as the Church of the New Jerusalem, was founded after his death in 1722. Many of his ideas influenced the later **spiritualist** movement.

Sources:
Encyclopedia Britannica. Chicago: William Benton, 1964.
Fishley, Margaret. *The Supernatural*. London: Aldus, 1976.
Fodor, Nandor. *An Encyclopedia of Psychic Science*. London, 1934.
Spence, Lewis. *An Encyclopedia of the Occult*. London: George Routledge & Sons, 1920.

SYCOMANCY

Sycomancy is divination by means of figs or fig leaves. In Sir Thomas Urquhart's *The Third Book of the Works of Mr. Francis Rabelais* (London, 1693) he comments: "By Sycomancy; O Divine Art in fig-tree leaves!" And Frederick T. Elworthy, in his *The Evil Eye* (1895), says: "Conjuring with fig leaves was called sycomancy."

It is said that questions or propositions on which the questioner wished to be enlightened were written on the leaves. If the leaf dried quickly after the question had been written, it was a negative reaction. If the leaf dried slowly, then it was a good omen. There are hundreds of species of fig trees, and in many different areas it is revered as a Tree of Life or Tree of Knowledge.

In **Greece** the fig was sacred to the god Bacchus, who was said to have created it, symbolizing procreation, fecundity, and wisdom. It is mentioned fifty-seven times in the **Bible,** testifying to its importance. It was under a fig tree that Buddha sat to first receive enlightenment. In Victorian England, for a woman to **dream** of figs meant she would have a long, happy life, with riches and all her wishes fulfilled. If a woman ever received a gift of figs that were dried out, it foretold bad luck and unhappiness to come.

Sources:
Cavendish, Richard (ed.). *Man, Myth & Magic*. London: BPC Publishing, 1970.
Oxford English Dictionary. Oxford: Clarendon Press, 1989.
Spence, Lewis. *An Encyclopedia of the Occult*. George Routledge & Sons, London 1920.

T

Table Tipping; Table Turning

(See also Radiestheia and Ouija® board)

Nandor Fodor described table tipping, or table turning, as "the crudest form of communication with the subconscious self or with extraneous intelligences." Yet tables have been used since antiquity for purposes of divination. Ammianus Marcellinus (330–395 CE), the author of a history of the **Roman** Empire, described a table with a slab engraved with the letters of the alphabet, above which a ring was suspended from a thread. The ring would swing to a succession of letters and spell out words. But table tipping was a little different and became very popular in the mid-nineteenth century, with the advent of **spiritualism.**

The usual form is for the sitters to be evenly spaced around a table and to sit with their fingertips placed lightly on the top edge (not the underside). One of the number may act as spokesperson and call out for a spirit to make contact. Very soon the table will start to move, sometimes quivering and shaking beforehand. It will often rise up on one or two legs and may actually turn, pivoting on a leg. The sitters invariably have to leave their seats and run around to keep up with the table. If questioned, the table will rear up on one or two legs and then drop back down again. Taking one thump as the letter "A," two as "B," three as "C," and so on, messages can be laboriously spelled out. An alternate (and faster) method is for the spokesperson to call out the letters of the alphabet and the table will drop down at the specific letter.

Table tipping originated in America. It rapidly spread to Europe, reaching England in 1853, where it quickly became very popular. One of the attractions of it was that there was no need for a professional **medium;** it could be done with any group of people and was usually done in someone's living room. Table tipping became such a phenomenon that scientists could not ignore it and felt they had to explain it. With the aid of the chemist Michael Faraday (1791–1867), they were able to show that the

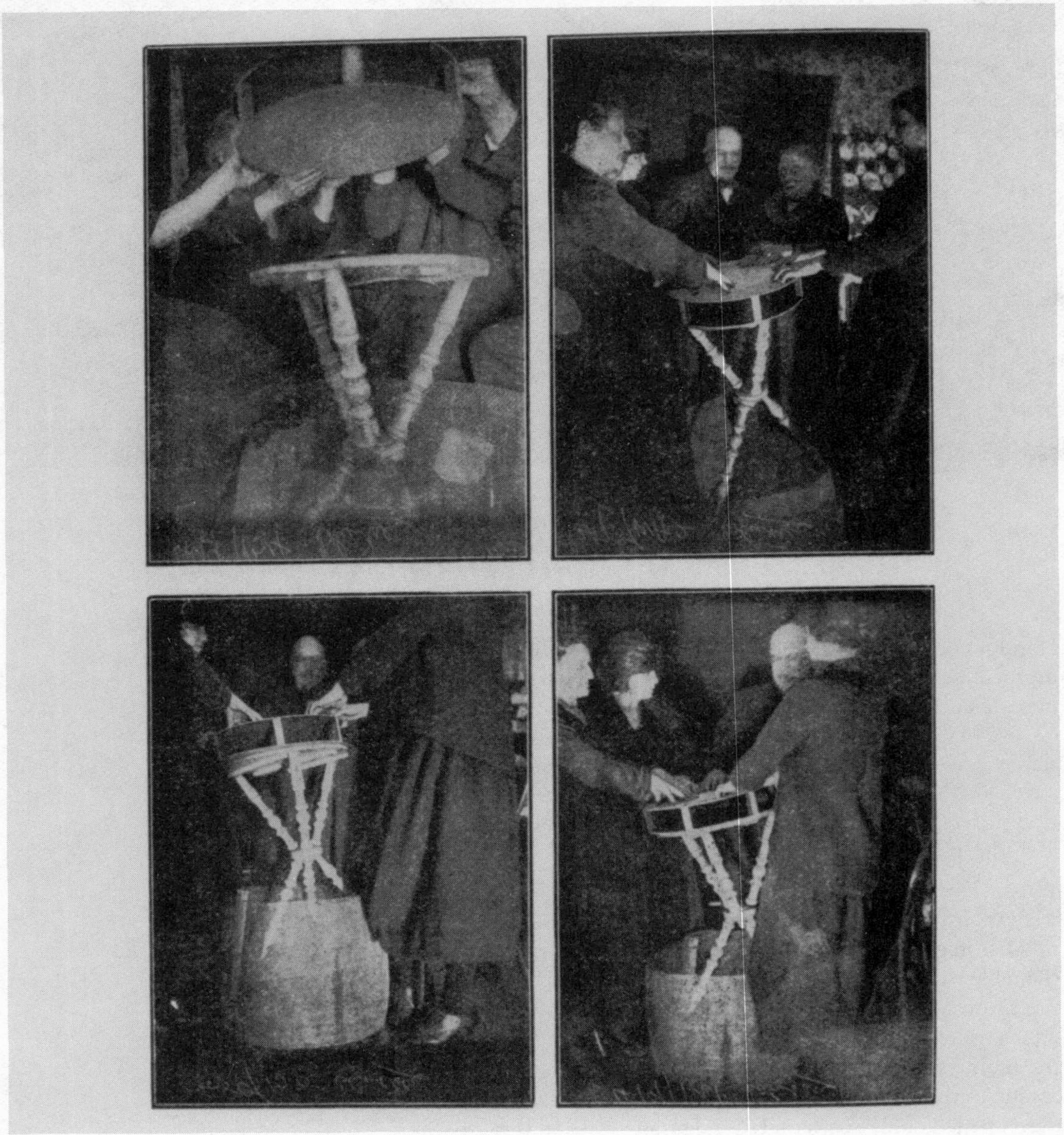

Images of a table levitation at a séance in October 1923. *Fortean Picture Library.*

actual movement of the table was due to the unconscious muscular action of the people with their fingers on it. While honestly believing they pressed downward on the table, in fact their pressure was oblique, causing the rotation of the table. The scientists seemed satisfied to have explained that (even giving the force a name: *ectenic force*), but they neglected to address the question of who or what was utilizing and directing this muscle power. How was the "table" able to give answers to questions that were unknown to those present?

Although most table-tipping **séances** are principally to communicate with the spirits of departed loved ones, they can also be for purposes of divination.

Sources:
Buckland, Raymond. *Doors to Other Worlds*. St. Paul, MN: Llewellyn, 1993.
Fodor, Nandor. *An Encyclopedia of Psychic Science*. London, 1934.
Owens, Elizabeth. *How to Communicate with Spirits*. St. Paul, MN: Llewellyn, 2002.

TAGES

A minor deity of the **Etruscans,** said to be a grandson of Jupiter. The Etruscans believed that it was Tages who had taught the art of **haruspicy,** or divination from the entrails of animals. The myth was that the god appeared from a newly plowed furrow and told the people many secrets of divination. These secrets were later written down in twelve sacred books. Tages apparently leapt from the furrow, "an infant in form but with an old man's head and wisdom," in front of Tarchon, the peasant working in the field.

Tages (also known as Tago) is often depicted as a young boy and described as "the wise Etruscan child plowed from the earth." He is said to amaze everyone with his **prophesies.** Some said that it was from his teachings that all **Roman** divination was drawn.

Sources:
Cavendish, Richard (ed.). *Man, Myth & Magic*. London: BPC Publishing, 1970.
Larousse Encyclopedia of Mythology, London: Paul Hamlyn, 1965.
Leland, Charles Godfrey. *Etruscan Magic & Occult Remedies*. New York: University Books, 1963.

TAOISM

Taoism originated in **China** and, together with Buddhism and Confucianism, is one of the three great religions of that country. It also flourishes in Singapore, Thailand and other countries of Southeast Asia. *Tao* means "the way," yet Taoism does not prescribe any particular way; it is simply "the uncomplicated essence of what is right." Chapter 37 of the *Tao Te Ching* (see below) says: "Tao does nothing, but there is nothing that it does not do."

Taoism was founded by Lao Tze, who was born in 604 BCE in Honan province of China. A predecessor of Lao Tze was the so-called Yellow Emperor Huang Ti, who lived about 2600 BCE. He has been referred to as a founder of the primary religion of the Chinese people. The names of the two are sometimes combined to give what is called the doctrine of Huang Lao.

In the first centuries of the Christian era, Taoism became a widely popular religion, associated with the practice of divination and sorcery and accepting the existence of ghosts and demons. A lot of magic was linked with the Yellow Emperor and at times Taoism is linked not only with the *Tao Te Ching* (the written teachings of Lao Tze) but also with the occult and even with the black arts, according to Benjamin

Walker. Certainly Taoism evolved an elaborate hierarchy of both male and female priest-magicians, who were specialists in various branches of Chinese occultism. They combined the roles of **medium, oracle,** sorcerer, and physician.

Various forms of divination, including both **astrology** and the **I Ching,** have become a part of Taoism, interpreted along Taoist lines. **Geomancy** is also used. In *The Concise Encyclopedia of Living Faiths* Werner Eichhorn says: "At the beginning of the present century we find Taoist religious beliefs and practices still carried on by numerous and mostly secret sects . . . much addicted to the use of charms, **planchette,** the practice of the 'three secrets' of finger signs, and magic phrases and incantations."

Sources:

Eichhorn, Werner. *The Concise Encyclopedia of Living Faiths*. New York: Hawthorne Books, 1959.
Lewis, John. *Religions of the World Made Simple*. New York: Doubleday, 1958.
Waley, Arthur. *The Way and Its Power*. New York: Grove Press, 1958.
Walker, Benjamin. *Man, Myth & Magic: Taoism*. London: BPC Publishing, 1970.

Tarot

The deck of cards known as the tarot is divided into two parts: the Major Arcana and the Minor Arcana. *Arcana* is from the Latin word for "secret." The two parts are dissimilar. The Major Arcana is a set of twenty-two distinctive cards, each separately titled. The Minor Arcana is a combination of four suits, each suit comprised of cards numbered from one (or Ace) to ten, plus court cards Page, Knight, Queen, and King. It can readily be seen that the Minor Arcana is the ancestor of our everyday playing cards, though the latter do not have the Knight and the Page has become known as the Jack.

The four suits of the Minor Arcana are most commonly known as Cups, Pentacles, Wands, and Swords (which became Hearts, Diamonds, Clubs, and Spades in the regular deck). However, they are variously known by other names such as cups, chalices, cauldrons, vessels, hearts; pentacles, coins, disks, wheels, deniers, stars, bells; wands, staves, batons, rods, scepters, leaves; swords, knives, blades, spears, acorns. Some decks are specialized in their art focus, thus producing yet other names for the suits. For divinatory reading of the tarot cards, the two Arcanas are usually intermixed, shuffled together and laid out in various spreads for interpretation.

The most common names for the twenty-two cards of the Major Arcana are: Fool, Magician, High Priestess, Empress, Emperor, Hierophant, Lovers, Chariot, Strength, Hermit, Wheel of Fortune, Justice, Hanged Man, Death, Temperance, Devil, Lightning-Struck Tower, Star, Moon, Sun, Judgment, and World. The order of these can vary slightly (in some decks Strength and Justice are reversed). The Fool may be placed at either the beginning or the end, and consequently is unnumbered. (The Fool became the Joker of the regular playing-card deck.) These cards depict symbolic figures, elements of nature, human experiences on the spiritual journey, and hopes, fears, joys, and sorrows. They are drawn from legend and myth, from universal symbolism, philosophies, religions, and magical beliefs. Some say they depict the grades or stages of the journey of an initiate. Some authors equate the Major Arcana with the twenty-two letters of the Hebrew alphabet and work them with the Qabbalah and the Tree of Life.

The French occultist known as Eliphas Zahed Lèvi (1810–1875), whose real name was Alphonse Louis Constant, was the first to do this.

In *A Complete Guide to the Tarot*, Eden Gray says:

> Symbolic keys, like material ones, are expected to fit locks and open doors. Systems such as the Kabalah or the Tarot, however, do not accomplish this in a simple or direct manner. Here we find keys that fit more than one lock and locks that can receive more than one key. The correspondence between the twenty-two Major Arcana Keys and the twenty-two paths on the Tree of Life and the twenty-two letters of the Hebrew alphabet, as well as astrological signs, evokes complex and subtle associations that can never be rigidly confined.

The first tarot cards were individually painted on thin sheets of ivory, parchment, silver, and gold. Later they were produced on card stock, though still individually painted. There was a set of tarot cards painted especially for France's Charles VI in 1392 (seventeen of these cards survive today in the Bibliothèque Nationale in Paris). With the coming of block printing, in Nuremberg c. 1430, they became more generally available and, eventually, quite popular. In fifteenth-century England, King Edward IV forbade the importation of tarot cards, but soldiers fighting in Normandy, Touraine, Anjou and Poitou smuggled back cards from France, and the decks found their way into the homes of the nobility. By the time of the French Revolution there was a grand revival of interest in esotericism and, with mystic lodges and secret societies springing up, the tarot came into fashion and more general use.

The actual origins of the tarot are lost in time. There is some evidence to show that the cards originated in the north of India and were brought out of that region by the Romany, or Gypsies, in their mass exodus. Certainly the Gypsies were responsible for much of the distribution across Europe. But there is also speculation that the cards originated in China, Korea or Northern Italy.

The cards may be used as personal, individual meditation tools. Some people draw a single card at the start of every day, and meditate on it, obtaining an idea of what the coming day will hold. But the most common practice is to use the cards to answer questions, or to glean an idea of what the future might hold for oneself or for another. There is a traditional way of doing this with a variety of spreads or layouts for the cards, with each card position having a specific meaning.

Querier

Usually a card is chosen to represent the querier, and this is laid down on the table with the other cards arranged around it. This is known as the significator card. It is best for the reader to go through all the cards in the deck to find one he or she feels is "right" to represent the querier. However, a faster (though not as accurate) method is to take a card from the court cards as follows: If the querier is male, choose from the Kings and Knights, with a King for an older man and a Knight for a younger one. If female, choose a Queen for an older woman and a Page for a younger one. If the person is dark, take from the Swords suit. If blonde, take from the Cups suit. If brown-haired, then choose from Wands and if light brown, from Pentacles.

Layouts

For any of the layouts, the cards are first shuffled by the querier, who concentrates on any question(s) to which an answer is sought. After the cards have been well mixed, the deck is cut into three piles, cutting to the left with the left hand. They are then picked up again in an order different from that in which they were laid down. Some readers do not like to have their cards handled by others and so they will do the shuffling and cutting themselves. They should still allow the querier to first place his or her hands on the cards, though, in order to transmit some personal energy into them.

Once the cards have been cut and restacked, they are spread across the table face down so that the querier may pick ten cards (or however many are called for in the particular layout). These are taken out in the order chosen and the rest put to one side. Some readers prefer to take ten (or however many) off the top of the shuffled and cut deck, rather than choose them at random.

The most popular layout is the Celtic Cross Spread, which utilizes ten cards. The significator is laid, face up, in the center of the table and the first card placed face down on top of it. The next card is laid across these two, forming a cross. Card Three is placed above these, Card Four below them, Five to the left and Six to the right. (Note that these positions may be reversed, depending on the preference of the reader, but their meanings are always the same.) Then, in a line upward and to the right of these cards, the remaining four are placed, with Seven at the bottom, Eight above it, Nine above that, and Ten at the top.

The meanings of the positions of the cards are as follows: The significator is the appearance of the querier or how he or she likes to be perceived. Card One is "what covers the querier"; that is, the forces currently at work around the querier. Card Two is that which "crosses" him or her: the forces, or people, working against the querier. Card Three is "above" the querier: what they aspire to; what they are capable of achieving. Card Four is "beneath." It is the querier's deep, inner, basic self. Cards Five and Six are what is behind (in the past) and in front (the immediate future). Moving now to the four cards on the right, Card Seven is a fuller picture of the querier and, as such, will probably reflect some of what has been seen in the significator, in One and Four. It also shows how the querier is likely to behave in the present circumstances. Above this is Card Eight, which is the querier's "House." This refers to those who are close to the querier; close friends and relatives who can be relied upon. Then comes Card Nine, which is "Hopes and Fears." If Card Two touched on some person or circumstance that was acting against the querier, then this may be seen reflected in Card Nine, if the querier is aware and afraid. Alternately, it may indicate that the querier is very much an optimist with few, if any, fears and many hopes. Card Ten is labeled the "final outcome," yet it must be remembered that tarot cards (or any form of divination) cannot see the far distant future, but only the situation with the forces currently at work around the querier. The extent of this is probably no more than a year at most. With this in mind, the "final outcome" is not truly final. Indeed, with this and any other form of divination, nothing is set in stone; it is within everyone to change what is indicated.

Another popular layout is the Horoscope Spread. This, as its name suggests, follows the houses of an astrological chart, so twelve cards are chosen and are laid

A tarot layout. ***Fortean Picture Library.***

down in a circle with the significator in the center. Following the numbering of the houses, the first card is placed on the left, just below the horizontal. Card Two is below it and so on around counterclockwise.

The houses are governed as follows, with their fields of interest and concern:

The Houses and Their Concerns

First house: Personal appearance and disposition; beginnings; childhood

Second house: Possessions; money; values; investing

Third house: Communication; brothers and sisters; close neighbors; short journeys; transport

Fourth house: Home; property; roots; real estate; underground places; a man's mother or a woman's father

Fifth house: Pleasure; love; sex; amusement; sensual pleasures

Sixth house: Domestic animals, health and conditions affecting health; clothing; servants; physical comfort

Seventh house: The spouse; partners

Eighth house: Death; losses; wills; legacies

Ninth house: Spirituality; religion; journeys to other lands; relatives by marriage

Tenth house: Business; business affairs; honors; earnings

Eleventh house: Friends and acquaintances; hopes; fears; wishes

Twelfth house: Confinements: prison, deportation, exile; enemies; large animals

The tarot cards are then interpreted with regard to these house meanings. This is a very good spread to use for a general reading to view a person's life circumstances.

A simple three-card layout is useful for a "past, present, future" look and is popular for very quick readings. The querier shuffles the cards and cuts, as usual. The reader then takes the top and the bottom card and places them to one side as the "surprise." Now three cards are dealt off the top of the deck and placed side by side, Card One being the past, Two the present, and Three the future. Three more cards are dealt on top of those, and then a final three on top of those. The result is three piles of three cards each. The first pile—the past—is turned over and the three cards spread out and interpreted, relating them to the past. Then the present three are read, and finally the future three. Last, the two surprise cards are turned over. These represent unexpected forces—which might be for good or ill—that may come into play at any time. There is no significator used in this layout.

Many more layouts can be used, and any good book on tarot will detail several of them.

Looking at the total cards in any spread can give some overall indications. A large number of Cups, for example, indicates a lot of love about the querier. Similarly, a large number of Pentacles shows the presence of money and/or intrigue. A lot of Wands shows change and possible obstacles. A large number of Swords shows suffering and possible sickness. A large number of court cards is indicative of the situation being in the hands of other people rather than the querier's. The presence of many Major Arcana cards shows that there are powerful forces at work, while a lack of Major Arcana cards indicates that the forces are slight and fragmentary and that the situation(s) may change quickly.

The cards should be read as they are turned up, which means that some of them will be upright while others will be upside-down, or "reversed." Usually the reversed meaning is a negative aspect of the upright meaning, though not always. For instance, sometimes it simply means that there will be minor problems and delays. With some decks, the Minor Arcana cards do not have full pictures but simply the designated number of symbols; for example: four cups or six swords, or three wands. With these decks it is not possible to tell when some of the cards are upright or reversed since they would look the same either way.

Some readers believe that it doesn't matter whether the cards are upright or reversed; the full meaning will come out just through the interpretation of the card itself, regardless of how it lies. Many readers will "read" the cards by saying what they feel about them, rather than by simply giving the traditional meanings as listed in most books. This is probably a better interpretation since it provides a much more personalized interpretation.

Below are the "traditional" interpretations for the Major Arcana.

0—FOOL. *Upright:* There is a choice to be made; one of vital importance to the Querier. Care must be used in making the choice; all powers are being brought to bear. *Reversed:* The querier is not taking the choice seriously and is not aware of the gravity of the situation.

1—MAGICIAN. *Upright:* Enlightenment. Mastery, skill, wisdom and occult knowledge. Power. The ability to direct power and control others. *Reversed:* The misuse of power. Weakness and indecision. Deceit and manipulation may be practiced. Possible egocentric control.

2—HIGH PRIESTESS. *Upright:* Hidden influences at work. Unrevealed future; mystery. Wisdom, sagacity. Objectivity. *Reversed:* Ignorance, conceit, shortsightedness. Surface knowledge. Lack of understanding.

3—EMPRESS. *Upright:* Material wealth, marriage, children. Fertility and fruitfulness. Feminine influence; female wiles. Mother; sister; comforter. Commitment; good union. *Reversed:* Loss of power, indecision, lack of harmony. Inaction. Possibility of poverty, war, destruction. Frittering away of resources.

4—EMPEROR. *Upright:* Authority, power, leadership, government. Control of the masses. Position of negotiation. Authority, confidence, stability. Attainment of goals. Male influence. *Reversed:* Loss of control. Insecurity, weakness. Lack of leadership, instability, vacillation. Domination.

5—HIEROPHANT. *Upright:* Ritualism, mercy, inspiration. Conformity. Religious leader. Preference for ritual. Bondage to convention. Appreciation of past heritage. *Reversed:* Unconventionality, unorthodoxy, openness to new ideas. Renunciation.

6—LOVERS. *Upright:* Attraction, harmony, beauty and perfection. Deep feelings, yearning, creating of bonds. Balanced opposites. Marriage of the feminine (receptive, formative) and the masculine (assertive, expressive) and of the conscious and unconscious. *Reversed:* Possibility of wrong choice, quarrels, need to stabilize emotions. Separation, frustration in love, fickleness.

7—CHARIOT. *Upright:* Triumph, conquest, success, mastering enemies through power and intelligence. Travel; triumph over financial problems. Rushing to a decision *Reversed:* Conflict, problems, loss of control. Victory slips through the fingers. An unethical victory.

8—STRENGTH. *Upright:* Determination; resolution. Conquest. Spiritual power overcomes material power. The triumph of love over hate; higher nature over carnal desires. Power of the personal will. *Reversed:* Weakness. Lack of faith. Tyranny. Domination of the material. Abuse of power. Personal weakness and failure.

9—HERMIT. *Upright:* Counsel, knowledge, wisdom. Withdrawal. A guide who will lead to spiritual goals. Possible journey. The lamp is sometimes seen as the Lamp of Truth. Solitary introspection may be needed. *Reversed:* Refusal to listen to advice. Imprudence. Haste; rashness. Rejection of knowledge. Childish acts.

10—WHEEL OF FORTUNE. *Upright:* Opportunity, success, increase, unexpected good fortune. Approaching the end of a problem. Progress; advancement, for better or worse. *Reversed:* Bad luck; failure. Unexpected interruption. Setbacks. Outside influences at work.

11—JUSTICE. *Upright:* Proper balance. Justice will be done. Harmony; equity. Good intentions. A balanced personality. A well-balanced mind. A fair and impartial outcome. Good education. A desire and a need for justice. *Reversed:* Injustice. Unfairness. Legal complications. Bias. A weighted balance. Unrevealed evidence.

12—HANGED MAN. *Upright:* Life suspended. Apathy, passivity, dullness. A respite between significant events. Suspended decisions. Self sacrifice; surrender; readjustment. Rebirth; regeneration. *Reversed:* Unwillingness to sacrifice or make necessary effort. Useless sacrifice. Wasted effort. False prophecy. Arrogance.

13—DEATH. *Upright:* Transformation, unexpected change. Destruction followed by renewal. Death (not necessarily physical) and rebirth. Loss; failure. Great change. *Reversed:* Stagnation; immobility; inertia. Partial change. Narrow escape.

14—TEMPERANCE. *Upright:* Modification, adaptation, coordination. Patience; self-control. Bringing together into perfect harmony. Good management. Expansion of the conscious mind into the metaphysical realms. *Reversed:* Separation. Quarrels, dissension, discord. Frustration. Inability to work with others. Competing interests.

15—DEVIL. *Upright:* Downfall, malevolence, domination of matter over spirit, black magic. Punishment, self-destruction, bondage, revolution. Unexpected failure. Inability to realize goals. *Reversed:* Overcoming handicaps, beginning of understanding, release from bondage. Divorce. Respite.

16—LIGHTNING-STRUCK TOWER. *Upright:* Change, in the sense of overthrowing the past. Conflict; catastrophe. Break-down of old beliefs. Disruption; misery; bankruptcy. Loss of love, money, security. Setback. *Reversed:* Oppression. Imprisonment. False accusations; entrapment. Living in a rut.

17—STAR. *Upright:* Inspiration, insight, hope, faith. Spiritual love. Astrological influences. Compassion, inner strength, guidance, spiritual enlightenment. *Reversed:* Doubt, pessimism, imbalance. Stubbornness. Lack of perception.

18—MOON. *Upright:* Deception, disillusionment, obscurity. Imagination, dreams and intuition. Warnings. Possible trickery and dishonesty. Latent psychic powers. Secret enemies. *Reversed:* Deceptions are not as bad as first feared. Temptations overcome. Getting off without having to pay the price.

19—SUN. *Upright:* Satisfaction, happiness, attainment. Love; joy. Pleasure in the simple way of life. Just rewards. Contentment. *Reversed:* Loneliness; unhappiness. Delayed victory (not necessarily lost). Loss of friendship.

20—JUDGMENT. *Upright:* Renewal. An awakening; a change of position; a change of consciousness. Development; promotion. A blending with the universe. Need to repent and forgive. *Reversed:* Disappointment, delay. Fear of death. Failure to find happiness. Self-doubt and self-judgment.

21—WORLD. *Upright:* Completion, attainment. The end result of all efforts. Triumph and just rewards. Assured success. Attainment of complete self-esteem. Capability. *Reversed:* Imperfection. Success yet to be gained. Failure; disappointment. Lack of vision. Refusal to learn.

Below are the traditional meanings for the Minor Arcana

ACE OF CUPS. *Upright:* Abundance, fertility, love, joy, nourishment. *Reversed:* Instability, revolution.

TWO OF CUPS. *Upright:* Partnership, cooperation, friendship, love, union. *Reversed:* False love, instability, broken partnership.

THREE OF CUPS. *Upright:* Perfection, conclusion, fulfillment, happy issue. A healing to come. *Reversed:* Excesses of pleasure, both physical and of the senses.

FOUR OF CUPS. *Upright:* Discontent, imaginary vexations, disgust, weariness, reevaluation. *Reversed:* Novelty, new instructions and relationships.

FIVE OF CUPS. *Upright:* Loss but not total, inheritance, not up to expectations, disappointing marriage. *Reversed:* Hopeful expectations, return of old friend, new alliance.

SIX OF CUPS. *Upright:* Past memories, renewed acquaintance, new knowledge and relationships, happiness. *Reversed:* Living in the past, gift from the past, renewal.

SEVEN OF CUPS. *Upright:* Multitude of ideas and interests, castles in the air, scattered forces, impermanence. *Reversed:* Will and determination, project about to be realized.

EIGHT OF CUPS. *Upright:* Leaving material success for new roads, abandoning present situation, disappointment in love. *Reversed:* Joy, feasting, celebration.

NINE OF CUPS. *Upright:* Material success, assured future, contentment, satisfaction, good health. *Reversed:* Overindulgence, mistakes, imperfections.

TEN OF CUPS. *Upright:* Happy family life, contentment, perfect love, lasting happiness, attainment of heart's desire. *Reversed:* Betrayal, loss of friendship, estrangement from family.

PAGE OF CUPS. *Upright:* Birth of a child or an idea, news, new proposals. A young person, often fair with light hair and light hazel eyes. *Reversed:* Obstacles, seduction, deception soon to be uncovered.

KNIGHT OF CUPS. *Upright:* Message, invitation, proposition. Coming love, advances. A young person with light brown hair and hazel eyes. *Reversed:* Trickery, duplicity, fraud. Propositions should be examined carefully.

QUEEN OF CUPS. *Upright:* Visionary gift, poetry, imagination, success, pleasure, wisdom. Often a fair haired woman with hazel eyes. *Reversed:* Good but perverse woman. Possible dishonesty, immorality.

KING OF CUPS. *Upright:* Business, lawyer, responsibility. Arts and sciences. Creative, liberal and generous. Light brown hair and hazel eyes. *Reversed:* Dishonesty, injustice, scandal, possible law suit. Man with violent temper.

ACE OF PENTACLES. *Upright:* Ecstasy, perfect attainment, felicity, bliss. Gold, prosperity. *Reversed:* The evil side of wealth, corruption of riches.

TWO OF PENTACLES. *Upright:* Agility at handling situations, harmony, difficulty in launching new projects, news and written messages. *Reversed:* Forced gaiety, exchange of letters, inability to handle situations.

THREE OF PENTACLES. *Upright:* Skilled labor, trade, master craftsman, apprenticeship. *Reversed:* Mediocrity in workmanship, puerility, pettiness.

FOUR OF PENTACLES. *Upright:* Possessiveness, inheritance, becoming attached to material possessions, miserliness. *Reversed:* Delay, opposition, suspense.

FIVE OF PENTACLES. *Upright:* Destitution, loneliness, poverty, love gone astray. *Reversed:* Disorder, good companionship, new interests.

SIX OF PENTACLES. *Upright:* Philanthropy, charity, gifts, success, sharing prosperity. *Reversed:* Envy, jealousy, desire.

SEVEN OF PENTACLES. *Upright:* Respite, growth after hard work, business, barter, possible delay. *Reversed:* Anxiety regarding money, impatience.

EIGHT OF PENTACLES. *Upright:* Craftsmanship, skill, apprenticeship, constant work. *Reversed:* Voided ambition, immodesty, vanity, cunning.

NINE OF PENTACLES. *Upright:* Material well-being, success, accomplishment, certitude. *Reversed:* Deception, bad faith, possible loss of material possessions.

TEN OF PENTACLES. *Upright:* Prosperous family, inheritance, riches, gains, family matters, real estate. *Reversed:* Loss of inheritance, robbery, family misfortune.

PAGE OF PENTACLES. *Upright:* Reflection, scholarship, messenger, study, news. Dark-haired, dark-eyed youth. *Reversed:* Unfavorable news, dissipation, opposition.

KNIGHT OF PENTACLES. *Upright:* Patience, responsibility, utility, black haired, black eyed young person. *Reversed:* Inertia, idleness, stagnation, carelessness.

QUEEN OF PENTACLES. *Upright:* Generosity, opulence, intelligence, magnificence, freedom from lack of material wealth. Black-haired, black-eyed woman. *Reversed:* Suspicion, fear, mistrust, neglected duties.

KING OF PENTACLES. *Upright:* Valor, intelligence, mathematical aptitude, wisdom, success. Black-haired, dark-eyed man. *Reversed:* Weakness, vice, corruption, perversity.

ACE OF WANDS. *Upright:* Enterprise, creation, invention, beginnings, virility, money, fortune, inheritance. *Reversed:* False starts. Fall, possible ruin, clouded joy.

TWO OF WANDS. *Upright:* Fortune, riches, real estate, interest in scientific matters. Plans for expansion. *Reversed:* Domination by others, suffering, sadness, trouble, fear.

THREE OF WANDS. *Upright:* Commerce, trade, cooperation and success in business, business partnership. *Reversed:* Caution, possible treachery and disappointment.

FOUR OF WANDS. *Upright:* Perfected work, bounty of the harvest home, coming romance, haven, repose, peace. *Reversed:* Prosperity, increase—as in Upright.

FIVE OF WANDS. *Upright:* Competition, struggle, battle of life, change for the better. *Reversed:* Litigation, disputes, contradictions.

SIX OF WANDS. *Upright:* Triumph, triumphal procession, victory, gain, good news, and advancement. *Reversed:* Fear of enemy, apprehension, delay, treachery.

SEVEN OF WANDS. *Upright:* Advantage, discussion from position of advantage, barter, competition, courage. *Reversed:* Perplexity, embarrassment, anxiety, caution.

EIGHT OF WANDS. *Upright:* Swift messenger, end of a journey, great haste, arrows of love. *Reversed:* Jealousy, quarrels, domestic disputes.

NINE OF WANDS. *Upright:* Preparedness, ready for fight, strength in reserve, defense. *Reversed:* Calamity, obstacles, delay.

TEN OF WANDS. *Upright:* Temporary burden, overreaching, success through effort, approaching solution to problem. *Reversed:* Separation, duplicity, treachery.

PAGE OF WANDS. *Upright:* Envoy, messenger, good news, faithful lover. Blond, blue- eyed young person. *Reversed:* Bad news, indecision, instability.

KNIGHT OF WANDS. *Upright:* Relocation, flight, absence. A fair-haired, blue-eyed young person. *Reversed:* Interruption, division, discord, frustration.

QUEEN OF WANDS. *Upright:* Honor, chastity, home loving, country dwelling, chaste. Often a blonde, blue-eyed woman. *Reversed:* Opposition, jealousy, strictness and economy, deceit, infidelity.

KING OF WANDS. *Upright:* Conscientious, honest, country dwelling, marriage, unexpected inheritance. Often a blond, blue-eyed man of authority. *Reversed:* Severity, unyielding, strict, stern judgments.

ACE OF SWORDS. *Upright:* Triumph by force, excess, fertility, dominance. *Reversed:* As Upright, but with disastrous results.

TWO OF SWORDS. *Upright:* Balance, equal forces, indecision, truce, impotence. *Reversed:* Movement sometimes in the wrong direction, falsehood, duplicity.

THREE OF SWORDS. *Upright:* Sorrow, unhappy love, separation, division, rupture. *Reversed:* Disorder, confusion, possible loss.

FOUR OF SWORDS. *Upright:* Exile, respite, retreat, solitude, convalescence. *Reversed:* Circumspection, precaution, social unrest, economy.

FIVE OF SWORDS. *Upright:* Conquest, defeat, degradation, dishonor, satisfaction. *Reversed:* Weakness, loss, defeat.

SIX OF SWORDS. *Upright:* Escape, attempted avoidance of danger, journey by water, eventual success. *Reversed:* Deadlock, no escape, stalemate.

SEVEN OF SWORDS. *Upright:* Partial success, attempt, partial loss, confidence, annoyance. *Reversed:* Good advice, counseling, slander.

EIGHT OF SWORDS. *Upright:* Crisis, bondage that is seemingly inescapable, waste of energy. *Reversed:* New beginnings possible, release, relaxation, meditation.

NINE OF SWORDS. *Upright:* Desolation, inability to make a decision, failure, despair, misery, suffering. *Reversed:* Imprisonment, shame, fear, doubt.

TEN OF SWORDS. *Upright:* Extreme burdens, great misfortune, pain, affliction, tears, not a card of violent death. *Reversed:* Advantage, profit, success, power.

PAGE OF SWORDS. *Upright:* Secrecy, espionage, vigilance, overseeing. A young person with dark hair and dark eyes. *Reversed:* Unexpected events, possible illness, unexpected state.

KNIGHT OF SWORDS. *Upright:* Bravery, skill, sudden appearance in querier's life, conflict, destruction, impetuosity. A dark-haired, dark-eyed young man. *Reversed:* Imprudence, extravagance, false bravado.

QUEEN OF SWORDS. *Upright:* Sterility, privation, widowhood, sadness, mourning. A dark haired, dark eyed woman. *Reversed:* Malice, artifice, bigotry, deceit.

KING OF SWORDS. *Upright:* Wisdom, authority, military or governmental intelligence, justice, power. *Reversed:* Cruelty, perversity, unjust, possible lawsuit.

Sources:

Buckland, Raymond. *The Buckland Romani Tarot: The Gypsy Book of Wisdom*. St. Paul, MN: Llewellyn, 2001.

Donaldson, Terry. *Step-by-Step Tarot*. London: Thorsons, 1995.

Gray, Eden. *The Tarot Revealed*. New York: Inspiration House, 1960.

Gray, Eden. *A Complete Guide to the Tarot*. New York: Crown, 1970.

Waite, Arthur Edward. *The Pictorial Key to the Tarot*. New York: University Books, 1959 (London 1910) .

Tasseography

Tasseography is divination by means of reading the pattern of tea leaves left in a cup. It was a big favorite around the turn of the last century and up to the 1930s and 1940s, when any number of "Gypsy Tea Rooms" sprang up in most large towns and cities. These establishments featured dubious "Gypsies" who would read the tea leaves for patrons. A true Romani (Gypsy) will make a ritual out of the reading, starting with making a pot of tea (*meski*) for the client and pouring a full cup. No strainer is used when the tea is poured, and it should be tea without milk or sugar added. The client should take at least three sips of the tea while concentrating on any question(s) he or she may have.

After the cup of tea has been poured and the tea is drunk, or at least sipped and poured away, very little liquid should be left in the bottom of the cup. What does remain is distributed around the cup by the client tipping it and rotating it three times before upturning the cup on the saucer. The cup is then turned right side up and the diviner studies the pattern of the tea leaves as they are distributed about the inner surface. Many diviners say that the cup should be turned counterclockwise, others say counterclockwise for females and clockwise for males.

Divination by reading tea leaves. *Fortean Picture Library.*

The tea most often used is China tea, but any large-leaf variety will do, such as Ceylon or even mint tea. Finer leaf tea can be used, as can coffee grounds, but these do not leave such interesting patterns. The clustering of the leaves is what makes the patterns that become symbols, as described below. The cup used should be a round one, pale colored or plain white on the inside, and with a handle. However decorative the cup might be on the outside, the inner surface should be clear and completely smooth, without grooves or ridges of any sort that might interfere with the casual distribution of the tea leaves.

To interpret, start at the top of the cup, by the rim, and work downward. The handle represents the client so those symbols closest to the handle will have the strongest influence on him or her. Those on the far side of the cup, away from the handle, will have the least influence. Those on the left are generally (though not always) negative influences, and those on the right are positive.

Time is judged according to the positioning of the symbol, top to bottom, in the cup. At or near the upper rim is the present. The further down into the cup, the further into the future. The very bottom of the cup represents the far future—up to a year away.

The symbols made by the groupings of tea leaves will not necessarily look *exactly* like the things they represent. Imagination must be used by the diviner. It will be found that there is the *suggestion* of, say, a bird or a rabbit. These suggestions should be enough to trigger the mind into seeing them fully and seeing all that they represent. Sometimes it happens that the symbols are very distinct, but it won't necessarily be so. As with so many forms of divination, what is actually seen is used as a focal point, as a "trigger," for the reader's inbred psychic power. Seeing and interpreting the symbols are best done when that interpretation comes from within the reader rather than from memorizing a list of shapes and symbols and their probable meanings. However, to start with here are some of the traditional meanings and interpretations.

Aces: The ace of any card suit indicates powerful forces at work. If Ace of Hearts, it will deal with domestic and social affairs; Diamonds, financial affairs; Clubs, business, especially contracts and lawsuits; Spades, sorrow, delays, upset.

Acorn: Near the handle indicates coming riches; far side, possible financial help through a second party.

Airplane: Swift journey; promotion. A biplane is success due to partnership.

Alligator: Great care is needed to avoid injury from those trying to harm you.

Alps: High ideals. Check other nearby symbols to gauge success and to get an idea of time.

Anchor: Settling down; establishing roots.

Angel: Good news on its way.

Ant: Industry; perseverance; thrift. Success through your own efforts.

Anvil: Financial gains following difficulties, with work needed.

Arc: Segment of circle—unfinished project or career. Premature retirement; possible accident.

Arrow: Bad news to come; disagreeable letter on its way. If dots around the arrow, it is connected with money. Note direction of arrow for indication of which direction the news will come from.

Asterisk: Immediate attention needed. Check other nearby symbols.

Axe: Danger and difficulties ahead. Possible separation or estrangement; loss of friends. Double-headed axe means there will be a choice.

Baby: New enterprise beginning. Possibly start of new troubles.

Bag: Secret enemies, plans, schemes, plots against you. The fuller the bag; the greater the problem.

Bagpipes: Difficulties in business. Discord. Excitement and high tension, bringing nervousness and ill health.

Ball: Various ups and downs to come, over which you will have no control.

Balloon: A rise in fortunes; a much-needed lift.

Barrel: Empty dreams and vain ambitions. You may have to serve when you'd rather be the boss.

Basket: If near a house it indicates an addition to the family. It can also mean a gift or legacy. Basket of flowers is good times ahead.

Bat: False friends. Need for caution, and prepare for the worst.

Bear: Could run into danger through your own stupidity. You may have to overcome obstacles through brute force.

Bed: Untidy bed is a poor state of mind bringing poor results. Tidy bed indicates that fortunes will be good.
Bee: Prosperity as the result of industry. Acquisition of fortune; wealth gained through trade. General change of fortune for the better.
Bench: Stability. Status quo.
Bird: Good news coming. Check other symbols nearby.
Boat: Possible journey; visitor from afar.
Book: Open book signifies some sort of revelation to your benefit. Closed book is need for research, with possible trouble and expense.
Boomerang: Retributive justice. You will gather the fruits of your actions; good or bad.
Boot: Protection from danger, if well formed. If rough it indicates disgrace and loss of position.
Bottle: Concerning your health. Check with your doctor.
Bow: Good sign, showing ability to grow. Hope.
Bracelet: Possible wedding, union, partnership.
Branch: Sign of birth. A new venture, when with leaves. Without leaves, disappointment; barren ambitions.
Bride: Symbol of sorrow. Possible troubles on their way.
Bridge: A way out of your difficulties; path over your problems.
Broken Lines: Uncertainty or broken promises.
Broom: Possible scandal or misrepresentation may be swept away. You can "clean up your act," your life, your job.
Buffalo: Exercise care and forethought. Danger through hazardous speculation.
Bull: Gain and prosperity.
Butterfly: Frivolity; vanity. Exercise caution.
Cabbage: Jealousy and spite.
Cage: Marriage.
Cake: Pleasure; celebration.
Camel: Progress, leading to a better position in life.
Candle: Doer of good deeds; philanthropist.
Canoe: Visitor from afar, or you will visit someone far away.
Carriage: Benefits coming from others.
Cart: Trade plentiful and profitable. Your burdens will be light.
Castle: High office for you, or you will find favor from those in high office.
Cat: Crafty nature. Beware of cheating in business. If cat is resting, then symbol of domestic comfort.
Chair: Position of trust and affluence; satisfaction and success. Can be change of estate or new occupation.
Chicken: Competence; completion; nervous energy.
Child: Progress and success through natural powers. Fresh enterprises will add to prosperity.
Chimney: Distinction through service. Expect changes in your environment.
Church: Ceremonial; formality. Possible connection with birth, marriage or death.
Cigar: Dreams of independence and luxury.

Cigarette: Don't be frivolous.
Circle: Work will come to completion and perfection.
Clock: Be attentive; time flies. Recovery from sickness. Possible death news.
Clover: Luck. Great luck if four-leafed.
Coffin: End of a plan or phase. Can be serious illness.
Column: Distinction and honors. Admiration.
Comet: Unexpected visitor or unexpected news.
Cornucopia: Freedom from want. Symbol of plenty.
Cow: Peaceful and happy existence. You may be asked for a donation; subscription.
Cradle: New projects; enterprises. Broken cradle indicates trouble.
Cross: Nucleus of energy; source for ideas; inspiration.
Crown: Ascendancy over difficulties. Elevation to higher position.
Cup: An offering. You may have to make a sacrifice but it will lead to an advancement.
Daffodil: Happiness. Plans fulfilled.
Dagger: Warning. Be careful.
Deer: Good news from the countryside, or from a distance. Quick decision may be called for.
Devil: Beware of false friends. Possible danger.
Dice: Possible losses from gambling.
Dog: Friendship. You can rely on the advice and assistance of friends. If dog is lying down, there will be a period of quiet and peace. If dog is leaping, there will be joyful news.
Door: Opportunity awaits.
Dot: Emphasizes the meaning and importance of symbols close by.
Dragon: New beginnings and opportunities ahead, but only after some challenges.
Drum: Publicity, not necessarily good. Can be riots and disturbances; domestic disputes.
Duck: Good news.
Dumbbell: Hard work for little profit. Rivalry.
Dwarf: Disappointment and failure.
Eagle: Aspirations will meet with tremendous success. Very fortunate sign.
Ear: Beware of scandal.
Egg or Oval: New projects and beneficial changes. Probable success.
Eight: Number of Uranus. Separation. Inspiration, invention, genius.
Elephant: Strength and wisdom. Success after some delay.
Explosion: Impending disaster. Violent upsets and disturbances.
Eyeglasses: Be extra careful in all business dealings.
Face, Head: Can be good or bad, depending on the type of face. Take note of which way the face is looking; toward or away from the handle. A full face that is pleasant indicates new discoveries.
Fan: False friends; flirtation; indiscretion.
Feather: Inconstancy. Levity: be more serious.
Fence: Obstacles and limitations.

Fire: Surprising news and hasty action. Be cautious in words and deeds.
Fish: A fortunate symbol. Increase and opportunities. Affluence.
Fist: Guard against impulses.
Five: Number of Jupiter. Good fortune and joy. Increase.
Flag: Can be a danger sign. Usually associated with duty. Possibly special honors.
Flower(s): A single flower shows a favor granted. A bunch of flowers is a sign of many benefits.
Fly: Annoyances, often connected with domestic issues. Can be a scandal.
Foot: Understanding. *Two Feet:* You can move in any direction you wish.
Fork: A dilemma from circumstances beyond your control.
Fountain: Great success and happiness.
Four: Number of Mercury. Reality; completion.
Fox: Possible treachery.
Frog: Wrong ideas and false outlook.
Fruit: Good sign, showing increase and profit.
Gallows: Extreme danger of financial or social failure.
Garland: See "Flower(s)."
Gate: If open, opportunities. If closed, a challenge or barrier.
Ghost: Possible danger form unexpected sources.
Girl: Happiness and prosperity.
Glass: Symbol of honesty but also fragility.
Goat: Misfortune due to obstinacy.
Grapes: Increase and prosperity but with accompanying burdens.
Grasshopper: News from a distant friend.
Grave: News of a death.
Guitar: Happiness in love.
Gun, Pistol, Revolver, Rifle: Need for unusual care. Possibility of hurt from a distance. If a heart is nearby, it symbolizes a rival for love.
Hammer: Stress and strain. Persistence is called for.
Hand: Friendship, assistance if extended toward handle of cup. Loss of opportunity if away from handle.
Handcuffs: Restraint. Difficulties and frustrations.
Harp: Harmony and concord. Happy union in a romantic situation.
Hat: A new occupation, fresh projects, new ambitions.
Heart: Happiness. Close friendship. Engagement or marriage.
Hill: Attainment. The higher the hill, the better your fortunes.
Hive: Symbol of the home. If with a swarm of bees, it is a symbol of great success.
Horn: Glad tidings.
Horse, Pony: Close friendships. A horse's head indicates a lover coming. A galloping horse is good news from someone dear.
Hourglass: You must act quickly, since time is running out.
House: Safety; possessions. A contented life.
Insect: Troubles and vexations. Small irritations.
Ivy: Loyal friends.
Jug: Influential friendships. You will help others and, in so doing, help yourself.
Kangaroo: Unexpected travel plans.

Kettle: Domestic happiness.

Key: Important decisions to be made. Possible new path ahead. Carefully consider any new proposals.

Kite: Unusual ambitions. You can reach new heights.

Ladder: Opportunities. If dots are near: opportunities to make money.

Lamb or Sheep: Changes coming. New ideas; innovations.

Lamp: Things previously hidden will be revealed. Lost property will be recovered.

Leaf: News, letters, messages. Many leaves mean good news and happiness.

Leg: Strength and fortitude. Note the direction in which the leg faces.

Letter: News coming, which could be good or bad. Look for other symbols nearby.

Lighthouse: Trouble ahead. Be cautious.

Lines: Straight or serpentine, they generally indicate roadways, rivers, directions; a course to be taken.

Lion: Supremacy. Your leadership will be recognized.

Loaf of Bread: Could mean happiness and plenty, depending on what is near.

Lock: An obstacle in the way of progress. A difficult problem that needs to be solved.

Man: A visitor. If facing the handle, the visitor will be staying for a while. If facing away, the visitor will only be there briefly.

Medal: Distinction and honor; recognition for work done.

Mermaid: Strength will be needed to resist temptation.

Monk: Deception and subterfuge. Be very cautious.

Monkey: Danger from flattery.

Moon: Possible romantic attachment. New ideas; new undertakings.

Mountains: Great ambitions and challenges. You will attain heights but only with much effort.

Mouse: Poverty. Neglected opportunities. Possible theft.

Mushroom: Advancement through expansion and growth.

Nail: Malice and cruelty may be directed against you. Your feelings may be hurt.

Necklace: If complete, a conquest and many admirers. If incomplete, danger of losing a loved one.

Nine: The number of Neptune. Spiritual perception.

Numbers are important and can refer to hours, days, weeks, etc. They should be applied to other symbols close by. They might also be tied into **numerology.** See actual numbers.

One: Number of the Sun. Happiness, success, dignity, honors.

Owl: A sinister omen. Possible failure of a new enterprise.

Ox: Prosperity and friendship of someone in a high position.

Pagoda: Traveling in distinguished company.

Palm Tree: Opportunity to retire wherever you wish.

Parachute: Escape from danger. You will always land on your feet.

Peacock: Elegance, splendor, and luxury.

Pig: Good luck. You will not want for food but beware overindulgence.

Pipe: Respite. Time to regroup; re-plan.

Pumpkin: Someone warmhearted and good natured. A diplomat.
Puppy: Frivolity. Insincerity. Indecision.
Pyramid: A secret will be revealed, which will help you advance. Coming good fortune.
Quiver: Ability to lead. You have a message to deliver.
Question Mark: The unknown. Frustration. Need to search for answers.
Rabbit: Timidity. A need to be more assertive.
Racquet (tennis): A coming contest. Possibility of trouble. If the handle of the racquet is toward the cup handle, you will triumph. If away from it; you will lose.
Rainbow: Hope and encouragement.
Rake: A careful and industrious nature.
Raven, Rook, or Crow: You have a roving nature. You tend to horde things. Your life could be shiftless, with illegal pursuits in it.
Ring: Goodwill and friendship, which can lead to important events. If initial(s) nearby, it could tie-in to partnership of some sort.
Rose: Possible marriage.
Saddle: A journey in the near future. You would be good at exploration.
Saw: Hard work.
Scaffold: Possibility of a law action against you.
Scales: Judgment is at hand. If the scales are tipped toward the cup handle, you will be favored.
Scissors: Misunderstandings; confusion. People working at cross purposes.
Scorpion: Danger. Be very careful, especially in business dealings.
Seven: The Number of Saturn. Wisdom, balance, perfection.
Shark: Someone of a predatory disposition. Note its proximity to the cup handle.
Ship: Success and good fortune. Efforts finally rewarded.
Shoe: A messenger is on the way with good news.
Six: Number of Venus. Cooperation, harmony, love, peace, satisfaction.
Skeleton: Possibility of sickness and want. Lean times coming.
Skull: Danger. Be careful in dealing with others.
Sleigh: Rapid progress with little opposition.
Snake: Healing and wisdom. Be cautious in business.
Spade: Steady work ahead, with ample compensation.
Spear: Wounding, either physically or from scandal.
Spider: Cunning, with possible entrapment.
Spiral: Slow and tedious progress, but you are slowly and surely working your way ahead.
Spoon: An energetic nature. You are not afraid to "stir things up" if necessary.
Square: Limitations. Exercise caution.
Star: Good fortune. Opportunities.
Steeple: High aspirations. Ambition.
Stocks; Pillory: Restraint, for your own good. Frustration.
Submarine: Hidden enemies. Be cautious.
Sun: Success with great happiness.
Swan: A lover; good luck in love. Look for an initial nearby.

Sword: Depending on which way it is pointing, it could be a menace (toward the cup handle) or a protection (away from handle).
Table: A reunion is coming.
Teapot: Consultations; committee meetings.
Tent: Temporary shelter. Coming troubles.
Three: Number of Mars. Possible accident, fire, or quarrel.
Torch: Progress. A pioneering spirit.
Tortoise or Turtle: Slow but steady advancement, with much hard work. Little to show immediately for your efforts but eventual rewards.
Train: Change. Probable travel.
Tree: A wish will be fulfilled. An oak tree is strength and protection.
Triangle: Always a good sign. Good luck and success.
Trident: Authority. Possible promotion to a position of respect.
Two: Number of the Moon. Relationship of opposites. Dualism.
Umbrella: If open, protection. If closed, frustration.
Vase: Service, by you, to others.
Violin: A reclusive and independent person. An individualist.
Volcano: A passionate person, possibly with an explosive temper.
Vulture: Cruelty and oppression. Possibility of theft.
Web: Tread carefully and listen to advice so that you don't get caught up in a difficult situation.
Whale: A big project that will not bring you returns for two or three years.
Wheel: Progress. A need for patience.
Wig: Deception.
Windmill: Grandiose plans may bring big rewards.
Wings: Mobility. Good news coming.
Wishbone: An inheritance.
Witch: Wisdom and sage advice is available.
Wolf: Great cleverness plus intrigue.
Woman: A visitor will come, bearing news.
Yacht: You will know that news is coming before you learn what it is.
Yoke: A position of submission and service.
Zebra: Special distinction. You are sought by a friend.

Often, when a younger person is having his or her tea leaves read, the question uppermost in the mind is "When will I get married?" To answer this, take a teaspoon and balance it on the edge of the cup. Then carefully drip tea into the bowl of the spoon, one drop at a time. After a number of drops, the balance will be broken and the spoon will drop into the cup. The number of drops that brings about the upset is the number of months or years the client must wait for marriage.

Sources:

Buckland, Raymond. *Secrets of Gypsy Fortunetelling*. St. Paul, MN: Llewellyn, 1988.
Complete Book of Fate and Fortune. London: Marshall Cavendish, 1974.
Gibson, Walter B. and Litzka R. *The Complete Illustrated Book of the Psychic Sciences*. New York: Doubleday, 1966.
Shepard, Leslie A. (ed.). *Encyclopedia of Occultism & Parapsychology*. New York: Avon, 1978.

TEA LEAVES *see* **Tasseography**

TEETH *see* **Odontomancy**

TELEPATHY *see* **Extrasensory Perception**

TEPHRAMANCY; TEPHROMANCY

In Sir Thomas Urquhart's *The Third Book of the Works of Mr. Francis Rabelais* (London, 1693), he says: "Have you a mind to have the truth more fully disclosed by tephromancy: thou wilt see the ashes thus aloft dispersed." Tephramonacy is divination by means of sacrificial ashes, though there seems to be some confusion on exactly how they were used. The above quote indicates that interpretation was based on the way in which the ashes rose in the air, carried by the heat of the sacrifice. When the rising ashes quickly dispersed, this was a favorable sign. When they seemed to hang in the air, making a confusion of soot and ash, then it was an unfavorable sign.

Charles Godfrey Leland quotes an old book titled *Trinum Magicum*, which refers to it: "And they were accustomed to divine sometimes with the ashes of the sacrifices. And to this day [in Italy] there is a trace of it, when that which is to be divined is written on the ashes with the finger or a stick. Then the ashes are stirred by a fresh breeze, and one looks for the letters which they form by being moved." This seems close to **spodomancy,** which is also divination using ashes of sacrifice and other ashes.

Some definitions differentiate between tephramancy and tephromancy, stating that the former makes use of the ashes of burned **tree** bark and the latter is the one that uses the ashes of a sacrifice.

Ashes in ancient symbolism signify that which is past and dead, or gone into oblivion. In Slavonia there was a form of divination similar to that in **Rome,** where women drew lines at random in the ashes of the fire. When these were counted, if the lines were even in number it was a propitious sign; if uneven in number, it foretold bad fortune. In Poland there was a similar practice wherein the ashes were strewn on the floor around the bed of an invalid. A "wise woman" predicted from the number of lines whether or not the invalid would recover.

Sources:

Leland, Charles Godfrey. *Etruscan Magic & Occult Remedies*. New York: University Books, 1963.
Oxford English Dictionary. Oxford: Clarendon Press, 1989.

TERAPHIM

(See also Idolomancy)

This is a plural form, and refers to household gods and objects of reverence; also to a form of divination among the ancient **Hebrews** and kindred people. In the **Bible**'s Hosea 3:4 there is mention of teraphim: "For the children of Israel shall abide many days without a king, and without a prince, and without a sacrifice, and without an image, and without an ephod (garment for the priest), and without teraphim."

A spirit house in Thailand, built as a shrine and spirit dwelling. Many Thai houses have such shrines. *Fortean Picture Library.*

Teraphim, then, were important items, obviously of a religious nature. In Judges 17:5 it says: "And the man Micah had an house of gods, and made an ephod, and teraphim." Edward B. Pusey goes on to say, in *The Minor* ***Prophets,*** *with a commentary* (1860): "The teraphim were used as instruments of divination." Unfortunately, nowhere are we told exactly what the teraphim were nor how they were used for divination.

THAILAND

Shaman diviners in Thailand pierce the ends of an egg and blow its contents onto the ground to be interpreted. They will also suspend an object—often a ring—on the end of a length of thread, and divine by way of **radiesthesia. Scapulomancy** is also practiced. They claim knowledge of helpful spirits, know the rules of sacrifices and rituals, and use shamanic paraphernalia such as drums, **mirrors,** and costumes. The shaman's instruments all have **Chinese** names.

The belief is that the first humans moved freely between Heaven and Earth but, as a result of "sin," the road became blocked. At death, however, the road is temporarily opened again if the priest-shaman performs the correct rites. The shamans will undertake **séances.**

Sources:

Eliade, Mircea. *Shamanism: Archaic Techniques of Ecstasy*. Princeton, NJ: Princeton University Press, Bollingen Series 1972.

Headon, Deirdre (ed.). *Quest for the Unknown—Charting the Future*. Pleasantville, NY: Reader's Digest, 1992.

THEOMANCY

William T. Brande's *A Dictionary of Science, Literature and Art* of 1842 refers to "Theomancy; a name given to that species of divination which was drawn from the responses of **oracles** . . . or from the predictions of **sibyls** and others supposed to be immediately inspired by some divinity." It is, then, the utterances of **prophets, seers,** sibyls, etc, and as such may cover many different types of divination, from **abacomancy** to **zoomancy,** so long as it is believed that those divinations are inspired by gods or goddesses.

Sources:

Oxford English Dictionary. Oxford: Clarendon Press, 1989.

Thomas the Rhymer and the Queen of the Fairies. ***Fortean Picture Library.***

THOMAS THE RHYMER (C. 1220–1297)

Thomas Rimor de Ercildun, or Thomas the Rhymer, was a Scottish **prophet,** almost as well known as the Brahan **Seer.** (*Ercildun* was the old spelling of Earlston, the name of a small village.) He was also one of Scotland's early poets and balladeers. Thomas lived in

The Egyptian god Thoth invented arts and sciences, including magic and soothsaying. *Fortean Picture Library.*

the thirteenth century in Learmont Tower in the west of the county of Berwickshire, close by the boundary with Roxburgh. He held several estates, which were not from the crown but from the Earls of Dunbar. His prophesies did not appear in literary form until the early fifteenth century.

Legend has it that Thomas met the Queen of the Fairies under a tree in the Eildon Hills, at Huntly Burn. She asked him to kiss her, which he did. He instantly fell in love with her and agreed to go with her and stay in her kingdom for seven years. It was on his return from this visit to the fairies that he began to exhibit his gift of prophesy.

One day the Earl of Dunbar asked Thomas what the following day would bring, and Thomas stated that it would bring the death of the king, Alexander III. Sure enough, the next day the old king died. Among many other things, Thomas prophesied the Jacobite uprisings of 1715 and 1745, the Battle of Bannockburn (1314), the union of the Scottish and the English crowns (1603), the Battle of Pinkie (1547), the banishment of the last Earl Marischal (1746), and the forfeiture of Marischal's lands of Inverugie.

A ballad of Thomas is included in Sir Walter Scott's *Minstrelsy of the Scottish Border*. For generations the local populations of Berwickshire have referred to Thomas as "True Thomas," because of the accuracy of his **predictions.**

Sources:

Buckland, Raymond. *Scottish Witchcraft*. St. Paul, MN: Llewellyn, 1992.
Shepard, Leslie A. (ed.). *Encyclopedia of Occultism & Parapsychology*. New York: Avon, 1978.
http://www.folklegend.com/article1066_2.html.

THOTH

Thoth (pronounced "Toe-th") was the **Egyptian** god of truth and patron of wisdom, learning, inventions, and literature. He was spokesman of the gods and keeper of their records. Thoth was known in **Greece** as Hermes Trismegistus—"the thrice greatest Hermes." He was the source of all mystic revelation. As "Scribe of the Gods," Thoth was responsible for all sacred writings. He is generally represented holding a reed pen and color palette, and he is often shown with the head of an ibis wearing a lunar disc in a crescent. Sometimes, however, he is shown as a dog-headed ape. Thoth recorded the verdict at the judgment of the dead, when the heart was weighed.

Endowed with complete knowledge and wisdom, Thoth invented all the arts and sciences: mathematics, geometry, surveying, astronomy, medicine, surgery, music, drawing, writing, and also magic and **soothsaying.**

Sources:
Cavendish, Richard (ed.). *Man, Myth & Magic*. London: BPC Publishing, 1970.
Larousse Encyclopedia of Mythology. London: Paul Hamlyn, 1965.

THRIOBOLY

(See also Pessomancy; Psephomancy)

Thrioboly is another name for pessomancy (or psephomancy). This is divination using pebbles or small stones, which are thrown onto the ground and then studied with regard to their positions and relationships. This would be a form of **geomancy.**

THUNDER ***see*** **Brontomancy; Ceraunomancy; Keraunoscopia**

TIBET

One of the main forms of divination in Tibet is the art of *tra*. It is, in essence, **scrying.** The diviner focuses his or her gaze on a **mirror, water,** or some other reflective surface. Or the sky may be looked at, if it is clear. The **seer** then empties the mind by repeating certain mantras until a vision appears. An example is given by Loewe and Blacker, in *Divination and* **Oracles**(1981), where they describe an instance of tra. A diviner in East Tibet was asked by a woman how many sons she would have. He used a mirror and had a vision of one red flower, one yellow flower, and one slightly damaged white flower. His interpretation was that she would have three sons: one would be a reincarnate lama, one a priest, and one would suffer a life of continual sickness. The **prophecy** proved to be correct.

Another form of scrying is known as *Dorje Yudronma*. This mirror divination is similar to other areas where the actual gazing is done by a young, virginal boy or girl.

Tibetans also perform is what is known as dough-ball divination. This latter involves writing all the possible answers to a question on pieces of paper and then rolling up the slips in lumps of dough. Great care is taken to see that all the dough-balls weigh the same. The balls are then sealed inside a jar that is set in front of a sacred object, such as an image or a painting. It is then prayed over for three days and nights, by lamas, with no one touching the bowl throughout. On the fourth day, the bowl is opened and a prominent lama will tip it up, rolling the balls around it as he does so. The ball that eventually falls out is the one containing the correct answer.

Cubomancy in Tibet uses three **dice.** It is stipulated that the diviner must have pure motivation and the questioner must have absolute faith in the diviner. Both pray to the Three Jewels, their root and lineage lamas, and their deities, asking for a clear answer. The diviner then pictures his or her special deity and requests a clear, true answer. The dice are rolled and the answer is taken from a book containing all possibilities for the various combinations of dots.

Tibetan Wheel of Life. ***Fortean Picture Library.***

It is felt that by looking into a person's future, the seer can assess situations and recommend remedial action if necessary, though performing divination for those who are sick is often considered tedious. Supposedly the invasion of Tibet by the **Chinese** was predicted and a number of rituals were performed, but they were ineffectual because of the great negative karma of the Tibetan people.

Scapulomancy is performed, as is **oneiromancy, lampadomancy,** and **causimomancy.** The lampadomancy is often performed with a butter lamp. Such a lamp should be as near perfect as possible, even made out of silver or gold. The wick should be a dry, odorless piece of wood placed in the center of the lamp. Barley is heaped on it, then melted, purified butter is poured over. The following is recited one hundred times: *Om ah hum vajra guru dhe vadakki nihum' od' od li sarva ah lo ke praha dhe naye svan bah.* While saying this, the question should be concentrated upon. The butter lamp is then lighted and the flame observed. The shape of the flame is considered significant, as is the brightness, and the steadiness..

Sources:

Headon, Deirdre (ed.). *Quest for the Unknown—Charting the Future.* Pleasantville, NY: Reader's Digest, 1992.
Loewe, Michael and Carmen Blacker. *Divination and Oracles.* London: Allen & Unwin, 1981.
http://www.tibet.com/Buddhism/divination.html.

TIME *see* Chronomancy

TIROMANCY; TYROMANCY

In Sir Thomas Urquhart's *The Third Book of the Works of Mr. Francis Rabelais* (London, 1693), he says: "To have the truth more fully disclosed by Tyromancy, whereof we make some Proof in a great Brehemont Cheese." Tyromancy is indeed divination by means of cheese. Lewis Spence remarks that "it is practiced in divers ways the details of which are not known." It seems probable that it was tied into the manner in which the cheese aged: the amount and appearance of mold, shapes seen in the mold, the depth of the mold, and so on.

Sources:

Oxford English Dictionary. Oxford: Clarendon Press, 1989.
Spence, Lewis. *An Encyclopedia of the Occult.* London: George Routledge & Sons, 1920.

TOADS *see* Batrachomancy

TOPOMANCY

Topomancy is divination using natural land forms. Hills, valleys, rivers, streams, and distant mountains all have their meanings. If the diviner is overly familiar with the scene before him, or her, then some action is taken to ensure a random view. This may take the form of spinning around with the eyes closed, and then stopping and opening them to interpret whatever happens to lie ahead. The presence or absence of **water** could be significant, as could the state of **trees,** the amount of open land, the number of hedgerows, and other factors.

TORCH *see* Lampadomancy

TRACKS, WHEEL *see* Trochomancy

TRANCE *see* Metagnomy

Trees

(See also Dendromancy)

There are representations of sacred trees on Assyrian and Chaldean engraved cylinders. The tree seems to have been the essential symbol of Chaldean religion. In ancient **Egypt** numerous deities were supposed to inhabit trees. In the Old Testament of the **Bible** are many references to sacred groves and to altars being set up in such areas, under trees such as the mighty oak. In **Rome** the tree omens were important. The withering of laurels foretold Nero's death. Similarly, the fall of a cypress was a presage of Titus Flavius Domitianus's death.

The tree was sacred to the **Celts.** In fact, they had a whole alphabet based on trees. The *Celtic Tree* ***Oracle,*** as presented by Liz and Colin Murray, aligns the trees with the ancient Beth-Luis-Nuin alphabet (also known as Ogham—pronounced "owam" or "ohm") of the Celts, and also gives individual meanings to them:

B—*Beith* Birch: New beginning; cleansing. First month—November

L—*Luis* Rowan: Protection against enchantment; control of all the senses. Second month—December

F—*Fearn* Alder: Oracular and protective. Third month—January

S—*Saille* Willow: Night vision; lunar rhythms; female aspects. Fourth month—February

N—*Nuin* Ash: Linking of inner and outer worlds; micro- and macrocosm. Fifth month—March

H—*Huathe* Hawthorn: Chastity; cleansing; protection. Sixth month—April

D—*Duir* Oak: Solid protection; strength; doorway to the mysteries. Seventh month—May

T—*Tinne* Holly: Best in the fight. Eighth month—June

C—*Coll* Hazel: Intuition; straight to the source. Ninth month—July

Q—*Quert* Apple: Choice of beauty.

M—*Muin* Vine: Prophesy. Tenth month—August

G—*Gort* Ivy: Spiral of the Self; search for the Self. Eleventh month—September

Ng—*NgEtal* Reed: Direct action. Twelfth month—October

Ss—*Straif* Blackthorn: No choice; cleansing.

R—*Ruis* Elder: The end in the beginning and the beginning in the end. Thirteenth (make-up) month—last three days of October.

A—*Ailim* Silver Fir: High views and long sight.

O—*Ohn* Furze: Magpie; good at collecting.

U—*Ur* Heather: Links to Inner Self; all heal.

E—*Eadha* White Poplar: Helps rebirth; prevents illness.

I—*Ioho* Yew: Rebirth and everlasting.

Ch—*Koad* Grove: Sacred place; all knowledge: past, present, future.

Th—*Oir* Spindle: Sweetness and delight; sudden intelligence.

Pe—*Uilleand* Honeysuckle: Hidden secret.

The oak tree represents solid protection, strength, and a doorway to mysteries. ***Janet and Colin Bord/Fortean Picture Library.***

Ph—*Phagos* Beech: Old knowledge; old writing.
Xi—*Mór* The Sea: Sea; travel; maternal links.

The letters of the tree alphabet originally were cut into the edges of square wooden sticks and along the edges of stone, being read from top to bottom. Nearly four hundred such stones have survived throughout Great Britain. A form of sortilege known as *Coelbreni* was performed by casting down sticks marked with the ogham letters. Liz and Colin Murray claim that the Ogham system of divination was created circa 600 BCE and was in use through at least the fourteenth century CE.

Throughout Eastern countries there has been a tradition of hanging gifts on sacred trees, or of attaching pieces of clothing to them, so that good luck and health may be enjoyed by the wearer. Similarly, in England and throughout the British Isles, many trees growing alongside sacred wells are decorated with pieces or cloth or even pieces of paper, asking for blessings and good fortune. Many early rituals for fertility were also centered on trees. Indeed, the traditional Maypole is closely connected to this association.

Among the sacred groves, one of the most notable was the grove of sacred oaks of Zeus at **Dodona,** in **Greece.** Also, the laurel tree at **Delphi** was famous. It was an oracle thought to be connected by its roots to the underworld, and therefore able to provide knowledge and connection to the world of the dead. The **Scandinavian** Tree of Life, or World Tree, named **Yggdrasil,** was one of the best known such trees, which reached down to the underworld and up to the heavens. Yggdrasil was an ash tree. In **India** the World Tree was a fig tree. For the **Mayans** it was the ceiba. All of these trees connected the everyday world with the underworld and the heavens through their deep-reaching roots and high-rising branches.

The Jewish Tree of Life is, in effect, a chart of reality, including the material Universe and its microcosm the human body. The Tree is based on ten *sephiroth*, or emanations. Masculine qualities are placed on the right and feminine ones on the left. They are combined and reconciled in the central sephiroth. There is an upper triangle formed of the Crown (*Kether*), Wisdom (*Kokhmah*), and Intelligence (*Binah*). Below it is another triad: Mercy (*Hesed*), Severity (*Geburah*), and Beauty (*Tifereth*). Then come Victory (*Netsah*), Glory (*Hod*), and Foundation (*Yesod*). At the very bottom is Kingdom (*Malkuth*).

Sources:

Huxley, A. J. *Man, Myth & Magic: Trees*. London: BPC Publishing, 1970.

Murray, Liz and Colin. *The Celtic Tree Oracle*. New York: St. Martin's, 1988.

Phillips, Stephen M. *Mysteries of Mind, Space & Time: The Unexplained*. Westport, CT: H. S. Stuttman, 1992.

Stuart, George E. and Gene S. Stuart. *The Mysterious Maya*. Washington, DC: National Geographic Society, 1977.

TRIGRAMS *see* I Ching

TRIPOD

The tripod (meaning "three-foot") was a form of **Greek** altar. The avenue leading to the sanctuary of Dionysus, in Athens, was known as the Street of Tripods, because of the number of small altars that lined the way. At the **oracular** sites, such as **Delphi,** the **Pythia,** and her sister **sybils** sat on the tripod while giving their oracular statements. When not in use, it was adorned with a laurel branch.

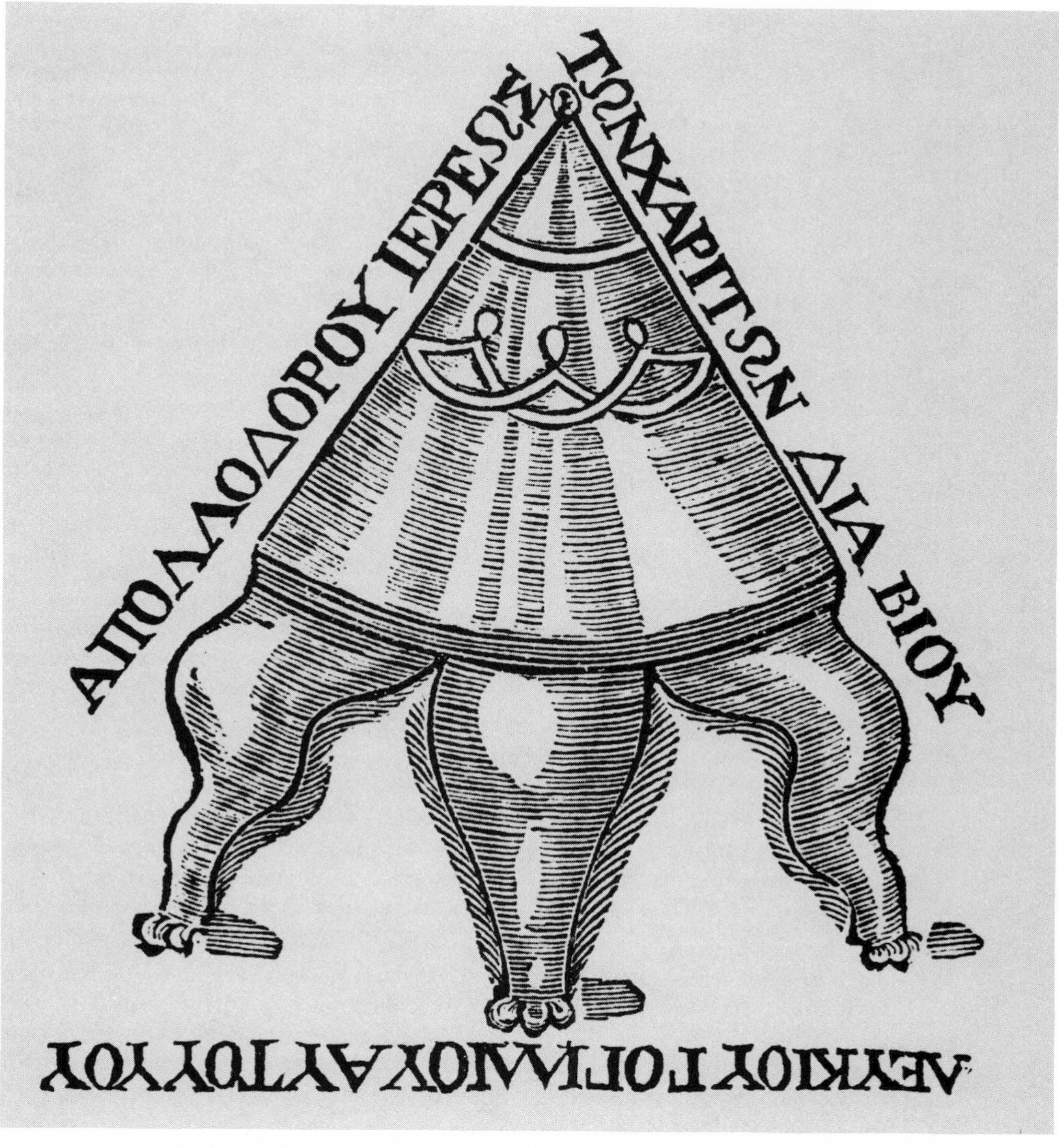

The sacred tripod from Delphi, Greece, on which the Pythia would make her prophetic utterances, 1724. *Fortean Picture Library.*

Sources:

Cavendish, Richard (ed.). *Man, Myth & Magic*. London: BPC Publishing, 1970.

Walker, Barbara G. *The Woman's Dictionary of Symbols and Sacred Objects*. San Francisco: HarperSanFrancisco, 1988.

Tripudiary; Tripudium

A form of divination where future events are divined by the actions of birds and, especially, of sacred chickens when they are fed. The actions of the birds are noted as is the way the bread that is thrown to them bounces when it hits the ground. Thomas Blount, in his *Glossographia, or a dictionary interpreting such hard words as are now used* (1656), states: "Tripudiary divination was by bread rebounding on the ground, when it was cast unto birds, or chickens." Also Sir Thomas Browne, in *Pseudodoxia Epidemica or enquiries into very many received tenets* (1646), speaks of "the conclusions of soothsayers in their auguries and tripudiary divinations, collecting presages from voice or food of birds."

The word also applies to sacred dancing, when the dancer leaps in the air and beats the ground with his or her feet, such as in ecstatic dancing. This is seen in such rites as are found in Voudoun.

Sources:
Oxford English Dictionary. Oxford: Clarendon Press, 1989.

Trochomancy

Divination by studying wheel tracks. The tracks of a four-wheeled vehicle (such as a farm cart) were best for this, since they provided meanderings of one set of tracks back and forth across the other set of tracks. The frequency of crossing and the variance were notable for divining.

Tympana

Tympana is drum divination. It is an adaptation of the drum divination of the **shamans** of Lapland. It is also found in Cornwall, England, and with some **Gypsies** in various countries. The Hungarian Gypsies refer to the drum as the *chovihanescro büklo*, or "witch drum." The English Roma would call it a *shuv'hani baulo tek*.

The Gypsies will usually use nine seeds (some use as many as twenty-one) from a thorn apple to cast into the tambourine. The skin head of the drum has been marked with nine stripes in a particular pattern. According to Leland, the stripe marked "a" is held closest to the diviner. When the seeds have been cast, the side of the instrument is tapped lightly with the heel of the hand, which causes the seeds to move about. Should all the seeds come within the four lines *a, d, e, f,* then all will be well. Even if only three seeds come within those lines, it is a good **omen.** However, if two roll into the space between *a* and *I* it is especially lucky for a woman; between *I* and *f* it is lucky for a man. If nearly all fall outside *b, c, g, h,* everything is unfavorable.

The same setup is found with the Laplanders. There three cowry shells are prepared by being marked with symbols. One has a star on it, another a **moon,**, and a sun symbol on the third. Each of these has particular meaning. For example, the star may represent present conditions and material gains. The moon may indicate occult knowledge and inner guidance. The sun may be connected to family and close friends.

Rather than the nine stripes there may be particular significant designs may be painted in the drum head and the shells read according to their correspondences and their area of landing.

Sources:

Katlyn. *Tympana: Drum and Tambourine Divination*. Long Beach, CA: Mermade Magickal Arts, 1991.
Leland, Charles Godfrey. *Gypsy Sorcery & Fortune Telling*. Fisher-Unwin, 1891.

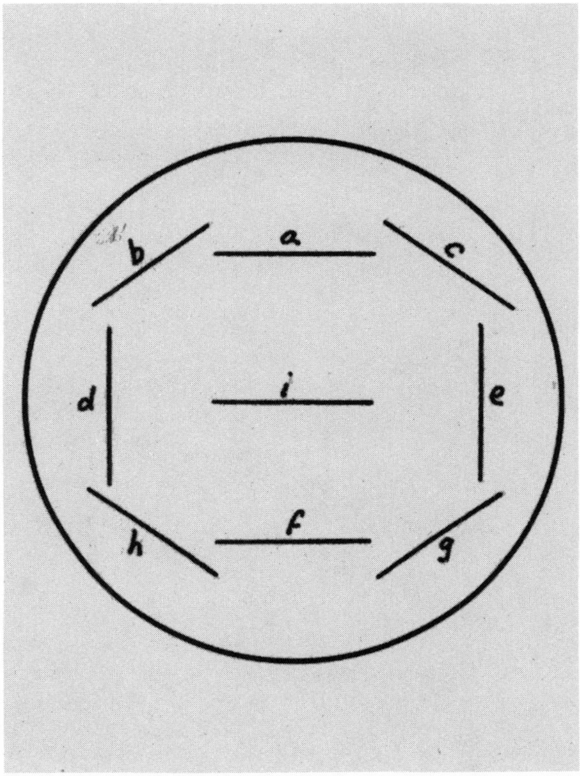

The skin of a tambourine, marked with nine stripes, used by Gypsies for divination. *Raymond Buckland.*

TYPTOLOGY

Typtology is the theory or subject of rapping in order to communicate with spirits. It was such rapping that led to the birth of **spiritualism** with the Fox sisters in Hydesville, New York, in 1848.

From the moment the Fox family moved into the house in Wayne County, on December 11, 1847, they experienced strange sounds that echoed through the wood-framed cottage. John Fox and Margaret, his wife, heard knockings and rapping the origin they could not trace. These continued. Some three months later, on March 31, 1848, Cathie and Margaretta, the two daughters, were lying in bed listening to the constant rapping when Cathie, the younger one, named the unknown "thing" causing the noise "Mr. Splitfoot" and started addressing it, telling it to knock to her count of "one, two, three, four." Surprisingly, the entity did just that. Eventually a full dialogue developed, with questions asked and answers coming by way of one knock for A, two for B, three for C, and so on. Neighbors were called in to verify what was happening, and eventually the phenomenon developed into regular "conversations." Over the years simple rapping was to expand and develop, with **mediumship, séances, clairvoyance, clairaudience, automatic writing,** and more, eventually growing into the spiritualist movement.

Sources:

Buckland, Raymond. *Doors to Other Worlds*. St. Paul, MN: Llewellyn, 1993.

TYROMANCY ***see*** **Tiromancy**

U

UMBILICAL CORD *see* **Omphalomancy**

URANOMANCY *see* **Ouranomancy**

URIMANCY; UROMANCY; URINOMANCY; OROMANCY

James Sanford, in *Agrippa's of the vanitie and uncertaintie of artes and sciences* of 1569, said: "For this cause **Scatomancie,** Oromancie, **Drymimancie,** be called the divinations or Prognostications of Physicians, gathered by odors and urines." Urimancy is divination by urine. As Agrippa suggested, it is done by odors and also by color. It was, in effect, an early form of urinalysis, albeit using the sample as an indication of what the future held rather than what was in the past.

Sources:

Oxford English Dictionary. Oxford: Clarendon Press, 1989.

URINE *see* **Urimancy**

URINOMANCY *see* **Urimancy**

UROMANCY *see* **Urimancy**

V

Vasiliev, Leonid (1891–1966)

Leonid Vasiliev graduated from Petersburg University in 1914 and became a teacher of biological sciences at Ufa, Bashkir, from 1914 till 1921. He later became the chairman of physiology at Leningrad University and was a pioneer in psychic research in the Soviet Union. He once told a meeting of Soviet scientists: "The discovery of the energy underlying **extra sensory perception** will be equivalent to the discovery of atomic energy." In 1961 he was made head of a special Parapsychology Laboratory at Leningrad University. His books included *Mysterious Manifestations of the Human Psyche* (1959) and *Suggestions at Distance: Notes of a Physiologist* (1962).

Sources:
Fishley, Margaret. *The Supernatural*. London: Aldus, 1976.
Shepard, Leslie A. (ed.). *Encyclopedia of Occultism & Parapsychology*. New York: Avon, 1978.

Vaticination

A vaticination is a prophetic utterance or forecast; a **prediction** of an oracular or inspired nature; a **prophecy** or prognostication.

Vedic Astrology

Vedic, or Hindu, **astrology** is also known as *Jyotish* and focuses on **predictions.** It uses the sidereal, or fixed, **zodiac** rather than the tropical, or moveable, one used by Western astrologers, and does not use house cusps the way Western astrologers do. Each house covers exactly 30 degrees and exactly one sign. In other words, if there is 12° Taurus rising, the entire house is regarded as Taurus (the second house Gemini, and so

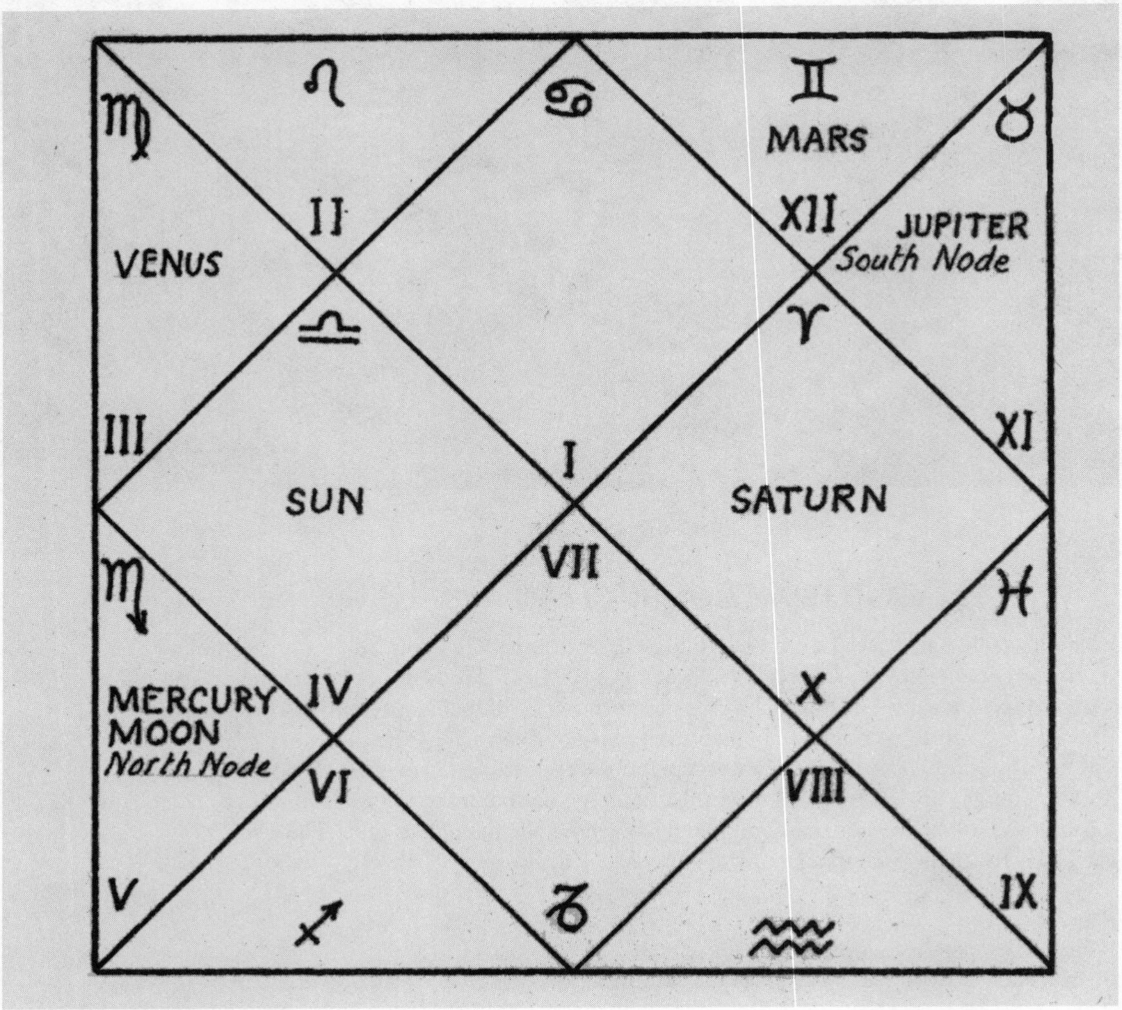

Vedic natal charts are done in a square format. *Raymond Buckland.*

on). Uranus, Neptune, and Pluto are generally ignored, with Saturn regarded as the ruler of Aquarius, Jupiter as the ruler of Pisces, and Mars the ruler of Scorpio.

Vedic charts are drawn up in a square format. Roman numerals are used to indicate House numbers.

Doing a natal **horoscope** can involve casting as many as sixteen different individual charts, each in a slightly different manner, in order to see the whole picture of past, present, and future. This is known as the *Vimsottari Dasha* system.

The Sun is considered a negative influence, as are Mars, Saturn, and the two **moon** nodes (*Ketu* and *Rahu*). Beneficial are Venus, Jupiter, Mercury, and the waxing moon. The moon and the ascendant are regarded as the most important parts of the chart. The 360 degrees of the zodiac are divided into twenty-seven lunar mansions, or *nakshtras*, each 13°20' long. Each of these nakshtras is associated with a planet, quality, deity, symbol, body part, sound, and so on.

Jyotish is a Sanskrit word derived from *jyoti*, meaning "light." It is referred to as "the science of the luminaries." Vedic astrology is based upon the statements of the Vedic literatures and Vedic sages, such as the Vedas, Puranas, Samhitas, and Rishivaakyas, and the statements of Maharishi Parashara, Vedavyasa, Narada, Garga, and others.

Sources:

Beckman, Howard. *An Introduction to Vedic Astrology: Spiritual Sscience of the Ancients*. London: Balaji Publishing, 1995.

Orion, Rae. *Astrology for Dummies*. Foster City, CA: IDG Books, 1999.

Virgilian Lots

(See also Runes)

Tacitus, in his *Germania*, mentions that in Teutonic divination, a rod cut from a fruit-bearing tree was cut into slices, or "slips." The slips were each marked with individual sigils and then thrown down, randomly, on a white cloth or garment. This cloth was taken up while making a prayer to the gods. The slips were then removed, three at a time, and interpreted according to the sigils on them. This was known as "Virgilian lots."

VISIONS *see* Metagnomy

Voudon; Voodoo

Voudon, or Voodoo, is a religion. It is not black magic and it does not consist of sticking pins into dolls. It is a religion of initiation; a mystery religion stemming from the kingdom of Dahomey, on the Ivory Coast of **Africa.** It was imported to the West Indies with the slaves at the latter end of the seventeenth century. The language of Dahomey was known as *fon*, meaning "king." The word *Voudon* is the fon word for "spirit" or "god," or for a sacred object.

The Republic of Haiti—the western part of Santo Domingo—is the island most often associated with Voudon and probably the place where it is practiced in its purest form. It is a religion in the sense of any other religion, with a system of beliefs, faith, and traditional rites. In *Religions of the World Made Simple*, John Lewis defines religion as "the attitude of individuals in community to the powers which they conceive as having ultimate control over their destinies and interests." This definition fits Voudon as exactly as it fits Roman Catholicism, Judaism, Witchcraft, Buddhism, or any other established religion.

In Voudon there are a number of gods, or *loa*. There is a priesthood and various festivals and ceremonies. The ceremonies are held at a sanctuary or temple known as a *hounfor* or *hunfo*. These sanctuaries vary greatly in size and style depending on the affluence of the immediate community. Some are very elaborate with a number of *peristyles* (covered altar areas) while others are small buildings with a rough cement block for an altar.

The priest in Voudon is the *houngan* and the priestess the *mambo*. Ceremonies are attended by initiated and noninitiated alike. However, the initial part of the ceremony is performed by the priests, the initiates, and the shortly-to-be-initiated only, while the rest of the congregation sits and watches. The two factors, participants and audience, tend to merge more and more as the ceremonies progress. The initiated are known as the *hounsi*, or "spouse of the god." They are dressed in white at the rituals and assist the houngan and mambo, whom they call "Papa" and "Mama." Those who are going through a training period for initiation are dressed in red and are known as the *hounsi-kanzo*.

The many gods, or loa, of Voudon have specific names and definite duties. They are invoked in ceremonies and make their presence known by possessing their worshipers and "riding" them like horses. There are two types of god: the *Rada*, who are chthonic deities known as "the Gentle Gods"; and the *Petro*, who are bitter, unyielding deities specializing in magic, charms, and cures. The Petro are feared and are named after a certain Don Pedro, who introduced the rites to Haiti from Santo Domingo. The more important loa are the Rada. The name Rada comes from the name of the ancient capital of Dahomey, Arada. Rada deities include:

DAMBALLAH-WÉDO—known as "the Ancient and Venerable Father." He is looked upon as the source of all wisdom; the origin and essence of life. Damballah is regarded as a serpent deity. The center post holding up the roof of the peristyle, and around which the altar is constructed, is regarded as Damballah's **tree,** and he is thought to be at the top of it during the rituals.

AYIDA-WÉDO—the wife of Damballah. She is also depicted as a serpent. The two together represent sexual totality. Their symbol is an egg, representing the world.

LEGBA—a most important loa, for he is the Guardian of the Crossroads (in this sense similar to the Greek goddess Hecate). He is sometimes referred to as *Maître Carrefour,* or God of the Crossroads. It is Legba who can remove the barrier between this world and the next, so he must be invoked first, of all the loa.

AGWÉ (or Agwé-Taroyo) is the Poseidon of Voudon. Called "The Shell of the Sea," "Eel" and "Tadpole of the Pond," he is lord of the sea and all that is in it: flora and fauna, ships and shipwrecks.

ERZULIE (or Ezilie)-FREDA-DAHOMEY is the counterpart of Aphrodite. She has an overabundance of love and is the Great Mother, a goddess of beauty. She comes from a family of sea spirits. She is extremely extravagant and loves beautiful clothes, makeup and perfume. Erzulie is very refined, sensual, and coquettish, always wearing three wedding bands.

OGOUN (or Ogu-Balindjo) is a storm god. Basically a sky deity, he is depicted as a wounded warrior and carries an enormous sabre. He is also known as "Blacksmith of the Gods," like the Greek Hephæstus.

ZAKA (or Papa-Azzaca) is in charge of crops and agricultural labor.

GUÉDÉ—the loa of Death and Sexuality. He is very much a chthonic deity. He is frequently obscene in both word and gesture. He is also a great healer. In his Petro aspect he is known variously as Baron Samedi, Baron La-Croix, Baron Cimitière, and The Three Spades, all of which are grave-digging tools.

Each of the loa has a symbol or emblem peculiar to him or her. These are known as *vévés* or vevers and are drawn on the floor of the hounfor during a ritual to invoke the specific loa.

There is one ritual in Voudon that is surprisingly similar to a **spiritualist séance.** It is called *Retraite de l'esprit de l'eau* or "Retreat of the spirit of the **water.**" A small canvas, tentlike, enclosure is erected in the hounfor. Inside are placed various offerings together with a tub of water and a stool. The mambo goes inside and the entrance flap is closed and secured. Several hounsi then sit or lie on the ground beside the structure, holding *govi* jars. These are earthenware jars that contain the spirits of the dead. As the people assemble, the mambo can be heard chanting in *langage*, the secret ritual language of the priesthood. There is a litany as she calls on the loa and the people respond. A sharp cry from the mambo is the signal for the first hounsi to slip her govi under the canvas into the tent. After a moment the sound of rushing water is heard, soon followed by a strained, hoarse voice. The voice will call the name of one of those assembled around the tent. It is invariably recognized as being the voice of a dead relative. A conversation will then ensue between the two, with the mambo interjecting a word here and there. It is not unknown for the mambo to be speaking *at the same time* that the dead ancestor is talking.

The ancestor may be consulted on family matters and advice may be sought on a variety of things. He or she may have some vital message to impart. There are even warnings of future problems divulged. All the while the voices are speaking, there is heard the rushing of water in the background. Although the mambo has a bowl of water in the enclosure with her, this background noise not something that can be reproduced using such a bowl. Occasionally during the ceremony, the mambo will give an example of glossolalia—speaking in tongues—though this is not common. When a number of voices have been heard, the govi is returned to the hounsi under the flap, and the next jar is taken in. Should the voices begin to fade at any time, the mambo will again chant in *langage* until the strength returns. When all govi have been used, there is a final song and then the mambo emerges from the tent. As with a spiritualist **medium** after a séance, the mambo invariably appears exhausted and has to be helped away.

There is a generous dose of Christianity mixed in with Voudon. This is from the fact that for years the Christian missionaries tried to stamp out Voudon and convert its followers from their ancestral religion. Not understanding the makeup of Voudon, the missionaries—fervent monotheists—persecuted the natives, burning peristyles, drums, flags, beads, assons, and all Voudon trappings, naively believing that by so doing they could stamp out beliefs that had been held for generations. The Haitians, for their part, eventually assumed a mask of Christianity in order to be left alone, but they continued to practice their own religion in secret. Since St. Patrick is often depicted surrounded by snakes, it seemed natural to the Haitians to use depic-

Mambo (Priestess) Miriam in her Voodoo Spiritual Temple in New Orleans, posing as incorporating the Voodoo deity Ogoun, a warrior god. *Dr. Elmar R. Gruber/Fortean Picture Library.*

tions of him to represent the Voudon serpent deity Damballah. Similarly, Mary was used to represent Erzulie, St. George to depict Ogoun, Jesus the plenipotentiary Legba, and so on. A Christian priest could go to a home in Haiti and happily see many Christian emblems and figures prominently displayed. He would leave not realizing that to the people in the house these were still their old pagan gods. In similar fashion, the Voudon followers could see the power of the Church and so adopted some of its ritual, believing it would add to their own power. In this way a typical Voudon ritual will include prayers, chants, Paternosters, and Ave Marias.

Voudon is found in places other than Haiti, though Haiti seems to be the main area for the religious emphasis. In New Orleans, for example—and in many large cities around the United States—there is a variety of Voudon but with more emphasis on the buying and selling of *gris-gris* (charms and spells), candles, baths, powders, and such. Here, also, may be found the Voudon "kings" and "queens." In the early nineteenth century the most famous of these was Marie Laveau, a free mulatto woman who would stage huge dances on the shores of Lake Pontchartrain.

Many South American countries have variations of Voudon. In Brazil the official religion is Roman Catholicism, yet, as with Haiti, it is only superficial for most. Macumba, Umbanda, Qimbanda, and Candomblé are the names of the varieties of Voudon found throughout Latin America. These are not dying out. On the contrary, even with the ever-increasing literacy rate in Brazil and the other South American countries, the followers of these different versions of Voudon are increasing in number. It has been said that the reason is the very personal nature of the relationship between the worshiper and the deities; the follower is not just a spectator but a participant. The communion with divinity is absolute.

Sources:
Buckland, Raymond. *The Anatomy of the Occult*. New York: Samuel Weiser, 1977.
Deren, Maya. *Divine Horsemen*. London: Thames & Hudson, 1953.
Lewis, John. *Religions of the World Made Simple*. New York: Doubleday, 1968.
Leybrun, J. G. *The Haitian People*. New Haven, CT: Yale University Press, 1941.
McGregor, Pedro. *The Moon and Two Mountains*. London: Souvenir Press, 1966.
Métraux, Alfred. *Voodoo in Haiti*. London: André Deutsch, 1959.
St. Clair, David. *Drum & Candle*. New York: Bell, 1971.

W

WAITE, ARTHUR EDWARD—"GRAND ORIENT" (1857–1942)

Arthur Edward Waite was born on October 2, 1857, in Brooklyn, New York. His father was a captain in the Merchant Marine who died at sea when Arthur was still a child. His English mother, Emma (née Lovell), then moved back to London. Despite having to live near poverty, Arthur and his sister were educated at Roman Catholic schools in North London. He eventually went to St. Charles's College. Growing up, Waite developed a great love for what were known as "penny dreadfuls" (cheap romance novels) and medieval fantasies that, apparently, fired his imagination. When he left school, he became a clerk and in his spare time wrote poetry. By the time he was twenty-one, he spent long hours in the British Museum Reading Room, studying esotericism. It was there that he met MacGregor-Mathers.

Waite grew up in the middle of the big renaissance of occultism, which stretched from the end of the nineteenth century through to the outbreak of World War I. Consequently he came to make the acquaintance of such notables as Arthur Machen, W. B. Yeats, **Helena Blavatsky,** Annie Besant, Aleister Crowley, Algernon Blackwood, MacGregor-Mathers, and Wynn Westcott. In 1885 he wrote his first book, *The Mysteries of Magic*.

In 1888 Waite married Ada Lakeman and they had a daughter. Ada was also interested in the occult and took the magical name "Lucasta." At the Mathers home, they were initiated into the magical order Isis-Urania. Ada was not enthused and Waite himself did not aspire to attain the Second Order. The same year he married, Waite wrote *The Real History of the Rosicrucians* and *Lives of Alchemystical Philosophers*, along with *Songs and Poems of Fairyland*, which he dedicated to his wife.

Waite contributed to Ralph Shirley's *Occult Review* and for twenty years anonymously edited the monthly *Review of Periodical Literature*, acquiring an unrivaled knowledge of major current occult works and the development of occultism around the world. He also edited the magazine *The Unknown World*. He joined the Order of the Golden Dawn in 1891, left shortly after but rejoined in 1896. He was admitted into the Second Order in 1899. Waite's writing embraced the translation and editing of alchemical manuscripts and treatises by Thomas Vaughan, Benedictus Figulus, Edward Kelly, and others. With the breakup of the Golden Dawn, Isis-Urania was split into the Isis Temple, which was still loyal and under the leadership of Dr. Berridge, and the Stella Matutina under Waite's own guidance.

It was about this time that Waite was initiated into Freemasonry, at the Runnymede Lodge No. 2430, Wraysbury, on September 19, 1901. He became master of that lodge in 1910. On October 28, 1914, he was provincial deputy grand director of ceremonies for Buckinghamshire. In 1921 he became a founder member and deputy vice president of the Masonic Study Society, resigning that post in 1924. In 1904 he founded his own Rectified Order of the Golden Dawn, and in 1915 founded his Fellowship of the Rosy Cross.

One of the most lasting effects that Waite had on the occult community was to produce the Rider-Waite **Tarot** Deck, which he did utilizing the artistic talents of **Pamela Colman Smith.** It has since become probably the most popular tarot deck in the world. Waite also wrote the book *The Pictorial Key to the Tarot* (1911). Two years earlier he had written *A Manual of Cartomancy*.

In 1924 Ada died, and Waite later married Mary Broadbent Schofield, whose magical name was "Una Salus." Waite continued writing, producing a tremendous number of books, most of them written with what has been described as "immense scholarship shrouded by a portentous and obscure style, deriving from the occult tradition of reluctance to reveal openly the esoteric mysteries, but instead [to] give hints and symbolic explanations." Waite died on May 19, 1942.

Sources:

Colquhoun, Ithel. *The Sword of Wisdom: MacGregor Mathers & the Golden Dawn*. New York: G. P. Putnam's Sons, 1975.

Shepard, Leslie A. (ed.). *Encyclopedia of Occultism & Parapsychology*. New York: Avon, 1978.

WALKING *see* Ambulomancy

WAND *see* Rhabdomancy

WATER *see* Bletonism; Dowsing; Hydromancy; Lecanomancy; Rhabdomancy

WATKINS, ALFRED (1855–1935)

Alfred Watkins was an English merchant, early photographer and amateur archaeologist. He was born in Hereford in 1855. On leaving school he was employed by his father as a brewer's representative, a position that brought him an intimate knowledge of the local countryside and the local customs and legends. Although he was wary of "the occult," Watkins did find that he had a close telepathic connection with his sister. As an inventor and photographer, he invented the pinhole camera and the Watkins exposure meter.

In later years, when he was in his mid-sixties, Watkins developed the theory of "ley lines," which were supposed lines of force linking various ancient sites such as mounds, stones, crossroads, churches, and holy wells. In the 1920s, while walking the hills of Herefordshire near Bredwardine, Watkins saw, in a vision, a vast network of straight lines. Checking an Ordnance Survey map, he found that ancient sites throughout the country were connected by such straight lines. He put forward his theory in an article in *Early British Trackways* in 1922. In the book he later wrote, *The Old Straight Track* (1925), he said: "I feel that the ley-man, astronomer-priest, druid, bard, wizard, witch, palmer and hermit were all more or less linked by one thread of ancient knowledge and power." His theory and book caused virulent controversy in archeological circles but has retained the interest of millions through to the present day. His book is still considered the most important source for the study of ley lines.

Alfred Watkins. F. C. *Tyler/Fortean Picture Library.*

Sources:

Fishley, Margaret. *The Supernatural*. London: Aldus, 1976.

Watkins, Alfred. *The Old Straight Track*. London: Methuen, 1925.

WAX *see* Ceromancy

WEATHER *see* Aeromancy

WHEAT *see* Aleuromancy

WHEEL *see* Cyclomancy; Trochomancy

WINDS *see* Austromancy

WINE *see* Œnomancy

WITNESS

A witness is a sample of something being looked for. For instance, in **dowsing** and **radiesthesia,** a hollow pendulum is frequently used, which allows a sample of the substance sought to be enclosed. If looking for gold, for example, a small piece of gold would be placed in the pendulum to make a psychic connection with the metal. Some pendula are made hollow and will unscrew, opening up into two halves, to accommodate a witness. If the pendulum is not of this type, then a witness can be attached to the pendulum by trying it on or other means.

In medical radiesthesia, when diagnosing a patient, a blood or urine sample might be used for a witness. When trying to trace a lost person, a sample of their handwriting or a piece of clothing might be attached to the pendulum or **divining rod** to make the connection.

Sources:

Buckland, Raymond. *Color Magic—Unleash Your Inner Powers*. St. Paul, MN: Llewellyn, 2002.

Wethered, Vernon D. *An Introduction to Medical Radiesthesia & Radionics*. London: C. W. Daniel, 1962.

De Wohl, Louis (1903–1961)

During World War II the British government briefly employed Louis de Wohl as an **astrologer.** In that capacity he was to check on what astrological information the German astrologers might be giving to Adolf Hitler as advice for war action. Louis de Wohl was born in Berlin, Germany, in 1903. His father was Hungarian; his mother was Austrian. He lived in Germany until 1935, when he moved to England because he could no longer accept the Hitler regime. By that time he had built up a career as a writer in Germany, with more than thirty novels published. However, he was unknown in England and could speak little of the language. Over the years he learned not only English but also French, Italian, Spanish, a little Latin, Greek, and Arabic. His method of learning English was to start with children's books and then work up from there, as any child might do in learning to read.

By the time war broke out, de Wohl could speak, read, and write reasonably well in English. He volunteered for the armed services but was declined because he was German. He eventually was accepted and given the rank of captain in a Department of Psychological Warfare. This came about because Virgil Tilea, the Rumanian minister in London, had heard that an acquaintance, famous Swiss astrologer Karl Ernst Krafft, had gone to work for the German High Command. Tilea suggested that the British government might use an astrologer of their own, to report on what advice Hitler might be getting from Krafft and thereby forestall German actions in the war. De Wohl was appointed in September 1940. As it happens, Krafft certainly was in Berlin, but he was working on giving the German High Command profiles of the British generals based on their horoscopes. He was not actually involved in suggesting dates and times for strategic operations, nor was he working for Hitler personally.

Whether or not the information that de Wohl produced was of any real use to the British government is a moot point. One comment he made was, "It is clear to me, as to every student of astrology who knew Hitler's **horoscope,** that he would launch his great attack against the West when Jupiter was in conjunction with his Sun, in May 1940." In fact, Hitler had no time for astrologers or any occultists. He equated astrologers with common fortune-tellers. De Wohl's employment by the British government lasted a very short time, as it quickly became apparent that he served no real purpose. De Wohl was, however, later employed on a casual basis by both the British and the Americans, on projects such as producing faked astrological predictions and bogus **Nostradamus** prophecies. After the war he went on to write a large number of novels, many of them about the lives of various Roman Catholic saints, and most with religious themes. One of his best-known novels was *The Spear* (1955). Louis de Wohl died in 1961.

Sources:

Hall, Angus. *The Supernatural: Signs of Things to Come*. London: Danbury Press, 1975.

Howe, Ellic. *Man, Myth & Magic: National Socialism*. London: BPC Publishing, 1970.

Wood, Robin (b. 1953)

The artist for one of the most popular modern **tarot** decks, Robin Wood was born November 24, 1953, in Syracuse, New York. After graduating from Michigan State University, she took a job teaching the visually impaired. At twenty-five, Wood encountered some modern Wiccans and began to study Witchcraft. The following year she met a military man, married him, and moved to Okinawa, Japan. Her husband was in the army and, with him, Wood formed an eclectic group called the Livingtree Coven.

Returning to the United States in 1982, Wood investigated a number of other Wiccan and Pagan paths. She divorced in 1987 and three years later married Michael Short, who had been her first love, following his divorce. They started their own tradition of Wicca with a group that lasted for a number of years. Wood was diagnosed with fibromyalgia, leading to the eventual breakup of the group in 1999 when she was unable to continue in the role of High Priestess.

Wood had begun illustrating books for Llewellyn Publications in the mid-1980s, focusing on Craft-related projects. In 1991 she produced the *Robin Wood Tarot*, which rapidly became popular, especially among Wiccan and Pagan people. It is today one of the most popular decks.

WORDS *see* **Logomancy**

WRITING *see* **Psychography**

XYZ

XENOMANCY

Xenomancy is divination by the action of strangers. The chance meeting with various people would also come under this heading, as an extension of **cledonomancy.** In **Greece,** to meet a priest is always considered unlucky, but for men more so than for women. The luck will be even worse if the priest happens to be riding on a donkey. It is also unlucky to meet someone physically disabled. However, to meet an insane person is considered a good **omen,** as is meeting a woman with a child.

The main aspect of xenomancy, however, is concerned with the action(s) of the person met. Actions, of course, can be many and various. A raised right hand, for example, would be a positive sign while a raised left hand would be unfortunate. Pointing would be significant, as would wild gesticulation. Interaction between two or more strangers would multiply meanings.

Sources:

Lawson, John Cuthbert. *Modern Greek Folklore and Ancient Greek Religion*. New York: University Books, 1964.

XYLOMANCY

Xylomancy is divination by the help of pieces of dry wood found on the road. It is also divination by the casual arrangement of sticks of firewood,and the way in which they burn, though this latter more correctly comes under the heading of **causimancy.**

Divination by reading **omens** from the positions of small pieces of dry wood found in one's path is practiced extensively in Slavonia, according to Lewis Spence. There the placement of the bits of wood is important, indicating good or bad fortune lying ahead, farther along the road. Large pieces of wood are seen as major obstacles while smaller pieces indicate minor irritations.

The relationship of various thicknesses and lengths of wood, when stacked for burning, is regarded as significant. This possibly originated with the building of pyres for the burning of bodies where related to the final destination of the corpse's spirit.

Sources:

Grand Orient (A. E. Waite). *The Complete Manual of Occult Divination: Volume 1—Manual of Cartomancy*. London: Rider, 1912.

Spence, Lewis. *An Encyclopedia of the Occult*. London: George Routledge & Sons, 1920.

YGGDRASIL

In **Scandinavian** mythology Yggdrasil, or Igdrasil, is an evergreen ash that is the world **tree,** overshadowing the whole planet. It is possible that the name comes from *Yggr*, which was one of the many names by which Odin was known. Yggdrasil is the guardian tree of the gods. Heaven and hell are bound together by its roots and branches, and the gods meet daily beneath its branches to sit in judgment. It was said to link together nine worlds, including those of the giants, the gods, and the dead.

Yggdrasil is fed by three main roots: one in Asgard, watered daily from Urd's fountain by the three Norns, who decide the destiny of men; one in Niflheim, watered by the spring Hvergelmir; and one in Midgard, watered by the underworld giant Mimir's well of knowledge. Odin's spear, Gungnir, was made from a branch of the tree.

Odin was the god of death and of battle. He was the Wodan of the Germans and the Woden of the Anglo-Saxons. He was believed to welcome into his halls those warriors who died a heroic death on the battlefield. The mythology says that Odin hung from the World Tree for nine days and nights while pierced with a spear. He fasted as he hung there as a sacrifice. At the end of that time he was able to bend down and lift up the magical **runes** that brought secret knowledge to humankind.

Vithofnir, a golden rooster, sits on top of the tree, and an eagle sits on the highest branch, with a falcon perched on its head. That highest branch shades Valhalla. The eagle and the falcon report all that they see to the gods who meet below. Gnawing at the roots of the tree is the serpent Nidhoggr, the World Serpent. A squirrel named Ratatosk runs back and forth between the serpent and the eagle, trying to stir up discord between the two.

Four stags—Dain, Duneyr, Durathor, and Dvalin—feed on the upper twigs of the tree while their antlers drop dew on to the world below. Odin's goat, Heidrun, the supplier of milk for the heavenly mead, browses on the tree branch Lerad.

Sources:

Davidson, Hilda Roderick Ellis. *Scandinavian Mythology*. London: Paul Hamlyn, 1969.

Leach, Maria (ed.). *Funk & Wagnall's Standard Dictionary of Folklore, Mythology, and Legend*. San Francisco: Harper & Row, 1972.

YIN AND YANG

In **Chinese** philosophy *yin* is the feminine or negative principle of two opposing cosmic forces. It is characterized by dark, wetness, cold, passivity, the **moon,** disintegra-

In Scandinavian mythology, Yggdrasil is an evergreen ash that overshadows the whole planet. *Fortean Picture Library.*

tion, shade, etc. Together with *Yang* it forms a combined creative energy whose fusion in physical matter brings the phenomenal world into being. Yang is the masculine, positive principle characterized by light, warmth, dryness, activity and so on.

The symbol for yin and yang, known as the *Ta ki*, is a circle enclosing an S-shape, one side of which is white and the other black. In the center of each is a "seed" of the other, symbolizing the relativity and inseparability of the two. There is an ancient belief that contrasting male and female forces are at work in all things. This lies at the heart of ancient Chinese thought. It is the cyclic alternation of all dualities. The two forces are held together in tension, not in antagonism but as mutually interdependent partners.

Every line of the sixty-four hexagrams that comprise the **I Ching** is either a yin line or a yang line. Basically the yin, the broken line, meant no and the yang, the solid line, meant yes. John Ogilby's translation of *Montamus' Atlas Chinensis* (1671) says: "The Chinese, by these Strokes, declare how much each Form or Sign receives from the two fore-mention'd beginnings of Yin and Yang."

Sources:

Cooper, J. C. *An Illustrated Encyclopedia of Traditional Symbols*. London: Thames & Hudson, 1978.

Headon, Deirdre (ed.). *Quest for the Unknown—Charting the Future*. Pleasantville, NY: Reader's Digest, 1992.

Oxford English Dictionary. Oxford: Clarendon Press, 1989.

ZENER CARDS

A deck of twenty-five cards designed in the 1930s by Dr. Karl E. Zener, an associate of Dr. **J. B. Rhine.** They are used in testing for **extrasensory perception.** In the deck there are five each of five different designs: a circle, a cross, three wavy lines, a square, and a star.

A subject going through the deck, trying to identify each card as studied by someone else, would be expected to score five hits out of the twenty-five, purely by chance. This gives a basis on which actual scores may be noted, no matter how many times the deck is gone through.

The procedure, as originally used by Rhine, was to have a subject guess the sequence of the symbols in the deck, after it had been well shuffled to ensure a random order. As mentioned, the expected average of correct guesses was five. This is known as the "mean chance expectation," or MCE. The point of the experiment is to see if the subject can guess significantly higher or lower than the MCE.

Sources:

Broughton, Richard S. *Parapsychology: the Controversial Science*. New York: Ballantine, 1991.

ZODIAC

In **astrology** and astronomy, the zodiac is a zone of the heavens along which lie the paths of the sun, **moon,** and principal planets. An earthbound observer sees the orbits of the planets as moving in a narrow zone, due to their very slight deviation from a common plane. The zone is about eight degrees either side of the ecliptic, or the path of the sun. Astrology is geocentric. The real orbits of the planets are around the sun in more or less the same plane.

Zener cards, used in testing for Extrasensory perception. ***Fortean Picture Library.***

As early as 3,000 BCE **Mesopotamia,** the various configurations of the fixed stars were grouped into constellations representing animals and objects. Since the majority of the constellations that were crossed by the paths of the planets represented animals, the **Greeks** called this zone "zôdiakos kyklos," or "circle of animals." From this comes the name "zodiac."

It was in Mesopotamia, some time before the Hellenistic period, that the development of mathematical astronomy resulted in accurate definitions of the boundaries and the number of zodiacal constellations. Equal arcs of the apparent orbital circle of the sun gave twelve "signs": Aries the ram, Taurus the bull, Gemini the twins, Cancer the crab, Leo the lion, Virgo the virgin, Libra the balance, Scorpio the scorpion, Sagittarius the archer, Capricorn the goat, Aquarius the water bearer, and Pisces the fish. In fact Leo is the only constellation that actually looks anything like its name so it is unknown how the signs got their names. The symbols for these signs first began to appear in Greek manuscripts of the late Middle Ages.

The concept of the zodiac reached **Egypt** around the third century BCE, when that country was under Greek domination. A rapid development of astrological doctrines occurred at that time, combining Egyptian, Greek, and Babylonian elements into a system regarding the powers of celestial bodies and their relationship to the

Representation of the zodiac at the Bracken House in London, England. ***Fortean Picture Library.***

zodiac. These ideas spread to **Rome,** Byzantium, **India,** and on to the West in general. Ancient **Mexican** codices include examples of astrology and its use.

Theories have been expounded linking various stone monuments around the world with astrology and astronomy, presenting the sites as ancient computer-like equipment. Stonehenge would seem the prime example, according to the research performed by Professor Gerald S. Hawkins in the early 1960s. The site at Mystery Hill, New Hampshire reflects this, on a smaller scale, as do the menhirs at Carnac and elsewhere. According to Derek and Julia Parker, the **pyramids** of Egypt still hold pride of place among ancient astronomical buildings, being oriented to the north pole of the sky that now lies close to Polaris.

Astrology is the study of the planets in relation to the earth, with regard to their influence on human life. *The Emerald Tablet of Hermes Trismegistus* (patron of the magical arts, associated with the Egyptian god **Thoth**) states: "That which is below is like unto that which is above, and that which is above is like unto that which is below, for the performing of the miracles of the One Thing." This is usually shortened to "As above, so below" or, what is found in the heavens is reflected here on earth.

Sources:

Encyclopedia Britannica. London: William Benton, 1964.
Fell, Barry. *America B.C.* New York: Quadrangle, 1976.
Hawkins, Gerald S. *Stonehenge Decoded*. New York: Dell, 1966.
MacNeice, Louis. *Astrology*. Garden City, NY: Doubleday, 1964.
Parker, Derek and Julia. *The Compleat Astrologer*. New York: McGraw-Hill, 1971.

ZOLAR *see* King, Bruce

Zoomancy

Zoomancy is divination by observing the actions of animals. This can vary tremendously from one part of the country to another, or even within one area. The best-known, almost universal, example of zoomancy is of a black **cat** crossing your path, which is usually thought to be a forecaster of bad luck to come. In some areas, for it to be the harbinger of bad luck the cat must be crossing from right to left. If it crosses from left to right, then it signifies the onset of good luck. In other areas these directions of travel are reversed.

Ailuromancy is divination by the movement of cats; **augury** is divining by the behavior of birds; **hippomancy** is based on the actions of a white horse; **myomancy** is the movement of rats and mice; **ophiomancy** covers snakes. All of these come under the general heading of zoomancy.

If horses and cattle refuse to drink in very dry weather, it is a sign that a cloudburst is on the way. Similarly, if horses suddenly stop feeding and start to scratch themselves on **trees** and fence posts, it means that heavy rain is coming. When chickens and turkeys stand with their backs to the wind, a storm is on its way. If a rabbit runs across your path from left to right, it is a sign of bad luck to come. But if it should be followed by a rabbit running the other way, then the bad luck is cancelled out.

In the Ozarks, if a bird defecates on a young girl's hat it is a sign that the girl's parents are stingy. In some areas it means that the parents will not accept the girl's suitor. When horses start running about for no special reason and neighing with no visible cause, it means there is going to be a death nearby in the very near future.

When a **dog** on a front porch howls four times and then stops, it is a sign of coming death.

There is a tremendous number of such signs and **omens** based on the behavior of animals.

Sources:

Randolph, Vance. *Ozark Superstitions*. New York: Dover, 1964.

Resources

Abbott, Arthur G. *The Mysteries of Color*. Chicago: Aries Press, 1977.

Adams, E. *Astrology for Everyone*. New York: Dodd, Mead, 1960.

Adkins, Lesley & Roy A. *Dictionary of Roman Religion*. New York: Facts on File, 1996.

Adkins, Lesley & Roy A. *Handbook to Life in Ancient Rome*. New York: Facts on File, 1994.

Agrippa, Henry Cornelius. *Fourth Book of Occult Philosophy*. Kila, MT: Kessinger, 1992.

Agrippa, Henry Cornelius (Donald Tyson, ed.). *Three Books of Occult Philosophy*. St. Paul, MN: Llewellyn, 1993.

Albertson, Edward. *Understanding the Kabbalah*. Los Angeles: Sherbourne Press, 1973.

Alexander, Paul Julius. *The Oracle of Baalbek: The Tiburtine Sibyl in Greek Dress*. Washington, DC: Dumbarton Oaks, 1967.

Almond, Jocelyn and Keith Seddon. *Understanding Tarot*. Wellingborough: Thorsons, 1991.

Altman, Nathaniel. *Discover Palmistry*. London: Aquarian, 1991.

Altman, Nathaniel. *The Palmistry Workbook*, Wellingborough: Aquarian, 1984.

American Federation of Astrologers. *Basic Principles of Astrology*. St. Paul, MN: Llewellyn, 1962.

Anderson, Russell K. *Biorhythm—Man's Timing Mechanism*. Park Ridge, IL: American Society of Safety Engineers, 1973.

Anderton, Bill. *Life Cycles* London: Foulsham, 1990.

Anderton, Bill. *Fortune Telling*. North Dighton, MA: JG Press, 1996.

Andrews, Ted. *Dream Alchemy*. St. Paul, MN: Llewellyn, 1991.

Angelo, Jack. *Your Healing Power*. London: Piatkus, 1994.

Angoff, Allan. *Eilen Garrett and the World beyond the Senses*. New York: William Morrow, 1974.

Aras, Evad. *Dream Book: Interpretations with Numerology*. New York: HC Publishers, 1969.

Arcati, Kristyna. *I Ching for Beginners*. London: Hodder & Stoughton, 1994.

Arcati, Kristyna. *Palmistry for Beginners*. London: Hodder & Stoughton, 1993.

Archer, F. *Exploring the Psychic World*. New York: Morrow, 1967.

Arlington. *The Complete Gypsy Fortune Teller*. London: Arlington Books, 1973.

Armstrong, Edward A. *Man, Myth & Magic: Sheep*. London: BPC Publishing, 1970.

Arrien, Angeles. *The Tarot Workbook*. Sonoma, CA: Arcus, 1984.

Ashby, Robert H. *The Guidebook for the Study of Psychical Research*. London: Rider, 1972.

Ashe, Geoffrey. *Man, Myth & Magic: Prophecy*. London: BPC Publishing, 1970.

Asimov, Isaac. *Asimov's Guide to the Bible*. New York: Avon, 1968.

Atkinson, W. *Mind-Power*. Chicago: Progress, 1908.

Atwater, P. M. H. *The Magical Language of Runes*. Santa Fe, NM: Bear, 1990.

Avenel Books. *The Prophesies of Nostradamus*. New York: Crown, 1975.

Bach, Marcus. *Miracles Do Happen*. New York: Waymark, 1968.

Baer, Randall N. & Vicki V. *Windows of Light: Quartz Crystals and Self-Transformation*. San Francisco: Harper & Row, 1984.

Bailey, Arthur. *Dowsing for Health*. London: Foulsham, 1990.

Balin, Peter. *The Flight of the Feathered Serpent*. Venice, CA: Wisdom Garden, 1978.

Bardon, Franz. *The Key to the True Quabbalah*. Wuppertal, Germany: Dieter Rüggeberg, 1971.

Barrett, Francis. *The Magus, or Celestial Intelligencer; being a complete system of occult philosophy*. London: Lackington, Allen & Co., 1802.

Barrett, Sir William and Theodore Besterman. *The Diving Rod: An Experimental and Psychological Investigation*. New Hyde Park, NY: University Books, 1968.

Barrett, W. P. (trans.). *The Trial of Jeanne d'Arc: The Original Latin and French Documents*. New York: Gotham House, 1932.

Barthell, Edward E. Jr. *Gods and Goddesses of Ancient Greece*. Coral Gables, FL: University of Miami Press, 1971.

Barton, W. G. (ed.). *Canada's Psi Century*. Metaphysical Society of Canada, 1967.

Bascom, William. *Ifa Divination: Communication between Gods and Men in West Africa*. Bloomington: Indiana University Press, 1969.

Bashir, Mir. *The Art of Hand Analysis*. London: Frederick Muller, 1973.

Baughan, Rosa. *The Influence of the Stars: A Book of Old World Lore*. London: George Redway, 1889.

Beasse, Pierre. *A New and Rational Treatise of Dowsing According to the Methods of Physical Radiesthesia*. Paris, France, 1941.

Becker, R. de. *The Understanding of Dreams*. London: Hawthorn Books, 1968.

Bend, Cynthia and Tayja Wiger. *Birth of a Modern Shaman*. St. Paul, MN: Llewellyn, 1988.

Benham, William G. *The Laws of Scientific Handreading*. London: Duell, Sloan & Pearce, 1900.

Benham, William G. *Playing Cards*. London: Rider, 1931.

Bentine, Michael. *The Door Marked Summer*. London: Granada, 1981.

Bentine, Michael. *Doors of the Mind*. London: Granada, 1984.

Bentov, Itzhak. *Stalking the Wild Pendulum*. New York: Dutton, 1977.

Berres, Janet. *Textbook of the Tarot*. Evanston, IL: Moonbeam, 1990.

Bessy, Maurice. *A Pictorial History of Magic and the Supernatural*. London: Spring Books, 1963.

Besterman, T. *Crystal-Gazing*. London: Rider, 1924.

Bevan, Edwyn Robert. *Sibyls and Seers: A Survey of Some Ancient Theories of Revelation and Inspiration*. Folcroft, PA, 1976.

Bird, Christopher. *The Divining Hand: The Art of Searching for Water, Oil, Minerals, and Other Natural Resources and Anything Lost, Missing, or Badly Needed*. New York: Dutton, 1979.

Black, David. *Ekstasy: Out-of-the-Body Experiences*. Indianpolis, IN: Bobbs-Merrill, 1975.

Blakely, John D. *The Mystical Tower of the Tarot*. London: Robinson & Watkins, 1974.

Blau, Didier. *Kumalak Mirror of Destiny*. Australia: Simon & Schuster, 1999.

Blavatsky, Helena Petrovna. *Isis Unvieled*. New York: J. W. Bouton, 1877.

Blavatsky, Helena Petrovna. *The Secret Doctrine*. London: Theosophical Publishing Company, 1888.

Blavatsky, Helena Petrovna. *The Theosophical Glossary*. London: Theosophical Publishing Company, 1892.

La Bleau, Madame. *Fortune Telling by Cards or Card Reading Made Easy*. Chicago: A. F. Seward, 1920.
Blofeld, John. *I Ching: The Book of Change*. London: Allen & Unwin, 1968.
Blok, Fritz. *I Ching: A Spiritual Guide*. New York: Stewart, Tabori & Chang, 1997.
Bloom, Harold. *Kabbalah and Criticism*. New York: Continuum, 1984.
Blum, Ralph H. *The Book of Runes*. New York: St. Martin's, 1982.
Blum, Ralph H. and Susan Loughan. *The Healing Runes*. New York: St. Martin's, 1995.
Boardman, D. *Defence of Phrenology: A Work for Doubters*. New York: Fowler & Wells, 1865.
Bonewitz, Ra. *Cosmic Crystals: Crystal Consciousness and the New Age*. Wellingborough: Turnstone Press, 1983.
Boos-Hamburger, H. *The Creative Power of Color*. Sussex: New Knowledge, n.d.
Bord, Janet and Colin. *Ancient Mysteries of Britain*. London: Guild Publishing, 1986.
Boswell, Harriet A. *Master Guide to Psychism*. New York: Parker, 1969.
Brandon-Jones, David. *Practical Palmistry*. London: Rider, 1981.
Branston, Brian. *Gods of the North*. Thames & Hudson, London 1980.
Branston, Brian. *The Lost Gods of England*. London:Thames & Hudson, 1957.
Brenner, Elizabeth. *The Hand Book*. Millbrae, CA: Celestial Arts, 1980.
Brenner, Elizabeth. *Hand In Hand*. Millbrae, CA: Celestial Arts, 1981.
Briggs, Katharine. *The Anatomy of Puck*. London: Hillary House, 1959.
Bringle, Mary. *Jeane Dixon: Prophet or Fraud?* New York: Tower Books, 1970.
Britten, Emma Hardinge. *Ghost Land, or Researches into the Mysteries of Occultism*. Chicago: Progressive Thinker Publishing House, 1909.
Broad, C. D. *Man, Myth & Magic: F.W. H. Myers*. London: BPC Publishing, 1970.
Brockman, Marcel. *The Complete Encyclopedia of Practical Palmistry*. Englewood Cliffs, NJ: Prentice-Hall, 1972.
Broughton, Richard S. *Parapsychology: The Controversial Science*. New York: Ballantine, 1991.
Brown, Rosemary. *Unfinished Symphonies: Voices from the Beyond*. New York: William Morrow, 1971.
Bryden, Dead. *Palmistry for Pleasure*. New York: Sully, 1926.
BSPR. *Catalogue of the Library of the (British) Society for Psychical Research*. Boston: G. K. Hall, 1976.
Buchanan, Joseph R. *Journal of Man*. Boston: Little, Brown, 1849.
Buchanan, Joseph R. *Manual of Psychometry*. Boston: Little, Brown, 1885.
Buckland, Raymond. *Advanced Candle Magick*. St. Paul, MN: Llewellyn, 1996.
Buckland, Raymond. *The Anatomy of the Occult*. New York: Samuel Weiser, 1977.
Buckland, Raymond. *The Buckland Romani Tarot: The Gypsy Book of Wisdom*. St. Paul, MN: Llewellyn, 2001.
Buckland, Raymond. *Buckland's Complete Book of Witchcraft*. St. Paul, MN: Llewellyn, 1986.
Buckland, Raymond. *Coin Divination: Pocket Fortuneteller*. St. Paul, MN: Llewellyn, 2000.
Buckland, Raymond. *Color Magic—Unleash Your Inner Powers*. St. Paul, MN: Llewellyn, 2002.
Buckland, Raymond. *Doors to Other Worlds*. St. Paul, MN: Llewellyn, 1993.
Buckland, Raymond. *Gypsy Dream Dictionary*. St. Paul, MN: Llewellyn, 1999.
Buckland, Raymond. *Gypsy Witchcraft and Magic*. St. Paul, MN: Llewellyn, 1998.
Buckland, Raymond. *A Pocket Guide to the Supernatural*. New York: Ace Books, 1969.
Buckland, Raymond. *Practical Candleburning Rituals*. St. Paul, MN: Llewellyn, 1982.
Buckland, Raymond. *Scottish Witchcraft*. St. Paul, MN: Llewellyn, 1992.
Buckland, Raymond. *Secrets of Gypsy Fortunetelling*. St. Paul, MN: Llewellyn, 1988.
Buckland, Raymond. *Signs, Symbols & Omens*. St. Paul, MN: Llewellyn, 2003.
Buckland, Raymond. *The Tree: Complete Book of Saxon Witchcraft*. New York: Samuel Weiser, 1974.

Buckland, Raymond. *Wicca for Life*. New York: Citadel, 2002.

Buckland, Raymond. *The Witch Book: The Encyclopedia of Witchcraft, Wicca, and Neo-paganism*. Detroit: Visible Ink Press, 2002.

Buckland, Raymond and Kathleen Binger. *The Book of African Divination*. Rochester, VT: Destiny Books, 1992.

Buckland, Raymond and Hereward Carrington. *Amazing Secrets of the Psychic World*. New York: Parker Publishing, 1975.

Budge, Sir E. A. Wallis. *Egyptian Magic*. New York: Bell Publishing, 1991.

Burt, Cyril. *Man, Myth & Magic: Jung*. London: London: BPC Publishing 1970.

Burton, J. *Heyday of a Wizard*. London: Harrap, 1948.

Butler, Bill. *Dictionary of the Tarot*. New York: Schocken Books, 1977.

Butler, William E. *How to Develop Clairvoyance*. New York: Samuel Weiser, 1971.

Butler, William E. *How to Develop Psychometry*. New York: Samuel Weiser, 1971.

Butler, William E. *How to Read the Aura*. New York: Samuel Weiser, 1971.

Cameron, Verne. *Map Dowsing*. El Carismo, 1971.

Campbell, John Gregorson. *Witchcraft and Second Sight in the Highlands and Islands of Scotland*. Glasgow: James MacLehose, 1902.

Carrington, Hereward. *Your Psychic Powers: And How to Develop Them*. New York: Dodd, Mead, 1920.

Case, Paul Foster. *The Tarot: A Key to the Wisdom of the Ages*. New York: Macoy, 1947.

Catholic Encyclopedia. New York: Encyclopedia Press, 1914.

Cave, Janet, and Laura Foreman and Jim Hicks (eds.) *Mysteries of the Unknown: Ancient Wisdom and Secret Sects*. Alexandria, VA: Time-Life Books, 1989.

Cavendish, Marshall. *The Book of Fate & Fortune*. London: Cavendish House, 1981.

Cavendish, Richard. *The Black Arts*. New York: G. P. Putnam's, 1967.

Cavendish, Richard (ed.). *Encyclopedia of the Unexplained*. London: Routledge & Kegan Paul, 1974.

Cavendish, Richard (ed.). *Man, Myth & Magic*. London: BPC Publishing, 1970.

Cayce, Edgar. *Auras*. Virginia Beach, VA: A. R. E. Press, 1973.

Cayce, Hugh Lynn. *Venture Inward*. New York: Paperback Library, 1969.

Celeste. *Astrology, Mythology and the Bible*. New York: Avon, 1969.

Chambers, Howard V. *Phrenology*. Los Angeles: Sherbourne Press, 1968.

Charboneau, Karen. *Crystal Gazing*. Los Angeles: Moon Magick/Glasscastle, 1981.

Cheasley, Clifford W. *Numerology*. Boston: Triangle, 1916.

Cheiro (Louis Hamon). *Cheiro's Book of Numbers*. New York: Arc, 1964.

Cheiro (Louis Hamon). *Cheiro's Complete Palmistry*. New York: University Books, 1968.

Cheiro (Louis Hamon). *Cheiro's Language of the Hand*. Chicago: Rand, McNally, 1897.

Chen Pin Hong. *Bian zheng bai nian li (Annotated 100-year Chinese Lunar Calendar)*. Taipei: Jing Kang, 1986.

Chesi, Gert. *Voodoo: Africa's Secret Power*. Perlinger, Austria, 1980.

Chetwynd, Tom. *Dictionary for Dreamers*. London: Aquarian, 1993.

Chetwynd, Tom. *Dictionary of Symbols*. London: Aquarian, 1993.

Christie-Murray, David. *Mysteries of Mind Space & Time: The Unexplained*. Westport, CT: H. S. Stuttman, 1992.

Christopher, Milbourne. *ESP, Seers, & Psychics: What the Occult Really Is?* New York: Thomas Y. Crowell, 1970.

Christopher, Milbourne. *Mediums, Mystics and the Occult*. New York: Thomas Y. Crowell, 1975.

Clark, John Grahame Douglas. *World Prehistory*. Cambridge University Press, 1961.

Clébert, Jean-Paul. *The Gypsies*. Penguin, 1967.

Cohen, Daniel. *E.S.P.: The Search beyond the Senses*. New York: Harcourt Brace Johanovich, 1973.
Colquhoun, Ithel. *The Sword of Wisdom: MacGregor Mathers & the Golden Dawn*. New York: G. P. Putnam's Sons, 1975.
Combe, George. *A System of Phrenology*. New York: S. R. Wells, 1876.
Complete Book of Fate and Fortune. London: Marshall Cavendish, 1974.
Cook, Mrs. Cecil. *How I Discovered My Mediumship*. Chicago: Lormar, 1919.
Cooper, D. Jason. *Using the Runes*. London: Aquarian Press, 1986.
Cooper, J. C. *An Illustrated Encyclopedia of Traditional Symbols*. London: Thames & Hudson, 1978.
Copen, Bruce. *Character Analysis with Color*. Sussex: Academic Publications, 1976.
Copen, Bruce. *The Modern Prospector*. Sussex: Academic Publications, n.d.
Cosmopolitan's Guide to Fortune-Telling. New York: Cosmopolitan, 1977.
Covina, Gina. *The Ouija Book*. New York: Simon & Schuster, 1979.
Cowan, Tom. *The Book of Séance*. Chicago: Contemporary Books, 1994.
Crawford, E. A., and T. Kennedy. *Chinese Elemental Astrology*. London: Piatkus, 1990.
Crawford, W. J. *The Reality of Psychic Phenomena, Raps, Levitations, Etc*. New York: E.P. Dutton, 1918.
Criswell, Jeron. *Criswell's Forbidden Predictions Based on Nostradamus and the Tarot*. Atlanta: Drake House/Hallux, 1972.
Crook, J. A. *Law and Life of Rome*. London: Thames & Hudson, 1967.
Crookall, Robert. *The Study and Practice of Astral Projection*. London: Aquarian, 1960.
Crookall, Robert. *The Techniques of Astral Projection*. London: Aquarian, 1964.
Crow, W. B. *A History of Magic, Witchcraft, and Occultism*. London: Aquarian, 1968.
Crow, W. B. *Precious Stones: Their Occult Power and Hidden Significance*. London: Aquarian, 1968.
Crowley, Aleister. *Aha*. Dallas: Sangreal, 1969.
Crowley, Aleister. *The Book of the Law*. Tunis, 1925.
Crowley, Aleister. *The Book of Thoth*. London: The O.T.O., 1944.
Crowley, Aleister. *The Confessions of Aleister Crowley*. New York: Hill & Wang, 1970.
Crowley, Aleister. *The Diary of a Drug Fiend*. London: W. Collins, 1922.
Crowley, Aleister. *Gems From the Equinox*. St. Paul, MN: Llewellyn, 1974.
Crowley, Aleister. *Magick in Theory and Practice*. New York: Castle Books, n.d.
Crowley, Aleister. ______*: The Holy Books of Thelema*. York Beach: Samuel Weiser, 1983.
Cunningham, Scott. *Art of Divination*. Freedom, CA: Crossing Press, 1993.
Cunningham, Scott. *Pocket Guide to Fortune Telling*. Freedom, CA: Crossing Press, 1997.
Cunningham, Scott. *Sacred Sleep*. Freedom, CA: Crossing Press, 1992.
Dale. *National Dream Book*. Philadelphia, PA: Dale Publications, 1933.
Da Liu. *I Ching Coin Prediction*. New York: Harper & Row, 1975.
DaEl (Dale Walker). *The Crystal Book*. Sunol, CA: The Crystal Company, 1983.
Dale, J.B. *Indian Palmistry*. London: Theosophical Publishing, 1895.
Davidson, Hilda Roderick Ellis. *Man, Myth & Magic: Freyr, Freyja, Frigg*. London: BPC Publishing, 1970.
Davidson, Hilda Roderick Ellis. *Scandinavian Mythology*. London: Paul Hamlyn, 1969.
Davidson, Victor S. *Iridiagnosis: Diagnosis from the Eyes*. Wellingborough: Thorsons, 1979.
Davies, Edward. *Celtic Researches*. London: Davies, 1804.
Davies, John D. *Phrenology: Fad and Science: A Nineteenth Century American Crusade*. New York: Archon, 1955.
Davis, F. *Myths and Legends of Japan*. London: Headland, 1917.
Deacon, Richard. *John Dee*. Muller, 1968.

Dee, Nerys. *Understanding Dreams*. Wellingborough: Thorsons, 1991.
Delmonico, Damyan. *I Was Curious—A Crystal Ball Gazer*. Philadelphia: Dorrance, 1972.
Delsol, Paula. *Chinese Horoscopes*. London: Pan, 1973.
Denning, Melita, and Osborne Phillips. *The Llewellyn Practical Guide to Astral Projection*. St. Paul, MN: Llewellyn, 1979.
Denning, Melita, and Osborne Phillips. *The Llewellyn Practical Guide to the Magick of the Tarot*. St. Paul, MN: Llewellyn, 1983.
Deren, Maya. *Divine Horsemen*. London: Thames & Hudson, 1953.
Deren, Maya. *The Voodoo Gods*. St. Albans: Paladin, 1976.
Dernay, Eugene. *Longitudes and Latitudes throughout the World*. Washington, DC: National Astrological Library, 1948.
Deutch, Yvonne (ed.). *Fortune Tellers*. London: Marshall Cavendish, 1974.
Dickinson, Peter. *Chance, Luck & Destiny*. Boston: Little, Brown, 1976.
Dietrich, C. *Diagnosis*. Sussex: Academic Publications, n.d.
Dingwall, E. and J. Langdon-Davies. *The Unknown—Is It Nearer?* New York: Signet, 1956.
Dixon, Jeane. *My Life and Prophesies*. New York: Bantam, 1970.
Doane, Doris Chase. *Time Changes in the World*. Hollywood: Professional Astrologers, 1971.
Doane, Doris Chase and King Keyes. *Tarot-Card Spread Reader*. New York: Parker, 1967.
Donaldson, Terry. *Step-by-Step Tarot*. Wellingborough: Thorsons, 1995.
Donnelly, Katherine Fair. *The Guidebook to ESP and Psychic Wonders*. New York: David McKay, 1978.
Douglas, Alfred. *The Tarot: The Origins, Meaning and Uses of the Cards*, Baltimore: Penguin, 1973.
Doyle, Sir Arthur Conan. *The History of Spiritualism*. New York: Doran. 1926.
Dropping Well Estate. *The Life and Prophesies of Ursula Sontheil Better Known as Mother Shipton*. Leeds: Arthur Wigley, n.d.
Drury, Nevill. *The Shaman and the Magician: Journeys between the Worlds*. London: Routledge & Kegan Paul, 1982.
Ducasse, C.J. *A Critical Examination of the Belief in Life after Death*. London: C. C. Thomas, 1961.
Dummett, Michael. *Game of Tarot: From Ferrara to Salt Lake City*. London: Duckworth, 1980.
Dunne, J. W. *An Experiment with Time*. New York: Macmillan, 1938.
Dupont, Ellen and Nance Fyson (eds.). *Quest for the Unknown: Life beyond Death*. Pleasantville, NY: Reader's Digest, 1992.
Eaglesfield, Francis. *Silent Union: A Record of Unwilled Communication*. London: Stuart & Watkins, 1966.
Ebon, Martin. *True Experiences in Communicating with the Dead*. New York: New American Library, 1968.
Ebon, Martin. *True Experiences in Telepathy*. New York: Signet, 1967.
Edward, John. *Crossing Over: The Stories behind the Stories*. New York: Princess Books, 2001.
Eichhorn, Werner. *The Concise Encyclopedia of Living Faiths*. New York: Hawthorne Books, 1959.
Eisenbud, Jules. *The World of Ted Serios*. New York: Morrow, 1967.
Eliade, Mircea. *Shamanism: Archaic Techniques of Ecstasy*. Princeton, NJ: Princeton University Press Bollingen Series, 1972.
Elliot, J. Scott. *Dowsing: One Man's Way*. London: Neville Spearmen, 1977.
Elliott, Ralph W .V. *Runes: An Introduction*. Manchester University Press, 1959.
Encausse, Gérard (Papus). *The Tarot of the Bohemians*. London: Arcanum, 1958.
Encyclopedia Britannica. Chicago: William Benton, 1964.
Epstein, Perle. *Kabbalah: The Way of the Jewish Mystic*. Boston: Shambhala, 1988.

Evans-Pritchard, E E. *Witchcraft, Oracles and Magic among the Azande*. Oxford: Oxford University Press, 1937.
Fairfield, Gail. *Choice-Centered Tarot*. Seattle: Choice-Centered, 1982.
Farb, Peter. *Living Earth*. New York: Harper Colophon, 1959.
Farber, Monte and Amy Zerner. *The Enchanted Astrologer*. New York: Thomas Dunne, 2001.
Fay, Anna Eva. *Somnolency and Guide to Dreams*. Boston: Fay, 1900.
Feher-Elston, Catherine. *RavenSong*. Flagstaff, AZ: Northland Publishing, 1991.
Feilding, Everard. *Sittings with Eusapia Palladino*. New York: University Books, 1963.
Fell, Barry. *America B.C*. New York: Quadrangle, 1976.
Ferguson, J. *Civilization of the Ancient Mediterranean. Greece and Rome. Volume II: Divination and Oracles: Rome*. New York: Charles Scribner's, 1988.
Ferguson, Sibyl. *The Crystal Ball*. New York: Samuel Weiser, 1979.
Fisher, Joe. *Predictions*. New York: Van Nostrand Reinhold, 1980.
Fishley, Margaret. *The Supernatural*. London: Aldus, 1976.
Fitzherbert, Andrew. *Hand Psycholog*. London: Angus and Robertson, 1986.
Fleming-Mitchell, Leslie. *The Language of Astrology*. London: W. H. Allen, 1981.
Fliess, Wilhelm. *Der Ablauf des Lebens* ("The Course of Life") Liepzig-Vienna: Franz Deuticke, 1906.
Fodor, Nandor. *An Encyclopedia of Psychic Science*. London, 1934.
Foli, Prof. P. R .S. *Fortune-Telling by Cards*. Philadelphia: David McKay, 1902.
Fontana, Marjorie A. *Cup of Fortune: A Guide to Tea Leaf Reading*. Madison, WI: Fontastic, 1979.
Fontenrose, Joseph. *Delphic Oracle: Its Responses and Operations, with a Catalog of Responses*. Berkeley: University of California Press, 1978.
Forbes, Alec. *Try Being Healthy*. Plymouth: Langdon, 1976.
Ford, Arthur. *Nothing So Strange*. New York: Harper, 1958.
Fortune, Dion. *The Mystical Qabalah*. London: Ernest Benn, 1935.
Fortune, Dion. *Practical Occultism in Daily Life*. London: Williams & Norgate, 1935.
Fortune, Dion. *Sane Occultism*. London: Rider, 1935.
Fortune, Dion. *The Training and Work of an Initiate*. London: Rider, n.d.
Fournier, D'Albe. *The Life of Sir William Crookes*. T. Fisher Unwin, London 1923.
Fowler, O.S. *The Practical Phrenologist; and Recorder and Delineator of the Character and Talents—A Compendium of Phreno-Organic Science*. Boston: Fowler, 1861.
Fowler, O.S. *Practical Phrenology*. New York: Fowler & Wells, 1866.
Fowler, O.S. *Self-Instructor in Phrenology and Physiology*. New York: Fowler & Wells, 1863.
Fox, Oliver. *Astral Projection: A Record of Out-of-Body Experiences*. London: Rider, 1939.
de France, Henry. *The Elements of Dowsing*. London: Watkins, 1971.
Fraser, Angus. *The Gypsies*. Oxford: Blackwell, 1992.
Frost, Gavin and Yvonne. *Astral Projection: Your Guide to the Secrets of Out-of-the-Body Experience*. London: Granada, 1982.
Fukuri, T. *Clairvoyance and Thoughtography*. London: Rider, 1931.
Galde, Phyllis. *Crystal Healing: the Next Step*. St. Paul, MN: Llewellyn, 1988.
Gauld, Alan. *The Founders of Psychical Research*. London: Routledge & Kegan Paul, 1968.
Garen, Nancy. *Tarot Made Easy*. London: Piatkus, 1990.
Garfield, Patricia L. *Creative Dreaming*. New York: Simon & Schuster, 1974.
Garrard, Bruce.*A Collection of Runic Lore*. London: Unique Publications, 1991.
Garrett, Eileen J. *Adventures in the Supernormal*. New York: Garrett, 1958.
Garrett, Eileen J. *Many Voices: the Autobiography of a Medium*. New York: G. P. Putnam's, 1968.
Garrison, Omar. *The Encyclopedia of Prophecy*. Secaucus, NJ: Citadel, 1978.

Gattey, Charles Neilson. *They Saw Tomorrow: Seers and Sorcerers from Delphi till Today*. London: Granada, 1980.
Gauld, Alan. *The Founders of Psychical Research*. London: Routledge & Kegan Paul, 1968.
Gearhart, Sally. *A Feminist Tarot: A Guide to Intrapersonal Communication*. Watertown, NY: Persephone, 1977.
Gebauer, Paul. *Spider Divination of the Cameroons*. Milwaukee: Milwaukee Public Museum, 1964.
Geddes, Sheila. *Art of Astrology*. London: Aquarian, 1992.
George, Llewellyn. *A to Z Horoscope Maker and Delineator*. St. Paul, MN: Llewellyn, 1970.
Gettings, Fred. *The Book of the Hand*. London: Paul Hamlyn, 1965.
Gettings, Fred. *The Book of the Zodiac: An Historical Anthology of Astrology*. London: Ward Lock, 1972.
Gibson, Walter B. and Litzka R. *The Complete Illustrated Book of the Psychic Sciences*. Garden City, NY: Doubleday, 1966.
Gittelson, Bernard. *Biorhythm: A Personal Science*. New York: Warner Books, 1980.
de Giustino, David. *Conquest of the Mind: Phrenology and Victorian Social Thought*. London: Croom Helm, 1975.
de Givry, Grillot. *A Pictorial Anthology of Witchcraft, Magic & Alchemy*. London: Spottiswoode, Ballantyne, 1931.
Goethe, Johann W. von. *Theory of Colors*, London: John Murray, 1840.
Goldberg, B. Z. *The Sacred Fire: The Story of Sex in Religion*. New York: University Books, 1958.
González-Wippler, Migene. *The Complete Book of Amulets and Talismans*, St. Paul, MN: Llewellyn, 1991.
González-Wippler, Migene. *Introduction to Seashell Divination*. New York: Original Publications, 1985.
Goodavage, Joseph F. *Astrology: The Space Age Science*. West Nyack, NY: Parker, 1966.
Goodman, Linda. *Linda Goodman's Sun Signs*. New York: Taplinger, 1968.
Grand Orient (A. E. Waite). *The Complete Manual of Occult Divination: Volume 1—Manual of Cartomancy*. London: Rider, 1912.
Grand Orient (A. E. Waite). *The Complete Manual of Occult Divination: Volume 2—The Book of Destiny*. London: Rider, 1912.
Graves, Robert. *The White Goddess*. London: Faber & Faber, 1961.
Graves, Thomas. *Dowsing*. London: Turnstone Books, 1976.
Graves, Thomas. *Elements of Pendulum Dowsing*. London: Element, 1991.
Gray, Eden. *A Complete Guide to the Tarot*. New York: Crown, 1970.
Gray, Eden. *Mastering the Tarot: Basic Lessons in an Ancient Mystic Art*. New York: New American Library, 1971.
Gray, Eden. *The Tarot Revealed*. New York: Inspiration House, 1960.
Gray, Magda (ed.). *Fortune Telling*. London: Marshall Cavendish, 1974.
Green, Celia. *Out-of-the-Body Experiences*. New York: Ballantine, 1968.
Green, Liz. *Saturn: A New Look at an Old Devil*. New York: Samuel Weiser, 1976.
Greenhouse, Herbert B. *Premonitions: A Leap into the Future*. New York: Bernard Geis, 1971.
Greer, John Michael. *Earth Divination Earth Magic: A Practical Guide to Geomancy*. St. Paul, MN: Llewellyn, 1999.
Greer, John Michael. *Paths of Wisdom: The Magical Cabala in the Western Tradition*. St. Paul, MN: Llewellyn, 1996.
Greer, Mary K. *Tarot for Yourself*. North Hollywood, CA: Newcastle, 1984.
Guiley, Rosemary Ellen. *The Encyclopedia of Ghosts and Spirits*. New York: Facts on File, 1992.
Guiley, Rosemary Ellen. *The Encyclopedia of Witches and Witchcraft*. New York: Facts on File, 1989.

Guiley, Rosemary Ellen. *Harper's Encyclopedia of Mystical & Paranormal Experience*. San Francisco: HarperSanFrancisco 1991.
Guirand, Félix. *Greek Mythology*. Paul London, 1963.
Gurney, Edmund, Frederic W. H. Myer & Frank Podmore. *Phantasms of the Living*. Society for Psychical Research, London 1886.
Gypsy Queen, A. *Zingara Fortune Teller*. Philadelphia: David McKay, 1901.
Hall, Angus. *The Supernatural: Signs of Things to Come*. London: Danbury Press, 1975.
Hall, Manly Palmer. *Astrological Keywords*. Totowa, NJ: Littlefield Adams, 1975.
Hall, Manly Palmer. *The Tarot*. Los Angeles: Philosophical Research, 1978.
Halliday, W. R. *Greek Divination*. London: Rider, 1913.
Hamilton, Edith. *The Greek Way to Western Civilization*. New York: W. W. Norton, 1942.
Hamilton, Edith. *Mythology*. New York: Little, Brown, 1942.
Hamilton, Edith. *The Roman Way to Western Civilization*. New York: W. W. Norton, 1932.
Hansel, C .E .M. *E.S.P.: A Scientific Evaluation*. New York: Charles Scribner's, 1966.
Hargrave, Catherine Perry. *A History of Playing Cards*. New York: Houghton Mifflin, 1930.
Harner, Michael. *The Way of the Shaman: A Guide to Power and Healing*. San Francisco: Harper & Row, 1980.
Harrison, Vernon. *H. P. Blavatsky and the SPR: An Examination of the Hodgson Report of 1885*. Pasadena, CA: Theosophical University Press, 1997.
Harold, Edmund. *Focus on Crystals*. New York: Ballantine Books, 1986.
Hart, H. *The Enigma of Survival*. London: Rider, 1959.
Hasbrouck, Muriel. *Pursuit of Destiny*. New York: Citadel, 1960.
Hawkins, Gerald S. *Stonehenge Decoded*. New York: Dell, 1966.
Headon, Deirdre (ed.). *Quest for the Unknown—Charting the Future*. Pleasantville, NY: Reader's Digest, 1992.
Heywood, Abel. *Mother Shipton's Prophesies*. Manchester: Abel Heywood, 1881.
Heywood, Rosalind. *Beyond the Reach of Sense*. New York: Dutton, 1961.
Heywood, Rosalind. *The Sixth Sense*. London: Pan Books, 1966.
Hickey, Isabel M. *Astrology: A Cosmic Science*. Watertown, NY: Hickey, 1970.
Hill, Douglas. *Man, Myth & Magic: Scrying*. London: BPC Publishing, 1970.
Hipskind, Judith. *Palmistry: The Whole View*. St. Paul, MN: Llewellyn, 1977.
Hitching, Francis. *Dowsing: The Psi Connection*. New York: Anchor Books, 1978.
Hoebens, Piet Hein. *Mysteries of Mind, Space & Time: The Unexplained*. Westport, CT: H. S. Stuttman, 1992.
Hoeller, Stephen A. *The Royal Road: A Manual of Kabalistic Meditations on the Tarot*. Wheaton, IL: Theosophical, 1975.
Hoffman, Elizabeth P. *Palm Reading Made Easy*. New York: Essandess, 1971.
Hoffman, Enid. *Huna: A Beginner's Guide*. Gloucester: Para Research, 1976.
Hollen, Henry. *Clairaudient Transmissions*. Hollywood: Keats Publications, 1931.
Holmes, Prescott. *The New American Dream Book*. New York: New York Book Company, 1913.
Holroyd, Stuart. *The Supernatural: Dream Worlds*. London: Aldus Books, 1976.
Holroyd, Stuart. *The Supernatural: Minds without Boundaries*. London: Aldus Books, 1976.
Holt, Peter. *Stars of India: Travels in Search of Astrologers and Fortune-tellers*. Edinburgh, Scotland: Mainstream Publishing, 1998.
Holy Bible—various editions.
Holzer, Hans. *Born Again—The Truth about Reincarnation*. Garden City, NY: Doubleday, 1970.
Holzer, Hans. *The Prophets Speak: What the Leading Psychics Say about Tomorrow*. Indianapolis: Bobbs-Merrill, 1971.
Holzer, Hans. *Psychic Side of Dreams*. St. Paul, MN: Llewellyn, 1992.
Hone, M. E. *The Modern Text Book of Astrology*. London: Fowler, 1955.

Honness, Elizabeth. *The Etruscans: An Unsolved Mystery*. New York: J. P. Lippincott, 1972.
Horwood, Harold. *The Conquest of Time*. London: Fowler, 1959.
House, Brant. *Strange Powers of Unusual People*. New York: Ace Books, 1963.
Howard, Michael A. *The Runes and Other Magical Alphabets*. London: Aquarian Press, 1978.
Howard, Michael A. *Understanding Runes*. London: Aquarian Press, 1990.
Howe, Ellic. *Man, Myth & Magic: National Socialism*. London: BPC Publishing, 1970.
Howe, Ellic. *Urania's Children*. London: Kimber, 1967.
http://dowsers.new-hampshire.net/.
http://mainportals.com/precog.shtml.
http://mayacalendar.com/mayadivination4.htm.
http://members.tripod.com/~rhazz/frobertson.html.
http://pages.britishlibrary.net/phrenology/combes.html.
http://allthingstarot.freeserve.co.uk/riderwaite.html.
http://www.angelfire.com/electronic/bodhidharma/bones.html.
http://www.awakenings-inc.com/academics/symbols.htm.
http://www.bbc.co.uk/so/weird/believe/composers2.shtml.
http://www.blavatskyarchives.com/.
http://www.bmlisieux.com/normandie/sybille.htm.
http://www.brihaspatinet.atfreeweb.com/.
http://www.britishdowsers.org/.
http://www.buddhistview.com/site/epage/7274_225.htm.
http://www.c-c-c.org/chineseculture/zodiac/zodiac.html.
http://www.cnn.com/SHOWBIZ/9701/26/dixon/.
http://www.denelder.com/tarot/tarot013b.html http://www.edgarcayce.org/.
http://www.esonet.at/groups/hartlieb.html.
http://www.esotericpublishing.com/pr/deunov.html. @resent:http://www.folklegend.com/article1066_2.html.
http://www.geocities.com/Athens/Acropolis/1896/crowhar.html.
http://www.geocities.com/HotSprings/Spa/2366/montgomery.html.
http://www.geocities.com/wolfreader/FunPage.html.
http://www.groundhog.org/.
http://www.hermetic.com/sabazius/papus.htm.
http://www.jrn.columbia.edu/studentwork/cns/2002-04-03/320.asp.
http://www.monroeinstitute.org/.
http://www.mysteriousbritain.co.uk/occult/drforman.html.
http://www.near-death.com/experiences/myers9.html.
http://www.news-journalonline.com/2002/Jun/10/NOTE1.htm.
http://www.serenapowers.com/.
http://www.serenapowers.com/mahjongg.html.
http://www.shades-of-night.com/aviary.
http://www.solsticemoon.com/spiritual.
http://www.solsticepoint.com/astrologersmemorial/cheiro.htm.
http://www.stargazers.com/raphael.html.
http://www.supertarot.co.uk/adept/friedaharris.htm.
http://www.tarotsociety.org.
http://www.tibet.com/Buddhism/divination.html.
http://www.urania.info/comments/2002/4/28/174740/593/0/post.
http://www.vedalink.com/.
http://www.yesterdayland.com/popopedia/shows/arcade/ag1256.php.
http://www.zolar-thoth.org./ .

http://www.zorrapredictions.com/5elements/palmistry.
Hunt, Stoker. *Ouija: The Most Dangerous Game*. New York: Harper & Row, 1985.
Hurkos, Peter. *Psychic: The Story of Peter Hurkos*. London: Barker, 1962.
Huson, Paul. *The Devil's Picturebook: The Compleat Guide to Tarot Cards*. New York: Putnam, 1971.
Hutchinson, Beryl. *Your Life in Your Hands*. London: Neville Spearman, 1967.
Huxley, A. J. *Man, Myth & Magic: Holly and Ivy*. London: BPC Publishing, 1970.
Huxley, A. J. *Man, Myth & Magic: Trees*. London: BPC Publishing, 1970.
Hyre, K .M. and Eli Goodman. *Price Guide to the Occult and Related Subjects*. Los Angeles: Reference Guides, 1967.
Innes, Brian. *Mysteries of Mind Space & Time: The Unexplained*. Westport, CT: H. S. Stuttman, 1992.
Iremonger, Lucille. *The Ghosts of Versailles*. London: Faber & Faber, 1957.
Jackson, Nigel and Silver RavenWolf. *The Rune Mysteries*. St. Paul, MN: Llewellyn, 1996.
Jaulin, Robert. *Geomancy: Formal Analysis*. Paris: Mouton, 1966.
Javane, Faith and Dusty Bunker. Numerology and the Divine Triangle. *Rockport, MA: Para Research, 1979*.
Jay, Roni. *Sacred Flowers*. Hillsboro, OR: Beyond Words, 1997.
Jensen, Bernard. *Iridology Simplified*. Escondido, CA: Iridologists International, 1980.
Jocelyn, John. *Meditations on the Signs of the Zodiac*. Blauvelt: Multimedia, 1970.
Jones, Ernest. *The Symbolic Significance of Salt*. New York: Spring Publications, 1995.
Jones, Mark Edmund. *Astrology: How and Why It Works*. London: Routledge & Kegan Paul, 1977.
Jones, Mark Edmund. *The Guide to Horoscope Interpretation*. New York: Sabian, 1961.
Jordan, Juno. *Numerology*. Marina Del Rey, CA: DeVorss, 1965.
Jordan, Michael. *Witches: An Encyclopedia of Witches and Witchcraft*. London: Kyle Cathie, 1996.
Kahn, Yitzhac. *Tarot and the Game of Fate*. San Francisco: Sebaac Publishers, 1971.
Kaplan, Stuart. *The Encyclopædia of Tarot*. New York: U.S. Games, 1978.
Kaplan, Stuart R. *Tarot Classic*. New York: Grosset & Dunlap, 1972.
Kaplan, Stuart R. *Tarot Cards for Fun and Fortune Telling*. London: Aquarian Press, 1978.
Kardec, Alan. *The Book of Oracles*. Summerland, CA: Kardec, 1984.
Kargere, Audrey. *Color and Personality*. New York: Wehman, n.d.
Kaster, Joseph. *Putnam's Concise Mythological Dictionary*. New York: G. P. Putnam's, 1963.
Katlyn. *Tympana: Drum and Tambourine Divination*. Long Beach, CA: Mermade Magickal Arts, 1991.
Keane, Jerryl L. *Practical Astrology: How to Make It Work for You*. West Nyack, NY: Parker, 1967.
Kelsey, Denys and Joan Grant. *Many Lifetimes*. Garden City, NY: Doubleday, 1967.
Kimmelman, Sydney (Omarr). My *World of Astrology*. New York: Fleet, 1965.
Kimmelman, Sydney (Omarr). *Sidney Omarr's Astrological Revelations about You*. New York: New American Library, 1973.
King, Bernard. *The Elements of the Runes*. Dorset, UK: Element Books, 1993.
King, Francis. *The Magical World of Aleister Crowley*. New York: Coward, McCann & Geoghegan, 1978.
King, Francis. *Man, Myth & Magic*. London: BPC Publishing, 1970.
King, Francis. *The Supernatural: The Cosmic Influence*. London: Aldus Books, 1975.
Kingston, Jeremy. *The Supernatural: Healing without Medicine*. London: Aldus Books, 1975.
Klimo, Jon. *Channeling: Investigations on Receiving Information from Paranormal Sources*. Los Angeles: Jeremy P. Tarcher, 1987.
Knight, David C. *The ESP Reader*. Secaucus, NJ: Castle Books, 1969.

Knight, Gareth. *A Practical Guide to Qabalistic Symbolism*. New York: Samuel Weiser, 1978.
Knight, Richard Payne. *A Discourse on the Worship of Priapus*. London: Knight, 1894.
Kraig, Donald Michael. *Modern Magick: Eleven Lessons in the High Magickal Arts*. St. Paul, MN: Llewellyn, 1988.
Krippner, Stanley and Daniel Rubin (eds.). *The Kirlian Aura*. Garden City, NY: Anchor Books, 1974.
Lakhovsky, Georges (tr. Mark Clement). *The Secret of Life: Cosmic Rays and Radiations of Living Beings*. London: True Health, 1963.
Lambert, R. S. *Exploring the Supernatural: The Weird in Canadian Folklore*. Toronto: McClelland & Stewart, 1955.
Lamont, André. *Nostadamus Sees All*. Philadelphia: W. Foulsham, 1942.
Lane, E .W. *An Account of the Manners & Customs of the Modern Egyptians*. London: C. Knight, 1856.
Langley, Noel. *Edgar Cayce on Reincarnation*. New York: Paperback Library, 1967.
Larousse Encyclopedia of Mythology. London: Paul Hamlyn, 1965.
Lau, Kwan. *Secrets of Chinese Astrology*. New York: Tengu Books, 1994.
Laurence, Theodor. *The Sexual Key to the Tarot*. New York: Citadel, 1971.
Laver, James. *Nostradamus: Or, the Future Foretold*. Maidstone: George Mann, 1973.
Lawson, John Cuthbert. *Modern Greek Folklore and Ancient Greek Religion*. New York: University Books, 1964.
Leach, Maria (ed.). *Funk & Wagnalls Standard Dictionary of Folklore, Mythology, and Legend*. San Francisco: Harper & Row, 1972.
Leek, Sybil. *The Complete Art of Witchcraft*. New York: Signet, 1973.
Leek, Sybil. *My Life In Astrology*. Englewood Cliffs, NJ: Prentice-Hall, 1972.
Leek, Sybil. *The Night Voyagers: You and Your Dreams*. New York: Ballantine, 1975.
Leek, Sybil. *Numerology: the Magic of Numbers*. New York: Collier, 1969.
Leek, Sybil. *A Shop in the High Street*. London: McKay, 1964.
Leek, Sybil. *The Sybil Leek Book of Fortune Telling*. Toronto: Macmillan, 1969.
Leland, Charles Godfrey. *Etruscan Magic & Occult Remedies*. New York: University Books, 1963.
Leland, Charles Godfrey. *Gypsy Sorcery & Fortune Telling*. Fisher-Unwin, 1891.
Lele, Ócha'ni. *The Secrets of Afro-Cuban Divination: How to Cast the Diloggun, the Oracle of the Orishas*. New York: Inner Traditions, 2002.
Lenormand. *Oracles of Mlle. Lenormand*. Switzerland: Urania Verlags AG, 1989.
Lerner, Isha and Mark Lerner. *Inner Child Cards: A Journey into Fairy Tales, Myth, and Nature*. Santa Fe, NM: Bear, 1992.
Lethbridge, Thomas C. *The Power of the Pendulum*. London: Routledge & Kegan Paul, 1976.
Lewi, Grant. *Astrology for the Millions*. St. Paul, MN: Llewellyn, 1969.
Lewi, Grant. *Heaven Knows What*. St. Paul, MN: Llewellyn, 1962.
Lewis, John. *Religions of the World Made Simple*. Garden City, NY: Doubleday, 1958.
Lewis, Ursula. *Chart Your Own Horoscope: For Beginner and Professional*. New York: Grosset & Dunlap, 1976.
Leybrun, J. G. *The Haitian People*. New Haven, CT: Yale University Press, 1941.
Lind, Frank. *How to Understand the Tarot*. New York: Samuel Weiser, 1969.
Line, David and Julia. *Fortune Telling by Dice: Uncovering the Future through the Ancient System of Casting Lots*. London: Aquarian Press, 1984.
Linn, Denise. *Past Lives, Present Dreams*. London: Piatkus, 1995.
Lipari, Paul. *The Mystery of Runes*. Kansas City, MO: Andrews McMeel, 1998.
Lissner, Ivar. *The Living Past*. New York: Capricorn Books, 1961.
Lissner, Ivar. *Man, God and Magic*. London: Jonathan Cape, 1961.

Litvag, Irving. *Singer in the Shadows*. Macmillan, 1972.
Llewellyn Editorial Staff. *The Truth about Astral Projection*. St. Paul, MN: Llewellyn, 1983.
Loewe, Michael. *Chinese Ideas of Life and Death*. London: Routledge, 1982.
Loewe, Michael and Carmen Blacker. *Oracles and Divination*. London: Allen & Unwin, 1981.
Lopez, Vincent. *Numerology*. New York: Citadel, 1961.
Lord, Walter. *A Night to Remember*. New York: Henry Holt, 1956.
Luck, G. *Arcana Mundi: Magic and the Occult in the Greek and Roman Worlds*, Baltimore: Johns Hopkins University Press, 1985.
Luckiesh, Matthew. *Color and Its Implications*. New York: Van Nostrand, 1921.
Lutoslawski, W. *Pre-Existence and Reincarnation*. London: Allen and Unwin, 1926.
Lystad, Robert A. *The Ashanti*. New Brunswick, NJ: Rutgers University Press, 1958.
Mackenzie, Alexander. *The Prophesies of the Brahan Seer*. Inverness, 1882.
MacHovec, Frank J. *Nostradamus: His Prophecies for the Future*. Mount Vernon, NY: Peter Pauper Press, 1972.
MacKenzie, Andrew. *Riddle of the Future*. London: A. Barker, 1974.
MacLeod, William ("Theophilus Insulanus"). *A Treatise on the Second Sight, Dreams and Apparitions*. Edinburgh, Scotland: Ruddimans, Auld and Co., 1763.
MacNeice, Louis. *Astrology*, Garden City, NY: Doubleday, 1964.
Macrae, Norman (ed.). *Highland Second Sight: With Prophecies of Coinneach Odhar and the Seer of Petty*. Dingwall: G. Souter, 1908.
Malinowski, Bronislaw. *Magic, Science and Religion*. New York: Doubleday, 1948.
Maltagliati, Raoul. *How to Dream Your Lucky Lotto Numbers*. St. Paul, MN: Llewellyn, 1990.
Mann, A. T. *Millenium Prophecies*. London: Element, 1993.
Maple, Eric. *Man, Myth & Magic: Necromancy*, London: BPC Publishing, 1970.
Martello, Leo. *Your Pen Personality*. New York: Hero Press, 1961.
Mathers, S. L. Macgregor. *The Book of Sacred Magic of Abra-Melin the Mage*. Chicago: De Laurence, 1932.
Mathers, S. L. Macgregor. *The Kabbalah Unveiled*. London: Routledge & Kegan Paul, 1951.
Mathers, S. L. Macgregor. *The Tarot*. New York: Wehman, n.d.
Matthews, John. *The Celtic Shaman*. Shaftesbury, UK: Element, 1991.
Maury, Marguerite. *How to Dowse, Experimental and Practical Radiesthesia*. London: Bell, 1953.
Mayo, Jeff. *Teach Yourself Astrology*. London: Hodder & Stoughton, 1992.
McGregor, Pedro. *The Moon and Two Mountains*. London: Souvenir Press, 1966.
McIntyre, Loren. *Incas and Their Timeless Land*. Washington, DC: National Geographic Society, 1975.
Mead, George R. S. *Apollonius of Tyana—The Philosopher-Reformed of the First Century AD*. London: Theosophical Publishing House, 1901.
Melville, J. *Crystal Gazing and Clairvoyance*. New York: Samuel Weiser, 1970.
Mermet, Abbé Alexis. *Principles and Practice of Radiesthesia*. London: Watkins, 1975.
Métraux, Alfred. *Voodoo in Haiti*. London: André Deutsch, 1959.
Miall, Agnes M. *Complete Fortune Telling*. London: C. Arthur Pearson, 1951.
Miller, Mary and Karl Taube. *The Gods and Symbols of Ancient Mexico and the Maya*. London: Thames & Hudson, 1993.
Minetta. *The Art of Tea Cup Fortune Telling*. London: W. Foulsham, 1958.
Mitchell, Edgar. *Psychic Exploration*. New York: G. P. Putnam, 1974.
Mitchell, Janet Lee. *Out-of-the-Body Experiences: A Handbook*. Jefferson, NC: McFarland, 1981.
Moakley, Gertrude. *The Tarot Crads Painted by Bonifacio Bembo*. New York: New York Public Library, 1966.
Moberly, C. A. E. and E. M. Jourdain. *An Adventure*. London: Faber & Faber, 1955.
Monroe, Robert A. *Journeys out of the Body*. New York: Doubleday, 1971.

Montgomery, Ruth. *A Gift of Prophesy*. New York: Morrow, 1965.
Montgomery, Ruth. *Here and Hereafter*. New York: Fawcett, 1968.
Montgomery, Ruth. *A Search for the Truth*. New York: Bantam Books, 1968.
Montrose. *Numerology for Everybody*. New York: Blue Ribbon, 1940.
Moses, William Stainton. *Direct Spirit Writing*. London, 1878.
Mühl, Anita M. *Automatic Writing*. Dresden: Steinkopff, 1930.
Muldoon, Sylvan J. and Hereward Carrington. *The Projection of the Astral Body*. London: Rider, 1929.
Muldoon, Sylvan J. *The Case for Astral Projection*. Chicago: Aries Press, 1936.
Murray, Liz and Colin. *The Celtic Tree Oracle*. New York: St. Martin's, 1988.
Murray, Margaret Alice. *The Witch Cult in Western Europe*. Oxford, UK: Oxford University Press, 1921.
Myer, Isaac. *Qabbalah: The Philosophical Writings of Avicebron*. New York: Samuel Weiser, 1970.
Myers, Frederick W. H. *Human Personality and Its Survival of Bodily Death*, New York: University Books, 1961.
Mysteries of the Unknown: Psychic Powers. Alexandria, VA: Time-Life Books, 1987.
Nash, Carroll B. *Science of Psi: ESP and PK*. Springfield, IL: Charles C. Thomas, 1978.
Neimark, Philip John. *The Sacred Ifa Oracle*. New York: Destiny, 1995
Newall, Venetia. *Man, Myth & Magic: Eggs*. London: BPC Publishing, 1970.
Nielsen, Greg and Joseph Polansky. *Pendulum Power*. London: Aquarian, 1986.
Niles, Edith. *Astrology and Your Destiny*. New York: HC Publishers, 1969.
Niles, Edith. *Palmistry: Your Fate in Your Hands*. New York: HC Publishers, 1969.
Noble, Vicki. *Motherpeace: A Way to the Goddess through Myth, Art and Tarot*. San Francisco: Harper & Row, 1983.
North, J. *Pagan Priests, Religion and Power in the Ancient World: Diviners and Divination at Rome*. London: Duckworth, 1990.
Northage, Ivy. *Mediumship Made Simple*. London: College of Psychic Studies, 1994.
Norton-Taylor, Duncan. *The Emergence of Man: The Celts*. Alexandria, VA: Time-Life Books, 1974.
Nostradamus, Michael de. *The Prophesies of Nostradamus*. New York: Avenel, 1975.
Offner, C. B. and H. van Straelen. *Modern Japanese Religions*. London: Twayne, 1963.
Oken, Alan. *Pocket Guide to the Tarot*. Freedom, CA: The Crossing Press, 1996.
Ophiel. *The Art and Practice of Astral Projection*. San Francisco: Peach Publishing, 1961.
Opie, Iona and Peter. *Children's Games in Street and Playground*. Oxford, UK: Oxford University Press, 1969.
Opie, Iona and Peter. *The Lore and Language of Schoolchildren*. Oxford, UK: Oxford University Press 1959.
Oppenheim, A. L. *Ancient Mesopotamia: Portrait of a Dead Civilization*. Chicago: Chicago University Press, 1964.
Orbis Publishing. *Mysteries of Mind, Space & Time: The Unexplained*. Westport, CT: H. S. Stuttman, 1992.
Orion, Rae. *Astrology for Dummies*. Foster City, CA: IDG Books, 1999.
Osborn, Arthur W. *The Future Is Now: The Significance of Precognition*. New York: University Books, 1961.
Osborn, Marijane and Stella Longland. *Rune Games*. London: Routledge & Kegan Paul, 1982.
Ostrander, Sheila and Lynn Schroeder. *Psychic Discoveries behind the Iron Curtain*. New York: Prentice-Hall, 1970.
Ostrom, Joseph. *Understanding Auras*. London: Aquarian, 1993.
Ouspensky, P. D. *The Symbolism of the Tarot*. New York: Dover, 1976.
Owens, Elizabeth. *How to Communicate with Spirits*. St. Paul, MN: Llewellyn, 2002.

Oxford English Dictionary. Oxford, UK: Clarendon Press, 1989.
Page, R. I. *An Introduction to English Runes*. London: Methuen, 1973.
Pagenstecher, G. *Past Events Seership*. Proceedings of the American Society for Psychical Research, v. 16, 1923.
Panchadasi, Swami. *A Course of Advanced Lessons in Clairvoyance and Occult Powers*. Chicago, 1916.
Papus. *The Tarot of the Bohemians: Absolute Key to Occult Science*. New York: Arcanum Books, 1958.
Paracelsus. *The Prophecies of Paracelsus*. Blauvelt: Rudolf Steiner, 1973.
Parke, H. W. *Sibyls and Sibylline Prophecy in Classical Antiquity*. New York: Routledge, 1988.
Parker, Derek and Julia. *The Compleat Astrologer*. New York: McGraw-Hill, 1971.
Parrinder, Geoffrey. *African Mythology*. London: Paul Hamlyn, 1967.
Paterson, Helena. *The Handbook of Celtic Astrology: The 13-Sign Lunar Zodiac of the Ancient Druids*. St. Paul, MN: Llewellyn, 1999.
Paterson, Jane. *Know Yourself through Your Handwriting*. London: Reader's Digest, 1978.
Pechel, Lisa. *A Practical Guide to the Runes: Their Uses in Divination and Magick*. St. Paul, MN: Llewellyn, 1989.
Pelton, Robert W. *Your Future, Your Fortune*. Greenwich, CT: Fawcett, 1973.
Pennick, Nigel. *Runic Astrology*. Chieveley, UK: Capall Bann, 1995.
Petulengro, Leon. *The Secrets of Romany Astrology & Palmistry*. London: Souvenir Press, 1969.
Phillips, C. Doreen. *The Autobiography of a Fortuneteller*. New York: Vantage Press, 1958.
Phillips, E. D. (ed.). *Man, Myth & Magic*. London: BPC Publishing, 1970.
Phillips, Stephen M. *Mysteries of Mind, Space & Time: the Unexplained*. Westport, CT: H. S. Stuttman, 1992.
Phrenological Journal. New York: Fowler & Wells, 1886.
Piggott, Stuart. *The Druids*. London: Thames & Hudson, 1968.
Pike, S. N. *Water-Divining*. London: Research Publications, 1945.
Piper, Alta L. *The Life and Work of Mrs. Piper*. London: Kegan Paul, Trench, Trubner, 1929.
Pollack, J. *Croiset the Clairvoyant*. New York: Doubleday, 1964.
Pollack, Rachel. *Sevety-Eight Degrees of Wisdom: A Book of Tarot—Part One: The Major Arcana*. Wellingborough, UK: Aquarian, 1980.
Pollack, Rachel. *Seventy-Eight Degrees of Wisdom: A Book of Tarot—Part Two: The Minor Arcana and Readings*. Wellingborough, UK: Aquarian, 1983.
Ponce, Charles. *Kabbalah: an Introduction and Illumination for the World Today*. Wheaton, IL: Theosophical Publishing House, 1973.
Potter, D. *Sibyls in the Greek and Roman World: Journal of Roman Archaeology 3*. Rhode Island, 1990.
Potts, Billie. *A New Woman's Tarot*. Woodstock, NY: Elf and Dragons, 1978.
Prince, W. F. *The Case of Patience Worth*. New York: University Books, 1964.
Puharich, Andrija. *Uri: The Journal of the Mystery of Uri Geller*. New York: Anchor Press, 1974.
Raine, Kathleen. *Yeats, the Tarot and the Golden Dawn*, Dublin: Dolmen, 1976.
Rakoczi, Basil Ivan. *Fortune Telling: A Guide to Foreseeing the Future*. London: Macdonald, 1970.
Rakoczi, Basil Ivan. *Man, Myth & Magic: Lots*. London: BPC Publishing, 1970.
Rakoczi, Basil Ivan. *Man, Myth & Magic: Palmistry*. London: BPC Publishing, 1970.
Rakoczi, Basil Ivan. *The Painted Caravan*. Holland: Boucher, 1954.
Randolph, Vance. *Ozark Superstitions*. New York: Dover, 1964.
Raphael. *Raphael's Astronomical Ephemeris of the Planets' Places*. London: W. Foulsham, annual.
Rawlinson, George. *History of Ancient Egypt*. New York: Dodd, Mead & Company, 1881.
Reed, Ellen Cannon. *The Witches Tarot*. St. Paul, MN: Llewllyn, 1989.
Reed, Henry. *Getting Help from Your Dreams*. New York: Ballantine, 1985.

Regardie, Israel. *A Practical Guide to Geomantic Divination*. New York: Samuel Weiser, 1972.
Renee, Janina. *Tarot Spells*. St. Paul, MN: Llewellyn, 1990.
Rennick, Nigel. *Games of the Gods*. York Beach, NY: Samuel Weiser, 1989.
Renzulli, Maria Letizia. *Zen Runes*. Shaftesbury, UK: Element Books, 1998.
Rhine, Joseph Banks. *New Frontiers of the Mind*. New York: Farrar & Rinehart, 1937.
Rhine, Joseph Banks. *New World of the Mind*. New York: William Sloane, 1953.
Rhine, Joseph Banks. *The Reach of the Mind*. London: Pelican, 1954.
Rhine, Louisa. *E.S.P. in Life and Lab*. New York: Macmillan, 1967.
Richards, Chris (ed.). *The Illustrated Encyclopedia of World Religions*. Shaftesbury, UK: Element, 1997.
Richmond, Olney H. *The Mystic Test Book: Or the Magic of the Cards*. North Hollywood, CA: Newcastle, 1983.
Robb, Stewart. *Prophecies on World Events by Nostradamus*. New York: Liveright, 1961.
Robbins, Rossell Hope. *The Encyclopedia of Witchcraft and Demonology*. New York: Crown, 1959.
Roberts, Estelle. *Fifty Years a Medium*. London: Corgi, 1969.
Roberts, Jane. *The Coming of Seth*. New York: Pocket Books, 1976.
Roberts, Kenneth. *Henry Gross and His Dowsing Rod*. New York: Doubleday, 1951.
Roberts, Kenneth. *The Seventh Sense*. New York: Doubleday, 1953.
Roberts, Kenneth. *Water Unlimited*. New York: Doubleday, 1957.
Roberts, Richard. *Tarot and You*. Hastings-on-Hudson, NY: Morgan & Morgan, 1971.
Roberts, Richard and Joseph Campbell. *Tarot Revelations*. San Francisco: Richard Roberts, 1979.
Rose, H. J. *Religion in Greece and Rome*. New York: Harper & Row, 1959.
Rougemont, Claire. *The National Dream Book*. Philadelphia: David McKay, 1901.
Rudhyar, Dane. *The Astrological Houses: The Spectrum of Individual Experience*. Garden City, NY: Doubleday, 1972.
Ryan, Mark and Chesca Potter. *The Greenwood Tarot*. Wellingborough: Thorsons, 1996.
Sagges, H. W. F. *Man, Myth & Magic: Mesopotamia*. London: BPC Publishing 1970.
Saltmarsh, H. F. *Foreknowledge*. London: G. Bell & Sons, 1938.
Sams, Jamie. *The Sacred Path Cards*. San Francisco: HarperSanFrancisco, 1990.
Sams, Jamie. *The Sacred Path Workbook*. San Francisco: HarperSanFrancisco, 1991.
Sams, Jamie and David Carson. *Medicine Cards*. Santa Fe, NM: Bear, 1988.
Sandback, John. *The Mysteries of Color*. Chicago: Aries Press, 1977.
Sara, Dorothy. *Personality & Penmanship: A Guide to Handwriting Analysis*. New York: HC Publishers, 1969.
Sauneron, Serge. *The Priests of Ancient Egypt*. New York: Grove Press, 1960.
Savage, Candace. *Bird Brains*. San Francisco: Sierra Club, 1997.
Scholem, Gershom. *Kabbalah*. New York: New American Library, 1974.
Schul, Bill. *The Psychic Power of Animals*. New York: Fawcett, 1976.
Schumann, Walter. *Gemstones of the World*. New York: Sterling, 1977.
Schwei, Priscilla. *The Solomon Manual of Divination and Ritual Spells*. St. Paul, MN: Llewellyn, 1988.
Schwei, Priscilla and Ralph Pestka. *The Complete Book of Astrological Geomancy*. St. Paul, MN: Llewellyn, 1990.
Scott's Bible; Old and New Testaments with Notes, Observations, and References. New York: Samuel T Armstrong, 1827.
Seal, S. G. and F. Bateman. *Modern Experiments in Telepathy*. London: Faber & Faber, 1954.
Sechrist, Elsie. *Dreams: Your Magic Mirror*. New York: Cowles, 1968.
Sepharial (Walter Gorn Old). *The Kabala of Numbers*. Philadelphia: David McKay, 1945.
Sepharial (Walter Gorn Old). *Sepharial's New Dictionary of Astrology*. New York: Arco, 1963.

Shakespeare, William. *The Complete Works*. London: Odhams Press, 1938.
Shannon, E. *Water Witching*. New Mexico: Shannon, 1967.
Sharpe, Eric. *Man, Myth & Magic: Birth*. London: BPC Publishing, 1970.
Shepard, Leslie A. (ed.). *Encyclopedia of Occultism & Parapsychology*. New York: Avon, 1978.
Sheridan, Jo. *The Wheel of Fortune*. New York: Popular Library, 1970.
Shipton, Mother. *Mother Shipton's Gypsy Fortune Teller and Dream Book*. New York: Wehman, 1890.
Showers, Paul. *Fortune Telling for Fun and Profit*. New York: Bell, 1985.
Shulman, Sandra. *The Encyclopedia of Astrology*. London: Hamlyn, 1976.
Simpson, J. W. *Mother Shipton: Her Life and True Prophecies Those Fulfilled and Those Yet to Be*. Bath, UK: West Country Editions, 1976.
Sinnett, A. P. *Incidents in the Life of Madame Blavatsky*. London: George Redway, 1886.
Skinner, Stephen (ed.). *The Magical Diaries of Aleister Crowley*. York Beach, NY: Samuel Weiser, 1979.
Skinner, Stephen. *The Oracle of Geomancy*. Bridport: Prism, 1986.
Skinner, Stephen. *Terrestrial Astrology*. London: Routledge & Kegan Paul, 1980.
Smith, A. W. *A Gardner's Handbook of Plant Names, Their Meanings and Origins*. Mineola, NY: Dover, 1997.
Smith, Christine. *The Book of Divination*. London: Rider, n.d.
Sneddon, Paul. *Self-Development with the I Ching*. London: Foulsham, 1990.
Solom, H. (ed.). *Studies in Item Analysis and Prediction*. Stanford, CA: Stanford University Press, 1961.
Somogyi, Imre. *Reading Toes*. Saffron Walden, UK: C. W. Daniels, 1997.
Sonero, Devi. *Phrenology: Secrets Revealed by Your Face and Head*. New York:Tower Books, 1970.
Sonetheil, Ursula. *Mother Shipton's Prophecies: The Earliest Editions*. Maidstone: George Mann, 1978.
Sophia. *Fortune Telling With Playing Cards*. St. Paul, MN: Llewellyn, 1996.
Soric, John. *The New Age Astrologer*. San Antonio, TX: Star Astrology, 1976.
Spence, Lewis. *An Encyclopedia of the Occult*. London: George Routledge & Sons, 1920.
Spence, Lewis. *The Magic Arts in Celtic Britain*. London: Rider, 1945.
Spence, Lewis. *Myth and Ritual in Dance, Game, and Rhyme*. London: Watts, 1942.
Spencer, Godfrey. *The Secret of Numbers Revealed*. Dallas: Dorene, 1969.
Spinden, Herbert J. *Ancient Civilizations of Mexico and Central America*. New York: American Museum of Natural History, 1946.
Spraggett, Alan. *The Unexplained*. New York: New American Library, 1967.
Squire, Elizabeth Daniels. *The New Fortune in Your Hand*. New York: Fleet Press, 1960.
St. Clair, David. *Drum & Candle*. New York: Bell, 1971.
St. Hill, Katharine. *The Grammar of Palmistry*. Philadelphia: Henry Altemus, 1893.
Stearn, Jess. *Edgar Cayce: the Sleeping Prophet*. New York: Doubleday, 1967.
Steiger, Brad. *E.S.P.—Your Sixth Sense*. New York: Award Books, 1966.
Steiger, Brad and Ron Warmoth. *The Tarot*. New York: Award, 1969.
Steinbach, Marten. *Medical Palmistry: Health and Character in the Hands*. Secaucus, NJ: University Books, 1975.
Stemman, Roy. *The Supernatural: Spirits and Spirit Worlds*. London: Aldus Books, 1975.
Stephensen, P. R. *The Legend of Aleister Crowley*. St. Paul, MN: Llewellyn, 1970.
Stern, Madeleine B. *Heads and Headlines: The Phrenological Fowlers*. Norman, OK: University of Oklahoma 1971.
Stevens, Jose and Lena S. Stevens. *Secrets of Shamanism: Tapping the Spirit Power within You*. New York: Avon Books, 1988.
Stewart, Bob and John Matthew. *Legendary Britain*. London: Blandford, 1989.
Stewart, R. J. *Elements of Prophecy*. London: Element, 1990.

Stone, L. A. *Story of Phallicism*. New York: Norton, 1927.

Stuart, George E. and Gene S. Stuart. *The Mysterious Maya*. Washington, DC: National Geographic Society, 1977.

Sugrue, Thomas. *There Is a River: The Story of Edgar Cayce*. New York: Dell, 1970.

Summers, Catherine and Julian Vayne. *Self-Development with the Tarot*. London: Foulsham, 1992.

Sutphen, Dick. *The Oracle Within*. New York: Pocket Books, 1991.

Swoboda, Hermann. *Das Siebenjahn* ("The Year of Seven") Vienna and Leipzig, Germany: Orion-Verlag, 1917.

Symonds, John. *The Great Beast*. New York: Roy Publishers, 1952.

Symonds, John. *The Magic of Aleister Crowley*. London: Frederick Muller, 1958.

Symonds, John. *Madame Blavatsky: Medium and Magician*. London: Odhams, 1959.

Tansley, David V. *Radionics & the Subtle Anatomy of Man*. Holsworthy, UK: Health Science Press, 1976.

Taylor, Ariel Yvon. *Character Grams: A Diving Rod to Human Nature the World Over*. New York: Ray Long & Richard R. Smith, 1934.

Taylor, John W. R. *A Picture History of Flight*. London: Hulton Press, 1955.

Telesco, Patricia. *A Victorian Grimoire*. St. Paul, MN: Llewellyn, 1992.

Terres, John K. *The Audubon Society Encyclopedia of North American Birds*. New York: Alfred A. Knopf, 1980.

Theobald, Robert (ed.). *Futures Conditional*. Indianapolis: Bobbs-Merrill, 1972.

Thommen, George S. *Is This Your Day?* New York: Crown, 1973.

Thomsen, Harry. *The New Religions of Japan*. New York: William Tuttle, 1963.

Thorpe, Charles. *Card Fortune-Telling*. London: Foulsham, 1989.

Thouless, Robert H. *Experimental Psychical Research*. London: Pelican, 1963.

Todeschi, Kevin J. *Edgar Cayce on the Akashic Records*. Virginia Beach, VA: A.R.E. Press, 1998.

Toland, John A. *A Critical History of the Celtic Religion and Learning: Containing an Account of the Druids*. Edinburgh, Scotland, 1815.

Tompkins, Peter and Christopher Bird. *The Secret Life of Plants*. New York: Avon, 1973.

Tomlinson, H. *Medical Divination*. Holsworthy, UK: Health Science Press, 1976.

Tooker, Elisabeth. *The Iroquois Ceremonial of Midwinter*. Syracuse, NY: Syracuse University Press, 1970.

Tope, M. *The Phrenological Era*. Bowerston: Tope, 1912.

Trevelyan, George. *A Vision of the Aquarian Age*. Bath, UK: Gateway, 1994.

Trinder, W.H. *Dowsing*. London: British Society of Dowsers, 1950.

Tseten, Dorjee. *Tibetan Art of Divination: Tibetan Bulletin*, March-April, 1995.

Tutuola, Amos. *The Palm Wine Drinkard*. New York: Grove Press, 1953.

Tyl, Noel. *The Principles and Practice of Astrology* St. Paul, MN: Llewellyn, 12 volumes, 1973–75.

Tyson, Donald (ed.). *Three Books of Occult Philosophy Written by Henry Cornelius Agrippa of Nettesheim*. St. Paul, MN: Llewellyn, 1993.

Tzu, Lao. *Tao Te Ching*. Harmondsworth, UK: Penguin, 1963.

Ulufudu (Brian Crowley). *The Zulu Bone Oracle*. Berkeley, CA: Wingbow Press, 1989.

Urquhart, Sir Thomas. *The Third Book of the Works of Mr. Francis Rabelais*. London, 1693.

Valcourt-Vermont, Edgar de. *The Practice of Palmistry for Professional Purposes*. San Bernardino, CA: Borgo Press, 1980.

Van Alen, R. *You and Your Hand*. New York: Greystone, 1948.

Vaughan, Alan. *The Edge of Tomorrow: How to Foresee and Fulfill the Future*. New York: Coward, McCann & Geoghegan, 1981.

Vaughan, Richard. *Numbers as Symbols for Self-Discovery*. London: CRCS, 1985.

Verner, Alex. *Practical Psychometry*. British Psychological Institute, 1935.

Verner, Alex. *Table Rapping and Automatic Writing*. London: Fowler, n.d.

Von Hagen, Victor Wolfgang. *The Aztec: Man and Tribe*. New York: New American Library, 1961.

Von Hagen, Victor Wolfgang. *Realm of the Incas*. New York: New American Library, 1957.

Von Hagen, Victor Wolfgang. *World of the Maya*. New York: New American Library, 1960.

Vore, Nicholas de. *Encyclopedia of Astrology*. New York: Philosophical Library, 1947.

Waite, Arthur Edward. *The Pictorial Key to the Tarot*. New York: University Books, 1959 (London 1910) .

Waley, Arthur. *The Way and Its Power*. New York: Grove Press, 1958.

Walker, Barbara G. *The Woman's Dictionary of Symbols and Sacred Objects*. San Francisco: HarperSanFrancisco, 1988.

Walker, Benjamin. *Man and the Beasts Within (The Encyclopedia of the Occult, the Esoteric, and the Supernatural)*. New York: Stein and Day, 1977.

Walker, Benjamin. *Man, Myth & Magic: Taoism*. London: BPC Publishing, 1970.

Wallechinsky, David; Amy Wallace and Irving Wallace. *The People's Almanac Presents the Book of Predictions*. New York: William Morrow, 1980.

Wallis, E.W. & M. H. *A Guide to Mediumship and Psychical Unfoldment*. Mokelumne Hill, CA: Health Research, 1968.

Wa-Na-Nee-Che with Eliana Harvey. *White Eagle Medicine Wheel*. New York: St. Martin's, 1997.

Wang, Robert. *An Introduction to the Golden Dawn Tarot*. New York: Samuel Weiser, 1978.

Wang, Richard. *The Qabalistic Tarot: A Textbook of Mystical Philosophy*. York Beach, NY: Samuel Weiser, 1983.

Ward, Charles A. *Oracles of Nostradamus*. New York: Charles Scribner's Sons, 1940.

Ward, Ritchier. *The Living Clocks*. New York: New American Library, 1971.

Waters, Frank. *Book of the Hopi*. New York: Ballantine, 1969.

Waters, Frank. *Masked Gods: Navaho and Pueblo Ceremonialism*. New York: Ballantine, 1970.

Watkins, Alfred. *The Old Straight Track*. London: Methuen, 1925.

Wavell, S. *Trances*. London: Dutton, 1967.

Webb, James. *The Occult Liberation*. London: Alcove Press, 1973.

Webster, Richard. *Revealing Hands*. St. Paul, MN: Llewellyn, 1994.

Wedeck, Harry Ezekiel. *Dictionary of Astrology*. London: P. Owens, 1973.

Wehman. *Practical Palmistry*. New York: Wehman, 1949.

Wells, Samuel Roberts. *How to Read Character: A New Illustrated Handbook of Phrenology and Physiognomy for Students and Examiners with a Descriptive Chart*. Rutland, VT: Tuttle, 1971.

Werblowsky, R.J. Zwi. *Man, Myth & Magic: Cabala*. London: BPC Publishing, 1970.

Weschcke, Carl L. and Stan Barker. *The Truth about Twentieth-Century Astrology*. St. Paul, MN: Llewellyn, 1989.

Wethered, Vernon D. *A Radiesthetic Approach to Health and Homeopathy, or Health and the Pendulum*. London: C. W. Daniel, 1950.

Wethered, Vernon D. *An Introduction to Medical Radiesthesia & Radionics*. C.W. Daniel, London 1962.

Wethered, Vernon D. *The Practice of Medical Radiesthesia*. London: C. W. Daniel, 1967.

Wheeler, Sir Mortimer. *Early India and Pakistan*. London: Praeger, 1968.

Wheeler, Sir Mortimer. *Man, Myth & Magic: India*. London: BPC Publishing, 1970.

White, Stewart Edward. *Excursions into the World of Other-Consciousness*. New York: Berkley, 1969.

White, Suzanne. *Chinese Astrology, Plain and Simple*. Boston: Charles E. Tuttle, 1998.

Wilhelm, Richard (Cary F. Baynes, tr.). *The I Ching*. Princeton, NJ: Princeton University Press, 1967.

Wilkinson, Sir J. Gardner. *The Ancient Egyptians: Their Life and Customs*. New York: Crescent Books, 1988.

Willey, Raymond C. *All You Need to Know about Modern Dowsing*. Cottonwood, CO: Esoteric, 1975.

Williams, Gertrude Marvin. *Priestess of the Occult: Madame Blavatsky*. New York: Alfred A. Knopf, 1946.

Willoya, William and Vinson Brown. *Warriors of the Rainbow: Strange and Prophetic Indian Dreams*. Healdsburg, CA: Naturegraph, 1962.

Wilson, Colin. *The Occult*. New York: Random House, 1971.

Wilson, Colin (ed.). *The Supernatural: Mysterious Powers*. London: Aldus Books, 1975.

Wilson, Colin (ed.). *The Supernatural: Signs of Things to Come*. London: Aldus Books, 1975.

Wing, R. L. *The I Ching Workbook*. New York: Doubleday, 1979.

Wosien, Maria-Gabriele. *Man, Myth & Magic: Slavs*. London: BPC Publishing, 1970.

Wright, Thomas (ed). *A Contemporary Narrative of the Proceedings against Dame Alice Kyteler*. London: Camden Society, 1843.

Xavier, F. C. and W. Vieira. *The World of the Spirit*. New York: Philosophical Library, 1966.

Yram. *Practical Astral Projection*. London, n.d.

Zolar. *The Encyclopedia of Ancient and Forbidden Knowledge*. Los Angeles: Nash, 1970.

Zolar. *Everything You Want to Know about Fortune Telling with Cards; Karma System, Gypsy System, Professional System, Palmistry*. New York: Arco, 1973.

Zolar. *Zolar's Ancient Mystical Prophesies*. New York: Zolar, 1971.

Zolar. *Zolar's Dreams*. New York: Zolar, 1969.

Index

Note: **Boldface** type indicates main entries and their page numbers; (ill.) indicates photos and illustrations.

D

E

N

O

R

S